XAVIER UNIVERSITY LIBRARY
NEW ORLEANS, LA. 70125

XAVIER UNIVERSITY LIBRARY
NEW ORLEANS, LA. 70125

D1451617

Perspective: An Introduction to Sociology

A 1.95

Perspective: An Introduction to Sociology

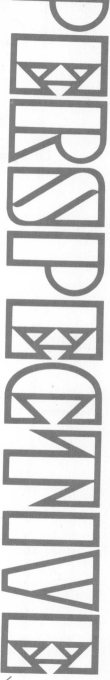

Burton Wright II
Florida Technological University

John P. Weiss
Rollins College

Charles M. Unkovic
Florida Technological University

The Dryden Press
Hinsdale, Illinois

Design by Stephen Rapley
Copy Editing by Ellen F. Farrow
Photo Research by Yvonne Freund

Copyright © 1975 by The Dryden Press,
a division of Holt, Rinehart and Winston, Inc.
All Rights Reserved
Library of Congress Catalog Card Number 73-13273
ISBN: 0-03-089170-1
Printed in the United States of America
5678 071 987654321

3-1303-00053-5381

301
W947p

To the late Joseph C. Byers,
Editor and Friend

Credits

Chapter 1 opener Photo by Lloyd E. Saunders
Chapter 2 opener Photo by James S. Soroka
Page 51 Photo by Geoffrey R. Gove
Chapter 3 opener Photo by Tim Eagan
Chapter 4 opener Photo by Tim Eagan
Chapter 5 opener Photo by Featherkill Studios
Page 134 Photo by Lynn McLaren
Chapter 6 opener Photo by Will Forbes
Page 157 Photo by United Press International
Page 166 Photo by United Press International
Page 182 © 1973 by The New York Times Company. Reprinted by Permission.
Chapter 7 opener Photo by United Press International
Chapter 8 opener Photo by Tim Eagan
Page 234 Photo by Winston Vargas
Page 235 Photo by Charles Gatewood
Chapter 9 opener Photo by Fred Leavitt
Chapter 10 opener Photo by Winston Vargas
Chapter 11 opener Photo by United Press International
Page 353 Source: U.S. Department of Commerce, Bureau of the Census
Page 357 Photo by United Press International
Page 359 Source: U.S. Department of Commerce, Bureau of the Census
Page 364 Source: U.S. Department of Commerce, Bureau of the Census
Page 365 Source: National Center for Health Statistics, Public Health Service, U.S. Department of Health, Education, and Welfare
Page 366 Photo by United Press International
Page 368 Source: U.S. Immigration and Naturalization Service
Chapter 12 opener Photo by The New York Times
Page 407 Source: *Statistical Abstract of the United States,* 1971, p. 112; Education figures are drawn from "Characteristics of American Youth, 1971," *Current Population Report, Special Studies,* S series P-23, no. 40 (Washington, D.C.: Bureau of the Census, 1972).
Page 408 Source: *Monthly Labor Review* and *Employment and Earnings Report on the Labor Force* (Washington, D.C.: Bureau of Labor Statistics, 1971).
Page 410 Source: "Spanish–American Survey," *Current Population Reports,* Series P-20, no. 238 (Washington, D.C.: Bureau of the Census, 1972).
Page 410 Source: "Spanish–American Survey," *Current Population Reports,* Series P-20, no. 238 (Washington, D.C.: Bureau of the Census, 1972).
Page 411 Source: "Spanish–American Survey," *Current Population Reports,* Series P-20, no. 238 (Washington, D.C.: Bureau of the Census, 1972).
Page 412 Source: "Spanish–American Survey," *Current Population Reports,* Series P-20, no. 238 (Washington, D.C.: Bureau of the Census, 1972).
Page 412 Source: "Spanish–American Survey," *Current Population Reports,* Series P-20, no. 238 (Washington, D.C.: Bureau of the Census, 1972).
Page 414 Source: "Minority Groups in California," *Monthly Labor Review* (Washington, D.C.: Bureau of Labor Statistics, 1966).
Chapter 13 opener Photo by Winston Vargas
Page 438 Photo by United Press International
Page 448 Photo by United Press International
Page 460 Photo by United Press International

In writing this book we considered not only the student majoring in sociology but also the thousands of students who will take only one or two courses in sociology and never be formally exposed to the discipline again. While we have a close, personal interest in our majors, it is our opinion that, in the long run, sociology will have its greatest effect through the general population. Since college students constitute an important part of the general population, we would argue that it is essential for students to somehow or other understand the importance of taking an analytical view of society. This cannot be accomplished either by polemics or requiring students to memorize innumerable facts derived from sociological research.

The general orientation of this book is analytical, by which we mean a functional analysis in the sense used by Robert K. Merton. We have interpreted Merton's concept to mean an analysis of society, not from any particular point of view—neither structural-functional nor conflict—but from the standpoint of manifest and latent functions. We have, of course, not avoided some consideration of dysfunctions. But we have indicated that to label something as "dysfunctional" is possible only with a value or values as a point of departure. While we recognize that complete objectivity is impossible, we have maintained explicitly and implicitly that sociologists should attempt to approximate objectivity. It seems to us that an overemphatic espousal of any one position renders any degree of objectivity not only unlikely but impossible.

Recognizing that sociology is a probabilistic science, we have concentrated on bringing to the student a reasonably adequate sampling of sociological knowledge with an emphasis on the *process* of analysis and those things that most sociologists would agree possess a reasonable degree of validity. In other words, we have tried not to make this book a mere compendium of facts. With respect to students, our intent has been heuristic; we have attempted to induce the students to discover for themselves the excitement and usefulness of an intellectual, objective, analytical approach to the study of society.

Implicit in this text is the belief (clearly a value judgement on our part) that objectivity coupled with rationality is by no means a dull, unexciting way to approach the study of sociology. It is, for example, essential to indicate that some segments of our society are denied equal opportunity to compete for the rewards available. This finding emerges clearly from an objective analysis of the relations between the dominant segment of a society and that society's minority groups. We would argue that any rhetoric about injustices, however understandable, is less likely to produce constructive changes than a careful analysis of the societal factors underlying discrimination and prejudice. For example, it has been widely assumed that merely bringing Black and white students together in schools will serve to reduce if not eliminate racial discrimination and prejudice. Yet as a recent careful study by Elizabeth

Cohen and Susan S. Roper indicates, it takes much more than social propinquity to solve the racial problem.*

In the early stages of this book, we asked ourselves this question: Did we want to stir up students and arouse their emotions? Did we want to get them angry about the many injustices and inequities that plainly exist in our own and other societies? Or did we want to give them the best information we have on culture and society, particularly the dynamics underlying the human interaction which produces both culture and society? We opted for a concentration on the latter while hoping for a leavening of the former. We do not argue for cold objectivity, but we would maintain that passion without knowledge is a source of trouble. Indeed many of the world's more serious problems can be traced to the autonomic nervous system functioning without any effective restraint from the temporal and frontal lobes of the brain.

As we said earlier, we were particularly mindful of the fact that the only formal exposure the vast majority of college and university students receive to sociology is in introductory courses. It is our belief that a knowledge of sociology is important to these young people specifically and society in general. It seems thoroughly reasonable to assume that some of these students will be leaders in future years and that many others will be in positions to exert some influence on the form of society. It seemed to us that the value and practical usefulness of the analytical approach to society and to people in groups was the essential idea we wanted students to take with them from a study of this text. While it would be foolish to argue that the analytical approach is any panacea for the things that ail men in particular and societies in general, it would seem correct to state that reasonably well developed habits of objective analysis are more likely to produce truly viable results than rhetoric, insults, and violence.

As the title of this book suggests ("perspective" purposely being in the singular), we have stressed the unique subject matter of sociology by emphasizing the approaches of such individuals as Emile Durkheim and Max Weber. With some minor variations, we have attempted to follow the example set by these two men by emphasizing the sociological method, the force of ideas, and the logic underlying inferences with respect to men in groups including societies. While far from social behaviorism, we have favored a mildly positivistic approach. Although the scientific method as utilized in the natural sciences transfers to some extent to sociology, it has been necessary to develop some research methods and techniques that are peculiar to sociology. Sociologists are, after all, part of the subject matter they are studying, a handicap from which natural and physical scientists do not suffer.

* Elizabeth G. Cohen and Susan S. Roper, "Modification of Interracial Interaction Disability: An Application of Status Characteristic Theory," *American Sociological Review* 37, no. 6 (1972), pp. 643–657.

In conclusion, we would like to acknowledge the important assistance we have received from a number of individuals who were concerned with bringing this book to its final form. First of all, there is a debt that we can never repay to the late Joseph C. Byers, the Dryden editor who worked closely with us from the inception of the book until it had neared completion. His intelligence, sensitivity, encouragement, and sound advice were assets the ultimate value of which can never be estimated. In addition, we want to specifically mention the skilled, perceptive, and enthusiastic assistance and expert help we received from Ray Ashton, Dryden editor; Stephen Rapley, art editor; Ellen F. Farrow, free lance editor; and Yvonne Freund, photographic consultant. We are also greatly indebted to Reece McGee who worked with us continuously during the preparation of this text. And our thanks to our two typists, JoAnn Russell and Sharon Wilson. We, of course, take full responsibility for any flaws that may remain.

Orlando, Florida
November 1974

Burton Wright II
John P. Weiss
Charles M. Unkovic

Contributors

Burton Wright II   Editor
Florida Technological University

Bruce W. Aldrich   Other Contributors
University of Miami
Alexander Bassin
Florida State University
Ronald A. Carriere
University of California at Los Angeles
Byron Coffman
Cleveland State University
Alan Horowitz
Yale University
Patricia Jette
Yale University
Hans Nagpaul
Cleveland State University
John D. Sorenson
Augustana College

Contents

Contents

xiv

Contents

xv

Development of the Sociological Perspective: An Ongoing Debate

INTRODUCTION

We could begin by saying that the *sociological perspective* is a way of looking at people in groups. But so simple a statement cannot begin to convey the totality of the sociological perspective, which, in essence, is the purpose of this book. But as finite beings, we always find it necessary to have some point of departure, a place of origin. In this case, we have chosen to begin an explanation of the sociological perspective with an account of the growth and development of sociology that, by implication, also covers the perspective used by sociologists.

Actually the sociological perspective has emerged from numerous questions that have been asked, researched, and argued many times over the past 150 years. During that time, some questions and methods have generated a continuing interest while others have withered on the vine. We might point out that the survival of ideas and methods is probably a good test of their validity; it is out of these surviving questions, attempted answers, and endless debates that the sociological perspective has developed. We would claim that the perspective is still developing although it is easy to agree with C. Wright Mills[1] who considered that the perspective was developed during the classic period of sociological inquiry (roughly from the second decade of the nineteenth century to the early 1920's).

We hope to introduce the reader to the work and thoughts of a number of individuals who attempted to view society objectively and who made use of the scientific method (discussed in Chapter 2) in their studies. Some of their findings can help and have helped people not merely to understand their own and other societies but also to take a hand in directing and shaping societies to be more responsive to their members.

In the next several sections, we will approach the sociological perspective by discussing the "core" ideas and problems of five figures prominent in the classical period of sociological thought. What this amounts to, of course, is a brief history of the beginnings of a scientific sociology and the development of the sociological perspective. By knowing something about the origins of sociology, it is easier to understand sociology as it is today. While we are not able to discuss all historical sociologists, that is not to say that their ideas have not remained useful, although some of their views and findings have been modified by those who came after them.

We will begin by briefly considering the work of the two traditional "fathers" of sociology, Auguste Comte and Herbert Spencer. Next, we will consider the work of Emile Durkheim, Karl Marx, and Max Weber. It should be noted that the work of the latter three is still very influential today, and the questions they raised still stand at the center of the sociological perspective.

1

Development of the Sociological Perspective: An Ongoing Debate

Sociological Perspective

2

AUGUSTE COMTE

Auguste Comte (1798–1857)[2] was born in Montpellier, France. For a time he was a student and collaborator of the early French socialist thinker Henri de Saint Simon, who heavily influenced Comte's work. Comte published three major works, a *Plan of the Scientific Operations Necessary for the Reorganization of Society* (1822), with Saint Simon; a *Course of Positive Philosophy* (6 vols., 1830–1842); and a *System of Positive Politics* (4 vols., 1851–1854).

Comte coined the term "sociology" and for that reason is known as the founder of the discipline. He was the first to argue that the study of society could be made into a science. He also divided his new science of sociology into two major parts

1. *social statics*, the study of the laws governing social order
2. *social dynamics*, the study of the laws governing social change

Three Stages of Development

Comte is principally remembered for his work in social dynamics, his *law of human progress*. Comte believed that the most important trends in history grew out of the human intellect, and he saw three stages in this process of development. Each stage had its own characteristic manner of understanding the world.

During stage one, the *theological stage*, man attempts to understand the nature of the world by likening the causes of natural phenomena to "acts of the human will."[3] Man sees a world full of mysterious, personalized forces and spirits that motivate the actions of people and inanimate objects alike.

During stage two, the *metaphysical stage*, man comes to see the causes of natural phenomena as resulting from the operation of more abstract, less personalized forces.

In the last stage, the *positive stage*, man understands the world in terms of the operation of scientific laws.

Comte believed that his three-stage scheme itself represented an "inevitable tendency," or scientific law, governing the development of all societies. He saw his own analysis as a model of the kinds of laws which would be found to govern both social order and social change when sociology finally became transformed into a "positive science."

Contribution to the Sociological Perspective

Comte made at least two major contributions to the sociological perspective: (1) he insisted that sociology could be made into a science by searching for the laws governing social phenomena; and (2) he outlined two major areas that continue to be of sociological interest, *social statics* and *social dynamics*. Most sociologists no longer give great weight to Comte's specific contributions in the area of the analysis of the three stages, although his notion that basic processes underlie human intellectual and social evolution is fundamental to the work of a number of recent sociologists.

HERBERT SPENCER

Herbert Spencer (1820–1903)[4] was born in Derby, England. He is often regarded as the second founding father of sociology, though most of his actual work is now seen as quite dated. Spencer's major works of sociological interest are *Social Statics* (1850), *The Study of Sociology* (1874), and *Principles of Sociology* (3 vols., 1886–1896).

Organic Analogy

While Spencer's work has had little direct influence on the work of modern sociologists, his use of the *organic analogy* and some of his notions about societal evolution may be regarded as forerunners of ideas central to the concerns of many social theories. Spencer believed that society resembled a biological organism. Like a living being, society has various parts—families, businesses, and political organizations, for example. He saw the various parts of society as performing specialized functions in a manner somewhat like the organs of a living body. Thus, government performs complex functions of coordination and control similar to the functions of the brain. Likewise, society is "integrated," or held together, by the complex relations, or interdependence, of each part with the others. When any major organ of the body fails to perform its function, death ensues; and so it is with societies according to the Spencerian view. Further, Spencer believed that social organizations respond to a gradual evolutionary process that results in the growing complexity of societies as the "parts" of societies become increasingly differentiated or specialized. For Spencer, the major dynamic behind this change was the greater efficiency resulting from the increased division of labor.

Although it cannot be said with certainty that Spencer actually foresaw the complex societies of today, it does seem clear that he did predict, in a general way, what has actually occurred. Societies have become more complex, and the various parts of modern societies are increasingly specialized and more dependent upon one another. One has only to envision the effects of a prolonged rail or trucking strike to appreciate just how dependent all members of a modern society are on its various operating parts.

EMILE DURKHEIM

Emile Durkheim (1858–1917)[5] was born in Epinal in the northeastern French province of Lorraine. He had a successful academic career, the high point of which was his appointment to the first French professorship in sociology and education at the Sorbonne in 1913. Earlier, in 1898, Durkheim had founded a journal of sociology, *L'Année Sociologique*, which became the center for the influential Durkheimian school in sociology. His most important works are *The Division of Labor in Society* (1893), *The Rules of the Sociological Method* (1893), *Suicide* (1897), and *The Elementary Forms of Religious Life* (1899). In this section we will discuss Durkheim's ideas in the following three areas: (1) *sociological realism*, one approach to understanding the nature of society; (2) *the problem of order*; and, (3) the requirements for a *scientific understanding of social life*.

Sociological Realism

Durkheim was a sociological "realist." He believed that society was *real*, not merely an abstraction meant to describe the behavior of masses of individuals. He was fond of saying that the whole (society) was greater than the sum of its parts (individuals and their characteristics). In attempting to convey this point he often made use of an analogy. Water is composed of two atoms of hydrogen and one of oxygen, but when these atoms are combined, something new and inexplicable, in terms of the properties of its constituents, emerges. In a like manner Durkheim argued that human group interaction and organization produces something new, that is, society. For Durkheim, society too is inexplicable in terms of the characteristics of its individual members.

Since most people find it easiest to conceive of "things" that have clear physical boundaries and most difficult to deal with abstractions, Durkheim's notion that society is real is sometimes difficult to grasp. But Durkheim's point is relatively simple. Social phenomena are "real" because communication and organization create properties that individuals do not possess. There are two fundamental reasons why this is so.

1. The structure of social organization creates situations that lone individuals never experience.

2. Participation in group life does much to alter the characteristics individual men bring to a social situation and thus *become something new as a consequence of that participation.*

This is so much the case, Durkheim argued, that the individual is in reality the creation of group life. Whatever characteristics men exhibit as members of social organizations are not so much *explanations* of those organizations as *creations* of them. In Durkheim's view, then, society preceded and created the individual; any understanding of individual phenomena would have to begin with an understanding of the social and *not* the other way around.

Problem of Order

Durkheim was very much concerned with what sociologists call the "problem of order," or the question "How is society possible?" Since this "problem" is not obvious we shall introduce it by way of example.

Several years ago my wife and I were traveling in Spain. We stopped at a small roadside restaurant and ordered a meal. When the bill was presented, we discovered that we had no Spanish currency. It was Sunday and the banks were closed, so we asked if the proprietor could cash a traveler's check. Since this particular restaurant was off the tourist beat, he was unfamiliar with both traveler's checks and exchange rates. To our surprise the proprietor asked me the correct rate of exchange and cashed a large check. The man's behavior showed considerable faith in the social order, which in most times and most places is justified. Why this faith should or can be justified has puzzled social philosophers since the time of Thomas Hobbes.

Hobbes, the seventeenth-century English philosopher, reasoned that the natural state of man was what he termed "a war of all against all." He concluded that since the desires of men are limitless and their resources limited, there will be countless situations in which men will find it advantageous to achieve a greater share of valued goods through force, violence, and fraud. For many men, these options of force and violence often present themselves as the most expedient means to the achievement of particular ends and, further, that what is expedient is rational (we may define rationality for our purposes as simply the efficient matching of means and ends without recourse to any questions of ethics or morality). Using as an illustration the case just given of the trusting Spanish innkeeper, it would have been quite simple to have stated a higher than actual rate of exchange and thus to have acquired a meal through fraud. Similar situations abound in modern societies. One modern case is a book written by Abbie Hoffman, *Steal This Book*, in which he suggests that

at take-out stands (like McDonald's, White Tower, and Chicken Delight), tell the counterman that you or your brother just picked up an order of fifteen hamburgers (or a bucket of chicken) and got shorted. We have never heard of anyone getting turned down using this method.[6]

Fortunately, few people take Hoffman's advice, for reasons that will become clear by the end of Chapter 5 on socialization. But for the present we can make the following general statement: If every individual in a group or if groups of individuals operated solely on the basis of his or her or their immediate self-interest, society would be impossible; and by society we mean a group of persons living out a particular culture (as opposed to Hoffman's "Counterculture"). In the long run, society *is* a rational enterprise —one that provides benefits for us all (even though this may not be readily apparent to some). In the short run, individuals will find it advantageous to break the rules that make long-range cooperation and, thus, society possible. Yet societies persist and most of us, most of the time, conform to the rules set up by the social order. Hobbes's answer to this paradox was that men conform because they fear the state.

But Durkheim—not to mention sociologists following him in time—could not accept Hobbes's glib and unsatisfactory answer. A moment's consideration should allow us to see why this is so—in most human situations the possibility and probability of official intervention is exceedingly remote. Thus, something other than "fear of the state" causes men to conform.

Durkheim provided two answers (or really two versions of the same answer) to the paradox raised by Hobbes. Durkheim's answers focused on forces much more pervasive and more powerful than the force of any political sovereign. Durkheim called these forces *solidarity*. He proposed two different types—mechanical and organic—to account for the general conformity to most rules on the part of the vast majority of the members of societies.

First Solution: Mechanical solidarity   Durkheim proposed that each society is held together by one of two kinds of social solidarity, depending on the society's social organization. "Simple" or "primitive" (terms which are definitely out of favor with modern sociologists) societies are held together by what Durkheim termed *mechanical solidarity*, or the solidarity of sameness. In societies characterized by mechanical solidarity, people all have pretty much the same experiences as a consequence of only a very rudimentary division of labor. Out of this sameness develops a force, which Durkheim termed the *collective conscience*, "the totality of beliefs and sentiments common to average citizens of the same society." [7] Durkheim regarded this collective conscience as a kind of impersonal force that operated independently of the wills of a society's members. The collective conscience kept primitive societies together by prescribing nearly all of the details of everyday actions. This was appropriate because in the absence of forces making for social change, behavior that is appropriate for older generations usually remains appropriate for following generations.

At this point Durkheim's sociological realism can create problems for the introductory student. People do not ordinarily think of customary ways of thinking and feeling as having an existence apart from individuals. It helps to understand Durkheim's point if it is recognized that systems of beliefs and values do exist prior to the existence of any particular person. Cultural systems do impose themselves on people. For example, very few strict Catholics are raised in the homes of Orthodox Jews and vice versa.

How did this, the collective conscience, solve the problem of order that Hobbes raised? It did so by prescribing the details of correct social practices in such a way that nothing was left for the individual's rational choice. Thus, Hobbes's paradox, that a society of rational men seemed impossible under conditions where all members act in accordance with their own self-interests, was eliminated by definition. Primitive men were not rational (in Hobbes's sense) decision makers; their behavior was so circumscribed by the force of the collective conscience that they could not even think of the individual advantages to be gained by the violation of the traditional order.

Organic solidarity Durkheim's solution to the problem of order for advanced societies with a more complex division of labor is not as neat as his solution for primitive societies. He proposed that such societies are held together by *organic solidarity*, or the solidarity of difference, a view quite similar to that of Spencer. Durkheim developed this notion through analogy to biological organisms.

This solidarity resembles that which we observe among the higher animals. Each organ, in effect, has its special physiognomy, its autonomy . . . Because of this analogy, we propose to call the solidarity, which is due to the division of labor, organic.[8]

Durkheim is referring to the fact that in more complex societies separation of societal "functions" creates relations of complex interdependence between the parts of society. In small, preliterate societies, all the functions of pro-creation, education, and production might be carried out by one social unit, the family. In modern societies specialization creates separate institutions to take care of many of these functions, for example, the church, the school, and the economy. Durkheim believed that such specialization created a new kind of solidarity based on the reciprocal needs of each part of society for the other parts. Out of this need, and in a way that Durkheim's treatment leaves unclear, there grows up a general body of rules that governs the kinds of relations the individual parts of society can enter into. This general body of rules serves the same function as the collective conscience in primitive societies—it solves the problem of order by sanctioning and prescribing some actions, but it does so in a different way. While the collective conscience prescribed the details of social relations in small, preliterate societies, the new body of rules is much more general in content. These rules are more like abstract ethical principles concerning justice, equity, and fairness. Durkheim believed that such principles solve the problem of order by making sure that the relations people can enter into are in the interest of society.

Second Solution Durkheim's second solution to the problem of order somewhat modified his original thesis that the social order emerged out of social constraint *apart from the wills of the members of society*. In his last book, *The Elementary Forms of Religious Life*, Durkheim proposed that social constraint operated by becoming a part of the personalities of society's members. People behave in accord with society's needs because they learn to desire conformity to those moral principles that symbolize those needs. Society's morality is "internalized," and society constrains, not from without, but from within.

Empirical Methodology

Durkheim was hopeful that sociology would make a contribution to the social problems of his day. He recognized that the recommendations of sociologists would have much greater weight if they had the force of science. For that reason Durkheim was very anxious to divorce sociology from social philosophy. He tried to develop an empirical methodology that, if followed, would guarantee that sociologists' recommendations concerning the health of the social order would have the same force as the physician's recommendations about biological health. While most sociologists have abandoned his search for a scientific morality, his methodology is still of interest.

Durkheim's methodological recommendations were published in his *Rules of the Sociological Method*, which had as its basis his principal prescription "to consider social facts as things." This statement expresses his sociological realism. Social facts, he argued, are as real as physical ones. They were, he said, *external* to the individual, and they "constrained" him. It is as if a person were born into two worlds, the physical and the social. The *physical world* consists of such objects as rocks, hot stoves, automobiles, streets, and so on. The *social world* consists of social objects, such as policemen, teachers, and even a particular property system. Durkheim's fundamental insight was that man behaves toward the second world much as he does toward the first. The social world "constrains" an individual as much as a hot stove, which forces him to retract his hand on contact. Acceptance of the social world is not a matter of individual whimsy any more than is acceptance of the physical world. Social life teaches that police authority and the rules governing a property system are inherent in the nature of things. In philosophical discussions we might recognize that things could be otherwise, but for the everyday actor this is simply not a possibility. The properly socialized citizen stops for the policeman's whistle as surely as if a huge rock had dropped in his path, and just as automatically.

Durkheim felt that his insistence on the reality of social facts was fundamental to transforming sociology into a science. If the objects of the sociologist's study—social facts—were real, outside of, and independent of the individual actor's will, it followed that the way to study social life was to look outside the individual for the sources of his behavior and not inside him. Durkheim added his own suggestions based on his positivistic view of the world. If you want to study the heavens you look through a telescope, you do not attend a roundtable philosophical discussion. If you want to look at social facts that constrain social life, you must abandon philosophical debate and look for real evidence of that constraint.

Since social facts are of a different order than physical facts, a special method is required. One cannot directly observe social facts, but their presence is clearly shown by *objective indicators*. An "indicator" is an *objective, observable measure of a variable not directly observable*. Thus, when Durkheim was studying the two types of social solidarity, he chose two types of law as *indicators* of the state of the moral order which held society together. Societies with mechanical solidarity were characterized by *repressive law*. Offenses against this type of law were dealt with as moral outrages and punished severely in accord with the degree of their offense to the collective conscience. Societies with organic solidarity were characterized by *restitutive law*, which did not require punishment for violation. Instead, only restoration of the principles of justice formulated in the law was demanded. Durkheim's methodological recommendations have had a lasting effect on most Western sociologists.

While much of Durkheim's work remains of importance, it is, perhaps, his concept and definition of "social facts" which has the most meaning for those beginning their study of sociology. In contemporary terms, much of what we do, our day-to-day behavior, is evidence of the existence of social facts, although these "facts" cannot be perceived directly. Most people in American society eat three meals a day at fairly regular intervals, but this is by no means the norm in other societies. Attempts to change our eating habits are usually strongly resisted despite the fact that there is no good physiological reason why one cannot just as well eat five meals a day. The majority of people in this and other modern societies arrive on time for work or other engagements even though no one is forced to do so. Only a very small proportion of the population ever commit a burglary, even though police are seen only infrequently in most residential areas. Incest—sexual relations between close blood relatives—is extremely uncommon in American society even though, for purely sexual purposes, blood relationship makes no difference. The important thing to note is that people do or do not do a wide variety of things *because they supervise themselves*. Their society has gotten inside them; they have *internalized* its values and norms and do more or less naturally what other people expect of them. But the process by which this comes about is far from natural in any genetic sense. Through an essentially continuous process of *socialization*, individuals learn what others expect of them and, in time, come to expect the same of themselves. It is those expectations and the fact that people tend to obey them that constitutes what Durkheim meant when he defined "social facts." In passing, it might be noted that what the society expects of an individual is not simply defined by the elders in that society but also, and to a much greater extent, by people who have been long dead.

KARL MARX

Karl Marx (1818–1883)[9] was born in the German town of Trier. He studied law and philosophy at various universities in Germany. In 1843, he immigrated to Paris and began an intensive study of economics which led the young Marx to a meeting with Friedrich Engels, who became his lifelong friend and collaborator. During the Paris years, Marx became a socialist revolutionary. Expelled from Paris in 1845 for his activities, he migrated to a number of European cities; then in 1849, he moved to London, where he lived until his death. During his life, he produced a great number of philosophical, economic, political, and sociological works including *The Economic and Philosophical Manuscripts* (written in 1844 but first published after Marx's death), *The Communist Manifesto* (1848), and *Das Kapital* (1867).

Karl Marx was an exceedingly complex thinker. There was Marx the economist, Marx the political scientist, Marx the historian, Marx the propagandist, and Marx the social philosopher and sociologist. Because his thought forms the basis of communist ideology, introductory treatments of Marx's work by Western sociologists often devote considerable attention to demonstrating the flaws in his system. That is in contrast to the treatment of Durkheim, Weber, and other "greats" of sociology, where the usual emphasis is on the positive contributions of each thinker. The emphasis on error in Marxian ideas is understandable (too much praise is often criticized as indoctrination), and we will try to avoid it. Aside from that, our interest is real because Marx posed some distinctly sociological questions that have remained at the center of sociological debate. This is so much the case that one sociologist has been prompted to characterize all late nineteenth-century and early twentieth-century sociological thinking as a "debate with Marx's ghost."

Economics

At the core of Marx's thought is the notion that the economic institutions of a society are basic; that the ways in which society produces and distributes economic goods determines the form and content of the rest of the institutional order; that the political, religious, educational, and artistic life of society is determined by the economic order; and, finally, that even the ideas that man holds are frequently merely expressions of economic interest.

The Marxian thesis rests on the fundamental axiom that economic power, or control over the means of production, is easily translated into power in other institutional orders—in political, educational, and even religious areas. We will attempt to illustrate Marx's point with reference to modern capitalist societies, the type of society in which he was most interested. For Marx, the rich and economically powerful, the capitalists, quite naturally believe that their wealth and power derive from their virtues. This group uses their economic power to gain ascendancy in the political, educational, and often religious areas. Schools teach that wealth is the reward that society provides to those who make important contributions to the good of all. Religious teaching reinforces this view and holds out the promise of compensation for injustice in an afterlife, or, in the words of an old Marxist song, "there will be pie in the sky by-and-by." Thus, the rest of institutionalized social life becomes organized as a kind of service sector for the capitalist class. The primary goal of this service sector is to assure continued and growing profits to the economically powerful. Since this group's primary concern is with profits, and not with religious, educational, or political questions, except as they affect possibilities for profit, the economic elite allows some independence to the other institutional sectors, to political, educational, and religious elites, for instance. Nevertheless, whenever this freedom threatens the system that generates the capitalists' profits, they intervene. Short of revolution, they always win.

Role of Ideas in History

Consistent with those ideas, Marx was a *historical materialist*: he denied that ideas have an independent effect on the course of history. One could not, according to Marx, understand history as the gradual unfolding of human consciousness as Comte had done. On the contrary, Marx viewed ideas as expressions of the material (economic) interests of actual social groupings. In this way, he read the whole of classical economic theory, with its defense of laissez faire (the doctrine that the state should not interfere in business) as an expression of the selfish interests of the capitalist class. It was his contention that the "ruling ideas" of any historical period were the ideas of the ruling class. By this he meant that the *core* values of any culture always served to support the interests of the economically privileged and powerful.

Forces Determining History

In Marx's view, the dynamic of history was a tension between what he termed *the forces of production* and *the relations of production*. The forces of production included natural resources, capital equipment, science and technology, the skills of workmen, and the division of labor. The relations of production referred to the distribution of economic power or, in the case of capitalist societies, to private property.

In Marx's view the actual "engine" of social changes was class conflict. He believed that the relations of production created groups with competing interests. In capitalist societies, for instance, the relations of production create two opposed groups, the workers, or *proletariat*, and the owners of the means of production, or the capitalists. As the forces of production develop, capitalist relations of production create more and more problems. The capitalist's desire for greater profits causes him to pay his workers wages barely sufficient to sustain life. In spite of increased productivity, the proletariat slips further and further into poverty.

Central to Marx's argument is the idea that the interests of the workers and capitalists are *objectively* opposed. The enlightened capitalist cannot decide to pay his workers more; to do so would mean that he would be forced out of business by unscrupulous competitors. But, there is no room for villains or heroes in Marx's analysis. The members of groups with objectively opposed economic interests are destined to play out the battle that is the dynamic of history. And, in Marx's view, the outcome is never in doubt. The inner logic of capitalism creates a larger and larger pool of impoverished workers and a smaller and smaller group of extremely wealthy capitalists. At some point along the way, increasing misery makes the workers aware of their plight; they are no longer fooled by the ideology of the ruling capitalist class. At that point they organize to overthrow their enslavers. The capitalists cannot win this battle, for in destroying the old independent groups of craftsmen and professionals, they have isolated themselves from potential support from other groups. After overthrowing the capitalists, the proletariat will organize themselves politically and use the State to wipe out the last vestiges of the class system. This period of the "dictatorship of the proletariat" will be short lived, for it will usher in the classless society in which the State will wither away for lack of any necessary functions.

Contribution to the Sociological Perspective

A good deal of Marx's thought has been negated by events. Workers in Western capitalist societies have not become increasingly impoverished. Class warfare does not appear to dominate the political arena. What then remains of Marx? What is left for the serious sociologist is a whole set of interesting questions and hypotheses. Presented as questions and hypotheses, many of Marx's core principles still serve to inform the sociological perspective. The three hypotheses that follow are an attempt to illustrate the continuing interest in a Marxian mode of analysis.

1. The economic base of society determines the form and content of the rest of the society's institutional order.

Certainly the economically powerful do attempt to translate their power into control in other institutional areas. In the flurry of campus activism during the 1960's, college presidents frequently found themselves under fire from those in control of the purse strings. Student activists were quick to note that college boards of regents and trustees were nearly always dominated by men who owed their allegiance to the business community. In spite of that, the assertion that the interests of the economic elite will always win out (short of revolution, that is) must be dealt with as a hypothesis. In reality this assertion rests on the unproven assumption that the only *real* power is economic. Perhaps a more realistic assumption is that there are many independent bases of power; some derived from the economic, some from the political, some from the military, and some from other institutional orders. There is no reason to suppose that any one need predominate. The question of whose interests win out becomes one for research. There is reason to expect the resolution of economic and other social problems to vary from society to society and from time to time. (That, incidentally, is the approach of Mills's attempt to analyze the structure of power in America in *The Power Elite.*)

2. Material interests determine the content of men's consciousness.

Marx's insight about the relationship between interest and belief is really fundamental. He is pointing to the fact that our beliefs often accord with our economic interests. In his central insight that economic interests often determine beliefs, Marx has been widely confirmed. But, in his belief that the basic wants of man are always economic, he makes an unwarranted assumption. Nevertheless, Marx's insights opened up the whole area that is now called the "sociology of knowledge." Sociologists working in this field are concerned with the relations between social conditions and intellectual trends within particular societies. For instance, they are concerned with such questions as what types of social conditions favor the development of science. In accord with Marx's insight, it seems that scientific progress requires the support of real groups with "objective" (but not merely economic) interests in scientific knowledge.

3. The dynamic of historical change is the tension between the forces and the relations of production which finds its concrete expression in class conflict.

There are two points of importance in the third hypothesis. First, it does appear that social change often begins in the area Marx termed the forces of production. Frequently, the introduction of some technical innovation works itself out through the rest of the social system, as with the manifold consequences of the introduction of the automobile in the American social system. Second, such changes have sometimes worsened class conflict, but sometimes they have moderated them. There are occasions when class conflict does seem to dominate the political arena, but people just as often divide over other issues. Again, Marx's assumption that the *only* real interests are economic is in error. There are other societal rewards for which men choose to compete. As will be discussed in more detail in Chapter 6 on stratification, sociologists now believe that the distribution of purely economic rewards is only one of several dimensions of social stratification. Other dimensions include the distribution of social status and of power. This complicates Marx's analysis because it blurs the lines of conflict. But it helps to explain the fact that poor white southerners have never formed a viable political alliance with their "objective" allies, the poor Blacks. There are other things to fight over —social status being one of them. In other words, without the poor Blacks, the poor white southerners would be at the very bottom of the socioeconomic hierarchy.

In brief, Marx's *economic determinism*—his argument that everything is determined by economics—while useful for analytical and polemical purposes, is not satisfactory if the purpose is either the analysis of the tensions and strains in society or the prediction of the ultimate outcome of social conflict. There is, it must be noted, an engaging simplicity in Marxian dogma which had and still has great appeal for some. It must be remembered, however, that the ultimate test of any theory, or model, is its ability to predict. Marxian theory, and it is not "theory" in the technical meaning of that word, fails almost completely to meet the empirical test.

MAX WEBER

Max Weber (1864–1920)[10] was born in Erfurt, Germany. He was trained in economics and law at the University of Heidelberg and later at the University of Berlin. Weber held several academic posts, but his health prevented him from a normal academic career. During most of his productive years he was a private scholar unable to stand the strain of academic life. His major works include *The Protestant Ethic and the Spirit of Capitalism* (1905), *The Methodology of the Social Sciences* (essays published at various times and translated into English in 1949), and an unfinished work, *Economics and Society* (published posthumously in 1922).

Weber was very much influenced by Marx but certainly not in a manner that would have delighted Marx. Weber took as his primary task the demonstration that Marxism was quite one-sided and that "ideas" had a rightful and necessary place in societal analysis.

Weber's work was characterized by early interpreters as largely an ongoing debate with Marx. Indeed, much of Weber's work strives to demonstrate the independent significance of ideas, particularly religious ideas, in the development of history. But Weber's thought is more complex than his early commentators recognized. His primary concern was not merely to refute Marx but also to build upon Marx's work by introducing new variables. Actually, there is as much agreement as disagreement in their descriptions of society. Weber, however, did agree with Marx about the struggle between workers and capitalists. Weber viewed the prospect of socialism with alarm. In his view, if capitalism was bad, socialism, by further extending the principles of the capitalist order (this point will become clear after we have discussed Weber's ideas on bureaucracy), would be worse. In this section we will discuss Weber's work in three principal areas: (1) the role of ideas in history, (2) rationality and bureaucracy, and (3) the methodology of the "ideal type."

Role of Ideas in History

Weber believed that ideas had an independent effect on the development of history. He recognized that ideas were conditioned by both material interests (from Marx) and what Weber called "ideal" interests. In introducing that category, Weber was recognizing what we have already pointed out with reference to Marx: people are "interested" in many things and not all of their interests can be explained in terms of a person's objective economic interests. Thus, Weber argued that an interest in religious salvation could be as real, as pressing, and as important as any economic interest.

Protestant Ethic and Spirit of Capitalism   Weber's starting point in that debate was his controversial and powerful book *The Protestant Ethic and the Spirit of Capitalism*. Weber argued that the rise of Protestantism, particularly in its Calvinist variety, was one of several independent variables which contributed to the rise of capitalism in Western Europe. An outline of his argument follows.

First, Weber attempted to show a psychological similarity between Calvinist religious doctrine and what he termed the "spirit of capitalism." This "spirit" was a set of attitudes, which he believed to be essential to Western capitalism:

1. A pursuit of money as an end in itself, rather than as a necessary evil or a means to other more important ends.

2. A pursuit of money without limit. Weber opposed this attitude to one he believed was much more common, namely, "traditionalism," or the pursuit of money to a level where it can support some traditionally defined standard of living.

3. An "ends justify the means" attitude toward the methods of acquiring money. That is, the capitalist spirit is not fettered by traditional ways.

4. Bound up with the third characteristic is the capitalist's individualistic tendency. In his dealings with others, the capitalist is not bound by traditional

obligations such as the *noblesse oblige* of the feudal lord (the obligations of high social rank that ideally included such behavior as humane treatment of social inferiors, bravery, and so on). If more profits can be had by introducing a mechanized process that does away with the usefulness of a group of craftsmen, that is a problem for the craftsmen, not the capitalist. For the capitalist, the breaking of traditional obligations results in an individualistic philosophy of every man for himself.

5. A sense of what Weber named a "calling" about one's work. The capitalist does not regard work as a necessary evil; rather, work is considered as a moral obligation.

6. The pursuit of gain in a rational disciplined manner. The pirate and the capitalist both pursue gain, but the capitalist does so every day in an organized way without the "speculative" spirit of the pirate.

The central beliefs of Calvinism, on the other hand, may be outlined as follows:

1. The ways of God transcend finite human understanding.

2. God's decisions, though incomprehensible, are made for all time. For reasons of his own, God has already decided the fate of each and every human soul. Some souls are already fated to be among the saved and some among the damned.

3. No behavior of the person during his time on earth can have any effect on God's decision in this matter.

4. In spite of this, God created the world for his own glory; and every person, whether among the saved or among the damned, is obliged to carry out God's will as revealed in the scriptures in order to further that glory.

5. The pleasures of the flesh and of this earth are to be shunned as wicked. Service, to be in accord with God's will, demands an active mastery of the things of the flesh and the world; the Calvinist *must* make the world over in accord with God's will.

After outlining the basics of the Calvinist and capitalist systems of thought, Weber argued that there is a special affinity between them:

1. Since service to God is conceived of in terms of control over the things of the flesh and the world, Calvinism is consistent with that aspect of the spirit of capitalism which calls for active mastery of the world. Even though the capitalist is concerned with mastery in the service of profit and the Calvinist with mastery in the service of God's will, both systems are similar in that they reject the contemplative, or passive, life in favor of the active life.

2. Since God's decisions stand for all time, there is a natural order of the universe governed by those laws set into motion by God's original decisions. The belief in this natural order is consistent with the capitalist drive to manipulate the world rationally rather than through magic and ritual. Though God's world cannot be manipulated through ritual supplications, his lawful order (but not his *reasons* for creating it) can be understood and manipulated

through the application of reason and ultimately through science and technology.

3. Calvinism, like capitalism, is individualistic. The notion that one cannot know whether one's friends are among the saved or damned creates a profound separation of each man from his fellow man. Weber felt this belief made the faithful wary of any close personal relations in this world because anyone, even one's closest relatives, might be among those fated for eternal damnation.

4. Weber theorized that the lack of certainty about whether one belonged to the chosen or to the damned created a strong need to know one's fate. This gradually led to the acceptance of the view that there were outward signs of God's grace. What were these signs? Principally, devotion and success in one's calling was a sign of grace; thus, eventually, monetary success came to be taken as a sign of God's grace.

5. Finally, Weber argued that the prohibitions against taking pleasure in the world forced the Calvinist to save and reinvest his earnings rather than to spend them on the pleasures of the world. This, of course, is consistent with the capitalists' drive to accumulate money and capital for its own sake rather than as a means to some other goal.

In concluding his argument, Weber attempted some sketchy empirical demonstrations of the association between Puritan beliefs and the growth of capitalism. His principle evidence was that capitalism began in countries of Protestant rather than Catholic predominance. In his later life he devoted considerable attention to the comparative study of religion in order to marshal greater empirical evidence for his thesis, but a consideration of these extensive studies is beyond the scope of this introductory treatment.

Direction of History

Rationality   While he viewed with suspicion the kind of historical prophecy that Marx had engaged in, Weber did believe that he had discovered a kind of general tendency which accounted for the drift of Western civilization. In his later work, the growth of the Protestant Ethic and rational capitalistic enterprise were treated as merely one aspect of the general process that he called *rationality*. Rationality referred to a long-term historical growth of a particular kind of world view. Weber termed behavior that involved this world view *Zweckrational* action, rational action in relation to a goal. When a person engages in that kind of action, he first conceives of a concrete goal. He then selects appropriate means to reach that goal. His selection of means is not governed by tradition, emotion, or by any values other than utilitarian ones, such as efficiency. Rationality in Weber's view involves a general disenchantment or demystification of life. Before the onset of the process, daily life was filled with mysterious forces, gods, and demons. For the truly modern man this air of mystery is gone. The world exists as a thing to be molded to man's purposes. Weber believed that the Western world had experienced a progressive rationalization of different areas of life. He believed that he saw this process operating in the religious, economic, political, and military areas.

Bureaucracy Weber viewed rationality with some ambivalence. On the one hand rationality permitted the more efficient adaptation of means to ends even if such efficiency were at the expense of tradition. Applied in the economic sphere, it had resulted in an enormous increase of productive power. Nevertheless, there were other aspects of the process which alarmed Weber. Applied rationality seemed to lead to certain rigidities. In illustrating this point, Weber pointed to *bureaucracies*. Bureaucratic organization, through the simplification of procedures for handling business, resulted in an enormous increase in efficiency, that is, in the ability to accomplish tasks from small to very large. But the adaptability of a bureaucratic organization to novel situations is limited largely because of the nature of its organization and because rules and regulations are not easily altered.

Anyone who has had the experience of pleading the merits of his "special" case before a bureaucratic official can understand Weber's point. A college student whose situation requires a waiver has had such an experience at registration. Because of this, Weber opposed Marx's vision of the future. He regarded socialism as merely a further extension of the rationality and bureaucratization of economic life. As explained shortly, Weber's model of bureaucracies was of an ideal situation and, as is now known, the reality is somewhat different. For example, all bureaucracies are marked by an informal structure that functions not only to protect the interests of individual members but to "get things done" even when bureaucratic organization and regulations (if strictly adhered to) would prevent attainment of the goals. The ideal model does not work for one very simple and sociological reason: there is no way to accomplish the work of a bureaucracy without some face-to-face interaction between individual workers. Out of this interaction develops the informal structure just mentioned; it is this structure that serves to humanize and, thus, to make working in a bureaucracy tolerable. Two things might be said to be characteristic of the experienced bureaucrat. He or she knows how to utilize both the formal and informal structure in order to protect individual interests and has ways of "bending" rules and regulations in order to accomplish necessary goals. In short, bureaucracies are not quite the soulless, impersonal, highly efficient organizations that they are imagined to be by those without experience in them.

Ideal Type

Weber believed that there is a fundamental difference between the natural and social sciences. He did not believe, as Durkheim did, that the social sciences could merely adopt the methods used by the natural sciences. The source of this difference lay in the concept that *we can understand the behavior of others in a sense in which we cannot understand the behavior of physical objects.* We *understand*, for instance, why a man takes his coat off when it gets hot. This type of understanding cannot apply to the behavior of one billiard ball when struck by another. We can describe the ball's behavior and show that it derives from general laws, but there we must stop. We cannot *understand* the ball's behavior because it does not have *motives* to understand. Because of this difference, that is, the presence or lack of motive, the task of social science is much more complex than that of the natural sciences. Explanation in the natural sciences need only be *causally adequate*, it need only show that a particular event follows from natural laws. Explanation in the social sciences must be both causally and *meaningfully* adequate; that is, it must create an *understanding* of the *motives of action.*

In the social sciences the role of general laws is replaced by what Weber termed *ideal types.* We are already familiar with three of Weber's ideal types: (1) the ideal type of Calvinism, (2) the ideal type of the spirit of capitalism, and (3) the ideal type of Zweckrational action. For Weber the ideal type is a one-sided exaggeration of certain features of social life. It is not a hypothesis, an average, or a complete description of reality. By exaggerating some features of social life, the ideal type helps us to understand the behavior of certain groups of people. Weber did not believe that such exaggeration meant the creation of abstractions without any correspondence to reality. Real Calvinists were *something* like Weber's ideal type. Indeed, even if they were only a little like it, the ideal type might help to explain the rise of capitalism. After the publication of *The Protestant Ethic*, Weber tried to show that the ideal type not only made sense but was also causally, that is, scientifically, adequate.

Contribution to the Sociological Perspective

Weber is considered by many to be *the* sociologist of the classical period. As a consequence, Weber has had lasting influences in many more ways than can be categorized here. But among those influences which have been most significant are: (1) a greater appreciation among sociologists of the complex connections between "ideal" and "real" (or economic) interests and the dynamics of history; (2) a lasting interest in bureaucratic organization and the process of bureaucratization; and (3) a clarification of the issues and difficulties confronting those who would seek to "understand" the meaning of social life.

We have dealt with some of the problems that were central to the thought of the nineteenth- and early twentieth-century sociologists. At this point it seems appropriate to consider some of the issues which hold the sociological center stage today. It would be difficult to pick a problem or issue that is really new. Recent meetings of the American Sociological Association have seen splits between those who have argued that social science should be "value free" and those, the "radicals," who believe that social science should be political to the core. The first group are direct descendants of Weber and the second, of Marx. There has also been a debate between those who would like to "reduce" sociological explanations to psychological ones and those who take Durkheim's sociological realist position. But perhaps the most fundamental debates have been between those who have been labeled *structural functional theorists* and those who call themselves *conflict theorists*. In the brief treatment that follows, we will outline the major issues that divide the two approaches and then attempt to illustrate the conflicting views by showing how theorists from each of the two groups approach one concrete sociological problem, that of *social stratification*.

Structural-Functional and Conflict Theorists

Social Integration   A key notion in the functionalist picture of society is denoted by the term *social system*. This school had as its model a conception of society similar to that of a biological organism. All the organs of the human body function together to keep the body alive. Functional theorists have argued that the "parts" (organs) of society form a complex integrated whole, or social system. The parts (that is, the institutions) of society somehow fit together, each part making some contribution to the maintenance of the social order. To take a modern example, the rapid growth of health and life insurance in industrialized countries *fits*, or makes sense, when one considers how different the role of the modern family is in providing for illness and death from the family of, say, a century ago. Then families were considerably larger, often with members of three generations living under one roof. When a member of a household became ill, there was always someone available to care for them. The difficulty of maintaining the ties of such *extended family relations* in the highly mobile, highly urbanized societies of the industrial West is directly related to the rise of the health and life insurance industry.

Coupled with the concept of the integration of parts is the implication that the social system tends to maintain some sort of *equilibrium*. Suppose some "part" fails to fulfill its function, that is, puts a *strain* on the system. Imagine, for example, that the formal school system is unable to adequately prepare and motivate the nation's youth for the kinds of careers that the economic system can provide. The social system (made up in this case of businessmen, personnel managers, and the students themselves) senses this inability to meet a necessary social function and moves to repair the damage. Businesses might set up their own training schools, as they actually do, to meet some deficiencies in public education. Pressure might be put on the government to provide some alternative to traditional education. Thus, the equilibrium principle operates so as to insure that such "strains" get taken care of and all the necessary functions (needs) of the social system are met.

Conflict theorists, on the other hand, believe that the case for societal integration and equilibrium is greatly overstated. In actual fact, they argue, society does not run smoothly. As often as not, the parts do not fit smoothly, and they have to be forced into place and held there by power. Conflict theorists see *people* and *interest groups* as the "parts" of the social system, not institutions. According to them, conflict is an ever-present aspect of social life, and the appearance of order is often only a temporary lull in the battle. The general orientation of those concerned with social conflict will be discussed in Chapter 13.

Social Needs versus Group Interests   The term "functionalism" derives from the idea that each part of the social system serves some function (as opposed to "purpose") in relation to the needs of the whole. The concept can be illustrated with a biological analogy. Biological systems, like the human body, have needs, for food, water, and rest, for instance. Such needs are recognized because when they are not met, the biological system breaks down. Ultimately the organism dies. In a similar way, failure to satisfy the needs of a social system is held to result in breakdown of the social system, although it is never clear when a social system dies. The belief that social systems have needs of their own has given rise to a search for a set of "minimum functional requisites," or requirements, for maintaining the social order. Within that framework functional theorists have analyzed the contribution that each part makes to the needs of the whole social order.

Conflict theorists have opposed that tendency and have focused on the interests of concrete groups. For the conflict theorist, things are as they are because of real group interests, not because of the abstract needs of society.

Value Consensus versus Value Conflict   Structural-functional theorists tend to stress the role of consensus through agreement on basic values as a key factor in the maintenance of the social order. This emphasis may be traced directly to Durkheim. Conflict theorists, on the other hand, argue that the vague consensus on general values actually conceals real conflicts of interest in concrete situations. Where the functionalists point to the role of value consensus in maintaining the social order, the conflict theorists emphasize the role of coercion in maintaining whatever order exists. For the conflict theorists, the social order is not held together because people agree; it is held together because some groups have more power or authority and are able to enforce their idea of the necessary order over those groups who might disagree.

Social Stability versus Social Change   Historically, the functionalists have been concerned with the problem of order. This has led to an emphasis on those social processes that maintain stability as opposed to those that lead to social change. Conflict theorists have emphasized the opposite. Furthermore, the conceptualization of the process of change has been different among adherents of the two views. Functionalists have spoken of gradual evolutionary change through such processes as "functional differentiation," which refers to the gradual division of necessary social functions among greater numbers of more specialized social units. Conflict theorists have emphasized sudden changes growing out of severe social conflict.

Liberal versus Radical   To a considerable extent, the differences between functional and conflict theorists are paralleled by differences in political orientation. Functionalists have tended to identify with political liberalism. Indeed, their emphasis on gradual evolutionary change seems congenial to the reformist approach of the liberal political movement. Conflict theorists, on the other hand, have been more likely to be radicals. Indeed, it is probably fair to say that most radical sociologists side with the conflict theorists, though by current standards two of the most prominent conflict theorists, Louis Coser and Ralph Dahrendorf, are anything but radicals.

Two Approaches to Social Stratification

The differences between the two approaches may be illustrated with reference to the work of modern theorists of social stratification working in each of the two traditions. *Social stratification* is the study of how society distributes rewards, such as money, power, and prestige, to different social groups. In our discussion of social stratification, we will consider the work of Talcott Parsons, a functional theorist concerned with the role of values in producing social integration, and Ralf Dahrendorf,[11] a conflict theorist who applies himself to the analysis of strain and tension produced by the authority structure of societies.

Functional Necessity   In his treatment of social stratification, Parsons stresses the notion that unequal distribution of rewards is *necessary* to social life. Some people receive more power, money, or prestige because it is necessary to provide greater rewards so that people will be motivated to work harder and make the sacrifices necessary to fulfill difficult and valued social roles. This would be the case with regard to doctors and statesmen, for instance. Then, too, it is often the case that the very nature of some roles requires that some people have more power than others. One could not expect doctors and patients to have the same power and authority in making diagnoses. In Parsons' view, differences in power, money, and prestige are necessary to get important jobs done. Society could not operate without such hierarchies.

Dahrendorf does not deny that hierarchies are necessary as society is presently organized. Instead he focuses on different aspects of the problem. While Parsons is concerned to show that stratification meets certain *societal needs*, Dahrendorf chooses to emphasize that since some groups get more than others, the members of those groups are better able to satisfy their *personal needs*. Dahrendorf is primarily interested in the distribution of authority in certain social organizations. He stresses that those who have authority can use it to meet their personal needs, not society's. Consequently, authority relations result in basic conflicts between those who have authority and want to keep it (for example, teachers in school systems), and those who do not but would like to have it (students). Those basic differences result in the formation of a network of conflict groups cutting through all those social organizations in which authority relations exist.

While admitting that social hierarchy may lead to social conflict, Parsons, as a functional theorist, calls attention to processes that allow social conflict to be moderated and social stratification to become a salient characteristic of a social system. Two mechanisms are of primary importance.

1. *Pluralism*, by which Parsons means that there are a variety of hierarchical principles operating in the modern society. A person has status because of the status of his parents, his ethnic identification, his numerous personal accomplishments, or his cultural and occupational skills. This variety of *hierarchical* principles means that any particular individual is subjected to a number of *cross pressures* when he tries to choose sides in any particular conflict. For example, a particular person may be a student and thus opposed to his teachers on the grounds of differences in authority. This same student may be from a wealthy family and thus have a stake in the system that those in authority represent. Additionally, he may be Black, knowledgeable about the fine arts, an expert on roller derbies, and so on. The point is that such cross pressures greatly moderate the potential for serious societal conflict. In fact, most individuals often do not know which side to choose in a social conflict. Consequently, many do not take action in any political conflict, remaining part of the "silent majority."

Dahrendorf does not deny the possibility of pluralism. In fact, his analysis attempts to provide an empirical measure of whatever pluralism exists in a society. But Dahrendorf's analysis does tend to stress other aspects of social stratification which make for greater possibilities for conflict. First, by concentrating on one aspect of social stratification, *authority relations*, Dahrendorf manages to ignore many of the pluralistic influences indicated by Parsons. Conflict theorists have always tended to simplify stratification analysis; functional theorists have tended to complicate it. Marx, the prototypical conflict theorist, dealt only with one dimension of stratification—*property relations*. In capitalist societies, one was either an owner or a worker. Dahrendorf's analysis retains much of the simplicity of Marx's original theory. Dahrendorf does not deny the reality of other bases for stratification, but his emphasis suggests that authority relations are of prime importance. Second, Dahrendorf's analysis is based on the principle that authority is not shared. One either has it or one does not. This clearly goes against Parsons' pluralistic emphasis.

2. *Social stratification becomes institutionalized into the social system.* Parsons contends that people come to accept inequality as normal, customary, and, more importantly, just and right. In some societies this is achieved by a value system that justifies hereditary privilege. Thus, in India, the rewards of the higher castes are presumed to be compensation for a ritually pure life in earlier incarnations. In American society inequalities are justified as rewards for greater effort and ability.

Dahrendorf recognizes the role of institutionalization but retains some of the earlier Marxian emphasis, which tends to see the self-serving (for members of elite groups) character of those values which institutionalize inequality.

Dahrendorf deals with change as it derives out of social conflict. For this reason, Dahrendorf deals with such variables as the "intensity" and "violence" of social conflict.

CONCLUSION

In this chapter we have spoken of the growth, or development, of the sociological perspective; in discussing the relations between the work of Marx and Weber, we illustrated the point that the perspective developed "dialectically," or through debate. A similar point could be made today with regard to the work of Dahrendorf and Parsons. What may not be clear is that no definitive treatment of the "perspective" is possible within the scope of an introductory text. But even if we could consider all the core sociological problems, some of the discussion would become obsolete as current sociological debate proceeds. Mindful of these difficulties, we have attempted to illustrate the perspective in this chapter by discussing some of those core problems which have been of continuing interest. The student should be aware that it is toward such big problems as "the problem of order" that much sociological thinking, research, and theorizing is directed.

Sociology and the body of knowledge that constitutes sociology is more than just the work and thinking of a few men such as Durkheim, Weber, or Marx. Particularly since World War II, many sociologists have performed research, argued conclusions, replicated each other's efforts, and in general made massive contributions to the body of sociological knowledge. Out of those few decades of progress have arisen some general orientations that constitute the modern sociological perspective. But it is not sociology alone that has progressed. The other social sciences too have been adding to their particular stores of knowledge, and there is increasing collaboration between all the social sciences to the benefit of each.

In Chapter 2, some attention will be given to the other social sciences so that the reader may not only appreciate the close relationship between the various sciences but also perceive the important differences. The discussion of the various social sciences will be followed by some of the general orientations which run through all of modern sociology and should further assist the reader in more fully understanding what *is* meant by the sociological perspective. All the social sciences contrast to some extent on the basis of the perspective peculiar to each. It is only through knowing these contrasts that the weakness, strengths, and limitations of the various social science perspectives—including the sociological—can be appreciated.

REVIEW QUESTIONS

1.1. In Marx's view, what is the relation between ideas and the course of history?

1.2. How does Weber differ from Marx in his analysis of the role of ideas in history?

1.3. How does Weber support his case for broadening the Marxian view of history?

1.4. Weber believed that he had discovered a process fundamental to the development of Western civilization. What was that process and how did it operate?

1.5. What are the three fundamental differences between functional and conflict theorists? How does the work of Parsons and Dahrendorf illustrate those differences?

1.6. What is the meaning of the term "sociological realist"?

1.7. What is the "problem" in the "problem of order"?

1.8. What is the meaning of the statement "Consider social facts as things"?

NOTES

[1] C. W. Mills, ed., *Images of Man: The Classic Tradition in Sociological Thinking* (New York: Oxford University Press, 1959).

[2] In addition to original sources, this section is indebted to all the general works noted in the bibliography at the end of this chapter, especially Coser's treatment of Comte in *Masters of Sociological Thought*.

[3] Auguste Comte, "On the Three Stages of Social Evolution," in *Theories of Society*, eds. Talcott Parsons et al. (New York: Free Press, 1961), pp. 204–221.

[4] This section derives in large part from the secondary sources listed in the bibliography, especially Timasheff's discussion in *Sociological Theory*.

[5] This section relies both on original sources and on numerous secondary analyses of Durkheim's work. Especially helpful in this regard was Talcott Parsons' *The Structure of Social Action*, to be found in the bibliography to this chapter.

[6] Abbie Hoffman, *Steal This Book* (New York: Grove Press, 1971), as quoted in *Moneysworth* 1 (July 1971), p. 1. It would have provided an interesting test of Hoffman's sincerity if large numbers of people had taken his advice and stolen the book. That would, of course, have affected his royalties adversely.

[7] Emile Durkheim, *The Division of Labor in Society*, paper ed. (New York: Free Press, 1964), p. 79.

[8] Ibid., p. 131.

[9] This section is indebted to C. W. Mills' *The Marxists*, cited in the bibliography to this chapter.

[10] Again, in addition to original sources, this section relies on Parsons' *The Structure of Social Action*.

[11] This section's treatment of Dahrendorf relies on his *Class and Class Conflict in*

Industrial Society (Stanford, Calif.: Stanford University Press, 1957). The portions on Parsons rely heavily on his own summary of his position, "Equality and Inequality in Modern Society," in *Social Stratification: Research and Theory for the 1970's* (New York: Bobbs-Merrill, 1971).

ANNOTATED BIBLIOGRAPHY

Aron, Raymond. *Main Currents of Sociological Thought*. Vol. 2. New York: Doubleday, 1970. Aron discusses the work of Durkheim, Weber, and others.

Coser, Lewis. *Masters of Sociological Thought*. New York: Harcourt, Brace, Jovanovich, 1971. Coser discusses the work of eleven sociologists important in developing the sociological tradition. The book emphasizes the connections between the work and the life of the man.

Inkeles, Alex. *What is Sociology?* Englewood Cliffs, N.J.: Prentice-Hall, 1964. One of the Prentice-Hall Foundations of American Sociology series. In 117 pages Inkeles manages to provide a concise overview of the field.

Loomis, Charles. *Modern Social Theories*. Princeton, N.J.: Van Nostrand, 1961. Loomis uses his own theoretical framework to categorize and discuss the work of nine social theorists. "Modern" in the title refers to the fact that most of the theorists were still living in 1961.

Madge, John. *The Origins of Scientific Sociology*. New York: Free Press, 1962. Madge discusses the development of the sociological perspective with an emphasis on the relations between the research and the theoretical traditions.

Martindale, Don. *The Nature and Types of Sociological Theory*. Boston: Houghton Mifflin, 1960. Martindale discusses five major schools, or types, of sociological theory. The treatment is sometimes difficult, so this book would be of interest primarily to students who plan to continue in the study of sociology.

Mills, C. W., ed. *Images of Man, The Classic Tradition in Sociological Thinking*. New York: Braziller, 1960. Selections from the writings of sociologists in the "classic" tradition in sociology.

———— *The Marxists*. New York: Dell, 1962. One of the best brief treatments of Marxist sociological thought. Mills's book is of special interest to sociology students because Mills, himself a sociologist, tends to emphasize the sociological features of Marx's work.

Parsons, Talcott. *The Structure of Social Action*. New York: Free Press, 1937. One of the best secondary interpretations of the work of Durkheim and Weber. An important work for its own contribution too.

Rex, John. *Key Problems of Sociological Theory*. London: Routledge, 1961.

A good introduction to the sociological perspective through a discussion of "key problems" central to the work of the sociological "greats."

Timasheff, Nicholas. *Sociological Theory, Its Nature and Growth*. New York: Random House, 1967. A very readable discussion of all the major sociological theorists up to the mid-twentieth century.

General Orientation to Contemporary Sociology: Framework for the Study of Human Behavior

INTRODUCTION

In Chapter 1 we were introduced to some of the significant historical figures in sociology and given a brief explanation of the contributions to sociology made by these men. Not all of the ideas important to sociology in its formative stages have survived, although many have, including a good deal of the work of Durkheim and Weber. But much new work has been done since then. And from that work have come some general ways of looking at men in groups —including whole societies—which form a pattern that we call a *general orientation*. That general orientation might also be termed "the modern sociological perspective." Therefore, before introducing the specifics of sociology, we will present the sociological perspective as it is generally understood by contemporary sociologists. And we hope that the general framework provided by Chapters 1 and 2 will serve to make the specifics of sociology more meaningful and, hence, more useful.

SOCIAL SCIENTISTS AND SOCIETY

If it were possible to communicate with fish in the various waters of the world, we would probably find that none of them have any real awareness or knowledge of "water," that is, of their *environment*. Even if fish were to develop language and a science of sorts, it would probably be some time before they became aware of "water." So it was with society and humans. It is only in relatively recent years, as recorded history goes, that man has discovered his *social environment*. Over the centuries, society has been seen as a *given*, not a problem. Most people did (and many still do) accept the values, norms, and folkways of their society as being the way things are; that is, whatever one's own society teaches is *the* truth and not to be disputed or discussed, and certainly not made an object of study. There were of course some individual exceptions to this, many of whom suffered unpleasant fates. For example, Galileo (1565–1642) avoided being burned at the stake by publicly recanting his scientific findings. Galileo's investigations indicated that the earth and the other known planets revolved around the sun. This concept ran counter to the accepted belief of the time that the sun revolved around the earth, which was the center of the universe. Today, of course, it is scientifically acknowledged that the earth is *not* the center of the universe but does, in fact, orbit the sun. Since this was a direct contradiction to both secular and religious beliefs of the time, Galileo was presented with a choice—recant or die. If this seems ridiculous today, remember that as recently as the 1960's people were being arrested and jailed for disseminating birth control information.

However, some conditions have changed since Galileo's time. Astronomers

General Orientation to Contemporary Sociology: Framework for the Study of Human Behavior

People have very little
emotional involvement
with molecular structure
but they do with the
subject matter of the
social sciences—human
behavior.

Copyright © 1973 by Playboy.
Reproduced by special permission of Playboy Magazine.

as well as physicists, chemists, botanists, and other physical and natural
scientists are free to pursue their studies unhampered and publish their
findings without fear of being forced to choose between death and denial.
Social scientists, while enjoying considerable latitude with respect to their
research and publication of their findings, are much more likely to be attacked or, at least, to be regarded with considerable suspicion. The reason
for this state of affairs is not too difficult to discern. As we noted earlier, what
one's own society teaches is often regarded, even today, as *the* truth and is
not to be disputed. Unfortunately (from some people's viewpoint), social
scientists have an uncomfortable habit of coming up with findings that run
counter to the accepted beliefs of the societies in which they live and work.
Social scientists, therefore, are people who, because they are seen as attacking
the eternal verities, are regarded if not with downright dislike at least with

Social Scientists and Society

33

some reserve. For example, many people *know* that life in the "good old days" was happier and freer of tension than life in modern societies. Then too, there are the Marxists who *know* just as certainly that the only good society is a classless one. Since the findings of social scientists tend to cast considerable doubt on the validity of both those propositions, social scientists are in the position of being attacked from both the left and the right. A certain amount of public abuse is probably an occupational hazard for social scientists as it is for politicians. People have very little emotional involvement with molecular structure but they do with the subject matter of the social sciences—human behavior. In the course of research, social scientists have discovered, and will continue to discover, that many of the things which various societies teach their members are not only in serious error but are also downright dangerous —for example, the notion that man is instinctively combative and pugnacious and, therefore, wars are inevitable, or that a Black ancestor makes one inferior. A less dangerous but also quite erroneous belief is that very bright people are neurotic and tend to be unhealthy. That notion was disproven by a long-range study of gifted children begun in the 1920's by the psychologist L. M. Terman.[1] As for the idea of man having any instincts including that of pugnacity, the vast majority of social scientists doubt that *Homo sapiens* has any instincts of significance. (We will discuss the subject of instincts in some detail in subsequent chapters.)

Although this book is about sociology rather than the social sciences in general, we will attempt to distinguish between sociology and the other social sciences by turning to a brief explanation of the individual social sciences.

THE SOCIAL SCIENCES

"Social science" is a generic term that includes, at present, six separate disciplines, all of which focus in one way or another on human behavior. Three of the social sciences, "anthropology," "psychology," and "sociology," are *general behavioral sciences*; that is, they study human behavior in a wide variety of contexts. Two others, "economics" and "political science," are concerned with *human behavior in limited contexts*, as their names imply. The final one, "communication," focuses largely on the *process* of communication rather than on the human actors.

Anthropology

Of all the social sciences, anthropology, particularly cultural anthropology, is the closest to sociology. The salient difference is that, historically, anthropologists are concerned with small, preliterate societies while sociologists direct their attention to large, complex modern societies. Because the societies they deal with generally have small populations, anthropologists study societies as functioning wholes. Sociologists cannot do this because modern societies are much too large in terms of populations and because they are too complex in terms of the number of differing and competing groups and the level of technology. We do not mean that the anthropologist studies "simple" societies, for there are no such things. Preliterate societies have complex cultures. It is their size and lower level technology that make it possible to approach them as functional wholes.

The field of anthropology is divided into several specialties. Archeology attempts to reconstruct man's past through a study of the evidence he leaves behind, such as the ruins of cities, burial mounds, wall paintings in caves, and so on. Physical anthropologists are concerned with physical types: modern man, Neanderthal man, Cro-Magnon, and so forth. Ethnologists study the life-styles of existing peoples often by living among them and acting as participant-observers. These studies are generally with preliterate peoples, although some contemporary anthropologists are turning their attention to modern societies including such diverse matters as "interracial and intercultural problems, child training, personality growth, questions of national character, and even . . . the complex and important problems of industrial relations . . ."[2] Linguists are concerned with the study of the structure of languages although other disciplines, including sociology, communication, and one of the humanities, English, are also concerned with linguistics.

Psychology

While psychology is closely related to sociology, there are some considerable differences. Both are concerned with human behavior, but psychology focuses on the individual and is concerned with such phenomena as motivation, attitudes, perception, and learning. Psychologists attempt to explain human events—from wars to small group formation—largely on the basis of individuals and individual personalities.

The concerns of psychology are widespread—ranging from general and experimental psychology through such subfields, or specializations, as clinical psychology, industrial and organizational psychology, and even military psychology. Currently, the American Psychological Association has thirty-two separate divisions, which gives some idea of the diversity within the field. Sociology and psychology converge in a subfield common to both, *social psychology*, which is the study of people in small groups.

Communication

In the formal sense, communication is a relatively new field of study. While the discipline tends to focus on the process of communication, those working in the field have a wide range of concerns overlapping the other social sciences. We find, for example, people in communication studying such phenomena as attitude change, persuasion, retention, decay, recall, and the individual personality—all matters of great interest to psychologists. Communication is also concerned with the influence of the group, mass media, and technological advances and with applying communication to advertising and politics—all matters of concern to sociologists. Finally, the process of communication is of great importance to all the social sciences—for example, for sociologists *interaction* is a fundamental consideration and it would be difficult to have human, social interaction without symbolic communication.

Economics

Economists are concerned with economics as being independent and autonomous. They study such things as "supply and demand," the operation of the "market place," and the economic system in general.

It should be recognized that for all societies there must be ways of meeting material needs and wants if life is to be sustained and any particular society is to remain viable. Food, clothing, and shelter are essentials that somehow or other must be made available. Economists are concerned with how this gets done and with the distribution of both goods and services. Economists, then, study activities of paramount importance to all societies.

The development of economic theory was originally based on a model of man which assumed that he behaved rationally at least with respect to purely economic activities. Stated simply, the rational man of economists will always act, when given an economic choice, in such a way as to maximize his own interests or economic position. Modern economists have considerably modified this view, and over the past fifty years, there have been evolving changes in both classical and Keynesian economic theory. While modern sociologists and economists dispute the early model of rational man because of evidence that man does *not* always act rationally, they admit that this model of rational man may represent an important institutionalized value or criterion that helps to direct behavior.[3]

When we consider that the economy is a *social institution* and, as such, also under the general purview of sociology, it should not be surprising that some economists would take positions that might be described as sociological. For example, speaking of Adam Smith, the author of the celebrated *Wealth of Nations*, Robert Weiss and David Riesman note that

at the beginning of the Industrial Revolution, Adam Smith was so impressed with
the stultifying nature of factory life that he could only hope that the hours away
from work might somehow maintain those qualities of character he regarded as
essentially human.[4]

Although it is probable that of all the social sciences anthropology is the closest to sociology, the contributions of economics to social theory and, indeed, to sociology as a whole has been and is significant. And it is worth noting that sociologists and economists cooperate in diverse ways. A most notable example of this is the research underlying Gunnar Myrdal's work some years ago on the racial problem in the United States.[5]

Political Science

Political science is concerned mainly with formal power and its uses. There are two main branches, or elements, in political science—theory and government administration. In recent years, political scientists have begun to emphasize behavior—for example, decision making with considerable attention being given to "nondecisions," that is, the use of power to prevent conflicts from becoming public decisions.

Political scientists are also beginning to emphasize the importance of symbol manipulation in the political process. The current attempts to present, via mass media, an altered or artificial symbolic representation of a candidate is a case in point. Other examples are the struggle of Blacks for political power, international relations such as the symbolic representations of East versus West, urban confrontations, and so forth. Along with other social scientists, political scientists are beginning to give increasing attention to that important development of the twentieth century—the mass media.

Although the attention of political scientists is focused on a single social institution and on processes within that institution, their interests are expanding. They are showing more interest in such things as the impact of public policies on societies, which means that they are becoming involved in such matters as pollution control, employment, inflation, and education.

With respect to formal power and its uses, sociologists concerned with political sociology have been mainly interested in political behavior. However, in pursuing this behavioral interest, political sociologists have also become involved with the subject matter of political science itself and with the other social sciences as well. This fusion has not escaped the notice of political scientists and possibly has been partly responsible for the fact that politcial scientists have vastly broadened the scope of their discipline.

Interrelationships

At this point in time, it can be stated accurately that cross-disciplinary interests and cooperation have begun to replace the rigid parochialism once characteristic of all the social sciences. Although it is doubtful that there will ever be a general merging of all of them into one social science, it is apparent that cross-disciplinary work and exchange of information is taking place and will continue to do so in the future—probably at an accelerating rate. In addition, *all* the social sciences are now using two important tools that mark them clearly as sciences: the *scientific method* and statistics or *statistical analysis*, to which the first is closely related.

There has been an enormous growth in information in each of the social sciences—not to mention what is aptly described as a general "knowledge explosion." The amount of time an individual must spend in simply learning his or her own discipline is formidable and is expanding. It would be impossible for anyone in each of the social sciences to be fully aware of the contributions by the other disciplines to their own. But, as John Diebold points out, new systems or new technologies, some already here in a rudimentary form, should make it possible for each of us to absorb *or* have readily available enormously more information than ever before.[6] When that situation is an actuality on a large scale, more meaningful cooperation between all the social, not to mention the natural and physical, sciences will become possible.

SCIENCE AND THE SOCIAL SCIENCES

The word "science" tends to conjure up images of people in white coats working in laboratories mixing chemicals and using various kinds of esoteric measuring instruments. Most laymen are quite certain that physics or chemistry, for example, are indeed sciences. They are less certain about the appropriate rubric under which to subsume the social sciences. Indeed, there is a general confusion about what science actually is—is it a body of knowledge or is it a series of activities that seem scientific? Many people equate the practice of medicine with science, which it assuredly is not, although some physicians are indeed scientists. However, when a physician is practicing medicine, he or she is functioning as a very highly skilled technician who is using the findings of medical science. The very nature of the *practice* of medicine and the ethics involved preclude the use of the *scientific method*. Science, then, is *not* merely a body of knowledge, although knowledge is certainly involved in science because empirically verified knowledge constitutes the results of scientific investigation. If knowledge and science were one and the same, then history would be a science which most agree it is not.

All humans continuously make any number of observations during the course of their lives. It is just such observations and the conclusions drawn from them that, over the centuries, have constituted much of the culture all of us experience in the societies into which we are born.

Copyright © 1972 by Saturday Review/World, Inc.
Reprinted by permission of the publisher and Laughs Unlimited.

"It's one of two things—either the great god of the inner earth, Timbuku, is angry with our last virgin sacrifice, or the enormous pressure of a formation of molten rock is breaking through a weak spot in the earth's crust."

Even social scientists have made the assumption that knowledge is science. Clifford T. Morgan, a psychologist, defines science as "a body of systematized knowledge," but he goes on to explain that this "knowledge is gathered by carefully observing and measuring events, sometimes, but not necessarily, in experiments . . ."[7] Morgan provides an important clue about what science really is when he mentions *careful observation and measurement of events*. Provided we understand fully what is meant by "careful," we begin to have some idea of what science is. The importance of the word "careful" can be made clear by discussing some of the important differences between "science" and "common sense."

Scientific Method versus Common Sense

All humans continuously make any number of observations and draw conclusions from these observations during the course of their lives. It is just such observations and the conclusions drawn from them that, over the centuries, have constituted much of the culture all of us experience in the societies into which we were born. Many of the conclusions so drawn are reasonably correct and, indeed, are fully or nearly fully consonant with facts uncovered by scientific investigations. If this were not true, there would be no societies. Human observations and what humans conclude to be reality from such observations must necessarily be at least sufficiently congruent with the real world to enable individual humans and societies to survive. For example, it was essential that our early ancestors recognized and correctly interpreted the sight of a large carnivore in search of food and acted upon that information. In the main, had this not been done, our species would not have survived and proliferated. A more modern example might be the individual who, under the influence of drugs, believes that he can fly. His interpretation of reality is quite in error as he would discover upon diving out a window that was, say, thirty-five or forty stories above the ground. That example is, of course, extreme. Most people are in sufficient touch with reality and their common sense observations work well enough to keep them alive for a number of years. In spite of this, the common sense approach has served to build in to most cultures a number of errors which, if not grave enough to cause the disappearance of the society concerned, are sufficiently grievous to render them less adaptive than they could otherwise be. One such "common sense" conclusion that has become part of many cultures concerns racial differences. For example, many Caucasians having only observed Black people in servile positions and listened to their "uneducated" speech reached the conclusion that Blacks are biologically inferior. But *careful* scientific investigation has determined that it is social environment that produces the apparently hereditary differences between Blacks and Caucasians, insofar as intelligence is concerned.[8] Some less damaging examples of common sense are given by Pierre Lecomte du Nouy who wrote that "common sense tells us that the edge of a razor blade is a continuous straight line, but if we examine it under a microscope it resembles the wavy line drawn by a child. Common sense tells us that a piece of steel is solid; x-rays show us that it is porous . . ."[9]

The findings of the sciences, including the social sciences, are not the same as those based on common sense observations, although they may sometimes coincide. The differences between common sense and science provide a reasonably accurate picture of what science really is.

Determining Reality   Both science and common sense are concerned with determining reality; that is, with knowing a situation as it exists. By employing certain methodological procedures, scientific research is able to produce verifiable conclusions about reality. Logic is employed in formulating a hypothesis, which is then subjected to empirical testing. The tests are conducted under rigidly controlled conditions designed to minimize "observer-caused effects"[10] as far as is possible. The data are then subjected to full statistical analysis, and the results of the analysis are then interpreted. The conclusions of the project are eventually presented to the scientific community. But that is not quite the end of the process. The publication of the findings in scientific journals, the presentation of new concepts at conventions, and so on, expose researchers' work to review and analysis by their peers. Any errors, specious reasoning, poor research techniques, any methodological lapses, are quickly discovered. That coupled with the requirement that experiments be replicated to insure that the same results are obtained as in the initial investigation permit science to be self-correcting. And the ultimate result of a research project or experiment is a proven, valid conclusion about reality.

Common sense evaluations about reality are subjective and personal. Even when people "check" their conclusions by discussing them with others, differing opinions are not likely to cause a change of mind. If logic is used, it is used to persuade and convince. The logic underlying common sense often functions under a set of rules which is not scientific. One such rule, which is also characteristic of a defense mechanism called "rationalization" by psychologists, is that every effort be made to find supportive evidence for a belief while ignoring or "explaining away" contrary evidence. A good example is the common sense reasoning favoring capital punishment that ignores the considerable body of evidence indicating that capital punishment is not an effective deterrent to murder. Further, common sense conclusions tend to be influenced and distorted by individual biases because no account is taken of those factors that scientists make the most rigorous efforts to control.

Statistical Analysis and Interpretation of Data   One of the requirements of science is that data be *quantifiable* and *quantified*—data must be expressible and expressed in numbers—so that statistical *analysis* is possible. Common sense evaluations tend to be impressed by the numbers themselves. For example, based on information in the FBI *Uniform Crime Reports*, it was widely believed that there was a serious increase in crime in the United States during the late 1960's and early 1970's. Even the press and politicians used such phrases as "a breakdown of law and order." Yet, after making a *careful analysis* of a series of the FBI reports, Albert Biderman concluded that

1. The errors and biasing factors affecting the Crime Index largely operate to show spurious increases rather than decreases in the rate.

2. The Crime Index does not provide a sound basis for determining whether criminal behavior is increasing or decreasing in the United States.

3. The Crime Index is highly sensitive to social developments that are almost universally regarded as improvements in the society. Thus, it is altogether possible

that year-to-year increases in crime rates may be more indicative of social progress than of social decay.[11]

Since the FBI *Uniform Crime Reports* present the best data *available*, they are an obvious authority to consult. And although the technical section warns against any improper interpretations, common sense conclusions were drawn by many.

It should be obvious now that when the data are all in and have been subjected to a full statistical analysis, *the necessity for interpretation remains—*what does it all mean? A researcher may discover a correlation between two variables—that is, changes in one variable are accompanied or followed by roughly equivalent changes in some other variable. But does that mean that the changes in one variable *cause* changes in the other? To use an extreme but highly illustrative example, it was discovered that there was a significant correlation between ice cream consumption and the incidence of sex crimes. In other words, it appeared that the more ice cream consumed, the greater the number of sex crimes. A "logical" common sense conclusion might be that sex crimes could be reduced by suppressing ice cream consumption. But that could not, of course, be the case. The correct, logical interpretation of the correlation was that *warm weather* is associated with both the eating of ice cream and the incidence of sex crimes and was therefore the cause of each.[12] So, the final step in the scientific process is the application of logic. Numbers, including statistics, *do not speak for themselves*, despite their misuse in common sense reasoning.

In comparing the scientific method to the more usual common sense approach, no attempt was made to provide information on the mechanics of the scientific method; only the general ideas and underlying philosophy were mentioned. It is important to recognize that sociologists, as well as other social scientists, are making increasing use of sophisticated scientific techniques and methods of statistical analysis because these have a high probability of ascertaining reality. We have attempted to make quite clear that the scientific method is important to all of us, not merely to scientists; that the social sciences, including sociology, are sciences; and that it is *not* subject matter but method that determines whether a particular discipline meets the criteria for being a science.

SOCIOLOGY: GENERAL ORIENTATION

The balance of this chapter will be devoted to providing an introduction to modern sociology itself in order that the detailed treatment contained in the following chapters will be more easily assimilated and, thus, more meaningful.

Subject Matter

It is the basic assumption of science that there is order in nature and regularities and relationships of various kinds which can be discovered. Indeed, there cannot be a science of *unique events*. It is quite apparent even to the most casual observer that there is much regularity and order in nature not to mention in daily human affairs. Most people can predict with some success the behavior of other people—in particular those close and well known, such as family and friends. These regularities of behavior are of two kinds: first, ways of behaving acquired in the process of socialization; secondly, the personal idiosyncracies and behavioral patterns of the individuals concerned. The first type is of primary concern to sociologists, for it is through observations of those behavioral regularities that society and culture are inferred.

Focus of Study and Research   The basic unit of sociological study is *human behavior as that behavior occurs in interaction with other humans*. For sociological purposes, human behavior is not studied in isolation, such as a man alone on a desert island. Instead, concentration is on humans in groups of three or more. But why three or more? Are not two people in interaction of interest to sociologists? Georg Simmel provided a succinct answer to this question when he wrote that "the sociological character of the dyad [two people] is characterized by . . . phenomena that are absent from it. One is the intensification of relations by a third element or by *a social framework that transcends both members of the dyad*."[13] The key idea here is that when there is a group of at least three persons the results are not simply additive but that something beyond just the three people is also present. That "something" is a *social framework*—a key concept in sociology. In moving to a consideration of this social framework within which men live and work, it should be kept in mind that this framework developed in and from human interaction. It must also be remembered that the framework of a society represents an abstraction from behavior and that no one has ever seen a society—only people behaving as if they were, in fact, part of this particular human concept.

Structure of Society

What do sociologists mean by the "structure of society"? The word "structure" has connotations of something firm and solid that can be both seen and felt. Buildings and other physical objects have structure, and so does society. However, the structure of society cannot be seen, felt (in the physical sense of touching), or otherwise *directly* observed. As with all the other concepts of sociology, social structure is an *inference from the observation of behavior of interacting humans*.

Man, Society, and Prehistory   We have no certain way of knowing just how human groups in the social sense got started. Anthropologists rarely give consideration to that matter, preferring to start with human groups, often called "bands"—that is with human social life already well under-way. That such bands possessed social structure seems obvious:

in . . . a band everyone knew everyone else and protocol was simple. Over the hundreds of thousands of years that man lived as a hunter he perfected his capacity to be intimate with the members of his band and formal with outsiders. Young men learned ways of behaving toward women, children, and old people which would make life easiest for all concerned, and hence would enhance the survival value of the band as a whole.[14]

Those ways of behaving which Coon claims served to aid in the survival of the band are commented on indirectly by V. Gordon Childe:

A doe rabbit may produce seventy offspring annually. As the rabbit population keeps fairly constant in the long run, the individual's chances of survival is clearly of the order of 1 in 70. A human pair does not produce more than one child a year, and families exceeding 10 are uncommon. Yet the human species is still increasing in numbers. The human child's chance of survival is incomparably greater than that of a young rabbit.[15]

Being a member of a human society, then, appears to enhance the probabilities of individual biological survival. Certainly the vast growth of human populations over the past few centuries, which has accelerated sharply in more recent times, provides ample evidence that societies more than adequately perform the function of survival claimed by both Coon and Childe. It should be understood that societies function in ways to enhance their survival which logically enough implies that the biological survival of individual members is also enhanced, as noted. However, society may and does function on occasion in ways inimical to the biological survival of individual members as in the case of war or the execution of individuals in rebellion against the polity.

Culture can be considered to be an *historically derived system* of explicit and implicit designs for living that tends to be shared by all or specifically designated members of a group or a society.[16] And it can be said that culture must be *cumulative*—that it grows and expands by successive addition. Some cultural elements are, of course, lost over time but, in general, more is added; therefore, culture becomes more complex with the passing of time.

Social Institutions   Although we have no way of knowing with any certainty just how a particular culture grew or a social structure developed, Coon's formulation of this process is worth noting.

As man progressively conquered the forces of nature, and as a division of labor on the basis of work techniques increased, more and more people were brought into mutual contact. For each type of organization that arose in addition to those of family and band, some kind of leadership and a pattern of orderly behavior created themselves.[17]

We perceive in Coon's words the formation of *social institutions*—that is, regular or conventional patterns of behavior and expectations that are characteristic of similar groups in societies and that are organized around some function or functions deemed of great importance to each society. From society to society institutions, from family to educational, provide regularized and predictable ways of behaving along with their accompanying expectations. This not only makes life tolerable but also makes life, in the social sense, possible. The alternative, of course, is epitomized by Jean-Jacques Rousseau's "natural man"—man divested of all that he has learned as a member of society. Such an imaginary individual would probably be brutish, solitary, and egotistical with an interest only in the present, for knowledge of the past or ideas of the future depend upon the acquisition of language.

The term "social institution" has a somewhat different meaning for sociologists than for laymen. For many, an "institution" means a group of people working in an organized way and dedicated to some common goal or goals. In the lay sense, then, institutions are planned, orderly, and goal-directed. The sociological meaning is more difficult to grasp because the concept is an inference. Furthermore, social institutions are *not* planned in the same way that, say, an institution for planned parenthood would be. Thousands of years ago when there was relatively little contact between societies, it was necessary for each society to work out its own solutions to those problems that confront all human groups. The institutions of each society represent its solutions to such problems and, as should be obvious, must differ, frequently in highly significant ways.

Let us take as an example the institution of marriage. In Vasilika, a village in modern Greece, courtship, in the sense of those activities leading to marriage, is carried out, not by the prospective marriage partners, but by intermediaries. And the success or failure of these negotiations usually hinges on the amount of the girl's dowry. Indeed, the key consideration is whether the marriage will be advantageous to the families of the couple, and the feelings of the potential marriage partners for each other are relatively unimportant. But, as has been noted,

The villagers are not callous about the matter of personal compatibility between spouses; they assume, however, that if the marriage conditions are right, a harmonious relationship will develop or, if it does not, the successful economic or

Sociology: General Orientation

45

prestige conditions of the marriage will help to allay sufferings arising from the lack of personal contentment.[18]

The custom in Vasilika provides a marked contrast with the norms for courtship and marriage in American society, where the compatibility of those entering into a marriage is the primary consideration.

Another example comes from the Dusun, a North Borneo society. There marriages are usually monogamous, not because the taking of more than one wife is forbidden, but because "a second marriage is exceedingly expensive . . . and therefore, most men cannot afford more than one wife."[19]

These are only a few examples of approaches to the institution of marriage that can be found in the various societies throughout the world. What may seem strange to the people of one society, with respect to the major institutions of that society, will be the norm in another. And it becomes evident that the working out of institutional arrangements is not an orderly, planned procedure but the result of arriving at the best solution for a particular group largely through trial and error. But all institutions and the norms and roles of these institutions have something in common: *they work for the people who adopt them.*

Dynamic Solidarity   In its own special way, the structure of any society has a dynamic solidarity beyond that possessed by physical objects. Taboos provide an excellent example of the solid character, or force, of social structures—and all societies have taboos. In American society, for example, the elimination of bodily wastes is considered a private matter, particularly with respect to the sexes, and private facilities are provided. Among the Trobriand Islanders of Melanesia it is taboo for brothers and sisters to have any sort of communication or contact past puberty. "From puberty until death they may not approach one another and may not therefore continue to inhabit the same household."[20]

All societies have taboos, and anyone violating them is subject to some kind of censure—anything from being thought seriously deranged to severe punishment. Few people, in fact, ever violate any of the taboos of their society which they accept as taboos. That most people would find it virtually impossible to do so provides evidence of the singular solidarity and force of the social structure. The overwhelming proportion of the population of all societies behaves, dresses, thinks, sleeps, eats, and, in general, conducts its affairs in the manner dictated by the structure of the society in which they live. Durkheim has said of himself:

I am not obliged to speak French with my fellow-countrymen nor to use the legal currency, but I cannot possibly do otherwise. If I tried to escape this necessity, my attempt would fail miserably. As an industrialist, I am free to apply the

It would seem that one cannot seriously doubt the reality of forces so powerful that they direct and constrain the behavior of almost all members of a society most of the time.

Copyright © 1973 by The New York Times Company.
Reprinted by permission.

technical methods of former centuries; but by so doing, I should invite certain ruin. Even when I free myself from these rules and violate them successfully, I am always compelled to struggle with them. When finally overcome, they make their constraining power sufficiently felt by the resistance they offer.[21]

In other words, people in society carry on their activities as they do because those are the solutions to a wide variety of problems worked out over the centuries by their society. Of course, as Durkheim observed, a person *can* successfully violate some of the rules, but he still feels resistance. And for many, this resistance becomes a matter of conscience. For example, the United States Internal Revenue Service has what might be called a "conscience fund." Every year, usually anonymously, come thousands of dollars

Sociology:
General Orientation

from taxpayers who deliberately and knowingly have, in the past, cheated on their income tax returns. This money provides a singular proof of the power of society over its members—a power that in this case is avoided only by making restitution.

It would seem that one cannot seriously doubt the reality of forces so powerful that they direct and constrain the behavior of almost all members of a society most of the time. To the argument that social rules are frequently broken, the sociologist can only reply that this rule-breaking may be more seeming than actual for there are also *rules for breaking the rules*. As an example, American society insists on monogamous marriage. Yet it permits divorce and remarriage, which makes for a kind of serial polygyny or polyandry. To take a lesser example, people can and do park in zones clearly marked "No Parking." But they usually recognize that they may well have to pay a fine for doing so. In other words, some rules may be violated if one is willing to pay some kind of forfeit, or acknowledges the possibility that one may have to do so.

Equilibrium or Conflict   In Chapter 1 we discussed the basic differences between the structural-functional and conflict theorists. Before going on to the discussion of social control, we should review those concepts and try to establish a synthesis of them.

The structural-functionalists based their ideas of society on a model of a biological organism. They stressed the idea of equilibrium and emphasized the importance of harmony, consensus, and equilibrium maintenance. They gave little prominence to conflict, strain, and change in social systems. To some extent, the functionalists were correct because there must be some equilibrium in all societies, otherwise they would disintegrate and disappear. But the conflict theorists have shown that strain and change are a part of social life. Therefore it is more meaningful to analyze the various ways developed in all societies for maintaining some uneasy state of equilibrium even while being subjected to conflict, tension, and change. Equilibrium in the social sense is not a static condition. One cannot imagine a real society free from conflict, although it is popular to visualize preliterate societies as being essentially harmonious. Every viable society must, in its own way, successfully cope with continuing conflict and strain in various of its parts because some change is endemic in all human societies.

Social Control

Social structure determines the way in which each person is going to behave and live out his life in the society of his birth. The force of social structure comes from the fact that the majority of the members of any society have *internalized* the culture—that is, the norms—of the society and exercise *surveillance over themselves.* Social structure is not something "out there," not some force emanating from an external place of origin, but is ultimately located within each individual.

To say that society is directly dependent for its functioning on the fact that its members exercise voluntary control over themselves raises some objections. Dennis Wrong objects to what he calls "the oversocialized conception of man in modern society." Wrong argues that men have not "been completely molded by the particular norms and values of their culture."[22] That contention seems to stem from the belief that man has certain natural biological tendencies, such as the sex drive, that bring him into conflict with the values and norms of his society. Wrong's position is similar to that of Freud, who assumed that man is by inheritance savage, lustful, quarrelsome, and rapacious.[23] The difficulty with such a stand is that it seems likely that such behaviors were *learned* by men as members of society. Speaking of the development of the atomic bomb, John Nef, an historian, is quoted as insisting that "our readiness to resort to ever more destructive warfare is not an inborn characteristic of human beings." Rather, Nef holds, it is a product of history.[24] Motivation for conflict or war does not spring from some savagery inherent in man's nature but from learned motives. As all those behaviors are learned, cultural, and not genetically transmitted, it is possible to argue that man's most destructive behavior—war—is part of cultural tradition and not the result of an inherited killer instinct. (We will discuss instincts, genetic transmission of behavior, and the biological foundations of human nature in greater detail in Chapter 3.)

It is important to understand that the well-balanced, socially adaptable, and well-socialized individual is produced by the same learning process that creates the deviant and troublesome individual. If, as we have said, conflict is endemic in society, then we must look to society itself for the source of this conflict and not to man's genetic inheritance. Wrong's argument that some sociologists have an oversocialized conception of man does appear to be basically correct. However, it is equally possible to err in the opposite direction and assume an undersocialized conception of modern man.

Wrong correctly argues that social control is not simply a matter of internal controls—that is, each man taking full responsibility for his own behavior. His contention that a good deal of appropriate social behavior is a function of coercion or the threat of punishment cannot be disputed. We would argue that people in all societies learn to obey some norms only under coercion or threat of punishment. Take, for example, the situation of speed limits on public highways. When there is no police vehicle in sight, statistical norms prevail—driving, say, five or ten miles above the posted speed limit. At the appearance of a police vehicle, the ideal norm—driving within the limit— tends to prevail until the police are out of sight.

The fact that people in modern, complex societies behave in diverse ways and often violate one or more norms in the process does not in any way demonstrate that they are poorly socialized. What it does show is that cultures and societies are full of inconsistencies and contradictions, as well as possessing ways of resolving those inconsistencies. But that does not deny that some members of any society are poorly socialized. This does account for some social conflict, but not, we suggest, for the greater part.

In all modern societies, some norms are codified into laws that are backed largely by a system of punishments under control of the polity. The very fact that norms have been codified is convincing evidence that the socialization of a significant number of individuals has not included internalization of some norms, and it probably indicates the internalization of norms that are in conflict with the official norms of the society. According to Judith Blake and Kingsley Davis, the sources of conflict and what *appears* to be contranormative behavior are to be found, not in man's biological drives, but in the complex relations between society and individual members and the norms of society.[25]

Sanctions   As used in sociology, "sanctions" refer to either rewards (positive sanctions) or punishments (negative sanctions). While there is little question that both negative and positive sanctions are effective, there is growing evidence to support the idea that reward is more potent than punishment.[26] And society uses those rewards that are available to it to motivate, direct, and constrain the behavior of its members, with negative sanctions or the threat of such sanctions being useful but less effective. And from this follows a concept of singular importance to sociology. Earlier, we noted that internalized norms have an important societal function—unless most people were reasonably well socialized, society as we know it would be impossible. Simply because someone believes a specific behavior to be right and proper does not necessarily impel that individual to perform the behavior in question. It seems, therefore, logical to assume that the performance of actual behavior which is consonant and in accordance with an internalized norm or norms is pleasurable and rewarding; thus it *constitutes a self-administered positive sanction*. As will be appreciated after reading Chapter 8, rewards for behavior are applied early in life by parents and others to the very young child. Such rewards often take the form of remarks such as "Good girl!" or "Good boy!" Later, youngsters develop the ability to regard themselves as an object and speak of themselves in the third person. When this occurs, the human concerned is from that time on in a position to apply positive sanctions to his or her own behavior, be that behavior overt or covert. And he or she is equally capable of administering negative sanctions—that is, guilt feelings, or pangs of conscience.

Sanctions are not only self-administered but are also applied by society at large or by others with whom one associates. There are four types of sanc-

tions: *informal positive sanctions*, such as a smile or a word of praise; *formal positive sanctions*, such as a military medal or job promotion; *informal negative sanctions*, such as a frown or sharp word; *formal negative sanctions*, such as a jail sentence or fine. It is through informal negative and positive sanctions that small, primary (and secondary for that matter) groups socialize into the group and maintain control over their individual members. The greater society has a system of formal negative sanctions ranging from a warning by a policeman not to, say, double park to a sentence of life imprisonment. But, as mentioned earlier, negative sanctions may not be as effective as is generally believed.

It is interesting to note that psychologists classify as *primary* reinforcers (that is, reward and punishment) such biological items as food, water, and sexual contact and speak of learned reinforcers, such as money, praise, social approval, attention, and so forth, as *secondary* reinforcers. Since all the biological drives with the possible exception of sex are adequately met in most cases, the reinforcers of real consequence to both sociologists and psychologists are the secondary reinforcers of the psychologists—that is, positive and negative sanctions. (We will discuss sanctions again, and more thoroughly, in Chapter 3.)

The greater society has a system of formal negative sanctions ranging from a warning by a policeman to a sentence of life imprisonment.

Sociology: General Orientation

Random Reinforcement   Societies control their members in diverse ways, which include the process of socialization and the concomitant internalization of norms; positive and negative sanctions administered by individuals to themselves; and positive and negative sanctions administered by others in the society. The total process of social control is further complicated by what may appear on an a priori basis to be irregularities in this process. As most of us clearly recognize, sanctions, either positive or negative, are not administered on a one-to-one basis—good deeds by no means always receive positive sanctions, and misdeeds are not always punished. In real life, both sanctions are given intermittently. Reasoning inductively from countless experiments, psychologists have determined that it is random reinforcement—both negative and positive—which is most effective in terms of obtaining a desired behavioral result.[27] What appears to be a certain haphazardness in the administration of positive and negative sanctions may well serve the ends of society much better than what would appear on a common sense basis to be more efficient—a reward for every correct response and punishment for each incorrect response. The power of intermittent and seemingly random reward (or, as the psychologists call it, "partial reinforcement") is illustrated by the so-called duffer at the game of golf who plays persistently over the years without any visible improvement in his game. Why does he do this? Possibly because of some peripheral rewards associated with golf such as using the golf course for business purposes. However, it is more probable that what happens from time to time is that he does play a good round of golf; his drives are long and right down the fairway; his approach shots are crisp, and his putting accurate. Because this happens randomly, it is enough to keep him coming back to the golf course over the years.

Human Element   While the control of society over individual members is indeed formidable, humans are not mechanically responding robots, if for no other reason than that each person is unique. The somewhat obvious basis for this statement is that it would be virtually impossible for any two persons to have not only identical heredity (which identical twins *do* have) but completely identical life experiences as well. In simpler societies individuals of the same sex and age were alike in many ways. But with the growing diversity of already complex modern societies, each member will have a wide range of educational and career opportunities from which to choose; great variation in possible life styles; and socialization into a number of subcultures having norms that conflict in a variety of ways with those of not only the larger society but other subcultures as well. This clearly increases the problems of social control, particularly if by "social control" we mean a certain uniformity in behavior. Such diversity both in individuals and groups within a larger society also presages increased conflict. But as a study of almost any modern society makes quite clear, intergroup and intragroup conflict is coming increasingly under sets of rules which keep this conflict within certain bounds and prevents the outbreak of actual warfare. As you will see in Chapter 9, this is what has been occurring in the institution of politics.

What we are implying is that societies are necessarily *self-correcting*—when something goes awry at least some members of the society perceive the difficulty and seek solutions to it. If these solutions work, if they meet the empirical test, they are likely to be used each time a like situation arises and eventually be incorporated into the culture of the society. That this invariable process is somewhat slow should be understood, but many neither comprehend nor appreciate how societies function. But their understandable impatience with a less than desirable speed of change hardly justifies some of the suggestions made for improving societies in particular or in general.

CONCLUSION

This chapter has presented concepts, facts, information, and ideas that should make the understanding of the following chapters easier and more complete. To briefly review some of these fundamental ideas that comprise the framework of sociology, we must first remember that while human nature does depend upon genetic inheritance, that dependence is largely a matter of limits that are imposed upon man because he is a physical organism. It is also true, as Theodosius Dobzhansky points out, that "culture has a genetic basis. Mankind is the sole possessor of culture because it is the sole possessor of a genetic basis for culture." But, at the same time, it must be kept in mind that technology has enabled man to transcend many of these limitations. In Dobzhansky's words, "man, by means of his culture and technology, changes his environment to fit his genes."[28] The majority of tools, from such commonplace things as a hammer or pliers to such sophisticated and complex inventions as computers, represent extensions of either the human body or the human nervous system. All these are social inventions and the result of humans interacting. Even human personality or, more generally "humanity," is a product of culture not merely for the entire species but for each individual. However, it must be noted that genetic inheritance *can* influence individual personality development; for example, some people inherit more pleasing looks, the tendency to larger muscles, a high level of energy, and so on; all of which influence individual personality.

The powerful forces available to and used by society to control and channel individual behavior were discussed at some length. Distinctions were made between positive and negative sanctions as well as the manner in which such sanctions were administered. Intentional emphasis was placed on the ideas that positive sanctions are more effective than negative sanctions and that individuals can and *do* administer both positive and negative sanctions to themselves. This latter process represents the *internalization* of society and culture and in a general way represents the most *powerful control* society has. and exerts over its members. In addition, mention was made of an important finding by psychologists that intermittent, random, or partial reinforcement (by which is meant positive and negative sanctions) are far more potent in terms of modifying or controlling behavior than regular reinforcement. Since society operates in such a manner as to make the applications of both positive and negative sanctions often if not usually random, intermittent, or partial, the power of any society to condition, direct, and modify human behavior is very great. People recognize that this is true but often express the view that such control was greater in the past and point to innumerable modern social problems as evidence that social control is becoming increasingly less effective. The sociological evidence indicates that control, while different in some ways, is becoming more rather than less effective. As societies grow more complex, more and more subcultures will appear and they will teach their members norms at variance with those of the larger society as well as those of other subcultures. This, of course, serves to make various kinds of conflict endemic in modern societies thus giving the appearance of a breakdown in social control. However, unrestrained and destructive conflict is one thing and conflict conducted under a set of rules is another. All societies tend to work out such rules. For example, the Indians of the American Plains conducted warfare in a manner that kept opportunities for enhancing a warrior's prestige at a maximum and the risk of getting killed at a minimum. While people were killed in these Indian wars, the chief merit was to count "coup," touch an enemy whether living or dead.[29] Such Indian "wars" are not dissimilar to political contests in which the winner gains both power and prestige and the loser retires from the field physically, if not psychically, unscathed, possibly to return and try again. What has happened is that norms regulating this kind of conflict are in operation. In all modern societies, codified norms (laws) regulate a considerable portion of the economy because it became apparent that a "free market place" was not free at all. Some regulation was required if business competition was to be kept within reasonable bounds. These and many other kinds and types of norms tend to proliferate in some as yet undetermined relationship to the division of labor —that is, with increased specialization comes the need for more norms. But as the normative system expands and becomes more complex, the possibility becomes greater for the appearance of norms that are in conflict to some degree with yet other norms. In other words, such conflict as we see among men is *normative conflict* and not dictated by *primeval, instinctual urges* that compel man toward aggression or the defense of his territory.[30]

It has also been stressed that society has structure which includes social institutions, values, norms, roles, and role sets. But society differs from physical objects in that its structure is necessarily *inferred*. Although quite invisible to the naked eye, the social structure is none the less potent and powerful and all must bend to it—gracefully or reluctantly. We are what we are because of our culture, which is expressed in living form by our societies. Both culture and society are an absolute necessary for mankind. "Man is the only species on earth . . . that relies for its adaptability mainly, though not exclusively, on culture learned by each individual in his or her lifetime and transmitted largely by means of symbolic language."[31]

In this chapter, some attention has been devoted to such aspects of society as social institutions, norms, social structure, social control, and so forth. These *social phenomena* are very much with all of us. And it would appear important, even essential, to inquire about the origins of what we call *culture*. The ways we have in our society of doing things, working together, and, in general, maintaining a viable society seem to many of us *the* right and proper way to live—the right way for a society to run. The ways of life that we call culture are discussed in Chapter 3.

REVIEW QUESTIONS

2.1. As noted in this chapter, sociology and sociologists may not be particularly popular because some of their findings contravene popular beliefs and ideas. You might consider the matter of "instincts" and see if you can find reasons why some—even many—people believe that there are significant human instincts.

2.2. Does the fact that sociology is based upon inferences make it any less a science than, say, physics or chemistry? Is it necessary in the physical or natural sciences to draw inferences, or is the subject matter of these sciences known by direct observation?

2.3. Other than inherited physical characteristics, can you think of any traits that are common to all men wherever they are found? General traits? Specific traits (by which is meant identical or nearly identical behaviors)?

2.4. What is *the* basic assumption of all sciences? Why is this a necessary assumption? Does it appear to be a *correct* assumption?

2.5. Why don't we know how human groups got started in prehistoric times? After all, sociology is based on assumptions.

2.6. We often refer to some particularly undesirable behavior on the part of humans as "animal-like." Is this really a correct analogy? Are animals, in general, really savage, lustful, quarrelsome, rapacious, covetous, and so forth? Do animals kill other animals for sport?

2.7. This chapter gives some examples of "rules for breaking the rules." Can you think of some other examples? (Note: You may have some difficulty doing this because breaking a rule usually if not always has some normative basis.)

2.8. As was noted, societies tend to be "self-correcting." Can we expect this process to be faster and more efficient in modern societies than in preliterate societies? Why or why not?

NOTES

[1] L. M. Terman and Melita H. Oden, *The Gifted Child at Mid-Life: Thirty-Five Years' Follow-Up of the Superior Child* (Stanford, Calif.: Stanford University Press, 1959).

[2] Ralph L. Beals and Harry Hoijer, *An Introduction to Anthropology*, 3d ed. (New York: Macmillan, 1965), p. 3.

[3] Neil Smelser, *The Sociology of Economic Life* (Englewood Cliffs, N.J.: Prentice-Hall, 1963), p. 34.

[4] Robert S. Weiss and David Riesman, "Work and Automation: Problems and Prospects," in *Contemporary Social Problems*, ed. Robert K. Merton and Robert A. Nisbet (New York: Harcourt, Brace, Jovanovich, 1961), pp. 580–581. For a modern view considered radical by some economists which is sociological in its analysis of the institution of economics in modern societies, see: John Kenneth Galbraith, *Economics and the Public Purpose* (Boston: Houghton Mifflin, 1973).

[5] Gunnar Myrdal, *An American Dilemma* (New York: Harper & Row, 1944).

[6] John Diebold, *Man and the Computer* (New York: Praeger, 1969).

[7] Clifford T. Morgan, *Introduction to Psychology*, 2d ed. (New York: McGraw-Hill, 1961), p. 2.

[8] See for example, Everett S. Lee, "Negro Intelligence and Selective Migration," *American Sociological Review* 16, no. 7 (1951), pp. 227–233.

[9] Pierre Lecomte du Nouy, *Human Destiny* (New York: McKay, 1947), p. 6.

[10] Julian L. Simon, *Basic Research Methods in Social Science* (New York: Random House, 1969), chaps. 5 and 6. "Observer-caused effects" are also called the "uncertainty" principle or "Heisenberg's principle" after Werner K. Heisenberg, a German physicist who discovered that his own body heat could influence the results of experiments and had, therefore, to be taken into account.

[11] Albert D. Biderman, "Social Indicators and Goals," in *Social Indicators*, ed. Raymond A. Bauer (Cambridge, Mass.: M.I.T. Press, 1966), p. 115. Biderman's conclusions are certainly surprising; but a reading of the entire article reveals that they are well supported—logically and factually.

[12] R. P. Cuzzort, *Humanity and Modern Sociological Thought* (New York: Holt, Rinehart and Winston, 1969), p. 43.

[13] Georg Simmel, "The Significance of Numbers for Social Life," in *Small Groups*, rev. ed., eds. A. Paul Hare, Edgar F. Borgotta, and Robert F. Bales (New York: Knopf, 1965), p. 15. (Emphasis added.)

[14] Carleton S. Coon, *The Story of Man*, 2d ed. rev. (New York: Knopf, 1965), pp. 6–7.

[15] V. Gordon Childe, *Man Makes Himself* (New York: New American Library of World Literature, Mentor Books, 1951), p. 17.

[16] Clyde Kluckhohn, "The Concept of Culture," in *The Science of Man in the World Crisis*, ed. Ralph Linton (New York: Columbia University Press, 1945), p. 97.

[17] Coon, *Story of Man*, p. 7.

[18] Ernestine Friedl, *Vasilika, A Village in Modern Greece* (New York: Holt, Rinehart and Winston, 1962), pp. 56–57.

[19] Thomas Rhys Williams, *The Dusun: A North Borneo Society* (New York: Holt, Rinehart and Winston, 1965), p. 52.

[20] Elman R. Service, *Profiles in Ethnology* (New York: Harper & Row, 1963), p. 242.

[21] Emile Durkheim, *The Rules of the Sociological Method*, 8th ed., trans. Sarah A. Solovay and John H. Mueller and ed. George E. G. Catlin (New York: Free Press, 1938), p. 3.

[22] Dennis Wrong, "The Oversocialized Conception of Man in Modern Society," *American Sociological Review* 20, no. 2 (1961), p. 192.

[23] The Freudian view of man is set forth in Sigmund Freud, *Civilization and Its Discontents* (New York: Norton, 1961). For an historically earlier position, see Thomas Hobbes, *Leviathan* (Oxford: James Thornton, 1881).

[24] As quoted in Meyer Weinberg and Oscar E. Shabat, *Society and Man*, 2d ed. (Englewood Cliffs, N.J.: Prentice-Hall, 1965), p. 598.

[25] Judith Blake and Kingsley Davis, "Norms, Values, and Sanctions," in *Handbook of Modern Sociology*, ed. Robert E. L. Faris (Chicago: Rand McNally, 1964), pp. 456–484.

[26] Ernest R. Hilgard and Gordon H. Bower, *Theories of Learning*, 3d ed. (New York: Appleton, 1966), pp. 135–136.

[27] Jerome Kagan and Ernest Havemann, *Psychology: An Introduction* (New York: Harcourt, Brace, Jovanovich, 1968), pp. 63–65.

[28] Theodosius Dobzhansky, "Genetics and the Diversity of Behavior," *American Psychologist* 27, no. 6 (1972), p. 528.

[29] George P. Murdock, *Our Primitive Contemporaries* (New York: Macmillan, 1934), pp. 283–284.

[30] Robert Ardrey, *African Genesis* (New York: Dell, 1961). This, as well as other books by the same author, makes the assumption that man is characterized by several instincts. Ardrey is obviously highly intelligent and writes exceedingly well, but he uses this excellent intelligence to defend a position that the overwhelming proportion of anthropologists and sociologists would consider untenable.

[31] Dobzhansky, "Genetics and Diversity of Behavior," p. 528.

ANNOTATED BIBLIOGRAPHY

Diebold, John. *Man and the Computer*. New York: Praeger, 1969. This work consists of a series of carefully edited lectures delivered by Diebold at various times in various places. *Man and the Computer* shows the accelerating nature of technological change and attempts to predict some further changes that will be the dynamic products or byproducts of today's technology.

Durkheim, Emile. *The Rules of the Sociological Method*. Translated by Sarah A. Solovay and John H. Mueller and edited by George E. G. Catlin. 8th ed. New York: Free Press, 1938. A good many of Durkheim's ideas and research results remain valid today and are worth the time of any serious student of sociology *and* the other social sciences. Durkheim argued that sociology has a subject matter all its own. Chapter 1, "What Is a Social Fact?," presents the very essence of sociology as Durkheim defined, explained, and illustrated what he meant by "social facts."

Gardner, Martin. *Fads and Fallacies in the Name of Science*. New York: Dover, 1957. Humorous, sad, and sometimes frightening, Gardner's book sets forth numerous examples of "common sense" disguised as science which, in some cases, have caused considerable harm. Those who read it will probably never again be comfortable around humorless individuals who see much if not most of the rest of mankind as being out of step with themselves.

McGee, Reece. *Points of Departure*. Hinsdale, Ill.: Dryden, 1972. A very well written, witty, and informative book which provides a better than excellent introduction to the sociological perspective.

Skinner, B. F. *Beyond Freedom and Dignity*. New York: Knopf, 1971. Skinner has made no secret that one of his principal interests (if not *the* principal one) is the control of behavior. This book is recommended reading but only for those with a solid grasp of the sociological perspective. It reveals, on the one hand, a very high level of sophistication with respect to operant conditioning. On the other hand, there is a considerable lack of sophistication, with respect not only to culture and society but also to *Homo sapiens*.

Culture: Fabric of Society

INTRODUCTION

It would be logical to begin this discussion of culture with a sociological definition of the term. But that is difficult to do. The concept is too wide, covers too much to allow for a concise definition. We will have to be satisfied with a brief examination of nine important aspects of culture.

Some of these aspects can be understood from a careful examination of a statement by Adamson Hoebel that culture "is the integrated sum total of learned behavior traits which are manifest and shared by the members of a society." [1]

One idea that comes through is that *culture is learned*. We turn to Edwin Guthrie for a definition of learned.

Changes in behavior which follow behavior we shall call learning. The ability to learn, that is, to respond differently to a situation because of past responses to that situation is what distinguishes those living creatures . . . [endowed] with minds. [2]

In other words, learning or learned behavior is quite different from instincts or instinctive behavior. (We will have more to say about instincts later in this chapter.) So we can say that culture is learned; it is not transmitted genetically.

From Hoebel's statement comes the idea that *culture is integrated*. Clifford Geertz has commented on that point and in doing so indicates two other aspects: *culture is cumulative* and *culture is a necessary condition for human existence*.

Undirected by culture patterns—organized systems of significant symbols— man's behavior would be virtually ungovernable, a mere chaos of pointless acts and exploding emotions, his experience virtually shapeless. Culture, the accumulated totality of such patterns, is not just an ornament of human existence but—the principal basis of its specificity—an essential condition for it. [3]

From Geertz's comments about significant symbols, that is, *language*, comes a fourth point: *culture depends on significant symbols*.

Another point contained in Hoebel's statement is that *culture is shared*. Clyde Kluckhohn agrees with that when he states that culture is "an historically derived system of explicit and implicit designs for living which tend to be shared by all or specifically designated members of a group or society." [4]

And out of Kluckhohn's statement comes yet another aspect of culture, as indicated by Reece McGee:

The really important [definition of culture] is explicit and implicit designs for living. Culture, then, refers to ways of behaving or doing things, patterns of

Drawing by Chas. Addams © 1973.
The New Yorker Magazine, Inc.

behavior for the members of a society. It is not the actual behaving or doing of things but the ways in which those things are done. Some of them are overt and explicit, and some are hidden and implicit.[5]

Implicit in Hoebel's statement is the idea that *culture is inclusive.* Robert Bierstedt elaborates on that idea: "Culture has come to mean not the so-called 'higher' achievements of group life—art, religion, philosophy, science and the rest—but *all* achievements of group life."[6] Anything and everything that man produces, uses, thinks, manufactures, devises *is* part of culture and, hence, culture. The works of Shelley, Vonnegut, Cleaver are no more (or less) cultural than the ill-spelled scribblings or explicit drawings on public lavatory walls.

But culture is even more. And we come to the final point: *Culture involves*

Introduction

63

the idea of self-identity. Anne Roe refers to the significance of socially transmitted *meanings* that make it possible for humans to become intelligible to themselves and to other humans.[7] (This will be discussed in the chapter on socialization.)

Because the concept of culture does not lend itself to a simple definition, let us review the nine aspects we have just identified. Culture is learned. It is integrated; the various segments of culture operate to function in an ordered manner. But it is not really culture that functions but the human beings for whom a particular culture is a way of life. Culture is dependent on language. It is cumulative; it grows by successive addition. Culture is essential for human existence. It is shared; nearly all members of any society know enough of its culture to survive. It provides a design for living, directing both overt and personal behavior. In various ways, culture provides each individual with some idea of personal identity and a means of identifying others in the society. Finally, culture is inclusive. It governs most of man's life—speech, everyday actions, motivations, and even private thoughts.

NATURE OF MAN

Any serious consideration of human culture must take into account the possibility that cultures are, at least partly, shaped by something called "basic human nature." Certain aspects of man's nature were implied in the preceding discussion of culture. And in the discussion of social control in Chapter 2 we advanced the idea that human nature depends in a limited way on genetic inheritance. But we have not actually answered the following important questions: What is man's fundamental nature? What would he be like stripped of the artificial trappings of what we call "civilization" (read "culture")? Is mankind predisposed (naturally inclined) toward good or evil? We will consider them now by examining various hypotheses that have been advanced over the years about the basic nature of man.

Instincts

Early Hypotheses   Most definitions of human nature have been based on a more or less tacit acceptance of the validity of evolutionary theory. But there has been a major dispute in the behavioral sciences focused on the existence and importance of *instincts* in human nature. Instincts have been defined as those basic traits with which an individual is born and which cannot be altered by environmental influences, such as the demand for food, the urge to reproduce, the need to survive, aggression, and so on. With that definition in mind, let us look at some of the early hypotheses about human nature.

Sigmund Freud recognized that society imposes cultural restraints on individuals through mechanisms he called the *ego* and *superego*. But he also saw another force involved in the shaping of human personality, the *id*. He presumed the id held, or consisted of, "unlearned physiological motives and *unlearned reactions for satisfying them*." [8] Freud held that each human is born with a certain amount of genetically transmitted information stored in the id, and this stored information, by implication, constituted man's basic nature (lust, greed, sex, and so forth). Thus he presents a none-too-sanguine picture of man's basic nature which culture and society, working in tandem, restrained within the bounds set by society.

Somewhat earlier, Thomas Hobbes asserted in his "problem of order" that man's actions come or stem from their "passions," and their passions are different and independent, not common. [9] Hobbes saw man's basic nature as selfish and brutal and held that without the restraints imposed by society the result would be what Hobbes called "the war of every man against every man." [10] (See Chapter 1, the section on Emile Durkheim.) In contrast, Jean-Jacques Rousseau thought that the nature of man was fine and noble but constrained or even chained and made corrupt by society.

Jean Piaget makes assumptions similar to those of Freud although by no means either as dramatic or as pessimistic. He said of the differences between directed, or conscious, thought and autistic thought:

Autistic thought is subconscious, i.e., the goals it pursues and the problems it sets itself are not present in consciousness. It is not adapted to external reality but creates for itself a reality of imagination or dreams. It tends, not to establish truth but to gratify wishes and remains strictly individual and incommunicable as such by means of language, since it operates primarily in images and must, in order to be communicated, resort to roundabout methods, evoking, by means of symbols and myths, the feelings that guide it. [11]

Implied by Piaget is the notion that there is a level of thinking that does not follow social teaching or learning but, rather, some mysterious, genetically transmitted rules of its own.

Contemporary Hypotheses   The evidence for any genetically transmitted patterns of behavior—overt or covert—is largely based on speculation rather than on empirical facts. There is, however, real evidence that humans are born with some very simple patterns of behavior; the suckling reflex among new-born children is an example of the level of complexity of those reflexes. But we are concerned with truly complex behavior patterns that, if instinctive, would function to direct the development of culture.

There is a fundamental distinction between nonhuman primate social groupings and human societies. The society of nonhuman primates is wholly dependent on anatomy and physiology; the society of man is largely governed by culture. Differences among human societies are not the concomitant expressions of variations in the biology of the organism. They are largely, if not entirely, independent of them.[12]

John Buettner-Janusch indicates in that statement the concept of man as being highly adaptable and plastic—free from the constraints of biologically determined behavioral patterns and free to develop a wide variety of cultures and culture forms. We agree with this. But we cannot side with Buettner-Janusch's ideas about human anatomy and physiology, as we will discuss in the next section.

Modern anthropologists are convinced that man cannot exist without culture. According to Geertz, noncultured adult humans do "not, in fact, exist, have never existed, and most important, could not in the very nature of the case exist." He continues by saying that "what sets him [man] off most graphically from nonmen is less his sheer ability to learn (great as that is) than how much and what particular sorts of things he *has* to learn before he is able to function."[13]

Let us make certain at this point that we differentiate between "society" and "culture." *Culture is nonexistent without a society*, but *societies do exist without culture*. There are, of course, many kinds of "societies" at differing levels among living things; such as societies of ants and bees. But none of those possesses culture—their behavior is essentially instinctive, although there is some evidence that animals do learn from each other. Culture is made possible, in part, because humans are relatively "free from a pattern of specific instincts."[14]

So far we have examined opposing views about whether man does or does not possess instincts. In order to decide, let us first recall that "instincts" were described as basic traits that are inborn and cannot be altered by external influences. If an instinct is basic to one member of a species, then it must be basic to all, since it is an unalterable aspect of inborn human nature. In order for such behavior as the demand for food, reproduction, survival, or aggression to be instinctive, each would have to be present in equal degrees in *every* member of a given species. And the instincts would have to be totally resistant to *any* environmental influences. From even a limited observation of the range of variation in human behavior among the many human societies, it is obvious that there is anything but uniformity in those patterns of behavior. For example, if sexual behavioral patterns are instinctive, how do we account for homosexuality? Or for celibacy? In other words, man *can* alter his behavior for any one of various external reasons. He is not forced to behave as he does because instincts tell him to.

Nevertheless, the arguments about whether or not mankind possesses innate, complex, unmodifiable traits goes on. We have pointed out that modern anthropologists do not find evidence for instincts in man. Our contention is that *man's basic nature consists of potentialities for a wide range of diverse behavior*, the specific realization of which depends upon the culture and society into which any particular human is born. Contrary views are held by Robert Ardrey and Konrad Lorenz who claim that man is more aggressive than other animals. Ardrey has referred to man as a "killer ape" based on an hypothesis that man emerged from an "anthropoid background for one reason only—because he was a killer." [15] Lorenz claims to have found evidence for some instinct of aggression or, as he calls it, the "killer instinct" in man. [16] If instinctive aggression were true of *Homo sapiens*, it would be found in all members of the species, and there would be no "peaceful" societies—societies in which the culture precluded, or at least greatly minimized, aggression and violence. Yet anthropologists have gathered impressive and extensive evidence of human cultures that are nonaggressive. [17]

Early in the twentieth century the psychologist William McDougall attempted to explain almost all human behavior on the basis of one instinct or another. [18] Had he been correct, our principal means of studying culture would be the development and definition of long lists of instincts. Since this does not appear to be the case, it would seem that we could now turn our attention to the primary source of human behavior—culture. But, when we examine several of man's more salient characteristics—none of which is exclusive to man in isolation—we find that there are biological and physiological sources for human culture (the instinct hypothesizers were right, in part). Therefore, before we analyze culture itself, we will take a look at those biological bases.

BIOLOGICAL FOUNDATIONS OF HUMAN CULTURE

First it is necessary to understand that man "is an animal, comparable organ for organ to other animals." [19] Insofar as biological classification is concerned, the relationship of the species man to the species ape is relatively close. "By 'species,' biologists mean an evolutionary unit composed of continuing populations, that regularly interchange genes by interbreeding and that do not or cannot have such regular interchange with other species." [20] When male and female organisms mate and produce fertile offspring they must be of the same biological species. Since men of all races mate with women of all races and consistently produce fertile offspring, it can only be concluded that all men belong to a single species.

While human look-alikes are relatively rare (except for identical twins), men do have considerable resemblances to one another. With some exceptions, all members of our species are born with similar physical bodies and nervous systems. Those physiological characteristics we all hold in common (and some we do not such as resemblances to fathers and mothers) are genetically transmitted—they are hereditary. But what does that have to do with human cultures? We have argued earlier that mankind has no significant instincts and implied that culture is very much a human product, so does it matter what our physiological or biological inheritance happens to be? In Geertz's view if we were to analyze man by "peeling off" successive layers— the various kinds and types of cultures, the regularities of social organizations, the psychological factors, and so forth—we would finally be "left with the biological foundations—anatomical, physiological, neurological—of the whole edifice of human life."[21]

The principal argument to be made in this section is that *human culture has biological foundations of such a nature that they not only made culture possible but were absolutely necessary for survival.* Beings coming into the world who are not initially "programmed" to deal with their environments must depend on some other source for that information. In the case of man, that source is culture which, of course, is conveyed to the new arrival by older members of societies.

But it is not only our species that is dependent upon culture, according to Hoebel:

It would be an error born of self-adulation were we to think that no traces of the culture-creating capacity occur below the level of man. Our near relatives in the primate family are capable of inventing new forms of behavior in the solution of some of the simpler problems that are posed to them by experimental animal psychologists. They apparently can also reason on very elementary levels.[22]

We noted earlier that, among other criteria, culture is a learned way of life shared by members of a group or a society. In this respect, a considerable amount of the overt behavior of primates can be considered as culture because it is apparently transmitted from generation to generation. That holds not merely for behavior that can be described as social but also for such a simple thing as the traditional home territory of a troop of apes.[23] Roe goes even further when comparing man to certain other species:

There is no single attribute which, if carefully examined, applies to all men and to no other creatures, unless, of course, you define attributes in a limited fashion. Certainly, only man has "language" but if one defines language as a means of communication or even as symbolic communication, there is no such clear-cut distinction. Tool-using and tool-making, intelligence and reasoning; social forms; culture; all the familiar points of distinction between man and non-man break down as all-or-none distinctions when they are carefully examined.[24]

Roe's comments are accurate but only, we would maintain, if one defines "attributes" in a limited fashion. Some apes do make and use crude tools—

rocks for crushing, sticks for prying—and other apes do observe and, learning, follow the example. But there is a vast gulf between even a pair of ordinary pliers and a stick used for prying. When tools are defined more generally in terms of the degree to which they effectively extend an organism's ability to accomplish some task, the gulf between *Homo faber* (man the tool maker) and the Pongidae (apes) becomes wider. But, in partial agreement with Roe, it is a difference in degree not kind. That apes make and use crude tools cannot be denied any more than the fact that they are social animals. And it seems that the survival of these close cousins to man depends to a considerable extent upon learned behavior. However, this learning is different from that of man. According to one anthropologist, cultural patterns in primates are transmitted, not by teaching, but by observation. Observation, or learning by observation, tends to go *down* the dominance hierarchy—when a dominant male ape overtly behaves in some way the other animals will tend to copy him. Learning by observation goes *up* the dominance hierarchy very slowly if at all.[25] The salient point is that among primates culture is *time bound*; the rudimentary culture of any primate group is a matter of the behavior of individual members at some given time. Behavior, however successfully performed in isolation, does not become part of the culture of primates because they have no *symbolic* means of passing it on to their fellows. Desmond Morris notwithstanding, man is not the "naked ape."[26]

According to John Doby, "the emergence and development of human culture is a direct result of phylogenetic [evolutionary] changes in man. The biological structures necessary for the capacity had to precede in development the products made possible."[27] Let us see what these changes were and how they were related to the development of human culture.

Prolonged Period of Dependency

Many life forms are born (or hatched) and are quickly able to function sufficiently well to survive in their environment. New-born primates, *in order to remain alive*, must be cared for by some competent older member of the group. That *dependency period*, which continues the longest for man, provides the framework within which humans become acquainted with some form of social living. But more important, that continuing contact prepares the young to deal with the problems of living. In other words, it is during that period of dependency that cultural learning takes place.

Unlike Cadmus, we cannot sow dragon's teeth and expect full-grown humans to spring from the earth.[28] An adult human capable of taking his place in a society is the product of a prolonged, complex, difficult, not always satisfying but necessary process of socialization. And socialization is the result of the long period of dependency. We should, perhaps, point out that one peculiarity of human existence is that in order to become competent, one must first be absolutely helpless.

Locomotion and Posture

The fact that modern man has upright posture and is bipedal—walks on two legs—is important to the development and maintenance of culture. The evolutionary change from quadrupedal (locomotion on all fours) to bipedal

must have introduced a marked perceptual change. The same eye can see considerably farther from five feet above the ground than it can from two feet, which is not only defensively useful in a plains living animal, but introduces a spatial extension of the world which may come to be associated with a temporal one. To see ahead is not only a figure of speech.[29]

But it did more than just extend the range of man's vision. Walking on two feet freed man's hands from locomotion. And, as Joseph Biegert said, the human hand is "an organ for culture."[30] With this remarkable tool, in conjunction with other characteristics, man was able to make other tools that served as further extensions of his physiological equipment (which is what any tool really is).[31] The tools that man makes are largely *specialized*—they are constructed to perform a limited range of functions. But man's hands are *generalized* tools able to perform a wide variety of functions. The impact of tool-using and tool-making on the evolution of culture is well presented by Ralph Beals and Harry Hoijer:

It seems very likely . . . that the beginnings of tool-using and especially tool-making greatly accelerated the evolutionary trend, already evident among the early primates, toward larger and more complex brains and nervous systems . . . In short, tool-making was probably the first step in the development of culture.[32]

Vision

Insofar as inherited physiology is concerned, no one characteristic made culture possible. Even with upright posture and the use of his hands, man still required good vision to make the most of those features. Beside extended range of vision, man needed sharp vision, color vision, and the ability to judge distances accurately simply to survive. Although man's visual characteristics were and are shared by all other primates, sight is significant because it "is associated with a very great enlargement of the brain area related to vision, a change that reaches its greatest development in man."[33] And it is because of his enlarged brain that man is distinct from nonhumans.

When we think of the brain, we almost automatically consider the matter of *intelligence*. In order to understand what we mean by intelligence, we shall look to psychology because the testing of intelligence is within their domain. Psychologists are in general agreement that intelligence is an adjustive capacity that is highly variable even in humans. That it is considered a *capacity* is borne out by two definitions. One, given by Jerome Kagan and Ernest Havemann, states that "intelligence is the ability to profit from experience, to learn new pieces of information, and to adjust to new situations."[34] In operational terms, an organism that persists in behavior that proves to be inadequate to a situation would be exhibiting less of this capacity than an organism that exhibited variable behavior until a successful one was discovered. Robert Woodworth and Donald Marquis provide the second, somewhat similar, definition:

As a word, intelligence *is closely related to* intellect, *which is a comprehensive term for observing, understanding, thinking, remembering and all the ways of knowing and of getting knowledge. Intellectual activity yields knowledge. Intelligent activity does this and something more. It is* useful, *helpful in solving a problem and reaching a goal.*[35]

Both definitions are helpful sociologically for they place the definition of intelligence in a *behavioral* context—given a problem to solve, what is the relative effectiveness of the solution from society to society or, for that matter, from species to species? (The determination of effectiveness, in the final analysis, involves making value judgments. Although we have tried to keep such evaluations to a minimum, on occasions such as this they seem unavoidable.) By implication, the majority of anthropologists hold that the solutions of *Homo sapiens* to the various problems of living are superior to those of other species. Certainly in terms not merely of survival but also of population growth, man has been successful— as we will discuss in Chapter 11 on population, much too successful. However, it is difficult to take the stand that man's adjustment to the conditions of living and his environment has not been more successful than that of other species. But at the same time, we ought to take note of Doby's comment that

man is so accustomed to his cultural forms of adaptation that most of us are unaware of the contradictions and stupidities that exist around us as cultural forms and hence the callousness and wastefulness of this form of evolution . . .[36]

There is some exaggeration in Doby's comment. We *are* becoming more aware of some of these cultural contradictions and stupidities—overpopulation, pollution, and so forth—and we call these "social problems." To be "aware" of complex errors in cultural ways is surely congruent with the definitions of intelligence we have been discussing. Man is not only perceiving problems but is also working toward some viable solutions.

We accept, then, that man's intelligence is superior to that of other species under most conditions. We now proceed to ask why this is so. The answer is necessarily biological and physiological.

In the last million years, our own genus Homo *has made considerable and apparently rapid evolutionary progress . . . Starting with a small brain of no more than pongid [apelike] proportions, there has been a three-fold increase in human brain volume . . . Truly, evolution has reshaped us . . . increasing our capacities to plan and to pursue . . .*[37]

Bernard Rensch notes that "the bigger the brain, the greater the brain power—this seems to be a general rule among comparable members of the animal kingdom."[38] Buettner-Janusch also argues that "man's capacity for culture depended on the evolutionary development of a brain of *sufficient size and complexity to enable him to symbol;*" he adds that "the development of culture also depended on culture itself. The filling of the tool kit depended on cultural traditions, on raw materials, and on the brain."[39] Beals and Hoijer emphasize both size and complexity stating that

Particularly important is the fact that not only is man's brain much larger than that of the ape but it is especially highly developed in the frontal region and has a much more complex convolutionary development of the cerebral cortex.[40]

But it is not mere mass or size that is really the significant element; it is the brain-to-body-size ratio, which is adjusted by a special formula for all sorts of factors, such as total body size. And by this method, mammals have been classified into five progressive classes of brain development. "Modern man alone occupies the top berth."[41]

Summary

Why all this material on biology, physiology, and evolution? The best answer to that question is that neither sociology nor any other science—behavioral, natural, or physical—can alone provide a complete explanation of the phenomena it studies. And, too, there has been a rash of popular books that either imply or directly state that significant aspects of human social behavior are instinctive in origin.[42] In view of that, it was considered important to

Copyright © 1972 by Saturday Review/World, Inc.
Reprinted by permission from the publisher and Herbert Goldberg.

"I'm overcome with despair. We've learned to talk, but we're further apart than before."

Complex organizations, human institutions, music, economics, politics would all be impossible without language.

provide information from more authoritative and scientific sources about the real origins of culture.

We have reviewed a number of human characteristics which are biologically, that is, genetically, inherited: the long period of dependence, upright posture and bipedal locomotion with a consequent freeing of the hands, sharpness of vision, and the human brain. Coon observed that man shared several of those characteristics "to some extent with the monkeys and apes, but the total combination was [man's] alone, and this combination of gifts became in itself something unique."[43] We might turn this around and look at it from another direction: "Man is highly flexible and adaptable because he *lacks* (1) the fixed, inborn patterns of behavior and (2) the specific biological adaptations to environment that other animals have."[44]

The "unique gift" of which Coon speaks is the possession of some things and the absence of others. The key word would seem to be *flexibility*, and "the human capacity for culture is a consequence of man's complex and plastic nervous system."[45]

One of the key elements in man's complex and plastic nervous system is another essential trait for the establishment of human culture—the capacity for language. As emphasized strongly by David Krech, no other animal has a brain that is capable of inventing and supporting language.[46] Since language is a component of culture, we will include a full discussion of language in the following section.

Biological Foundations of Human Culture

73

COMPONENTS OF CULTURE

Culture has a social base, by which we mean that culture develops from *social interaction*. In the case of apes that culture is, as we noted in the preceding section, rudimentary and limited to current life situations—the *temporal present*. But human culture is a product of a different kind of social interaction, symbolic interaction.

Symbolic Interaction: Language

Symbolic interaction among humans involves two kinds of signs, natural signs and conventional signs. Alfred Lindesmith and Anselm Strauss present helpful definitions of both. *Natural signs* consist of movements, sounds, smells, gestures, or any other stimuli that are "perceived regularly to precede or be connected with something else." In contrast, a *conventional sign*

derives its meaning from social consensus and is "movable" or arbitrary in the sense that different signs (for example in different languages) may mean the same thing, and that the sign (for example, a word) may be used in situations in which the object referred to is not present. Conventional signs are relative to social groups or language communities in which the same signs are interpreted in the same ways by a plurality of persons.[47]

Without going into the various hypotheses concerning language (and there are many), it will be merely noted that language is a by-product of two things: (1) the *capacity* (biological and physiological capacity) to develop language, and (2) the opportunity to do so through human interaction. With respect to the second point, it is important to remember that a certain amount of interaction is forced upon humans by the long period of dependence when they are young.

Lindesmith and Strauss in defining conventional signs mention that "the same signs are interpreted in the same way," from which it follows that language involves *consensus* about the meaning of words. This consensus on *meaning* extends to agreement on *grammar*—overall agreement on language usage—and especially on *syntax*—the arrangement of word forms to show their relationship in a sentence. Once all these agreements were made among the plurality of a society and became part of the culture, many things became possible. Doby contends that "the development of human speech and language were tremendous steps in evolution. This gave man the power to organize his thoughts and to objectify these through the creation of organizations of all kinds."[48] To this idea Noam Chomsky, a noted linguist, adds that although the users of language are constrained by the rules of language, they are "free to express new thoughts."[49] The "new thoughts" are a product of yet another function made possible by the human invention of language. Once a language is learned, along with its grammar and syntax, it is possible for people "to manipulate objects *imaginatively* and to convey the results of such imaginative manipulations to [others]."[50] These manipulations, these new thoughts, and most importantly, the ability to create many different kinds of organizations are possible for all human societies because "every human society has a well-developed language."[51]

While there is some organization among nonhumans who cluster together in what might be called societies, none of them is organized in the same sense that human societies are. The difference between the organization in nonhuman societies and that in human societies is a matter not of degree but of kind.

The relationship between language and culture is a direct one, and all human culture is dependent upon language. Language, a product of social interaction, made culture possible. Complex organizations, human institutions, music, economics, politics would all be impossible without language. Language makes culture both progressive and cumulative.

But since all societies are organized in different ways by the components of their culture, we will now turn our attention to these other elements. Emphasis will be placed on not merely the relationship of each element to all other elements of society but also the dynamic aspects of each.

Social Status

"Status" is often misused and incorrectly taken to mean much the same thing as "prestige." But in sociology, status is synonymous with "category." Each individual has a number of statuses at any given time—male or female, child or adult, married or unmarried, and so forth. Each of those statuses has certain roles attached to them. We would, for example, expect a middle-aged woman to behave differently from a young man and engineers to act as engineers and not physicians. In other words, all social statuses have sets of *expectations* attached to them.

There are two types of statuses, *ascribed* and *achieved*. Ascribed statuses are those assigned to all individuals by others, and the most obvious are sex, age, and race. Achieved statuses possess a voluntary aspect. A person can choose to marry or not to marry, or he can work to become a physician or an engineer: he thus acquires an achieved status as husband or as engineer or physician. Both ascribed and achieved statuses are very important to an individual's sense of self. In other words, "Statuses are what we are."[52]

Social Class

"Social class" is used to classify people according to the rewards and privileges they possess as a consequence of their economic standing in society."[53]

Class is a matter of the rankings that people assign one another on the basis of economic factors and is directly concerned with life style—the way one lives—and life chances—which include such things as the opportunities for a long and healthy life, a college education, entry to the more desirable and remunerative professions and occupations, and so on. While class is a significant sociological variable in modern societies, it is also a factor in some preliterate societies; there is no known society in which some members have not been able to obtain more of the rewards available than others in that society.

Social Roles

The "unit of human society is not the 'individual' but the social role which is taken by the individual." [54] McGee defines "roles" as

the parts we play in life as actors where the drama engaged in is defined by group memberships, e.g., "father," "teen-ager," "Methodist," etc. Roles are always attached to groups and are reciprocal in that group members have mutually understood expectations for each other's behavior. Many roles are also complementary, i.e., to be a father, one must have a child, etc. [55]

That definition makes clear that social roles do not function in a vacuum. They get their meaning from the fact that the people in different social statuses share mutual expectations about how they will behave toward others—be they in a similar or different status—and how others will behave toward them. It is in knowing something about others—their social position, status, and so forth—that enables people to carry on meaningful social interaction. Without knowledge of many different roles in modern society and the expectations attached to each of them, it would be difficult for an individual not merely to stay out of serious difficulties but also to survive. Even in traditional societies, members play several roles—warrior, husband, hunter, herdsman, and so forth. In modern societies, the opportunities to play more roles are greater because modern societies are more complex. While it is probable that roles were more sharply defined in preliterate societies, roles are nonetheless well defined in modern societies. All statuses have roles—how one is expected to behave in such positions and how others are expected to behave toward the role-player. Without those expectations, any kind of social organization would be impossible.

Social Norms

A general definition of social norms is that they prescribe the proper way of behaving. But a moment's reflection will tell us that this is too sparse to be satisfactory. Certainly there are proper ways of behaving for almost any *Culture* situation of which one can think. Yet for some situations it would seem to be unimportant whether the norms were followed or not. In others, it would appear prudent to behave according to what is known to be the proper way. Then, too, some norms can be violated with no subsequent punishment. And for ignoring others, the penalty could be as severe as imprisonment.

Glenn Vernon distinguishes between two kinds of norms.[56] *Mores* are those norms the group or society considers as particularly important, and any deviations are likely to be severely punished. *Folkways* are general rules —for example, etiquette—and any deviation is regarded with considerable tolerance, although those who consistently violate folkways are likely to suffer some kinds of sanctions. However, some human behavior is not *normative*—that is, it is under the control of the individual concerned. But such behavior tends to be largely trivial. To illustrate behavior not under the control of norms, we might point out that the movie one attends or whether one stays home and watches television is largely a matter of personal decision.

It is likely that in preliterate societies mores were a more significant factor in directing behavior than in modern societies. Mores are associated with morality to a much greater extent than other norms, and certainly folkways do not involve any marked degree of morality. For example, consider what Durkheim asks in a comment about morality in simpler societies.

What social danger is there in touching a tabooed object, an impure animal or man, in letting the sacred fire die down, in eating certain meats, in failure to make the traditional sacrifice over the graves of parents, in not exactly pronouncing the ritual formula, in not celebrating certain holidays, etc?[57]

All those behaviors were subjected to severe and cruel punishments in many preliterate societies. But each of them could be violated with impunity in a modern society.

Has the moral order declined in modern societies? Many would claim that it has. Durkheim, however, saw a different kind of force holding society together as a society grew more complex (Durkheim was referring to the increasing division of labor). What he saw as replacing "moral force" as the cohesive element in society, was increasing *interdependence*. Few if any people are self-sufficient in modern societies, and their behavior is governed by norms that, if not mores, are stronger than folkways.[58] Norms in modern societies, then, take on more of an element of rationality and are keyed to the needs of industrialized societies. Although tradition is still a force, because norms change very slowly, modern norms tend to be based on reality rather than to have their origin in mythology. In fact, there are few mores at all in modern societies. To make this clearer, we might ask ourselves what norms in modern societies can be considered *universals*—norms that "apply to all the members of the society and from which there is no permissible deviation . . . [59] Incest, murder, and treason might be called universals, but there are exceptions even to those. There is, for example, the so-called unwritten law, that allows a husband who catches his wife and another man in the act of sexual intercourse to shoot the man and stand a chance of being acquitted on the basis of justifiable homicide. In addition to universal norms, there are also *alternative* norms. Ralph Linton describes these as being attached to certain activities that may have two or more possible norms with approximately the same value and degree of preference. [60]

Another way to view norms is to consider that all norms can be placed on a continuum. At one end would be mores—norms having a sacred quality for the members of the society, violation of which would be punished with the utmost severity. At the other end would be the most minor folkways that could be flouted with virtual immunity, such as the requirement that when a gentleman and lady are walking in the street, the gentleman walks on the side nearest the curb. We may also think of single norms as falling on a continuum with the ideal norm falling in the center. It should be apparent that except for few mores, some latitude is permissible with the great majority of norms. For example, college students are supposed to study hard and obtain high grades. The grading systems in effect at colleges and universities rather directly recognize that the ideal will not be met by most students and permits *some* variation. A system using A as the highest and F to indicate failure considers C as being satisfactory. But students cannot stray too far from the ideal norms. Any significant number of D's or F's results in probation and, if work does not improve, eventually expulsion. The same situation prevails in many aspects of life. Some deviation from the ideal is permissible, but too much invites sanctions of one kind or another. What constitutes permissible variation is usually based on what has been called *modal* behavior, or the most frequent behavior observed. [61]

Finally, it is essential to emphasize the significance of norms for human groups and for the formation of groups. In this respect, George Homans defines norm as "an idea in the minds of the members of a group, an idea that can be put in the form of a statement specifying what the members or other men should do, ought to do, are expected to do under given circumstances." [62] Norms, then, make group activity and cooperation possible by defining those tasks appropriate to different groups. Roles, according to John Kinch, can be considered as "those norms that refer to expectations for individuals because of some characteristic that an individual possesses or a position he holds in a group or society." And he says that group norms (be the group small or very large, such as a society) take two general forms, (1) *rights and privileges*, and (2) *duties and obligations*. [63] Then when a particular "label," or role, is assigned to an individual, it immediately brings into play certain norms relating to that label or role out of which come *expectations* about individual behavior in a variety of group contexts.

There are few groups in which the role of male or female is not significant. This is true even in a symphony orchestra where musical skill is relevant but the sex of the musicians ought not to be. Age, too, is a factor in group roles. Interaction for age, sex, and race are broad cultural roles that are present in the role definitions of most groups.[64]

Sanctions

All cultures are marked by a variety of sanctions, which may become operative when norms are violated. We say "may" because norms can be, and often are, violated privately. But even then, negative sanctions may come into play because, as indicated in Chapter 2, individuals can apply sanctions to themselves. Preliterate cultures, although they generally have no formalized sanctions, apply them more evenly than large, complex modern societies because in small societies most members are under close observation much of the time.

Modern cultures are marked by two kinds of sanctions: (1) *formal*, and (2) *informal*.

Formal Sanctions Formal sanctions are applied for violations of those norms that have been codified into written laws. Such norms are enforced by separate individuals and bodies, which include the police and the courts (the codification of norms into laws being a function of legislative bodies). It might be well to note that some laws do not represent the norms of the culture. An outstanding example from American history is the Volstead Act, or Prohibition Amendment of 1919, which made the consumption of alcoholic beverages illegal. The norms that decried the drinking of alcohol were far from being universal.

Supporting the dry crusade was, roughly, the small town, farming, middle-class tradition infused with the radical Protestant ethic that sought to make men better by legislation. The opposition to the Volstead act drew much of its strength from the newer urban groups, mixed in religious affiliation or secular-minded and devoted to a much freer, tolerant, and often sybaritic way of life.[65]

While severe, almost barbaric sanctions—very long jail sentences, for example—were meted out to violators of the Volstead Act, the well-publicized arrests and convictions were ineffective in stopping the use of alcohol. To this case, the Latin phrase *Quid leges sine moribus?* (to what avail are laws without the support of the mores?) can be applied. In Philadelphia alone, there were 16,819 arrests for drunkenness in 1919. Six years later and in the face of

3 1303 00058 5381

great activity by prohibition agents, arrests had grown to 51,361.[66] Sanctions, then, are effective only under circumstances in which there is cultural support for their use. More recently, the controversy over drug use, particularly of marihuana, is an analogous case. As was stressed in Chapter 2, social control very largely rests on the *internalization of culture by a substantial majority of the members of any society.* Insofar as the norms of modern societies are concerned, the increasingly pluralistic trend of such societies virtually insures on-going conflict about what a society's norms are.

Informal Sanctions Informal sanctions, contrary to what is usually thought, are unquestionably the more potent form of coercive control over behavior. It is the family, friends, and acquaintances who "keep one in line" to a far greater extent than either officially applied sanctions or the *threat* of them. The range of informal sanctions is unknown but undoubtedly extensive. We say "unknown" because what is or is not a sanction depends very much upon the persons involved. For example, a sadist could apply a sanction to a masochist simply by *withholding* "punishment." The sanction could be made even severe were the sadist to treat the masochist with great kindness. Persistent violators of norms close to the folkways end of the continuum often suffer sanctions without knowing it. Television advertisements promoting the use of preparations to make one pleasanter to be near are an example of an emergent norm in modern society. For some individuals, failure to use such preparations may well involve sanctions of a particularly cruel nature— people tend to avoid the individual; he or she may have difficulty obtaining social companionship or even a job.

Another set of informal sanctions revolves around behavior that might be considered as "swimming upstream when everyone else is going with the current." Prodigious effort is expended, but little progress is made. In American society, an individual fluent in French but who could also speak English could probably "get by," after a fashion, if he or she insisted in speaking only French. But the difficulties would be obvious. So in thousands of ways all of us function quite informally to maintain surveillance over the behavior of others and apply sanctions when we feel that it is necessary to do so. The difference between a mother spanking a small boy for some misdeed or a wife withholding sexual favors from her husband for some misdeed is a matter of degree, not kind. But most of the time for most of the people the "garden variety, everyday type" norms are followed with reasonable consistency. This holds true even for those norms we defined earlier as folkways. According to Robert Nisbet, "the power of habit and custom are great because they are reflections of adaptation or control which make the hard work of thought, of *attention* unnecessary."[67] Looked at in that way, norms provide directions for carrying on those numerous, routine details of everyday life without having to devote too much thought to it. In this context, norms serve a function not often considered—they make life simpler and easier.

There can be little doubt that sanctions constitute an essential element of culture. When deviant behavior is punished, the actual social function of punishment is, as Durkheim and George Mead pointed out, to affirm moral standards. Punishment functions to distinguish, or set off, wrong from right. The purpose of punishment is to reform the erring individual. Arnold Green contends that arguments against punishment of any kind because it often does *not* reform the "criminal" are overlooking an essential cultural function of punishment. What the application of severe sanctions to individuals strongly implies is that individuals bear a certain responsibility for their acts.

Whether or not a man is responsible for what he does, he must be held personally accountable for what he does. Only on the basis of mutual accountability can mutual prediction of behavior take place, without which all social relationships would be impossible.

Green continues by saying that the manifest or stated purpose of the administration of sanctions, be they informal or formal, is "always rationalized with some symbolized purpose, such as reform, the good of the soul, or the protection of the membership of society."[68] But the latent function is to maintain the general predictability of most of the behavior within any given society. To the extent that unpredictable behavior is either rewarded (which it is sometimes) or not negatively sanctioned, the likelihood of unpredictable behavior is increased, and with this comes a reduction in the cohesion of society. We do not mean to imply that the tendency of most people to adhere most of the time to most norms is a mechanical or forced process whereby man is a slave of a particular culture and living in a society that gives behavioral expression to that culture. In modern societies, people *are* asking questions about traditional norms, and these norms are changing, as we will discuss in Chapter 13.

Material and Nonmaterial Culture

Material culture consists of "things" produced by people which are tangible; they can be seen, touched, measured directly, felt, and so forth. Items of material culture have a concrete existence. *Nonmaterial culture* consists of the concepts discussed earlier in this section—statuses, roles, norms, and so forth. "Strictly speaking, material culture is not really culture at all. It is the product of culturally determined activity. Behind every artifact [a man-produced thing] are the patterns of culture that give form to the idea for the artifact and the techniques of shaping and using it."[69] Sociologists tend to restrict the meaning of the term "material culture" to only those products of human manufacture which have some *meaning*, that is, to those that take on some aspects of nonmaterial culture:

A material object is a part of culture only insofar as one person can expect another person to act toward it in a certain way under certain circumstances. If a person makes something unique and no one sees him use it so that it has no meaning to other people, it is not a cultural object.[70]

Since it *is* difficult to find a single object manufactured by man (except in isolation of course) which does *not* have some meaning, virtually all artifacts can be considered as material culture.

The relationship between material and nonmaterial culture is complex. There can be no question that certain inventions or innovations of a material kind have had profound effects on nonmaterial culture—the wheel, the plow, the steam engine, and so forth. The development of material culture proceeds more predictably than that of nonmaterial culture. Inventions and innovations tend to be combinations of earlier material culture—for example, the steamboat combined two material items already available, the hull of a boat (or ship) and a steam engine.

While nonmaterial culture does not progress in quite the predictable manner of material culture, some inventions belong distinctly within the realm of the nonmaterial, such as religion, democracy, Einstein's theories, paperback books, the germ theory of disease, social security, the Peace Corps, and a host of others.[71] On the other hand, nonmaterial culture *is* less consistent. "Some contemporary norms are not demonstrably superior to those of two thousand years ago, whereas the automobile is patently superior to the oxcart as a means of transportation."[72] While the distinction between material and nonmaterial culture should be made, it is the linking together of norms relating to each that is important—the cultural patterns that function in an integrated fashion to meet social requirements.[73] The distinction between material and nonmaterial culture is an artificial one; both kinds of culture are highly integrated and constantly interact in a dynamic fashion to mold, influence, and change each other.[74]

Cultural Persistence

While all cultures depend for their existence on living human beings, the life-span of a culture is not limited in the same sense as that of their carriers. People are born, live out their lives, and die; the culture that shaped their lives existed before they entered the world and remains long after their deaths. Cultures do not die, but they do change over time, as we have noted in this chapter and will discuss in detail in Chapter 13. While cultures tend to persist in single societies as well as in nations composed largely of one culture, they can also persist among peoples who are widely scattered such as the Jewish Diaspora. These are people who have lived for hundreds of years scattered throughout the world and yet retain their distinctly Jewish culture, although there are, of course, cultural differences between European and Asiatic Jews. And we can say that very few cultures have ever disappeared entirely. The so-called tribal instincts or tribal memories of which some writers speak are probably nothing more than cultural traits that have persisted over time in cultures far removed from those in which the trait originated. Linton makes a convincing case that a great many material elements in modern American culture are, in fact, diffusions from other cultures and some very ancient ones at that.[75]

Cultural persistence depends upon two principal factors: (1) recruitment of new members, and (2) the socialization of new members into the culture (to be discussed more fully in Chapter 5). If a society were to become suddenly sterile—if no new members were recruited by birth—and there was no in-migration, it would, as an entity, disappear except for those cultural traits that had diffused to other and more viable societies. Culture, then, exists before the birth of individuals, is acquired by individuals, and persists long after their deaths.

Ethnocentrism

Ethnocentrism is defined as the belief that the ways of doing things peculiar to one's own culture are the only right, proper, and moral ways of behaving.[76] That is a general characteristic of all human groups, from the small to the very large. Societies appear to somehow or other indoctrinate new members to regard whatever is practiced in their own culture as being not merely superior in terms of efficiency but also more proper in terms of morality.

As a phenomenon, ethnocentrism has some variable qualities. It can be thought of as a series of concentric circles each having a larger diameter than the one preceding it. At the center of these circles and represented by the circle with the smallest diameter are such small human groups as the family. Since people tend to most strongly internalize (make their own) the values and norms of those with whom they are in the closest personal association and continuing interaction, ethnocentric feelings regarding such groups are apt to be the strongest. The next circle could represent the neighborhood; then the city or town in which an individual resides. From that circle we move on to other circles representing states, regions, the nation, its allies, and finally all of mankind (as compared with other species).

Another characteristic of ethnocentrism is that views can change. Groups previously viewed with deep suspicion as being seriously "different" can

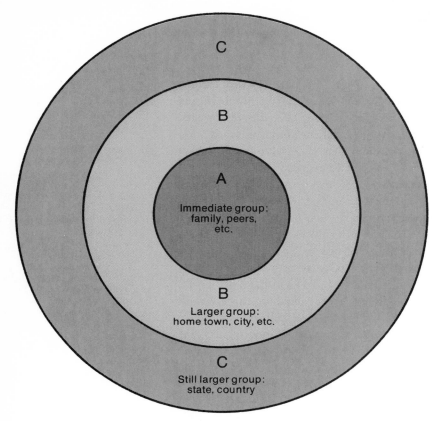

A

Immediate group:
family, peers,
etc.

B

Larger group:
home town, city, etc.

C

Still larger group:
state, country

Ethnocentrism is dynamically incremental. Members of group A may well be ethnocentric with respect to all larger groups of which they are actually members. But should there be some threat to groups B or C, then loyalties will tend to shift to these larger groups.

suddenly be considered not so different, with obvious dissimilarities viewed as "quaint" or "interesting." For example, prior to being attacked by Nazi Germany, the USSR was regarded by most Americans as representing a monolithic conspiracy to take over the world, and it was widely believed that Russians were brutal, godless, given to sexual excesses, and so forth. Suddenly they were attacked by Germany and her allies, and things changed overnight. The brutal dictator Joseph Stalin became kindly Uncle Joe, and the brutal Russian soldiers and enslaved civilian population became the "kindly Ivans." Things, of course, have changed several times since then. Immediately after World War II the earlier ethnocentrism returned with all its dark suspicions of the Russians and their ways. And more recently, there has been a softening of this attitude toward the USSR, both politically and culturally.

In an extreme form, ethnocentrism is referred to as *phenomenal absolutism*, which is "the tendency to assume that the world is exactly as one sees it, and that all other persons (other groups, other cultures) really perceive it in the same way but behave the way they do out of a perverse wickedness or in-

Culture

84

competence."[77] From this follows the idea that others need to be punished or, if judged incompetent, to be taught more efficient ways.

It is tempting to question the purely cultural nature of ethnocentricism because this trait appears to be characteristic of human groups wherever they are found. Is there something within mankind—genetically passed on from generation to generation—that compels man to behave ethnocentrically? Lorenz, for example, claims that if some intelligent observer from another world were to observe our species, "he would unavoidably draw the conclusion that man's social organization is very similar to that of rats, which, like humans, are social and peaceful beings within their clans but veritable devils toward all fellow members of their species not belonging to their own community."[78] And Ardrey maintains that man is instinctively compelled to protect his own "turf" against encroachments from others, which he calls the "territorial imperative." He regards "the territorial imperative as no less essential to the existence of contemporary man as it was to those bands of small-brained proto-men on the high African savannah millions of years ago."[79]

The trouble with Lorenz's view is that men do not *necessarily* behave like "veritable devils" toward those not having membership in their own community. And Ardrey's view, aside from assuming some territorial instinct in man, is in error in failing to define how much territory is involved. If men did, and we can assume that this was so, defend their territory in prehistoric times it was probably less a matter of real estate than it was of protecting their own lives and the lives of their women and children. Then, too, how does Ardrey explain the increasingly large amounts of territory man seems willing to protect? In World War II, men were fighting for continents, not just a few hundred square miles of arable land. And, if they did go into combat for territory, it was usually because the territory in question possessed some tactical or strategic advantage. It seems highly doubtful that ethnocentricism, whether the belief in the superiority of one's group or some genetically inherited feel for the earth around where one was born, is anything but a learned cultural trait that varies in its force from culture to culture.

Arnold and Caroline Rose suggest one explanation for ethnocentricism:

If one surveys the cultures of the world, he finds that human beings are behaving in almost every way that they can possibly behave. What is indecent in one culture is proper and expected in some other culture. What is humorous or ridiculous in one culture is serious and profound in another culture. What is a religious act in one culture is a criminal act in another culture.[80]

Ethnocentricism is, then, nothing more (or less) than the learned reaction toward deviance within a social group turned outward, or against other groups, on the basis of deviance from real or suspected norms. It is, in effect, a tendency to see the world in moral terms. This moralistic outlook is applied not only to group members but also to the rest of the world. Robin Williams points out that the value of "moral orientation"—some systematic way of judging conduct—is a characteristic of the American value system.[81] And Rose and Rose observe that "Americans, along with the French, the Arabs, the ancient Greeks, and the ancient Hebrews, and a few other peoples, have cultures that are particularly characterized by ethnocentrism."[82]

If ethnocentricism has some negative aspects, such as encouraging conflict between groups, it has the positive feature of contributing to in-group cohesion. This would clearly have been an important survival mechanism for the mechanistic type societies described by Durkheim in times of crisis. Today among modern societies, there is not only less evidence of virulent ethnocentrism (phenomenal absolutism) but also less need for it in terms of promoting in-group cohesion.

CONCLUSION

This chapter was intended to provide some idea of the bases for human cultures and the principal components, traits, and characteristics of culture. Some aspects of culture not treated in this chapter, for example, the family, social institutions, values, social and cultural change, and race and ethnicity are considered in detail in subsequent chapters.

It has been necessary to perform that artificial operation of segmenting the subject into various parts. This is not unlike taking apart a reciprocating gasoline powered engine and leaving the parts strewn around—one knows what the parts are and where they go but the engine as a totality has disappeared. Continuing with the engine analogy, if we consider the engine to be society, then surely that which gives direction to its power is culture.

Culture is not, it must be emphasized, something that operates independently. It is absolutely dependent upon human beings. People often reify culture—that is, they endow it with life and regard it as if it had corporal substance, which it does not. Culture exists only inside people. As we observed, material culture *is* cultural only insofar as manufactured objects have *meaning*. And meaning can only be given by humans. Culture, then, is very much a human product.[83] "Only members of society plan, decide, and act. Society does nothing."[84] The same is true of culture.

We have mentioned the artificiality of any analysis of culture, but we maintain that some understanding of the parts is a prerequisite for a comprehension of the whole. In conclusion, our emphasis must be that culture is meaningful only insofar as it is related to, either as an independent or dependent variable, behavior of some kind. An important contribution of

Parsons to sociological thinking has been his emphasis on actors and situations. However, he makes a distinction between behavior and action. It should be recognized that while all action *is* behavior, not all behavior can be viewed as action. Edward Devereux has said that

if the flight of a moth toward a candle is conceived simply as a mechanistic response of its organism to the stimulus of light, there is behavior but not action. On the other hand, if we were to conceive of some subjective process of orientation as an essential link in the chain ". . . as if the moth, for example, were to reason with itself: 'What a pretty light! I would like to move closer to it. I will fly there as directly and quickly as possible . . .'" then we should be dealing with action.[85]

If we agree with that statement, then there is very little human behavior but much action, and what makes this difference between behavior and action is what we call *culture*.

In the following chapter we will devote our attention to one aspect of culture that we have not as yet examined—values.

REVIEW QUESTIONS

3.1. Would you expect to find cultural change proceeding more rapidly in some kinds of societies than others? Explain your answer and give real-life examples of some extant societies in which culture change might be expected to proceed somewhat slowly.

3.2. What is the Hobbesian "problem of order," and is this problem *really* a problem to modern sociologists? Why or why not?

3.3. Could man exist without culture? Defend your answer?

3.4. What do we mean when we say that societies can and do exist without culture but that culture cannot exist without societies?

3.5. If human culture has biological foundations, then what particular biological facts made culture an imperative for human survival?

3.6. Present an argument supporting the idea that some animals other than man possess rudimentary culture. What animals? Be sure to define first what you mean by "true culture."

3.7. In terms of culture, what are some of the more important consequences of the prolonged period of dependency in human young?

3.8. What was probably the most important result of upright posture and bipedal locomotion in man? Why?

3.9. If we grant that men, in general, are more intelligent than other animals, how do we define intelligence?

3.10. What is man's most important general characteristic?

3.11. What is the difference between *natural* and *conventional* signs? Which are the more important insofar as human communications are concerned?

3.12. What is the source of meaning for social roles?

3.13. What function do norms perform for members of a society?

3.14. Differentiate between *mores* and *folkways*.

3.15. Why did the Volstead Act fail in its purpose to bring an end to the consumption of alcoholic beverages in the United States?

3.16. In modern societies, which are the most potent form of social control, *formal* or *informal* sanctions? Why? What is the essential social function of punishment?

3.17. Differentiate between *ascribed* and *achieved* statuses. Give some examples of each in modern societies.

3.18. What is the essential difference between material and nonmaterial culture? Can inventions be considered part of nonmaterial culture? If no, why not? If yes, provide examples.

3.19. In simple terms, describe or explain why cultures outlast their individual human carriers.

3.20. Define *ethnocentrism*. As a cultural component it has at least two significant, variable features. What are they?

3.21. What is meant by the term *phenomenal absolutism*? Do we find much of this in the world today? Give some examples.

3.22. First defend the assertion that ethnocentrism might be a human instinct. Then present an argument that it cannot be instinctive.

3.23. What do we mean when we say that people *reify* culture? Is reification likely to lead to a better understanding of culture? Why or why not?

3.24. In the Parsonian view, what is the difference between *action* and *behavior*? Which is the more characteristic of humans?

NOTES

[1] Adamson E. Hoebel, "The Nature of Culture," in *Man, Culture, and Society*, ed. Harry L. Shapiro (New York: Oxford University Press, 1956), pp. 168–182.

[2] Edwin R. Guthrie, *The Psychology of Learning*, rev. ed. (New York: Harper & Row, 1952), p. 3.

[3] Clifford Geertz, "The Impact of the Concept of Culture on the Concept of Man," in *Man in Adaptation: The Cultural Present*, ed. Yehudi A. Cohen (Chicago: Aldine, 1968), p. 25.

[4] Clyde Kluckhohn and William Kelly, "The Concept of Culture," in *The Science of Man in the World Crisis*, ed. Ralph Linton (New York: Columbia University Press, 1945), p. 97.

[5] Reece McGee, *Points of Departure* (Hinsdale, Ill.: Dryden Press, 1972), p. 19.

[6] Robert Bierstedt, *The Social Order*, 3d ed. (New York: McGraw-Hill, 1970), pp. 122–123.

[7] Anne Roe, "Psychological Definitions of Man," in *Classification and Human Evolution*, ed. Sherwood L. Washburn (Chicago: Aldine, 1963), p. 329.

[8] Clifford T. Morgan, *Introduction to Psychology*, 2d ed. (New York: McGraw-Hill, 1961), pp. 489–490.

[9] Talcott Parsons, *The Structure of Social Action* (New York: Free Press, 1949), pp. 89–94.

[10] Thomas Hobbes, *Leviathan* (Oxford: James Thornton, 1881), p. 95.

[11] Jean Paiget, *Le Langage et la pensée chez l'enfant* (Neuchatel-Paris: Delachaux and Niestle, 1923), pp. 59–60.

[12] John Buettner-Janusch, *Physical Anthropology: A Perspective* (New York: Wiley, 1973), p. 324.

[13] Geertz, "Impact of Culture," pp. 18, 25.

[14] Hoebel, "Nature of Culture," p. 147.

[15] Robert Ardrey, *African Genesis* (New York: Dell, Delta, 1961), p. 29.

[16] Konrad Lorenz, *On Aggression*, trans. Majorie Kerr Wilson (New York: Bantam, 1963).

[17] See, for example, John Beatty, "Taking Issue with Lorenz on the Ute"; Edmund R. Leach, "Don't Say 'Boo' to a Goose"; Omer C. Stewart, "Lorenz-Margolin on the Ute"; all in *Man and Aggression*, ed. Ashley Montagu (New York: Oxford University Press, 1968).

[18] William McDougall, *Social Psychology*, 13th ed. (Boston: Luce, 1918).

[19] Ralph L. Beals and Harry Hoijer, *An Introduction to Anthropology*, 3d ed. (New York: Macmillan, 1956), p. 61.

[20] George G. Simpson, "The Biological Nature of Man," in *Perspectives on Human Evolution*, ed. S. L. Washburn and Phyllis C. Jay (New York: Holt, Rinehart and Winston, 1968), pp. 6–7.

[21] Geertz, "Impact of Culture," p. 20.

[22] Hoebel, "Nature of Culture," pp. 145–146.

[23] Allison Jolly, *The Evolution of Primate Behavior* (New York: Macmillan, 1972), p. 350.

[24] Roe, "Psychological Definitions of Man," p. 320.

[25] D. Miyadi, "Differences in Social Behavior among Japanese Macaque Troops," in *Neue Ergebnisse der Primatologie*, ed. D. Starck, R. Schneider, and H. J. Kuhn (Stuttgart: Fischer, 1967).

[26] Desmond Morris, *The Naked Ape* (New York: Bantam, 1969).

[27] John T. Doby, "Man the Species and the Individual: A Sociological Perspective," *Social Forces* 49, no. 1 (1970), p. 13.

[28] The story of Cadmus, the founder of Thebes, and the dragon's teeth comes from Greek mythology. According to the legend, Cadmus sowed the dragon's teeth, and armed men sprang up who immediately began fighting until only five were left.

[29] Roe, "Psychological Definitions of Man," p. 324.

[30] Joseph Biegert, "The Evolution of Characteristics of the Skull, Hands, and Feet for Primate Taxonomy," in *Classification and Human Evolution*, ed. S. L. Washburn (Chicago: Aldine, 1963), p. 133.

[31] A good example of this is the stone or flint axe, a simple tool that marked a considerable advance. Around 7500 B.C. the Ahrensburg folk used such axes to cut down trees. As an extension of the human body, a stone or flint axe is not to be denigrated. In terms of elementary physics, a stone axe consisting of a 5-pound axe head lashed to a stick approximately 18 inches long could deliver a blow with some ten times the force of one delivered by the naked fist. Such basic tools, whether used for cutting down trees or in warfare, vastly augmented the energy available to the Ahrensburg folk. (We are indebted to William O. Oelkfe, Department of Physics, Florida Technological University, for this information.)

[32] Beals and Hoijer, *Introduction to Anthropology*, p. 63.

[33] Ibid., p. 55.

[34] Jerome Kagan and Ernest Haveman, *Psychology: An Introduction* (New York: Harcourt, Brace, Jovanovich, 1968), p. 504.

[35] Robert S. Woodworth and Donald G. Marquis, *Psychology*, 5th ed. (New York: Holt, Rinehart and Winston, 1947), p. 32.

[36] Doby, "The Species and the Individual," p. 13.

[37] Stanley M. Garn, *Culture and the Direction of Human Evolution* (Detroit: Wayne State University Press, 1964), p. 1.

[38] Bernard Rensch, *Psychobiology* (San Francisco: Freeman, 1967), p. 158.

[39] Buettner-Janusch, *Physical Anthropology*, p. 322.

[40] Beals and Hoijer, *Introduction to Anthropology*, p. 53.

[41] Carlton S. Coon, *The Story of Man*, 2d ed. (New York: Knopf, 1956), p. 16.

[42] Antony Jay, an intelligent and perceptive Englishman, read three of Robert Ardrey's books—*African Genesis, The Territorial Imperative*, and *The Social Contract* —all of which deal with human instincts and human behavior. Jay was so impressed with these writings that he wrote *Corporation Man*. Jay describes "who he [corporation man] is, what he does, and why his ancient tribal impulses dominate the life of the modern corporation." Like Ardrey's books, *Corporation Man* is a remarkable edifice erected on a shaky foundation.

[43] Coon, *Story of Man*, p. 12.

[44] Mavis H. Biesanz and John Biesanz, *Introduction to Sociology*, 2d ed. (Englewood Cliffs, N.J.: Prentice-Hall, 1973), p. 57.

[45] Hoebel, "Nature of Culture," p. 145.

[46] David Krech, "Coming—A New Breed of Brain Changers?" *California Monthly*, June–July 1969.

[47] Alfred R. Lindesmith and Anselm L. Strauss, *Social Psychology*, 3d ed. (New York: Holt, Rinehart and Winston, 1968), p. 31. (Emphasis added.)

[48] Doby, "The Species and the Individual," p. 61.

[49] Noam Chomsky, "Form and Meaning in Natural Language," in *Communication*, ed. J. D. Roslansky (Amsterdam: North-Holland, 1969), p. 84.

[50] Buettner-Janusch, *Physical Anthropology*, p. 326.

[51] Biesanz and Biesanz, *Introduction to Sociology*, pp. 59–60.

[52] Reece McGee, *Points of Departure*, alt. ed. (Hinsdale, Ill.: Dryden, 1973), p. 120.

[53] Ibid., pp. 129–130.

[54] Ritchie P. Lowry and Robert P. Rankin, *Sociology: The Science of Society* (New York: Scribner, 1969), p. 104.

[55] McGee, *Points of Departure*, pp. 204–205.

[56] Glenn M. Vernon, *Human Interaction*, 2d ed. (New York: Ronald Press, 1972), pp. 229–231.

[57] Emile Durkheim, *The Division of Labor in Society* (New York: Free Press, 1960), p. 72.

[58] Ibid., p. 227.

[59] Hoebel, "Nature of Culture," p. 147.

[60] Ralph Linton, *The Study of Man* (New York: Appleton, 1936), pp. 272–273).

[61] Everett K. Wilson, *Sociology: Rules, Roles, and Relationships* (Homewood, Ill.: Dorsey, 1966), p. 63.

[62] George C. Homans, *The Human Group* (New York: Harcourt, Brace, Jovanovich, 1950), p. 123.

[63] John W. Kinch, *Social Psychology* (New York: McGraw-Hill, 1973), p. 44.

[64] James A. Schellenberg, *An Introduction to Social Psychology* (New York: Random House, 1970), pp. 233–234.

[65] Charles Merz, "The Crusade Starts," in *The Twenties: Ford, Flappers, and Fanatics*, ed. George E. Mowry (Englewood Cliffs, N.J.: Prentice-Hall, 1963), p. 89.

[66] Joseph K. Willing, "Profession of Bootlegging," in *The Twenties: Ford, Flappers, and Fanatics*, ed. George E. Mowry (Englewood Cliffs, N.J.: Prentice-Hall, 1963), pp. 101–102.

[67] Robert A. Nisbet, *The Social Bond* (New York: Knopf, 1970), p. 317.

[68] Arnold W. Green, *Sociology: An Analysis of Life in Modern Society*, 6th ed. (New York: McGraw-Hill, 1972), pp. 43–44.

[69] Hoebel, "Nature of Culture," p. 151.

[70] Arnold M. Rose and Caroline B. Rose, *Sociology: The Study of Human Relations*, 3d ed. (New York: Knopf, 1969), pp. 47–48.

[71] Francis R. Allen, *Sociocultural Dynamics* (New York: Macmillan, 1971), pp. 254–255.

[72] Francis E. Merrill, *Society and Culture*, 4th ed. (Englewood Cliffs, N.J.: Prentice-Hall, 1969), p. 85.

[73] Joseph S. Himes, *The Study of Sociology* (Glenview, Ill.: Scott, Foresman, 1968), p. 75.

[74] Allen, *Sociocultural Dynamics*, pp. 267–268. See also, William F. Ogburn, *The Social Effects of Aviation* (Boston: Houghton Mifflin, 1946).

[75] Linton, *Study of Man*, pp. 326–327.

[76] McGee, *Points of Departure*, p. 198.

[77] Robert A. Levine and Donald T. Campbell, *Ethnocentricism: Theories of Conflict, Ethnic Attitudes, and Group Behavior* (New York: Wiley, 1972), p. 14.

[78] Lorenz, *On Aggression*, pp. 326–327.

[79] Robert Ardrey, *The Territorial Imperative* (New York: Atheneum, 1966), pp. 6–7.

[80] Rose and Rose, *Study of Human Relations*, p. 49.

[81] Robin M. Williams, Jr., *American Society*, 2d ed. (New York: Knopf, 1960), pp. 424–425.

[82] Rose and Rose, *Study of Human Relations*, p. 53.

[83] Morris E. Opler, "The Human Being in Culture Theory," *American Anthropologist* 66 (June 1964), pp. 507–528.

[84] Green, *Life in Modern Society*, p. 45.

[85] Edward C. Devereux, Jr., "Parsons' Sociological Theory," in *The Social Theories of Talcott Parsons*, ed. Max Black (Englewood Cliffs, N.J.: Prentice-Hall, 1961), pp. 20–21.

ANNOTATED BIBLIOGRAPHY

Bierstedt, Robert. *The Social Order*. 3d ed. New York: McGraw-Hill, 1970. Part 3, "Culture and Socialization," discusses the meaning, content, and acquisition of culture and is well written, exceedingly informative, and thoroughly sociological in its approach.

Garn, Stanley M., ed. *Culture and the Direction of Human Evolution*. Detroit, Mich.: Wayne State University Press, 1964. This short symposium (less than 100 pages) contains seven articles. Considerable understanding of the relationship between man's biological heritage and cultural evolution can be gained by reading the first three: Stanley Garn, "Culture and the Direction of Human Evolution"; William Etkin, "Social Behavioral Factors in the Emergence of Man"; and Theodosius Dobzhansky, "Summation."

Keesing, Robert M., and Keesing, Felix M. *New Perspectives in Cultural Anthropology*. New York: Holt, Rinehart and Winston, 1971. Chapters 1–6 are particularly germane to this chapter. They provide a more detailed account of culture, its beginnings, evolution, and content than was possible in a single chapter.

Lenski, Gerhard. *Human Societies*. New York: McGraw-Hill, 1970. Lenski's approach is essentially macro-level—he concentrates on *total* societies rather than the constituent parts. A reading of Chapters 3–6 should assist the student in gaining a "feel" for the dynamic nature of societies and the culture that guides individual and group behavior within a society.

Lowie, Robert H. *An Introduction to Cultural Anthropology*. New York: Holt, Rinehart and Winston, 1940. Although this work was published many years ago, it is still very much worth reading. It is devoted to many of the details of preliterate cultures, such as hunting, fishing, gathering, language, knowledge and science, and so forth. In addition, some widely different cultures are treated separately. There is also, by way of contrast, a final section on western culture.

Washburn, Sherwood L., ed. *Classification and Human Evolution*. Chicago: Aldine, 1963. Four articles that are particularly relevant to the subject matter of this chapter are: Joseph Biegert, "The Evaluation of Characteristics of the Skull, Hands, and Feet for Primate Taxonomy"; John Napier, "The

Locomotor Functions of Hominids"; Anne Roe, "Psychological Definitions of Man"; and Theodosius Dobzhansky, "Genetic Entities in Hominid Evolution." While several of the articles are somewhat technical, they can be read easily with the help of a dictionary of biological terms.

Values: **Invisible Threads**

INTRODUCTION

In a modern society such as America there are many values and objects to value. At the same time, there are other things that are not valued, such as pollution, noise, overcrowding, racial discrimination, and so on. Paradoxically, dislike or disapproval of some person, behavior, thing, or condition implies the holding of values. For example, one must value clean air and an uncluttered landscape to disapprove of pollution. On the other hand, factory chimneys pouring black smoke into the air and a landscape dotted with debris may be highly valued as signs of industrial progress. Given a specific set of values, any position becomes tenable.

All over the world there are individuals and groups engaged in conflict of all kinds up to and including warfare. It may well be that war is economically based as some maintain, but people could not be brought to fight in wars unless their values and value systems somehow made it important to do so. Although some might disagree, it seems reasonable to state that one set of values was responsible for involving the United States in Southeastern Asia and another set, partly responsible for bringing that war to its somewhat uncertain close. That men *will* go forth to do battle even when they are personally unwilling to risk their lives provides some compelling evidence of the power of held values. That is, of course, not completely accurate for all instances. Some support for war probably arises because war is "exciting," which is why social scientists concerned with doing away with war speak of "psychological alternatives to war."

All around us is evidence of values in operation. Some people picket buses carrying children to integrated schools while others agitate for integration. Most people in the United States marry, but some never do. Some individuals seek careers in one of the professions. A small proportion take to religious life; while others profess atheism or agnosticism. All of those behaviors provide evidence of the existence of something we have called "values."

As with other sociological concepts, values per se are invisible. No one has ever seen, touched, or directly measured a value. Yet, as the physicist who has never seen electrons and protons infers their existence from certain evidence, the social scientist has valid reasons for knowing that values *must* exist.

What, then, are values? We cannot attempt an inclusive review of values because that would be beyond the scope of an introductory textbook. Instead, we will concentrate on certain aspects of values which will give us the most insight: (1) sociological definitions, (2) functions and dysfunctions, (3) value conflict, and (4) value change. And we should, perhaps, preface the discussion with Kluckhohn's view of values: "Each way of life is a pattern . . . each pattern depends to a considerable degree upon the underlying system of ideas and particularly of ideas about values." [1]

4

Values: Invisible Threads

SOCIOLOGICAL DEFINITIONS

Most dictionary definitions of "value" are couched in economic terms—the monetary worth of some object, thing, service, and so on. There are even some sociologists who conceive of values in such terms: "Anything that is prized or of benefit."[2] Unfortunately, although many texts written in the field of sociology contain references to values, the literature devoted explicitly to values is scanty, fragmentary, and sometimes seemingly contradictory. But despite the confusion in the sociological approaches to values there is a certain order and logical coherence.

Obviously, then, the concept of "value," like that of "culture," does not lend itself to concise definition. So we will, again, examine various characteristics in an attempt to understand the sociological meaning of "values."

Seven Initial Characteristics

Superficially there are different ways of looking at values depending on the kind of society in which one lives. But the standard by which an individual values some object, thing, or service is not the entire story. Kurt Baier recognized an important distinction:

The value *possessed by things must be distinguished from the values held by people. The former is an* evaluative property *whose possession and magnitude can be ascertained by appraisals. The latter are* dispositions to behave *in certain ways which can be ascertained by observations. The former are* capacities of things to satisfy desiderata. The latter are *tendencies of people to devote their resources (time, energy, money) to the attainment of certain ends.*[3]

Implicit in that statement are two important ideas. First, value does not reside in some object or service but is the result of *appraisals of value* by people; second, values serve to determine how hard people will work or how many resources they will expend in order to reach certain goals. In other words, values are not something "out there" but the learned social attributes of people. Let us see what this might mean in terms of a real-life example. All of us know that diamonds are valuable and occasionally people will pay large sums of money to possess a diamond. But supposing that an individual's resources will not permit him to purchase a large diamond without forgoing something else, say a new automobile to replace an old one that had become unreliable. Under such circumstances, which will have the greatest value, the diamond or the automobile? Because values are often powerful enough to override rational decisions, it is probable that some individuals would opt for the diamond. However, it is more likely that most would choose the automobile. That conclusion leads us to the conclusion that *value is a relative*

Drawing by Alan Dunn © 1973. The New Yorker Magazine, Inc.

"And now, on your right, one of nature's wonders—the famed Palisades of New Jersey."

matter; it depends upon situations and is a matter of individual or group determination. Value, then, is not something inherent in an object, thing, service, or even behavior. *Values underlie judgments* and, with some exceptions, involve some degree of relativity—some things, objects, services, or behaviors are more valuable than others. It should be understood that any determination of value at any given time under a given set of circumstances is subject to change at different times under differing circumstances—an individual desiring a large diamond who has a trouble-free automobile will value the diamond higher than a new car. In other words, *judgments of value change as circumstances change.*

"The value possessed by things must be distinguished from the values held by people."

Values

Now let us look at another definition from the literature. Walter Gold-schmidt defined values as "those recognized qualities that persons in societies should possess and the symbolic representations by which these desirable qualities are given overt expression."[4] In that definition are three important ideas. First, values involve *symbolic representation*, second (implicitly), objects provide a means for identifying what is valued by humans—objects are merely a *means* through which values are expressed and, third, *values are social*. And from the idea that values are social we can draw still another implication—*values are learned*. According to J. D. Cardwell:

Value is typically defined as the learned meaning *of relative worth of ends, objects, acts, and combinations of these. "Relative worth" is understood to convey the notion of good–bad, pretty–ugly, expensive–inexpensive, and so forth. The key word contained in this definition of value is "learned." It is important because it alerts us to the fact that humans must learn the value of objects, acts, ends, and so on.*[5]

Because the subject is so complex, we will summarize the initial characteristics before going on.

1. Values underlie appraisals or judgments; values are *not* either appraisals or judgments but the genesis of both.
2. The value of anything is a function of its assessed capacity to satisfy.
3. Values are *not* properties of things, services, or anything else except as such is imputed to them by humans either individually or in groups.
4. Values vary in intensity depending on circumstances; the relationship between values and specific situations is reciprocal.
5. Values are social.
6. Values are symbolic; they involve symbolic representation.
7. Values are learned; they are not part of man's meager instinctive equipment.

Eight Additional Characteristics

Biological drives can certainly cause persons to behave positively or negatively toward objects, persons, things, or behavior. To return to our example of the diamonds, a man dying of thirst in the desert would probably give up a fortune in diamonds for a drink of water. But he might not, in which case we would have an example of learned values overriding physiological drives. The manner in which biological drives are satisfied by humans is clearly overlaid with cultural learning. But the force and direction of such drives is to a considerable extent physiological—if one is hungry one seeks food; if thirsty, water; and so forth. But drives are *not* the same thing as values, as Kluckhohn makes clear:

Biological drives and environmental pressures are only obliquely pertinent to the realm of values. Indeed I would assert that the category of "value" becomes useful only when we are dealing with behavior that is influenced by perduring, i.e., long-lasting standards which do not arise from and may be in conflict with the individual's desires at a specific moment in a particular situation. To speak of values is one way of saying that human behavior is neither random nor . . . "instinctual." [6]

Kluckhohn is saying that not only are *values different from biological drives* but that values may function to control, direct, or even thwart such drives. This can be illustrated by pointing to what has been described as a sexually permissive age (modern times), and noting that the sex drive is still controlled to a considerable extent by social norms. Clearly something that can control biological drives to the extent of thwarting them is a powerful determinant of behavior. Most of us would be inclined to feel that the repression of a biological drive, even temporarily, constitutes objective evidence for the existence of values. In other words, *values can be inferred from positive or negative behavior of individuals or groups toward other persons, situations, objects,* and so forth.

William Scott, in a definition that is partly psychological and partly sociological, defines values as representing "the individual's standards for judging the 'goodness' or 'badness,' the 'rightness' or 'wrongness,' of his own and other people's judgments." [7] That definition locates values within the individual and also recognizes the societal implications of the concept. Kluckhohn specifically recognized that *both the individual and social groups are involved* when he defined values as "a conception, explicit or implicit, distinctive of an individual or characteristic of a group, of the desirable which influences the selection from available modes, means, and ends of action." [8] Values, then, are characteristic not only of individuals but of groups as well, which implies that values have both psychological and sociological aspects.

With only slight changes in wording, Kluckhohn's definition of values could serve as a definition of norms. Do not norms also influence behavior in much the same way as Kluckhohn claims for values? The distinction is made clear by Blake and Davis who state that "values . . . are the goals or principles in terms of which the specific norms are claimed to be desirable." Further, they observe that values and norms are inseparable and "disembodied values, i.e., values without any norms through which they can be collectively achieved are . . . sociologically irrelevant." [9] Other authorities show agreement with Blake and Davis; the weight of opinion appears to be that behavior is specified by norms, which, in turn, have their genesis in values. [10]

Earlier we pointed out that under some circumstances diamonds might be willingly exchanged for a drink of water. If values function in a relative manner, it may be possible to differentiate between values in both qualitative and quantitative terms. As Cardwell observes, "a person who is defined as a social deviant in one society could be behaving in a manner consistent with the prevailing values of another society," and "value definitions can be conceptualized as falling along a continuum from high intensity . . . to low intensity . . ."[11] The connection between judgments of behavior as being deviant or nondeviant and norms and values should be clear. Values determine norms, which, in turn, specify behavior that is appropriate. Thus judgments about whether behavior is normative or deviant are a function of held values.

Although each individual probably feels that he or she is making independent and individual judgments of the behavior of others or the worth of objects, things, and so forth, each individual's values must necessarily come from somewhere and that "somewhere" is *not* genetic inheritance. That is, *values are nonbiological in origin*. The source of individual values is, of course, culture, which implies that there must be some *general consensus on values* within any given society. Otherwise there would be no society. A unique value held by a single individual may indeed be a value, but it has no significant societal consequences. (A unique value held by a single individual is an abstraction and quite likely unknown in the real world.) Goldschmidt stresses that "values are culturally established; that is, they are a part of tradition and are inculcated in the process of growing up. The deeper-seated and presumably more basic values are acquired without awareness and are held without self-consciousness."[12] In addition to emphasizing that values are part of tradition and, hence, resting on some general consensus, Goldschmidt also makes the point that values are acquired *without awareness*. We are not conscious of learning values as such; by implication, they function below the conscious level. This is borne out by the fact that when asked what their values are, most people are unable to give any detailed explanation. Yet the behavior of clinically normal people over time yields quite valid inferences that they do have values and, more than that, *systems* of values. The concept of the unconscious as influencing overtly observable behavior is not commonly encountered in sociology. Without going into a detailed discussion of behavior that is unconsciously motivated and directed, let it suffice to say that there is ample psychological evidence to indicate that such behavior is commonplace.[13] We can, therefore, accept even with some reservations the idea that values are or may be unconscious and function at that level to influence human behavior. That well-known question "What's a nice girl like you doing in a place like this?" is loaded with value implications and is rarely if ever answered in a psychiatrically acceptable fashion. The "nice girl" does not always consciously recognize the factors, including values, that brought her to "a place like this."

We can now summarize eight additional aspects of values:

1. Values are nonbiological in origin: they are not instinctive and are not to be equated with biological drives.
2. Values are assumed to exist on the basis of observable positive or negative behavior toward objects, persons, situations, behavior, and so on.
3. Values are peculiar to social systems; values and value systems differ from society to society.
4. While values are social in origin, once internalized, they become an individual matter in the sense that they serve as society's surrogates to direct and organize the behavior of individuals.
5. Values are not the same thing as norms; values are general, abstract standards, whereas norms are behavioral prescriptions and proscriptions specific to specific situations.
6. Values, to be defined as values in the societally meaningful sense, require consensus.
7. Values are acquired and held without full awareness; such unconsciously held values function to direct human behavior.
8. Aside from any situational aspects, it seems reasonable to assume that values can be conceived of as falling on a continuum of intensity; some values are held more strongly than others.

A Working Definition

Can we, at this point, be satisfied that we have covered the major aspects that identify values? Very nearly so, but there yet remains one matter that requires some clarification. Lenski observed that

it is important to distinguish between two sets of values which are often lumped together and treated as though they were the same. These are (1) pragmatic values and, (2) ideal values. Pragmatic values are at the core of all popular moral codes and are based on the recognition that members of the group need one another. Therefore, they condemn those kinds of activities that threaten to undermine the unity of the group (e.g., dishonesty, violence against fellow members, etc.) and encourage those actions that enable the group to satisfy its needs (e.g., hard work, honesty, etc.). Ideal values go much further. They define how the ideal man should act, but it is taken for granted that few if any group members will be able to live up to this standard (e.g., the Christian Church has always taught that men should love their neighbors as themselves).[14]

Lenski questions whether or not a value has any social meaning if it is not represented by an active component, that is, by a norm or norms. Ideal values do, indeed, have social meaning because they are represented by norms that prescribe ideal behavior even though that behavior is rarely seen in real life.

It should by now be obvious that any definition of values, such as "anything that is prized or of benefit,"[15] is not acceptable. The following definition attempts to take into account the complexity of values and valuing and the aspects we have discussed:

> Values are hypothetical, inferred constructs assumed to exist on the basis of observable positive or negative behavior toward objects or symbolic representations of objects, persons and situations and which, further, are learned, social in origin, enduring, variable in intensity, nonbiological and noninstinctive, and which provide socialized individuals with bases for making judgments or selections from or on a wide range of objects, persons, situations, and behaviors.

That definition is, of course, too complex and involved for convenient use so we will attempt to put it in plainer language. Man's general behavior, the direction of society, the groups to which an individual belongs, and the nature of each individual's life stem from values and value systems. The values that trigger a person's judgments and assessments of the worth of some object, person, behavior, and so forth, tend to function at some level below that of immediate awareness. An understanding of human behavior ranging from total societies through groups down to individuals requires an appreciation of values and value systems. To describe the behavior of a group or individual as "irrational" means that one is ignoring values and, thus, delivering no explanation at all but only a description, which is itself based on some value, or value system.

FUNCTIONS

Stability

As we have done with other concepts, we will determine the functions (and dysfunctions) of values by inferences made from observations of behavior.

If we take an overview of the world and the human societies in it, we will observe that societies appear to possess a certain measure of stability and that most of them survive for long periods. In Chapters 7–9 we will see that social institutions give structure and form to societies and that norms, roles, role sets, sanctions, and so forth, function to keep societies reasonably stable. And values, as the anchoring points for social institutions, serve not merely as stabilizing factors for societies but also provide their vitality, direction, and purpose. It is in values that individuals look for answers to such philosophical questions as the meaning of life. Societies have what is

Values, then, function to give a general thrust, or purpose, to societies as a whole and, hence, to individual members of societies.

Copyright © 1973 by Playboy.
Reproduced by special permission of Playboy Magazine.

"Here comes my country right or wrong."

often called their "ethos," by which is meant their "distinguishing character." For example, being the victor in any sort of competition is highly valued by Americans; Britons, on the other hand, emphasize "playing the game"— that is, proper form and obeying the rules is more important than mere victory. Both points of view appear to be based ultimately on values. Values, then, function to give a general thrust, or purpose, to societies as a whole and, hence, to individual members of societies.

This general thrust of a society carries with it strong overtones of value consensus, which, if not entirely universal, is characteristic of some majority. Values plus norms constitute "social facts" as defined by Durkheim. The directing and constraining forces of any society function to compel some minimal level of adherence that, as we have emphasized, does not come from without but from within. Internalized norms serve to produce voluntary obedience to the norms of society. It is, of course, the sharing of similarly internalized values—"a common set of representations"—which is of singular importance with respect to the cohesiveness, vitality, and thrust of a society.[16] Because norms are inferences from specific behavior, the importance of norms is somewhat easier to perceive. But as we observed earlier in this chapter, *norms have their genesis in values*; therefore, values are what provide the common set of representations. Societies, then, depend for orderly pat-

Values
104

terning on an underlying system of values without which social life could not exist.

We must not, however, overlook the fact that values function in a continuously dynamic way and are related and interrelated to all facets of society. Philip Bock stressed this stating that "ideology, technology, language and social structure all interact to produce a living changing culture."[17]

Science provides an example of the profound interaction between values and other aspects of society. The variable place of science from society to society and from one historical period to another illustrates clearly that there is such a relationship. For example, the majority of Americans take science as a source not merely of improved technology but also of answers to difficult questions.[18] Nevertheless, early in 1973 the state of California agreed to present the theory of evolution in textbooks so as to indicate that the theory had not been fully validated. That action was in response to pressure from religiously conservative citizens.[19]

A second example should make clear the relationship between values and other aspects of society. In the United States the values of achievement and success are often measured in economic terms and *are* values for the majority. Yet a general finding from a study conducted by Albert Mayer and Harry Sharp indicates that

religious preferences appear to have meaningful consequences for economic success, quite apart from other background factors associated with religion. It would seem, therefore, that religion continues to play an essential role in controlling, limiting, and guiding economic behavior.[20]

Thus, even in a society that, by and large, adheres to the value of achievement, other values function to either promote or inhibit economic success as that is evaluated and determined in a competitive society.

Predictability

From time to time in this book we consider the matter of predictability, which refers to the ability to predict within a reasonable margin of error the behavior of both individuals and groups. Norms, roles, role sets, and the institutions of society serve to make behavior predictable. It is no exaggeration to say that unless a good deal of human behavior was, is, and continues to be, predictable, societies could not and cannot continue to exist. It is essential, then, that most people in a society play their various roles as these roles are understood by all concerned. Social roles, as defined by David Popenoe, "denote the part, or pattern of behavior, which one is expected to play in social interaction."[21] But what determines the essence of social roles, the manner in which they are enacted? John Spiegel's reply is that "roles are patterned in accordance with the value orientations of a culture or sub-culture."[22] Values, then, function to provide significant clues for the prediction of behavior.[23] Predictability, if it is to be meaningful, must be more than simply chance. When a young man asks a young lady for a date, and a time is agreed upon, each can reasonably expect that the other will be at the appointed place at the time specified. When someone is employed to perform the tasks of a particular position, the employer has some expectation that the employee will perform as anticipated. And the employee has reason to believe that the employer will fulfill his part of the bargain, particularly with respect to salary or wages. John Glidewell puts this in sociological parlance: "For the members of the system, the significant predictability for social roles is the forecast of immediate performance in relation to ultimate values and immediate goals."[24]

Successful prediction of the behavior of those not known to an individual personally rests upon such things as status and role; knowing those enables one to predict the behavior of others and, in turn, informs one of how to behave toward them in one's own role or roles. But predictability is greatly improved when a person has knowledge of how others (individuals or groups) define their values. With this kind of information in hand, it is possible to predict the behavior of others relative to many things. It is through this process-learning that a person is able to anticipate the behavior of others and, thus, interact with them in a consistent manner.[25] As an example of human interaction that rests on knowledge of both role and status, consider the physician-patient relationship. The behavior of both, when interacting, is highly predictable. Rarely do patients question the diagnoses and prescriptions of their physicians, partly because they believe that physicians are competent (a value judgment) and partly because they believe that physicians hold to the value of life (a value judgment about a value).

Summary

The essential functions of values are to (1) provide a general stability to societies; (2) equip individual members with standards or sets of standards for judging, assessing, and evaluating a wide range of things, objects, persons, behaviors, situations, and choices in accordance with the cultural values of the society of which they are members. Values are fundamental to societies, which could not survive without them. It is from values that norms, mores, folkways, social institutions, roles, and role sets draw their particular character.

DYSFUNCTIONS

The preceding section indicated that even though some values are characteristic of any particular society, not all members hold identical values. Since value conflict will be discussed later in this chapter, consideration at this point will be given strictly to the matter of dysfunction excluding conflict. (We will argue shortly that conflict is not necessarily dysfunctional. Such a statement, of course, constitutes a value judgment and helps to show the ubiquitous nature of values. There are those who, holding different values, find all conflict dysfunctional.)

Differences between Classes

All societies are *stratified* to some extent. All societies provide for various statuses and, beyond the subsistence level, become hierarchical. Eventually social classes emerge. In Chapter 6 we will emphasize that modern societies are stratified, and we will provide evidence to support that view. For the purposes of this discussion of values we shall have to accept two facts about stratification in modern societies—it requires value consensus, and it produces certain value phenomena that appear to be dysfunctional if one is looking for consistency within a society. Jackson Toby finds that

lower-class families are not fully included in the societal community because they do not learn the values and skills they need to participate effectively in the highly symbolic culture of urban industrial societies. Sometimes this deficit in values and skills is due to a history of exclusion of certain ethnic groups from the mainstream, as with the burakumin *in Japan, or the Negro in the United States. Whatever the genesis of the deficit, however, its existence is an obstacle to full membership in an urban industrial society, and thus to the solidarity of the entire society.*[26]

The value differences between classes are both subtle and pervasive. They extend to the college or university attended, some of which are understood to both recruit and graduate students who, in general, represent an elite. Such institutions of higher learning will clearly have a much greater impact on the values of their students than others whose graduates are considered as eligible for more limited societal roles.[27] In essence, people in the different strata of society are marked to some extent by differing values; the holding of a certain hierarchy of values can serve to inhibit *or* facilitate full participation in a society. For example, if one places more value on immediate gratification, opportunities for upward mobility are much less than if one emphasizes (that is, values) delay of gratification in order to achieve some greater reward after a time.

It must be emphasized, however, that there is a core of similar values running through all strata of viable societies. To the extent that values differ from stratum to stratum, the society is less well integrated than otherwise, and values serve a dysfunctional purpose. But there are limits to the degree to which any society can tolerate differences of values, that is, the degree of dysfunction arising out of value differences. If these limits are exceeded, the society concerned is likely to disappear.[28]

Determination of Dysfunctionalism

Can the values of an entire society be dysfunctional? If we agree that the disappearance of a society as a society *is* dysfunctional, then we have implied that there must be some general agreement about the values permeating all strata of any society. But a viable society that evidences no dissolution can have a value system that, while promoting survival of the society as a society, is dysfunctional *provided we can agree that economic progress is desirable.* T. R. Fillol claimed that "the basically passive, apathetic, value-orientation profile of the Argentine society must be regarded as the critical factor limiting the possibility of steady, long-run economic development."[29] Let us emphasize that Fillol is implicitly making a value judgment—economic progress is "good" and lack of economic progress is "bad." There are others, including some in American society, who would take just the opposite value position. And now we arrive at an important attribute of values: they are not right or wrong, immoral or moral *except from a frame of reference* provided by still other values. So, with the single exception of a society and its culture, it must be stressed that the determination of whether or not a value, or value system, is dysfunctional is a matter of value judgment.

The great majority of humans live in societies that value such things as good health, longevity, comfort, entertainment, and, in general, the enjoyment of life. While the judgment of those things rests ultimately upon values, values that serve to diminish those objectives can be considered as dysfunctional for human purposes.

To illustrate, let us consider a traditional American value, success. Because the indices of success in modern societies are always relative, it is impossible for everyone in a modern, achieving society to attain the goals set by the value of success. There have to be not only some losers but also others, such as racial and ethnic minorities, who (as we see in Chapter 12) are not even allowed to play the game. It is reasonable to surmise that the losers may suffer some psychic damage along with those who were not allowed to compete for the rewards that distinguish successes from failures in American society. But from a different value perspective, it is possible to view such competition as a necessary, although not sufficient, condition for modernization, progress, and affluence.

Thus, to establish what is or is not dysfunctional with respect to any value or value system is far from an absolute matter; one cannot simply establish criteria that indicate whether a particular value is dysfunctional, or not without resorting to another value or value system. We must, as humans, make assessments and judgments on many matters both within and outside of the society in which we live. It is such judgments that contribute to national and international ferment. It is also those same judgments that are at the root of many, if not most, conflicts.

VALUE CONFLICT

Any observer of the contemporary scene would concede that conflict is endemic throughout the world. Historians know that has been the case since the beginning of recorded history, and archeologists believe there was much conflict prior to the invention of writing.

The word "conflict" includes situations in which violence is used or occurs. But it also covers less dramatic disagreements in which the contending parties do not utilize force or violence but seek by relatively peaceful means to change the points of view of others in a direction more congruent with their own. Conflict of all kinds takes place between individuals, within families and small groups, in corporations, in government, and, in general, wherever there are humans.[30] In this section, we will be concerned with the functions played by values as independent variables (causes) of conflict.

There are many explanations for the pervasiveness of conflict in human affairs, and most follow one of two general orientations. One views aggression and conflict as being essentially physiological in origin and largely a function of inherited instincts.[31] The other views conflict as being cultural in origin.[32] It is the second orientation that we will take. The arguments that man is instinctively aggressive are simplistic and are attractive because they allow one to be aggressive and blame it on one's genes. However, there are too many exceptions, not merely in individuals but also in whole societies, for instinct as a basis for aggression and conflict to be acceptable.

Earlier in this chapter we showed that an important function of values was to provide a certain stability for societies. But values can also function to cause disequilibrium. While there is much consensus on values within societies and even between societies, there is also much intrasocietal dissensus. For example, the latter half of the 1960's was marked by much unrest, particularly the protest movements on college campuses, some of which ended in violence and tragedy. Observing what was going on caused many people to assume that the younger generation had acquired values different from those of the parental generation. But to assume that parents and their offspring hold disparate values overlooks the fact that the family remains a significant socializing agent even in modern societies. Parents and their children are more likely to hold the same values than not, as we shall see in Chapter 8. And to assume that conflict arises largely out of situations in which different values are held may be seriously in error. It does seem, however, that when different values *are* held, conflict is likely to ensue. But

DUNAGIN'S PEOPLE

"Dunagin's People" by Ralph Dunagin.
Courtesy of Publishers-Hall Syndicate.

"When are you going to get a haircut, dad?"

To assume that parents and their offspring hold disparate values overlooks the fact that the family remains a significant socializing agent even in modern societies. Parents and their children are more likely to hold the same values than not.

let us consider all possible explanations of conflict where such conflict relates in one way or another to held values.

Goals

Goal-directed behavior constitutes an objective, behavioral manifestation of held values. When individuals or groups, or whole societies, can be observed working assiduously toward some objective, it can be concluded that the objective *is* valued. But the determination of what values are held by individuals or groups attempting to attain a goal cannot be made simply on the basis of what *appears to be the goal*. For example, education is highly valued in the United States, but is the held value really learning or something else? The actual values underlying the considerable expenditures required to obtain a baccalaureate degree may not be (and often are not) the value of "love" of learning but, rather, the traditional American values of achievement and success. Most Americans are aware that education is an important key

Values

to upward mobility. To the extent that this is the case, attending university and college may be viewed by students as a necessary evil that must be completed successfully if the held values of achievement and success are to be realized. Since some (but by no means all) university professors do value learning for its own sake, a disinterest in learning may bring students into conflict with faculty members. In other words, the value for which education is a surrogate may not always be learning but achievement and success.

Another value commonly held by many in the United States is "external conformity"—that is, within a certain range, individuals are expected to dress and behave in public in accordance with accepted beliefs and practices. On an a priori basis, it would appear that many young people reject this particular traditional American value—long hair, no shoes, and so forth. Yet, one cannot help observing that among themselves they tend to dress and behave very much alike. Again, it is not the value of external conformity itself that is the crux of the situation. Rather, it is who determines the nature of the external conformity. On the one hand, adolescents show that *they* do hold the value of external conformity by dressing and behaving as do other members of their age cohort. On the other hand, they are not behaving and dressing as their elders feel is appropriate. Both generations are giving clear-cut evidence of adherence to the traditional American value of external conformity.

Means to Goals

Here we are concerned with the *means* of goal attainment under conditions where values and goals are the same or nearly so. For example, one value that many hold might be called "peace" or the "elimination of war." There are two general orientations to the means by which peace can be obtained. One school of thought holds that the best way to prevent war is to be so strong that others will not dare to attack. A quite different orientation is represented by the suggestion that the United States (or another great power) disarm unilaterally.[33] Considerable conflict is inherent in these opposed views even though the values and goals are virtually identical.

Inherent Conflict

Conflict *is* inherent in some values, for example, achievement and success. Williams, speaking of American society, stated "our society has been highly competitive . . ." He noted that conflict engendered by that value (competition) requires considerable regulation in order to minimize the "persistent strain upon institutional regulations of means used to attain this goal."[34] Achievement and success are relative goals; success is defined by nonsuccess or lesser success, and achievement is measured in the same fashion. A good deal of competition arises because, among all those striving for the rewards of American or any other society, some will get less than others. That knowledge, coupled with the valuing of achievement and success, easily produces conflict. Then, too, there is the matter of rules. How *is* competition to be conducted? In business, sports, and, indeed, any area in which individuals and groups compete for scarce rewards, conflict arises not merely from competition but also in the determination and enforcement of the rules. If all who hold a particular value were assured of being able to attain a goal exemplifying that value, there would be no conflict. But that is virtually never the case in the real world. We can expect conflict to be inherent in some values because goal attainment is a relative matter under some circumstances and because societal rewards are in scarce supply.

Differing Interpretations

Even when there is consensus on values or value orientations, they may be interpreted differently by various individuals, groups, or whole societies. For example, Williams points out that "progress . . . has permeated a wide range of behavior patterns."[35] Individuals and groups can agree that "progress" is a good thing but disagree sharply about how it ought to be behaviorally expressed. Daniel Fusfeld specified one criticism of such concrete means for expressing the value of progress:

Modern marketing and advertising techniques are used by business firms to mold consumer spending to their needs as producers, instead of adjusting production to match a pristine pattern of consumer wants. The system as a whole operates for the benefit of producers rather than consumers . . . and its goal is the aggrandizement of business wealth instead of the individual's welfare.[36]

Even by implication, that statement does *not* deny the value of progress; it only claims that progress is being achieved for a few (businessmen) to the detriment of the many through advertising. There are those who take an even more extreme view and regard the economic and political systems—indeed much of human culture—as essentially malign and antagonistic to human values.[37] But such views of the American economic system or human culture in toto, do not imply a negation of the value of progress. Indeed, the powerful emotionality underlying sharp criticisms such as those provides implicit evidence that the value of progress is held but that the *interpretation* of what constitutes progress is quite different.

Perhaps the most dramatic example concerns a value that has shaped much of the recorded history of mankind—religion. From differences in interpretation of that value, much historical and current conflict has arisen.

On the evidence, it would appear that religion is extremely important to the human psyche, and differing interpretations are seen as dangerous threats by individuals, groups, and entire societies. Thus the religious wars of previous centuries, the *auto da fé* of the Spanish Inquisition, and the "wars" between the Hindus and Moslems in Pakistan and the Catholics and Protestants in Northern Ireland in the twentieth century have occurred.

Summary

It seems apparent that a good deal of human conflict, from minor disputes between friends to war between nations, is related, however subtly, to values or value systems. Indeed, the more serious and more prolonged a conflict, the more likely it is that values are involved. In a general way, it is possible to perceive why this is so. Values are purely cultural and entirely symbolic. Furthermore, keeping in mind the elaborate definition of values given earlier, values are highly abstract. Aside from knowing that values *must* exist in order to explain human behavior, people are usually unable to verbalize their own values. Therefore, since values clearly influence human behavior, values must be held largely on the unconscious level. From that it follows that values are not susceptible to logical analysis by the value holder. Values are felt rather than being objective or logical. All humans utilize values as a basis for making judgments or selections from a wide range of objects, persons, situations, behaviors, and so on. Since values or value systems ultimately dictate a judgment, objectivity and logic are used to defend the judgment. But in such a situation a *genuinely* objective and rational judgment is unlikely. Instead of seeking the truth (insofar as this can be known), individuals and groups defend *their* values, *their* interpretations of values, or *their* means to goals, which produces conflict.

A contemporary example will make this clear. It is apparent that both those who favor abortion and those who are opposed to it hold substantially to the value of "life." But the arguments and discussions appear to take place in an intellectual vacuum with neither side appearing to understand the arguments of the other. The proabortionists center their arguments about the value of the prospective mother's life and her right to have her body under her jurisdiction (a complicated argument that really involves two values, life and individuality). In opposition is the argument of those who insist, on religious and other grounds, that the child *in utero* has rights too, including the right to life.

The conflict over abortion is essentially a matter of values. Logic and objectivity do not enter into the matter except as they are used to defend either position. Pure value differences can be settled in either of two ways.

Value Conflict

There must be some sort of agreement worked out that, while satisfactory to neither side, is something that both sides can accept. Or one side must muster sufficient power to impose its point of view. Since the second alternative is unlikely, it can be predicted that the uneasy agreement will continue to be the most likely solution.

Values are purely social, not transmitted hereditarily; they likely produce, directly or indirectly, most human conflict. Arguments suggesting that human aggression has an instinctive basis lack any basis in fact. Curiously enough, however, analysis of values leads to similar conclusions by both schools of thought: Conflict is part of the human condition, and will remain part of the human condition.

Is a society that is marked by an absence of conflict possible? The answer is, of course, no. Granting that, what prescription should societies follow to reduce or contain value-caused conflict? Part of the answer is for a society to follow the course it is on. As societies become increasingly complex, part of that complexity lies in the numerous rules developed for containing conflict within reasonable bounds. Another possibility would be the development of greater tolerance for judgments and behaviors that are not congruent with those of the majority—in other words, the development of a pluralistic society in terms of values, which is essentially what is meant by the term "pluralism." In brief, then, since conflicts arising out of values cannot be eliminated, the best solution is to work in the direction of containment.

VALUE CHANGE

In discussing the functions of values, we observed that values serve to stabilize societies, provide continuity, and furnish an ethos. From that it follows that values must necessarily be resistant to change *if* they are to operate effectively as stabilizing forces for societies. But, as even a cursory reading of history demonstrates, societies *do* change, which stimulates at least two questions about values. First, to what degree are values susceptible to change? Second, does value change precede or follow social change—that is, is value change an independent variable of social change or a dependent variable?

Attitude Change

We begin the discussion of value change both indirectly and inferentially with an examination of the possibility of changing attitudes. Attitudes are generated by values; if attitudes can and do change, it would seem logical to make the same assumption about values. But how easily are attitudes changed? Clifford Morgan, for example, considered them somewhat inflexible:

Once formed, attitudes are relatively resistant to change. They tend to be preserved by (a) selective interpretation and perception of information, (b) avoidance of information conflicting with existing attitudes, and (c) social disapproval of one's associates.[38]

There is, however, a considerable body of evidence to indicate that attitudes can be and are changed both deliberately and through general life circumstances, for example, the particular college attended. One famous study determined that in a certain women's college, most of the matriculating students came from the upper and middle socioeconomic classes and generally held the conservative economic views of their parents. Over a period of several years, attitude surveys revealed that the longer the young women remained in the politically liberal atmosphere of the college, the more liberal their political and economic attitudes became.[39] The change in attitude was the result of the women being introduced into a milieu in which different values predominated. And various studies of deliberate attitude change indicate that it *is* possible to modify or even drastically change attitudes although neither quickly nor easily.[40]

Susceptibility of Values to Change

If attitudes are subject to modification or change, does it also follow that values are subject to alteration? To say that values are not would require the assumption that societies are static. But that is empirically and logically untenable. Since "no living culture is static,"[41] we can say that values can and do change.

Now let us consider the question of the *degree* to which values are susceptible to modification or change. The definition of values given earlier in this chapter used the word "enduring." William Catton noted that "the noun 'value' has usually been used to imply some code or standard which persists through time . . ."[42] To the extent that values function in such a manner as to cause societies to *resist* change, it can be assumed that values are resistant to change. And Elbert Stewart and James Glynn have indicated that "sacred values and beliefs often cause resistance to change."[43]

Historical evidence indicates that social change does involve a shift from simple to complex societies. But such change is never accomplished without resistance. In addition to sacred values and beliefs, Parsons appears to have assumed that resistance to social change is immanent in social systems. He postulated "the law of inertia" in the social process, which he described as a conception "similar to that of homeostasis in physiology."[44] "Homeostasis" as applied to societies describes a pronounced tendency for societies to attempt to maintain some state of equilibrium.

Regardless of the orientation taken toward the *causes* and functions of value conservatism, there is general agreement that values are not easily changed or modified. For example, Peter Gutkind found, in a study of urban-born Africans living in East London, South Africa (an urban area), that certain traditional values were expressed in the observance of such customs as boys' initiations and *lobolo* (bride price). Adherence to those and other customs still had considerable "emotional importance contributing to the status and role of the African urban resident who knew no other social environment but urban life."[45]

Environmental factors   Gutkind's study indicates that at least some values are highly resistant to change and tend to be perpetuated even in environments highly dissimilar to that in which the values originated. And that raises the question What kinds of environment are most conducive to value stability? Allen Edwards contends that within an *isolated* social system, correlations between a society's values and individual, personal desires tend to increase over time. There is, essentially, some strain or tendency toward the alignment of personal desires with socially acquired values.[46]

It appears that Edwards, a psychologist, assumed that personal desires, in some fashion, come from *within* individuals; in isolated societies, personal desires become increasingly congruent with the values of the society. In more sociological terms, it can be said that in isolated societies there tends to be far less intrasocietal, interindividual, and intraindividual value conflict than in more complex societies. When a particular society becomes less isolated or when the structure of such a society begins to move toward a division of labor, values will begin to change: "As long as the structure of society is simple and static, established valuations will last for a very long time, but if society changes, this will immediately be reflected in changing valuations."[47] Under circumstances where a previously isolated society has come into contact with other societies and is showing the beginnings of more complex organization, the old values (or some of the old values) will be subjected to pressures for change. Whether or not the values of any society with a simple technology, small population, and heavy emphasis on tradition will resist change depends upon several factors, particularly the cohesiveness of the society. But, in general, when such a society has frequent contact with a more technologically advanced and complex society, the simpler society's values and norms will change. There are some exceptions, of course, including the community of Tristan da Cunha, located on an island in the Atlantic Ocean.[48]

Value Change and Social Change

There are, however, forces, including values, within some simpler societies which function to impede change, such as that associated with industrialization. Everett Hagen theorized that "a person with a normal traditional childhood cannot set a high value on using his energies in attacking the problems of industrial production or other varieties of modern business activity."[49] Yet, Goldschmidt observed, "it is possible for values, as for any other part of culture to change. There is a tendency for them to change under the pressure of such forces as the development of new technologies."[50]

Here, then, is a quandary. If values are conservative and, as Parsons indicated, some are not conducive to the development of modern societies,[51] do values change in such a way as to *stimulate industrial development* or does industrial development *compel value change?*

Max Weber in *The Protestant Ethic and the Spirit of Capitalism,* a classic study of economic motivation, meticulously documented the way in which religious interests, or values, unintentionally encouraged the development of capitalism. Such values as hard work, ascetic living, and material success were intended to demonstrate to individuals that they were of God's elect, predestined to go to heaven.[52] By implication, Weber appears to have believed that value change *precedes* significant social change.

David McClelland provided a socio-psychological explanation of economic development by asserting that the entrepreneur is a product of a particular kind of childrearing that emphasizes such things as the value of independence and assertiveness.[53] By implication, McClelland also appears to hold that value change precedes significant social change, particularly with respect to modernization and industrialization. He and an associate have, in fact, attempted to teach a value they call the "need for achievement" (nAch) to certain businessmen in India.[54]

The most notable opposition to those views is the arguments of Karl Marx, discussed in several parts of this book, particularly Chapters 1 and 9. He insisted on the priority of economic and social structural factors in social change.[55]

There is a lack of consensus about whether value change precedes or follows other kinds of social change. Science, for example, could not flourish in a society having a value system inimical to science (recall Galileo). While values cannot be described as the independent variables (causes) of the development of science, certain values surely made such development possible. What we can conclude is that value change and social change are inextricably related in a dynamic way with changes in values encouraging or producing social change and vice versa.

Summary

When we attempt to synthesize the discussion of value change it becomes apparent that the relationship between a society and its basic value structure is dynamic. Values influence societies and vice versa, with a possible intervening variable being the cohesiveness of a society. By "intervening variable," we mean one that monitors the reciprocal effects of values on societies and societies on values. In small societies with populations of up to two or three thousand persons, cohesiveness is likely to be greater than in larger societies. Smaller societies are also apt to be subsistence-level, mechanistic societies in which tradition is highly valued and changes in both the society and its values proceed very slowly. With the beginnings of division of labor, growth in population size, increasing complexity, and a move toward social pluralism, various segments of a society internalize values that are peculiar to those segments. Value-based conflict between the various segments of more complex societies do function to bring about social change. Further, the continuous interaction between segments of modern societies (such as social strata, political parties, economic organizations, and even age cohorts) serves to modify both the values of all concerned and the goals or goal objects deemed appropriate for those values.

We can say that values have been and are changing and that such change is associated with the modernity of societies—the more modern, complex, and industrialized a society, the more rapid is value and other kinds of change. But specific, empirical evidence is lacking on the extent to which values have changed over recent years in modern societies. Indeed, we have suggested the possibility that it is not so much values per se that change as the definitions of goals or objectives that fulfill such values.

In summary of this section on value change, we can conclude that (1) Attitudes are subject to modification and change; therefore, it is appropriate to assume that values also change. (2) While values doubtless do change, they are highly *resistant* to change. (3) A general tendency toward homeostasis may be immanent in social systems, and this tendency would logically apply to values as the important source of any homeostatic tendency. (4) The more isolated and simple a social system, the more likely there is to be a condition of general stability, including stability of values. (5) When a society changes in the direction of greater complexity, values also tend to change. (6) Whether or not value change is a prerequisite to societies becoming more complex, the evidence is not conclusive. But it is in the direction of value change being an initial, important independent variable of social change with social change, in turn, becoming an independent variable of value change.

CONCLUSION

Implied in this chapter has been the premise that values are an important, if not a principal, source of stability for societies. But the final section pointed out, with some reservations, that values can and do change. Unless they did, modern societies as we know them could not possibly have come into existence. Those general conclusions appear contradictory: if one accepts them both, a seeming paradox develops. Yet the paradox is not genuine but is rather a function of a human tendency to view things in an either-or fashion. That values can serve both as a stabilizing function for societies and as agents of change is evidence of the dynamic nature and complexity of values. For example, it is fashionable to speak of "the meaninglessness of modern life" or of "a search for true meaning." But one could not refer to modern or any other kind of life as "meaningless" without some value or values as a standard for judgement. Those "searching for true meanings" are attempting to find goals or goal objects that satisfy criteria determined by *their* values. It is evident that dissatisfaction with the way things are has its genesis in values and, in the long run, will serve to alter what are considered suitable goals for satisfaction of values. Ultimately, changes in value-determined goals can reciprocally change some values. For example, if the value called "humanitarianism" is extended beyond the bounds of a single society, it is likely to have some effects (in terms of modification) on another value called "patriotism"—at least to the extent of bringing into doubt the value-based belief that killing for one's country is a good thing. If another value called "equality" is altered in terms of its goal from "equality of opportunity" to some kind of genuine equality, then we can anticipate changes in other values called "achievement" and "success," which, for goal attainment, require that there be losers, obviously a violation of a value of generalized equality.

Values, then, as sociological phenomena are not well understood. And because they are held somewhat unconsciously, they are difficult to study empirically and objectively. Nonetheless, values are of singular importance to men in all societies, and they must be studied, if only indirectly and inferentially.

To this point we have been mainly concerned with the setting in which man enacts his role in society. In the next chapter we will deal with man himself or, rather, with the process through which man is transformed from a biological entity into a social being—socialization.

4.1 The traditional American value of "progress" appears to be undergoing modification. Is it the value per se that is changing *or* the criteria for determining what really constitutes progress *or* both? Be able to defend your answer and cite examples in support of it.

4.2 Make up a list of what you consider to be the traditional American values (you should be able to come up with fifteen or more). Does it appear that any of the values on your list are less significant than in the past? Why?

4.3 Explain why value is *not* inherent in an object or objects, such as gold or diamonds (or an expensive, new sports car).

4.4 The value attributed to anything is a function of what?

4.5 Human behavior with respect to powerful biological drives, for example, sex, provides considerable evidence for the existence of values. Explain that statement and cite some real-life examples in support of your explanation.

4.6 Are values and norms essentially the same thing—sociologically? Why or why not?

4.7 Is it possible to make a case for the contention that the same values are common to humans everywhere? Why or why not?

4.8 This chapter contends that values are unconsciously acquired and also function at the unconscious level to influence behavior. How can this be true? Are we not always conscious of our reasons for doing things? Cite some examples from your personal experience to support your answer.

4.9 Lenski mentions two sets of values—"ideal" and "pragmatic." Which set of values is more likely to be characteristic of college students? Explain your answer.

4.10. Cite several values that would tend to inhibit an individual's full participation in modern society. At the same time, select certain values that would make it difficult to participate fully in a traditional society. Explain the reasoning underlying your selection of values in each case.

4.11. When we decide that a certain value is good or bad, what are we providing evidence of in terms of values?

4.12. What are two or three value-determined goals underlying efforts towards a college degree? One of these is obviously obtaining a degree, but there are others. Do those value-determined goals all stem from the same value? Explain your answer.

4.13. Consider the traditional American value of "humanitarianism." How could conflict arise between persons, groups, or societies holding this value?

4.14. What logical and empirical proof exists that values *must* change over time?

4.15. Does the fact that values function to both stabilize societies and cause social change constitute a genuine paradox? Why or why not?

NOTES

[1] Clyde Kluckhohn, "The Scientific Study of Values and Contemporary Civilization," *Zygon* 1 (September, 1966), p. 231.

[2] Leonard Broom and Philip Selznick, *Principles of Sociology*, 4th ed. (New York: Harper & Row, 1970), p. 54.

[3] Kurt Baier, "What Is Value? An Analysis of the Concept," in *Values and the Future*, ed. Kurt Baier and Nicholas Rescher (New York: Free Press, 1969), p. 40.

[4] Walter Goldschmidt, *Man's Way* (New York: Holt, Rinehart and Winston, 1959), p. 66.

[5] J. D. Cardwell, *Social Psychology* (Philadelphia: Davis, 1971), p. 19.

[6] Kluckhohn, "Values and Contemporary Civilization," p. 239.

[7] William A. Scott, "Psychological and Social Correlates of International Images," in *International Behavior*, ed. Herbert C. Kelman (New York: Holt, Rinehart and Winston, 1966), p. 447.

[8] Clyde Kluckhohn, "Values and Value Orientations," in *Toward a General Theory of Action*, ed. Talcott Parsons and Edward A. Shils (Cambridge, Mass.: Harvard University Press, 1954), p. 394.

[9] Judith Blake and Kingsley Davis, "Norms, Values, and Sanctions," in *Handbook of Modern Sociology*, ed. Robert E. L. Faris (Skokie, Ill.: Rand McNally, 1964), p. 456.

[10] See, for example, Bernard S. Phillips, *Sociology: Social Structure and Change* (New York: Macmillan, 1969), p. 46; Robert C. Atchley, *Understanding American Society* (Belmont, Calif.: Wadsworth, 1971), p. 9; and Richard T. Morris, "A Typology of Norms," *American Sociological Review* 21, no. 4 (1956), p. 612.

[11] Cardwell, *Social Psychology*, pp. 27 and 62. With respect to the relativity of values and the observation that values differ in held-intensities, see also Robert B. Taylor, *Cultural Ways* (Boston: Allyn and Bacon, 1969), p. 131.

[12] Goldschmidt, *Man's Way*, p. 74.

[13] As, for example, Freud's theory of the unconscious, which holds that there are forces, inclinations, influences, impulses, and attitudes of which the individual is unaware but which modify behavior. See Kenneth Appel, "Psychiatric Therapy," in *Personality and Behavior Disorders*, ed. J. McVey Hunt (New York: Ronald, 1955), vol. 2, pp. 1107–1163.

[14] Gerhard Lenski, *Human Societies* (New York: McGraw-Hill, 1970), p. 46.

[15] Broom and Selznick, *Principles of Sociology*, p. 54.

[16] As quoted by Jesse R. Pitts, "Introduction to Personality and the Social System," in *Theories of Society*, ed. Talcott Parsons et al. (New York: Free Press, 1961), p. 686.

[17] Philip K. Bock, *Modern Cultural Anthropology* (New York: Knopf, 1969), p. 369.

[18] Robin M. Williams, Jr., *American Society*, 2d ed. (New York: Knopf, 1967), pp. 454–456.

[19] As widely reported in the press.

[20] Albert J. Mayer and Harry Sharp, "Religious Preferences and Worldly Success," in *Life in Society*, rev. ed., ed. Thomas E. Lasswell et al. (Glenview, Ill.: Scott, Foresman, 1970), p. 456.

[21] David Popenoe, *Sociology* (New York: Appleton, 1971), p. 32.

[22] John P. Speigel, "The Resolution of Role Conflict Within the Family," in *The*

Planning of Change, ed. Warren Bennis et al. (New York: Holt, Rinehart and Winston, (1961), p. 391.

[23] Harold G. Pauling, *The Sociology of Behavior* (New York: Columbia University Press, 1969), p. 318.

[24] John G. Glidewell, "The Entry Problem in Consultation," in *The Planning of Change*, ed. Warren Bennis et al. (New York: Holt, Rinehart and Winston, 1961), p. 654.

[25] Cardwell, *Social Psychology*, p. 25.

[26] Jackson Toby, *Contemporary Society*, 2d ed (New York: Wiley, 1971), p. 564.

[27] John W. Meyer, "The Charter: A Condition of Diffuse Socialization in Schools," in *Social Processes and Social Structure*, ed. Richard W. Scott (New York: Holt, Rinehart and Winston, 1970), p. 569.

[28] Williams, *American Society*, p. 414.

[29] T. R. Fillol, *Social Factors in Economic Development: The Argentine Case* (Cambridge, Mass.: M.I.T., 1961), p. 3.

[30] Robert A. Nisbet, *The Social Bond* (New York: Knopf, 1970), p. 76.

[31] See, for example, Konrad Lorenz, *On Aggression* (New York: Bantam Books, 1969); Desmond Morris, *The Naked Ape* (New York: Dell, 1969); and Robert Ardrey, *The Territorial Imperative* (New York: Atheneum, 1966).

[32] An example of this orientation is provided in Ashley Montagu, ed., *Man and Aggression* (New York: Oxford University Press, 1968).

[33] An excellent discussion on this and other aspects of international behavior is contained in Herbert C. Kelman, ed., *International Behavior* (New York: Holt, Rinehart and Winston, 1966), pp. 385–386.

[34] Williams, *American Society*, pp. 417 and 418.

[35] Ibid., p. 431.

[36] Daniel R. Fusfeld, "Post-Post-Keynes: The Shattered Synthesis," *Saturday Review*, 22 January 1972, p. 38.

[37] Jules Henry, *Culture against Man* (New York: Random House, 1963).

[38] Clifford T. Morgan, *Introduction to Psychology* (New York: McGraw-Hill, 1956), p. 560.

[39] Theodore M. Newcomb, *Personality and Social Change* (New York: Holt, Rinehart and Winston, 1943).

[40] See, for example, C. I. Hovland, "Effects of Mass Media of Communication," in *Handbook of Social Psychology*, ed. G. Lindzey (Reading, Mass.: Addison-Wesley, 1954); J. Hyman, *Political Socialization* (New York: Free Press, 1959); and D. Krech and R. S. Crutchfield, *Theory and Problems of Social Psychology* (New York: McGraw-Hill, 1948).

[41] Melville J. Herskovits, "The Processes of Cultural Change," in *The Science of Man in the World Crisis*, ed. Ralph Linton (New York: Columbia University Press, 1945), p. 143.

[42] William R. Catton, Jr., "A Theory of Value," *American Sociological Review* 24, no. 5 (1959), p. 311.

[43] Elbert W. Stewart and James A. Glynn, *Introduction to Sociology* (New York: McGraw-Hill, 1971), p. 303.

[44] Talcott Parsons, *The Social System* (New York: Free Press, 1951), pp. 46–51 and 58–67.

[45] Peter C. W. Gutkind, "African Urban Family Life and the Urban System," *Journal of Asian and African Studies* 1, no. 1 (1966), p. 39.

[46] Allen L. Edwards, *The Social Desirability Variable in Personality Assessment and Research* (New York: Holt, Rinehart and Winston, 1957), chap. 3.

[47] Karl Mannheim, "Roots of the Crisis in Evaluation," in *The Planning of Change*, ed. Warren Bennis et al. (New York: Holt, Rinehart and Winston, 1961), p. 102.

[48] In a direct encounter between the ethos of modern, rational economic man and a small, subsistence-level community, the small community essentially prevailed. (Peter A. Munch, "Economic Development and Conflicting Values: A Social

Experiment in Tristan da Cunha," *American Anthropologist* 72, no. 6 [1970], pp. 1300–1318.)

[49] Everett E. Hagen, *On the Theory of Social Change* (Homewood, Ill.: Dorsey, 1962), p. 47.

[50] Goldschmidt, *Man's Way*, p. 78.

[51] Parsons, *Social System*.

[52] Max Weber, *The Protestant Ethic and the Spirit of Capitalism*, trans. Talcott Parsons (New York: Scribner, 1930).

[53] David C. McClelland, *The Achieving Society* (Princeton, N.J.: Van Nostrand, 1961).

[54] David C. McClelland and David G. Winter, *Motivating Economic Achievement* (New York: Free Press, 1969).

[55] Karl Marx, *Das Kapital*, trans. Samuel Moore and Edward Aveling and ed. Friedrich Engels (London: G. Allen, 1946).

ANNOTATED BIBLIOGRAPHY

Bronfenbrenner, Urie. "Responses to Pressure from Peer Versus Adults Among Soviet and American School Children." *International Journal of Psychology* 2, no. 3 (1967), pp. 199–207. This article is concerned with types (and orientations) of school systems as such systems serve to minimize or increase conflict (including value-conflict) between adults and children. It provides some illustrations of the essentiality of the learning process in the acquisition of values and values systems.

Cantril, Hadley, and Allport, Gordon W. "Recent Applications of the Study of Values." *Journal of Abnormal and Social Psychology*, October 1944, pp. 259–273. Although this article is somewhat dated, it sheds some light on attempts to measure values—particularly those in the Allport-Vernon study of values. The student may find it interesting to learn about the psychological approach to the study of values. Some of the difficulty of measuring values is implicit in this article.

Carter, Roy E., Jr. "An Experiment in Value Measurement." *American Sociological Review* 21, no. 3 (1956), pp. 156–163. Carter reports a most ingenious experiment designed to measure values across different cultures. His conclusions may surprise the student.

Catton, William R., Jr. "A Theory of Value." *American Sociological Review* 24 (1959), pp. 310–317. Catton has done a considerable amount of work in the area of values, and his attempt to build a theory of values is worth reading.

Eisenstadt, S. N. *From Generation to Generation*. New York: Free Press, 1956. For an understanding of the complex relationship between "ideal" and "pragmatic" values and homogeneous and heterogeneous age groups, this book is probably the best available. Further it contributes to an understanding of the seeming generation gap with respect to values.

Goldschmidt, Walter. *Man's Way*. New York: Holt, Rinehart and Winston, 1959. This book could serve as a general introduction to the study of either anthropology or sociology. It is replete with material on values, is extremely well written, and contains many valuable insights on the species Man.

Hofstadter, Richard. *The Age of Reform*. New York: Vintage, 1955. This work is an account of corruption, mismanagement, political chicanery, and other signs of "moral decay" and "loss of values" (particularly in chapter 5). The judgments made by Hofstadter are, of course, based on his own values and value system. The reader might well consider whether or not the examples of chicanery given really constitute signs of moral decay, loss of values, and so on, *or* indicate either different values or different criteria for goals satisfying values.

Kluckhohn, Clyde. "The Scientific Study of Values and Contemporary Civilization." *Zygon* 1 (September 1966), pp. 230–253. Kluckhohn presents as good an account of values as is available from the standpoint of providing some "feel" for the dynamics of values.

Maslow, Abraham. *Eupsychian Management*. Homewood, Ill.: Irwin and Dorsey, 1965). This book is particularly well worth reading once one has acquired some knowledge of values and their varied functions in society. It represents, of course, a particular value orientation toward management and management policies with respect to personnel.

Wheelis, Allen. "The Quest for Identity." In *Analyses of Contemporary Society*, edited by Bernard Rosenberg, vol. 1, pp. 1–38. New York: Crowell, 1966. "Knowledge of one's identity" as a value appears to be a matter of considerable contemporary concern. Wheelis explores it in a well-written and humanistic fashion.

Socialization and Human Development: Cutting a Pattern

INTRODUCTION

The process of *socialization* is the process of social interaction through which the individual acquires the ways of feeling, thinking, and acting (the capabilities) essential for effective participation within a society. Through the learning process the individual is transformed into a *social being*. The content learned through this process constitutes what we have called "culture." (You may want to refer to Chapter 3 for the definition of culture.) While it is apparent that no individuals acquire all the ways of adapting—the total culture possessed by a society—socialization is successful if individuals learn enough to participate at a minimum level in the society. Beyond this minimum level, there are vast differences between people in both their ability to learn the culture of their society and their motivation to do so.

Recognizing that there are those individual differences, we find ourselves confronted by a series of questions about this learning process. What are the essential features of the socialization process throughout the life cycle? From whom is the necessary information acquired that allows the individual to participate in society? What are the minimal levels of participation expected of individuals at various points in the life cycle? When, or under what conditions, could we conclude that socialization has been ineffective? Is any ineffectiveness of socialization attributable to inadequacies in ability or motivation of the person, or can it be traced to defects or inconsistencies or both in the process of socialization? Which is to blame when socialization fails: the individual attempting to adapt to demands of society, or the society attempting to mold the individual? We will propose some answers to those questions as we probe crucial issues in the study of the development of the individual within the framework of human society.

But before beginning our investigation about the nature of socialization, we should briefly consider the nature of man. As we discussed in Chapters 2 and 3, the human being is a product of two basic forces: (1) biological, or hereditary, factors; and (2) social, or environmental, factors. While individuals vary in the extent to which they possess basic biological capabilities, such as longevity or intelligence, social factors will determine to a considerable degree whether the biological capabilities are ever expressed or utilized. Both heredity and environment are powerful influences, but which is more important in producing the social being, the individual who has acquired the capability to adjust to a changing social world?

In chapter 3 we examined in some detail the role of heredity and environment in determining human nature and in shaping human behavior. We concluded that, while the human organism does possess innate characteristics, these inborn elements of human nature can be modified substantially by the social environment. There is a dynamic interplay between heredity and environment such that environment makes substantial alterations on

5

Socialization and Human Development: Cutting a Pattern

hereditary potential. At the same time man, employing his hereditary potential, modifies his environment. That reciprocal relationship operates so that changes in human nature or the social environment produce effects on the other. Man looks to the environment for the satisfaction of his basic drives. And the environment determines whether man will have to devote the majority of his time to satisfying these drives or can readily find the satisfaction in the environment. Thus, while man can apply his capabilities toward altering the environment, the environment places limitations on the range of expression of human nature.

CONTINUITY

The process of socialization is directed at the problem that every society of men has had to solve—continuity. The problem of continuity can be solved only when children are reared to become productive adult members of the society of which they are members and in which they are expected to reside. Socialization is considered effective when the product of the process—members of succeeding generations—assume appropriate social roles. The process is considered ineffective when large numbers of the members of succeeding generations do not assume these roles for some reason, either personal inadequacy or the presence of some social defect. Because there is always the possibility that socialization will fail, there is substantial concern in most human societies with the child-rearing process. Most of this concern is directed at how to elicit the desired behavior from those being socialized with the least possible resistance to the demands being imposed by the socializers. In order to insure continuity, it is essential that the process of socialization takes place in a social environment that is conducive to conformity. When the social environment promotes deviance, resistance to the demands of the socializers, and intergenerational conflict, the socialization process is disrupted, and the question of whether continuity will prevail becomes crucial.

EARLY SOCIALIZATION

Development of Self-Awareness

The aim of socialization from the viewpoint of society is to insure continuity. For the individual, the heart of the matter is the emergence and development of the *self*. The self consists of all ideas, feelings, and conceptions that the individual associates with himself as a result of social interaction with others in his environment. As self-awareness develops, the individual becomes able to differentiate clearly between himself and others in his social environment. This emerging self is a psychic entity; it is acquired within a social frame of reference; and it is reflexive, that is, the self can become the object of personal appraisal.

At birth, the human organism has no concept of self, no awareness of self as a psychic entity apart from others in the environment. He (or she) acquires this awareness of self only as his perceptual facilities develop so that he is aware of the presence of others. During the first few months of life, the human infant receives a wide variety of physical stimuli from many sources. The initial relationship established between the infant and the mother serves as the basic social contact upon which subsequent socialization depends. While the infant responds primarily to physical needs and stimuli, during the first year of life the initial contacts with the mother provide the organism with the first distinction between self and another human being. As the infant's perceptual capabilities develop and he is able to manipulate objects in his surroundings, he becomes aware gradually of the difference between self as an entity and objects as distinct from self.

The emotional gratification and sensorimotor experiences the infant receives during the initial year of life are essential to the subsequent development of the self. Without these initial human contacts the individual will suffer severe sensory and psychic damage. W. Sluckin, Lorenz, and other scientists have asserted that the first year of life may constitute a "critical period" in which certain basic human contacts must be made or the child suffers permanent retardation in psychological development.[1] Inferring from animal studies, these researchers suggested that a phenomenon called *imprinting* takes place during this period. Imprinting in man, they contend, consists of basic recognition and visual following of other persons in the child's immediate environment—that is, following with the eyes other persons as they move about. Without these simple, initial forms of perceptual contact with other persons, the child is unable to differentiate between self and other objects. Thus the initial stages in the development of the self are delayed and psychological functioning is considerably impaired. Research on this topic has been difficult to perform with human subjects (few parents are willing to subject their children to long periods of sensory deprivation which could produce permanent psychological damage). But case studies of emotionally disturbed children who were neglected during the earliest stages of life tend to confirm the "critical period" hypothesis. Whether the damage suffered by the child experiencing early sensory deprivation is permanent has yet to be confirmed.

During the first year of life, the child gradually, but not completely, develops an awareness of a distinction between himself and the external world. However, self-awareness in the sense of his being able to distinguish between

When language facilities
develop and
communication improves,
the child will be able to
differentiate more sharply
between self and others.

Reprinted by permission of The Kappan and Bardulf Ueland.

"After 'like' and 'man'—what do you articulate guys do for an encore?"

himself and other persons as distinct *social* objects has not emerged to a
significant extent. The major social relationship developed during the first
year of life is the dependency on the mother. When language facilities
develop and communication improves, the child will be able to differentiate
more sharply between self and others. And when the child acquires the ability
to refer to himself and to others as objects, he is well along in the process of
self-development.

There are a number of divergent views on how the self develops and what
stages in self-development can be isolated. Each theory emphasizes some
particular stage more than others. Consequently greater stress is placed on
the experiences received during that stage and its relationship to maturation
and personality development. But all agree upon one point: The essential
characteristic of self-development lies in the emergence of *the ability to
reflect upon the self as an object, and not only as a subject.*

The process of self-development occurs in infancy and can be said to have
begun when the individual develops the ability to view himself *reflexively.*
That ability develops out of increased experience with those in his environment, as well as from an increase in communicative ability. Only when we

Early Socialization

are able to conceive of ourselves as others do will we achieve this reflexive ability. The self develops according to the ability of the individual to perceive of himself in this reflexive and objective fashion.

In reviewing the various theories of self-development, we shall note the *importance of early childhood experiences* in determining the direction of self-development and the emergence of individual personality.

Cooley's Looking-Glass Self Charles Cooley advanced the theory that self-development depends upon the ability of the person to view and judge himself in the way that he imagines others would.[2] By assuming the position of others in the social environment, the individual is able to gain a view of his "self" which is partially free from the distortion and error of purely personal appraisals. Cooley called that process the "looking-glass self." And he believed that self-development followed a distinct set of steps.

Appearance to others First, one must gain some idea of how he appears to others. Obviously, a person must first have had some contact with other people. A knowledge of how he appears to others depends on the *experiences* a person has with others—how others have reacted to him—and on the ability to *communicate*. Language provides the person with a wealth of information on the various ways he appears to others in given situations. Language also supplies knowledge of how he should behave in certain situations *in order to elicit a favorable response from others*. Extensive experience and communicative facility are essential in order to acquire accurate conceptions of how one appears to others.

Judgment by others After one has acquired some knowledge about how he appears to others, he must gain additional knowledge of how others judge him in order to gain an objective appraisal of the self. This information is derived from human experience in which that person has been rewarded by others for certain behaviors and punished for inappropriate behaviors. On the basis of how a person imagines others are judging him, he may experience some kind of response, particularly an emotional one such as guilt, love, hate, envy, or embarrassment. An individual judges himself on the basis of what he imagines are the judgments of others. In this sense he is making a reflexive response to the self based upon external, social criteria of judgment. When this ability to judge the self on the basis of *social standards* emerges, the social self has developed.

Modification of behavior In arriving at some indication of how others are actually judging one's behavior, a person becomes highly sensitive to cues, gestures, and other stimuli which may indicate approval or disapproval for a given course of action in a certain situation. Once some indication of these is acquired, the individual reacts to that imagined judgment by modifying his behavior. In this way the self is responsive to *social controls*. In this case the social controls are the judgments that the person believes others are making on him and on his behavior.

Importance of early experiences Cooley felt that these early impressions of how others were judging an individual were highly important in shaping an enduring personality in early childhood. He asserted that the imagined judgments of others acquired *early in life* were more durable than those acquired *in later life*. For example, if a person experienced rejection often enough in childhood till he felt others had negative judgments of him, he might regard himself as inferior regardless of whether in later life he was regarded by others as a superior person. While Cooley admitted that the self was capable of vast change, he felt that the initial impressions upon which the self was originally constructed were those most resistant to eradication. That is, one's initial estimates of how others judge one are the hardest to change and the most persistent elements of personality.

Mead's social self George H. Mead, a social psychologist, agreed with Cooley that the self arises in a social context out of an estimate of the judgments of others. But Mead added that the most important factor contributing to the development of the self was *language*.[3]

Language facility Language enables a person to determine *how* appropriate or inappropriate his behavior in specific situations is regarded by others, and it enables him to gain a more refined conception of how others are judging him. Once the person acquires extensive language facility and considerable experience with the judgment of others in a wide variety of situations, he has the basis for determining which of his actions would be judged as particularly bad or exceptionally good or somewhere in between. He develops the ability to assess his own behavior in terms of the standards through which and by which it would be defined by other people. Thus, he has the basis for acquiring a *moral hierarchy* by which he can judge his actions. He can assign degrees of appropriateness or condemnation to his own behavior through the use of language. In this way, the person acquires a knowledge of the range of behavior available to him in any given situation, and he has some basis for anticipating the action of others. Particularly, the person has some ability to predict how others will make public judgments of his behavior and the degree of reward and punishment to expect from them.

Role playing Initially, according to Mead, the judgment of particular persons, such as parents, are acquired as the criteria by which to judge one's own behavior. Once knowledge of what behaviors would be regarded as appropriate or reprehensible is acquired, the child is then able to act out the role of the parent with considerable accuracy. In fact, that is what often happens when the child acts out the role of the parent with some inanimate object representing a child, such as a doll. The child playing the role of

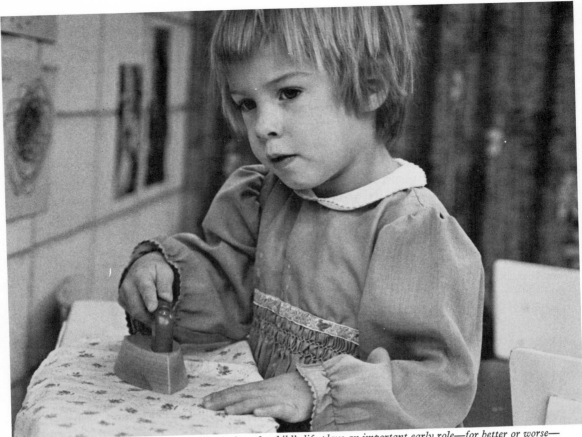

The introduction of "sex appropriate" toys into the child's life plays an important early role—for better or worse— in the socialization of sex identification.

the parent will employ the same language of praise and punishment used by the parent. By doing so the child learns the breadth and depth of the role of parent beyond what would be gained through mere observation of the parents alone.

The generalized other   As a person's experience widens, the number of persons whose judgments are acquired as standards through which to assess one's own behavior increases dramatically. As the child's experience widens, he comes to see commonalities in the judgments of others. Eventually the child judges his behavior on the basis of what he feels to be the standard of the *generalized other*. In his thinking, the child has fused all of the particular judgments of "others" into a diffuse external standard. It is at this point that the individual adjusts his concept of his "self" according to what he feels to be the judgment of external and organized society. He makes *moral* judgments regarding his own behavior on the basis of whether "society," or some diffuse external force, would approve or

Once knowledge of what behaviors would be regarded as appropriate or reprehensible is acquired, the child is then able to act out the role of the parent with considerable accuracy.

disapprove. By this time in the developmental process, the person has acquired a sense of morality. He is able to evaluate his own behavior independently of whether he will be directly rewarded or punished for it by someone in the immediate social environment. In other words, he has acquired what we call a *conscience*. He chooses what behavior is appropriate on the basis of his perception of the overall reaction of society to such behavior.

Internalized morality With the acquisition of conscience, or the beginnings of such acquisition, the child begins to decide on actions or behaviors that are in accord with the ideas of right and wrong he has internalized. This implies that the partly socialized child is developing *self-control*; he is selecting behaviors as appropriate or nonappropriate less on the basis of whether or not they will be punished by others and more in accordance with what might be called *internalized morality*. Unless socialization were generally successful in developing *some* measure of self-imposed control, society would obviously be an impossibility. To imagine a society in which individuals conformed only because of the hope of external rewards or the fear of punishment is to compound an absurdity.

Rules of the Game Mead notes that the child begins to acquire such a general basis for morality when he enters into play with other children in organized games. In such situations, the child may play a wide variety of roles, and he acquires the knowledge of what behavior is allowable and what is not. He judges the performance of others in the game situation on the basis of an external set of rules that govern the game. And those rules were not developed by the participants at hand but provided by an external authority. The game is governed by the behaviors that are expected of persons in given positions, regardless of the identity of the persons "playing" those positions. He learns, therefore, that expectations depend upon a *person's position* rather than on the *identity of the person* occupying that position. He also learns that the judgments he may expect from others depend heavily on whether he fulfills the expectations associated with occupancy of that position. This enables him to conform successfully to whatever the current expectations are for many roles throughout the life cycle, such as son, student, single adult, married adult, parent, employer, employee, grandparent, and so on. In short, according to Mead, knowledge of this kind is absolutely essential in order for the person to assume productive roles in an organized social order later in his life.

Freudian Views Freud's views have had a profound impact upon the field of psychology; since psychoanalysts and psychiatrists often employ his theories to treat problems arising during the developmental stages, his contribution to the study of socialization has been considerable.[4] Freud viewed socialization primarily as a process characterized by an internal struggle between biological impulses and culturally established inhibiting rules of behavior. He held the view that normal children passed through four stages of development, each of which had distinctly different characteristics, features, and patterns of human relationship. Each also required different forms of gratification. The first is the *oral* phase, lasting from birth until about the age of eighteen months. Behavior centers around sucking activity, with the mouth, lips, stomach, and tongue serving as the primary sensorimotor sources of gratification. Following this is the *anal* phase, lasting until about three years of age. At this time parents make the first substantial demands on the child, demands focused largely upon the control of elimination. It is at this time that the child begins to perceive himself as a distinct entity from the parents. In the next stage, the *phallic*, or *genital*, phase, autoerotic sexual behavior begins. According to Freud, male children experience a sexual love of the mother coupled with hostility for the father, while female children feel a sexual love for the father and hostile rivalry with the mother. Those psychological relationships are referred to as the *Oedipus* and *Electra complexes*, respectively. In the *latency* stage, which normally follows, those complexes are resolved, and sexual interests recede until puberty. When sex interest re-emerges, it is directed toward members of the opposite sex of the same age group.

Freud felt that early childhood was crucial in normal psychological development. The frustration of a pattern of gratification in early childhood eventually would manifest itself in an adult neurosis. In Freud's view all adult neuroses could be traced to some early frustration of the normal sequence of gratification.

Freud's contribution to the study of socialization rests primarily on his emphasis on the importance of infancy and early childhood in personality development. His description of the life cycle as being composed of distinct stages led researchers to look for points of major transition in the life cycle and to discover the importance of these transition points for personal development. Much of his thinking is, either directly or indirectly, incorporated into stage-developmental theories depicting the process of socialization and human development. While there has been widespread criticism of many of his assertions, his work did alert behavioral scientists to the importance of isolating phases of human development and studying their impact upon the person throughout the life cycle.

Summary

Throughout this review of the major contributions of some key theories about the process of self-development, a number of dominant themes emerged. Emphasized in each was the importance of early experiences in shaping the nature of the self. In Cooley's account of the development of the looking-glass self, the early impressions of how others are judging one's behavior were the most important bases of personality development. And those impressions were the most strongly resistant to eradication and change. Freud's view was that any frustration in the pattern of gratification occurring early in life would manifest itself later as an adult neurosis. Mead stressed the importance of language acquisition and facility early in life as a significant factor in human development. Without linguistic facility, the child would be unable to gain knowledge regarding the *degrees* of rightness or wrongness associated with given behaviors. In other words, the individual's knowledge of the expectations associated with various social roles would be severely limited.

According to Mead, one of the most significant events occurring early in the socialization process involves the transfer of the source of others' judgments from the parents to the generalized other, or to society as a whole. When the child governs his behavior on the basis of standards attributed to an external source of such a diffuse nature as "society," he has the basis for the development of a standard of morality. When a child's behavior depends upon the immediate reward or punishment administered to him by a parent or other authority figure, the type of behavior he will emit in a given situation will depend upon the presence or absence of that authority figure. However, when the child governs his own behavior with reference to the standards of a generalized other, this insures that his behavior will be reasonably consistent with these standards, *regardless of whether authority figures are present or not.* Generally, behavior consistent with a set of standards is required of persons holding certain positions in human society. Adherence to a given set of roles, standards, ethics, and obligations is an indispensible aspect of playing adult social roles in a competent manner. When a child begins to use the generalized other as his standard for judging his behavior, he has taken the first major step toward adulthood. That transition is one of the most critical steps during early socialization, for it assures that the child will be able to perform a role that is governed by abstract rules in a setting in which others are doing likewise. Indeed, no society can continue to exist unless that stage is reasonably well attained by a majority of its population. The alternative would, of course, be the necessity for complete external and coercive control of all members by a society. Since this is a manifest impossibility, there must be a considerable degree of self-regulation. To understand this in a practical way, consider the control of traffic on the streets and highways. Even though there usually is no traffic policeman in sight, the majority of people stop when a traffic light is red and proceed when it is green. Now and then, of course, some people do fail to follow the traffic rules—fail to govern their own behavior properly—often with catastrophic results. So while self-regulation is never complete, it must attain some minimum level for society to function at all.

Perspectives on the Learning Process

Since much of what is learned during the process of socialization involves the development in the child of the ability to exercise internal control over his own behavior, there has been substantial speculation regarding just how these internal controls emerge. We have seen that the development of the self as a separate psychic entity involves the ability to adopt external standards as internal guidelines for behavior. This ability is acquired via learning. Since facets of the learning process are so crucial in the early stages of socialization, we shall review some perspectives on the learning process in order to gain a fuller understanding of what actually takes place during the period in which internal controls over behavior are acquired.

Instrumental Learning Theory   The perspective that has contributed a vast amount to our knowledge of early socialization and the learning process is that of *learning theory*. In contrast to the Freudian view, this school of thought stresses the paramount importance of the social environment in determining the direction and course of human behavior and the development of internal controls. Freud emphasized that socialization involved a constant struggle between man's inherent nature and the constrictions of the social environment. Learning theorists, on the other hand, regard the child as essentially a passive organism that is subject to the controls that others exercise over him. Through manipulating these controls, others in the environment are able to shape the child's behavior.

The chief assumption underlying the major contentions of learning theorists is the principle of *hedonism*. Briefly stated, this principle asserts that men act in order to maximize pleasure and minimize pain. Also built into the assumptions of learning theory is the *principle of rationality*. This principle rests on the contention that, given a situation in which a person knows what behaviors will bring reward and avoid punishment, he will choose the option that minimizes punishment. Learning theorists view the developing individual as one who chooses the available alternatives that will bring about the greatest volume of reward. Since the alternatives of reward and punishment are largely controlled by adults or other authority figures, learning theorists maintain that they can exercise almost complete control over the behavior of the child, particularly in the early stages of socialization.

Learning theory is sometimes called *stimulus-response* theory. A *stimulus* may be broadly defined as anything that rouses an organism to activity—an incentive to action. According to learning theorists, *responses* follow stimuli in a time sequence. When a person perceives a stimulus, he responds in a certain manner. If he is rewarded for responding to that stimulus in that manner, then, when the individual is presented with the same stimulus sometime in the future, he will respond in the same way as the first time. In the terms employed by learning theory, that response comes under the *control* of the stimulus; when that stimulus is presented to the organism, it is likely that he will respond to it in the way he did when he received a reward.[5]

Patterns of reward and punishment are referred to as *reinforcement* in the jargon of learning theory. Behavior can be shaped according to the patterns of reinforcement that are applied to people following their exposure to stimuli and their reactions to those stimuli. The child's behavior is shaped gradually through the applications of reinforcement. Some responses he makes are followed by a high level of reward, others by varying degrees of reward or punishment. This is a conscious effort on the part of parents and other authority figures to direct behavior. The process of shaping the behavior of a child by the parents is called *conditioning*. Through the process of conditioning, a child learns which responses are regarded as appropriate and inappropriate in specific situations. The situations themselves become stimuli that elicit a whole range of responses that have been rewarded in the past.

Obviously, the learning theorists place strong emphasis on the past history of the child. Learning theorists study past histories of reinforcement patterns in order to explain why the child behaves in a certain way when confronted with specific stimuli. In addition, learning theorists are interested in determining who it was who dispensed this reinforcement. They argue that rewards and punishments administered by persons who are important to an individual are likely to shape behavior more readily than those dispensed by others. Not only are the patterns of reinforcement important, but also the *sources* of that reinforcement.

Another challenge facing parents and other agents of socialization, according to learning theorists, is one that involves attempting to insure that the child will respond appropriately in the absence of direct reward and punishment. Rewards and punishments must be dispensed consistently and often enough so that eventually children will conform to expectations on their own. Learning theorists emphasize that conformity in the absence of reinforcement will not occur until the child acquires the ability to *reinforce himself*. This requires the capacity to view the self as an object: to reward the self for appropriate behavior and to punish the self for transgressions.

Social Learning Theory   While learning theory has contributed a great deal to our understanding of how children develop and how behavior is acquired, the emphasis it places on external reinforcement as the main determinant of behavior overlooks a number of alternative influences. Recent research on how children learn has suggested that there are instances in which striking changes in behavior occur in the absence of direct reinforcement. A major modification of learning theory has emerged in the last few decades which has called attention to these alternative sources of influence on human behavior.

Although continuing to emphasize the importance of external reinforcement in learning, the *social learning* theories note the significance of such factors as modeling, imitation, and vicarious learning independent of direct external reinforcement.[6] The theories recognize that certain classes of behavior, particularly moral behavior, often require the performance of noxious, definitely nonhedonistic activities such as hard work, discomfort, and delay of gratification. Why would the individual choose to perform such behaviors in the absence of direct reward?

The answer to that important question began to form from the conclusions of the work of Albert Bandura and Richard Walters.[7] They demonstrated that behavior can be acquired through the *observation of models,* without direct reinforcement being given to the observer. A model, of course, is some other person, generally someone admired by the child, whom the child uses as a guide for his or her own behavior. The child is likely to adopt a mode of behavior if he sees a model rewarded for doing that particular activity. The strongest degree of imitation of observed behavior occurred in situations in which the model was seen by the observer as having been essentially like him in many respects or as having possessed desired attributes such as power, status, wealth, and the like.

Further inquiry into the question of why certain activities are performed in the absence of immediate reward, or even under substantial discomfort, showed that a number of additional factors were involved in the process of learning by observation. Bandura and Walters demonstrated in a series of studies that, while children were likely to *acquire* the behavior of models that they saw rewarded, they were not likely to actually *perform* those behaviors unless some reward would be forthcoming for so doing. Actual performance of the observed activity depended on whether there were any rewards for successfully *imitating* the model's behavior. This evidence implied that, while parents and other agents of socialization may not have too much control over what a child may observe in his environment, they can exert considerable influence on his behavior *by rewarding only the successful imitation of desired responses.*

Apparently, a child can acquire moral behavior and can learn to participate in unpleasant activities and delay gratification in the pursuit of a long-term goal if he sees others being rewarded for doing so *and* if he feels that he will be similarly rewarded. Social learning theory proposes that successful learning of such patterns of behavior will depend upon the characteristics of the model, the kind of reward the child sees received by the model, and the kind of reward the child actually expects to receive for successful imitation of the model's behavior. Since so many adult roles require effort and often entail some discomfort and delay of gratification, each of these elements of the process of *learning by imitation* assumes great importance in early stages of socialization. In order for the essential features of adult roles to be learned and learned well, children must be exposed to an environment in which they will not only see models rewarded for displaying the activities associated with adult roles, but also be rewarded for successfully imitating those models. As we shall discuss in the material on adolescent socialization, successful acquisition and performance of adult role behavior should occur relatively early in life if a person is to be able to adjust to and meet the rapidly increasing demands made on him or her in late childhood and adolescence.

Developmental Approach While instrumental and social learning theories have contributed immensely to our understanding of the learning process in early socialization, they are limited in application to the study of how one particular class of behaviors is acquired. However, one might ask how is the acquisition of one set of responses, say moral behavior, related to overall mental and cognitive development? In order to gain some perspective on this question, it will be necessary to turn to the work of another group of scientists who propose what might be called the *developmental* viewpoint.

The principal contribution to the developmental approach to studying mental development during childhood was provided by the Swiss social psychologist Jean Piaget. He was concerned most notably with how the child acquired concepts of right and wrong—so basic for membership in human society.[8] He believed that the child's ability to comprehend society's demands and moral rules did not depend on the history of reinforcement or on observation of moral behavior but was limited by the level his thought processes had attained. He proposed a theory of stages in human development which illustrated how the overall level of mental development determined the kind of moral behavior and internal controls the child would possess.

Among young children, Piaget contended, there was a tendency to view the world from an *egocentric* position. At this stage, the child is unable to take the role of another person; he does not have the ability to see the world from another's perspective. The child regards rules of conduct as external and unchangeable, being imposed upon him from the outside, but not standards that should draw any allegiance or support from him whatsoever. Later in the developmental sequence, he gradually accepts obligations to conform to the rules, even though he still regards them as external and outside of his control. He applies rules to specific situations, but still regards moral authority as being external. The individual does not reach the stage of substantial cognitive development until he recognizes that rules are imposed upon persons for the good of society as a whole and are necessary in order to promote the general welfare of all. At this point, the child begins to perceive that, if rules are so essential for his and others' welfare, he has a stake in preserving the social order. He feels that rules are maintained by his assent, not imposed by some external source of authority as he did earlier. The child's actions will reflect greater maturity in judgment and far greater concern for the welfare of others. When this stage in mental development is reached, the individual forms concepts of equality, fairness, reciprocity, and other aspects of human social relationships essential for functioning in a social order.

Piaget's major contribution to our understanding of early socialization derives from his emphasis on the overall mental and cognitive development of the child, rather than from his focus on specific learning sequences as do the instrumental and social learning theorists. One should not consider the learning process independently of the total development of the person. The successful learning of moral rules and internal controls is possible only when the child attains the level of development where he is able to realize that his own well-being and the welfare of others depends on the orderly operation of human social relationships and the exercise of control over one's own behavior.

Summary

In concluding the review of some of the theories concerning socialization and the development of self, it appears desirable to point out that none of these represents a mutually exclusive position with respect to any of the others. Both Cooley and Mead stress the *process* of socialization and how individual perception of others and then the self emerges. Freud was concerned with the appearance of certain *stages* of development, but he was even more concerned with providing a basis for understanding and alleviating various neuroses than the process of socialization itself. Freud's position opposes Mead's in only one particular. Mead conceived the "I" and "me" aspects of individual personality as not necessarily at war or in conflict with one another. Freud conceived the id, which corresponds roughly with Mead's "I", as eternally at war with the supergo, which Mead called the "me" part of the individual personality.

Instrumental learning theorists appear unconcerned with the social aspects of the process of socialization but devote their attention to explaining how *learning takes place*. The concept of *reinforcement* is not some theoretical abstraction but has great practical consequences for all humans. For example, if a young child can satisfy its own needs only through throwing a temper tantrum, then it can be reliably predicted that frustration will be followed by another temper tantrum. Or should a husband ignore a wife's excellent cooking efforts but be quick to comfort her when she is in tears, the husband will end up with a wife who is an indifferent cook but a highly skilled producer of tears.

Likewise, as Bandura and Walters indicate, *models* play an important role in development and socialization. Admired individuals often play a key role not only in general behavior but also in such things as choice of occupation or profession.

Too literal an acceptance of the ideas of those theorists may lead to the conclusion that individuals are born into a society and are shaped pretty much by that society without volition or conscious involvement on their part—that is, that man is, after all, an organism that responds in a mechanical fashion to forces beyond his control. But Piaget, while going along with the fact that the process of socialization does proceed in general along the lines laid down by a particular society, does introduce the very human element of *reasoning*—that is, that internal controls are possible only when a child reaches that level of development where he or she begins to consider the significance of norms for society. In other words, normal humans develop some concern for others and the society in which the individual and others live.

It should also be noted that if socialization were a purely mechanical process in and by which each of us is passively taught the values, norms, and roles of our society, it would be without the pain and anguish that so many experience during the period of adolescence.

ADOLESCENT SOCIALIZATION

Adolescence, or that period of transition between childhood and adulthood, is a time in which the individual is faced with massive problems of adjustment. At the onset of adolescence, there is a shift in expectations toward more independence which many societies impose upon their formerly dependent children. The importance of the peer group increases dramatically, largely because the child's position in the educational system usually entails attending a secondary school that may be some distance from home. As a result, overall contact with the family diminishes. Increasing peer demands upon the adolescent's time and energy further reduce the volume of contact between the child and his family, particularly in urban areas. The person is faced with the problem of adjusting to these increased demands of the outside world and modifying these when they conflict with the expectations of his family.

Another critical problem often facing children emerging into adolescence is the changing school environment. In many elementary schools, children are treated as dependent creatures. In such an environment, children's particular personal idiosyncracies are likely to be tolerated to some degree. In the secondary school, the child faces a "universalistic" environment in

In school, the child faces a "universalistic" environment in which everyone is treated according to the way he is able to compete successfully against uniform standards.

Reprinted by permission from Sidney Harris.

"I don't care if he does have an I.Q. of 169—I still think he's faking."

which everyone is treated according to the way he is able to compete successfully against uniform standards. At this time, if he has not encountered them already, the child comes to grips with the realities of race, social class, religion, and ethnic status. And these factors assume more importance in determining who one's peers are and whether some potential peer groups will accept him. Add to these problems and complexities of assuming a sex role, for which the individual probably has had little if any preparation, and some idea of the dilemmas of early adolescence become apparent.

Demands for Achievement

In adolescence the individual encounters for the first time the problems of having to accomodate fantasies to reality. This calls for a major alteration in one's self concept. And the individual must come to grips with the often disagreeable fact that his concept of himself may have no counterpart in the external world. Suddenly, demands intrude on him from all directions— family, peers, school, and other institutions—which force him to make concrete choices and formulate definite aspirations. As Piaget notes, adolescence is likely to be the first time that the individual is confronted with real demands for *achievement,* and it is during this period that most individuals attempt to become an achiever in a socially significant sense. Achievement in

Socialization and Human Development

school quickly becomes relevant for such future pursuits as college, occupational goals, and career planning. For the first time, essentially adult standards are applied to his performance. Demands are made for his commitment to long-range goals, and pressures toward acceptance and conformity emerge from peer groups and from the community at large.

Adolescence is a period in which individuals are expected to express *achievement motivation* in some concrete fashion. Whether this entails academic success, athletic prowess, or social competence will vary from person to person. The general features of achievement motivation, such as autonomy, planning for the future, mastery of socially relevant skills, a devotion to effort and hard work, ambition, and a desire for upward mobility, all comprise a set of expectations that intrude heavily upon adolescents. Studies have demonstrated that social pressures toward the demonstration of achievement motivation are applied, often abruptly, early in adolescence and increase substantially throughout this period. Aversive behavior, such as the postponement of work activities, tardiness, erratic habits, and other forms of avoidance of responsibility, which would have been condoned in childhood are often severely punished in adolescence. He is expected to be an achiever, and to achieve consistently in many fields.

As adolescents come to perceive social realities more accurately, advantages that are seen to accrue to some on the basis of race, social class, ethnic, and religious status will play an increased role in how the adolescent perceives the world and his chances in it. Young adolescents are likely to be quite idealistic; older adolescents, through experience, tend to perceive social realities more clearly and are likely to have more realistic career plans and future ambitions. Among adolescents from disadvantaged groups, it is not unusual for expectations to decline with age; older adolescents are far more aware of the limitations that are imposed upon them and respond accordingly. By contrast, among more advantaged youth expectations remain constant and even increase with age as they become more aware of their relative advantages over others.[9] Future choices of activities, then, are more and more conditioned by social realities as one proceeds through adolescence.

Demands for Assumption of Sex Roles

While the onset of puberty signals the beginning of sexual maturity, there are attempts in all societies to impose restrictions on the sexual behavior permissible for adolescents. For many years in American society the ideal norm was complete sexual abstinence outside of marriage. This ideal, was of course, far from realized. But while deviations from it were at least tacitly condoned when committed by young males, any female who deviated risked the loss of her "reputation" and faced difficulties in obtaining a suitable spouse. More recently, there has been much greater sexual freedom not only in the United States but in other parts of the world as well. And this change has obviously had some effects on sexual behavior among adolescents. While various studies give conflicting estimates of increases in sexual behavior among adolescents, there can be little question that adolescents do engage in such behavior, including sexual intercourse, with greater frequency than in the past. That the advent of the "pill" has had considerable behavioral consequences for human sexual behavior, particularly of females, can not seriously be questioned.

The problem for adolescents is not simply the avoidance of pregnancy or venereal disease but also the resolving of an intense conflict being waged in the larger society over sex and sexual behavior. A considerable segment of American society still adheres to the earlier norms and holds that a continued deterioration will result in the further breakdown of the American family and the ultimate ruin of society as we know it. Another large segment takes an almost mutually exclusive view, namely, that sexual freedom constitutes progress and that the older norms constitute unnecessary and indeed unhealthy restrictions on human freedom and happiness. Where previously the values and norms with respect to sexual behavior were reasonably well understood, they are now confused and ambiguous. When it is considered that the sexual drive is a powerful one and that adolescence is often considered, in the physical sense, as being the period of greatest sexuality, the problems of the adolescents are obviously severely compounded.

Demands of the Youth Culture

As John Clausen notes, no peer socialization pressures are stronger than those demanding that the adolescent be emancipated from the restrictions of his parents.[10] Particularly among adolescent males, being under the control of parents (particularly of the mother) shows a lack of demonstrated independence and masculinity. The peer group savagely enforces conformity to these age-appropriate activities and norms and usually makes acceptance in the group contingent upon near total adoption of these practices. As a result of an increase in peer interaction, there is a greater *convergence of attitudes* among members. This pattern of convergence often produces a substantial divergence from the norms of the parents. This is most likely when the youth culture is opposed in many respects to the culture of the parents, as among immigrant groups in which the parents are foreign-born and cling to the ways of the old country while their American-born progeny reject all things foreign in favor of the American youth culture. Parents during this period feel, for the first time, the loss of control over the activities of their children, a fact which, in itself, sets the stage for intergenerational conflict. Peer group activity and selection revolves around the school environment, which may be far removed from the home. For children living in slum areas

Copyright © 1972 by Saturday Review/World, Inc.
Reprinted by permission from the publisher and W. Von Riegen.

"You mean you hated your father too? When did you turn square?"

There is the tendency of adolescent peer groups and adult authority figures to confront one another in ideological rhetoric regarding the extent of the "generation gap."

in which delinquent gang activity is frequent, the loss of control over the activities of the children is very threatening for parents and portends later trouble with the law.

One of the major contemporary problems associated with the loss of parental control involves the emergence within the overall youth culture of the drug consuming subculture. It was during the late 1960's that some adolescents began consuming drugs with which their parents had little, if any, experience and that are illegal for all citizens. (In the case of alcohol, many parents have had experience with it, and it is legal for those over the age of majority in most states.) There is considerable anxiety among parents and other authority figures about the influence that certain adolescent peer groups exercise over the behavior of their members. The fact that there is a drug subculture points up the serious error inherent in treating the youth culture as though it were monolithic and standardized. In most adolescent youth groups, parental values are not so much totally rejected as partially recast. Despite the publicity regarding the extent of the "drug scene," it remains a distinct and recognizable subculture *within* the overall world of adolescent youth.

There is, of course, the tendency of adolescent peer groups and adult authority figures to confront one another in ideological rhetoric regarding the extent of the "generation gap." But adolescent peer groups provide their members with a standard against which to compare the life style and values of the parent generation, and they provide a basis on which individual adolescents can recombine aspects of each culture in order to produce a viable synthesis which will enable them to live in the future.[11] These peer groups give the adolescent information about how members of his or her generation perceive the major social problems confronting their society, and they give some indication of what solutions might work. While many of these solutions consist of little more than idealistic dreams, they at least may serve as the basis for the moral philosophy of the upcoming generation and give some indication of the direction that social change might take in succeeding generations.

Changes in Parent-Child Relations

Adolescence poses quite a problem for the parent: How much autonomy should he grant to his offspring and how much and what type of control should he exercise? These are questions facing parents at all points during the socialization process. But they become particularly acute during adolescence owing to the rapid onset of this period of development and the rapid physical, mental, and social changes occurring in children. Direct power and coercion may be applied in order to exact compliance from adolescents. But this strategy is likely to produce alienation and possibly rebellion, particularly if the culture of the youth peer group is widely at variance with the parents' norms and its pressures for independence are strong. Generally, parents solve this problem of autonomy versus control by allowing adolescents freedom commensurate with physical, psychological, and social maturity. When both parents and children take advantage of this newly granted autonomy, the parents may feel rejected by their children and the children feel that the parents have suddenly become distant. Since there is a substantial reduction in the time spent in the home as both parents and children increase their activities outside, these feelings often have basis in fact. There appear to be socioeconomic differences in the extent to which there is decreased parent-child interaction during adolescence.[12] In working class families, the economic needs often force adolescent children into the job market, granting them a measure of economic independence and increasing the time spent outside of the home. By contrast, in middle-class families the long-range educational aspirations of both the parents and children involve greater convergence of interest in the child's activities, since they are instrumental for the goals of all parties concerned.

In the early 1970's, the unrest among youth, particularly college youth, appeared to have dissipated somewhat. To interpret this as meaning that significant changes have taken place in the adolescent subculture would probably be in error. Intergenerational conflict appears to be especially endemic in industrial societies. In a society in which violence remains a suitable instrument for overcoming opposition, it can be anticipated that various groups—including youth groups—will resort to it from time to time. However, protest and the use of violence are not peculiar to young people and should not be regarded as some special behavioral characteristic of the adolescent subculture.

The continuing problems of the adolescent in modern society, with emphasis on American society, have been noted. These problems can be expected to continue. The problems facing young people in the transition from elementary school to high school and college cannot simply be dismissed as part of growing up. Indeed since the adolescent subculture is in large part a function of the greatly extended period of formal education in most modern societies, but particularly in the United States where so many young people go on to college, it seems obvious that more attention must be given to utilizing the powerful forces inherent in such a subculture rather than dismissing or ignoring it.

ADULT SOCIALIZATION, MATURITY, AND OLD AGE

While the age of eighteen is considered as majority for voting, the draft, and the consumption of alcohol and tobacco, *legally* the age of majority is twenty-one. At that age a person can enter into a legal contract and is therefore subject to the full weight of the law if he breaks the terms of a contract. There are no significant restrictions on marriage, and many of the protections afforded adolescents by the law no longer apply.

Even though many people delay entry into the occupational structure until their late twenties or early thirties because of the length of time required to prepare themselves for professional status, adulthood is considered to be the period in which one assumes his major occupational and marital roles. Socialization during this period, therefore, relates directly to these various roles. What is learned are the particular behaviors necessary to perform these roles. Rarely does the content of adult socialization include the moral training so characteristic of childhood and adolescence. By early adulthood the person is expected to have acquired enough internal control over his behavior to guide him for the rest of his life. Following marriage and procreation, the individual is expected to have sufficient purpose and moral development to enable him to impart moral principles to, and instill internal controls in, the succeeding generation of children. In fact, there are stern legal proscriptions regarding what are and what are not fit parenthood and parental practices. In addition to the strong emphasis on the marriage and parental role, self-determination and self-actualization are important features of the expectations which define adulthood. Devotion of substantial effort to professional, occupational, and developmental activities is virtually required of adults. During this period the major achievements of life are expected; the person's ultimate occupational, social, and economic status will depend almost entirely upon activities demonstrated during this period.

Termination of active parental and occupational but not necessarily marital roles determine the beginning of the transition from adulthood to old age. Among women, this transition often occurs with the menopause. When the physical and psychological problems associated with menopause are coupled with the departure of the children from the home, the effects of this discontinuity in roles can be profound. Among men, the transition from active adult status to retirement often is even more traumatic, especially if the transition entails a drastic loss in economic status. And retirement often requires a significant change in life style, owing to the economic realities of senior citizenship—pension and Social Security payments rarely approach a mature man's yearly income.

Special problems are faced by the elderly in American society. The labels "old" and "elderly" carry negative connotations in a society, such as America, where youth and all its appurtenances are regarded as the ideal. Since occupational activity is the prime determinant of personal competence and social status among males, loss of this role often leaves the retired male with little basis for identification. He is just a senior citizen, nothing more. When this retirement is accompanied by relative poverty and deprivation, older people experience an even greater loss of identity and personal worth. Only through the attention of younger family members and interaction with others sharing their problems can older people maintain the sense of worth and identity which supported them through their productive years. People who prepare for their retirement with advance knowledge that they will have to cope with those problems make the most successful transition to retirement. It appears that some amount of *anticipatory socialization* (and financial preparation) is required prior to retirement in order to circumvent the major discontinuities associated with the cessation of "productive" (in the sense of occupational or parental) activity.

CONCLUSION

In this chapter we have reviewed in some detail the process of socialization throughout the life cycle, and considerable attention has been given to early socialization. We have found that both *heredity* and *environment* have influences on human nature and that there is a reciprocal relationship between each factor. Examination of various formulations dealing with the *development of the self* disclosed that the perceptions of others play a crucial role in the type of self concept which emerges. *Language* is essential for a wide knowledge of how others perceive one and is an invaluable aid in the refinement of, and increasing complexity in, the developing self. In discussing the *processes of learning* we obtained a better understanding of how internal control over behavior is acquired. Since these controls are so important in adult life for successful functioning, *learning theory* approaches aid greatly in our understanding of how morality is acquired and cognitive development proceeds. Jean Piaget provided substantial information on how the total development of the person proceeds. Problems of adolescent and adult socialization were discussed in some detail, with emphasis on the problems of discontinuity experienced by adolescents preparing for adulthood as well as by those retiring from active adult roles.

A major theme of this chapter has been that socialization proceeds *throughout the life cycle* from birth to death. While the behaviors and knowledge acquired early in life play an important role in shaping that life, the high degree of adaptability of the human organism insures that major problems during life can be met by adjusting to new demands and new environments. The considerable adaptability man possesses and his vast ability to learn new ways of adjusting to changing situations comprise man's major resources for solving the problems of continuity and of survival.

In this chapter we have discussed how man is transformed into a social being. We have seen how he acquires the capabilities necessary for him to participate effectively in his society. In the next chapter we will discuss that society and see how it operates in relation to the socialized individual.

REVIEW QUESTIONS

5.1 Which is more important in producing the social being, heredity or environment? Why?

5.2 From society's point of view, the task of socialization is to insure continuity. What constitutes success, and where is the greatest concern focused?

5.3 Compare and contrast the personality theories of Freud, Mead, Cooley, and Piaget. What are the major similarities and differences?

5.4 What are the major sources of discontinuity within the adult phase of the life cycle? What major social problems are produced due to these discontinuities? How might our society deal with these problems?

5.5 What are the major demands placed on the child as he enters adolescence? Give a general description of the changes in parent-child relations during this period.

NOTES

[1] W. Sluckin, *Imprinting and Early Learning* (Chicago: Aldine, 1965).

[2] Charles Horton Cooley, *Human Nature and the Social Order* (New York: Scribner, 1902). This pioneer American sociologist provided an important perspective on the development of the self.

[3] George Herbert Mead, *Mind, Self, and Society* (Chicago: University of Chicago Press, 1934). Originally published over 40 years ago, this work has great relevance today, particularly for those who seek ideas on the formation of human personality.

[4] Sigmund Freud, *A General Introduction to Psychoanalysis* (New York: Horace Liveright, 1920). This volume contains most of Freud's ideas on the development of human personality.

[5] Clark L. Hull, *A Behavior System: An Introduction to Behavior Theory Concerning the Individual Organism* (New Haven: Yale University Press, 1952). A more modern work which is highly recommended is Ernest R. Hilgard and Gordon H. Bower, *Theories of Learning*, 3d ed. (New York: Appleton, 1966).

[6] See Albert Bandura and Richard H. Walters, *Social Learning and Personality Development* (New York: Holt, Rinehart and Winston, 1963), where personality development is discussed from the perspective of social learning theory. See also J. Dollard and N. E. Miller, *Personality and Psychotherapy* (New York: McGraw-Hill, 1963); and J. M. W. Whiting, "Resource Mediation and Learning by Identification," in *Personality Development in Children*, ed. I. Iscoe and H. W. Stevenson (Austin, Texas: University of Texas Press, 1960), pp. 112–116.

[7] Bandura and Walters, *Social Learning*.

[8] Jean Piaget, *The Moral Judgment of the Child* (New York: Collier, 1962). Piaget's thinking dominates the developmental school of thought on the processes of cognitive development.

[9] R. M. Dreger and K. S. Miller, "Comparative Psychological Studies of Negroes and Whites in the United States: 1959–1965," *Psychological Bulletin* 72, no. 3 (1968), pp. 1–58. Dreger and Miller review the conclusions of six years of study on the psychological characteristics of both races.

[10] John A. Clausen et al., "Perspectives on Child Socialization," in *Socialization*

and Society, ed. John A. Clausen (Boston: Little, Brown, 1968), pp, 130–182; socialization is treated as a cumulative process.

[11] While there is much talk about a "generation gap," it may be that this "gap" is superficial and not the deep, ideological gulf supposed by so many to exist. In a recent comparative study of the values of college students as compared with those of their parents, it was dicovered that the students tended, by and large, to have the same values as their parents. Differences tended to be differences in degree and not kind. In other words, college students are probably somewhat more idealistic than their parents but the values actually held are much the same. See, Burton Wright II, "The Generation Gap: An Intergenerational Comparison of Values" (Ph.D. diss., Florida State University, 1972).

[12] Mirra Komarovsky, *Blue-Collar Marriage* (New York: Random House, 1964), provides a major inquiry into family life and personality development in working class families.

ANNOTATED BIBLIOGRAPHY

Kohlberg, L. "Development of Moral Character and Moral Ideology." In *Review of Child Development Research*, edited by M. L. Hoffman and L. W. Hoffman. pp. 383–431. New York: Russell Sage Foundation, 1964. Kohlberg emphasizes the view that moral development and conformity rest on the desire of the child to avoid punishment for deviance from parental desires.

Mead, George Herbert. *Mind, Self, and Society*. Chicago: University of Chicago Press, 1934. Mead belongs with a few other "timeless" sociologists, such as Durkheim and Weber. His thoughts on socialization read as well and truly today as they did when written. It should be noted that the material for this book was gathered together from Mead's notes and other sources by his students and friends after his death.

Service, Elman R. *Profiles in Ethnology*. New York: Harper & Row, 1958. Those who are interested in seeing the varied forms taken by different cultures and societies will find this work particularly valuable. Without knowledge of at least some other societies, it is difficult, if not impossible, to obtain a full appreciation of the socialization process.

Stratification: One for You, Two for Me

INTRODUCTION

The Declaration of Independence, written by Thomas Jefferson, says in part, "We hold these truths to be self-evident, that all men are created equal . . ." But Jefferson's words, embodying John Locke's philosophy of the social contract, refer to equality before the law and to equal treatment by governments. Jefferson did not, so far as we can judge, imply that all human beings are born with an equal biological endowment or equal opportunities to obtain prestige, wealth, or power. Literate human beings with a grasp of the principles of democracy can agree that equality before the law is a most desirable ideal, but an ideal that has not yet been achieved. To state the matter directly, the law, as represented by the legislators, the judiciary, and the police, does not accord all citizens equality of treatment.[1]

But inequality involves more than the well-documented failure of the law to accord all citizens the same treatment. Inequality is a fact of life and ranges from those inequalities occuring almost at the instant of conception to widespread differences in education, income, life styles, and life chances. Even in athletics, where the assumption underlying contests is that the participants are of roughly equal talent, coaches, managers, and athletic directors make continuing efforts—recruiting superior athletes, for example—to ensure that victory does indeed accrue to the better team.

Inequality is pervasive—not merely in the United States and other democratic countries but also throughout the world wherever humans are found in groups. We are not surprised when we note vast differences among people in other nations, but we attempt to gloss over these facts in the United States. As W. Lloyd Warner remarked, "the primary and most important fact about the American social system is that it is composed of two basic but antithetical principles: the first, the principle of equality; the second, the principle of unequal status and of superior and inferior rank."[2] The concern in this chapter is with inequality as it relates to the stratification of social systems.

There are, of course, many questions concerning stratification. One that is of considerable relevance to many students is this: Does an individual born into a relatively poor family have a *real* opportunity in American society to improve his or her position—that is, to attain a level above that of his or her family? Stated in another way, Is the United States still a "land of opportunity" for those who are motivated to work hard and persevere?

SOCIAL STRATIFICATION AS A SOCIAL PROBLEM

Before considering stratification as a social problem, we ought to understand the meaning of *social stratification* and of *social problem*. For purposes of this chapter, we will use Bernard Barber's definition of social stratification

Stratification: One for You, Two for Me

Inequality is a fact of life and ranges from those inequalities occurring almost at the instant of conception to widespread differences in education, income, life styles, and life chances.

as "a structure of regularized inequality in which men are ranked higher and lower according to the value accorded their various social roles and activities."[3] Keeping in mind Warner's comment about the conflict between the American values of equality and the principle of unequal status, it is easy to see that this very contradiction in values poses a *social problem*. Paul Horton and Gerald Leslie define *social problem* as "a condition affecting a significant number of people in ways considered undesirable, about which it is felt something can be done through collective social action."[4]

Keeping in mind those definitions, it would seem that two groups of people, one large and the other relatively smaller, would see stratification as posing quite different social problems. The reasons are both sociological and psychological. First, modern societies in general and American society in particular socialize most members with ideas about the value of competition; competition not merely for the sake of playing the game but *also for the purpose of winning*. Satisfaction, or, to use the psychological term, reinforcement, from vigorous competition involves a demonstration of superiority over the losers. While some think of competition mainly in terms of athletic contests, competition actually ranges across all kinds of social activity, from getting good grades in school to building up a successful business enterprise. The way competition is structured divides competitors into two groups—winners and losers. When this competition involves the considerable societal rewards available to people in modern societies—wealth, status, power, and material comforts— it follows logically that losers will see their social problem as involving a *change* in their condition, and winners will see it as a problem of *maintaining* the status quo.

Although modern American society is the wealthiest in the history of mankind, vast inequities exist between the various social classes in power, income, material comforts, and life styles, all of which affect life chances. In competitive terms, some members obtain a greater share of the rewards than others. The dissatisfactions inherent in losing not merely breed tensions and discontent (social problems in themselves) but also tend to divide many societies into "haves" (winners) and "have-nots" (losers). The haves, of course, see the social problem as one of maintaining their own preferred position, and the have-nots see it as one of improving theirs. In addition to the losers, there are also those who have not been permitted to play in the game at all. Until recent times, nonwhite Americans have not often been in a position to compete for significant societal rewards.[5] The invidious distinctions inherent in any system of stratification are tension and conflict producing, even when all members of a society are given an opportunity to compete on some kind of equal terms. But in a society such as in America, which still practices active discrimination against nonwhite Americans, the social problems inherent in all systems of stratification are further exacerbated. It is one thing to be at the bottom of the hierarchy but believe that one has an opportunity to better one's condition. It is quite another thing to be at the lowest point without any real hope of improvement.

In American society some of the severe problems so evident in developing countries have been at least partially alleviated. We are referring here to the very clear distinction in many developing countries between a small minority at the top of indigenous stratification systems and the great mass of people trapped at the bottom. In the United States, the largest of all societal groups—often referred to as the "middle class"—has, in fact, gained access to a substantial amount of societal rewards. While middle-class Americans aspire to improve their position and certainly to maintain it, there is less bitterness and hostility in the class than in the large sectors of the poor in Latin America, the Middle East, the Orient, and so on.

If we define "power" as the ability to gain one's own objectives in the face of opposition, it is evident that an important concomitant of stratification is that some people—those at the top of the hierarchy—have or tend to have more power and influence than those further down in the stratification system. Without becoming involved in any psychological considerations about why men desire power, it is reasonable to state that many do simply because it works to satisfy wants. In the United States, the decade of the 1960's witnessed a growing disenchantment on the part of some youth with the power structure. They claimed that it was unresponsive to the real needs of the great mass of people. On the basis of age alone, the young do not occupy positions in the stratification system where they wield any real power—they are relatively powerless to change things as they feel things ought to be changed.[6]

Inherent, then, in systems of stratification are a number of real problems. And these are social problems because "they are conditions affecting a significant number of people in ways considered undesirable, about which it is felt that something can be done through collective social action."[7] Not all people, of course, regard all aspects of stratification as social problems. *Fatalism,* characteristic of many preliterate cultures, is found even in modern societies.[8] By fatalism is meant a general belief that everything is preordained and that the individual is, therefore, powerless to do anything to alter his condition or the condition of others. From this extreme, we find people holding all degrees of opinion, up to and including the modern Marxists, who hold that stratification is wrong and unnecessary, and should (or will) be replaced by a classless society.[9]

Having seen that stratification generates a host of social problems, we should now consider the theories held by sociologists about this social phenomenon.

THEORIES OF SOCIAL STRATIFICATION

There are three ways of looking at stratification—the *functional,* the *conflict,* and a combination of the two, or the *eclectic.* Those approaches provide considerably more understanding of this phenomenon than any single perspective could.

Functional

When contemporary sociologists speak of a *functional theory of stratification,* they most likely have in mind a seminal and controversial point of view put forth by Kingsley Davis and Wilbert E. Moore.[10] The view maintains that stratification is based upon, or arises out of, the needs of societies and not the needs of the individual members of societies.

Three Assumptions The starting point for Davis and Moore was their observation that *no society is unstratified.* And there is no question that all societies are differentially ordered in some ways. Anthropologists, implicitly or explicitly, hold that rank differences and unequal rewards are characteristic of human societies wherever they are found.[11] The initial assumption of Davis and Moore is that, if all societies are stratified, there must be reasons for such a general state of affairs. And it is with those reasons that they are concerned.

The second assumption is that there is considerable uniformity in the distribution of prestige between the major types of positions in various similar societies. From the highest and most important position in any society to the very lowest, there is a roughly proportional decrease in prestige as one descends the stratification hierarchy. In American society, for example, one can readily grasp the considerable prestige differences between the president of a corporation and a stock clerk; and one can see as well that a much smaller difference exists between the president and a company vice-president.

Third, between societies there are differences in the degree and type of stratification. In relatively simple societies, stratification may be along age and sex lines with, perhaps, a few males holding the important positions of high prestige and leadership. But the vast majority of adults would be classified either along sex lines or on the basis of such criteria as skill as a hunter, the number of cattle or horses, and so forth. In modern societies, stratification is infinitely more complex. For example, status distinctions are made among skilled, semiskilled, and unskilled workmen in a particular plant.

Davis and Moore begin their argument by detailing their basic assumptions (none of which is disputed by anthropologists or sociologists) and indicate that they are hopeful of explaining two phenomena: "one to understand the universal, the other to understand the variable features of stratification."[12]

Before discussing the details of the Davis-Moore position, one important point must be made. The reader, his or her family, friends, relatives, and, in fact, all humans are involved in some system of stratification. For the moment at least, the reader must not become personally involved in the argument. What Davis and Moore are talking about are status positions, *not* the people who fill the positions. "It is one thing to ask why different positions carry different degrees of prestige, and quite another to ask how certain individuals get into these positions."[13] For example, if we were to ask why Woodrow Wilson or John Kennedy became president of the United States, we would tend to get a set of answers revolving around the life history of the men concerned. But if we ask why is there a *position* of president of the United States, quite another set of answers is generated. Davis and Moore address themselves to the latter type of question.

The essentials of the Davis-Moore position are not at all difficult to grasp. They possess a certain degree of highly persuasive, logical appeal.

Society as a Machine   While analogies are risky, we will, for the purposes of argument, view society as a sort of machine. Machines have some genuine utilitarian purpose. If we view society as a machine, that purpose is the survival of society. Note particularly that the purpose of society is not the survival of the individual members but the survival of society as a whole.

Machines, of course, have parts all of which must perform their necessary function if the machine is to be kept running and do what it is designed to do. Similarly, society is composed of parts—institutions, norms, strata, roles, and so forth—all of which must function at some minimal level if any society is to survive.

The smallest parts of the societal machine are roles which, of course, are occupied by people. Although people may be considered to require fuel, that is, nourishment, they also must be motivated if they are to function as necessary in light of societal goals.

Motivation   Davis and Moore consider motivation as a key factor and point out that motivation functions in two diverse but related ways: (1) to cause people to want to fill certain positions; (2) to insure that the incumbents of positions function both initially and continuously in such a way as to meet some minimum necessary standard of performance.

The situation for an entire society is in some ways, not too much different than for a corporation. Any business, if it is to stay in business, requires employees who are somehow motivated not only to apply for work but, once hired, to perform that work with reasonable efficiency. The differences between societies and corporations, however, are important. The corporation has some directive authority over its employees; within limits, it can discharge unsatisfactory employees. Society lacks this kind of precise control over its members. Motivation both to seek a certain vocation or profession and then to work at it effectively must necessarily be immanent in society itself—that is, society must somehow be organized so that these ends are accomplished.

But, as we know, jobs are different in many ways, including the fact that various kinds of prestigious work are not referred to as "jobs"—we speak of "positions" or "professions." The work necessary for societal survival differs in at least four ways.

1. Work varies in importance. For example, if retrenchment or cut-backs were necessary in a company, it would not fire all the executives leaving only the clerks.

2. Work varies in terms of intrinsic enjoyment.

3. Some kinds of work require greater natural talent or native ability to accomplish than others. As can be readily appreciated, it takes much less native ability to work on an assembly line than it does to plan and supervise the delivery of the necessary materials to that assembly line.

4. Much more than motivation is required for many kinds of work. Varying periods of education and training are needed for all but the most unskilled. As is obvious, it takes only a few hours of on-the-job training to perform competently on some kinds of work. But to be a physician necessitates many years of education and training prior to entering practice.

Rewards In complex societies, particularly if all members chose their work on the basis of such criteria as pleasantness, ease, and minimum educational and training requirements and if many wished to work only to gain the necessities of life, a great many important functions would not be performed. Therefore it follows that societies, particularly *modern* societies, must (1) have available meaningful and desirable rewards to persuade people to fill all necessary positions and perform all vital functions; and (2) distribute societal rewards differentially, since the different positions have differential societal importance and require varying degrees of native talent, education, and training. Society's rewards—sustenance, diversion, self-respect, material comforts, luxuries, ego-expansion, and so forth—tend to be built into positions and consist of certain rights for the incumbents of these positions. Although Davis and Moore do not say so explicitly, it appears reasonable to assume that this "built-in" feature of rights to rewards is essential for the purpose of providing a certain stability for motivational purposes. For example, if the prestige accorded physicians were constantly shifting from high to low while the period of education and training remained constant, it would be difficult to motivate sufficient numbers of persons to seek a career in medicine.

Rebuttal The Davis-Moore position does have a certain persuasive, logical appeal. If all work in a modern society were to be rewarded in an identical fashion, there would be little incentive for individual members to seek a career in areas where the work was unpleasant, difficult, or required long periods of preparatory training and education. It seems, therefore, that the societal rewards that include rights to rewards *must* be distributed unequally in order for society to function with minimal effectiveness. Since stratification is institutionalized inequality, it follows that all societies must be stratified. In the words of Davis and Moore, "social inequality is thus an unconsciously evolved device by which societies insure that the most important positions are conscientiously filled by the most qualified persons."[14]

But as logical and persuasive as the Davis-Moore argument appears to be, it is too neat and too tidy to represent the real world. Earlier several questions were asked that have a bearing here. For example, What is the relationship between life styles, life chances, and stratification? Even the most cursory inspection of any modern society shows that a large number of management positions are filled by those whose fathers were themselves part of management. Professional fathers tend, by and large, to have sons who themselves become professionals. Are these sons initially as well or better qualified in terms of native intelligence than the sons of men further down the stratification hierarchy? Furthermore, taking biases into account, the public press contains reports of behavior by men in responsible positions which range from the merely foolish to the psychotic. While allowances must be made for mistakes and lapses in judgment, an important question still can be raised. Are the thousands of truly important positions vital to any modern society actually being filled by the *most* qualified persons? On the evidence, the answer is no.

The Davis-Moore point of view on stratification does provide a framework for a general understanding of stratification. But their orientation raises a number of new questions. We turn now to a quite different orientation to stratification.

Conflict

The conflict theory sees stratification as the result of the striving by groups within a society for power, with power determining the distribution of those rewards available to members in a society. The functionalists consider stratification of societies as not only inevitable but also necessary. In contrast, those holding the conflict orientation, while admitting that stratification is indeed ubiquitous, argue that stratification is neither necessary nor inevitable. Considering the flexibility and adaptability of *Homo sapiens*, it is difficult to refute that contention. To resort to the argument that since all known societies are stratified, stratification is necessary and inevitable would be analogous to someone saying that since no man has ever landed on Mars, no man ever will. One of the strong points of the conflict position is that it considers the realities of power distribution and then attempts to explain them. Aside from the predictions of Karl Marx (thus far demonstrated to be in some error), or Plato's hypothetical construct of an ideal society set forth in *The Republic*, few satisfactory alternatives to stratification have been offered. But, upon further thought, it seems obvious that inequality alone is not enough to fill many necessary positions. Just as plausible is the argument that the positional structures of society could be rearranged to be more in keeping with available talents and skills.[15]

Competition Much conflict arises out of competition for things of value that are in short supply. If stratification is ubiquitous, so is conflict. The functionalists have tended to ignore the part that conflict plays in determining the form, shape, and operation of systems of stratification. When an individual's socially learned aspirations are blocked, it can be anticipated that frustration, aggression, and, hence, conflict will ensue. Even when aspirations are not blocked in the absolute sense, competition for scarce rewards will inevitably occur; this competition is a salient feature of American society.[16]

The functionalist position is perhaps most vulnerable in its contention that inequality functions to ensure that important positions are filled by the best qualified. This is obviously *not* the case in the real world. Indeed, there are currently no measuring instruments available that would enable us to determine just who *is* the best qualified. It is probable that in competition for almost any position in almost any modern society there are a number of people capable of performing its functions and tasks with reasonable competence. Just who finally gets a particular desirable position involves many factors including power. But ability does play some part; even in ascribed societies, incumbents of high positions were expected to meet certain obligations of which noblesse oblige is an example.

Every Man against Every Man   A good starting point for developing an understanding of the conflict perspective is with Thomas Hobbes, who saw men's actions as stemming from their different, independent, and individual passions. Granted that in Hobbes's view man is essentially self-seeking and egocentric, it nonetheless follows that any individual is in a position to thwart any other individual. This clearly would result in what Hobbes called "the war of every man against every man."[17] In order to avoid this "war" it has been necessary for man to invent society, which is, in effect, a mechanism for controlling and regulating conflict. The conflict view, then, is that society evolved out of a need to control primitive, atavistic, and aggressive elements in human nature. Speculating further from the Hobbesian premise, it can be imagined that certain groups of men combined, entered into agreements with one another, and, by virtue of the strength of combination, gained power. This in turn led to stratification which emerged as an essential element of that entity we call society.

Stratification and Societal Rules   Hobbes as well as others are probably in error regarding man's basic nature. It is generally agreed by contemporary sociologists that men are what society makes them. All societies, preliterate to modern, have numerous rules for the conduct of their members. In modern society the rules (or laws) regulating commerce, many of which are designed to keep competition on some roughly equal plane, do testify in partial support of Hobbes. It is also clear that many societal rules have a direct bearing on stratification and stratification systems, with some rules tending to maintain the status quo and others having a different effect. For example, up until recently, stratification and justice were closely related when in theory they ought not to be. In the United States and other countries, for example, types of crime and imposed sanctions very often vary according to the social class of the offender.[18] Considerable conflict has arisen out of this disparate treatment alone. It seems clear that this has produced efforts to provide more equal treatment before the law—for example, the ruling that the state must provide an attorney for those too poor to afford one. Even questions of life and death are involved in stratification. It has been reliably reported that the quality of treatment in some hospital emergency rooms may well depend on the evaluation by the physicians and nurses of the social status of the patient.[19]

Access to Resources Considering the foregoing comments, high status in a stratification system is something earnestly to be desired and, perhaps, fought for. Since such positions are as scarce as the societal rewards connected with them, it is not surprising that competition and conflict are involved as able individuals compete with one another for the limited supply of higher positions. If obtaining valued positions was simply a function of merit or ability, then conflict and competition would not be quite as relevant in shaping stratification systems. While merit may be a factor in upward mobility, other variables may be of equal or even greater importance. One such factor is the matter of access to resources based on birth. What are the class, resources, and power of the family into which one is born? If it is high or even middle-class, then sons (and increasingly daughters) are afforded an opportunity for that advanced education that has become important if one is not only to improve one's condition but also to maintain it. Further, having parents or other relatives in positions of power and influence in business or government automatically opens doors to applicants that, except for unusual circumstances, would be barred to other eligibles. The predominance of graduates of the Ivy League universities in some governmental and business areas is a good case in point.

A criticism of aristocratic societies by democratic societies is that in the former merit counts for little and birth for much. But as sociologists know and citizens in democracies can perceive, *ascription*—the placement of offspring based on family rather than ability—is present even in American society. Parents do use a variety of methods and techniques, occasionally unethical, to insure that their offspring have an opportunity to maintain or better parental status. These ascriptive practices are contrary to the value of equality. And it is not surprising that tension, frustration, and the conflict born of these psychological phenomena are generated in those denied status positions by what they see, often correctly, as unfair means. Thus in terms of the occupants of roles in a stratified society, it seems clear that conflict does play a role.

Conflict between Groups Conflict between individuals in modern societies is sharp, real, and of importance to those concerned. But of more far-reaching social significance is the conflict between groups. Although some of this group conflict may appear to be primarily economic, ideological, or both, it is generally a *struggle for power*. There are, of course, those who would argue to the contrary, including more than a few politicians. But political parties are less concerned with the promotion of a particular ideology than they are with the acquisition and maintenance of political power. This

In the United States, an excellent example of group conflict is the historic battle between management and labor. The unions have been successful in raising the wages, living standards, and, hence, life chances of many Americans.

is not to say that members of one political party or another are not sincere in their ideological belief. Rather, the end goal is election to public office and the acquisition of the power that such office confers on the holder. Revolutionaries preach their ideologies in order to obtain the necessary support for overthrowing a government. But once in office, they often behave, in terms of power, much like their predecessors.

In the United States, an excellent example of group conflict is the historic battle between management and labor. The unions have been successful in raising the wages, living standards, and, hence, life chances of many Americans. But the unions (perhaps we should say "union leaders") have also obtained considerable power that hitherto had been the prerogative of management—the ability to influence elections. Labor-management conflict has abated somewhat in recent years, especially in terms of physical violence. But management is now faced with a new adversary in the form of environmental protection groups particularly concerned with pollution. And unions have lost some of their power owing to the intervention of the federal government in their activities.

While it can be anticipated that individuals will continue to seek power, the conditions of modern social life make it almost mandatory that success can be gained only by being a part of a group or, at least, through the support of some group. Because people in modern societies have learned how to organize and because modern societies have developed norms for regulating group conflict, it can be anticipated that there will be more rather than less group conflict. But it can also be anticipated that such conflict will, in general, be in accordance with developed norms—the game will be played according to the rules.

Conflict is influenced by stratification and, in turn, influences stratification. While the precise role of conflict in determining the form of systems of stratification is not clear, it is evident that the functionalists have failed to take conflict into account in devising an explanation for stratification and systems of stratification. But do we have to accept completely either the functionalist perspective or the conflict point of view in seeking to understand stratification? This question will be explored in the following section.

Eclectic Approach

It does not seem reasonable that either the functionalist or the conflict orientation provides a fully acceptable explanation of stratification. Unfortunately, the assumption is frequently and incorrectly made that by accepting one point of view, one automatically rejects another. With respect to the functionalist and conflict of views, they should be seen as complementary rather than as alternative concepts of society.[20]

Reciprocative Distribution Systems Stratification systems are related to the distribution to members of those rewards available in societies. Obviously the amount and quality of rewards varies greatly from society to society. In simple, subsistence societies, distribution is primarily reciprocal—there is rarely any large *surplus* of food or other commodities and what there is, to a considerable extent, is shared in response to need. A modern example of such a society is found on the island of Tristan da Cunha. There "when a man kills a bullock, he distributes probably more than half the meat as gifts to other members of the community."[21] In modern societies, however, it would be highly unusual for one family to share its income or the contents of its deepfreeze with another family.

Gerhard Lenski has developed what is called a *distributive theory of stratification,* and the following is a paraphrase of his "first law."[22]

Reciprocative distribution systems, then, are very common in those societies in which a surplus of any kind is uncommon.[23] Such societies are stratified largely in terms of age and sex, and elaborate stratification is the exception rather than the rule. The very survival of the society is dependent upon the existence of norms that provide for reciprocative distribution. This is particularly true when the availability of necessities is at or below some minimum level. To make this clear, consider a hypothetical case in which a number of persons are adrift in a lifeboat with a supply of food and water sufficient to keep them alive for thirty days. If the supplies are equitably shared, all will live for that period. But, should some of the castaways have a gun or superior physical strength and choose to deprive the others of any food or water, those with power would stay alive on a more than minimum diet for longer than thirty days and the rest would perish in less time. Any society whose technology is at a low level of development and whose supply of food is rarely above the minimum subsistence level would not long survive without a system of reciprocative distribution. In other words, when necessary for survival, men will share the products of their labors with others.

Development of Surpluses What happens in preliterate societies when a surplus *is* accumulated and is regularly available? To arrive at some answer we will consider preliterate societies that have had or do have continuing surpluses. Most such societies are found in areas where there is an abundance of food and materials, such as the Nootka, a people of British Columbia. While the Nootka had little organization above the level of kinship ties, the society was far from egalitarian; the members had a powerful interest in wealth and engaged in what clearly deserved to be called "conspicuous consumption." While it would probably be incorrect to say that the Nootka were marked by the kind of grouping we call social classes as such, each individual was ranked according to a somewhat rigid system from the highest to the lowest.[24]

Is it then the development of a *continuing surplus* which marks the origin of the kind of complex stratification systems found in all modern societies? On the available evidence, the answer appears to be in the affirmative. But what are the processes involved?

Societies such as the Nootka had been in existence for a long time prior to contact with Western explorers and adventurers. While their artifacts were by no means primitive—for example, the Nootka built substantial wooden houses of considerable size—that specialization of labor so closely related to the development of vast surpluses and a true class society had not appeared. The explanation may be that societies having an abundance of food and material resources easily exploited for human use had little *need* to evolve a sophisticated technology.

Need for Organization The archeological record of Egypt around 3000 B.C. reveals the existence of a state having a complex organizational structure with such classes and specialties as royalty, priests, artisans, soldiers, and craftsmen. Could the circumstances of the Nile Valley itself help to explain this elaborate development?

The Nile Valley, while rich in foodstuffs, lacked building materials such as were readily available to the Nootka. Regular agricultural use of the land made it important that the precise time of the regular flooding the Nile be determined, leading to the development of astronomy. Furthermore, some kinds of public works were required to drain and irrigate the land in order to make efficient use of the rich soil.

What seems to have occurred is that the agricultural surplus, coupled with a need for materials unavailable locally, made the development of

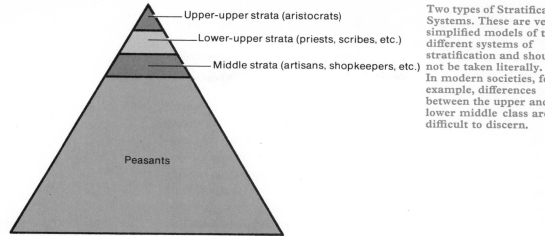

Upper-upper strata (aristocrats)

Lower-upper strata (priests, scribes, etc.)

Middle strata (artisans, shopkeepers, etc.)

Peasants

A. The pyramid shaped system is characteristic of peasant societies.

Two types of Stratification Systems. These are very simplified models of two different systems of stratification and should not be taken literally. In modern societies, for example, differences between the upper and lower middle class are difficult to discern.

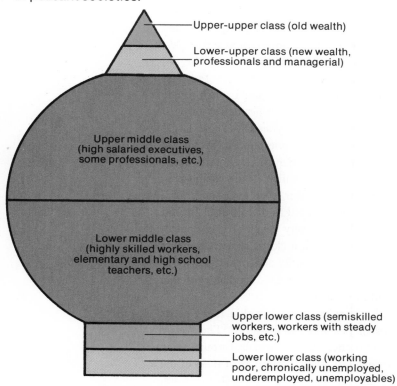

Upper-upper class (old wealth)

Lower-upper class (new wealth, professionals and managerial)

Upper middle class (high salaried executives, some professionals, etc.)

Lower middle class (highly skilled workers, elementary and high school teachers, etc.)

Upper lower class (semiskilled workers, workers with steady jobs, etc.)

Lower lower class (working poor, chronically unemployed, underemployed, unemployables)

B. A system shaped like a reversed top is characteristic of many modern societies.

Theories of
Social Stratification

169

extensive foreign trade both necessary and possible. This, in turn, led to a loss of individual economic self-sufficiency. For example, extensive trade fosters the growth of a number of specialists, from those concerned with keeping accounts to those who sailed the trading ships. Necessarily, these specialists had to rely on others for the satisfaction of many of their needs.

As the productivity of agriculture rose, the proportion of the population concerned directly with food production decreased. There are two important and powerful independent variables of population increase. One, a recent factor, is the control of death. The other is an increase in the food supply. Ancient Egypt doubtless experienced a phenomenon currently found in developing countries. As agricultural efficiency increased, so did the population; at the same time, fewer workers were required for agricultural purposes. Vast numbers of rural dwellers were forced to move to the cities, which were quite different from the agricultural settlements. People in the cities, producing no food, could not simply use the available surplus of food in order to stay alive; they had to work for it.

Development of Leadership It can be shown that Egypt, like other developing societies, was marked by a growth in organization as individuals learned through experience how to work together. Concurrent with this co-operation, societal norms appeared that authenticated the authority of royalty, priests, and lesser officials. The evidence for this lies not only in such public works projects as extensive irrigation but also in the construction of such nonutilitarian structures as temples and the great Pyramids. These large-scale public works would not have been possible without the accrual of very real power to certain limited segments of Egyptian society—particularly to the royalty and the priesthood. Once a dominant ruling class is established, such a class makes every effort to legitimate its power, such as the successful efforts of the pharaohs to have themselves regarded as divinities.[25] Insofar as Egyptian society was concerned, a closed society developed which led, in turn, to the establishment of an aristocracy. In a closed society, the elite become imbued with notions of their own superiority and the inferiority of the subordinate classes. This is further buttressed by providing that legitimate succession can be only by birth within its own ranks.

It should be mentioned that such a system contains within it the seeds of its own decay and eventual loss of position and power.[26] The reason why closed elite systems eventually decay and collapse—usually through some form of revolution—is that they are small in relation to the great mass of the population beneath them. Within this larger and underprivileged mass, there are always men of intelligence, ability, and motivation who, themselves, aspire to privileged position. Unless a ruling elite provides for *cooptation*—a mechanism for absorbing new elements into the leadership structure and thus maintaining and stabilizing the society—it will be unable to successfully resist onslaughts from below. A possible reason for the stability of the British system, for example, has been that in addition to a gradual diminution of the power of the aristocracy, the ruling class coopted many commoners of ability who then became, if not supporters of the system, at least neutral rather than rebels.

Iron Law of Oligarchy   Ancient Egypt provides an excellent example of what happens when a reliable and continuing agricultural surplus becomes a reality and when such a surplus is at least partially dependent on some kind or type of organizing or organizations. The change from a relatively simple, undifferentiated society to one marked by a more complex division of labor, referred to by Durkheim as organic, clearly occurred in Egypt. But does it *necessarily* have to develop in this manner? Robert Michels set forth his "iron law of oligarchy," which claims that organization *always* produces the rule of the few (oligarchy), making the rule of the many (democracy) impossible. He presents two arguments: (1) leadership is necessary for any kind of organization of human endeavor; (2) such leadership always becomes an oligarchy.[27]

It can be argued that leadership is necessary; but why does this lead to the formation of an oligarchy? The best answer may be found in the nature of the leadership process and what it does—not only for leaders but also for followers. Leaders gain a knowledge of the workings of the entire organization not ordinarily available to those specialists further down the chain of command. Leaders tend to promote or otherwise immediately surround themselves with men loyal to their leadership. Leaders have control over communications, records, and, indeed, over who will or will not be a member of the organization. Furthermore, the vast majority of followers are indifferent to running the organization and may well feel indebted to the leaders for providing them with a livelihood however meager.

A psychological explanation might be that a taste of power causes a particular form of intoxication, the symptoms of which are a desire to remain in such a position. From the sociological perspective, however, those in positions of power are seen to desire power because they then have the ability to maintain the status quo, to control their own life styles, and to provide better life chances for their children. This practice of ascription is a most important factor militating against the establishment of a truly open system.

Conflict versus the Status Quo   To recapitulate the discussion thus far, the development of surpluses—reliable surpluses—necessitates some kind of organization. Organization requires leaders. From the processes of leadership, oligarchies develop concerned with maintaining the status quo. Aside from the pleasures of authority, "power will determine the distribution of nearly all of the surplus possessed by a society."[28] Power then is not something to be desired for the purely psychic rewards involved. It has practical consequences in terms of the distribution of relatively scarce societal rewards. As history can testify, those at the top of any stratification pyramid in a society have always obtained a disproportionate share of whatever rewards the society has to offer.

Modern history, however, suggests that a status quo is not the entire picture. For example, a study of British history shows that the status quo was maintained over a very long period. But there have been considerable changes, not only in the direction of more democracy but also in the government becoming more directly responsive to the needs and wishes of the mass of people.[29] Long-term maintenance of the status quo is possible under conditions where the people of a society are generally satisfied with their life styles but where this satisfaction may stem in part from a lack of knowledge of any alternatives. When there is widespread dissatisfaction, ruling elites attempt to maintain things as they are by becoming increasingly repressive. Ultimately, repression becomes counterproductive, and the elites either modify their behavior (which is rare) or are overthrown by force.

Oligarchies can be expected to attempt to maintain their position not merely for the individual membership of any oligarchy at any given moment of time but also for future generations. Again, calling on the evidence of history, it is evident that with very few exceptions successful maintenance of the status quo over very long periods has been the rarity. Equally, history provides repeated examples of how resistant societies in general, and stratification systems in particular, are to rapid change. It has been largely only since the breakdown of feudalism that any remarkable alterations in stratification began to occur in European history. And much that was true of stratification centuries ago is still true today in Europe. Struggles for power took place, for the most part, among the same people—those of the ruling or aristocratic class. However, the French Revolution did depose an outmoded monarchy and, except for the rule of Napoleon III, brought to France some semblance of democratic government. But the class system is still viable in France, and class endogamy is widely practiced.

Synthesis of Functional and Conflict Orientations In light of this kind of evidence, a coherent explanation of the genesis of stratification and of the forms it takes and the persistence of such forms requires a synthesis of the functionalist and conflict orientations, or perspectives. The argument for such a synthesis is recapitulated in brief as follows:

    1. The appearance of a surplus of the necessities of life in a society

frees some of the population for activities not connected with maintaining a minimum subsistence level.

2. In ways that are not understood completely, because the evidence is unclear or lacking, some individuals in a society gain control of the surplus. In doing so they gain control of political, economic, and social institutions and, therefore, of power in the society.

3. In time, a division of labor begins to appear. With it comes the beginnings of more complex forms of organization—the work of specialists requires coordination, for example, the obtaining of raw materials, the marketing of products, and so forth.

4. In the fluid, early periods of change from the preindustrial to industrial type of society, the greater rewards of becoming a specialist or a leader doubtless attract individuals of ability, which is in accordance with the functionalist point of view. But once stratification begins to appear, individuals at or near the top of such stratification systems begin subverting the pure functionalist model.

5. Recognition of the subversion of the functionalist model clearly involves a partial acceptance of the conflict model. As was noted earlier, oligarchies may be counted upon to take steps to secure their positions not merely for themselves but also for their children and grandchildren.

6. Closed stratification systems begin to appear—for example, Egypt, Sumer, Crete—but, history shows, not all possess an indefinite life span. They fall either to outside conquerors or from internal disabilities. Those closed systems that have persisted over time—England, for example— were not entirely closed systems as they did provide for some limited access to higher status on bases other than the purely ascriptive.

7. In a rigidly closed system with a very small ruling class, it is obvious, merely on the basis of what is known about genetics, that in several generations a certain proportion of individuals of low ability will appear among the ruling group. If no new "blood" is brought in, the ruling class will eventually be unable to protect its position; a new set of rulers will supersede it.

Those seven points represent an over-simplified view; nevertheless, it is accurate in essentials. It tends to bear out the functionalist position that societies operate to fill their necessary positions with qualified individuals. But it also bears out the conflict orientation. For example, no known group in power has ever willingly relinquished control. Taking control from it requires the application of force.

This synthesis, while focusing on the growth and development of stratification in ancient societies, does not furnish any real explanation of what has occurred in recent years, particularly in complex modern societies. The functionalist perspective provides for little, if any, change; the conflict orientation largely provides for only that sort of change set forth by Vilfredo

Pareto when he wrote of the "circulation of elites." But changes in the twentieth century, particularly following World War II, involve more than merely an exchange of one elite for another.

Although there is some merit in the functionalist position, its proponents essentially envision a perfect system operating at some high level of efficiency to maintain societies. Similarly accurate in other respects, the conflict perspective provides no other explanation for stratification than human greed and a desire for power. To the conflict theorists change is more seeming than real. As the conflict theorists see it, change essentially involves only the substitution of one set of masters for another.

DYNAMICS OF CHANGE IN MODERN STRATIFICATION SYSTEMS

But stratification systems have changed. Elites have become more responsive to demands from the masses, and new faces and new names move into and out of positions of power and responsibility in modern societies. Competition may explain some of this, but much competition appears to be in accordance with social norms. If the dynamics of older societies rested on conflict— that is, change in the stratification system could only be produced through conflict, generally between elites—the dynamics of newer and more modern societies appear to rest on something else again. Clearly there are many countervailing forces to the stability of stratification systems in modern societies. Let us now see how what Comte called the "dynamics" of society apply to stratification systems in modern societies.

Rapid change, including changes in stratification systems, is a relatively recent phenomenon in human history. And the holding of egalitarian values by entire societies is quite rare in the 5,000 or so years of recorded history. The ideals of democracy now include the belief in upward social mobility. And the idea that economic success can be gained through conscientious effort, thrift, and hard work is clearly a function of variables that have begun to operate significantly only in the last century. Therefore the dynamics of change in modern stratification systems must be sought in modern societies.

It has been observed that societies tend to be stable and resistant to change. Understandably, power elites behave in such a way as to perpetuate their positions and perquisites. Change in societies and stratification systems, therefore, can result only through the applications of countervailing power—that is, power that will result in concessions by original power elites. Note in particular the use of the word "concessions." If those in power, when confronted with substantial countervailing power, do not make concessions, then the usual result is a revolution of some kind and the substitution of one power elite by another. This does not necessarily result in any substantial change either in societies or stratification systems. It has frequently been simply a reshuffling of individuals; the structure remains much as before, although changes can and do occur. For example, the overthrow of the Batista government in Cuba was followed by considerable change in both the society as a whole and the stratification system in particular. Certainly the ideology of Castro and his followers was a large factor in bringing about the tremendous changes. But of possibly even more significance was the elimination from the society of the former Cuban elites by execution, imprisonment, or exile. To allow them to remain in possession of their considerable economic assets would have invited counterrevolution or, at the very least, strong resistance to the social and economic changes that have taken place. What we are concerned with, however, are those relatively peaceful changes in stratification systems and in whole societies being experienced at the present. Such changes involve concessions. And it is the development of the requisite power to bring about such concessions that we will now consider.

Elites without Formal Power

The Marxian position on social change including stratification systems is often described as "economic determinism." While economic in a large part, Marx's position has sociological and psychological implications. As we discussed in Chapter 2, Marx saw the Industrial Revolution as dividing modern industrial societies into two classes—the bourgeoisie and the proletariat—who were in conflict. The bourgeoisie, controlling the means of production, would behave in ways calculated to increase their profits through raising prices and lowering the costs of production, which includes wages paid the proletariat. This would result in increasing misery for the proletariat leading to the development of a class consciousness. That would finally lead to revolution, with the proletariat winning. A brief dictatorship of the proletariat would be established. Afterwards a classless society would develop in which all would be equal and in which, presumably, a formal government would be unnecessary. Thus far in time, Marx has proven to be a very bad prophet. Those who look at the Bolshevik revolution in Russia in 1917 may conclude that *this* revolution verifies Marxian dogma. It does not. Russia at the time of the revolution was not heavily industrialized with the mass of people working in factories.[30] Indeed as the fifty-odd-year history of the USSR demonstrates, modern Russia is far from being a communist state as Marx defined it. It is somewhat rigidly stratified. Political, economic, and social factors prevent the USSR from being the class-free meritocracy that Soviet propaganda would have the rest of the world believe it is.

Industrialization in the USSR proceeded quite rapidly before, but particularly after, World War II. A consequence of this has been the creation of a large class of middle-managers, or as John Kenneth Galbraith calls it the "technostructure." These men are gaining for themselves an increasing measure of autonomy insofar as the management of industry is concerned. "In sum, it seems likely that the Soviet resolution of the problem of authority in the industrial enterprise is not unlike that in the West . . ."[31]

An irresistible effect of industrialization is the creation of an elite class that lacks *formal* political power but that is nonetheless a force to be reckoned with by those in political power. The technostructure is in a position to cooperate fully or minimally with the objectives of those having political power. In the USSR, industrial objectives, such as the number of tons of steel to be produced per year, are determined by politicians for political purposes. But the expertise required to produce *any* steel is held by the experts and technicians. And the politicians, in order to achieve their goals, must obtain the cooperation of middle management. Coercion is ineffective, because managers in prison are not liable to produce much of anything. Therefore, what often results is a *quid pro quo*—literally "something for something"—between industrial management and the Communist Party.

In the United States, there has been the creation not only of a powerful technostructure but also of elites not found in the USSR—labor unions. The genesis of labor unions in the United States was due to at least four important factors:

1. The egalitarian value of American society.

2. Legal limits placed on the coercive powers of management.

3. Rank-and-file workers, by virtue of being part of an organization, learned something about organizations and organizing. Since individual workers are helpless to bring about change, it is only through organizing that workers gain power and, hence, the ability to influence management decisions in their favor.

4. Considerable disparity between the goals of management and the goals of workers.

In respect to the fourth factor, Marx was an accurate prophet. Business management, with some rare exceptions, is concerned with growth in terms of increased production and more sales. Since an increase in sales depends on articles or goods being competitive in price, production costs are important considerations. One way to cut costs is to increase worker production without any increase in worker costs. In opposition, workers desire higher salaries and shorter working hours and, in particular, object to some measures instituted in the name of efficiency, for example, time clocks.[32]

In the early days of the Industrial Revolution in the United States, companies were managed by their owners. In owner-run companies, there is often a certain element of paternalism that at least blunts some of the feelings of frustration and anger of the workers. With the turn of the century and the advancing age of the original owner-managers, companies came to be run increasingly by hired management whose positions depended upon their performance—specifically as measured by profits. Hired management lacked the paternalistic attitude of the owners toward the rank and file. And such managers resorted to measures and practices that were not merely often dysfunctional in terms of production but also designed, albeit unconsciously, to irritate workers. As contemporary Black Americans can testify, being treated as second-class citizens is an aggravating experience. And workers, particularly prior to the growth of unions, were often so treated.

The development of the countervailing elites called labor unions occurs under the conditions of what might be called "a law of large numbers." It has been hypothesized that "industrial disputes and work stoppages increase with the size of the establishment."[33] It seems likely that rapport through personal contact becomes less as organizations grow in size. And the result is a polarization between workers and management which sets the stage for the development of unions, particularly if management is concerned only with profits.

Could management, apprised of the conditions inherent in large organization, take steps to effectively inhibit the development of countervailing elites? The answer is yes. But the very measures employed would constitute concessions in response to "power in being"—that is, to potential rather than actual power. The success of a management would depend on its recognizing that there is a direct relationship between the actual organization and the development of countervailing elites (unions) and two aspects of management orientation: (1) emphasis on the profits of a business organization; and (2) degree of lack of recognition of the power-in-being of the rank and file.

Other things being equal, it should be noted that the relationship between organizational size and the development of countervailing elites appears to be a direct one—the larger the organization the more likely the development of such elites.

Level of Literacy

The power elites, or ruling classes, in peasant societies may have taken actions or behaved in ways inimical to their own status. But they were not required to do so by the very nature of the situation in which they existed. Peasant societies *were* maintained in Europe from the fall of the Roman

Empire to the Renaissance. And that is evidence of the general success of the aristocracy in retaining their power and, hence, ability to distribute the rewards of their societies predominantly among themselves.

With the advent of the Industrial Revolution a change occurred. Large numbers of jobs could be filled with the illiterate. But as production became more complex, some level of literacy in the labor force became necessary. In addition, while one could comfortably perform the aristocratic role without being able to read and write, literacy and other skills were required in managing an industry or business of any size. By and large, the aristocracy did not meet the demands of the Industrial Revolution, and their places were taken by a new class of middle-class managers who were, for the times, educated men. Because of this, the conditions necessary for the establishment of schools for the general population became increasingly common. Education—the ability to read, write, and use simple arithmetic—gained in economic importance. For the new power elites of business, it was rational to encourage public education in order to ensure some minimal level of literacy in the labor force. The paradox in this is that, if we accept the proposition that elites tend to behave in such a manner as to preserve their status, the encouragement of the development of mass education was dysfunctional for the elites in a personal way. C. Harold Anderson gives two cogent reasons for this.

[1] *Even a modest schooling makes people more alert to opportunities and equips them to articulate their ideas over a wider range of topics.*
[2] *A literate populace is more capable of checking up on the operation of the elites.*[34]

Education, which must be considered to include the acquisition of what is called training or "know-how," is a source of power. Positions in industry from semiskilled work up to president all require varying kinds and degrees of education. In addition, all but the very lowest jobs in industry necessitate functional literacy—the ability to read and write well enough to take selection tests, take courses of training, read written instructions, understand machinery dials, and so on.

The relationship between an expanding economy and the educational level of a society is close and reciprocal. The phenomenal increase in the percentage of young people graduating from high school is well known in the United States—not to mention an equally dramatic increase in the proportion of young people attending and graduating from institutions of higher learning. That widespread and general increase in the educational level of citizens has consequences for power elites in accordance with Anderson's two points. The ultimate consequences of education for the masses—the sharing of power—will be dealt with in more detail in the conclusion to this chapter.

Surplus of Nonfunctional Needs

All that mankind requires for physical survival is a sufficiency of food, shelter, and clothing. While a disturbing proportion of the population in the United States still lives at or near this subsistence level, the largest proportion of Americans subsist far above it. Not too many years ago, for example, bathing was done on Saturday night in a washtub in the kitchen. Yet today in many residential areas it is difficult to sell a house with only one bathroom. Citizens in the United States, and some other modern countries, are experiencing a surplus of not merely those things requisite to the support of life but also comforts and luxuries that until recent years were *nonfunctional*—that is, their need was not recognized. Hot and cold showers, other indoor plumbing, television sets, central heating, air conditioning, and telephones are commonplace items that even King Midas with all his gold could not have purchased. This means that a high standard of living is no longer the prerogative of power elites but is seen by the masses as being both their need and their right.

Technology in conjunction with highly efficient industrial organizations has made it possible to develop, produce, and market a wide range of items hitherto unknown and, for that reason, undesired. The role of advertising has been to create demands for nonfunctional goods, although its function may have been more informative than creative with respect to some items.

The effect of this general rise in the standard of living has been to blur class lines. Previously, only the traditional upper classes had sufficient power to inequitably distribute societal rewards. While it is true that such status symbols as yachts and Lear jets are available only to the very wealthy, it is rarely possible to distinguish between a middle-class business man and a corporation president by the way they dress or the type of car they own. The blurring of class distinctions which accompanies the vast improvement in the standard of living for so many has had a psychological by-product—the diminution of envy and hatred on the part of the middle class for the power elites.

Mass Media

As we observed earlier, power elites have used a variety of techniques to buttress their positions, including the notion of the "divine right of kings" doctrine—a legacy to political thought from Alexander the Great.[35] The effectiveness of pretensions to divinity or to intelligence and powers of judgment not accorded other people is possible today only under conditions in which eccentricities, weaknesses, and other deficiencies of those in power are unknown to those subject to their authority. The vast proliferation of mass media—television, newspapers, radio, magazines—over the past century coupled with a growth in the freedom of the press have made it difficult for those in high positions, particularly politicians, to conceal mistakes and misdeeds. Just such a situation prevailed during the "Watergate affair." The majority of Americans, at the beginning of the disclosures about illegal actions by President Nixon's political associates, did not hold the president responsible. As more facts became known, through the papers and the televised Senate hearings, more and more Americans came to hold President Nixon at least partially culpable. Dictators, such as Adolf Hitler, who attempt to tightly control the mass media are behaving sensibly *from the point of view of their interests*.

In 1971, the United States was stirred by a considerable controversy over what came to be known as the "Pentagon papers." The papers, a study instituted by Robert MacNamara, secretary of defense under President Johnson, were intended to reveal the underlying causes of United States involvement in Vietnam. Surprisingly, a Republican administration attempted to prevent the *New York Times* and other newspapers from printing excerpts from the papers. On Friday, 2 July 1971, the United States Supreme Court ruled in favor of the media.

Aside from matters of national security, the power structure in the government was behaving quite logically from its own viewpoint. Governmental decisions at the highest level are all too often made on the basis of inadequate or incorrect information or even personal prejudice. The prestige of governing elites may suffer from *any* exposure. It is accurate to say that no elite is unaware of the consequences of public disclosure of its decision-making processes. Therefore, there should be no particular surprise at the reaction of the Nixon administration to the publication of the Pentagon papers.

It is plain, then, that mass media operating under conditions of freedom serve to erode the real power of elites. It becomes increasingly difficult to arrive at decisions of importance either in secret or to feel confident that secrets will be kept. This knowledge operates to inhibit the power of the elite because it acts as a constraint on the individuals involved. To stay in power they must make decisions that are defensible in terms of the public interests.

In concluding this section, an additional point needs to be made. The power of the mass media, or rather the power elite who control the mass media, is itself countervailed by other societal forces. The power of all mass media stems, to a considerable extent, from their *credibility*—whether readers, viewers, and listeners believe the media. Any particular segment of any of the various media which becomes identified with a particular political party loses credibility and thus power with respect to members of another political party. It is the same for issues of national or local importance. If the mass media act to dampen the power of other elites, their own power is also lessened by the difficulty (perhaps impossibility) of gaining a reputation for being completely objective on all issues.

Technology

Many years ago an American anthropologist cum lawyer, Henry Lewis Morgan, named technology as *the* independent variable of social change.[36] Morgan's oversimplified conception of man's progress as going through three regular stages fell into disrepute along with that of Herbert Spencer. Recently there has arisen a much more sophisticated version of social change as a function of technology under the leadership and guidance of the anthropologist Leslie A. White.[37]

Social change, including changes in systems of stratification, can be attributed to many causal factors, or independent variables. Although factors other than advances in technology doubtlessly do influence stratification and systems of stratification, technological advances are of great importance in this respect. Indeed, had technology not progressed beyond the wheel, the plow, simple weapons, sailing ships, and several of the arts, it is likely that stratification systems for the most part would have remained rigid. However, with the advent of the first suggestion of steam as a motive power by Christian Huygens in 1666, technology, or rather new technology, has grown almost geometrically. If the steam engine and some uses of electricity marked the nineteenth century, such advances as wireless transmission, television, atomic power, the computer, the transistor, cryogenics, genetics, and the laser have characterized the twentieth century.[38] Each of these depended on earlier technological discoveries and sometimes on the implementation of subsequent discoveries—for example, the microscope, which was known for a long time, did not get wide use until after the development of the bacterial theory of disease.

Technology has created a host of new conditions for mankind. The automobile, for example, has made possible the development of a much maligned suburbia with consequences for stratification. Before the development of the automobile, people were forced to live close to their work in crowded cities. Residential class lines were sharply drawn on an economic basis; only the wealthy could afford either property or a dwelling of any size. Less expensive land away from the center cities became practicable for living only with the advent of the automobile. The move to the suburbs and to more comfortable and luxurious housing blurred the previously sharply drawn class lines and clearly contributed to the identification of what some call the great American middle class.

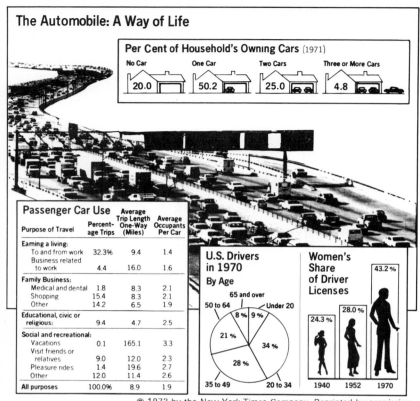

The Automobile: A Way of Life

Technology has created a host of new conditions for mankind. The automobile, for example, has made possible the development of a much maligned suburbia with consequences for stratification.

© 1973 by the New York Times Company. Reprinted by permission.

Vast organizations have grown around various new or improved technologies. The proliferation of the sheer number of large organizations tends to create groups of people with considerable personal power to challenge established elites. And each new large organization inevitably adds to the growing technostructure found in all modern societies, the influence of which should not be underestimated.

In essence, as we discussed earlier, technology functions to affect not only stratification but also societies as wholes. Briefly, let us review the four general functions of technology in this respect.

1. As technology proliferates, it makes possible the creation of vast surpluses; these surpluses are not merely the essentials of life but also the items and services that contribute to a higher standard of living.

2. Control over a surplus is at least partial control over other members of society. Such control, however, is diminished when a power elite no longer holds a monopoly over surpluses or does not control some kinds of surpluses at all.

3. The production of many technologically based surpluses is accompanied by the development of new power bases and new elites. Historically this can

be seen in the loss of power by an aristocratic elite to the new rising class of bourgeois capitalists during the early part of the Industrial Revolution.

4. Immanent in technological development is the appearance of not only some education for the masses but a growing class of highly educated persons. Since education per se functions to produce a questioning attitude among the educated, power elites failing to function effectively for what is considered the common good will arouse opposition and countervailing applications of power in the educated and their followers.

Modern revolutions have been marked by the fact that the leaders of such revolutions are members of the middle class and are usually *not* members of the upper class in the sense of wielding real power in the society concerned. In this regard, many names come to mind, among them Lenin, Trotsky, Castro, Mao Tse Tung, and Ho Chi Minh. On the basis of this evidence, it is incorrect to consider technology per se, as the independent variable for either the genesis of stratification systems or changes in already established systems. Technology is a *catalyst*. The appearance and diffusion of some important item of technology promotes societal reactions, sometimes with profound consequences for stratification not to mention societies. Technology causes reactions in human societies, reactions often serving to change societies but not the technology concerned. The plow is an early example, high-speed computers a recent one. Of course, in the case of computers, these useful machines have been greatly improved since their inception. But the computer fits the definition of catalyst, for it is society that has altered and perhaps will continue to alter, not the computer.[39]

SOCIAL CLASS

For a long time any real sociological examination of *class* and *status* was inhibited by the fact that the two were considered to be virtually inter-changeable or that status was an attribute of class. While it is accurate to say that the two do coincide in some societies, they are quite separate and distinct phenomena.[40] It is vital to understand why class and status are different in order to perceive some specific contemporary changes in modern stratification systems but particularly in the United States.

Concept

Walter Goldschmidt defines social class as a division of "the whole society into a series of social layers, the members of each sharing general hierarchical status, each ranked according to the value system prevailing in the society."[41] This definition is satisfactory as far as it goes, but it lacks operational utility— it would be difficult to design a research project to test the definition. However, by adding certain criteria of class to Goldschmidt's definition, the meaning of the concept can be made clear.

Dress

In a class society, the various strata—working class, middle class, aristocracy, and so on—are distinguishable to a considerable extent simply by the clothing worn. No one walking the streets of London at the beginning of the twentieth century could possibly mistake a commoner for an aristocrat and vice versa. But it was not simply a matter of the richness or plainness of apparel but the *manner* in which it was worn. As an example, men not actually in one of the Armed Services will, for reasons best known to them, don a uniform and attempt to pass themselves off as members, sometimes as officers and sometimes as non-commissioned officers. They are often caught, not because any part of the uniform was being worn incorrectly, but because something about them invited a closer and more critical inspection. That something was the manner in which the uniform was being worn. People of low birth have worn the apparel of the upper or aristocratic class and managed to masquerade successfully, but not often in the society in which they claim noble birth. One man who did succeed was Johann Kalb (1721–1780), a major-general in the revolutionary army of George Washington. He is better known in American history books as the Baron de Kalb.[42]

The manner of dress is important in a society marked by well-drawn class lines for at least two reasons. First, with respect to the upper classes, richness of apparel serves to emphasize the possession of both wealth and power. Second, visible class differences in dress serve to indicate appropriate behavior when individuals come into contact with one another. Class societies are marked by patterns of deference and dominance based on class. Thus it is possible for an individual to recognize his betters and defer to them and to know his inferiors from whom he expects deference.

Language

British society provides an excellent example of language differences between the various classes. There are considerable and very obvious differences between the speech of upper-class Englishmen and that of the lower classes. George Bernard Shaw's famous play *Pygmalion* has as its theme the proposition that even a young woman with a cockney accent could, if taught to speak the language of the upper class, successfully pass as a well-bred, aristocratic young woman. Modern theater and movie goers will know Shaw's play as *My Fair Lady*.

Easily discernible language differences in accent and word usage between classes are clearly a function of a rigidly drawn class system. Under such a system, close association is maintained among members of each class, which tends to not only perpetuate but also sharpen language differences. For a commoner, however gifted, to move upward in class while still speaking with the inflections, accents, and vocabulary of the lower class, is still difficult in English society. That this language distinction remains important in England today is evidenced by the fact that there are schools that attempt to teach those with lower class language habits, particularly the cockney, to effectively mimic the speech of the upper class.

In some cases two or more languages are spoken in a particular society with one language having become associated with higher class position. Africans of the Rhodesian Copperbelt have accepted the importance to status of education and have come to associate the speaking of English with higher status. For this reason, many adults go to school at night for the purpose of learning English.[43] Since all known languages are complete languages, there is no logical reason why any language is superior as a means of symbolic communication. However, a language or specific language habits can become associated with social class and thus function as prestige symbols.

Life Style

Weber, who may have coined the term "life styles," used it to indicate differential opportunities to attain social honor, or, as we call it today, prestige. Weber saw differences in life style as primarily a matter of differences in education.[44] In the example of the English class society, formal schooling served to establish life styles and provide for recognizable class differences in education. But Weber may have meant the total process of education that sociologists usually refer to as "socialization." Almost at birth, members of English society are still taught those behaviors, including the speech, dress, bearing, and attitudes, characteristic of the class into which they are born. It should be mentioned that attitudes include not only attitudes toward others but attitudes toward self. The arrogance and self-confidence of the English aristocrat is the product of a socialization of considerable consistency.[45]

When life styles are characteristic of social classes, it follows that the class structure will be somewhat rigid and social mobility difficult although not impossible. Such a class structure will be maintained until such time as substantial numbers of individuals born into lower strata are able to obtain a sufficiency of education to blur distinctions between their life styles and those of the upper classes. That this process is taking place in modern England is evidenced by the fact that each year's "honors list" contains the names of commoners being elevated to a titled status.

Economic Basis

The basis for social class distinctions is essentially economic. As one ascends higher in the class structure of a society, one finds that those at higher levels enjoy a more favorable economic position than those below them and a less favorable economic position with respect to those above. People in the upper classes of a society (for example, the middle class) have much better "life chances" than, say, the working poor. These improved life chances are, in the main, a matter of economics. Children born into families living in a middle-class suburb, for example, attend good schools, get prompt medical attention when they are ill, usually (although not always) eat better, and can count on being able to attend college.

Individuals in the middle or higher classes live more comfortably and have longer life expectancies than do those further down the social class hierarchy, largely because they have the economic resources to make their lives more pleasant and to pay for the skills of others which can serve to keep them healthier. These factors make it more likely that middle or upper class individuals will maintain their class position. And they guarantee that the children, by virtue of good life chances, will do so likewise. Conversely, working class individuals find difficulty in moving upward, and this handicap is transmitted to their children.

Can social class or the social class structure be altered by deliberate social policy? In other words, can the life chances of the poor be improved so that they or their children can move significantly upward in the class structure? The history of the United States makes it clear that the answer must be affirmative. A simple and well-known illustration of this is the system of mass education. Although mass education is not the sole reason for the burgeoning of the American middle class, it undoubtedly has been a significant factor. Theoretically, at least, it is possible to eliminate most of the poor by improving their life chances. But this would require considerable upgrading of schools; provision of medical services for all, including the availability of preventive medicine; attending to matters of nutrition; providing full training programs and retraining programs to insure that all employable adults were possessed of a needed skill; and so on. From this brief list, it is obvious that the elimination of the poorer classes is, to a considerable extent, a matter of economics. It follows, then, that social class is largely a matter of economics, and it is primarily economic considerations that determine the all important life chances.

SOCIAL STATUS

In Chapter 3 we explained that social status is a category, either ascribed or achieved, that tells each member of society what he or she is. In the classless society envisioned by Marx, the word "status" lacks some of the meaning it has in both modern and preliterate societies. Statuses possess certain attributes; people are accorded or not accorded prestige and ranked on the basis of their statuses. But in a classless society, all members would be on an absolutely equal footing. Such commonplace features as stratification, rank, and hierarchies would be absent. In other words, status necessarily includes considerations of rank, hierarchy, and stratification. Since social class includes the same concepts, what then is the distinction between class and status? The question can best be answered by considering *status inconsistency*.

Status Inconsistency

A prominent feature of a rigid class society is the general absence of status inconsistency. While there may be more than one hierarchy, for example, political and military hierarchies, only the upper classes are represented at the top of the various hierarchies. But in societies where class lines are blurred, it is possible for the same individual to be at or near the top in one hierarchy and very near the bottom in another. The almost classic example of this is a Black physician in American society.[46] The profession of physician *ranks* high— it has high status in American society. Being a doctor was ranked near the top in a survey, second only to being a United States Supreme Court Justice.[47] It is almost superfluous to point out that even today race places a Black physician at the bottom of other hierarchies. That is status inconsistency.

Status inconsistency can also be subjective. When a person high in, say, politics or industry considers his or her own social status to be middle class, then status inconsistency is, in part, subjective. As Richard Centers found in a survey done in the United States some years ago, only 3 percent of his respondents rated themselves as upper class. This latter group included many men who by objective standards were at or near the top of one or more hierarchies.[48] In a truly class society no such inconsistency would appear except in the rarest instances; individuals at the top of any of the various hierarchies would consider themselves as belonging to the upper classes.

Social class and social status are not, then, the same phenomenon. Even in a tightly knit class society it is possible to have status inconsistencies. A person born into an upper social class has automatic high status because of his birth. But this ascribed high status is not necessarily permanent. An upper class individual might well commit an act that would seriously depress his high status, thus introducing an element of status inconsistency. It should be noted that high social class did and does function to protect members from a loss of status under circumstances in which socially disapproved behavior is brought to public attention. A case in point is that of Oscar Wilde, who was not a member of an upper class. He was tried on a charge of homosexual activity and sent to prison. However, two young aristocrats involved in the same kind of behavior suffered no formal punishment at all, although there was some loss of status.[49]

Whether the distinction between social class and social status is evident depends upon the degree of social mobility in a society. Under circumstances in which individuals can progress from some lower strata of society to or near the top of one or more hierarchies, class declines in importance while status increases. For both social class and social status, kinship or birth is important; it is of less importance in modern societies. Indeed a hallmark of American society is that status has become increasingly a matter of personal characteristics and attributes. *What* one is is more important than *who* one is. While sex and kinship (two "who" attributes) are still significant as status determiners, of greater importance in modern American society are wealth, political authority, education, and occupation.

Wealth

While inherited wealth is a criterion for determining high status today, personal income gained through individual efforts is highly significant. High income acts in at least two ways to confer honor and higher status. First, the possessor of wealth is able to acquire significant status symbols, such as a large and well-furnished house, expensive automobiles, a swimming pool, and so forth. Second, ordinarily, high income is associated with an equally high position in some hierarchy, such as business or politics. The very possession of such a position implies at least some power. The possession of power automatically carries with it considerable prestige.

Wealth alone, however, is no guarantee of high status. In the United States at least, certain remnants of the so-called Puritan ethic result in a downgrading of those individuals, usually with inherited wealth, who spend their time seeking amusement and excitement. While the modern "jet set" receives considerable publicity, a distinction must be made between *notoriety* and high status.

Political Authority

Upper level political positions in the United States usually carry with them comfortable salaries. Yet, it is often true that the men who accept these posts do so at considerable financial sacrifice. Aside from a laudable desire to serve their country, a voluntary sacrifice of considerable income in order to gain a high political post tells us something about the relative status values of being high in the industrial as opposed to the political hierarchy. Relative power, too, may be a factor. It seems reasonable to say that, for example, Robert S. McNamara wielded considerably more power as secretary of defense than he did as president of the Ford Motor Company.

In a society thoroughly sensitized to status and status symbols, it is, therefore, not too suprising that members would seek political power. Mills spoke of "status panic," by which he meant, with reference to white-collar workers, that concern with status is a central characteristic.[50] Mills may well have overlooked something very important in his somewhat pessimistic analysis of the lot of white-collar workers. While it is a fact that only a very few individuals can ever occupy the highest political positions in any given period of time, satisfying political power can be gained in many other ways. State, city, and county governments all require leaders and have a number of posts of local importance (and carrying local prestige and status). Should these be closed to status seekers, a modicum of political power resides even in community associations and special interest groups, not to mention a considerable variety of other organizations whose purpose may be fraternal or recreational. Unless one aspires to the presidency of the United States or, perhaps, to the Supreme Court, there are countless avenues to higher status through countless organizations.

Education

It is generally believed in the United States that *the* key to upward mobility is education—specifically a college education. This belief coincides reasonably well with available data for those who are Caucasian and come from middle-class families. But for ethnic minorities, particularly Black Americans, a college education is not an automatic guarantee of future social class or upward changes in their status. In terms of income, the differences between white college graduates and those with a high school education are considerable—roughly $2,000 annually. But even white high school graduates receive better incomes on the average than do average Black college graduates.[51] There are, then, social factors that tend to depress the financial and status advantages of a college education.

In spite of the occasional self-made millionaire who was "a grade-school dropout," the odds are against success for the individual with below average formal education. The complexity of modern society, the so-called knowledge explosion, the increasing demand for people educated and trained in a wide variety of specialties, and so on, are designed to make formal education (and individual teachers) gatekeepers insofar as raising or even maintaining status is concerned. The term "gatekeeper" was coined by Kurt Lewin[52] and refers to those forces that determine who or what passes through a particular gate—for example, education.

The relationship between education and status is, in spite of the inequities mentioned, a direct one. As one ascends the status hierarchy, increasing amounts of education are required if one is to qualify for many positions and are certainly necessary if one is to perform competently. Only the uninformed would claim that all children in the United States start out with equal chances for a college education, even if genetic differences in endowed intelligence are overlooked. On the other hand, the virulent critics who see American education as a failure lack a balanced perspective. If we compare the United States with modern European nations, we see, as Arnold Rose points out, that lower class and low-income children in the United States do attend institutions of higher learning whereas in Europe "they do not think they can do so."[53] Education in the United States is clearly an important gate to high status. Even if that gate is not wide open, it is ajar.

Occupation

When is a job an occupation or an occupation a profession? The very question, and it is asked frequently, reveals that the work one does is related to status—that is one's status is determined in part by the kind of work one does. Few question the high status of medicine as a *profession*. But what about pharmacists, school teachers, morticians, engineers?[54] For some time the question of what is and what is not a profession has generated considerable emotionality. The reasons underlying the desire to identify so many jobs as professions are probably based on a desire for high status. And the resistance to admitting all claiming membership to the status of professional is undoubtedly based on the desire not to lose status—unlimited "membership" would detract from the status of those occupations already accorded recognition as professions.

Competition for status through the sort of job one has is a fact of American society. It would not be a fact *if* American society were organized into stratified and rigid classes because the general type of work done is determined by ascription in closed societies. Insofar as stratification is concerned, the most important point is that the very competition for status has its genesis in the fact that the competitors believe that higher status can be gained.

Caste

If competition for achieved statuses and social position is a fact in modern American society, the caste system, theoretically at least, does away with that sort of competition by ascribing, not only the usual statuses—sex, age, race, and so forth—but also social position on the basis of birth. One is born not only into the usual statuses but also into a social position that, because of genetic inheritance, is presumably unchangeable. One notable modern example of this is India, where only partial success has been achieved in doing away with the caste system by legislation. Another example closer to home is the color caste system that still exists in the United States although with much less effect than in the past.

Examples of at least a rudimentary caste system are found in all modern societies and are identifiable whenever individuals are assigned statuses and social class on the basis of genetically inherited characteristics or family of birth. Subtler examples of a caste system are found, for example, in the United States where admission to certain private preparatory schools is open only to those from certain families or where private clubs bar from membership those persons with certain racial or religious attributes.

In the 1970's, it can be anticipated that a somewhat different rudimentary caste system will function with job preference being given to certain minority groups and to women simply because they are from a particular minority group or are female. While it can be argued that such procedures have been instituted to right long-standing wrongs, they still very much represent a viable caste system and produce the discrimination found in all such systems.

Class and Prestige

In concluding this section, we will emphasize the dynamic relationship between class and the prestige accorded some statuses. In a clearly stratified society, social class is the determiner of prestige, with some exceptions. But, as in the United States, and to a lesser extent in other modern countries, class lines are becoming indistinct. Prestige is no longer an attribute automatically acquired by virtue of being born into a family of high social class. Increasingly prestige relates to the personal attributes of wealth, education, and so on.

The closed or nearly closed class system has given way to what Ralph Turner calls "contest mobility," a system in which accession to elite status (or simply higher status) is a prize in an open contest to be won by the aspirant's own endeavors. Turner adds that "since the prize of successful upward mobility is not in the hands of the established elite to give out, the latter are not in a position to determine who shall attain it and who shall not."[55]

The real-life situation is not, obviously, quite as Turner describes it. The matter of birth, determining as it does life chances and life styles, is still significant in terms of upward mobility. The burgeoning middle class had made contest mobility an activity for a significant portion of the population in the United States. But for the poor, particularly the poor Black, it is still far from a reality.

CONCLUSION

In concluding this chapter, it is appropriate to comment on two matters of considerable contemporary importance. Some people argue that mankind's most serious problems could be automatically eliminated with the establishment of the classless society envisioned by Karl Marx. Others are disenchanted with modern society and see it as a "closed corporation," particularly with respect to opportunities for upward mobility. What is the sociological perspective with respect to these two points of view?

Is Stratification Necessary?

The Davis-Moore arguments are difficult to refute. If nature were entirely bountiful and all of mankind lived in a climate where food was readily available and the need for clothing and shelter was minimal, very little organized effort would be necessary to sustain life comfortably. However, this is not often the case. To wrest even the basic necessities of life from most environments requires considerable organization. Certainly, to provide the scale of living enjoyed by so many in the United States necessitates the most complex industrial and political organizations. The problems of efficiently running any large organization include the necessity for specialists of all kinds, not to mention leaders. In the modern world, the effort, energy, time, and motivation required to provide these specialists seem to lie to a considerable extent in systems of stratification and an unequal distribution of societal rewards. Perhaps the best answer, and this may beg the question, is that no one has yet devised any workable means other than a system of stratification. As numerous experimental and research projects have demonstrated, even in small groups leaders and some ranking by status always appear.[56]

Finally, as a function of biological transmission, ability is not distributed equally among human populations. For example, consider the "intelligence quotient" (IQ) made famous by Alfred Binet and Theodore Simon. When tests of intelligence are administered to large samples, they usually show a normal distribution of IQ's. This distribution indicates that only about 12 percent of any human population rates as superior or very superior.[57] Owing to purely genetic factors, some individuals are clearly more able than others. It is difficult to imagine that some of those "superior" individuals would not be able to obtain more than their proportionate share of any available societal surpluses and establish by this behavior a system of stratification. There are two general reasons why stratification systems will always be present in human societies, the second of which constitutes compelling evidence that stratification systems may be necessary.

1. Stratification systems are ubiquitous, in part, because of the fact that humans do differ in genetic endowment.

2. Stratification systems appear to be necessary because without an hierarchical arrangement in society as a whole and in organizations within each society, the accomplishment of societal goals would be impossible.

At the time of the American Revolution, class strata with fairly clear lines of demarcation did exist. This class system continued in a recognizable form until well after the Civil War. But as even a cursory reading of American history reveals, powerful forces were at work to erode the rigid class system and establish a more "open" one. In other words, over the two centuries of existence of the United States of America, the shift has been from a heavily ascriptive society to one in which achievement criteria largely apply.[58] This process, while not completed, is ongoing. To the extent that a shift from ascription to achievement continues, American society becomes more and more one of opportunity for those having superior ability though born into families of low status.

Changes in stratification systems such as have taken place in the United States are, to a considerable extent, a function of enormous surpluses. If for any reason, such as too large a growth in population or the exhaustion of raw material, this massive surplus were to decline, it can be anticipated that a closed class system might reappear, perhaps with a totalitarian system of government. The reason for this is obvious. The greater the scarcity, the more potent, in terms of power, is the possession of any surplus. If in early societies a monopoly of scarce surpluses led to not only stratification but also the establishment of a class society, there is no reason to expect that any other result would occur, even in modern societies, under conditions of a drastic shrinkage in available surpluses. The possibility that economic disorganization and a drop in production could lead to a totalitarian government is borne out by what happened in Germany in the period between World War I and World War II.[59]

In the United States, the Great Depression saw power become greatly concentrated in the hands of the federal government. Only a tradition of democracy and the presence of countervailing groups served to moderate the growth of this concentration of power. But it is clear that federal power has continued to increase since 1932, when Franklin Delano Roosevelt became president for his first term.[60]

But the struggle for power is not a zero-sum game, a game in which any gain by one player is offset by exactly the same loss to another player or players, as in table-stakes poker. Within any society, there is not some fixed amount of power that would mean that a gain in x units by one organization would necessarily involve an equivalent loss by another. Power makes possible increasing organization and more efficient direction of human effort in diverse areas including government. While it is true that the power of the federal government has increased, there has been a concomitant growth of power in many other, nonpolitical sectors of American society.

Although there are few exceptions, such as individuals with exceptional personal appeal or charisma, the creation of power follows only after the development of some kind of organization. While the growth of labor unions did indeed weaken certain of the powers of industrial management, the power gained by labor unions was certainly not the equivalent of what management lost.

In older societies power and the application of power was virtually a monopoly of the ruling elites, with the chief check on such power being other groups drawn from the same social class as the elites. But the situation has changed drastically in modern societies, particularly in the United States. The principles of organization are known at status levels well below the very highest. People continually organize for a variety of purposes, ranging from an interest in bird watching to bringing pressure to bear in connection with a governmental issue. The net effect of this has been to not only greatly increase power but also move the entire society more in the direction of a complex and dynamic relationship of *shared power*. Barring some economic catastrophe or the holocaust of a nuclear war, this process can be expected to continue. That power will be increasingly shared by all strata of society does not mean, necessarily, that social class and prestige will become any less significant in American society. It will only mean that the acquisition of high social class does not free the holder of such a high position from the necessity of considering the rights and views of others further down the stratification hierarchy.

We should also note that it is not unreasonable to recognize that human progress is necessarily slow. Stratification is institutionalized inequality. If we measure one aspect of human progress, not so much as the elimination of inequality per se, but as the reduction of *inequalities in opportunity*, then a survey of current modern societies in general and in the United States in particular provides evidence that such inequalities for all members are less than at any time in history. We must, of course, acknowledge that this is not entirely true for nonwhites although their lot has improved in recent years.

That setbacks will occur in progress, however defined, needs to be accepted along with the truth that human progress is never as fast as we would like it to be. Some commentators agree that *Homo sapiens* faces long-term success and short-term disaster. What do we mean by long-term success? Many centuries ago Aristotle said, "It is clear that some men are by nature free, and others slaves, and that for these latter slavery is both expedient and right."[61] That almost no one today would agree with Aristotle does indeed constitute a long-term success.

In this chapter we have prepared the groundwork for an intensive consideration of the principal institutions found in modern societies: the family, politics, economics, education, and religion. In Chapter 7, we will be introduced to social institutions in a general way after which, in the following two chapters, the social institutions themselves will be discussed in detail.

REVIEW QUESTIONS

6.1. Are rank and privilege as consequential today as they were when most nations were ruled by an hereditary aristocracy? Defend your answer.

6.2. Are modern stratification systems simply carryovers from the past? Did modern societies simply inherit them, or is stratification really functional in modern societies such as the United States? Explain your answer.

6.3. Are stratification systems necessary? Would it be possible to have a viable society in which all members were truly equal? Why or why not?

6.4. Can it be said that systems of stratification simply represent the relative positions of the "winners" and the "losers" in an ongoing battle for power and the societal rewards that accompany power? Back up your answer with illustrations.

6.5. Is the concept of "class," as defined by Weber, meaningful in modern societies, particularly in the United States? What about the concept of "status honor"?

6.6. What is the relationship among life style and life chances and stratification?

6.7. Do such variables as race, ethnicity, and religion have any bearing on stratification and stratification systems? If so, in what ways?

6.8. Are stratification systems dynamic or static and what do these words mean as applied to stratification systems?

NOTES

[1] Paul B. Horton and Gerald R. Leslie, *Studies in the Sociology of Social Problems* (New York: Appleton, 1971), pp. 126–128. For a more complete account of "unfairness," see "President's Commission of Law Enforcement and Administration of Justice," in *The Challenge of Crime in a Free Society* (Washington: U.S. Government Printing Office, 1967).

[2] W. Lloyd Warner, *American Life* (Chicago: University of Chicago Press, 1953), p. 104.

[3] Bernard Barber, *Social Stratification: A Comparative Analysis of Structure and Process* (New York: Harcourt, Brace, Jovanovich, 1957), p. 7. Written some fifteen years ago, this book is still current in most respects and particularly well worth reading for the interested student of stratification.

[4] Paul B. Horton and Gerald R. Leslie, *The Sociology of Social Problems*, 4th ed. (New York: Appleton, 1970), p. 4. For a complete definition and discussion of social problems, read chapter 1.

[5] Although no one who has not personally been subjected to discrimination can ever fully understand what it is like, *some* comprehension can be gained through reading Andrew Billingsley, *Black Families in White America* (Englewood Cliffs, N.J.: Prentice-Hall, 1968).

[6] A completely new model of an "ideal" society is to be found in Amitai Etzioni, *The Active Society* (New York: Free Press, 1968). This book is so rich in detail that it is often difficult to read. But it is well worth the intellectual effort required and

should be read by all who believe that *they* know how modern societies should be changed.

[7] Horton and Leslie, *Sociology of Social Problems*.

[8] A characteristic of many preliterate societies is that the members of these societies do not feel that they have any significant control over the course of their own lives much less over society. To gain some idea of fatalism, see George P. Murdock, *Our Primitive Contemporaries* (New York: Macmillan, 1934), pp. 393, 585, 592–593.

[9] There are innumerable accounts of Karl Marx's theories and of Marxianism in general. A particularly well written and lively account is contained in Irving M. Zeitlin, *Ideology and the Development of Sociological Theory* (Englewood Cliffs, N.J.: Prentice-Hall, 1968), chap. 10.

[10] Kingsley Davis and Wilbert E. Moore, "Some Principles of Stratification," *American Sociological Review* 10 (April 1945), pp. 242–249.

[11] The reader will gain some understanding of the rank differences and unequal rewards in preliterate societies by reading almost any ethnographic report by a competent anthropologist. Recommended are Ronald Cohen, *The Kanuri of Bornu* (New York: Holt, Rinehart and Winston, 1967); Norman A. Chance, *The Eskimo of North Alaska* (New York: Holt, Rinehart and Winston, 1966); and Elman R. Service, *Profiles in Ethnology* (New York: Harper & Row, 1963).

[12] Davis and Moore, "Some Principles of Stratification," p. 242.

[13] Ibid.

[14] Ibid., p. 243.

[15] Richard D. Schwartz, "Functional Alternative to Inequality," *American Sociological Review* 20 (August 1955), p. 430. It should be noted that Schwartz's conclusions were drawn from a study of two middle-size Israeli settlements, which obviously provided for greater ease of manipulation than would a complex society. For an earlier and quite different view of the kibbutzim, see Eva Rosenfeld, "Social Stratification in a 'Classless' Society," *American Sociological Review* 16 (December 1951), pp. 766–774.

[16] Kenneth D. Benne, "An Approach to Problems of Inter-Religious Conflict," in *The Planning of Change*, ed. W. Bennis et al. (New York: Holt, Rinehart and Winston, 1961).

[17] An essentially psychological approach to society would be that societies are formed out of the characteristics of individual members. This point of view plus a decidedly pessimistic opinion of man's basic nature is contained in Thomas Hobbes, *The Leviathan* (Oxford: James Thornton, 1881), p. 95. Students of Freud will recognize certain basic similarities between Hobbes and Freud.

[18] Horton and Leslie, *Sociology of Social Problems*, chap. 5.

[19] The naive belief that hospitals and, in particular, hospital emergency rooms treat the sick or injured with equal medical skill and compassion is rudely dispelled in an article by David Sudnow, "Dead on Arrival," in *Sociological Realities*, ed. Irving L. Horowitz and Mary Symons Strong, with the assistance of George A. Talbott (New York: Harper & Row, 1971), pp. 225–232. A much earlier work with similar conclusions is August B. Hollinshead and E. C. Redlich, *Social Class and Mental Illness* (New York: Wiley, 1958). This latter work, of course, covers mental rather than only physiological trauma.

[20] Full information on this point can be found in Ralf Dahrendorf, "Integration and Values versus Coercion and Interests," in *Social Stratification in the United States*, ed. Jack L. Roach et al. (Englewood Cliffs, N.J.: Prentice-Hall, 1969), p. 59. The original version appears in Ralf Dahrendorf, *Class and Class Conflict in Industrial Society* (Stanford, Calif.: Stanford University Press, 1959).

[21] Rarely do subsistence-level economies survive unchanged in competition with a modern, technological society. A compelling sociological drama of one that did survive is in Peter A. Munch, "Economic Development and Conflicting Values: A Social Experiment in Tristan da Cunha," *American Anthropologist* 72, no. 6 (December 1970), p. 1303.

[22] Gerhard Lenski, *Power and Privilege: A Theory of Social Stratification* (New York: McGraw-Hill, 1966), p. 44.

[23] An excellent general discussion of economics in preliterate societies is contained in Ralph L. Beals and Harry Hoijer, *An Introduction to Anthropology*, 3d ed. (New York: Macmillan, 1965), chap. 14.

[24] Service, *Profiles in Ethnology*, chap. 10, p. 215. For other chiefdoms see chaps. 11–13; for primitive states, chaps. 14–17.

[25] A useful discussion of the behavior of those in power is found in Gaetano Mosca, *The Ruling Class* (New York: McGraw-Hill, 1939).

[26] See Vilfredo Pareto, *Mind and Society* (New York: Harcourt, Brace, Jovanovich, 1935).

[27] A complete account of the iron law of oligarchies is given in Robert Michels, *Political Parties* (New York: Free Press, 1949).

[28] Lenski, *Power and Privilege*, p. 44.

[29] Interested students can acquire a knowledge of the sweep of English history and the emergence of democratic processes by reading Sir Arthur Bryant, *Makers of England* (New York: Doubleday, 1962).

[30] Robert Payne, *The Life and Death of Lenin* (New York: Simon and Schuster, 1964). For more information, see Leon Trotsky, *My Life* (New York: Scribner, 1930).

[31] John Kenneth Galbraith, *The New Industrial State* (Boston: Houghton Mifflin, 1967), p. 107. Students would do well to read this entire book. It provides a lucid and logical model of the inherent dynamics and consequences of industrialization and how these dynamics operate to move the societies concerned toward more viable democracy.

[32] Arnold S. Tannenbaum, "Unions," in *Handbook of Organizations*, ed. James G. March (Skokie, Ill.: Rand McNally, 1965), pp. 733–734. In addition to the pages cited, students will do well to read the entire section on union-management conflict, pp. 720–736.

[33] Ibid., p. 732.

[34] C. Harold Anderson, "The Impact of the Educational System on Technological Change and Modernization," in *Industrialization and Society*, ed. Bert F. Hoselitz and Wilbert E. Moore (UNESCO-Mouton, 1966), pp. 266–267. This article also considers some of the possible dysfunctions of educational systems in developing countries. For a full and scholarly explanation of resistances to change, see Francis R. Allen, *Socio-Cultural Dynamics* (New York: Macmillan, 1971).

[35] T. Walter Wallbank and Alastair H. Taylor, *Civilization: Past and Present*, 4th ed. (Chicago: Scott, Foresman, 1960), vol. 1, p. 124.

[36] Henry Lewis Morgan, *Ancient Society*, ed. L. A. White (Cambridge, Mass.: Harvard University Press, 1964; originally published in 1877). Morgan spent many years in self-financed anthropological research and travel among the American Indians. The value of his writing has continued in the ethnographic sphere. And Morgan's contributions should not be narrowly evaluated on the basis of his three-stage theory of social evolution.

[37] Leslie A. White, *The Evolution of Culture* (New York: McGraw-Hill, 1959). A more recent discussion of technology and human societies written by a psychologist is Robert L. Schwitzgebel's "Behavioral Instrumentation and Social Technology," *American Psychologist* 25, no. 6 (June 1970), pp. 491–499.

[38] A lively and perceptive account of technology and social change with emphasis on the computer is to be found in John Diebold, *Man and the Computer: Technology as an Agent of Social Change* (New York: Praeger, 1969).

[39] Ibid.

[40] English society at the turn of the twentieth century is vividly brought to life in Barbara W. Tuchman, *The Proud Tower* (New York: Macmillan, 1966). Chapter 1 provides a description of a society in which class and status did, to a considerable degree, coincide.

[41] Walter Goldschmidt, *Man's Way* (New York: Holt, Rinehart and Winston, 1959), p. 88.

[42] Samuel Eliot Morison, *The Oxford History of the American People* (New York: Oxford University Press, 1965), p. 231.

[43] Hortense Powdermaker, *Coppertown: Changing Africa, The Human Situation on the Rhodesian Copperbelt* (New York: Colophon Books, 1965), p. 274.

[44] H. H. Gerth and C. Wright Mills, eds. and trans., *From Max Weber: Essays in Sociology* (New York: Oxford University Press, 1946), p. 300. Their introduction contains an informative biography of Max Weber.

[45] Tuchman, *Proud Tower*, chap. 2. The author conveys, better than many conventional sociological writings on the same topic, the attitudes toward self, class, and the rest of humanity of the English aristocracy in the period 1890–1914. For a study of more recent class attitudes and values, attention is invited to Herbert Hyman, "Value Systems of Different Classes: A Social-Psychological Contribution to the Analysis of Stratification," in *Class, Status and Power*, 2d ed., ed. R. Bendix and M. Lipset (New York: Free Press, 1966).

[46] This situation is particularly clear-cut in the case of Black Americans. Recommended reading in this respect is Everett Hughes, "Dilemmas and Contradictions," *American Journal of Sociology* 50 (1945), pp. 353–359.

[47] Robert W. Hodge et al., "Occupational Prestige in the United States," *American Journal of Sociology*, November 1964, pp. 286–302.

[48] Richard Centers, *The Psychology of Social Classes* (Princeton, N.J.: Princeton University Press, 1949), p. 77.

[49] Tuchman, *Proud Tower*, pp. 32–33.

[50] C. Wright Mills, *White Collar: The American Middle Classes* (New York: Oxford University Press, 1951), p. 247.

[51] It will be instructive for the reader to inspect the United States Bureau of the Census, *Current Population Reports* for several years and note that while the incomes of college educated Black Americans *are* improving, those of white American college graduates is increasing at a relatively higher rate—the gap is increasing rather than narrowing.

[52] Kurt Lewin, "Group Decisions and Social Change," in *Readings in Social Psychology*, ed. Theodore M. Newcomb et al. (New York: Holt, Rinehart and Winston, 1947), p. 333.

[53] Arnold M. Rose, "The Concept of Class and American Sociology," in *Life in Society*, rev. ed., ed. Thomas E. Lasswell et al. (Glenview, Ill.: Scott, Foresman, 1970), p. 576. (Emphasis added.)

[54] A new and illuminating discussion of the differences between professions and occupations (the occupation-profession continuum) is presented by Ronald M. Pavalko in *Sociology of Occupations and Professions* (Itasca, Ill.: Peacock, 1971), chap. 2.

[55] Ralph Turner, "Modes of Social Ascent through Education: Sponsored and Contest Mobility," in *Education, Economy, and Society*, ed. A. H. Halsey et al. (New York: Free Press, 1961), p. 122.

[56] For a useful account of social interaction in small groups, see A. Paul Hare et al., eds. *Small Groups* (New York: Knopf, 1965).

[57] W. Edgar Vinacke, *Foundations of Psychology* (New York: American Book Co., 1968), p. 653. For a more complete discussion of the characteristics of the normal curve, see Allen L. Edwards, *Statistical Analysis*, 3d ed. (New York: Holt, Rinehart and Winston, 1969), pp. 117–119.

[58] Ascription and achievement are one pair of Parsons's "pattern variables." For a more complete discussion of three of the five pattern variables, see Bert F. Hoselitz, "Main Concepts in the Analysis of the Social Implications of Technical Change," in *Industrialization and Society*, ed. Bert F. Hoselitz and Wilbert E. Moore (UNESCO-Mouton, 1966), pp. 16–19.

[59] For a complete and chilling account of the relationship between economic factors

and totalitarianism, see William L. Shirer, *The Rise and Fall of the Third Reich* (New York: Simon and Schuster, 1960). A more recent work, emphasizing both sociological and psychological factors, is Joachim C. Fest, *The Fall of the Third Reich* (New York: Random House, Pantheon Books, 1970).

[60] The relationship between economic depression and the increase in power of the federal government is brought out implicitly in David A. Shannon, *The Great Depression* (Englewood Cliffs, N.J.: Prentice-Hall, Spectrum Books, 1960).

[61] Aristotle, *Politics*, trans. Benjamin Jowett (New York: Modern Library, 1943), p. 60.

ANNOTATED BIBLIOGRAPHY

Bierstedt, Robert. *The Social Order*. 3d ed. New York: McGraw-Hill, 1970. On stratification, this text devotes several chapters to a number of topics including "Women and Men," "Class and Caste," "Color and Creed," and others, all of which provide information in some depth concerning various aspects of stratification. The chapter on women and men is particularly timely, in view of legislation attempting to provide economic and legal equality for women, not to mention the activities of various groups agitating for women's rights.

Broom, Leonard, and Selznick, Philip. *Sociology*. 4th ed. New York: Harper & Row, 1968. This is a popular text in introductory sociology courses. For an excellent treatment of status consistency and inconsistency, see chapter 6, pp. 170–173.

Lenski, Gerhard. *Human Societies*. New York: McGraw-Hill, 1970. While the treatment of stratification is somewhat brief, there are several chapters on preindustrial societies. Students are urged to review chapters 7–10 in order to gain an appreciation of the dynamics underlying the shift from mechanical to organic type societies, with consequent effects on systems of stratification.

McKee, James B. *Introduction to Sociology*. New York: Holt, Rinehart and Winston, 1969. This is a scholarly and well-written text. The entire chapter on stratification is worth reading. Of particular value is the section in chapter 10 on social mobility.

Merrill, Frances E. *Society and Culture*. Englewood Cliffs, N. J.: Prentice-Hall, 1969. Chapters 9–12 on stratification are excellent; chapter 9, "Race," is especially well organized.

Peacock, James L., and Kirsch, A. Thomas. *The Human Direction*. New York: Appleton, 1970. The authors describe this book as "an evolutionary approach to social and cultural anthropology." Those interested in social change can gain an interesting perspective from reading it. Of particular importance to students of stratification are the chapters on the evolution of society and culture and on sociocultural evolution and the future.

Popenoe, David. *Sociology*. New York: Appleton, 1971. Particularly recommended is what the author calls "Topic 5: The Consequences of Stratification." Attention is invited to the inclusion, under "Some Related Resources," of both fiction and films as sources for understanding the consequences of stratification.

Toby, Jackson. *Contemporary Society*. New York: Wiley, 1971. Chap. 12. Germane to the study of stratification are techniques for measuring status, a discussion of which is provided in this book. In addition, Toby provides a relative perspective in that he contrasts stratification in the United States with stratification in other industrial societies.

Introduction to Social Institutions: A Question of Survival

INTRODUCTION

In 1872, Karl Marx stood up before a public meeting of the Hague and uttered the following words: "We know that the institutions, manners and customs of the various countries must be considered, and we do not deny that there are countries like England and America where the worker may obtain his object by peaceful means." It is remarks like this which turn scholarly heads grey. For in the space of several seconds, Marx tore an all but fatal gash in the theory of history he had so painstakingly developed in his formal writings.[1]

In this and the next two chapters we will be concerned with *social institutions*, which are present in all societies, modern and preliterate. In part, an institution can be seen as a simple concept that provides a way of doing things in a society. But, in fact, institutions do much more. If, as we said in Chapter 6, socialization provides society with a means for assuring its continuity, then social institutions provide society with some means for assuring its survival. While there are many things that may drive a society out of existence, there are others that can protect it from collapse. We call those *functional prerequisites.*[2] The version of the functional prerequisites that we will present at this time is a somewhat idealized version. Because the prevailing attitude of the majority of the population of any society toward that society's institutions is somewhat idealized, threats to any institution either from outside or inside are generally reacted to in terms of ideals rather than actualities. We will proceed from the generally held views about society and its functioning to an objective, analytical discussion about the specific prerequisites that must be met by social institutions if a society is to survive.

Functional Prerequisites

For a society to be viable, it must have an adequate relationship to its environment, to both human and nonhuman aspects. There must be a provision for adequate sexual reproduction to meet the problems created by the deaths of a society's members. It must define and assign roles to its members so activities that must be performed regularly are carried out with significant motivation and ability. If there is adequate communication between members of the society, then a common value structure can be maintained, socialization can take place, and role differentiation can be implemented. There must be a shared orientation that allows members to adapt to the society's social institutions in such a way that there is adequate protection and control to sustain and not destroy motivation. A shared set of goals that members can articulate among themselves can serve as alternatives for which the individual may work. And there must be some kind of normative regulation of the means by which people are told *how* to accomplish those goals. Society must have a

Introduction to Social Institutions: A Question of Survival

way to regulate and control affective feeling between members so certain destructive forms of social reaction do not take place. Society must be able to transmit the structure of action to new members through socialization. And, finally, there must be a way to exert social control over those members who deviate by engaging in disruptive forms of behavior and endangering the survival of the society.

Institutions represent patterned and regularized ways of meeting those sets of problems. For example, it is a function of the economy, as a social institution, to provide for an adequate relationship between a society and its physical environment through agriculture, mining, lumber, manufacturing, and so on. This is not to say that for each set of functional prerequisites there exists only one institution or that each institution fulfills only one set of functions. The institution of the family, for example, attends to vital aspects of several of those functions in societies having low-level technologies. Nonetheless, if a society is to continue to exist, it must have some *ready-made solutions* to the problems of survival available on a daily basis.

INSTITUTIONAL COMPLEX

Institutions provide the means for mankind's survival as do instincts in lower forms of life. Don Martindale has stated the significant distinction between man's solution to survival problems and those based on instincts: "That man lacks the biological foundation of instincts gives an experimental property to behavior arising in response to his needs. It also makes possible a wide range of behavioral solutions to the problems presented by the need." [3]

To think of institutions in the United States as having an "experimental property" is difficult. As a function of ethnocentrism, most people in any society feel that their forms of religion, family, state, education, and so forth have a quality of not only permanency but also *rightness*—other ways practiced by other peoples seem odd or wrong. But institutions were not planned in the sense that our early ancestors sat down and decided on the ideal model for their institutions and then proceeded to set them up. What institutions do represent are solutions to various survival problems that proved successful. When a particular situation recurred, it is likely that our ancestors tried various solutions until they found one that worked for each occurrence. Such a successful solution tended to become "stamped-in" to human behavior patterns and eventually institutionalized. Given widely separated groups spread over considerable parts of the earth's surface and without communication with one another, it is quite understandable that quite different but workable solutions evolved in the various ancient societies. From this it can be seen that dissimilar institutions could arise in as many different societies; this, of course, is what happened. It is not that any institution in any society represents the best possible or most efficient form such an institution could have taken. The principal point is that human institutions, differing as they still do from society to society, all have one feature in common—utility for survival. Value judgments of the institutions of our own or other societies are sociologically irrelevant. If a society persists over time, then its institutions are performing their essential function.

Reciprocal Relationships

The institutions of any society do not operate in a vacuum; they are linked by reciprocal relationships to all the other institutions. In the United States, for example, the amount and quality of formal education any individual is likely to obtain is closely related to his or her position in the stratification system. Further, the reciprocal relationships between institutions may carry with them tensions, discrepancies, and strains. In some developing countries where efforts are made to move the economy in the direction of industrialization, considerable tension and discrepancies arise between the economy and the institution of religion, in which the emphasis is not on this world but on the world to come.

Ability to Change

Institutions can and do change. But for a society to move toward any significant modification in existing institutions, there must be some conscious recognition of the need for change. Beyond this recognition, which may be somewhat vague, there must also be an *articulation* of the situation.[4] What is necessary is the development of goals or of ways and means of remedying a situation. Once this is done, new patterns of action can be established which will meet the needs better than did the old patterns. However, it must also be recognized that institutional changes of a gradual kind do take place without any conscious design or intent on the part of people in a society.

Institutional change is not brought about automatically because people consciously or unconsciously desire change. It is almost axiomatic, as will be discussed in Chapter 13 ("Social Change"), that some people in any society will resist any attempts to bring about change however slight the change. But when resistance is minimal, new patterns introduced into an institution are legitimized more readily. When resistance is considerable, institutional changes are more difficult to accomplish and require more time. In England, for example, the change from autocratic government and the predominance of the House of Lords to a social democracy and the predominance of the House of Commons took several centuries and the shedding of much blood.

On the surface, the problem of bringing about desired changes in an institution seems clear-cut. A fairly large group of people within a society

Copyright © 1972 by Saturday Review/World, Inc.
Reprinted by permission of the publisher and Bernard Schoenbaum.

". . . and do you promise to love, honor, and cherish each other even though the institution of matrimony may become obsolete . . ."

feel that a change is necessary; end goals of change and the means to attain these goals are agreed upon; ipso facto, the institution is changed. But it is far from that simple or logical. People resist, sometimes vigorously, any attempt to alter what they regard as *the* right and proper way. Then, too, there are vested interests who have something to lose if the change is made and who will oppose with whatever resources they have any attempts to alter what they regard as a favorable situation. When we add *inertia*—a tendency to resist change because it requires learning new ways of behaving and the extinction of well-established habits—it can be appreciated that the impatient reformer faces a formidable task.

In simple societies, institutions are, for the most part, in harmony with one another. One paradox of modern, complex, and highly integrated societies is that there appear to be general strains and inconsistencies between the various institutions. Changes in any one institution affect to some extent all the other institutions. For example, in the United States the gradually increasing power and authority of the federal government has had considerable ramifications for the institution of education, such as scholarships, grants to colleges and universities, busing and so forth. And other American institutions have similarly been influenced and modified by this change in the polity. Based on historical evidence, it would seem that societies tend in the direction of bringing institutions into consistency with one another:

By and large actions consistent with the established forms are favored over inconsistent ones. Hence, in all man's institutional spheres rays of inconsistency radiate from the established solutions to collective problems like waves from the impact point of a stone in a quiet pond.[5]

Consistency

A major theoretical problem is how stability is worked out within a society between the forces created by the various institutions. This has led to the assumption of a certain degree of stability, or equilibrium, and a concentration on stability and equilibrium by the structural-functionalists. That school, which we discussed in Chapters 1 and 2, has concentrated on attempting to understand the way institutions are able to accomplish their ends and, at the same time, tailor their solutions to fit the solutions posed by other institutions. A problem such as the military-industrial complex is worked out by the ability of the economy and the polity to arrive at mutually agreeable solutions to problems created by international tensions.

But we must be careful not to overstate the case for institutional consistency because it is also quite possible for institutional arrangements to exist side by side even though they may make conflicting demands upon the individuals involved. As long as there are enough "safety-valves" to allow for the meeting of institutionally unmet needs, the institutions can continue to function. In his analysis of prostitution, for example, Davis argues that prostitutes play a positive role in the maintenance of the monogamous family institution. They allow the need for sexual variety to be met by another institutional arrangement (prostitution) that does not affect the basic structure of the family or its main operating features.[6] And it is interesting to see how the prostitutes themselves are concerned with keeping the demands made upon them within the confines of their definition of the prostitute-client relationship. From both sides in such a relationship there are processes that help to keep the norm of monogamous marriage intact.[7]

Even though the relationship between institutions may be one of conflicting purposes, most functional theorists assume that

1. any one structure is more likely to persist if it is engaged in reciprocally functional interchanges with some others;

2. *the less reciprocal the functional interchanges between structures, the less likely is either structure or the patterned relationship between them to persist.*[8]

Conformity

Along with a tendency for consistency, another interesting feature of an institution is that so few people ever think to question it as a solution to the problems of day to day living. Part of this is because the solution becomes internalized as part of what W. I. Thomas has called "the definition of a situation." A social situation often is only what it is defined to be by the participants, a point we hardly realize as we move through our daily lives. One perceives part of a definition of a situation from one's contemporaries, but a significant part of one's definition is handed down to us from the past. Peter Berger has said that

our lives are not dominated by . . . our contemporaries, but also by those men who have been dead for generations . . . This is important to stress because it shows us that even in areas where society apparently allows us some choice, the powerful hand of the past narrows this choice even further.

Berger also notes that most of the time many of the ways we are to behave are established before we are even born, and often "all that is left for us to do is to play [the game] with more or less enthusiasm."[9]

The German sociologist Arnold Gehlen, along with Don Martindale, conceives of an institution as a regulatory agency that channels human action in much the same way as instincts channel animal behavior.[10] Since those institutions are learned and *not* instinctive patterns, we must ask at this point how it is that there is such a high degree of seeming inevitability in the demands made on members to conform to institutional solutions. Part of the answer lies in the understanding that there is a kind of push and pull to all institutions. It takes the form of a set of rewards attached to the performance of activities that are institutionally approved and a set of punishments that are part of what the nonconformist must face in his search for new solutions.

Rewards often take the form of the enhancement of status through recognition, the granting of material rewards, and the accomplishments of other goals that may be important to the individual. For example, the businessman who performs in accord with society's expectations will receive a promotion, a greater salary, and the increased ability to send his children to college. For a violation of society's expectations, he can expect to be greeted with ridicule, humiliation, and other forms of social control including loss of employment. Yet, as we have discussed, those social controls are often so informal in the ways they work, they are hardly recognized by the participants. "The choice of an occupation inevitably subordinates the individual to a

THE NOW SOCIETY

Rewards often take the form of the enhancement of status through recognition, the granting of material rewards, and the accomplishments of other goals that may be important to the individual.

Reprinted by permission from Chronicle Publishing Company.

"I'm going places at Global, Irma. They've put a document shredder in my office."

variety of controls, often stringent ones."[11] Books like William Whyte's *The Organization Man* fascinate readers because they reveal the sanctions and rewards built into the engineering of human motivation in accord with the goals of the organization.[12] And today it is often a person's organizational affiliations that determine where he may live, the schools he may send his children to, and the informal organizations he is permitted to join. Thus many groups the individual uses for his essential self-definition are opened or closed to him as the result of his conforming to the demands made upon him by society. This is part of the power that institutions have over individuals. Man derives his very sense of self from his involvement with socially prescribed ways of doing things.

When an institution is fully developed in a society, the norms that tell an individual how to behave are (1) widely known and generally accepted; (2) enforced by strong sanctions that are continuously and widely applied; (3) based on honored and revered sources of authority; (4) internalized by individuals and thus made part of their personalities; (5) learned early in life largely on the basis of continuous reinforcement; (6) conformed to by most individuals in the society.[13] As true as those six points may be, we must not overstate the case for institutional determinism of behavior. Society is not a prison where the most minute details of life conform to a rigid time schedule. Social norms today often are plastic and vague, lack strong internal consistency, and contradict each other in the behavior they demand. In realizing that, we are closer to a definition of "modern" as applied to complex societies where the degree of heterogeneity precludes the demands for stricter conformity more traditional societies are able to make. Rather than there being a rigid set of institutional norms in modern American society, there is a certain variability in behavior which is tolerated as long as it does not violate the outer limits of society's normative boundaries.

Nonconformity

One way a society can define its boundaries is not in a physical sense but in terms of the behavior it is willing to tolerate as a departure from the institutional structure of society. In *Wayward Puritans* Kai Erikson defines deviance as that behavior falling outside the boundaries of a society.[14] And those boundaries are normative; within them the institutions exist with a greater ability to tolerate deviance in a modern, complex society than is possible in a highly integrated, relatively simple social system.

In dealing with the issue of nonconformity in American society, Williams points out that

in the United States nonconformity to nominally accepted norms partakes . . . of the intrinsic sources of ambiguity and deviation found in all cultures, as well as the differing standards of relatively separate subcultures. Also, a relatively high rate of certain types of nonconformity is expectable because of rapid social change.[15]

Consistent Value System

There is a certain willingness to tolerate nonconformity by institutions of American society. But another basic feature of the institutional complex is that a fairly consistent set of values serves as the core upon which these institutions are built. Seymour Lipset characterizes the enduring basic American values by using Parsons's "pattern variables." Parsons designed the pattern variables to reflect dimensions along which an actor had to make certain choices before he entered into interaction. In looking at those choices, not only individuals but also societies are forced to choose between the alternatives. For example, a societal value system may choose to emphasize individual performance or it may stress ascribed qualities in the assignment of individuals to social roles.

The first Parsonian pattern variable Lipset uses to characterize American social institutions is the emphasis on individual performance and not on nepotism for the filling of social roles. The great outcry when President John F. Kennedy appointed his brother Robert to the position of attorney general arose largely because nepotism is so frowned upon.

A second pattern variable Lipset uses is the *universalism-particularism* distinction, which he says

> may emphasize that all people be treated according to the same standard (e.g., equality before the law) or that individuals should be treated differently according to their personal qualities or their particular membership in a class or group.[16]

There is a great emphasis in American culture on universalism, transmitting it to the young largely through the educational system. Teachers are supposed to treat each child according to the same set of standards and to avoid the playing of favorites, which is characteristic of particularism. A great deal of the trauma of a child's first day in school stems from the fact that often for the first time he finds himself confronted by universalistic standards. In school he is not someone's well-loved son but merely one child among many.

The last of the Parsonian pattern variables Lipset uses is the *specificity-diffusion* distinction. Specificity refers to the treatment of individuals only in terms of the roles and statuses they occupy. This can be contrasted with a diffuse relationship in which a great number of an individual's characteristics can be used as the basis for interaction. An emphasis on specificity limits the range of interactions that can take place between individuals and has led to many segmented relationships in American society.

Lipset adds to the three Parsonian pattern variables one he calls the *egalitarian-elitist* distinction. In doing so, he raises the question To what extent can emphasis on status, power, and privilege be used as the basis for other social relationships? In American society, with its stress on egalitarianism, the differences between high and low statuses are not the general determinants of most other forms of social relationships. An important aspect of American ideology is the denial that any real status differences exist between individuals, often in situations where it is patently absurd to do so. Lipset summarizes his position in noting that "the United States, more than any other modern non-Communist industrial nation, emphasizes achievement, egalitarianism, universalism, and specificity. The four tend to be mutually supportive."[17]

Conflict and Tension

The importance of Lipset's work is that it stresses an underlying consistent value system common to many, if not all, American institutions. Even within an institution such as the family, there are strong threads of this basic value system. The emphasis by many husbands and wives on equality in decision making can be viewed as a strong carryover from other institutional complexes such as the economy.

Despite the underlying consistency in values, there are conflicts and tensions in and between the various institutions. Let us continue with the family to illustrate this point. Much of the strain in familial relations is due to the opposing value orientations that govern family life operating in conjunction with the fact that the family is the only institution still based on diffusion and particularism. In other words, the family stresses a different set of values from other institutions in society. This puts the family in competition with some other institutions and directly contributes to the difficulties experienced by many individuals during adolescence. During that period, each individual must somehow learn to reconcile the values of his or her family with the often contradictory values of the larger society.

The interaction and relationships between the family and the other institutions are not, of course, the only ones marked by some tension and conflict. Another example is the conflict between the institutions of economics and religion—in spite of the Marxian view that religion necessarily supports the established order. Such conflicts and tensions are by no means dysfunctional. As we will discuss in Chapter 13, social change is, in part, a dependent variable of such conflict and tension.

FUNCTIONS OF INSTITUTIONS

Thus far in this chapter, we have discussed social institutions with some emphasis on ideal, rather than actual, functioning. This is not to imply that our ideals may not someday be approximated; history (and Max Weber) have well demonstrated the force of ideas and, by implication, ideals. But we will now turn our attention to a more objective analysis in order to place institutions in an empirical rather than idealized perspective.

It should be clear by now that the individual cannot exist outside of society, and we must therefore ask What are the real requirements a society must meet in order to survive? There are at least six functions necessary to the vitality and continued existence of all societies.

Reproduction

History shows that societies do not always survive. Those societies that disappeared probably did so because one or more of their institutions was not functioning adequately. The example of the Cathars will somewhat dramatically illustrate that point. During the twelfth century there was a great movement for Church reform in Europe in the direction of asceticism and unworldliness. Among the groups that sprang up in France were the Cathars. Their extreme beliefs led them to an extreme of asceticism. Flesh was evil, and propagation of the flesh was a sin. Thus sexual intercourse and marriage were sins. As Cuzzort comments, "had the Cathars been completely successful, the consequences would have been the loss, in a generation or two, of the total society . . ."[18] In order to survive, then, a society must be able to recruit, by birth or other means, sufficient numbers of *persons to replace those who are lost* through death or otherwise.

But physical replacement of lost members is not the whole story. Society must also be able to *reproduce the individual culturally and socially*. Let us suppose that an American family consisting of a father, mother, and several young children were transported lock, stock, and barrel to the Kalahari Desert in South Africa. Would they survive for very long without assistance from the native Bushmen? It is doubtful. All the sophistication gained from their experiences in a complex modern society would be of little avail in such a region. There knowledge of such things as the location of water holes or the ability to imitate certain animals in order to facilitate the hunting of game is essential.[19] Even if Bushmen did appear, would our American family know the tribal customs and etiquette necessary to establish a friendly relationship? Most serious of all would be the language barrier, which would make all but the simplest communication impossible. One cannot, then, become a Bushman simply by going to the Kalahari Desert. It is necessary to be born into the society and have that society reproduce the individual culturally and socially so that, in time, the individual will be able to function as an adequate adult.

In modern society, as we will discuss in Chapter 8, the family performs a considerable amount of the function of socialization. But, except for the physical reproduction of humans, this function could be performed by individuals or agencies other than the family, as for example, the Israeli kibbutz. Socialization does remain an important aspect of the human family in all societies. But it is the *function* of socialization, not the family, that is essential to society. This is said, not to indicate agreement with Barrington Moore that the family is archaic and outmoded[20] but, rather, to place stress on function.

Production and Distribution

In subsistence-level societies basic requirements are obviously simple— enough food and water to sustain life, and clothing and shelter as necessary.[21] But if we consider the survival of any particular society as not merely the physical survival of its members but also the structural survival of the society, the picture becomes considerably more complicated. The more complex a society becomes, the greater the volume and variety of basic requirements. Here we mean basic to the existence of a society *as it has come to be constituted*. What the members of a particular society have come to regard as essential to their needs must be made available—must be *produced and distributed*—by the institutions that have developed in that society for meeting those needs. For example, any extreme and continued failure in the production and distribution of such basic "needs" as electricity, television programs, automobiles, indoor plumbing, and so forth, would not destroy a modern society in the sense that all the members would perish. But that society would be so drastically changed that it could be said to have failed to survive.

Maintenance of Order

Part of the function of maintaining order is carried out through the socialization process. But socialization, in the sense of producing amiable, cooperative, norm-abiding members, is never perfect. Therefore, one or more institutions of a society must be prepared to deal with behavior that is sufficiently annoying or deviant to be inimical to the better interests of the society as a whole or the individual concerned. Commonly, we look to political institutions as the means of maintaining internal and external order, but the responsibilities borne by all the institutions of a society are considerable. In modern societies, for example, the family and the educational system bear a large responsibility for effectively socializing young individuals into their society. At the same time, socialization goes on for adults who have obtained employment; this is carried out mainly by the institution of economics. Whatever the roles may be and in whatever the institution, deviant behavior is subjected to pressure for conformity from other role-players in that institution.

We must also consider any dysfunctioning of any institution with respect to order. Should any institution fail significantly to meet those of its functions essential to a society, disorder within that society is sure to follow. During the Great Depression in America (1929–1937), a failure of the economic institution, there were many disorders, although remarkably little violence. But that failure of the economic institution, which reached as far as Europe, also produced considerable social change.[22]

Provision for Physical Welfare

Without living humans, no society can exist. This may seem to be a tautology, but it bears some thought. Except for plagues, famines, or other such disasters, viable societies have been characterized by death and fertility rates that maintained and usually increased their populations and by enough healthy individuals to meet their basic needs. A situation peculiar to modern times (which is discussed in considerable detail in Chapter 11) is that the lowering of the death rate can and does have dysfunctional consequences for societies. Since the health of most members of modern societies is sufficiently good for them to play their necessary roles and since enough people live long enough to reproduce themselves, physical welfare may appear, from a functional standpoint, to be moot. This may have been true prior to the development of science and of medical practice based on science. Today people see physical health as a need that can in most cases, be fulfilled—poor health is rarely regarded as an affliction to be borne with resignation. The physical welfare of members has become critical to societies that are advanced enough to have significantly reduced fatalities.

Satisfaction of Indispensable Needs

There are some authorities who feel that "the society's members must see enough meaning and purpose in life to be motivated to perform their various tasks."[23] But it is difficult to take any *sociological* position. It can be argued that certain tasks must be accomplished if a society is to survive; therefore the members of a society must see enough meaning and purpose in life to be impelled to undertake the necessary tasks. It would, however, appear more appropriate to say that sufficient numbers of persons in any society must be sufficiently motivated to undertake the necessary tasks of that society but without specifying just how they are or become motivated. (We have discussed this in detail in Chapter 6.) Guthrie stated, somewhat facetiously, that "the hen lays her egg, not because it has reached an embarrassing size, but because the species must be preserved. She is aiming at motherhood and carrying a torch for her species, not just laying an egg."[24] That, as Guthrie intended, is ridiculous. And it is equally ridiculous, even dangerous, to assume that institutional tasks get done only if people see enough meaning and purpose in life. A good many institutional tasks are probably performed out of habit or because it is easier to do them than to avoid doing them.

But people's values, attitudes, beliefs, and opinions are very closely related to the shape, form, and tasks of institutions. What is or is not *indispensable* (with the exception of those things vital to sustain life) is a matter of cultural determination. And if those culturally determined needs are not adequately met by the institutions of a society, that society can be greatly affected. It might, for example, become disorganized while corrective measures are taken. Or a gradual blurring of the outlines of the society could lead to a situation where the society ceases to exist in the sense that it once did. This does not mean that the people who once constituted the members of that society necessarily die or are killed. They may adjust to the loss of their society by fragmenting into isolated or semi-isolated groups lacking the structure of the original society. Some of the American Indian tribes reacted in just that way.

There are, of course, other kinds of adjustments. John Bushnell suggests that the Hupa should be called "Indian Americans" and not "American Indians" because they have acquired an American culture while managing to retain some ethnic identity.[25] It would appear that so long as the individual members of a particular society do not perish in the face of a societal breakdown, a new, although not necessarily entirely different, society can emerge.

In the case of modern societies, such as the United States, what could be expected to happen if one or more institutions failed to fulfill their tasks on a continuing basis? Aside from predicting some disorganization, it would be impossible to state with any certainty that some redefinitions of what is indispensable to the society would occur. In the early 1970's, for example, it became apparent that the energy requirements of the United States were not being fully met—a task of the economic institution. If, for example, there should be a continuing shortage of gasoline, can we safely predict that there will be some disorganization with respect to certain sectors of the institution of economics? The answer to that surely must be yes. But can we also predict that the members of American society will drastically redefine what they consider as at least two of the indispensable tasks of that institution— the supplying of automobiles and the supplying of fuel to run them? The safest prediction (as of this writing) appears to be that measures will be taken to ensure that the institution of economics fulfills its indispensable tasks, as "indispensability" is defined by the members of American society.

REQUIREMENTS OF INSTITUTIONS

Having discussed the essential *functions* that are performed by social institutions, we will now turn our attention to an examination of the requirements of social institutions.

Essentiality

Social institutions, as timeless and permanent as they may seem, did not simply happen. They arose in answer to the survival requirements of societies. But this, as we have tried to emphasize, did not necessarily mean the physical survival of members, although that was surely involved. For example, the economic system of a society might effectively supply and distribute the necessary food and clothing to sustain life in that society. But, if the institution failed to meet what the society had defined as indispensable, then disorganization and conflict would follow. The first essential for the functioning of institutions, then, is one belonging to the society at large—the definition of some task, thing, service, or product as being *essential*. It is this quality of essentiality around which institutions are organized and from which they develop the characteristics peculiar to each. There is considerable disagreement *between* societies about the various definitions given for what is truly essential to a society. And *within* some modern societies there is considerable discussion about what is essential. From the sociological point of view, when something *is* defined as essential, it will be institutionalized.

Roles and Status

Roles, as we have indicated earlier, can be defined as "the conceptions and implied expectations that people always have of other people's behavior."[26] The majority of males in American society play the role of husband, and many will play the role of father. The majority of women will become wives, and many will become mothers, grandmothers, and so forth. What is important to understand is that most Americans know quite well what is expected of them when they are playing a particular role; they conform, within fairly broad limits, to their own and others' expectations with respect to that role.

Similarly, all institutions are characterized by a network of roles, mutually supporting and interacting in such a way as to enable the institution to fulfill its societal functions. In any institution there are a number of clear-cut roles that are filled by persons who, knowing those roles, behave so as to meet the expectations of others, not only those in similar roles in the same institution but also others in other institutions.

Within institutions, roles are associated with statuses. Within the family, for example, the status of "child" is an ascribed status and carries with it relatively low prestige, with the behavioral norms for "child" being somewhat broadly defined. Statuses with high prestige—corporation president, federal judge, state governor, and so on—carry connotations of high prestige. As one ascends the prestige hierarchy in most societies, roles become increasingly well-defined, and there is less and less latitude for the player. In other words, high-prestige roles require closer adherence to the expectations others have of the role and the role player. Any role player in such a position can expect to encounter negative sanctions for deviations from the expectations, even for minor deviations.[27] A physician who worked shoeless and wore only denim trousers and a t-shirt could find himself with very few patients because he was not living up to the expectations others had of him in his role as physician.

While statuses are institutionalized, they are mainly concerned with "position or location of individuals, vis-à-vis others . . ." Institutionalized roles, "on the other hand, [have] an operational connotation; [they are] . . . what the actor does in his relations with others as seen in the context of . . . functional significance for the system . . ."[28] In other words, social institutions are highly organized with differing levels of status; statuses vary in prestige and in the roles that are necessary for meeting the particular functions of each institution. Roles and status in most institutions are not as well or neatly defined as they are in the military; nonetheless they do exist and do fulfill their functions, at least at the minimum level necessary for both the continuance of the institution and the survival of the society.

Resources

Certain resources must be available to an institution for it to accomplish its functions. A socialization process that prepares children for assuming appropriate adult roles in the institution and value and belief systems are a few of the "necessary" resources of any society. Except for those things necessary to support life itself, what is essential to a society is defined by that society. From this it follows that the institutional functions must be considered as essential if the institution is to perform its functions. For example, most people living in modern societies support a formal education system because they consider it to be essential for their societies. While there is difference of opinion about *how* the institution of education should perform its various tasks, there is virtual *unanimity* that these tasks must be performed. It is such unanimity of opinion that makes it possible for the institution of education to obtain tax money to build and maintain schools and to pay teachers and other necessary personnel. It is this same unanimity that functions in the polity to make laws regulating and requiring the attendance in school of all individuals until a certain level or age has been reached.

It is our contention that the matter of resources is largely a by-product of the value and belief systems of societies. If a majority of the society defines a function as critical to that society, the resources—in terms of material, humans to play the necessary roles, and all other necessary requirements—will be met.

CONCLUSION

In this chapter we have been introduced to the general nature of institutions. First we examined the ideal functional prerequisites of institutions. Then we moved to an objective empirical analysis of institutions as they actually exist and function in living societies.

Social institutions are, in a real sense, *the* principal social structures and, hence, tend to be highly stable and resistant to change. Nonetheless, institutions do change with the passage of time. Over the years and with increasing complexity, societies have redefined what is essential to them; this redefinition has often been in the direction of increasing the tasks that social institutions perform.[29] Once a society progresses beyond the bare subsistence level, institutions change toward greater complexity of functions as societies begin to redefine what is essential for their survival. We must remember that societies are living people acting out a particular culture. Cultures are, in the simplest definition, a way of life. What we find is that institutions must support ways of living. What it takes in terms of fulfilled functions to meet the requirements of a society, is considered essential and thus becomes institutionalized. For example, as Americans, we might ask some questions about the automobile. Is it simply a convenient mode of transportation that could be dispensed with if fuel were to suddenly become scarce, as some believe may happen? Or is the automobile too institutionalized? Would any sudden change that made it impossible for Americans to use their cars cause widespread disorganization and confusion? Would that disorganization and confusion seriously imperil the American way of life and, hence, the integrity of the society *as it has come to be constituted*? In other words, is the automobile *essential* for the survival of the *society*?

We have also examined the complex, necessary, and continuing inter-relationship and interaction between the various institutions of society. Nearly all humans play roles in all social institutions. The relationships between roles within and between institutions are generally well understood by all concerned. Within fairly broad limits, most people in society play their roles in accordance with the expectations attached to them. Any general failure to do so would lead to the disintegration of the society concerned.

In the following chapter, we will discuss in detail the institution of the family. The family is undoubtedly the chief agent of human socialization, the process so necessary to society for its continuity. We will discuss the forms family structure can assume. And we will be concerned with both American family types and types found in various other cultures.

REVIEW QUESTIONS

7.1. Considering the differences between agrarian and industrialized societies, does the same definition of "social institution" hold for both? Why or why not?

7.2. Draw up two lists of functional prerequisites for the modern family—one an ideal list; the other a list of the functions in the real world. Note the differences between the two lists. Can you explain these differences? But, more importantly, are these differences having any effects on real families, for example, divorce? Explain your answer.

7.3. How can an individual's life be dominated by people who have been dead for centuries?

7.4. Most of us can perceive some ways in which one (or more) of our social institutions is dysfunctional. Cite several examples of such dysfunction and *then* explain why such obvious deficiencies are not corrected.

7.5. Lipset contends that one Parsonian "pattern variable" that characterizes American social institutions is *universalism*. Do you agree or disagree? Fully or in part? Why?

7.6. Does the size and complexity of a society have any relationship to what a society considers as *essential* for survival? Explain your answer.

7.7. Can you think of any role in any society which is not an institutional role? Defend your answer.

7.8. Make a list of the various roles *you* are currently playing and indicate the social institution under which each role principally belongs. Do you find any roles that appear to either overlap or belong about equally to two or more institutions? Specifically, which of your roles?

7.9. Those who have attained a high-prestige status in American society have gained much. But they have also lost something they had when in lower prestige statuses. This "something" is highly valued in American society. What is it?

NOTES

[1] A. Hacker, "Sociology and Ideology," in *The Social Theories of Talcott Parsons*, ed. M. Black (Englewood Cliffs, N.J.: Prentice-Hall, 1961), p. 289.

[2] D. F. Aberle et al., "The Functional Prerequisites of a Society," *Ethics* 60 (January 1950), pp. 101–111.

[3] Donald Martindale, *Social Life and Cultural Change* (Princeton, N.J.: Van Nostrand, 1962), p. 44.

[4] J. Zollschau and W. Hirsch, *Explorations in Social Change* (Boston: Houghton Mifflin, 1964), p. 90.

[5] Martindale, *Social Life and Cultural Change*, p. 45.

[6] Kingsley Davis, "The Sociology of Prostitution," *American Sociological Review* 2 (October 1937), pp. 744–755.

[7] "Streetwalker," in *In Their Own Behalf: Voices from the Margin*, ed. C. McCaghy et al. (New York: Appleton, 1968).

[8] A. Gouldner, "Reciprocity and Autonomy in Functional Theory," in *System, Change and Conflict*, ed. N. Demereth and R. Peterson (New York: Free Press, 1967), p. 151.

[9] P. Berger, *Invitation to Sociology* (New York: Doubleday, Anchor Books, 1963), pp. 85, 87.

[10] For a more complete discussion of Gehlen's work, see Ibid., p. 87ff.

[11] Ibid., p. 75.

[12] William Foote Whyte, *The Organization Man* (New York: Doubleday, Anchor Books, 1956).

[13] Robin M. Williams, Jr., *American Society: A Sociological Interpretation*, 2d ed. (New York: Knopf, 1960), p. 31.

[14] Kai Erikson, *Wayward Puritans* (New York: Wiley, 1966).

[15] Williams, *American Society*, p. 377.

[16] Seymour Martin Lipset, *The First New Nation* (New York: Doubleday, Anchor Books, 1967), pp. 240.

[17] Ibid., p. 244.

[18] R. P. Cuzzort, *Humanity and Modern Sociological Thought* (New York: Holt, Rinehart and Winston, 1969), pp. 77–78.

[19] Ralph L. Beals and Harry Hoijer, *An Introduction to Anthropology*, 3d ed. (New York: Macmillan, 1965), p. 373.

[20] Barrington Moore, *Political Power and Social Theory* (Cambridge, Mass.: Harvard University Press, 1958), pp. 160–178.

[21] For an excellent account of the biological need for nutrition and how culture determines what and how people eat, see Marston Bates, "Man, Food, and Sex," in *Life in Society*, rev. ed., ed. Thomas E. Lasswell et al. (Glenview, Ill.: Scott, Foresman, 1970), pp. 43–48.

[22] David A. Shannon, *The Great Depression* (Englewood Cliffs, N.J.: Prentice-Hall, 1960).

[23] Melvin M. Tumin, *Patterns of Society* (Boston: Little, Brown, 1973), p. 272.

[24] Edwin R. Guthrie, *The Psychology of Learning*, rev. ed. (New York: Harper & Row, 1952), p. 5.

[25] John H. Bushnell, "From American Indian to Indian American: The Changing Identity of the Hupa," *American Anthropologist* 70, no. 6 (1968), pp. 1108–1116.

[26] Kurt Lang and Gladys Engel Lang, *Collective Dynamics* (New York: Crowell, 1961), p. 8.

[27] It is probably correct to say that the president of the United States, in terms of public appearances and his image, is highly constrained. For example, when the late Harry S. Truman was running for reelection in 1947, a woman heard him use the word "damn." She was so shocked, she stated that from that day forward she would never again believe in a president of the United States.

[28] J. O. Hertzler, *American Social Institutions* (Boston: Allyn and Bacon, 1961), p. 46.

[29] In Chapter 9 we will discuss the possibility that the institution of religion is an exception to this statement.

ANNOTATED BIBLIOGRAPHY

Hertzler, J. O. *American Social Institutions*. Boston: Allyn and Bacon, 1961. Even if there were a great many books devoted to social institutions (which there are not), this work would remain highly recommended. The approach is sociological, and Hertzler makes clear that social institutions are the major agencies by which society is organized, patterned, stabilized, and made predictable.

Miner, Horace. "The Folk-Urban Continuum." In *Social Change: Sources, Patterns, and Consequences,* edited by Amitai Etzioni and Eva Etzioni, pp. 147–158. New York: Basic Books, 1964. Although this article is largely concerned with a critique of the folk-urban continum, it richly describes changes in social institutions when moving from folk to urban society. The use of a continuum to discuss change of any kind is particularly useful. Change in social institutions is rarely drastic or sudden but takes place slowly and can be studied and understood more easily in terms of a continuum of considerable length.

Ross, H. Laurence, ed. *Perspectives on the Social Order.* New York: McGraw-Hill, 1963. Chapter 17 on society and its institutions is informative and readable and deals with the economic and political institutions.

Weinberg, Meyer, and Shabat, Oscar E. *Society and Man.* 2d ed. Englewood Cliffs, N.J.: Prentice-Hall, 1965. The introduction to chapter 5 and the material in it, drawn from W. P. Webb, *Great Plains* (Boston: Ginn, 1931), constitute real-world illustrations of both the resistance to change and the modification of social institutions that will take place when clearly indicated by circumstances.

Williams, Robin M., Jr. *American Society: A Sociological Interpretation.* 2d ed. New York: Knopf, 1960. Chapter 10 discusses institutional variation and the evasion of normative patterns. It makes explicit some of the factors leading to changes within institutions and the interaction and interdependence of all the institutions of a viable society upon one another.

The Family:
Society's
Life-Line

8

The Family: Society's Life-Line

INTRODUCTION

Of all the social institutions, the family probably performs functions that are the most critical to society. Since the human species has no instincts of significance, infants are helpless at birth and remain dependent for several years. Therefore infants and young children must *learn* how to survive. The only source for such learning is other humans, which presupposes that these "other humans" have workable solutions to pass on to the young of their species. We have called those solutions "culture," and the persons living out a particular culture constitute a "society." The chief agent for passing on each society's culture to newly born members is the *family*. Without that function being met, man would not have survived. William Goode notes that the central significance and importance of the family is verified by the fact that "the family is the only social institution other than religion which is *formally* developed in all societies." [1]

We have discussed the power of society to enforce its demands upon individual members. And nowhere is that power more evident than with respect to the institution of the family. In order to survive, most individuals in modern societies are compelled by circumstances to conform to the demands of other institutions, such as economics and the polity. As adults they are not compelled to participate in family activities, yet all but a small proportion do so, even to the point of establishing families of their own. Nonparticipation in family activities is not punished by any formal negative sanctions. There are no real demands to talk to parents or siblings or to marry, but most people do. "So pervasive and recurrent are the social pressures and so intertwined with indirect or direct rewards and punishments, that almost everyone either conforms, or claims to conform to family demands." [2]

If asked to define the word "family," most of us would not hesitate. The standard reply in American society would be that a family consists of father, mother, and their children, plus, but only sometimes, other near blood relatives such as grandparents, aunts, and uncles, cousins, and so forth. This does not, however, tell us much because it defines the family only in terms of *relationships*. Such a definition is not satisfactory because it provides only a framework that tells us nothing about *interdependencies* and *functions*. We need a definition that tells us what a family is in a dynamic sense.

Definition of the Institution

As we discussed in the last chapter, social institutions are organized around at least one function of importance to society. If we consider what functions the family performs, we should arrive at a definition of the institution. What, then, does the family do for society beside preparing new born humans for survival in their environment? Morris Zelditch suggests four functions and provides a workable definition:

[1] *A family is a social group in which sexual access is permitted between adult members,* [2] *reproduction legitimately occurs,* [3] *the group is responsible to society for the care and upbringing of children, and* [4] *the group is an economic unit at least in consumption.*"[3]

There is considerable agreement among sociologists that those four functions are universal. Therefore, we should establish why they are important and whether it is the family as *we* know it that performs all of them in all societies. Note, in particular, that Zelditch's definition says nothing about mothers, fathers, and children. It merely says that a group that fulfills the functions *is* a family. When we think in terms of "functions" rather than blood "relationships," we see that some of the functions of the family can be and are performed by social units that are not called families, such as orphanages. Or consider the function of the permission of sexual access between adult members, that is, between husband and wife. In a society where sexual access is permitted between consenting adults in general, it follows that no small group fulfills this function and therefore the definition given does not hold. That, however, is purely hypothetical, for all known societies place some restrictions on sexual behavior many of which are unwritten. In other words, mere legal permission for sexual access between consenting adults does not take away the power of society to punish sexual relations that violate social mores. There can be no doubt that there is some sexual misbehavior in all societies. But whether or not such behavior is formally punished does not change the fact that all societies provide for some form of *regulated* access. And the group that meets the criteria for family is usually *the* vehicle for granting such access.

It is possible to find societies that do not have groups fulfilling all four family functions. In Israel for example, the *kibbutz* (collective farm) is, in the ideal form, marked by characteristics that appear to have eliminated the family as an identifiable group. There are husband-wife units who do have sexual access to one another and who produce legitimate offspring. But the children live on the kibbutz, not with their parents, and economic cooperation is carried on by the kibbutz as a whole. In other words, two of the family *functions* are carried out by the family (sexual access and legitimate offspring), and two by the kibbutz (upbringing of children and economic consumption).

While it is not necessary for any particularly small group to perform all the functions specified, it does appear that all these functions are *necessary* and *critical* to societies. Even in the radically different society proposed by Plato in *The Republic*, we find all the functions of the family being carried out although not by any arrangement with which we are familiar.[4] Changes that have occurred over time in the institution of the family have not, we suggest, represented changes in functions. Rather, they represent changes in who or what performs the functions. In preliterate societies, for example, families are production as well as consumption units. Modern families, for the most part, perform only the consumption function inasmuch as working adults are employed outside the place of residence and outside of family activities.

APPROACHES TO THE STUDY OF THE FAMILY

As any number of ethnographies (accounts of societies) make clear, it is the *nuclear family*—mother, father, children—that predominates in both pre-literate and modern societies. There are, of course, many variations, some of which will be mentioned later. But the family, as a *set of functions*, is not always easy to identify. What the ethnographer concludes may depend directly on the method of research or study used.

Reuben Hill and Donald Hansen have pointed out that there are at least five basic approaches that are used in research on the family: (1) inter-actional, (2) situational, (3) developmental, (4) structural-functional, and (5) institutional.[5] Three of these are of particular interest: (1) and (4) because they tend to focus upon and emphasize the functional perspective; and (3) because it is concerned with the way the family, as a social institution, fulfills one of its significant missions for societies.

Interactional

If the family as a social institution is to fulfill the functions that constitute the criteria for its existence, considerable interaction must occur *within* the family. A number of researchers have chosen to concentrate on intrafamilial processes and study in detail psychological and interpersonal interrelation-ships. This approach can be subsumed under *social psychology*—the study of human interaction in small groups. If we consider the human family as defined to be at least generally represented by the nuclear family, then it follows that at least some of the interactions in the family are sociological in origin—they come from society at large—and others are primarily psycho-logical—personal adjustments, attitudes, and so forth. While this particular framework is of interest and importance, it does not provide too much material upon which to base any assessment of the functional relationship between society and the family. Indeed, those concentrating on intrafamilial relationships must necessarily start with the assumption that the groups do in fact represent families. That, as illustrated by the kibbutz, may be invalid.

Developmental

The focus of the developmental approach is on the individual as he or she passes through his own life span. Characteristic of this approach is the concept of "life stages" through which the individual passes. One of the particular concerns of this approach is what are often called "developmental tasks," those things that must be accomplished at each stage of life if the individual is to pass on to the next. This "stage" approach provides some means of assessing the general effectiveness of the family in terms of how well the family socializes the young.

Structural-Functional

From the structural-functional perspective, the family is studied in relation to and with the larger society. Interest is shown in the family structures found in various types of societies. This approach is based on the assumption that the constituent parts of societies—particularly the social institutions—perform specific, essential functions at any particular time. The further assumption is made that institutions that do *not* perform specific, necessary functions are dysfunctional and that such institutions either change or disappear. Focus here is on the dynamic relationship between the institution of the family and the greater society. That relationship is *reciprocal*; the society influences the family and vice versa. In passing, it might be noted that the structural-functional approach can also be used to describe the relationship of individuals to the family, which is referred to as *microfunctionalism.*

The approach in this chapter will be essentially structural-functional. And a *caveat* with respect to "pure" structural-functionalism is in order. It is a highly artificial model of society, the purpose of which is to make clear the relationships between the various parts of societies. While recognizing that there is conflict between and within social institutions and that societies, including their parts, do indeed change, we will ignore both change and conflict and concentrate instead on the relationships between the family, other institutions, and the society at large. Our concern for pedagogic purposes is with *integration*, and the structural-functionalist approach is competent to deal with the problem of integration.[6]

It may be difficult to conceive of the family being studied by this approach. Most of us are aware that conflict does take place in families and that families change. One of the considerable problems in studying the family scientifically (and, by implication, objectively) is that while most of us are "experts" on only a few families, we feel that our data permit us to generalize to all families. The very idea of "families" involves some degree of emotionality for most people, and it is difficult to be coolly scientific. In order to establish some objectivity, let us consider that the family, as viewed in a modern society, is not the same thing as that institution in a preliterate society. Indeed, the family can take a variety of forms and still fulfill the functions outlined earlier.

FORMS OF FAMILY STRUCTURE

There are at least three major ways of describing family structure. Each has several varieties that can be subsumed under it.

Adult Membership

In order to have a family, a husband and wife must be *physically* capable of reproduction. Using sexual access as *the* criterion, we might ask What does sexual access have to do with family structure? In modern societies, including the United States, both formal and informal norms support *monogamous* marriage—one man married to one woman at a time and vice versa. But monogamy is not characteristic of marriages in all societies. There are two other forms of marriage and consequent family life that *seem* to revolve around sexual access between adult members of the family. In some societies, *polygyny*—where one man can take two or more wives at the same time—is permitted.[7] In terms of actual practice, polygyny is relatively rare even in those societies in which it is condoned. When polygynous marriages are entered into, it is only by the affluent and not infrequently at the behest of the first wife who desires not merely to emphasize her husband's affluence but also to provide herself with a house servant.

The third form of family life concerned with sexual access is extremely rare. *Polyandry* refers to one woman having two or more husbands at the same time. This particular practice is usually associated with female infanticide, as in the case of the Toda, a people of southern India.[8] That is, any widespread practice of polyandry would be associated with a shortage of marriageable females. Similarly, the practice of polygyny usually reflects a shortage of marriageable males, as among the Baganda where for various reasons, there is a high mortality rate among the males.[9]

There remains one other possible but not probable form of marriage in which sexual access is the key factor, *group marriage*. Described in *The Harrad Experiment*,[10] a novel popular some years ago, group marriage is the simultaneous marriage of several men to several women at the same time with all having the right of sexual access to all others in the group. It is a popular belief that prehistoric peoples practiced considerable promiscuity, with a sort of group marriage developing at some later time. Group marriage, in turn, gave way to polygamy which evolved into the "highest" form of marriage, monogamy. Beals and Hoijer have this to say about that exceedingly flimsy hypothesis:

Evidence . . . was sought in "primitive" cultures on the assumption that these preserved ancient forms relatively unchanged. But . . . polygamy is by no means general among so-called primitives. Rather, monogamy occurs far more often, if only for the reason that polygamy is impossible except under rare and special circumstances.[11]

In recent years, there have been attempts to form communes and experimental living arrangements marked by group marriage. But these are likely to end in failure unless they are drastically modified. Unfortunately, a full discussion of this topic is not possible because of space limitations. Let it suffice to say that individuals from modern societies who participate in a group marriage will probably experience failure for three significant reasons.

1. The participants come from societies in which monogamy is the norm; this norm, as well as those associated with it, have been internalized to an extent not realized by the participants. Group tension and personal difficulties will arise, and these tend to bring about either eventual breakup or modification of such experiments.

2. Marriage is more than simply a matter of sexual access; there are many problems connected with family living for which solutions exist in the usual forms of marriage. However, problems arise in experiments in group marriage for which no ready-made cultural solutions exist. For example, in the case of pregnancy in a group situation, *who* is the father? This might be decided by blood tests but the evidence could be inconclusive. The few societies practicing polyandry have worked out ways of deciding this, but individuals from modern societies experimenting with group marriage have not.

3. The economic factor may also be critical. To the extent that experimenters in group marriage have come from societies where private ownership of various kinds of property is the custom, conflict can be expected to develop very quickly in group marriage over the question of who owns (or controls) what?

Once individuals have been reasonably well socialized into a culture, it is difficult to adopt practices that are proscribed by that culture. It can be done, of course, but the costs in terms of various kinds of conflict are high.

There are some who argue that monogamy is an "unnatural state" imposed on men by some societies—such societies being marked by highly puritanical standards of sexual behavior. Monogamy may well be a function of a number of factors, but one of the more significant is that population is roughly divided equally between the sexes. The fact remains that even where polygyny is permitted, it is the exception rather than the rule; it is much more closely tied to personal wealth and prestige than to sex and sexual behavior.[12] And this argues against the supposition that men have greater sex drives and require greater sexual variety than do women.

Household Living Arrangements

Most Americans are familiar with the nuclear family because it is the most common family structure in modern countries. For the purposes of this discussion, we will extend the definition of nuclear family to mean the marriage partners along with their children living under one roof. Although less frequent, the *extended family* is known in America and was quite common in the early years of the Republic. An extended family is a basic nuclear family to which is added grandparents, from one or both sides of the family, also living under the same roof. This is more characteristic of families in the lower social strata. It is often in such cases a matter of economics and involves a pooling of resources between the parental and grandparental generations. Extended family systems are also found in other societies. Two principal forms, other than the three-generational type just described, are the *polygynous nuclear family*, which consists of the adult male and his wives and their children; and the extremely rare *polyandrous nuclear family*, which consists of the adult female and her husbands and their children.[13] Such families are referred to as "extended" because they represent *extensions* of the basic nuclear family unit. Extended families usually represent a realistic adjustment to situational circumstances that are usually economic in nature.[14]

Another type, essentially rare in modern societies, is the *joint family*, which represents several nuclear families residing under the same roof. Where they are found in modern societies is in the ghettos of large cities. Joint families are related to one another usually by consanguinity but sometimes by marriage.

Joint families can be organized along either paternal or maternal lines which involves the matter of "residence." Sociologically, the type of residence has implications for the other institutions of society. (We will discuss residence shortly.) When we find an extended family in modern society, it is usually a matter of economics. Joint families may represent the fact that in preliterate and primarily agricultural societies, families are not merely consumption units but *production units* as well. Since the economic self-sufficiency of a nuclear family depends to a considerable extent on the health and longevity of the adults, joint extended families may represent practical provisions against an uncertain future—the loss of one member of either a joint or extended family is not so critical a matter. Furthermore, such families also have the added feature of providing a form of "social security" for the aged.[15] In modern societies a multitude of agencies serve the functions of providing some measure of security, and the working members of the family tend to be employed outside the home. Therefore the family ceases to be a production unit and is no longer needed to protect the aged or otherwise incapacitated. Under such conditions we would expect the nuclear family to predominate, and it does. Although family forms vary in technologically simpler societies, the self-interests of members of these societies make extended or joint families a logical adjustment to situational conditions.[16]

The concern that some in modern societies show for what they call the disappearance of the *kinship system* is misplaced. That disappearance was a function of the changing institutions of society, particularly the economic institution. There is no longer any need for either extended or joint families, except in some isolated instances. As Goode has emphasized, the conjugal, or nuclear, family pattern is part of a change that is taking place all over the world as a function of increasing industrialization.[17]

Location of Residence

Location of residence is not a structural principle but is determined by the structure of the family in any given society. It is concerned with the way in which newly married individuals establish their place of residence with respect to their families of origin. In primarily agrarian societies, the most common practice is that of *patrilocality*, where newly married couples move into residence with or near the parents of the husband. Patrilocality serves several functions, one of which is economic. It also keeps a number of fighting males (warriors) together for purposes of defense against attack from other groups or for purposes of offense. *Matrilocality* is the practice of newlyweds living with or near the parents of the wife. Neither patrilocality nor matrilocality is basically a matter of sentiment (although sentiment is involved); they reflect the interests of those concerned. Neither custom, except incidentally, is practiced in modern countries. When human interests are better served by the introduction of new norms and customs, the old ways will disappear.

In modern, industrial countries the usual residence practice for young couples is *neolocality*; young couples choose their place of residence without reference to the parental residence of either the husband or the wife. With the extended period of education required in modern countries, a temporary form of patrilocality or matrilocality may operate while young couples finish graduate and postgraduate studies. But it appears that it will become more common for economic ties to be maintained between newlyweds and both sets of parents until the bridegroom or bride become economically self-sufficient.

We begin this section with another *caveat*. The average American family is a statistical artifact; no such family exists in the real world. Try, for example, to picture a family with 2.7 children or 1.4 automobiles. And such an "average" family would be meaningless unless one cited further specifics, such as social class. Establishing an "average" family for the upper, the middle, and the lower class might have some usefulness in terms of providing some crude idea of what is typical. But establishing some "average" family for all of the United States would be futile.

But it is possible to speak of the American family as having *general characteristics*. Indeed, it is necessary to assume that the American family can be spoken of in this way. As we observed earlier, a science of unique events is impossible. However, in discussing these general characteristics, it must be kept in mind that not all families are marked by one or more of them. The notion of deviance applies to families as well as to individuals.

Geographic Mobility

Geographic mobility has been a characteristic of man since our remote ancestors roamed their terrains in search of game and wild fruits. And those early hunters were socialized humans with complex cultures. Take, for example, the people who lived between 12,000 and 15,000 years ago in the Kostenki-Borshevo sector of the Don River Basin (now part of the USSR). Based on the material evidence of their culture, F. Clark Howell feels that:

> *their substantial size, complexity, and persistence through time surely indicates a pattern of cultural adjustment and elaboration in a harsh but potentially rewarding environment, which reflects human inventiveness and adaptability quite independent of and prior to the agricultural revolution.*[18]

Nomadic peoples, whether prehistoric or contemporary, move around in groups larger than the family. But the underlying purpose is much the same as that which has resulted in the considerable geographic mobility of the modern American family—self-interest. In other words, *self-interest dictates mobility*.

The emergence of the nuclear family and the general disappearance of the extended and joint families has freed the family to respond to the exigencies of modern, industrial societies. Possibly the most significant factor is the family's ability to respond to the demands of the economic system. Many large corporations have a policy of rotating executives from plant to plant, which are most often in different states. And the ambitious executive is compelled to go along with company policy. The Armed Forces move their personnel from base to base, sometimes transferring them to foreign countries. Skilled as well as semiskilled and unskilled workers move around in response to the demands for their services; the construction industry, for example, fluctuates both seasonally and geographically in demand for workers. Farm hands move seasonally, following the crops as they ripen in different parts of the country. Still others, under no compulsion, move because they have decided, realistically or not, that doing so will improve some aspect of their lives, usually the economic. The modern geographic mobility, and we mean *voluntary* mobility, of families that takes place in industrialized countries is fundamentally similar to other kinds of mobility found in different periods of history. The similarity lies in the fact that mobility in modern societies is dictated by self-interest (or what is presumed to be self-interest). Modern American geographical mobility demonstrates the interrelationship and reciprocity between the institution of the family and the institution of economics, which is another way of saying that a large proportion of American families do tend to move about in response to economic pressures. Such a relationship clearly exists with respect to the family in most modern societies, as it has in the past and in preliterate societies.

Critics of modern society claim that geographic mobility contributes to a breakdown of all kinds of personal ties with family and friends and neighbors. While this may be true, especially in terms of family ties, the critics overlook a very important point. The mass media coupled with this mobility have tended to standardize American culture wherever it is found; individuals can adjust to the circumstances in different localities with a minimum of psychological disorientation. Societies function, however imperfectly, to meet the needs of their members. And this is quite evident in organizations such as Welcome Wagon. Those groups, while having a basic economic motive, serve to bring new arrivals in a community into quick contact with other residents thus accelerating the assimilation process. In terms of social adjustments, a society such as the United States has a mechanistic flavor reminiscent of Durkheim's mechanistic, rather than organic, societies. People who move out of an American community are easily and quickly replaced by newcomers to that community.

Social Mobility

Social mobility is something quite different from geographic mobility. Since the United States is a stratified society, movement from one stratum to another is not only possible but likely. Historically, of all the factors influencing individual upward mobility, the family of birth is probably the most important. While there are dramatic instances of some individual making the transition from working class to upper class (in economic terms), such cases are rare. According to Joseph Kahl, in the years 1920–1950, there was a high degree of intergenerational mobility (67 percent of the sons moved to occupations higher than those of their fathers). But most of this mobility was on a modest order—from low level blue- or white-collar categories to a semiprofessional level.[19] It would seem that one's family of birth and attendant socialization can serve to both limit and stimulate upward mobility. As each generation comes of age, and if the working members of that generation have improved their position with respect to the preceding generation, then the following (or third) generation should have some chance of moving further up the socioeconomic ladder. The key to this, aside from the general matter of life style, appears to be education. Research in the late 1960's indicates that education does determine an individual's chances for upward mobility. *But* the research implies that an individual's education "depends to a considerable degree on the socioeconomic status of his father."[20] Families in which the principal wage earner has not improved his position vis-à-vis his family of origin also inhibit all but the most modest upward movement of any children.

An expanding economy functions to create opportunities for, and motivation toward, upward movement, and the shift from an agrarian to an industrial economy has some effects on the type of family. One of the by-products of the Industrial Revolution was to change the family from being both a consumption and a production unit to being simply a consumption unit. This did away with the need for having as many family "hands" available as possible because the production of necessary goods and services was provided by organizations outside the family. Further, the need to move geographically in order to obtain work made the extended and joint family forms impractical. The expense and difficulty of moving from one locale to another favors the nuclear family form. There have also been qualitative changes in the American family. Parental authority is no longer absolute. The family, as a socializing agent, is in competition with the homogeneous age groups characteristic of modern society with its extended period of formal education. And the system of mass education functions to socialize the young as well. All those factors serve to weaken the effects of tradition—sons no longer expect to follow in the occupational footsteps of their fathers and daughters do not compliantly prepare for lives as only wives and mothers. The result has been to weaken the psychic barriers to upward mobility.

As older cultural traditions vanish, except as historical curiosities, the family changes. It seems probable that many American families now socialize their young, at least to some extent, for upward mobility. It is probably true that the influence of the family has waned somewhat in comparison to the family in preliterate or primarily agrarian societies. However, that does not ignore the fact that the family still has great influence on children. During the late 1960's it was widely assumed that a serious gap existed between parents and children. More recent research, however, casts doubt on the belief that young people—particularly those in college—hold greatly different values from those of parents.[21]

But the family is no longer the chief socializing agent for modern societies; it shares the task, to some extent, with the institution of education and with peer groups. Moral judgments to the effect that such sharing weakens the family are probably incorrect. Sharing of the socialization function may, in the long run, serve to strengthen it. Individuals who reach the age where procreation is possible have not necessarily acquired the wisdom to rear their own children so that they are realistically prepared to take their places in society. What Jules Henry refers to as "lethal child-care practices" can be counteracted to some extent by the other agents of socialization.[22]

Our emphasis in this section has been on the considerable flexibility of the family in adjusting to societal changes. A significant change relative to upward mobility has been the weakening of traditional family norms. And the family, as an institution, has responded to an increasingly open society by such actions as socializing the young to both the *possibility* of upward mobility and the realistic preparation for such mobility—for example, an emphasis on more education. That and such other factors as industrialization, geographic mobility, the shift to the nuclear family form, and the sharing of the socialization function have served to increase the probability of individuals not merely aspiring to upward mobility but also achieving some vertical movement however modest. In the past, such factors as the greater influence of the family as a socializing agent, lack of geographic mobility, less open societies characteristic of agrarian economies, and reliance on tradition functioned to socialize individuals into a certain social stratum—into the stratum into which they were born. And that acted to limit both upward mobility itself and the motivation essential to the attempt to move upwards.

Open Mate Selection

You will recall that earlier we said that in some societies marriages are arranged. The couple concerned have little voice in the matter, marriage being a matter of considerations other than compatibility between prospective marriage partners. In American society, the assumption is made that mate selection is a reciprocal process under the control of the individuals concerned. "Romantic love," a phenomenon based on unattainability, has been presumed to be the general basis for mate selection in the United States and other parts of the world.[23] But it is likely that contemporary Americans, while looking for something called "love," are just as interested in compatibility when considering marriage. Such an emphasis would appear to be congruent with what the sociologist Nelson Foote terms "familism": "the self-conscious recognition of family living as a distinctive and desired activity—

Reprinted with permission from Family Circle Magazine.

"Twenty-five years ago I was Juliet to your Romeo, 15 years ago I was Harriet to your Ozzie, now I'm Dingbat to your Archie."

"Romantic love," a phenomenon based on unattainability, has been presumed to be the general basis for mate selection in the United States and other parts of the world. But it is likely that contemporary Americans, while looking for something called "love," are just as interested in compatibility when considering marriage.

quite different from operating a family business, 'raising a family,' or visiting relatives . . ."[24]

   If that change in emphasis from "love" to compatibility has occurred, it follows that, during the courtship period, an attempt will be made to observe the prospective marriage partner under various *situations*, including sexual behavior, in order to determine the degree of compatibility. We would expect, then, to find, not a general promiscuity among young people, but a less restrictive framework; "a general shift from relatively puritanical, absolute standards to a set of more flexible, *situational* standards."[25] There is some evidence available that suggests strongly that this may be the case. In a study by Eleanor B. Luckey covering a representative selection of some twenty-one American colleges and universities, the majority of students took a situational view; fewer than one out of six college males considered it "appropriate" for couples between the ages of fourteen and seventeen to engage in coitus. However, reactions were somewhat more favorable toward older couples, particularly if engaged, having sexual relations. This is far from promiscuity and does represent a partly moralistic and partly situational approach to sexual behavior. Quite significant was the finding that six out of ten coeds felt that sexual intercourse should be reserved for marriage.[26] To the extent that those results represent actual rather than idealized behavior, the family remains functional to a large extent as a means of providing sexual access.[27]

But mate selection is by no means as completely free as might be imagined, even in American society. Certain factors function to delimit the number of potential marriage partners. To begin with, there are legal and normative restrictions sufficiently powerful to be called taboos—marriage between brother and sister is tabooed almost universally and is illegal in some states. There are also legal restrictions on marriages between individuals of certain relationships such as first cousins, although these may not be tabooed. Such restrictions fall into the category of *exogamy*, which forces people to marry *outside* their group. Exogamy can apply to one's local unit or be very widespread, as with the Chinese who forbid marriage between individuals of the same surname.[28]

Endogamy, which forces individuals to marry *within* their group, usually functions simultaneously with exogamy. Both rules are followed in the United States, although only the prohibition against individuals related by blood—brothers and sisters—marrying is backed by legal sanctions. But endogamy prevails in a de facto manner thus limiting mate selection as, for example, by *propinquity*. That refers to the tendency to marry individuals who live within reasonable proximity of one's own home. The reason for this is obvious—one is simply more likely to have contact with those living in one's own community. Propinquity is not a hard and fast rule, particularly since families as well as individuals are highly mobile and because travel for pleasure is common in America. But it is probably nearly as true as it was more than thirty years ago that "one-third of the couples who applied for a marriage license lived within five city blocks of each other and more than one-half lived no more than 20 blocks apart."[29]

Homogamy describes the tendency to choose a mate from the same general social background when possible. Homogamy, then, also operates to produce and enforce a de facto endogamy. In the United States most marriages are between individuals of the same socioeconomic level, the same religious preference (or lack thereof), and the same racial background. While interracial marriages are probably increasing, they are still fairly uncommon. Homogamous marriages very likely reflect the situation that people of similar backgrounds tend to have similar values and to have been socialized in much the same fashion. A little reflection is sufficient to remind us that we are generally not drawn to individuals for marriage or friendship whose values, norms, and customs are very much at variance with our own.[30]

It seems clear that the American family is somewhat different from that institution as represented in earlier societies and in other contemporary societies—yet that the American family, for the most part, does meet the functional criteria we outlined earlier in the chapter. If several of the earlier family functions have been somewhat attenuated, the American family has taken on an additional function that James McKee calls the *affectional* function. He suggests that the modern family may be the most important single source for affection and emotional support for people in American society.[31] Whether or not people find warmth, affection, and emotional support is by no means a moot point. As Marshall Clinard observes, the high divorce rate in the United States today, as compared with the rate at the turn of the century, is no evidence that marital unhappiness has increased to the same extent. He goes on to point out that:

divorce laws have become more liberal . . . and the grounds for divorce have broadened . . . Moreover, there has been a decided change in public opinion about divorce. Many persons who formerly continued unsatisfactory marriages, or separated, or were deserted, now secure a divorce.

Clinard adds that public attitudes toward divorce are much more tolerant than in the past and that "these changes in public opinion seem to reflect more fundamental transformations in values and norms relating to the nature of marriage and divorce."[32] When married people in modern societies do not find the affectional function to be present in their marriages, they are more likely to consider divorce than to "muddle along" for the sake of the children or because society disapproves of divorce or for any other reasons.

This discussion has not meant to imply that all is necessarily well with the American family. As just noted, and as Parsons observed some years ago, a large proportion of the population does marry and people who get divorced remarry.[33] We would merely argue that the social institution of the family in the United States appears to have the stability that comes only from the flexibility to adjust to changing situations.[34]

CROSS-CULTURAL PERSPECTIVES

An attempt has been made to indicate that the most common form of the family—the nuclear family—in the United States is not the only form in which the family *as a unit fulfilling certain functions* exists (or existed) in societies around the world. Because we are most familiar with the nuclear family and because some degree of ethnocentricism is inevitable, we tend to regard those whose way of life and family type is different as being *untermenschen,* or less than human or subhuman. The following discussion is an effort to demonstrate that other ways of life and family types have logics of their own; we have, in fact stressed the idea that the family type is an adjustment to varying life situations.

What we are leading up to is a point of view called *cultural relativism.* An implicit assumption of cultural relativism is that truth is relative in terms of time and place. Therefore, social scientists should avoid making value judgments about cultures and societies different from their own. Carried to extremes, cultural relativism would require that no moral, ethical, or value judgments of any kind be made about the behavior of peoples living in societies other than one's own. But, as Robert Redfield made clear, this is not merely impossible but undesirable as well.[35] In the brief discussion that follows, we shall, however, attempt to avoid making value, moral, or ethical judgments and will try to relate family forms to the two societies to be discussed.

Purposes of Cross-Cultural Studies

Before we begin a discussion of specific peoples, we should arrive at some understanding of the purposes of cross-cultural studies. One aim of such studies is to determine whether there are any universals in terms of the way the functions of the family are carried out in the various societies. In American society, for example, functions are carried out by the nuclear family, with notable assists from other social institutions such as education. The importance of determining universals has considerable implications in terms of defining human nature. To the extent that any are discovered, it is possible to state that some behaviors are characteristic of man wherever he is found and, thus, are attributes of human nature.

Second, cross-cultural studies provide useful information about the intricate relationships between the various elements of social structure. We have, for example, already pointed out the interrelationship between the family and the institution of economics.

Cross-cultural studies are also concerned with social change and how such change affects the family. By studying various societies and their cultures, it should be possible to arrive at testable hypotheses regarding the dynamics of the family and society at large as they influence each other reciprocally. Such information could be useful for, among other things, predicting the shape of the family in the future.

Finally, purely intellectual curiosity motivates studies of the family as it exists in the various societies. With several experiments going on at present, such as group marriage, communes, and so forth, it would be interesting to know whether human values and happiness (as defined by American society) are better served by family forms other than those with which we are most familiar. We have heard and read so much about families in the "good old days" that it is advisable to determine whether or not such families (and such types are available for study in various parts of the world) really provide greater satisfaction and meet human needs better than the modern nuclear type.

Because of space limitations, we will consider briefly the matter of universals in respect to the purposes of cross-cultural studies. In order to demonstrate the difficulty of determining universals and, hence, human nature, we will consider something that is both of concern in terms of the family and considered to be a human universal—the incest taboo.

Incest Taboo In every society there are certain prohibitions against sexual relations between those defined as close members of a kinship group, even though for purely sexual purposes kinship is irrelevant. In the United States, for example, it is unlawful to have sexual relations between parents and children and between siblings. Even if there were no laws against such relations, the majority of individuals would not engage in them because all known cultures, in general, contain and teach an aversion to such practices.

The incest taboo does appear to be nearly universal, and many theories have been advanced to explain the phenomenon. In the 1920's Edward Westermark suggested that there was an instinctive aversion to incest in the human race which was aroused by familiarity with those in close proximity— such as among members of a family.[36] Somewhat later, and with no reference to the fully discredited belief in human instincts, Brenda Seligman hypothesized that the incest taboo arose out of jealousy. The father protected his sexual rights to the mother by forbidding sexual relations with the son. Likewise, the mother protected her rights with her husband by forbidding him access to any daughters. Further, since the father was denied sexual access to his daughters, he also denied it to his sons. The mother's motivation with respect to sons and daughters was similar; hence, both parental and sibling incest was controlled.[37]

Neither of those explanations is satisfactory—Westermark's because of his reliance on some "instinct"; Seligman's because it is not logically defensible, if for no other reason that in the early days power was by no means equally shared between husband and wife and it seems doubtful that the wife, in particular, could have denied her husband sexual access to his daughters had he really desired it. Furthermore, the incest taboo is not fully universal; while it appears to be universal with respect to cultures and societies, it is not always observed by individuals within the societies. Russell Middleton, in examining data on the eighteenth and nineteenth dynasties of ancient Egypt, noted that there were frequent cases of brother-sister and father-daughter marriages among ruling families. Based on this and on other exceptions to the incest rule, Middleton concluded that "either the aversion to incest is not as great as Westermark thought, or if Seligman is right, the parents must have suddenly lost their jealousy."[38] Such explanations are not merely unsatisfactory, as we have already observed, but they are also unproven and very likely unprovable.

A somewhat different explanation is provided by Parsons's attempt to explain both the near universality of this taboo *and* the known deviations. He hypothesized that the incest taboo operates in such a way as to literally propel individuals out of their immediate families and into marriages of their own. From these marriages, of course, new families are formed; in Parsons's view, this is to society's benefit.[39] The trouble with Parsons's hypothesis is that it ignores the fact that in society after society marriages are arranged. And these arrangements are designed to improve the relative positions of the families concerned through such things as dowries, bride price, the forming of alliances, the acquisition of new "hands," and other similar reasons. While the sex drive is assuredly a factor in promoting marriage, it can be doubted that the principal factor driving men and women to marriage is sexual frustration brought about by the incest taboo.

In bringing this discussion to a close, it seems reasonable to state that the incest taboo is generally universal but that there are also violations; violations not only in ancient times among royalty but at all times among individuals at all socioeconomic levels. Why does this taboo exist and why is it as strong as it is? The best answer to that is that no one really knows. That it is most probably a *learned* aversion can hardly be doubted, but why all societies appear to teach it is a matter for speculation. Possibly, it would have had its origins in the fact that when close relatives have sexual relations resulting in pregnancies, the children of such pregnancies are more often than usual defective in some way. Humans do observe and draw correct conclusions from such observations. And it could be that the incest taboo represents a logical adjustment to the mechanics of genetics.

Turning now from the question of human universals, we will examine two family types that are different from those common to most modern societies.

Nayar of India

The Nayar,[40] who live in the southwestern corner of the Indian subcontinent, are a caste in which the males were mostly warriors. Their life style was molded by the necessity for having family continuity in spite of the fact that the men were often absent for long periods of time. The Nayar, as we are describing them, no longer exist. Their particular life style began to change with the British colonization and rule over India, and it has continued to change in modern-day India. Understanding the Nayar marriage practices and the family type and organization of the past and knowing how they changed over time will help us to gain some understanding of the flexibility of the institution of the family.

Before the British gained control of India, the traditional Nayar family performed three of the functions of that institution (as given earlier in this chapter). As Linton notes, it did not perform the fourth, the satisfaction of sexual needs.[41] The social system of the Nayar was based on the *taravad*, in which all of the matrilineally related kin, both male and female, lived in one house. The property of this extended family was held jointly by the taravad in the name of the oldest surviving male in the matrilineage. The typical household was composed of a woman, her children, and any grand-children or great-grandchildren in the matrilineal line.

The Nayar women married following Hindu law. But the marriage, curious according to modern views, was with a stranger and was ended after three days by a formal divorce. The legal husband played no further role in the life of the wife. Sexual needs of both men and women were provided by informal love affairs, which might be of short or long duration and could be ended by the woman simply dismissing her lover by returning his latest gift.

The influence of the Nayar males appeared somewhat transitory insofar as families were concerned. They did not head up households and depended for sexual access on finding women willing to have an affair with them. The *pater role*—the father role ordinarily played by the male biological parent in most societies—was assumed by the brother of the mother. It was the male sibling of any woman having children who regarded his sister's house as his home and took an interest in her children.

The rationalization given for this arrangement of family is neither illogical nor impracticable considering the chief occupation of the males. Not only were they primarily warriors but they were also mercenaries—they were available for hire as fighting men. Because it was necessary for them to leave their homes on short notice, the Nayar family type made it possible for them to be free to pursue their vocation without regrets. Considering their "line of work," their safe return home was consistently in doubt.

What has happened since British rule was established? Although fighting continued for some years, the demand for mercenaries eventually ceased and the basic reason for the traditional Nayar family type no longer existed. If, as has been claimed, the institution of the family is flexible, some changes should have occurred. Although there is still some emphasis on matrilineage, nuclear family units are becoming more usual in Nayar society. As men began to earn independent incomes without leaving their place of residence for protracted periods of time, they also started to establish separate house-holds. Initially these were for their sisters and the sisters' children, but in fairly recent years there have been the beginnings of separate families of the nuclear type—a male, a female, and *their* children.

Clearly, the family is flexible and will change as circumstances dictate. It is instructive to note a general albeit slow movement in the direction of the nuclear family once the necessity for the male to leave the home and be gone for long periods ended.

The history of Nayar society and the institution of the Nayar family represent an actual case. Thanks to reports about them covering a long period, researchers have been able to draw some conclusions about the family, in particular about the manner in which the family type, values, and associated norms are altered according to situational aspects both internal and external to any particular society.

Israeli Kibbutz

The Israeli kibbutz was a deliberate attempt at group living based on the belief that the family, as it is known in the vast majority of societies, is subversive to any truly communal form of living. The early founders of the kibbutz were German, Russian, and Polish socialists seeking a new Zion. To these idealists, the family clearly constituted a threat to an ideal way of life. Aristotle much earlier had recognized that the family made a *meritocracy* impossible. A meritocracy is a society in which all positions are assigned purely on the basis of merit. And able and successful parents will use their influence to obtain advantages for their children without regard for whether or not such children are well or even minimally qualified. In *The Republic*, Plato wrote of an ideal society that no longer had the family, as we know it, although the *functions* of the family were to be carried out.

The kibbutz is basically a communal way of life in which the production of goods and services and the rewards of these endeavors are communally organized. The members of the kibbutz (called *kibbutzim*) were to be equal. Government was in the hands of a general assembly and various committees that had responsibilities for specific areas of community life.

We are concerned with the attempt to turn this ideal into a reality as Israel began to fill with Jewish immigrants.[42] The organizers of the early kibbutz acted deliberately to weaken family loyalties. Husbands and wives were alloted independent jobs, and there were prohibitions against members of the same family working together. Since all were theoretically equal in the kibbutz, women were to be treated the same as men and to participate in all the activities connected with communal living.

The rearing of children was to be entrusted to the community. After birth, children were to live apart from the parents in special children's houses under the direct care and supervision of a nurse-teacher. Outside of normal working hours, children could be with their parents but were to spend most of their time in *age cohorts*—that is, with children of the same or very nearly the same age. Youngsters were, by this process, to be socialized in such a way as to fit them for adult life in the kibbutz. In many ways the kibbutz marks an ideal form of communal living advocated by some people in modern societies, and the organization of the kibbutz implicitly recognizes that the traditional family forms represent a threat to communal living. Therefore, it is of particular value to consider what actually occurred when the experiment was made by individuals *who accepted the values and ideals of the kibbutz* and who clearly desired to implement these ideals and values in an actual communal situation.

When the experiment first started, couples did not have to be married in order to cohabit. Any couple wishing such an arrangement had only to request that they be assigned a room together and, with the approval of the council, could set up a one-room flat for themselves. Couples did legally marry, but the ceremony ordinarily did not take place until the woman was pregnant with the couple's first child. While the community did approve couples living together, there were informal sanctions to encourage individuals to spend considerable time with other community members. Meals were taken in community dining halls, and there were forms of group recreation in which all members were expected to participate. The basic idea was clearly to maximize group contact and, hence, group influence, and to minimize family contact in order to render the conventional family form, if not fully obsolete, at least relatively impotent.

The communal living went generally according to plan until the second generation began to come of age. Those who had started the kibbutz—the original settlers—had left their families behind them. But the second generation now had relatives living in the kibbutz. Quite possibly because of that, some practices began to change.[43] Some of the couples along with their children began to exercise the more traditional functions of housekeeping. Some families began eating the evening meal in their own quarters. There was a growing tendency to use personal funds and free time to make living quarters more attractive and *a place for the family*. This move toward family, rather than communal, living served to alter the kibbutz ideal of living arrangements. Rather than single rooms in barracks type housing, apartments began to be built with cooking facilities, private baths, and two or three rooms. With the construction of apartments, children began to spend more and more time at home with their parents and less with their peers.

The result of that closer and more protracted contact between biological parents and their children was, of course, to return a good part of the socialization function to the parents. While much of the education was still left to the teachers in the kibbutz, there was more cooperative planning between parents and teachers. Pressures also arose to reduce the number of hours that women, particularly married women with children, worked on communal enterprises.

More recently, with three and four generations living together in the kibbutz, there have been further changes. It has been noted, for example, that there is considerable interest in visiting and spending time with family members. What has happened, in effect, is a growing trend toward returning to the kinship and kinship organization characteristic of the societies from which the pioneer members of the early kibbutz were drawn. However, as Yonina Talmon-Garber observes, there is some ambivalence toward the family. While the strong antifamilism has abated, there is some bias against the family form found in most societies. The former strong bias against the family has been "superseded by a moderate collectivism which regards the family as a useful though dangerous ally."[44]

CONCLUSION

We have seen how the polygamous, matriarchal type of family developed by the Nayar in response to situational circumstances changed when those circumstances changed. The Israeli kibbutz, an experimental way of living that sought to abolish or at least weaken the family as a viable social institution was unable to do so. Indeed, the trend all over the world, as more societies begin to industrialize, has been toward the nuclear family form, very likely because that type appears to be most suited to industrialization. If society were to alter radically in some unpredictable way, it is possible that the family would change as necessary to conform to such different circumstances. It can be said that history has amply demonstrated that the human family, as a central institution of society, is remarkably durable. In general, some form of the nuclear family has been the norm (we include both joint and extended family in the phrase "some form of nuclear family").

The functions of the family must be performed in some minimally efficient manner if society is to survive. To date, at least, it seems that the family as we know it, or some variant, has been successful in meeting the demands society has placed on that institution. But does the historical record mean that the family is both necessary and enduring? Barrington Moore does not think so. He criticizes the family on the basis that there is no need for this institution in modern society and that many of its features are useless, outmoded, or worse. He sees affection among kin as "a true relic of barbarism."[45] Some of Moore's criticism is based on accurate observations that not all families properly prepare their children for taking their places in society. However, he misses the very important fact that the *majority* of families do prepare their children properly even if, at times, somewhat indifferently. But Moore's diatribe against the family can be criticized on other grounds as well. His whole position is based on a set of value judgments[46] that are seriously in error. Goode provides trenchant, if unintended, criticism of Moore's position when speaking of the "fit" between industrialism and the conjugal family:

Without a family unit to deal with the idiosyncracies of aged parents, the emotional needs of adults, or the insecurities of children, very likely not enough adequately functioning people would be produced to man the industrial system.[47]

It would appear that the family is society's most valued and valuable primary group even though it shares some socialization functions with the adolescent peer group and the social institution of education. It can only be predicted that, if the family as we know it should disappear from human society, the functions presently performed by that institution will continue to be performed. But we can be reasonably certain, based on the empirical evidence, that the family has a significant and probably enduring place in the society of the future.

In Chapter 9 we will be concerned with the other social institutions with which we all have contact throughout our lives—politics, economics, education, religion.

REVIEW QUESTIONS

8.1. What family functions can you perceive as being performed by an orphanage? Do you see this as being advantageous or disadvantageous to the children concerned? To society at large? To both?

8.2. Some interactions *within* the family are sociological in origin. Can you think of some examples of family interaction that quite clearly appear to be sociological in origin? What criteria would you use to distinguish between psychological and sociological interaction within the family?

8.3. Male students should make up a list of what they conceive to be the wife's duties in the family; female students should do the same with respect to the husband's role. Discuss these lists and their differences and similarities. Or both male and female students should prepare lists on the role of either the husband or the wife and see how these compare.

8.4. Why would it be important to determine paternity—the identity of the biological father—in an experiment in group marriage taking place in a modern society? To whom would this be of the greatest importance?

8.5. In modern societies, do nuclear families assume any responsibilities for the care and support of the aged? How do the customs and practices in modern society compare with those in preliterate societies insofar as old people are concerned? Aside from such fundamentals as food, clothing, and shelter, in what type of society would an aged person probably have the greatest psychological satisfactions—modern or preliterate?

8.6. If there is no such thing as the average American family in the "real" world, to what use can such a statistical abstraction be put?

8.7. Is it an advantage or disadvantage to complex modern societies *and* their individual members to have the socialization function shared between the family, the institution of education, and adolescent peer groups?

8.8. Can you think of any taboos, other than the so-called incest taboo, characteristic of modern societies? Of just the United States? Of subcultures within American society?

8.9. Could the communal idea as represented in an ideal form by the early kibbutz ever be made to work and at the same time retain its purely communal norms? *Or* is the development of a shift to the nuclear family more or less inevitable? Defend your answer.

NOTES

[1] William J. Goode, *The Family* (Englewood Cliffs, N.J.: Prentice-Hall, 1964), p. 4. (Emphasis in the original.)

[2] Ibid.

[3] Morris Zelditch, Jr., "Family, Marriage, and Kinship," in *Handbook of Modern Sociology*, ed. Robert E. L. Faris (Skokie, Ill.: Rand McNally, 1964), p. 681. (Emphasis in the original.)

[4] Plato, *The Republic,* trans. Benjamin Jowett (New York: Modern Library, n.d.).

[5] Reuben Hill and Donald Hansen, "The Identification of Conceptual Frameworks Utilized in Family Study," *Marriage and Family Living* 22 (1960), pp. 299–311.

[6] Ralf Dahrendorf, "Toward a Theory of Social Conflict," in *Social Change,* ed. Amitai Etzioni and Eva Etzioni (New York: Basic Books, 1964), p. 104; originally published in the *Journal of Conflict Resolution* 11, no. 2 (1958), pp. 170–183.

[7] Many members of modern societies endow the sexual side of polygynous marriages with imaginative and prurient aspects. The realities of such marriages are seldom congruent with the fantasy.

[8] Robert H. Lowie, *An Introduction to Cultural Anthropology* (New York: Holt, Rinehart and Winston, 1940), p. 245.

[9] Ralph Beals and Harry Hoijer, *An Introduction to Anthropology,* 3d ed. (New York: Macmillan, 1965), pp. 524–527.

[10] Robert H. Rimmer, *The Harrad Experiment* (New York: Bantam Books, 1966).

[11] Beals and Hoijer, *Introduction to Anthropology,* pp. 527–529.

[12] For data and other information on actual rates of polygyny in societies where it is permitted, see Vernon Dorjahn, "The Factor of Polygyny in African Demography," in *Continuity and Change in African Culture,* ed. William Bascom and Melville Herskovits (Chicago: University of Chicago Press, 1959), pp. 88–112.

[13] Beals and Hoijer, *Introduction to Anthropology,* pp. 478–480.

[14] The very rich are also marked to some extent by a form of extended family. There is great pride in lineage and concern with blood relatives; sometimes the family is dominated by a patriarch or matriarch. While such families do not usually live under one roof, they appear to have sociological and psychological characteristics of extended families who do share the same dwelling.

[15] What happens to the aged in a preliterate society in which the nuclear family predominates? Among the Copper Eskimos, the nuclear families live at a bare subsistence level in a harsh environment. They lack the resources to care for sickly or deformed children or for the aged. And mercy killings under dire conditions are reported to have taken place.

[16] An excellent discussion that implicitly covers economics as a key independent variable in the formation and proliferation of extended and joint families is contained in Ralph Linton, *The Study of Man,* (New York: Appleton, 1936), pp. 160–161.

[17] William J. Goode, "The Family as an Element in the World Revolution," in *The Study of Society,* ed. Peter I. Rose (New York: Random House, 1967), pp. 528–538.

[18] F. Clark Howell, introduction to *Man and Culture in the Late Pleistocene,* by Richard G. Klein (San Francisco: Chandler, 1969), p. xxv.

[19] Joseph Kahl, *The American Class Structure* (New York: Holt, Rinehart and Winston, 1961), pp. 257–262.

[20] Peter M. Blau and Otis D. Duncan, "Occupational Mobility in the United States," in *Structured Social Inequality: A Reader in Social Stratification,* ed. Celia Heller (New York: Macmillan, 1969), pp. 340–352.

[21] Burton Wright II, "The Generation Gap: An Intergenerational Comparison of Values" (Ph.D. diss., Florida State University, 1972).

[22] Jules Henry, *Culture against Man* (New York: Random House, 1963), p. 331.

[23] Guthrie, whom we discussed in Chapter 3 in reference to his contiguity theory of learning, was fond of saying that what Americans call "love" is nothing more than the tensions aroused by unfulfilled sexual desires. He may have been correct. The increase in sexual freedom in recent years seems to have been accompanied by the disappearance of the romantic novel and of romantic themes from motion pictures.

[24] Nelson Foote, "Family Living as Play," *Marriage and Family Living* 17 (November 1955), p. 297.

[25] Philip K. Bock, *Modern Cultural Anthropology* (New York: Knopf, 1969), p. 420. (Emphasis added.)

[26] Winfield Best, "Teensex: How Far do They Really Go?" *Ladies Home Journal* 90, no. 2 (1973), pp. 76, 78–79, 128.

[27] The actual degree of sexual relations outside of marriage of young people is, of course, impossible to determine objectively. However, venereal disease reports, the number of legal abortions performed on unwed girls, the extensive use of the "pill" and other contraceptives make it clear that there is considerable sexual activity. But such behavior has always been, and remains, much sought after by humans. Any claims that sexual activity has increased significantly in recent years is unproven. One thing is clear: there is less need or desire to conceal that behavior than in the past.

[28] Lowie, *Introduction to Cultural Anthropology*, p. 232.

[29] H. S. Bossard, "Residential Propinquity as a Factor in Mate Selection," *American Journal of Sociology* 38 (1932), pp. 219–224.

[30] There is a sociological reason for this. People whose socialization and, hence, internalized norms and values are the same or closely akin tend to be more comfortable with one another because reciprocal behavior is more predictable.

[31] James B. McKee, *Introduction to Sociology* (New York: Holt, Rinehart and Winston, 1969), p. 362.

[32] Marshall B. Clinard, *Sociology of Deviant Behavior*, 3d ed. (New York: Holt, Rinehart and Winston, 1968), pp. 543–544.

[33] Talcott Parsons, "The Stability of the American Family System," in *A Modern Introduction to the Family*, ed. Norman W. Bell and Ezra F. Vogel (New York: Free Press, 1960), pp. 93–94.

[34] Value judgments about whether or not the American family as a whole is good or bad will have to be left to others. To argue, for example, as Gresham Sykes does, that the American family is "a small fragile unit . . . without more extensive kinship ties," is probably correct in part, considering human mortality. But Sykes goes on, speaking of the "great loneliness that afflicts Americans," to conclude that "central to that loneliness is the isolation of the smallest unit of family structure—the nuclear family— with all other kinship ties so often stripped away or converted to an empty gesture." But Sykes's comments constitute value judgments based on an assumption that may be quite invalid. He assumes that in the "good old days" the joint or extended family and the small community provided companionship, love, and the feeling of belonging- ness. That, however, is doubtful, just as it can be doubted that the American family and community are any more fragmented or lonely than others have been over the centuries. Community cohesiveness, such as that in Durkheim's mechanical societies, involved a considerable loss of individuality and personal freedom; there is no evidence that this cohesiveness necessarily provided for an idyllic life in the emotional sense. See Gresham M. Sykes, *Social Problems* (Glenview, Ill.: Scott, Foresman, 1971), pp. 73–89.

[35] Robert Redfield, "A Critique of Cultural Relativism," in *Readings in Sociology*, 4th ed., ed. Edgar A. Schuler et al. (New York: Crowell, 1971), pp. 36–42.

[36] Edward Westermark, *A Short History of Marriage* (New York: Macmillan, 1926), p. 80.

[37] Reo Fortune, "Incest," in *The Family: Its Structure and Functions*, ed. Rose Coser (New York: St. Martin's Press, 1964).

[38] Russell Middleton, "A Deviant Case: Brother-Sister and Father-Daughter Mar- riage in Ancient Egypt," *American Sociological Review* 27 (1962), pp. 603–611.

[39] Talcott Parsons, "The Incest Taboo in Relation to Social Structure," *British Journal of Sociology* 5 (1954), pp. 101–117.

[40] This account is based in large part on the discussion in Joan P. Mencher, "The Nayar of South Malabar," in *Comparative Family Systems*, ed. M. F. Nimkoff (Boston: Houghton Mifflin, 1965).

[41] Linton, *Study of Man*, pp. 154–155.

[42] Yonina Talmon-Garber, "Family vs. Community: Patterns of Divided Loyalties in Israel," in *Comparative Perspectives on Marriage and the Family*, ed. A. Kent Geger (Boston: Little, Brown, 1968), pp. 47–67.

[43] In an economic sense, many of the kibbutzim were quite successful. As economic pressures weakened, the group may well have lost some of its cohesiveness. Formal and informal sanctions designed to weaken the family lost some of their force. We say

this not to indicate that notions that the nuclear type family, or family living in general, arises from some instinctive drive are tenable. One of the things that all societies teach is attachments to in-group members. It is difficult to find an in-group with more significant, learned ties than the family related by blood or marriage. The first kibbutz members had received just such socialization in their societies of origin.

[44] Talmon-Garber, "Family vs. Community," p. 56.

[45] Barrington Moore, *Political Power and Social Theory* (Cambridge, Mass.: Harvard University Press, 1958), pp. 160–178.

[46] He has, of course, a perfect right to make such value judgments as a private citizen but not, we would argue, as a sociologist or behavioral scientist. It is one thing to criticize society in general or any of its institutions in particular. But critics ought to be prepared to offer viable alternatives, which they usually fail to do. Insofar as sociology or any of the other social sciences is concerned, criticism based on value judgments is likely to confuse rather than clarify issues. If the family as we know it does change or even disappear, this change will take place because the present forms of family have lost their social utility, not because someone finds things to criticize. In the long run and often in extremely subtle ways, not only is society its own critic but it also acts as an agent of its own change. A close observation of how that process works is more likely to enable us to gain some control over society in general and social change in particular than angry words or criticisms leveled from some particular value position.

[47] Goode, *Family*, p. 109.

ANNOTATED BIBLIOGRAPHY

Cox, Frank D. *American Marriage: A Changing Scene?* Dubuque, Iowa: Brown, 1972. This book of readings attempts with some success to present a diversity of views on the institution of the family in general and marriage in particular, with the general concentration being on the changes that have taken place and are occurring in the institution of the family in America. No value position is taken with respect to the family in modern societies. There is a good, somewhat speculative, section on the family of the future.

Fullerton, Gail Putney. *Survival in Marriage.* New York: Holt, Rinehart and Winston, 1972. The author conceives of this book as a means of setting forth to students marriage as "a unique setting for the satisfaction of human needs, an opportunity not to be lightly dismissed in our increasingly dehumanized society." A considerable amount of real-life material on marriage gathered during interviews serves to enliven the book and make it more personal and meaningful. While the author has her own ideological point of view, which she frankly admits, she has nonetheless produced a book that should be useful for both those who have not yet married and those who have but are experiencing some difficulties in adjusting. There are several chapters that are particularly excellent: one concerning marriage in the culture of poverty, and one entitled "Love as Myth."

Goode, William J. *The Family.* Englewood Cliffs, N.J.: Prentice-Hall, 1964. This is about as good a general treatment of the family as can be found in a relatively few pages (120 pages). The treatment attempts with some success to combine sociological theory with the family and family relations.

Goode has written an analytical treatise on this important human institution which utilizes data from other societies both contemporary and historical.

Klemer, Richard H. *Marriage and Family Relationships*. New York: Harper and Row, 1970. This work reflects the growing interest in psychic satisfactions (or lack thereof) in marriage; it also approaches marriage from the institutional perspective and discusses such matters as endogamy, social factors in mate selection, and changes over time in the institution of the family. It contains much useful and pertinent information about commonly encountered problems in marriage as, for example, the budgeting of family income. The book offers students "a way of studying marriage and family relationships that can have direct pertinence in their own living experiences."

McKee, James B. *Introduction to Sociology*. New York: Holt, Rinehart and Winston, 1969, chap. 13. There is a scholarly and useful chapter on the family, with an excellent set of references to still other works on the family.

Miller, Daniel R., and Swanson, Guy E. *The Changing American Parent*. New York: Wiley, 1958. A well written work that considers a topic of considerable interest, particularly since many authorities are concerned with interclass differences in families and child-rearing practices. Miller and Swanson have some interesting things to say about *intra*class differences based on their study in the Detroit area.

Parsons, Talcott. *Family, Socialization, and Interaction Process*. New York: Free Press, 1955. This book utilizes psychodynamic theory (and indeed reformulates this theory) as a means of interpreting family interactions.

Toby, Jackson. *Contemporary Society*, 2d ed. New York: Wiley, 1971. Chapter 4 is concerned with initial socialization in the family of orientation. It provides a section on child socialization in industrial societies of great value in terms of providing an analysis of the nuclear family in modern, complex societies.

Westoff, Leslie A., and Westoff, Charles F. *From Now to Zero*. Boston: Little, Brown, 1971. Dealing with fertility, contraception, and abortion in America, this work is useful with respect to an important element in modern American families, the control of fertility. The thrust is generally sociological, and the discussions of factors conducive to fertility control as well as those militating against it are especially enlightening.

Yang, Martin C. *The Family in the Chinese Revolution*. Cambridge, Mass.: Harvard University Press, 1961. This presents not merely an excellent cross-cultural perspective on the family but also what the Chinese revolution has meant to the traditional Chinese family.

Zelditch, Morris, Jr. "Family, Marriage, and Kinship." In *Handbook of Modern Sociology*, edited by Robert E. L. Faris, pp. 680–733. Skokie, Ill.: Rand McNally, 1964. This article, although a trifle dated, remains an excellent review of the literature on family and marriage. It is highly readable and provides one of the better discussions on the subject of legitimacy.

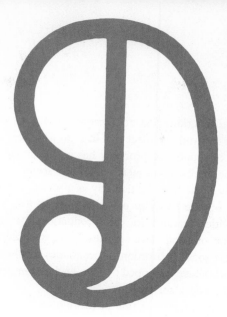

Economics,
Politics,
Education,
Religion:
The Rest
of the
Life-Support
System

Economics, Politics, Education, Religion: The Rest of the Life-Support System

Introduction

All social institutions perform functions that are considered vital to society. But it can be said that some institutions affect our lives to a greater extent than others. The institution of economics probably has an affect second in importance only to that of the family on all members of any society.

What, then, do we mean by economics, particularly as a social institution? Remembering our emphasis on the *functions* of social institutions, we will define economics as "activities leading to the production, processing, distribution, and consumption of goods and services." [1] If we accept that definition, we can see that the social institution of economics touches all of our lives, even those people who have "dropped out" to lead communal lives free from the complexities of modern societies.

In order to appreciate the essentiality of this institution—as determined not only by modern societies but also by subsistence-level societies—we will need to know something about how economics functioned in earlier periods. The development of economics follows similar stages as did culture, society, stratification systems, and so on. We begin again with the early hunting and gathering societies. Those nomads were constantly on the move in search of wild game, berries, and so on; they required fairly large territories for their subsistence. They had no need to build permanent structures. And the acquisition of material possessions was made difficult by the need to carry possessions with them as they moved around. Clearly such groups had (and have) relatively simple economies.

The "neolithic revolution"—domestication of animals and the cultivation of edible plants—was necessary for a marked change in the direction of economic complexity to occur. Either domestication or cultivation would create a change in the economic system, which in turn would produce changes throughout the society. Domesticated animals allow nomadic peoples to carry their possessions more easily, and they are able to acquire more material goods. As people spend more time cultivating crops, more permanent shelters become common. And cultivation leads to a more reliable food supply and eventually to a surplus of food.

However, the greatest changes in the economic system and, hence, the society as a whole, occur when the constant movement of the group becomes unnecessary and there is also a food surplus.

In the "Old Stone Age" [paleolithic] . . . men relied for a living entirely on hunting, fishing, and gathering wild berries, roots, slugs, and shellfish. Their numbers were restricted by the provisions of food made for them by nature and seem actually to have been very small. In the "New Stone Age" [neolithic] . . .

men control their own food supply by cultivating plants and breeding animals. Given favorable circumstances, a community can now produce more food than it needs to consume and can increase its production to meet the requirements of an expanding population . . . As a result of the neolithic revolution, the population had increased enormously. From the biological standpoint, the new economy was a success; it had made possible a multiplication of our species. [2]

The significance of a food surplus and its attendant increase in the populations is brought out by Lowie when he speaks of ancient Peru:

The tremendous importance of farming . . . lies not in what it did for mankind when first introduced but what it was capable of achieving after being itself greatly improved. The expert farmers of Peru could maintain a population of possibly three million. This meant a chance for more geniuses to be born, and for part of the people to enjoy leisure during which able craftsmen might perfect their art. [3]

In addition, more people brings about more human interaction, out of which arises even greater complexity.

Perhaps the most significant changes in human affairs, including life style, life chances, and economic complexity, were the result of the Industrial Revolution, which had its beginnings in the eighteenth century.

The sweeping changes in material culture and equipment, the new social forces of production, the economic reorganization that is termed the Industrial Revolution, reacted upon the whole mass of . . . people as no political or religious event had done. One effect obviously was to render possible a gigantic increase in their numbers. [4]

For the first time in history, the agricultural sector was not the prime center of human endeavour. The Industrial Revolution paved the way for the emergence of possibly the most significant aspect of modern society, the middle class.

This discussion has, of necessity, been brief. We have focused only on the two most significant stages in the development of the institution of economics, the neolithic and industrial revolutions. Both have had the greatest effects on the institution. And as economic complexity increased, societies changed and developed to meet the new situations.

Comparative Perspectives on Modern Economics

In examining the modern institution of economics, we will emphasize the American system. Our view will be essentially sociological. But we will also discuss evaluative judgments of the economy in order to highlight some criticism of the institution. As might be expected, the sociological approach differs from that of the economic, particularly traditional economics. Because these differences are important to any understanding of the sociological view of ceonomics, we will discuss them briefly.

Rational Economic Man   The assumption of rational economic man can be traced to Adam Smith's emphasis on individual self-interest as the foundation upon which market structure was built. Yet, as Weber noted, economic rationality itself cannot be based on irrational assumptions. Weber defines rationality as "the matching of means to a given set of ends." A person is rational if he takes the most efficient course of action in accomplishing his goals. But this still leaves the problem of choosing between different ends.

There often is difficulty in dealing with non-Western cultures because of the American assumption of a certain kind of economic rationality. A great many case studies have shown that when improved techniques are introduced into non-Western societies, people do not always respond by increasing their output. They may, instead, take the extra time to enjoy their easier lives. From the Western point of view, that is not rational economic behavior. Yet, in America, with an economy devoted to meeting a high level of consumer demands, is it rational to produce hula hoops to the neglect of basic housing or to produce military weapons while cities rot and decay? Current evidence seems to indicate that America is coming to realize that rationality does, in fact, involve a series of choices in accord with varying priorities.

Functional Interdependence   Robert Heilbroner offers three solutions to the economic problem. The first two are tradition and command. The third, he says, "is the market organization of society which . . . allows society to insure its own provisions with a minimum of recourse to either tradition or command." [5] Heilbroner's view that the "market mechanism" of the economy is largely isolated from other aspects of society is inadequate from the sociological position. Tradition, for example, still determines a large number of the more basic economic relationships. And command of political power does lead to economic privilege, as close examination of various political careers shows.

Given American society, reliance on market mechanisms to meet social objectives and needs may be unrealistic in the practical sense. According to Robert Ross,

Business cannot, and will not, move into housing or vocational education or preventive medicine unless it can make a good or sure profit. To insure profit means . . . that high risk sections—in this case, social reconstruction—must be

baited with government guarantees (tax incentive, cost plus contracts, and the like). It means that most intolerable social ills—more often than not directly traceable to the antisocial priorities of the profit motive itself—will now be sought for a price. It means that over and above immovable or inept municipal government a far more cynical and politically alien system of power will hold sway. But equally pervasive is the simple fact that modern industry presently organized has little or nothing to offer the angry poor.[6]

Ross points out that one cannot deal with the economy as a separate entity having a set of unique rules that govern its existence in isolation from other social realities. And functional inter-relationships and interdependence of all institutions forms an important part of the sociological perspective.

Quantifiable Variables   In dealing with the economy as an isolated institution, economists have relied on analysis based on a group of quantifiable variables. These *economic models* provide information about variables that allows government policy to be oriented toward accomplishing important economic and noneconomic goals. But many variables, once known and understood, become subject to some manipulation by the government. Today decisions on government expenditures, interest rates, the flow of gold abroad, antitrust legislation, and so on, are largely under government control. The American economy can no longer be seen as a free market. The notion of a free market represents an ideology, and the sociologist can study the way it operates in the same way he studies other things. However, he must look behind economic decisions for the groups who hold political power and at the consequences the decisions they make have on other parts of society.

Economics as a Set of Means   The sociologist views the economy as a set of means to accomplish the goals important to American society. Here again we must ask which goals have priority in that extremely complex and heterogeneous society. For example, resources allocated in 1965 to the Military Space Program would have built 3,469 elementary schools or provided 71,317 new hospital beds or built 143,688 units in low-rent public housing.[7] While traditional economic analysis may have the ring of cold value neutrality, the alternatives raised by America's ability to produce a trillion dollar gross national product requires seeing the economy as a means for accomplishing goals. Costs for goods and services cannot be measured in terms of dollars alone but must be thought of in terms of the alternatives that the means of production can provide.

Objectivity   The last point that seems to separate economists from sociologists is whether a genuinely objective assessment of the economic institution is possible. There has been a long debate over whether the functionalist approach to society is essentially conservative or radical. Some see functional analysis as the basis for a kind of status quo preservation because of its emphasis on equilibrium and integration, while others see in it the possibility for a critique of any institution. Since sociologists begin with a series of problems (the functional prerequisites), they can choose different ways of approaching and solving each of the different system problems. There is no need to structure an institution in any particular way as long as it meets the criterion of successfully fulfilling human needs. Yet, even when an alternative pattern for producing goods and services and for distributing them can be shown to meet human needs more adequately, society most often insists upon retaining the traditional ways. Simple inertia, value systems and beliefs, psychological resistance to alteration of established behavior patterns, and vested interests operate to maintain the status quo. Functionalism does, however, suggest that a departure from established structures is possible, but it is certain to be a gradual process. According to Durkheim, once something has become institutionalized, it may take on a "sacred" quality; any attempts at modifying it become unthinkable. And that is one of the reasons why institutions change slowly, even when rapid change would be beneficial. However, since relatively moderate changes often take place unnoticed, they do not rouse strong resistance.

World of Work

There are a number of other sociological issues concerning the way the economy works which are not contained in the economic perspective. "The promise of material well being is one thing . . . [and] the way the economic order operates is another." [8]

In our introduction to social institutions, we discussed how the institutions of a society help it survive by meeting certain functional prerequisites. But it does not necessarily follow that a pattern of behavior that is beneficial to a society is also beneficial to the individuals who are expected to carry out that action. War, for example, is beneficial to a society when it creates an expanded material resources base. War is, obviously, harmful, even lethal, to the men conscripted to do the fighting. With that discrepancy in mind, we can now begin a sociological examination of the economic institution.

Many authors have been concerned with how the millions of men and women who are employed in America feel about their work. Mills, writing in the early 1950's, set the tone for almost all the more recent commentaries when he said that "underneath virtually all experiences of work today, there is a fatalistic feeling that work per se is unpleasant." He acknowledges that when people were asked if their jobs were interesting and enjoyable, 64 percent of the white-collar workers, 85 percent of the professionals and executives, and 41 percent of the factory workers responded that it was.

But, as Mills notes, "these figures tell us very little since we do not know what the question meant to the people who answered it, or whether they mean the same thing to different strata."[9]

In our analysis we will separate the blue-collar from the white-collar workers in order to see if any real differences exist between the two groups in their attitudes toward work.

Blue-collar Attitudes Mills observed that workers in factories were much less satisfied than were those who worked in white-collar occupations. He felt that work for most blue-collar employees has little if any meaning other than the monetary rewards, which led him to comment that

the only significant occupational movement in the United States, the trade unions, have the pure and simple ideology of alienated work; more and more money for less and less work. There are, of course, other demands but they can be only "fixed up" to lessen the cry for money. The sharp focus upon money is part and parcel of the lack of intrinsic meaning that work has come to have.[10]

Employers have made several responses to those feelings on the part of workers, although mostly owing to union activity. But it can be said that, first, employers have been meeting the demands for increased wages; second, management is trying a wide variety of "human relations" approaches in an effort to improve worker morale and job satisfaction. But, as Argyris noted, when workers were told of the importance of their jobs, the reaction was not quite what management hoped for:

As the workers told me later, "How would you like to get up in the morning, look at yourself in the mirror, and say to yourself, 'The most important thing I can do is place four bolts in the right rear end of a car'?" He was asked, "But what would you want management to do? Tell you that it is a dull, boring, uninteresting job?" The worker's eyes lit up and he replied, "If they did, it would be the first time in eight years they weren't lying!"[11]

Mills's argument may seem to overstate the case for the blue-collar worker's feelings of hostility toward his work. So let us consult the writings of Harvey Swados, himself a worker in factories on and off for thirty years. He documents the feelings of factory workers he personally encountered in his assembly line experience:

The plain truth is that factory work is degrading. It is degrading to any man who ever dreams of doing something worthwhile in his life: and it is about time we faced that fact . . . Almost without exception the men with whom I worked on the assembly lines last year felt like trapped animals . . . Sooner or later, if we want a decent society, by which I do not mean a society glutted with goods or one maintained in precarious equilibrium by overbuying and forced premature obsolescence—we are going to have to come face to face with the problem of work.[12]

Patricia Sexton, also an assembly line worker for three years, echoes exactly the same sentiment with greater feeling:

Factories are like this in most places, I guess . . . But still if you work there, you don't like it, not one damn bit . . . The noise, dirt, and confusion drained off surplus vitality. Continuous supervised manual work produces a dull, deadening fatigue which you must experience to know.[13]

If the workers do feel this way about their jobs, can they do anything other than to demand higher wages? Many withdraw from their work by limiting their involvement in it. Studies over the past twenty years document the strategy for restricting output. In a factory, few are more despised than the "rate-buster" who seeks to prove that he is superior to the rest of the workers by putting out significantly more work than they do. The ways the informal social system of the factory controls this type of individual would make for good comedy, if the issues were not so real to those concerned. Sending defective parts to his bench, sabotaging work he has already done, refusing to talk to him, and in general making his life miserable are only a few of the tactics a work crew can use to bring a deviant member back to meeting, but not surpassing, accepted work norms.

Outside the factory, workers are finding that their increased leisure can make up for some of the things they are forced to endure as part of their jobs.

Each day men sell little pieces of themselves in order to try to buy them back each night and weekend with the coin of fun. Work is split from the rest of life, especially from the spheres of conscious enjoyment: nevertheless, most men and many women must work. So work is an unsatisfactory means to ulterior ends lying somewhere in the sphere of leisure.[14]

To modern man, if leisure is the way to spend money, work is the way to make it. When the two compete, leisure wins hands down.

White-collar Attitudes   On the surface, it would appear that white-collar workers are more satisfied with their occupations. But there is a growing body of literature to show that even without the physically tiring labor of the factory, there are equivalent problems for the white-collar employee. Joseph Bensman and Bernard Rosenberg notice that many white-collar workers in large bureaucracies evidence the same kinds of reactions blue-collar workers do: "overwhelmed by the impersonality of their work, [white-collar workers] give up the idea that it is meaningful or a suitable medium for their self-realization. By denying the meaningfulness of their work, they become less devoted and less efficient."[15]

Bensman and Rosenberg also point out the tendency of white-collar workers to overidentify with the organizational rules and purposes. This overidentification, while serving as a defense mechanism, precludes the recognition of what is happening in the larger social context. The following example gives a dramatic insight into the basic notion of the problem:

Nazi documents captured after World War Two indicate that on the day Adolph Hitler committed suicide and Russian troops were marching through the streets of Berlin, officials of the Reich chancellory were too busy to look out the windows. They were engaged in estimating and ordering paper clips for the next fiscal year![16]

That bizarre example illustrates the tendency, inherent in large organizations, of employees to get involved in their own routine to the point of blinding themselves to other events that greatly influence their lives. Being authoritarian to subordinates and overidentification with organizational purposes are part of the pattern with which individuals respond to the stress created by their jobs. In a poll conducted by the *Federal Times* (an employee-oriented government newspaper), "sixty-nine percent of the employees questioned said they would not go to work for the government if they had it to do over again, and seventy percent said they would advise their children to stay out of federal service." The reasons given for this negative attitude were that employees were discouraged from airing their gripes and that they found it difficult to get a satisfactory hearing from the Civil Service Commission if they were fined and punished. In addition, "the nation's biggest employer, the federal government, subjects its 2,500,000 workers to conditions that are rampant with back biting, rumor mongering, character assassination, and promotion by favoritism."[17] These conditions may well be what prompted Willard W. Wirtz, secretary of labor from 1962 to 1969, to remark at a trade union convention that employee relations in the government are thirty years behind those in private industry.

Future prospects   In order to be fair in our assessment of the situation workers face in modern America, we must acknowledge that any bureaucracy is neither as limiting as some have portrayed it nor as efficient as its champions claim it to be. Clearly, not all employees are frustrated by the kinds of conditions that we have discussed. However, such problems do exist on a large scale and have done much to downgrade the feelings of accomplishment that white-collar employees get from their work. Regarding the future, many authors doubt that they will be lessened. The increased use of electronic computers, operations research, and decision theory all point to still greater emphasis on the bureaucratic organization. There is a growing concern with the impact of data processing, the alienation of white-collar men, and "the slavery that chains the exurbanite to a commuting timetable."[18] These have led many to predict that the white-collar employee is entering the grey world of the working man. Argyris notes that

problems of today affect white-collar workers as well as blue and the signs are that they will grow worse as advancing technology and a rise in leisure time threatens to leave employees less involved in their work often without other interests to help them compensate.[19]

Argyris' view is balanced somewhat by his admission that America, as a society, has made progress toward helping employees meet their physical needs and achieve security and stability of employment. But there is a real need for attention to be given to the assembly line as well as to the management side of the giant corporation of tomorrow.

In spite of the genuine problems that work presents to many, workers both in factories and in large bureaucracies have often been able to shape a tolerable life style for themselves, based in large part on their relatively high wages. Money has made a real difference to these people, giving them the ability to compensate through leisure time activities for problems faced on the job.

In this context, it is interesting to consult the study that Eli Chinoy made of the American automobile worker in the 1950's. He found that many of the assembly line workers proposed to get off the line by opening small businesses of their own—gas station, grocery store, bar, and so on.[20] But statistics show that one out of two of these small businesses go into bankruptcy within the first two years. So chances for permanent escape from the factory by setting up a business are not good.

Historical view   The discussion has, so far, been somewhat one-sided because it neglected the historical view. To understand what is meant by the historical view, let us try to determine whether the lot of the greater part of the population of modern societies, including that of the United States, improved or worsened with respect to the way life was lived in peasant or preliterate societies. That much of the work in modern societies is dull, repetitious, and routine cannot be questioned. But can it be said that life in a nonindustrialized society is any more creative or fulfilling? In the main, life in preliterate societies was far from idyllic. Those who imagine pastoral scenes filled with happy, healthy people who do a little hunting and fishing to meet their needs and spend the rest of the time in joyful play are simply naive. Transgressions against the norms of such societies were often punished with great brutality. It is doubtful that, given a few ethnographies to read, many in any modern society would willingly trade places with those living in less complex societies. In passing, it should be noted that a common characteristic of people living in peasant societies is "fatalism," that is, a resigned acceptance of the way things are. But people in modern societies do find much wrong with their societies and, more importantly, insist that conditions be remedied. This change in attitude alone constitutes evidence that the present may be preferable to the past and that the future may be marked by societies more fully responsive to the needs of their members.

Extent of dissatisfaction Some comment seems advisable about the reports we have been discussing about widespread dissatisfaction with work. Many contend their work is unsatisfying, boring, repetitious, and deadening, and fails to fulfill people or give meaning to their lives.

Historically, it would seem that work per se has not been held in high esteem at least in Western nations. Aristotle, for example, considered work as distasteful and justifiable only as a means to the enjoyment of leisure. The early Christians regarded work as a form of penance. American society makes a clear distinction between "work" and "leisure" although, at times, more energy is expended in the pursuit of leisure than in activities called work.

In modern societies work is more than simply a way to earn sufficient money to meet one's needs, whatever they may be. Work is also tied to social position and the prestige accruing to social positions. Considering the low regard in which work is held in American society it is not surprising that workers with relatively low-status jobs report dissatisfaction. However, some of the reasons are unrelated to the actual position or job. Management is doing many things to increase job satisfaction by providing more pleasant work environments, regular rest periods, and a host of fringe benefits. The considerable commentary about the unpleasant and unfulfilling work in modern society can be criticized on at least four counts.

1. No viable alternatives are offered. It requires no great acumen to speak of work in modern societies as dehumanizing. Even if this were true, we look in vain to the critics for any constructive suggestions about how this might be remedied.

2. All the independent variables that could account for the subjective reports of high job dissatisfaction are not considered. In a society that views *any* activity labeled "work" as distasteful and that ties in the kind of work done with social position, factors other than the work performed affect judgments.

3. Much of the criticism of work in modern societies concerns the lack of fulfillment and meaning. That fulfillment and meaning can be brought back into one's life only through a return to an ancient pastoral way of life appears to be a romantic myth.

4. There is a failure to recognize that work, subjectively unpleasant or not, must be done if modern society is to continue.

The Poor in American Society

War on Poverty   Although many workers face the unpleasant realities of work, there is another segment of American society whose survival is often marginal: the poor who, either unemployed, on relief, or marginally employed, find themselves with barely enough money on which to live. Fortunately, there is a growing recognition of this poverty, and the concern has been the basis for the federal programs designated as the War on Poverty.

In beginning the poverty programs, it was first necessary to define who was eligible for aid, and some attempt had to be made to look into the problems of the poor. Mollie Orshansky of the Department of Health, Education, and Welfare attempted an objective measure of the people who inhabit this "other America." In 1964, she calculated the poverty line to be at $3,130 or less, a figure accepted by the Social Security Administration.[21] But Michael Harrington challenged the notion that progress has been made in dealing with the poor.

By 1966, the poverty line had risen to $3,335. While this index went up by nine percent, the average income of four-person families in America had increased by thirty-seven percent, so the new criteria meant that the poor had even less of a share of affluence.

He did not deny that some advances had been made but remained skeptical that the progress had more than scratched at the surface. Blacks and children of the poor were relatively worse off than before the War on Poverty began, and *subemployment* figures from the Department of Labor indicated that rates of 30 percent in New York ghettos and 50 percent in New Orleans ghettos existed as a major source of frustration. This may have contributed to urban riots. Even though there was a drop from 25 to 18 percent in the segment of the population still classified as poor, according to Harrington,

the War on Poverty has never been more than a skirmish and this provision for more feasible participation of the poor was quickly subverted by hysterical mayors. In theory, the country wants the disadvantaged to stand up and fight for their rights as all the immigrant groups did; in practice, we have knocked people down by taking this pious myth seriously.[22]

Harrington also pointed to some factors that give cause for a degree of hope in this situation. The "other America" has become more assertive in its demands for a part of America's promise, a factor that can serve as the basis for real political and economic advance. Behind this greater self-assertion is a sense of alienation based on the rhetoric of unfulfilled promises and poorly conceived plans for progress. The essential problem remains that poverty is a creation of the current American economic system.

The entire concept of welfare has become the center of an economic controversy concerning, among other things, the rights of the poor and the necessity for their working. In New York City alone, for example, the number of people on welfare has tripled since 1960. The city is going bankrupt in part because its contribution to these programs, at only 25 percent, represents about a third of a billion dollars annually. In addition wage supplements are available in New York to help raise the income of a family, where one member makes the minimum wage ($3,120 annually), as high as $6,000, $7,000, or $8,000 depending on the number of dependents and their ages. But oddly, hundreds of millions of dollars available to the poor by way of these supplements are unclaimed each year. Farmers, construction unions, the middle-income groups, and the wealthy all enjoy a host of tax breaks, housing and transportation benefits, and wage supports that are available to the poor but not used by them out of ignorance, fear or dislike of official involvement, or both.[23]

As the poor are called the "other Americans," there is a vast stratum just above them, the lower echelon of the working class, whom Peter Schrag has called the "forgotten Americans."[24] These are the workers who become the "heroes" of films such as *Joe*, hold down two jobs, hate hippies and Blacks, and live in white working-class districts of major cities. While sociologists have been busy finding out the attitudes of the unemployed and Blacks, virtually no one has paid attention to the people in the 18 million families who make between $5,000 and $10,000 per year, many of which have two or more wage earners. As Nicholas Kisburg, a research director for the Teamsters Union Council in New York, was reported as saying:

I do not think anybody has a single job anymore. All the cops are moonlighting and the teachers; and there's a million guys who are hustling, guys with phony social security numbers who are hiding part of what they make so they don't get kicked out of a housing project, or guys who work as guards at sports events and get free meals that they don't want to pay taxes on. Everyone of them is cheating.[25]

The reaction of these workers to the increase in welfare payments, greater taxes, and the like is reaching the point where they are refusing to appropriate new money for schools, roads, and hospitals. From their viewpoint, which emphasizes the values of hard work, authority, order, and self-reliance, what is going on in American society borders on the criminal. Thus, antagonisms between economic strata in society seem to be sharpening during a time of fairly widespread prosperity.

Assessment of the Government's Approach   As part of this assessment of the War on Poverty, a series of articles has been written pointing to the failure of the government's approach. Problems have arisen because most of the people involved in planning were neither poor nor had any real power to implement alternatives for changing the economic system. One example, provided by David Wellman, supports the hypothesis that certain individuals in American society are most concerned with keeping the present social system intact and not with changing it to meet the demands of marginal subgroups. From his study of a federally sponsored program called TIDE, designed to help Blacks in West Oakland, California, Wellman concludes that

> the program aimed to change the youngsters by making them more acceptable to employers. Their grammar and pronunciation were constantly corrected. They were indirectly told that in order to get a job, their appearance would have to be altered. It asked that they change their manner of speech and dress, that they ignore their lack of skills and society's lack of jobs, and that they act as if their arrest records were of no consequence in obtaining a job. It asked most importantly that they pretend that they, and not society, bore the responsibility for their being unemployed. TIDE didn't demand much of the men, only that they become white.[26]

In the end, the Blacks who were to be helped by the program ended up considering it as a $5-a-day job and viewing the whole effort as a big put-on by white society.

There is evidence that this has been the direction in which much effort by the War on Poverty has gone. Even the cautious *Reader's Digest* has featured biting and cynical stories. One, "Laredo Learns about the War on Poverty," describes the feelings of the ungrateful poor. After $630,000 had been spent for a civic and convention center and $752,000 for a building to house all the county and city welfare agencies, they found little change in their own condition. A total of more than $5,500,000 was spent to aid the poor in Laredo; about all it seems to have accomplished was to bring an end to the cheering, leaving poverty in the town as acute as ever—except for the War on Poverty job holders. "We are a demonstration city, all right . . . We're a demonstration of how to shatter high expectations and pass our problems over to a new Federal hierarchy."[27] The attempt to end poverty, while keeping the usual system of economic priorities intact, has proven an impossible dream because of certain unresolved issues. These involve an understanding of how the economy is controlled and where the centers of economic decision making lie.

The War on Poverty has not been lost for the rather obvious reason that it continues. But it will probably never be won unless some ideal society is established on a global basis. Since this seems unlikely, attention should be directed to the matter of improvement. Just what constitutes "improvement" is not only a relative matter but also depends on value judgements. An evaluation of the success or failure of some program designed to alleviate poverty may tell us much more about the evaluator than the program.

While remaining unsatisfied with progress toward improving the lot of the poor, it should be remembered that mankind has had very little experience with trying to remedy this particular situation and that even abortive attempts to aid the poor represent an improvement over the past. From the purely sociological point of view, trial-and-error efforts to alter a part of society should be examined. From the historical perspective, it should be appreciated that any such efforts are always marked by many failures and much dissatisfaction.

Integration and Conflict in Modern Economies

Competition In subsistence economies, in which little or no surplus is produced, conflict that is based in the institution of economics is absent. Although there are certain quarrels about many things including material objects, potables, and edibles, reciprocal giving is a general characteristic, as we have already seen. Speaking of the Hopi, Beals and Hoijer state:

When by reason of crop failure or lack of success in hunting or gathering, a family is unable to sustain itself, food and other necessities are provided by related families as gifts, these imposing on the recipients the obligation to give similar aid when it may be required. No family may hoard foods or other necessities when others are in want.[28]

In modern societies in which the business and industrial portion of the institution of economics is essentially competitive, the behavior of the Hopi would be difficult to understand. For example, when there is some rumored shortage of a particular foodstuff or desired commodity, it can be observed that buying of that item increases considerably over what is normal. *Scarce* items are not necessarily bought for use but to be hoarded against some possible need.

Most modern societies are highly competitive, and this competition filters down and includes competition between individuals. Some of this competition is, of course not necessarily related to economics. Amateur sportsmen, for example, compete, not for tangible reward, but for the satisfaction of winning. But most competition in modern societies is related quite directly to the institution of economics. For example as Ronald Pavalko makes quite clear, one's occupation is not merely a matter of pleasant working conditions and remuneration. One's occupation in modern societies pretty much determines one's prestige. That is, one's place in the socioeconomic strata is a matter of one's occupation. For example, "to refer to an individual as a professional is to accord him a high degree of prestige and respect."[29] Competition is not, then, simply a matter of fighting to get enough to eat or some kind of shelter but is also deeply concerned with such things as dignity, respect, prestige, and so forth. Since people often estimate class position by visible possessions, something that Thorstein Veblen called "conspicuous consumption" occurs with great regularity. What Veblen meant is that people "consume"—buy and use—visibly in such a manner as to indicate to others their social position and, in fact, to lay claim to such position.[30]

Private Property   Competitive economic institutions have as their base the cultural concept of private property that, in turn, rests upon the conception of scarce resources. There are two obvious features and one common misconception with respect to property. The obvious features are: (1) property *is* limited. There is only a certain amount available, an amount that is clearly exhaustible;[31] and (2) the available property varies considerably in the degree of desirability; this desirability is almost invariably expressed in monetary terms.

The common misconception is that the individual or group owning the property has certain absolute rights with respect to the use and disposal of it. But the ownership of a gun, for example, does not permit the possessor to fire the weapon where and when he pleases and at any target. Nor can the owner of a piece of real estate erect any sort of building on it that he desires. Ownership confers certain rights on the owner, but these rights are circumscribed by values and norms (some in the form of laws and regulations).

With respect to competition, it is the finite amount of available property that is important when we consider the institution of economics and conflict or integration. In a competitive society, there is constant conflict for those things—concrete and abstract—that are in limited supply. Members of modern societies compete individually and in groups for scarce rewards, which include real property, money, the various appurtenances of rank and privilege, and such abstractions as prestige and high status.

Sociologists have come to recognize that conflict is endemic in complex modern societies. In Chapter 13 ("Social Change") mention is made of Wilbert Moore's view that society is in essence a tension-management system.[32] The institution of economics in modern societies is concerned with both tension- and conflict-management.

Integration   The shift from subsistence-level societies to industrialized, complex societies, such as the United States, is highly dependent on functional integration not merely within the institution of economics but also between economics and the other institutions of society. In Chapter 8 we indicated that the extended family type, common in agrarian societies, has shifted to the nuclear form in industrialized societies. Durkheim's contrast between the mechanical type of society characteristic of agrarian societies and the organic form found in industrial societies serves to illustrate the importance of

Copyright © 1972 by Saturday Review/World, Inc.
Reprinted by permission from the publisher and Mort Gerberg.

"There's just one problem—getting parts."

In modern societies, highly specialized groups contribute to the needs of the society, with each group being dependent upon many others to meet its own requirements. If there were not considerable and continuing integration, modern societies would cease to function as industrialized societies.

integration in industrial societies. While some cooperation among members was essential in subsistence-level societies—for example, reciprocal giving— each family was an independent economic entity and depended upon its own members for most of its needs. In modern societies, highly specialized groups contribute to the needs of the society, with each group being dependent upon many others to meet its own requirements.[33] If there were not considerable and continuing integration, modern societies would cease to function as industrialized societies.

Normative Nature of Conflict Conflict is much easier to recognize in the economy than is integration. It is more dramatic and more personal. With rare exceptions, most of us have some stake in such conflict. The early structural-functionalists tended to view conflict as dysfunctional and societies as essentially equilibrium-maintaining systems. Even if, as we have observed, the structural-functionalists are wrong to view conflict as essentially dysfunctional, there *is* validity in their concept of societies as being essentially equilibrium-maintaining systems. This can be appreciated best when one considers the types of conflict that characterize modern societies.

Williams notes that "American culture is marked by a central stress upon personal achievement, especially secular occupational achievement."[34] As we pointed out earlier, one's prestige is very much tied to one's occupation, from which it follows that Americans tend to be highly interested in upward mobility if they occupy a low or intermediate position in the stratification system. It further follows that those having high socioeconomic status are interested in maintaining the status quo. Since "room at the top" is limited, there is a certain amount of on-going conflict, or competition, for highly valued statuses. Such high statuses with their concomitant prestige also involve other significant societal rewards such as access to money and the power associated with money.

Conditions in the latter half of the nineteenth century in America favored a laissez-faire system for business. Further, large businesses were the exception rather than the rule. Thus, the individual entrepreneur could, with relatively little capital, set himself up in business. But conditions changed; during the last two or three decades of the nineteenth century, exposés of the corruption and unfair practices of American businesses bred a new kind of journalism called "muckraking." As Richard Hofstadter pointed out, speaking of such famous muckrakers as S. S. McClure, Ida Tarbell, and Lincoln Steffens, "they were able . . . not merely to name the malpractices in American business . . . but to name the *malpractitioners* and their specific misdeeds, and to proclaim the facts to the entire country."[35]

Nothing illustrates the highly complex and interactional nature of the institution of economics better than the difference between the contemporary and the early twentieth-century interpretations of the concept of "free enterprise." The contemporary interpretation put forth, in general, by conservatives, argues that business and private enterprise generally suffer if overregulated by government; therefore, they should be left to their own devices as much as possible. In 1912, campaigning for the presidency, Woodrow Wilson claimed to be engaged in

a crusade against powers that have governed us—that have limited our development—that have determined our lives—that have set us in a straitjacket to do as they please . . . This is a second struggle for emancipation . . . If America is not to have free enterprise, then she can have freedom of no sort whatever.[36]

Today's conservatives would have cheered that speech, but they would have been laboring under a serious delusion. What Wilson was talking about was the *power of monopolistic business*, not interference and *regulation of business by government*. Since the beginning of the twentieth century, the institution of economics has come increasingly under normative regulation, which stems from two sources: (1) the laws and attendant regulations that govern the conduct of business in myriad ways, and (2) greater control of the significant products and markets by large corporations and the norms attendant upon such control. Currently, then, while conflict within the institution is a matter of competition between individual businessmen or business, there is also *conflict between the institution of economics and the institution of politics*. Essentially, the struggle is one between two institutions or, rather, individuals and groups representing these institutions in terms of functions, in which clear-cut victory is unlikely. Victory is unlikely (in any practical sense) because economics and politics have numerous interests in common; for the foreseeable future, any "victory" would not be in the interests of those representing either institution.

The struggle for both autonomy and legitimate power continues and can be expected to continue for a long time. Yet, it is only a "half-hearted" struggle conducted in accordance with norms that tend to create more of a *modus vivendi* in which businessmen bewail high taxes and government interference while politicians rail against vested interests and the power of monopoly. In a real way, this interinstitutional struggle is highly economic because it involves any number of quid pro quos. Realistically, when a corporation contributes funds to the campaign treasury of a candidate for high office, the corporation expects some political restraint with respect to that corporation should the person be elected. But, if corporations seek to influence politicians by contributing to election expenses, incumbent politicians are in a position to pressure corporations into making contributions to reelection funds. That this is done and that some politicians and business-men see nothing improper about it was made abundantly clear during the Senate inquiry into the Watergate in 1973.

What has occurred, particularly during the twentieth century, is that conflict within the institution of economics and interinstitutional conflict between economics and other institutions have come more and more under the control of norms that have emerged from widespread and continuous interaction. Conflict and competition are tolerated so long as they are controlled by some set of norms or rules which keeps them within reasonable bounds. In almost every case in which conflict goes outside normative bounds, some norms will emerge, however slowly, that have as their function the control of unrestrained conflict. Let us emphasize, in concluding this section, that the development of norms is a function of social interaction and the greater the amount of such interaction, the more normative will become the interactional behavior concerned.

Summary

So far we have emphasized the centrality of the social institution of economics. At the same time, we have avoided taking an economic determinism position. The on-going conflict between the institutions of economics and politics makes it clear that economics is by no means the decisive institution in all matters although its role and functions are of great significance. Essentially, we have taken the Weberian position that ideas (as well as ideals) are powerful forces in all societies, preliterate as well as modern. For example, power is by no means a matter of only economic resources in modern societies. The late Henry Luce, although he did have considerable economic resources, wielded great personal power through his ownership of *Time Magazine*. A story on Luce in *Der Spiegel* makes quite clear the force and power of ideas:

No one man has, over the last two decades, more incisively shaped the image of America as seen by the rest of the world, and the Americans' image of the world, than Time *and* Life *editor Henry Robinson Luce . . . No American without a political office—with the possible exception of Henry Ford—has had greater influence on American society. Luce . . . was the first—between the wars—to use the term American Century. Recently, at a party on board Onassis' yacht* Christina, *Winston Churchill counted him among the seven most powerful men in the United States, and President Eisenhower, while still in office, called him "a great American."*[37]

Finally, we would argue that even within the institution of economics, it is not matters of economics pure and simple that necessarily prevail. Indeed, ideas, if they are good ones, have a lifetime well beyond that of the originator. Who, for example, knows the names of any businessmen of ancient Athens? Yet literate people know of Socrates, the ancient Greek whose economic position was precarious but whose ideas have persisted over the centuries.

The rest of the chapter will discuss three more social institutions—politics, education, and religion. Politics and education are of singular importance in modern societies. However, all three are essential to modern societies. The word "modern" is used to indicate that the institution of education, as a separate institution, exists in only a rudimentary form in preliterate societies. Thus, as an institution, it is not essential to such societies, although it clearly is essential for modern societies. It must be kept in mind that *essentiality* is a key criterion in the definition of what constitutes a social institution.

POLITICS

Introduction

Political processes in the United States are closely associated with other normative patterns of behavior, including the economy, social stratification, and the increased use of bureaucracy as a tool of social organization. Since all institutions fulfill more than one function for the society, all evolve patterns of actions which are compatible among themselves, even though this integration may sometimes be incomplete. In a sociological framework, the study of politics cannot be done in terms of a conceptual scheme divorced from concerns about the larger social system. Many authors feel the line between the economy and the polity has become blurred, and they have coined the phrase "political economy." In fact that is one of the major differences between political sociology and political science. For the political scientist, the stress on such subjects as "forms of government" and the "dimensions of political power" is in terms of the internal processes and not the social system as a whole. Sociologists, especially those who favor the functional approach, focus on the "integration of all its analytically distinguished components, not of a specially differentiated class of these components."[38]

Concepts of Social Power

The study of social power involves more than simply the study of political power. It must incorporate economic, financial, industrial, and military decision making as well:

Power, in short, is a universal phenomenon in human societies and in all social relationships . . . Power supports the fundamental order of society and the social organization within it, wherever there is order. Without power there is no organization and without power there is no order.[39]

The working out of conflicts and the means of attaining some balance between opposing interest groups is one important concern of the sociology of politics. Much conflict takes place within a framework provided by society for disputes concerned with politics. But the maintenance of the general peace and the protection of lives and property is also a political matter because in some cases the law and the police are involved. Indeed, disputes of many kinds involve political considerations to a greater or lesser degree. A society without quarrels, disputes, or some open conflict is hard to imagine except as an ideal. Therefore, a key concern of political sociology is the maintenance of a reasonably stable society without the need of applying authoritarian control.

Since the political institution is primarily concerned with power and the exercise of power, let us now define power—power is the ability of an individual or group to attain goals in the face of opposition. That does not imply that the use of force or the threat of force is *necessary*. In a society where all individuals were well socialized and duly elected leaders behaved honestly and responsibly, no force or threat of force would be required; leaders would not exercise absolute power because they would be under compulsion to use their power in a responsible manner.

At the opposite end of the continuum, the exercise of power is closely tied to the use or threat of physical force—that is, to assassination and terror. As Mao Tse-Tung has said, "power comes from the muzzle of a gun." The speech of the late Black leader Malcolm X demanding either the "ballot or the bullet" [40] is a statement of one kind of underlying relationship between political power and the application of physical force. But the control of any society where such control is based *solely* on physical force or the threat of physical force appears impossible. No society could, in the long run, maintain the police, military, or paramilitary units necessary to keep control. Under conditions in which a substantial proportion of a society at least acquiesces to a ruler or set of rulers, sufficient force to keep dissidents in line may be available and practicable for a time. But to maintain power, there must be a gradual shift away from "terror tactics" toward less restricted policies. And Rousseau points out that "the strongest is never strong enough to be always master unless he transforms his strength into right, and obedience into duty." [41] The amount of time and effort spent on political indoctrination by the People's Republic of China, for example, shows that the leaders are very much concerned with establishing belief in their system of government. Force alone would not have been sufficient to keep this leadership in power, much less to bring about the changes that have transformed the face of China. It is true that the army in China has been the vehicle for much of the political indoctrination, and this use of the army is strange to Western observers from countries in which the army is under civilian control. The army in China has been very crucial to the establishment of respect for the government in power, and this has been accomplished for the most part with words, not bullets. The Chinese leadership, it seems, is aware of the truth contained in Rousseau's statement.

Legitimacy   In stable societies political and other power has been transformed into the right to use force under certain conditions, even if that power was originally obtained through force. Nations have a monopoly of the use of force within their own borders. This monopoly comes from the granting of the right to exercise power by others, and power takes on a new dimension called *legitimacy*. When power is granted legitimacy, *it is transformed into authority*. Even Hitler's Third Reich paid careful attention to presenting some semblance of legitimacy, even though active opposition was often silenced by force or the threat of force. The Nazis understood that authority, the only kind of power that can become institutionalized, serves as a basis for gaining conformity when any kind of opposition appears.

Legitimacy is at the heart of understanding the contemporary American political situation. The extent to which various groups accord to the political leadership the right to exercise power over their lives concerns political sociologists because of certain changes that have been occurring. Democratic stability requires a situation

in which all the major political parties include supporters from many segments of the population. A system in which the support of different parties corresponds too closely to basic social divisions cannot continue on a democratic basis for it reflects a state of conflict so intense and clear cut as to rule out compromise.[42]

In American politics various coalitions have been assembled, such as Franklin Delano Roosevelt's New Deal, or Lyndon B. Johnson's Great Society, that for a while reflected a high degree of legitimacy granted by very different kinds of social groups. But perhaps the best example of coalition formation occurred during the administration of Mayor Fiorello H. La Guardia of New York City. La Guardia appears to have had considerable personal appeal to a variety of groups in New York City, and this influence enabled him to govern a city that, according to some politicians, is essentially ungovernable.[43] Clearly, the mayor of New York or any other city governs by law. But if any elected official is really to control all the elements under his legal jurisdiction, he must also have de facto control. His authority must be accepted by the governed. For example, in 1973, the Watergate affair appeared to have weakened the power of President Nixon to govern effectively even though his legal powers were not greatly affected.

Distribution of Wealth

The distribution of wealth in complex societies is the most important source of a conflict of interests. According to some authors, economic development in Western societies has meant prosperity for a large enough number of people so that a stable democratic political coalition has been worked out.[44] This prosperity has made any violent social revolution impossible and unnecessary. An essential point in our analysis of contemporary political institutions is that one functional prerequisite any society faces is the need *to handle the conflict among opposing interests in distributing economic wealth.* In discussing his feelings about that basic requirement and the benefit provided by democracy, Lipset remarked:

My commitment to democracy as a political system does not rest solely on the belief that free debate and institutionalized conflict among opposing interest groups are the best way for society to progress intellectually as well as materially, but also on the assumption that only a politically democratic society can reduce the pressures endemic in social systems to increase the punitive and discriminatory aspects of stratification.[45]

Lipset has linked the workings of the stratification system (as one institution) with a system of political control, democracy. Stratification involves institutionalized inequality between people in a society, which is, according to some theorists, an effective and necessary way to get certain roles filled and the duties involved in these roles carried out on a day-to-day basis. But, given the system of rewards that are desired by the members of a society, there has to be some means to counteract the pressure toward inequality derived from the stratification process. "Pressure toward inequality" means more than merely that stratification systems involve inequality. Since it follows that in a stratified society some individuals and groups have more power than other individuals and groups, the more powerful will act to maintain and enhance their present positions. On a personal basis, power is directly related to life style. Life chances involve some fundamental things such as health, a long life, and opportunities for one's children. In a society that places a premium on achievement and success, people will tend to contest vigorously for available rewards and to take advantage of and utilize any power accruing to their present position in a stratification system. That those who are economically well off possess advantages in competition should be obvious. People already having power have a better chance of increasing it or, at least, retaining it than those lacking power have of obtaining it. To assume that there is some national or even worldwide conspiracy on the part of the powerful to retain and buttress their positions is nonsense. That they act in concert toward such ends is obvious.

Lipset recognizes the social pressures brought about by stratified inequality. He further notes the tendency by those at the top of a stratification system to endeavor to maintain an ongoing system for their benefit and the benefit of their posterity. But Lipset holds that such tendencies must be countered by some means and that the political institution must serve this purpose.

Democracy and equality are not simply ideological propaganda phrases for Americans. Democracy is not simply a means to the end of the good society, it is the only *society in which the social tendencies that press man to exploit man may be restrained.*[46]

Economic Decision Making and Control

Much of the criticism of the American political system has centered around the relationship between that system and economics. One key political problem in any society is who controls the allocation of resources. Who gets the benefits is largely determined by who controls the firms and businesses doing the actual production and who directs the government decision making under which they operate. The control of American corporations is a complex question. Some observers have argued that, in fact, no one controls the corporate economy; others have seen the board of directors and trustees as the chief control agents; and a third group feel it is middle management that retains the real power. Part of this disagreement stems from the fact that (1) there are over 24 million people who hold stock in American corporations;

Copyright © 1972 by Saturday Review/World, Inc.
Reprinted by permission of the publisher and Jeffrey J. Monahan.

"But if we rob from the rich and give to the poor, then the former poor will be rich and the rich will be poor, so then we'll have to rob from the former poor who are now rich and give it to the former rich who are now poor. Somebody ought to be able to figure a way out."

There is adequate substantiation that some small proportion of the population of America, as well as of other modern countries, receives a percentage of income far out of proportion to its numbers relative to the rest of the population.

(2) there has been a steady rise in a managerial group who manage but do not own businesses; and (3) there is documentation of the appearance of a "power elite" who retain control although not ownership or management.

Ownership of Stock   When we talk about "people's capitalism," with a large number of people owning stock in American enterprises, there is good evidence to support the position that this is, indeed, the nature of American stock ownership. But sociologists find it necessary to look at the issue of stock ownership as only one aspect of the control of economic resources. According to G. William Domhoff, there are four easily confused issues: the number of stockholders, the distribution of wealth, the distribution of income, and the standard of living.[47]

Distribution of Income and of Wealth   It seems that the majority of Americans do have consumer goods in sufficient quantities for an adequate standard of living. Many of the people in the top salaried professional positions enjoy life styles not too different from those in what has been traditionally called the upper class. There is adequate substantiation that some small proportion of the population of America, as well as of other modern countries, receives a percentage of income far out of proportion to its numbers relative to the rest of the population.

In the United States, while income tax is a major source of revenue for the federal and state governments, it was, at its inception, seen as a leveler of income. For various reasons, including the fact that only the wealthy have access to tax shelters,[48] it is questionable that income taxes have had any significant effect on the equalization of wealth, although they may have had some leveling effect on income.[49] "Income" refers to that which is earned in exchange for services or monies accruing from such sources as interest on savings accounts, dividends from stock and bonds, rental from property, and so forth. "Wealth" is what has been amassed as assets, such as savings accounts, stocks and bonds, land, buildings, machinery. It is important to distinguish between income and wealth in order that the relationship between the two can be understood. It would seem that those who pay a higher proportion of their income in taxes are less likely to accumulate wealth. Equally obvious is the fact that someone with an annual income of $100,000 who pays an income tax of 50 percent has a greater chance of accumulating wealth than the individual who earns $10,000 annually and pays 25 percent in income taxes. In actuality, the real-life situation favors those with higher income to an even greater extent. For example, a study done by Keyserling indicates that those who make under $2,000 yearly pay about 38 percent of their income in taxes of all types while those who had income in excess of $18,000 paid a smaller 31.6 percent.[50] The important factor is the obviously greater income remaining after taxes. The low income person is likely to have to use the remainder to meet the costs of living whereas high income individuals are apt to have some residue that becomes wealth.

Robert Lampman concluded in 1962 that wealth is much more unequally distributed than income.[51] For example, the amount of wealth held by the top 1 percent of adults in 1956 was 26 percent of the estimated total wealth of the country. In 1971, Domhoff wrote:

It seems certain that there has been very little reason to believe that there is any change in wealth distribution in the past several decades. Nor is there any reason to believe that there is any tendency whatsoever toward increasing equality.[52]

Number of Stockholders Other examples of a monopoly of wealth include the matter of stock ownership. In 1959, Heilbroner quoted a United States Senate committee report estimate that less than 1 percent of the families owned over 80 percent of the stock publicly held in industrial corporations. This is in accord with the findings of a trio of Harvard economists who have established that 0.2 percent of the "spending units" (meaning families) own between 65 and 70 percent of the publicly held stock.[53] That reinforces the conclusion drawn by Mills, who estimated that 0.2 or 0.3 percent of the adult population owned the bulk of the shares of the corporate world.[54]

Standard of Living   Other authors have examined the life styles of many of those who control the economic institutions in the United States. E. Digby Baltzell, for example, reasoned that the existence of an upper class establishment helps to provide the basis for leadership in a variety of different areas: "It is my central thesis that in order for an upper class to maintain a continuity of power and authority, especially in an opportunistic and mobile society such as ours, its membership must in the long run be representative of the composition of society as a whole."[55] Baltzell presents evidence that there is an "Establishment," the majority of whose members are in fact white Anglo-Saxon Protestants (Wasps); since the year 1880 they have tried to limit membership in this Establishment to their own kind. Baltzell saw the election of John F. Kennedy, a Catholic, in 1961 as the opening of the Establishment to the admission of certain minority groups. In 1968 a series of articles in *Look* magazine appeared to argue against Baltzell's optimism:

Of the 790 directorships of the fifty largest corporations, eighty-eight percent (88%) are held by apparent Wasp's; of 241 directorships of the ten largest commercial banks two hundred or eighty-three percent (83%) are held by Wasp's; and in life insurance companies, of the five largest with 131 directorships, one hundred or over eighty percent (80%) are held by Wasp's.[56]

Some authors view the progress made in civil rights legislation, fair employment practices, and the pressure on Congress for admitting Blacks as part of the process through which the Establishment is opening its doors. Yet for those trapped in the ghettos of the urban centers, this promise is so remote as to be within the reach of perhaps the next generation. And the realities have often led to riots and the looting of stores within the ghetto itself. If we want to understand what the economic control processes really mean to the poor, Black and white alike, let us look at the reasons that are part of the background of recent urban riots.

The numerous articles on the looting that took place during the riots of 1966–1968 pointed out the counterproductive aspects of rioting and other violence. But as some sociologists are beginning to recognize, there are often fundamental, unresolved issues concerning property rights that come to the forefront when the right "opportunity" presents itself: "The looting that has occurred in recent racial outbreaks is a bid for the redistribution of property."[57] However, one somehow doubts that those carrying away television sets, furniture, or liquor were thinking in such ideological terms of the redistribution of property. They were taking advantage of an opportunity as their way of life had taught them to do. Certainly, one of the independent variables of rioting is hatred and hostility fostered by envy of those who lead affluent lives. But riots are not a matter of economics alone; there is no instance of a riot by the white poor in the United States exclusively for economic reasons.

Economics may provide a precipitating cause for Black rioting and other violence but only when economics constitute a form of active discrimination. Black Americans are aware that a small minority of whites make considerable profit from stores owned and operated in the ghettos—a condition not unlike the exploitation of native populations by European colonizers prior to World War II. A recent review of the Kerner Commission Report about the causes of urban civil disorder noted that

what makes the Kerner report a less-than-radical document is its superficial treatment of racism and its reluctance to confront the colonized relationship between black people and the larger society. The report emphasizes the attitudes and feelings that make up white racism rather than the system of privilege and control which is the heart of the matter.[58]

Another surprising, well documented fact is that the poor pay more for shoddy merchandise than people living in the more prosperous suburbs pay for better merchandise. In suburbia, stores must compete with each other; are more selective in the giving of credit (so they can limit their losses); and, in general, sell better, more durable goods for lower prices than in the ghettos. The following example of a television set sold in a ghetto area will illustrate the point.

Base price of television set	$285.00
Ninety-day warranty	14.95
Selling price	$299.95
Tax	12.00
Total	$311.95
Down payment	−31.95
Balance	$280.00
Carrying charge (24 months)	88.42
Grand total	$368.42

The merchant who had figured out the cost of the television set revealed

that grand total is a real gimmick—my own thinking. You subtract the down payment so that doesn't figure in at all—otherwise it comes to over $400.00 and that would be no good, no good—they wouldn't buy. And the ninety-day warranty, *that's pure gold. The carrying charges, well if you want to know the truth, after you take the down payment away, they are between 25% and 38% a year. But you've got to do it . . .* [59]

And there are cases where the customer cannot meet the monthly payments, even over a 36-month period. Often the final payment is a "balloon payment." If the buyer cannot make this large final payment, then refinancing is necessary; such refinancing is, of course, expensive.

Obviously, the desire to own such things as television sets, washers, dryers, automobiles, and so forth, create a vicious circle for all poor people. With much less income, they are compelled by the exigencies of the credit system to pay more for a similar article than middle-class persons. While doubtlessly poor whites resent this, the situation is highly explosive with Black Americans because they feel that they are paying these higher prices because they are not merely poor but also Black.

If this situation is to be remedied not merely for poor Blacks but for all poor people, political remedies must be sought; and this involves political power. In the preceding discussion we have attempted to look at the structure of economic power in terms of the distribution of income and wealth, the presence of an establishment, and the reactions of people outside the system to the way it distributes goods and services. Now we will look at the political decision making process.

Political Decision Making

Politics and the Poor A vanishing breed in American politics is the "boss." This individual, in return for votes, made it his business to look after his constituents—sometimes in personal ways. The boss was someone the poor could turn to; with his disappearance, the poor are left more powerless than before. We note the almost total absence of people of low social rank in positions of leadership in the United States. Although the white poor have not begun organizing for political purposes, the Black poor have done so. And they may unintentionally aid the white poor in the process. There are two reasons why there is more political organization from the Black poor. First, Black poor have recently developed the "class consciousness" that Marx predicted for the proletariat as a whole. Second, active discrimination has prevented the cooptation of any sizeable proportion of able Black Americans by the affluent middle class. These factors taken together mean that Black Americans have not only a strong sense of identity but also individuals who are able to provide organization and skilled leadership. It may well be that effective organization by Black poor and group participation in the political process will do more for the poor in general than the numerous and uncoordinated programs presently in operation. The disenchantment of affluent young whites with the system and their un-willingness to work in it may serve to create opportunities for Black poor in the United States; such opportunities will be eagerly grasped.

Alleviation of the plight of the poor in the United States is largely political. Within the framework of the extant political system, it is possible to organize successfully for such purposes as the attainment of power by the poor themselves. To be sure, considerable power may be and often is held by elites. But in an atmosphere of what Jean-François Revel calls "constitutional benevolence,"[60] changes can be made within the system. The long struggle between the British House of Lords and the House of Commons for real political power, which was "won" by the latter, epitomizes this essentially peaceful "revolution."

Power Elite: Military-industrial complex   Sociologists see the amassing of power in a few hands as a consequence of the ways in which complex societies organize their institutions to (1) meet the challenge of technology, (2) benefit from the economics of mass production, and (3) cope with the scale of modern living in general. Sociology rejects the extremist contention that there is some secret conspiracy to remove power from the people and to place it in the hands of a few elites. But even without a conspiracy theory, sociology does acknowledge that institutions can become unresponsive to the wishes of a sizeable proportion of the population. One major contemporary problem, the so-called military-industrial complex, illustrates the thrust contained in those statements.

One could support a view of the American political process as controlled largely by men who make up a small elite if the tie between governmental power, military power, and economic power was strong. But, as Dwight D. Eisenhower, in his farewell speech as president in 1960, indicated, decisions in one of those areas seem to call for and reinforce decisions made in the other two. The federal government has taken over a great deal of the responsibility for national planning. And that has required, in the postwar period, a vast increase in the public subsidy of the corporate world partly through the defense budget. In light of this, Richard Flacks sees that drastic changes are needed to avoid increasingly concentrated power exercised through elite control. He concludes that the further development of the trend toward merging political and economic control, if it continues un-abated, will preclude the possibility of achieving a more open, participatory democracy: "The two governments, political and corporate, are merged and this merger approximates an elitist corporationist model, hence breaking down even the modest pluralism which once characterized the system."[61]

During the build-up of American forces in Vietnam, there was the appearance of a merger between what Flacks called the two governments, political and corporate. But to assume that this is a permanent condition that marks the beginning of an elitist corporationist model and the end of viable democracy ignores situational aspects. During any national military build-up, the interests of government and certain parts of the industrial complex are convergent. Industry furnishes the military hardware and other supplies needed by the military. With the withdrawal from Vietnam, a somewhat different situation existed. While it was very much in the interest of certain industries to maintain orders for their products at a high level, it was no longer in the interest of politicians to provide orders at the previous level. There are some who advocate maintaining a strong military defensive posture, but others resist that attitude, at least in its extremes. To the extent that the government is responsive to the part of the electorate that is sufficiently vocal and organized to make known its opposition to large military expenditures, the merger cited by Flacks ceases to exist.

Civilian control Traditionally the armed forces have been under and responsive to civilian control in the United States. Since the commander-in-chief of all the armed forces is the president of the United States, in a nominal sense the armed forces are under the control of the voting public. In practical terms, the military bureaucracy is partly autonomous. It is not subject to any continuing civilian scrutiny, although the mass media do occasionally focus on the armed forces. But there is another source of scrutiny that may be less obvious. Through the enlisted ranks of all the services and, to a lesser extent, through the officer corps, flow thousands of young men and women who remain in service for only a few years. To assume that all or even a large proportion of them leave as staunch supporters of the various services is not logically possible. The various services also have reserve units, which consist of thousands of civilians who participate in military activities for only short periods on a weekly or monthly basis. These reserve units are comprised of people from all strata, including the high echelons of government. In 1959, for example, a Senate subcommittee disclosed that seventy-four senators and representatives had held or were holding reserve rank in the armed forces while serving as legislators.

Continuing contact between civilians and the military is also evident in other spheres, for example, research undertaken for the military. According to Marc Pilisuk and Thomas Hayden,

more than three hundred universities and non-profit research institutions supply civilian personnel to and seek contracts from the Department of Defense. Approximately half of these institutions were created specifically to do specialized strategic research, probably the most influential of these is the Rand Corporation.

Another example, which Pilisuk and Hayden view with some alarm, concerns the thousands of military offers who are assigned to nonmilitary duties in various departments of the government. According to them, "these trends clearly demonstrate that the traditional American separation of military and civilian is outmoded."[62]

But has there been a traditional American separation of military and civilian? Until World War II, the United States had traditionally relied upon a civilian militia. What has been traditional has been *civilian control* of the armed forces. Any separation of the military and the civilian would tend to create a military elite with considerable real power over both military and civilian population.

Other checks on freedom of action   Aside from situations in which something akin to a military-industrial complex does appear, it can be argued that the pluralism in American society places certain checks on the freedom of action of military, political, and industrial elites. Two celebrated cases are the CBS television documentary "Selling of the Pentagon" and the publication of classified Pentagon papers by the *New York Times*.

Summary

"Vested interests," and there are many with considerable power in the United States and other countries, often operate successfully to protect their own interests. Nevertheless, there has been much legislation in the United States which has taken vested interests into account and attempts to place legal constraints on their operations in an effort to protect the public good.

As an institution, the economy will always be marked by considerable tension and conflict. Each citizen is personally involved in economic matters. When individuals and groups are locked in a struggle for economic advantage or economic survival not only life styles and life chances are involved but power as well. To the extent that the personal fortunes of individuals are linked to some organization, they will behave in ways to further that organization even to the detriment of other organizations and individuals. The principal problem, then, is to establish and enforce rules that keep competition within reasonable bounds. Although the "games" analogy cannot be strictly applied to the institution of economics, there are parallels that seem to apply. For example, it would be difficult to imagine a football game without rules or referees or a boxing match without some equality of weight between the contestants.

A democratic society requires that the institution of economics be subjected to continuous scrutiny and that the gaining of too much power or misapplications of power be checked as necessary. The increasing pluralism of American society should produce increasing scrutiny of and checks on the economy.

Drawing by Stevenson; © 1973.
The New Yorker Magazine, Inc.

Education can play a key role in producing and directing social change, and that aspect of the schools' relationship to society is currently receiving increased attention.

"What do you want to be when you grow up?"
"A sub-systems communications engineer in synchronous-satellite development, establishing module design and defining internal-external interface requirements and performing breadboard and flight-hardware tests."

EDUCATION

Introduction

The educational institutions of a society fulfill a variety of the functional prerequisites. At one time, the most important prerequisite was thought to be the provision of the skills and training required by technology. The writings of such educators as Max Rafferty, Admiral Hyman Rickover, and James Conant have stressed the need for education to be useful to a society —that is, to have "practical" applications. After the Russian satellite Sputnik was launched in 1957, there was an intensive examination of the American philosophy and system of education to determine how and why it had "failed." So, in the decade of the sixties, America made a commitment to put a man on the moon, which it has since fulfilled. But there is now a move to re-examine the American system of education and its goals, not in terms of an expanding space technology, but in terms of a rapidly shrinking world. Education can play a key role in producing and directing social change, and that aspect of the schools' relationship to society is currently receiving increased attention. Universities, for example appear to be responsive to whatever society wishes. Provided sufficient funds are furnished, universities will attempt to carry out what they perceive to be the desires of the society in which they are located. That and other factors, including desegregation, have made schools very much a political issue.

As a nation, America has a strong tradition of keeping education under local, community control. In New York City, for example, with over 1,000,000 children in schools, there are over 5,500 full-time administrators, including 2,200 principals and assistant principals. The board of education controlling this bureaucracy consists of nine members, *all serving part time*. They exercise power through their representative, the superintendent.[63] One study indicated that superintendents are often caught by conflicting demands made by people external to the schools.[64] Parent-teacher associations, school board members, taxpayers, town financial committees, church and religious groups, and so on, have tried to influence educational decisions by putting pressure on the superintendents. And in recent years, the federal government has also pressured the schools to implement part of the federal desegregation policies. Many parents moved their families to the suburbs in order to avoid racial mixing. Integration aroused the fear that educational quality would be lowered for all.

Maintaining the Stratification System

Among the powerful influences the schools exert on all other institutions in society is the maintenance of the economic and political power dimensions of the stratification process. According to Dan Dodson, a major function of the school is "to take the children of the community and teach them their place in the power order. They are taught in such a way that all will understand their failures as their own rather than those of the system. Otherwise they would rebel and blow the system apart."[65] It is an important function of the institution of education to socialize children into the larger society. For a variety of reasons too complex to be considered in this book, children are often indifferently or even destructively socialized by the schools. This is particularly true of the poor in general and Black Americans in particular. In his writing about the education of Blacks in Boston, Jonathan Kozol illustrates how education can function to keep minority groups "in their places." Some Boston school teachers spoke of their school as a "zoo" and the Black children in their charge as "animals."

In discussing how the economics involved in making school decisions reflect the power structure of Boston, Kozol tells of the decision not to integrate the Black children of one area into existing white facilities. Instead the Boston school system decided to buy a forty-year-old abandoned Hebrew school and refurnish it at a cost of $240,000 when, in fact, there was an adequate school with space for the children a couple of miles away.[66]

In 1937 August B. Hollinshead did the first major study that related the treatment of children in school to their position in the stratification system. Since then, much research has been carried out in that area. The conclusion of another author summarizes the vast body of literature that has developed.

In molding children to a stratified society, the school engages in continuous sorting and selecting of students—rating, ranking, and separating them into quality groups. Children from higher social strata usually enter the "highest quality" groups and those from lower strata the "lower" ones. Schools' decisions about a child's ability will greatly influence the kind and quality of education he receives as well as his future life, including whether he goes to college, the jobs he will get, and his feelings about himself and others.[67]

Preparation for Higher Education

Schools, then, are faced with the problem of sorting out students for different kinds of treatment. Large schools often resort to the "track system," which groups students together largely on the basis of test scores although some other criteria may also be used. The children of the poor are more often found on the lower tracks. Aside from the fact that the children are very much aware of the significance of each "track," the category into which a child is placed determines who goes where—on to college or out into the larger society to seek unskilled or semiskilled jobs.

The matter of higher education is an important one in any modern society. Aside from the prestige still conferred by a college degree, it is clear that income and amount of education are positively correlated. While not all high school students go on to university, a sizeable proportion do. In the past, it was not always possible for all who wanted to go to college or university to gain admittance. More recently state-supported junior colleges and universities, with low tuition for state residents, have been established making it economically possible for many more people to matriculate. But admission to a college or university is not the only problem a high school graduate faces. He or she must be able to complete the course of study.

Equal Opportunity

The attrition rate at most colleges and universities for first-year students is high. There are several reasons for that: (1) Some come from elementary and high schools where their academic preparation was inadequate for successful college work. (2) Some are insufficiently motivated or are attending college for reasons unrelated to obtaining an education, for example, at the insistence of parents. (3) Lack of ability. (4) Combinations of those three factors.

In a democratic system and under the ideals by which state university and junior college systems are conducted, admission must be open to all who desire to attend. The rigors of college life, however, are often too much for some students, and they drop out and pursue other activities. Colleges and universities are under no compulsion to promote students to the next highest grade, which is often the case in elementary and high schools. Nor do universities and colleges present instruction at the level of a common denominator. The student who lacks ability, who is unmotivated, or who lacks adequate preparation tends to hinder the operation of college classes. And he or she must be persuaded to leave voluntarily. This process, called "cooling out" by Burton Clarke,[68] involves getting a student to acknowledge that his failure on examinations and in course work is not the fault of the college or university, but, rather, his own lack of ability.

In American higher education the aspirations of the multitude are encouraged by open-door admissions to the publicly-supported colleges. The means of moving upward in status and of maintaining high status now includes some years in college, and a college education is a prerequisite of the better positions in business and the professions. The trend is toward an ever tighter connection between higher education and higher occupation as increased specialization and professionalism insure that more persons will need more preparation.[69]

That equality of opportunity to enter a junior college or university creates serious educational problems because, as we have shown, not all entering students have equal ability. The junior college has an important series of functions to perform aside from preparing some students for further education at a four-year college or university. For those who do not intend to continue their education beyond a junior college, some opportunity for upward mobility is provided. Junior colleges also help to cushion the ego-bruising effects of failure by suggesting alternatives to the failing student. There is a reorienting process that involves essentially the restoring of feelings of personal worth to failing students through the use of guidance and counseling, remedial instruction, and so forth.

Martin Trow attempts to clarify this issue by considering the problems of making the most of abilities of two different but related groups—children from *culturally deprived* backgrounds and children *lacking adequate academic preparation* for higher education. The "culturally deprived" are made up largely of Black and white lower class children. For them, real problems exist in their home life, in their attitudes toward work in school, and in the reaction of teachers to them. An increasing number of authors are taking a strong stand against the argument that such children cannot learn in the schools because of their deprived backgrounds. Some research complements Kozol's in showing that the schools themselves compound the problem of achievement and that poor children fall farther behind the others the longer they stay in school.

"In contemporary America," says Trow, "potential talents are not often realized unless they are developed and certified through formal education and increasingly through higher education."[70] The realization of talent in lower class children has been far lower than in the middle-class child. The inability of the educational system to develop existing talent in all segments has been justified by the argument that the poor child has less potential talent available. However, frequently bright children from the lower classes are not *encouraged* in the same way as those from higher strata. The enormous impact that encouragement seems to make in changing a child's IQ in the early years of school was shown in the remarkable study *Pygmalion in the Classroom*. The effect of teacher expectation, a social variable of importance in how children develop, was shown to account for a seventeen point increase in IQ in the first grade. In other words, when teachers expected children to be bright, their IQ increased sharply.[71]

A host of studies have shown that intelligence-test scores are greatly influenced by environment. And some social scientists feel that IQ is largely environmentally determined, with those from certain backgrounds being favored and those from others being hurt.

Intelligence tests are constructed by psychologists who are largely middle-class individuals. These tests are, for the most part, based on the kinds of information, values, and attitudes to which middle-class children are likely to be exposed. Poor children simply are not familiar with the middle-class experiences on which the tests are based. It is not surprising, then, that poor children tend to do poorly on such tests. Nearly all psychologists hold that the races do not differ significantly in terms of *inherited* ability. Since the majority of Black children come from poor families and since poor children tend not to perform well on intelligence tests, there are those who hold that Blacks are less intelligent, which is not the case. However, from the purely practical standpoint, intelligence-test scores can be used to predict success and nonsuccess in school because most schools are run by middle-class individuals who expect students to have middle-class knowledge and to behave in middle-class ways.

It is now recognized that intelligence tests cannot be relied on to measure *innate* learning capacity in all children. While it seems as though the IQ question may never be closed completely, the problem now is no longer one of low intelligence-test scores. If it is assumed that intelligence is a relatively fixed entity in children, then the best that can be done is to tailor the education of a child to fit his abilities. That is what Trow refers to as the older "liberal" view of education which seeks to

reduce or remove all external handicaps of birth or poverty which interfere with the translation of intelligence into academic achievement, and thus into social, political, and economic leadership. In this view, intelligence is largely genetically given and substantially fixed.[72]

LAUGHING MATTER

$$\frac{1}{+1}$$

© 1973 by The Chicago Tribune
World Rights Reserved   9-18

Reprinted through the courtesy of the
Chicago Tribune—New York News Syndicate, Inc.

"Look, I'm no Einstein!"

It is now recognized that intelligence tests cannot be relied on to measure innate learning capacity in all children.

Radical Perspective With a change in the basic assumption about the nature of intelligence from a fixed, measurable entity to one capable of growth, there develops what Trow has called a "radical perspective" on the role of school in society. This perspective stresses that the problems a poor child faces are not only financial and cultural but are also motivational and emotional. And it is up to the school system to find a way to meet and solve all dimensions of the problem, not simply those with which it has been traditionally willing to deal—financial and cultural deprivation. It has been the failure of programs based on the liberal position that over the past several decades has caused a more radical view to develop among some educators.

A basic distinction between the liberal and radical concepts of equality of educational opportunity is the demands they make on the school for the success of the student. Under the liberal concept, responsibility for the student's success or failure is placed largely on his own shoulders; although the quality of the school and the teachers is thought to have some bearing in the matter, the primary cause of success or failure in schools seem to be the student's own moral and intellectual resources. Under the radical concept, the student's success, or more commonly failure, is seen as a failure of the school or the teachers, a failure to create in the child the moral and intellectual resources that lead to academic success.[73]

The radical perspective would shift the onus for failure from the student to the school. Extending this view to cover all of society would have appalling consequences. No failure, no crime, no sins of omission or commission could be held as a matter of individual responsibility; society would be to blame. Since a large part of the socialization process in all societies functions to prepare members for taking a responsible and integrated part in their own society, it is difficult to perceive how any society could survive that freed its members from policing their own behavior and accepting responsibility for their own actions.

There is no question that American schools do not function as effectively as they could in helping students to realize the fullest possible potential. But the realization of the potential of any individual depends on a complex of factors and circumstances including socialization by the family, early child-hood experiences, inherited aptitudes, and personality structure, not to mention the experience or lack of experience of success. To hold the schools responsible for the total life experiences of their students would be not merely impossible but foolish.

Summary

The institution of education is growing not merely in the modern, industrialized nations but also on a world-wide scale. This applies to both formal schooling of children and continuing education of adults. Industry conducts considerable in-house training and schooling for employees and often subsidizes their education at universities and technical schools. Night schooling for employed adults at both the secondary and college levels continues to grow. Not too long ago, a college graduate could expect his education to last a lifetime. In many areas, this is no longer the case. But perhaps the most important educational reform required is a change in emphasis on what is taught. John Diebold has said that "there must be fundamental changes in our educational methods to enable students to learn how to learn instead of only acquiring specific skills that are subject to obsolescence." [74]

RELIGION

Introduction

Religion is an ancient institution, quite possibly predating *Homo sapiens*. In the Middle Paleolithic epoch, characterized by the Mousterian cultures, Neanderthal man left some evidence of religious beliefs. "Intentional burials with offerings and altarlike assemblages of the skulls of cave bears suggests the existence of religious ideas."[75] With respect to these Mousterian burial practices, Childe wrote:

This ceremonial bears witness to the activity of human thought in unexpected and uneconomic directions. Faced with the terrifying fact of death, their primitive emotions shocked by its ravages, the . . . Mousterians had been roused to imaginative thinking. They would not believe in the complete cessation of earthly life, but dimly imagined some sort of continuance thereof in which the dead would still need material food and implements.[76]

Functional Utility

While we have no way of knowing what the Mousterians actually believed, Childe's evaluation seems reasonable. And that leads us to consider the *functional utility of religion.* And we must remember that human institutions are constellations of values, norms, behaviors, roles, and folkways organized around some function deemed to be of critical importance to the society.

Psychological Functions Even to modern man there is much that still defies scientific explanation. The vastness of the universe, its ultimate boundaries, and its very beginnings are still mysteries. How much more confusing the world must have been for our progenitors. Religion has provided, and still provides, many orderly and coherent explanations of the universe. Aside from such metaphysical matters, as Francis Merrill noted,

the function of religion is to reconcile man to his fate. Human beings need some assurance in order to bear the human condition, as they see their loved ones suffer and die and know that they themselves will ultimately meet the same fate. Man lives under conditions of uncertainty, when his well being, safety, and even his life may be lost at a moment's notice.[77]

To the extent that Merrill is correct, we could expect religion to be of more critical importance to societies that lack even a rudimentary science—such societies would, of necessity, need to rely on religion for explanations of many phenomena in addition to death. Parsons notes, in speaking of criteria for societal primitiveness, that in primitive societies, religious orientations to the world are of overwhelming importance.[78]

Those functions, however, are largely psychological; they are functions performed by religion for individuals. Does religion have recognizable functions for societies?

Societal Functions Durkheim, whose work is often regarded as the classic study of religion in society, contends that:

all known religious beliefs, whether simple or complex, present one common characteristic. They presuppose a classification of all things, real and ideal of which men think into two opposed classes or opposed groups, generally designated by two distinct terms which are translated well enough by the words profane *and* sacred.[79]

According to Durkheim, there is no common quality of things treated as sacred that could account for the attitude of respect or veneration shown them. For example, there is no intrinsic value in two pieces of wood, one shorter than the other and crossed at right angles to one another. But to a Christian two such pieces have great sacred significance. And there is no intrinsic value to a certain cultivated pungent, marsh herb of North Borneo. But to a female Dusun specialist in divination and curing rituals, it is known as kAmbarANun and has great sacred significance. A principal difficulty for sociologists, anthropologists, and students of religion is identifying the *referents* for sacred symbols—that which in a particular culture gives sacred meaning to a particular symbol or set of symbols. To illustrate, *Das Kapital* may be merely a book to some or a work of the devil to others; to the dedicated communist, the writings are highly sacred.

The Supernatural

For Durkheim, society was the real object of religious veneration. Since the attitude of respect for sacred things is essentially identical with the respect for moral authority, religion *in one form or another* serves to buttress the authority of society by making adherence to its values and norms a sacred duty. The very concept of honor, seemingly a personal matter, involves behaving correctly, that is, with a somewhat rigid adherence to the code of a particular society. Honor, then, is considered to be either upheld or lost depending upon whether one adhered or not. The force of such feelings and the high regard for the sacred should not be underestimated in terms of directing and compelling human behavior.

But how is the leap made from respect for moral authority, as epitomized in the values and norms of a society, to a concept of the supernatural? Durkheim believed that the relation of men to their society is akin to the worshipper before his God. A society is seemingly supernatural because it dominates its members by closely controlling their thoughts and desires. Men feel confident and at peace with themselves when fulfilling their society's conventions.[80] Durkheim, in explaining the transition from society to the supernatural, explained

that men develop a concept of personified supernatural beings directly from the model that their society provides. Unaware as they generally are of the extent to which overt behavior and inner impulse are formed by relations with other people, men find themselves in the hands of mysterious forces. Unlike other forces, these social customs seem to speak to individuals, chiding them for misbehavior, directing them to choose some goals rather than others, and rewarding their conformity. The thoroughly socialized individual has so acquired these social standards that they are effective in directing his conduct even when he is quite alone.[81]

Religion and Modern Societies

Durkheim's views, while likely in consonance with the realities of simpler societies, are not satisfactory for modern, complex, industrialized societies. As Weber (and later David McClelland and others) demonstrated, ideas can serve as prime causes of change.[82] It was the so-called Protestant Ethic, especially as developed by the Calvinists, that led to the value that hard work and frugality had merit. Both attributes are closely related to the growth of modern industrial economies, and achievement in this world through hard work is a value characteristic of almost all Western nations. Some research has strongly suggested that in the United States there is a specific relationship between religious preference and economic success. Albert Mayer and Harry Sharp, using data collected by the University of Michigan, showed that religion as a social factor is related to "this-worldly" achievement and success:

From one perspective, life in a modern community may be viewed as a hotly contested foot race in which families vie with each other in the hope of material reward. The rewards are rather well defined in Western society; they include such achievements as economic success, collection of worldly assets and status to be derived from the attainment of these culturally approved goals.[83]

Mayer and Sharp emphasize the competition for material rewards; they have stated that success, as measured in American society, is related to religious preference. But to accept this conclusion uncritically conceals that formal religion is exercising less and less influence with respect to other institutions including the economic. If the original stimulus for the Industrial Revolution came in substantial part from Calvinism (as epitomized by the Protestant Ethic), the current stimuli are found in society itself. The values and norms of the Protestant Ethic have been incorporated into modern societies. Very few achievers are concerned with demonstrating to themselves or others that they are one of God's elect. This drive for achievement and success exists because men find themselves in the hands of mysterious forces; these "mysterious forces" are, according to Durkheim, society itself.

But the process in Western societies has been more than the incorporation of essentially religious values and norms into society as a whole. The process has been and is one of *secularization* (or desacralization)—that is, the elimination of religion as a symbolic representation of social integration. In other words, religion per se is no longer the force that binds a society together. Instead, a modern society is held together by a mutual interdependence of the parts of that society including its institutions.[84] A salient characteristic of modern nations and of the modernization of developing nations is the increasing differentiation of institutions. Politics, education, economics, and to some extent the family have become increasingly interdependent upon one another and increasingly *less* dependent upon religion. Man's understanding of himself, the values and norms that regulate the various institutions of society (other than religion), and the world in general is viewed and regulated less and less in religious terms or in a religious framework and more and more in terms of natural processes. This does not mean, as it did in the nineteenth century, that there is a general hostility toward religion but, rather, that religion is ceasing to be a viable social institution in modern societies. Organized religion is no longer clearly involved with meeting functions deemed to be of critical importance to the society.

Failure as a Social Institution There are at least four reasons why religion no longer meets the criteria for an institution in modern societies.

1. The power of religion stems directly from belief. For example, among the Dobu, a people of northwestern Melanesia, incantations and charms are bought and sold. If the buyers did not believe in the efficacy of these charms and incantations, they would be valueless. Similarly, if any substantial proportion of a society does not believe in religious dogma or that priests, rabbis, or ministers are intermediaries between them and a supreme being, the ability of those functionaries to control or direct other institutions of society or the behavior of members of that society is lost.

2. Coercion in the form of sanctions applied or threatened is necessary if the behavior of members of a society is to be constrained within approved limits. The sanctions available to modern religious authorities are relatively few—for example, expressions of disapproval, or in extreme cases, excommunication from an established church. In the past, excommunication was a terrible punishment; now it is relatively ineffective. The excommunicant can, if interested, find other denominations willing to accept him or her as a member.

3. Religion no longer pervades all aspects of life including other social institutions. Economics, politics, education, and even the family are now geared much more to this world than the next.

4. Many aspects of organized religion seem to be dysfunctional. With respect to the population explosion, for example, many hold that the stand of the Roman Catholic Church against contraception is harmful to mankind. Other examples, and there are many, revolve around the unreasoning ethnocentricism of many religious groups which results in an institutionalized

and continuing hatred of other religious groups. Clinical psychologists and psychiatrists point to rigid religious codes of conduct, particularly in regard to sexual matters, and the serious personality problems arising out of a concept of sin.

Power of Organized Religion   The fact that organized religion is being subjected to secularization has not escaped the notice of theologians and ecclesiastical authorities. In an attempt to counteract or at least retard this process, many churches have made considerable efforts to make religion more relevant to modern life. It is argued here that most of those efforts have not succeeded in maintaining religion as an institution of society. Rather, the efforts have tended to accelerate the process of secularization as, for example, with respect to youth. Many churches have formed youth groups, not for the purpose of religious study or religious indoctrination, but for the purpose of providing young people with amusement and recreation of various kinds under the supervision of the church. This has had the effect of developing within organized religion a considerable number of organizations whose chief function is only peripherally religious. While youth organizations and activities may maintain formal membership in organized churches, such membership serves functions that are not in the main religious.

Many Black churches in particular are more of this world than the next. Most of the leadership for Black Americans in the struggle for civil liberties has come from their churches. In this, of course, they have been joined by white clergymen from a wide variety of denominations. That considerable success has marked these efforts for civil rights is less because the leadership was religious than because leaders and followers were organized. The various churches concerned provided the framework for such organization, but when working for civil rights, the thrust was clearly secular and not religious.

Organized religion or religion in general would no longer seem to be a social institution in modern societies. But religion is not necessarily passé. Americans do place some emphasis on religion in their daily lives although much of this emphasis may be superficial. Still, millions of Americans are involved actively with organized religion even if some of the involvement is of a secular nature. Lipset, for example, has noted that the number of clergymen per thousand population, per capita donations to churches, per number of available church seats, and so forth, has remained consistent with population growth. Relatively, religion appears to be holding its own in terms of membership. While it seems that organized religion is serving certain functions for society, it is much less clear than in the past just what these functions are.

Organized religion does have some power simply because it is *organized*. Churches also possess additional power to the extent that their congregations believe in their dogma. There is much general support for religion on a pro

Copyright © 1972 by Saturday Review/World, Inc.
Reprinted by permission of the publisher and Robert Hageman.

"It's not the sinners that worry me as much as competing with the Jesus freaks."

In addition to large-scale ideologies, it can also be anticipated that many small sects and cults will continue to appear and either become established denominations or vanish.

forma basis, as exemplified by the official addition of the words "under God" to the Pledge of Allegiance by the Congress of the United States some years ago. But, unlike those of other institutions in modern society, norms peculiar to the institution of religion have not been institutionalized as such. Although there are laws that do apply to religion, particularly to organized religion, these are mainly concerned with certain obligations of recognized clergy and conscientious objectors with respect to military service. While canonical law depends for enforcement on belief and on those few sanctions available to ecclesiastical authorities, the entire force of society is available to administer sanctions for violations of the institutionalized norms of other social institutions.

Religion and Science

Modern man often finds himself caught between science and religion. While such conflict continues, it does appear that some contemporary interest in religion is concerned with reconciling science and religion. "If people could see that to explain the origins of man and the universe in scientific terms does not necessarily destroy the concepts of respect for the individual, love, trust, justice, and the historical background from which these ideas grew, the conflicts between science and religion would be less intense."[85] In that statement, John Wood implies a kind of emotionality that we tend to associate with religion but not with science.

Science has created a value system of its own based on objectivity, logic, research methodology, the presentation and analysis of evidence in a certain format, and a considerable skepticism about accepting things on "faith." Many of these elements are so fixed that they have not only become characteristics of an ideology but also assumed a sacredness akin to a religion. This sets science up in competition with other ideological systems including religion. Of course, not everyone in modern society accepts science as a form of religion or necessarily considers science and religion to be in conflict. But for those in conflict, be they theologians or scientists, the emotional involvement characteristic of all conflicts tends to indicate some commitment to an ideology.

Future of Religion

It can be anticipated that the secularization of religion in the United States and other modern countries will continue. In time, religion will cease to be a major institution of society and, instead, will become a matter for groups and individuals. Sacredness in the general sense will become an element of society and not the exclusive property of organized religion.

If pluralism is a general characteristic of modern societies, it will continue to be a characteristic of organized religion as well as of other ideologies that have some of the characteristics of religion. The "little red book" of Chairman Mao, Marx's *Das Kapital*, and the Communist Manifesto represent, in a real sense, dogma so sacred that adherents are ready to fight and die for them.

In addition to large-scale ideologies, it can also be anticipated that many small sects and cults will continue to appear and either become established denominations or vanish. One contemporary cult has been called the Jesus Movement and its adherents, Jesus Freaks. They have attempted to put their beliefs into a workable form by establishing communes, coops, and organizations aimed at reforming or completely changing modern life styles. Their ideas are based on a return to "pure" Christianity as preached by Christ and recorded in the Bible. They have many followers. And even people who are not members are in agreement with their ideals and aspirations. Whether the movement will survive and grow is anybody's guess.

For the time at least, it seems reasonable to hypothesize a continuing future for organized religion, although with ongoing changes. Organizations tend to develop a certain functional autonomy; they tend to persist because they are in existence. But religion's future appears dependent upon man's need for answers, solutions, understanding, and explanations. Without passing judgment on the truth or error of any religion, it should be pointed out that religious authorities and writings supply answers to questions that are unanswerable by scientists, at least at the present time. For the dedicated scientist, there may well be complete emotional security in science; for many people, this is not sufficient. They want security, and religion is a readily available source of security. Speaking of the Jesus Movement, James Nolan states the emotional situation for some young people (and we suspect older people as well) when he writes:

Intuitively I realized what a Jesus trip really meant to a lot of these kids; it is a way of getting back to Kansas from the tortured and confused psychedelic world of surreal low-life munchkins, witches and wizards, back to the comfort and reassurance of your own back yard. Back from the drop-a-tab crash pad spirituality of cross country hitch hiking, of protesting and confronting, of wide-open grooving that somehow always ended with the needle, getting busted, having your head swaggersticked opened, or getting pregnant.[86]

Thus, if religion is no longer an institution in modern societies, if religion is no longer a central focus of human thought and existence, it is at least a lively social phenomenon. Religion is very much in the mass media and is a subject of conversation. On Sabbath days or other Holy Days, it is a matter of some formal observance for a large proportion of American society.

As Beals and Hoijer point out, the functions of religion have important psychological and sociological implications. Psychologically, ritual and ceremony appear to allay fears and anxieties. Sociologically,

the individual participant in such occasions [religious rituals and ceremonies] experiences a variety of emotional satisfactions, not the least of which is in his more complete identification with the group and consequent enhancement of his own security.[87]

CONCLUSION

Chapters 7, 8, and 9 have examined several social institutions. Since these institutions constitute the very structure of human societies—at least the more permanent and enduring parts of that structure—it is essential to have some understanding of the functions performed by them if we are to exert even minimal control over both the rate and the direction of social change. The contemporary citizen needs a combination of many things at his immediate disposal, including sound ideas of how his society functions. Such knowledge provides the basis for a more realistic appraisal of both what is sound and what is unsound with regard to social institutions. We have also tried to counteract the fatalistic orientation that little or nothing can be done about society by pointing out that institutions do change but that whether they change haphazardly or in an orderly way depends very much on knowing something about society *and* having faith that it can be subjected to planned change.

In Chapter 10, we will consider a problem that is endemic in all social institution—crime and deviance. By now the reader should be aware that societies are orderly enough to survive because the majority of members exhibit behavior that conforms closely enough to the values and norms of the society and the institutions of the society. But as a scanning of the daily news makes clear, there are those whose behavior deviates beyond the acceptable limits—the statistical limits—as defined not merely by law but also by the mores of society.

9.1. Is there any escape (outside of death) from social institutions? Think carefully before answering this question.

9.2. With a growing population, a society will grow more complex. Is this simply a result of there being more humans or of some other factor or factors? Explain.

9.3. From the sociological perspective, how did early economists err in their notion of "rational man"?

9.4. In modern societies, does it appear possible to plan the institution of economics to work in a fully rational manner? Why or why not?

9.5. Recognizing that some elements of the institution of economics are under government control, how would you classify this control? As absolute, perfect, imperfect, subject to informal negotiation between government and business, or what?

9.6. Why do nations who attempt to modernize insist on adhering to traditional ways of doing things in the face of the fact that the traditional ways are often dysfunctional for modernization?

9.7. What are some factors, historical and otherwise, that would tend to make most work in American society seem unsatisfying? Before answering this question, make clear the difference between "work" and "recreation."

9.8. Is poverty an absolute or relative condition? Could it be absolute under some conditions and relative under others? Explain.

9.9. Do you see any problems arising out of the fact that recent efforts to alleviate poverty in the United States have been called the War on Poverty? In answering, you might think of the slogan "Fight Mental Illness." What does that tell us about American society?

9.10. Is it really paradoxical that in modern societies that require a high degree of cooperation there is also a considerable amount of conflict? Explain your answer.

9.11. Can you think of any economic conflict (that is, conflict within the institution of economics) in America that is not normative to some extent?

9.12. The meaning given to "free enterprise" by Woodrow Wilson in 1912 is quite different from that given the same term by conservatives today. How and *why* has the meaning changed?

9.13. Consider a relatively low level political organization—a club of one of the major American political parties at the county or small city level. Does such an organization possess any real political power, potential or actual? What are the limits on the exercise of that power?

9.14. Realistically, should a pluralistic society attempt to end political conflict of all kinds? (For purposes of answering this question, assume that political conflict stops short of physical violence.) If not, can you define some appropriate objectives with respect to political conflict?

9.15. The poor pay more for merchandise than do middle-class persons. Is this entirely because the poor tend to be more gullible or are there other reasons? What are they? You might consider the matter of credit and installment purchasing in preparing your answer.

9.16. When power is distributed inequitably in a society, efforts will be made by those out of power to obtain it. Looking back in history, can you identify any *violent* revolution that resulted in a more equitable distribution of power?

9.17. If society should not put an end to economic competition, what must be done to prevent one group from gaining unfair advantages in this competition? Can you think of specific things that have been accomplished toward this end?

9.18. Economic determinists hold that the entire explanation for society is a matter of economics. How might an economic determinist explain the ban on cigarette advertising on television in the United States?

9.19. If intelligence tests are unfair to lower class and poor children, what are some things that could be done to remedy the situation in the schools? If it were decided to do away with psychological tests entirely and place children purely on the basis of actual school performance, would the present situation be altered significantly? Why or why not?

9.20. The "cooling out" process appears wasteful in both human and economic terms. Can you propose any viable alternatives that do not involve radical changes in American society?

9.21. Men in all societies hold some things as sacred. Does it follow that anything held as sacred is also religious or an element of religion? Explain.

9.22. Make a list of what religious belief can do for the individual. Do the purely personal benefits of religious belief serve any important function or functions for society as a whole?

9.23. According to Durkheim, what is the source of human conceptions of a supernatural deity or dieties? Do you agree with Durkheim? Defend your position.

9.24. Is religion still a significant cohesive force in modern, complex societies? Why or why not?

NOTES

[1] Francis E. Merrill, *Society and Culture,* 4th ed. (Englewood Cliffs, N.J.: Prentice-Hall, 1969), p. 259.
[2] V. Gordon Childe, *Man Makes Himself* (New York: New American Library, Mentor Books, 1951), p. 35.
[3] Robert H. Lowie, *An Introduction to Cultural Anthropology*, new, enlarged ed. (New York: Holt, Rinehart and Winston, 1940), p. 25.
[4] Childe, *Man Makes Himself*, p. 18.

[5] Robert Heilbroner, *The Making of Economic Society* (Englewood Cliffs, N.J.: Prentice-Hall, 1962), p. 14.

[6] Robert Ross, "Is Planning a Revolution?," *Viet Report,* Special Urban Issue (Summer 1968), p. 11.

[7] Seymour Melman, *Our Depleted Society* (New York: Holt, Rinehart and Winston, 1965), p. 38.

[8] Carlo Oglesby and Richard Shaull, *Containment and Change* (New York: Macmillan, 1967), p. 187.

[9] C. Wright Mills, *White Collar* (New York: Oxford University Press, 1951), p. 229.

[10] Ibid., p. 230.

[11] Chris Argyris, "We Must Make Work Worthwhile," *Life,* 5 May 1967, p. 56.

[12] Harvey Swados, *A Radical's America* (Boston: Little, Brown, Atlantic Monthly, 1957), p. 117.

[13] Patricia Sexton, "The Auto Assembly Line: An Inside View," *Harper's,* June 1962, p. 54.

[14] Mills, *White Collar,* p. 237.

[15] Joseph Bensman and Bernard Rosenberg, "The Meaning of Work in Bureaucratic Society," in *Identity and Anxiety,* ed. M. Stein et al. (New York: Free Press, 1960), p. 187.

[16] Ibid., p. 189.

[17] Robert G. Sherril, "Washington's Bland Bondage," in *Society As It Is,* ed. G. Gaviglio and David Raye (New York: Macmillan, 1971), pp. 95 and 98.

[18] Swados, *Radical's America,* p. 118.

[19] Argyris, "Make Work Worthwhile," p. 50.

[20] Eli Chinoy, *Automobile Workers and the American Dream* (New York: Doubleday, 1955).

[21] Michael Harrington, "The Other America Revisited," in *Society As It Is: A Reader,* ed. G. Gaviglio and David Raye (New York: Macmillan, 1971), p. 184.

[22] Ibid., pp. 185 and 187.

[23] Richard A. Cloward and F. Pivan, "The Poor Against Themselves," *The Nation,* 25 November 1968, p. 56.

[24] Peter Schrag, "The Forgotten American," *Harper's,* August 1969.

[25] Ibid., p. 28.

[26] David Wellman, "The Wrong Way To Find Jobs for Negroes," *Transaction,* April 1968, p. 10.

[27] Kenneth O. Gilmore, "Laredo Learns about the War on Poverty," *Reader's Digest,* January 1967, pp. 44 and 49.

[28] Ralph L. Beals and Harry Hoijer, *An Introduction to Anthropology,* 3d ed. (New York: Macmillan, 1965), pp. 459–460. (Emphasis added.)

[29] Ronald M. Pavalko, *Sociology of Occupations and Professions* (Itasca, Ill.: Peacock, 1971), p. 16.

[30] Thorstein Veblen, *The Theory of the Leisure Class* (New York: Random House, 1931).

[31] This is dramatically illustrated by the so-called energy crisis. From the sociological point of view, the exhaustion of fossil fuels is not expected to bring modern economic systems to a halt. Alternative forms of energy are already available. What can be predicted, however, is that some complex technological (and social) changes will accompany the shifts in energy sources.

[32] Wilbert Moore and A. Feldman, "Society as a Tension-Management System," in *Behavioral Science and Civil Defense Disaster Research Group,* ed. G. Baker and L. Cottrell, National Research Council Study no. 16 (Washington, D.C.: National Academy of Science, 1962).

[33] Emile Durkheim, *The Division of Labor in Society,* trans. George Simpson (New York: Free Press, 1949).

[34] Robin M. Williams, Jr., *American Society,* 2d ed., rev. (New York: Knopf, 1960), p. 517.

[35] Richard Hofstadter, *The Age of Reform* (New York: Knopf, Vintage Books, 1955), p. 188.

[36] Arthur S. Link, *Wilson: Road to the White House* (Princeton, N.J.: Princeton University Press, 1947), p. 514.

[37] William A. Swanberg, *Luce and His Empire* (New York: Scribner, 1972), p. 473.

[38] Talcott Parsons, *The Social System* (New York: Free Press, 1951), p. 127.

[39] Robert Bierstedt, "An Analysis of Social Power," *American Sociological Review* 15, no. 6 (December 1950), p. 735.

[40] Malcolm X, *Malcolm X Speaks* (New York: Merit, 1965), p. 27.

[41] Jean-Jacques Rousseau, *Social Contract,* trans. Charles Frankel (New York: Hafner, 1947), p. 8.

[42] Seymour Martin Lipset, *Political Man* (New York: Doubleday, Anchor Books, 1963), pp. 12–13.

[43] For a good analysis of La Guardia's ability to put together a coalition, see E. E. Digby Baltzell, *The Protestant Establishment* (New York: Random House, Vintage Books, 1964).

[44] See Ralf Dahrendorf, *Class and Class Conflict in Industrial Society* (Stanford, Calif.: Stanford University Press, 1959).

[45] Lipset, *Political Man,* p. xxii.

[46] Ibid., p. xxxii.

[47] G. William Domhoff, "The Control of the Corporate Economy," in *Society As It Is: A Reader,* ed. G. Gaviglio and D. Raye (New York: Macmillan, 1971), pp. 218–219.

[48] For example, tax-free municipal bonds are sold only in large amounts; they can be purchased only by those with considerable resources.

[49] Herman Miller, *Rich Man, Poor Man* (New York: Crowell, 1964), p. 53.

[50] Leon Keyserling, "Taxes from Whom, for What," *The New Republic,* 23 April 1966, p. 18.

[51] Robert Lampman, *The Share of Top Wealth-Holders in National Wealth* (Princeton, N.J.: Princeton University Press, 1962).

[52] Domhoff, "Control of Corporate Economy," p. 224.

[53] Robert Heilbroner, *The Future as History* (New York: Harper & Row, 1959), p. 125.

[54] C. Wright Mills, *The Power Elite* (New York: Oxford University Press, 1956), p. 122.

[55] E. E. Digby Baltzell, *The Protestant Establishment* (New York: Random House, Vintage Books, 1964), p. 180.

[56] Fletcher Knebel, "The Wasps," *Look,* 23 July 1968, p. 70.

[57] Robert Dynes and Ernest Quarantelli, "What Looting in Civil Disturbances Really Means," *Transaction,* May 1968, p. 13.

[58] Robert Blauner, "Internal Colonialism and Ghetto Revolt," *Social Problems,* Spring 1969, p. 406.

[59] Robert Conot, *Rivers of Blood, Years of Darkness* (New York: Bantam Books, 1967), p. 299.

[60] Jean-François Revel, *Without Marx or Jesus,* trans. J. F. Bernard (New York: Doubleday, 1970).

[61] Richard Flacks, "On Participatory Democracy," *Dissent,* November-December 1966, p. 708.

[62] Marc Pilisuk and Thomas Hayden, "Is There a Military Industrial Complex which Prevents Peace?," *Journal of Social Issues* 21, no. 3 (1965), pp. 83 and 86.

[63] For an analysis of the problems this creates, see Maurice Berube and Marilyn Gittell, *Confrontation at Ocean-Hill Brownsville* (New York: Praeger, 1969).

[64] Neal Gross, *Who Runs Our Schools?* (New York: Wiley, 1959), p. 50.

[65] As quoted by Patricia Sexton, *The American School* (Englewood Cliffs, N.J.: Prentice-Hall, 1967), p. 32.

[66] Jonathan Kozol, *Death At an Early Age* (New York: Bantam Books, 1967), pp. 7 and 36.

[67] Sexton, *American School*, p. 57.

[68] Burton Clark, "The 'Cooling-Out' Function in Higher Education," *American Journal of Sociology* 65 (May 1960).

[69] Ibid., p. 570.

[70] Martin Trow, "Two Problems in American Public Education," in *The Sociology of Education*, ed. Robert Bell and Holger Stub (Homewood, Ill.: Dorsey, 1968), p. 11.

[71] Robert Rosenthal and Lenore Jacobson, *Pygmalion in the Classroom: Teacher Expectation and Pupils' Intellectual Ability* (New York: Holt, Rinehart and Winston, 1968).

[72] Trow, "American Public Education."

[73] Ibid., p. 15.

[74] John Diebold, *Man and the Computer* (New York: Praeger, 1969), p. 17.

[75] Ralph L. Beals and Harry Hoijer, *An Introduction to Anthropology*, 3d ed. (New York: Macmillan, 1965), p. 82.

[76] V. Gordon Childe, *Man Makes Himself* (New York: New American Library, 1951), p. 50.

[77] Francis E. Merrill, *Society and Culture*, 4th ed. (Englewood Cliffs, N.J.: Prentice-Hall, 1969), p. 261.

[78] Talcott Parsons, *Societies: Evolutionary and Comparative Perspectives* (Englewood Cliffs, N.J.: Prentice-Hall, 1966), p. 33.

[79] Emile Durkheim, *The Elementary Forms of Religious Life* (London: G. Allen, 1912), p. 37.

[80] It has been suggested that any number of Americans tend to suffer from headaches on Sunday; headaches that could be cured or avoided by attending church. To the extent that this is true—and it seems to have some merit—it is an illustration of the power society exerts over its members. That would apply, of course, to those whose socialization involved regular church attendance.

[81] As quoted by Guy Swanson, *The Birth of the Gods* (Ann Arbor, Mich.: University of Michigan Press, 1960), p. 16.

[82] Max Weber, *The Protestant Ethic and the Spirit of Capitalism* (New York: Scribner, 1958; London: G. Allen, 1930); and David I. McClelland, *The Achieving Society* (Princeton, N.J.: Van Nostrand, 1961).

[83] Albert Mayer and Harry Sharp, "Religious Preference and Worldly Success," *American Sociological Review* 27 (1962), p. 220.

[84] Harvey Cox, *The Secular City*, rev. ed. (New York: Macmillan, 1966), p. 2.

[85] John K. Wood, "The Nature of Conflicts between Science and Religion," in *The New Technology and Human Values*, ed. J. Burke (Belmont, Calif.: Wadsworth, 1966), p. 55.

[86] James Nolan, "Jesus Now: Hogwash and Holy Water," *Ramparts*, August 1971, p. 24.

[87] Beals and Hoijer, *Introduction to Anthropology*, p. 602.

ANNOTATED BIBLIOGRAPHY

Beale, Calvin L. "Rural Depopulation in the United States: Some Demographic Consequences of Agricultural Adjustments." In *Population and Society*, edited by Charles B. Nam, pp. 415–423. Boston: Houghton Mifflin, 1968. The move from rural to urban areas is a phenomenon not confined to the United States. It can be fully understood only as a function, in part at least, of changes in the institution of economics resulting from technological advances, particularly with respect to agriculture. This short, highly readable article illustrates the close relationship between society as a whole and the single institution of economics with, as we always find, some complications arising out of the ongoing interaction with and between other institutions.

Berger, P. *Invitation to Sociology*. New York: Doubleday, 1963. Berger has put together one of the most enjoyable and readable introductions to sociology that is available. His chapter "Man in Society" fits in especially well with the concerns developed in this chapter.

Dalton, Melville. "Conflicts between Staff and Line Managerial Officers." *Social Processes and Social Structures*, edited by Richard Scott, pp. 356–366. New York: Holt, Rinehart and Winston, 1970. This article is an excellent account of a type of conflict that appears to be endemic *within* the institution of economics. The author makes it quite plain that this intrainstitutional conflict has as its sources variables outside the institution of economics per se. While worthwhile merely from the standpoint of illustrating internal conflict, it is especially useful, as well, in showing the interdependence and interaction between all the institutions of modern societies.

Demereth, N. and Peterson, R. *System Change and Conflict*. New York: Free Press, 1967. This book provides a variety of theoretical orientations to the study of institutions. It has the advantage of looking at problems of system change and stability, not as separate processes, but as part of total system dynamics.

Domhoff, G. *Who Rules America?* Englewood Cliffs, N.J.: Prentice-Hall, 1967. An excellent work for those interested in the question of control over the political economy. Domhoff asks significant questions and provides some very illuminating answers about who makes the decisions that affect all of our lives.

Galbraith, John Kenneth. *The New Industrial State*. Boston: Houghton Mifflin, 1967. This book is highly sociological in its treatment of both capitalistic and communistic industrial societies, even though Galbraith is, by profession, an economist. Chapter 6, "The Technostructure," is of particular significance because it illustrates a kind of change that is immanent in large corporations once they move from private to public ownership. Most important, perhaps, the identification of the "technostructure" as a new, countervailing power not merely within the institution of economics but also in whole societies.

Gaviglio, G. and Raye, D., eds. *Society As It Is: A Reader*. New York: Macmillan, 1971. This reader contains many of the most provocative articles about the institutions in American society to come out in the past several years. These articles were written by a variety of authors, and the book reads very quickly and enjoyably.

Goulden, Joseph C. *Monopoly*. New York: Putnam, 1968. Written somewhat in the style of the "muckrakers" mentioned in this chapter, this work concentrates on one very large business, American Telephone and Telegraph Company. While written from the author's point of view, it is a useful book because it presents a picture of the relationship between the institutions of the economy and the polity. Further, it presents some idea of the influence of large businesses on the daily life of average citizens.

Hofstadter, Richard. *The Age of Reform*. New York: Knopf, Vintage Books, 1955. The author, who was awarded the Pulitzer Prize for history in 1956, presents a historical account of social change starting with the William Jennings Bryan campaign of 1896 and continuing through the "New Deal" of Franklin Delano Roosevelt. Because much of the book is concerned with the institution of economics and its relation to the institution of politics, it is particularly useful for obtaining an historical background for sociological analysis of institutional change.

Lipset, Seymour Martin. *Political Man*. New York: Doubleday, 1963. This book is written with the sophistication that pervades all of Lipset's work. It is a good basic introduction to the political system in American society.

McKee, James B. *Introduction to Sociology*. New York: Holt, Rinehart and Winston, 1969. "Economy and Society" is one of the better chapters in an excellent introductory text. It is highly sociological and is written, in part, from the standpoint of the economy as a sociological problem.

Williams, Robin R. *American Society*, 2d ed. New York: Knopf, 1960. Even though this work is over ten years old, it provides an indispensable foundation for both the understanding of American institutions and the changes that have occurred within the recent past.

10

Crime and Deviance: Flaws in the Fabric

INTRODUCTION

One of the things that Americans often do is talk about other people who do not conform to the acknowledged way things are done in society. At cocktail parties and other social gatherings, conversations often turn to some "public outrage of the day." Homosexuals may have demonstrated for gay liberation, or the son of a local minister may have been "busted" for dope. Much newspaper, television, and radio news is concerned with the latest murders, rapes, or frauds. Although people appear to express shock over such happenings, there is often a certain fascination with deviant behavior. While some persons may be expressing secret wishes and desires when they talk about deviance, others can, as part of their discussion, reaffirm to themselves and to the others present who they are and what they stand for.

It will be our purpose in this chapter to outline the major approaches to deviance. And we will present some of the tools that the sociologist uses to understand this interesting dimension of human behavior.

It might seem to be easy to designate who the deviants in American society are: a sinister minority slinking through the rat-infested alleys of urban ghettos breaking the rules that respectable members of society hold most dear. Yet a closer look shows that even professionals have a hard time deciding who the deviants really are. A recent experiment by D. L. Rosenhan regarding schizophrenic behavior dramatically illustrates this.[1] Rosenhan had eight *sane* persons gain admission to twelve different mental hospitals by claiming that they heard voices. As soon as they all were admitted to a psychiatric ward, the pseudopatients began to act normally, and they even made notes in the ward of their experiences. None of the pseudopatients was detected by hospital staff members as being sane, and they remained in the hospital for seven to fifty-two days each, with an average stay of nineteen days. All were treated exactly like their supposedly insane fellow patients. They gave their life histories as they had actually occurred; these histories were not used to show how the pseudopatients were mentally healthy but, rather, how their family dynamics produced their supposed schizophrenic state. Yet, remarkably, it was common for other patients to uncover the pseudopatients' sanity, and many voiced suspicions that they were journalists or professors posing as patients.

Rosenhan's study is important for its implications about the defining of deviant behavior in general. It shows how certain forms of deviance are difficult to define and how normality and abnormality can often be interchangeable. Furthermore, the study points up how simply being in a certain environment, in this case a psychiatric hospital, may in itself be enough to label persons as deviant, regardless of any characteristics the persons themselves may have.

Even if we limit the designation "deviant" only to people who have engaged in obvious manifestations of deviancy specified in criminal law, most of us would be guilty. A study that dramatizes this proposition was performed by James Wallerstein and Clement Wyle, who distributed questionnaires listing forty-nine offenses under the penal law of the state of New York.[2] All the offenses were considered sufficiently serious at the time (1947) to draw a maximum sentence of not less than one year. Subjects were requested to check each offense they had committed and indicate if the act took place before or after the age of 16, the upper limit for juvenile court jurisdiction. Some 1,698 individuals answered the questions—1,020 men and 678 women—many of them residents of the New York City metropolitan area. The mean number of different offenses committed in adult life by men in the population ranged from a low of 8.2 offenses per person for ministers to a high of 20.2 for laborers, with a mean of 18 for all men. For women, the range was from a low of 9.18 for laborers to a high of 14.4 episodes per woman for those in military and government work. The mean for all women was 11. Men reported a mean of 3.2 and women 1.6 juvenile offenses. But of most importance, very few of the incidents ever came to police or judicial notice.

Similar findings materialized from a number of other studies of "hidden offenses."[3] Does that mean there is no difference between offenders who escape detection and those who are caught? These studies suggest that, on the average, those who get into trouble with the law are likely to have committed more offenses, more serious offenses, and the same offenses more frequently. But there is a substantial and impressive amount of overlap between those who get caught and those who do not. "In brief, we are all offenders, but we differ in the patterns into which our offenses fall."[4]

CONCEPTIONS OF DEVIANCE

Those studies point out that it may be difficult to judge whether or not a person is really deviant and that all supposedly normal people commit deviant acts at some point in their lives. In addition, different groups judge different acts to be deviant. The fraternity brother who breaks windows on a Saturday night drunk may be seen by his friends as just having a good time, while his stricter classmates may see him as a drunken vandal. It should be apparent that it is likely that the person making the judgment, the process by which the judgment is arrived at, and the situation in which it is made may all be intimately involved in the deviance phenomenon. Behavior is deviant not because of something inherent in the act but because of the definitions, expectations, and viewpoints that others apply to the act. Sometimes entire groups become labeled as deviant, such as some religious sects, extremist political organizations, hippies, motorcycle gangs, and so on.[5]

Statistical Approach

With these considerations in mind, we will review the most common conceptions of deviance and see the different ways deviance may be viewed. The statistical view of deviance is the simplest one. It sees deviance as essentially a *statistical matter*—to be left-handed, redheaded, or cross-eyed is to be deviant because such traits appear in a minority of the population. Clearly, this view is not concerned with rule-breaking and is overly simplistic.[6] For example, the majority of persons may run stop signs or exceed speed limits sometimes, but that will not stop them from being punished if they are caught. In addition, studies such as the Kinsey reports show that a vast proportion of Americans have extramarital sexual relationships or homosexual liaisons at some point in their lives, yet these acts are still considered deviant by most people in the society.[7]

Pathological Approach

A less simple and more common view of deviance is the *pathological approach*, which sees deviance as something indicating the presence of a "disease." It may take either a psychopathological view, which sees "sick" individuals as committing deviant acts; or a social pathological view, which sees deviant behavior, such as high rates of crime, alcoholism, or suicide, as the product of a "sick" society. This view rests on a medical model and makes medical analogies. But this definition soon gets us into hot water because it is hard to find a definition of healthy behavior that would satisfy even a small group of psychiatrists let alone a less homogeneous group of citizens.[8] Defining a healthy society is an even harder task.

The noted psychiatrist Thomas Szasz has shown how such a view has grown to cover many forms of deviance and pointed out the flaws in looking at deviance as a form of pathology. In *The Myth of Mental Illness*, Szasz writes that originally only such diseases as syphilis, tuberculosis, typhoid fever, carcinomas, and fractures, each clearly involving a disordered physiochemical structure or function of the human body, were included in the category of "illness." Then physicians redefined their criteria and began to include disability and suffering. Finally, physicians and especially psychiatrists began to apply the label of "illness" to anything and everything in which they could detect any sign of malfunctioning, no matter what its basis. Thus, Szasz continues, agoraphobia became an illness because one should not be afraid of open spaces. Homosexuality became an illness because heterosexuality is the social norm. Divorce became an illness because it indicates the failure of marriage. "Crime, art, undesired political leadership, participation in social affairs, or withdrawal from such participation—all these and many more have been said to be signs of mental illness."[9]

The trouble with the pathological conception is that by using a medical analogy it locates the source of deviance within the individual and prevents us from seeing *the judgment itself* as a crucial part of the phenomenon. For instance, today a cocaine addict may be seen as deviant and in all probability as "ill", yet at one point in America's history, such addiction was common and respectable among the middle class.[10]

Functional Approach

A third view looks at the functions that deviance fulfills for the society. As opposed to the pathological view, this approach generally emphasizes the positive aspects of deviance for social groups. Deviance, when it occurs in large enough quantities, becomes a threat to social organization. In limited amounts and under certain circumstances, however, it may actually make an important contribution to the validity and efficiency of organized social life; even conforming members of a society may neither wish to see deviance totally eradicated nor the deviant performer exiled. Some functions of deviance are examined in the following discussion.

Cutting Red Tape   In a bureaucratic organization it is often necessary, in the best interests of efficiency and orderly progress, to violate some rules and regulations. Someone must have the courage to cut through the red tape in an emergency, such as when a military unit, railroad, or sales office needs supplies in an unanticipated situation or in excess of normal quota. If rule-based procedures are followed, the material will arrive too late or in insufficient amount. So, out of a sense of identification and concern for the welfare of an organization, some daring soul will violate its rules. In contrast, a rigid and slavish adherence to the letter of each rule and regulation can effectively paralyze an organization.

Acting as Safety Valve   If rules are so rigorously enforced that people are handicapped in their access to the legitimate means to satisfy their wants, accumulated frustration and discontent may lead to an attack on the rules themselves and on the social institutions they support. A certain amount of deviance, disparaged but not vigorously repressed, may thereby perform as a "safety valve" and reduce a dangerous strain against the legitimate order. It may be argued, for example, that pornography performs such a function with respect to unsatisfied sexual needs without threatening the legitimate institution of marriage.[11] Pornography, by providing an outlet for socially illegitimate sexual desires, prevents "freaky" sexual interests from becoming real and thus allows persons to restrict their actual sexual behavior to the marital relationship. In that way, a supposedly deviant activity may actually act to promote the well-being of a valued institution, in this case marriage, which it is supposedly subverting.

Clarifying Rules   The precise meaning of a rule is seldom obvious. Many rules emerge as crude indicators of a general understanding between people. The boundaries of rules are established by testing the limits and observing if the action is met by chilly looks or raised eyebrows. When a rule is formulated, it is fuzzy around the edges; there is no general agreement on the limits of its application. Very often, especially when the stakes are high, special procedures are invoked to consider the problem and generate an authoritative opinion. One of the main functions of courts is to reduce the ambiguity of laws; appellate and supreme courts, in particular, provide a conclusive definition of a law. But the process requires a deviant as a sort of "guinea pig" to challenge the system and obtain a ruling.[12] The persons who participated in the lunch counter sit-ins in the 1950's were initially punished and ostracized but their behavior eventually led to a court ruling that segregation in public eating places was unconstitutional.

Promoting Social Solidarity   Nothing appears to unite a group as well as a common enemy—be he devil, spy, or criminal. The ability of people to forget or overlook petty internal squabbles and arguments in the face of a community danger is a phenomenon of long standing. The appearance of a deviant considered likely to cause pain and injury can solidify a community with lightning speed. A radio warning that a "homicidal maniac" has escaped from a nearby institution brings neighbors together and makes friends out of strangers, all united *against* the deviant intruder. As Mead noted more than half a century ago, "the criminal does not seriously endanger the structure of society by his destructive activities, and on the other hand he is responsible for a sense of solidarity aroused among those whose attention would otherwise be centered upon interests quite divergent from those of each other."[13]

Accentuating Conformity   Deviance provides the contrast that makes conformity something "special," a source of gratification and satisfaction. There is little distinction in being saintly within a community consisting only of certified saints. Even in a community of saints, as Emile Durkheim pointed out, someone would be labeled a sinner. One aspect of payoff for conforming is the opportunity provided for censuring another's misbehavior and, by implication, congratulating oneself for his own superior attributes. A certain amount of deviation may provide the reference point against which conformity can shine; a good deed seems better when done in a bad world. Deviance provides the tape with which to measure the merits of conformity, especially when conformity is commonplace rather than unique.

Providing Innovation and Creativity   Finally, deviance may serve to bring innovation and creativity to society, which needs a certain amount of deviance if it is to remain flexible and open to change and adaptation. Many historical figures, such as Jesus and Socrates, were considered deviants by their societies; yet their actions helped to shape the course of history. If society is to remain open to change, certain individuals must be willing to accept a deviant label, as when some women are labeled "sluts" when they attempt to change the double standard of sexual behavior. This function of deviance is summed up in Eric Hoffer's comment that the future of a nation depends on the nature of its misfits.

The functional approach to deviance is useful in providing a remedy to the more usual conceptions that emphasize only the negative aspects of deviance. However, it often tends to become too one-sided and neglects the very real and harmful aspects of many forms of deviance. In addition, it neglects the fact that a form of deviance that is functional for one group may have negative consequences for another. For example, a rape of a white woman by a Black man may function to solidify the white community but only at the expense of the Black community.

Labeling Approach

A final conception of deviance is the labeling view. It argues that social groups create deviance by making the rules whose infraction constitutes deviance and by applying those rules to particular people and labeling them as outsiders. From this viewpoint, deviance is not the quality of an act a person commits but, rather, the consequence of the application by others of rules and sanctions to an "offender." The deviant is merely one to whom the label has successfully been applied; *deviant behavior is behavior that people so label.*[14]

That definition goes a long way toward removing the confusion raised by the "hidden offender" surveys of Wallerstein and Wyle, Kinsey, and others, which would classify "everyman" as a deviant because we have all, at some time or other, displayed grossly deviant behavior.[15] But most people were never caught, condemned, and labeled; they escaped the *stigma* that a deviant label brings. Just because one has committed an infraction of a rule does not mean that others will respond, and, conversely, just because one has not broken a rule he may be treated, in some circumstances, as though he had. Furthermore, the reaction to deviance varies over time. Someone drinking alcoholic beverages during Prohibition was subject to arrest while before or after that period such behavior was legal.

The degree to which an act will be treated as deviant also depends on who has committed the act and who feels harmed by it. Studies of juvenile delinquency make the point clearly. Boys from upper and middle-class homes do not get in as much trouble with the legal process when they are apprehended as do boys from slum areas. Albert Cohen and James Short conclude that the middle-class boy is less likely to be taken to the station house; less likely when taken to the station to be booked; and extremely unlikely to be convicted and sentenced.[16] Similarly, the law is applied differentially to Blacks and whites. A Black man believed to have attacked a white woman is more likely to be punished than a white man who commits the same crime. Interestingly, a Black who kills another Black is less likely to be punished than a white man who commits murder.[17] And more than thirty years ago, Edwin Sutherland, a leading American criminologist, pointed out that crimes committed by corporations are almost always prosecuted as civil cases, but the same offense committed by an individual is ordinarily treated as a crime.[18]

There are rules enforced only when their breakage results in certain consequences. For example, illicit sexual relations seldom result in severe punishment or social censure for the offenders. But if a girl becomes pregnant as a result of such activities, reaction is likely to be severe. Howard Becker uses these commonplace observations to emphasize his contention that, taken together, there is good support for the proposition that deviance is not a simple quality, present in some kinds of behavior and absent in others.[19] It is, rather, *the result of a process that involves responses of other people to the behavior*. The same behavior may be

a. an infraction of the rules at one time and not at another
b. an infraction when committed by one person and not another
c. related to a rule that can be broken with impunity or to another that cannot
d. an infraction in one place and not in another
e. an infraction with one group and not with another

An interesting study that shows the importance of those propositions is F. K. Heussenstamm's experiment on how rules are applied more to some people than to others.[20] Heussenstamm recruited fifteen college students of different races, all of whom had exemplary driving records, and pasted Black Panther party bumper stickers on their cars. While none of the subjects had received any traffic citations over the previous year, with the bumper stickers supporting that deviant group, their citation record was nothing short of remarkable. The first subject received a ticket for making an "incorrect lane change" less than two hours after leaving school. Eight more tickets were collected over the next two days for such things as "following too closely," "driving too slowly in the high-speed lane of the freeway," "driving erratically," and "failure to observe proper safety of pedestrians using a crosswalk." In all, the participants received thirty-three citations in seventeen days, when the experiment was ended because the funds for paying fines were exhausted. That study gives dramatic evidence of the importance of looking not only at deviant activities but also at the responses to them, and it shows how those responses themselves may often create the deviance.

Whether a given act is deviant or not does depend in part on the nature of the act (whether or not it violates some rule) and in part on what other people do about it. It would thus be best to speak of *rule-breaking behavior* and reserve the term *deviant* for those people or groups so labeled by some segment of society. "Deviance," Becker concludes, "is not a quality that lies in behavior itself, but in the interaction between the person who commits an act and those who respond to it."[21]

The labeling approach has, as have the other approaches we have discussed, certain shortcomings, especially in its extreme versions. If we are to view as deviant only those persons who are actually labeled as deviant, we are unable to study one of the most interesting questions in the sociology of deviance— why some persons are labeled as deviant while others, the secret deviants, are not. Also, some types of deviance do not easily fit a labeling framework. A murderer, for example, does not murder because a certain label has been applied to him, but psychological and sociological factors can be used to explain his behavior apart from the label that has been applied to him. The labeling approach is a very valuable one but should be used with caution and not accepted uncritically.

A Case in Point: Prostitution

It might, at this point, be useful to take one form of deviance, say prostitution, and see how it would be approached by each conception we have been discussing. A statistical approach would regard prostitution as deviant simply because only a small minority of women engage in it. That view, however, does not add much to our knowledge or allow us to ask any interesting questions about prostitution. A psychopathological view would see the prostitute as a disturbed individual and attempt to find the background personality and family patterns that led her into this deviant occupation. Similarly, a social pathological view would see the prostitute as a product of her environment, most likely from an area marked by high rates of drug addiction, broken homes, inferior education, and generally unhealthy social surroundings. The functional conception would see prostitution as contributing to the maintenance of the social institution of marriage.[22] Prostitution may function to provide an outlet for sexual tensions that are not satisfied in marriage. A relationship with a prostitute does not threaten the stability of the family since the sex involved is a strictly commercial transaction, and neither party is permitted to become emotionally involved or attached. Without prostitution, the argument goes, the family system would be weakened, since persons would find other outlets for their sexual needs which may be more threatening to the marital relationship. A labeling approach would shift the focus to the definition of prostitution itself. Why, it might ask, is a woman who accepts money in exchange for sexual intercourse labeled a prostitute and ostracized from respectable society while the mistress of a rich man may be held in high esteem? Why are lower class streetwalkers routinely arrested and held in jail while call girls operating in fancy hotels are often allowed to ply their trade unmolested by the law? Indeed, the labelers might say, prostitution is legal in Nevada (and in many other nations), and madams have risen to respectable positions in different historical eras, such as during the American frontier days. Finally, why is prostitution considered to be a deviant act at all?

We can see that each of these conceptions of deviance emphasizes very different aspects of the phenomenon. If we want to know why some persons become deviant and others do not, it may be most useful to use the pathological approach. If we wish to find out what deviant behavior contributes to the society, the functional approach is called for. The labeling approach is best suited for asking why some persons are punished for committing deviant acts while others are not or why an action is considered deviant in the first place. Whichever conception of deviance we adopt, however, it should be remembered that it is never a straightforward matter to define a particular type of behavior as deviant and that definitions of what constitutes deviance are constantly changing. Just as a sane person may be seen as mad if he is put in a mental hospital, today's deviant may become tomorrow's model citizen. How we regard deviance determines, to a large extent, what we will find out about it. And our conceptions of what constitutes deviance must be formed with caution.

THEORIES OF CRIME AND DEVIANCE

Keeping in mind that the nature of what constitutes deviant behavior is problematic, we will now turn to some of the major theories of deviance. While each of these theories is based on one of the conceptions of deviance we have discussed, they are not identical to them. A *conception* of deviance defines what deviant behavior is and locates its general features. A *theory* goes beyond a conception and attempts to *explain* the causes of deviant behavior and to *predict* which persons or social groups are likely to become deviant and which are not. In this section we will review the major biological, psychological, and sociological theories of deviance, focusing in particular on criminal behavior.

Biological Approaches

Commentaries on deviance are nearly as old as writing itself. But the scientific investigation of deviance dates mainly from the nineteenth century, when the theory of evolution inspired efforts to ascribe criminal behavior to hereditary differences. Nineteenth-century researchers presumed behavioral variations to have correlates in the physique, and physical anthropology was the major focus for the scientific study of crime. The study of criminal deviance from that point of view ultimately becomes a branch of biology, and the chief tools of research become calipers, scales, and cameras. Criminal biology is still a dominating theory in Europe today and emphasizes the inheritance of weakness or proneness toward crime and delinquency, plus pressure from a bad environment.[23]

Cesare Lombroso   Criminal biology—based on the pathological conception of deviance—takes as its focus of study the individual deviant, explaining his behavior in terms of fundamental biological characteristics that differentiate him from "normal" people. An Italian physician, Cesare Lombroso, is credited with founding this school, called the "positive school of criminology," as a reaction to the "classical school." The classicists had argued that man calculated the advantages and costs of any course of action; based on free will, he chose that course in which the advantages outweighed the costs. The sources of variance in conforming or deviating were to be found in the rewards and penalties persons could reasonably anticipate. Social control, on this basis, could be most effectively achieved by instituting punishments sufficiently swift, certain, and severe to counterbalance the expected gratification.

The positive school, in contrast, presented a rigorous determinism that insisted that men had been shaped by biology or social circumstances or both into a certain mold and were then moved irresistibly to act as they did. On the basis of body measurements of Italian prisoners, Lombroso described the "born criminal" whose criminality and bodily structure were both manifestations of his underlying "atavistic" traits. Those traits were thought to be characteristic of a more primitive stage of the biological evolution of the race. During roughly the last third of the nineteenth century when this position dominated European criminology, Lombroso changed his ideas several times, largely in response to criticism. But the centrality of biological predisposition to his writing was evident until the end.

In the early years of this century, Lombrosian criminology took a severe critical battering, culminating in a devastating critique by Charles Goring, an English prison medical officer. He carefully compared large samples of English prisoners with noncriminals and concluded that there was no evidence of the "stigmata" of atavism and degeneracy related to a distinct criminal type. His work has since been accepted by most criminologists as the definitive refutation of the Italian school.[24]

Ernest A. Hooton   In 1939, the distinguished Harvard anthropologist Ernest A. Hooton published a study based on countless anthropometric measurements of prisoners. These led him to the conclusion that different types of offenders yielded different measurements as a group. And those measurements could be used to show that prisoners were morally, intellectually, morphologically, and genetically degenerate when compared to noncriminals. The logical conclusion he drew was that the key to a decisive attack on crime lay in eugenics, or social control over who would be allowed to reproduce.[25] Hooton's vogue was brief; his research was eventually disclaimed because of dubious sampling methods and imperfect controls—a defect frequently encountered today in criminological research.

William H. Sheldon Another Harvard faculty member, the psychologist and physician William H. Sheldon, is responsible for another attempt along biological lines. Sheldon created a typology of body types, which he called *somatotypes*, based on the relative predominance of digestive viscera, bone and muscle, and neural and cutaneous tissue. *Endomorphs*, according to his classification system, are soft and round; *mesomorphs* are hard, rectangular, athletic; *ectomorphs* are lean and fragile. Sheldon suggests a variety of ways in which his body types might affect delinquency.[26] Despite his array of data, including photographs of each of his 200 subjects from three angles, and an intricate and sophisticated manipulation of statistics, "the logic of proof is no stronger—indeed is perhaps weaker—than that of Lombroso almost 80 years earlier."[27]

Eleanor and Sheldon Glueck The last of the trio of Harvard faculty to be involved in bioanthropological studies of deviance is the husband-wife team of Sheldon and Eleanor Glueck. They investigated the relationship between Sheldon's somatotypes and juvenile delinquency. The complaints and strictures made about Sheldon's methodology do not apply to the Gluecks, who generally displayed more careful and responsible methods in their comparison of 500 delinquents and 500 nondelinquent controls. They discovered that significantly more of the delinquents were predominantly mesomorphic. (However, 40 percent of the delinquents were not predominantly mesomorphic or athletic in body build.)

The Gluecks, in keeping with their generally eclectic theoretical orientation, made no such sweeping claims for inherited constitutional factors as did Sheldon, Hooton, and Lombroso. Nor do they arrive at conclusions for social control through selective breeding. They assert that there are other ways of becoming a delinquent. They suggest that the mesomorphic constitution provides merely a *delinquent potential* that is likely to be activated in an appropriate environment.[28]

Cohen points out that the somewhat disproportionate representation of mesomorphs among labeled juvenile delinquents may occur not because of some special inherited feature associated with mesomorphy, but because the street life of which delinquency is a part is socially organized to reward and prize strength, agility, physical toughness, and athletic competence. Observation reveals that people generally gravitate toward those occupations and activities for which they are best equipped; it may, therefore, be anticipated that the athletically built mesomorph will be more attracted to certain forms of delinquency than the plump endomorphs and the skinny ectomorphs. "We would expect mesomorphs to have a higher 'delinquency potential' for the same reason we would expect them to have a higher 'high school athletic potential.' In both cases, 'the rules of the game' confer an advantage on the mesomorph."[29]

Summary Biological theories of criminality have involved studies of identical (one-egg) and fraternal (two-egg) twins, glandular malfunctions, EEG abnormalities, chromosomal anomalies, and family lineage. These studies, it is now generally agreed, have been inconclusive at best. Nevertheless, the suspicion that there may be heredity factors at least partially involved in the determination of psychological traits—emotionality, impulsivity, general abilities and limitations—appears worthy of still further study. However, modern biology is very clear about the inheritance of traits. Genetically determined attributes are specific; eye and hair color, for example. But "criminality" is not specific at all. There is murder, burglary, rape, tax-evasion, draft-card burning, embezzling, pickpocketing, indecent exposure, drunk driving, and so forth. If criminality were inherited, the genetic factor would likewise have to be specific. The criminal should inherit the behavioral trait driving him to burglary rather than to forging checks or stealing hubcaps. Studies using this approach have, as a rule, merely compared "criminality" with "noncriminality" with no concern about whether or not the alleged genetically determined crime patterns could possibly be as specific as the Mendelian mechanics of inheritance require. Nor do such studies provide an answer to the question: If individuals are biologically fated to be burglars or rapists, then do genetic factors also determine the occupations of noncriminals? Is a man as surely fated to become a computer programmer as he is to have blonde hair?

The fact is that almost all biological theories of crime overlook some obvious points—criminality, whatever else it may be, is a status conferred by society; many people who break laws avoid the status; the vagaries of law enforcement and judicial conviction can hardly be explained on a biological basis. In this context, we can agree with Sutherland that "this school [the Lombrosians], by shifting attention from crime as a social phenomenon to crime as an individual phenomenon, delayed for fifty years the work which was in progress at the time of its origin and, in addition, made no lasting contribution of its own."[30]

Copyright © 1970 by Playboy.
Reproduced by special permission of Playboy Magazine.

"You can't talk to that crowd—they've all got extra Y chromosomes."

The fact is that almost all biological theories of crime overlook some obvious points—criminality, whatever else it may be, is a status conferred by society; many people who break laws avoid the status; the vagaries of law enforcement and judicial conviction can hardly be explained on a biological basis.

Psychological Approaches

Intelligence Criminals, second only to college freshmen, have been favorite subjects for study and experimentation by psychologists, particularly in relation to intelligence testing and personality evaluation. In 1904, at the request of the Paris school authorities, the French psychologist Alfred Binet devised a series of questions that tested the intelligence of retarded children. Soon after, IQ testing of criminals began, and hundreds of studies were conducted. There are few areas of research into deviance more instructive, and more alarming, than the history, findings, and conclusions about the intelligence of criminals.

It is understandable that the followers of Lombroso, still battered by Goring's devastating critique, would find the IQ concept highly palatable, as would those who were searching for a biological basis for criminal behavior. It seemed to them that criminals might well have insufficient intelligence and therefore be less capable of mature judgment and less able to understand the consequences of antisocial behavior and the significance of rules and laws.

Crime and Deviance

Armed with various adaptations of the original Binet scale, psychologists tested juvenile and adult prisoners all over the world. The results appeared to confirm fully the hypotheses of the testers—findings of mental deficiency in as high as 90 percent of certain criminal populations were made. In a study of sixteen early reports, R. Pintner found a median of 64 percent feeble-minded in a criminal population against 2–9 percent in the general population.[31] In a survey of 350 reports made between 1910 and 1914, Sutherland found that an average of 50 percent were diagnosed as mental defectives.[32] The evidence seemed to provide conclusive corroboration of a relationship between crime and low intelligence. Henry Goddard, the author of the study of the notorious Kallikak family, testified in 1921 that it could no longer be denied that the "greatest single cause of crime and delinquency is low-grade mentality, much of it within the limits of feeble-mindedness."[33]

Contemporary findings are of the opinion that there is no support for those sweeping judgements about the intellectual inferiority of criminals. World War I provided the forum for large-scale intelligence testing of adults. The massive test programs revealed that the true adult mental age was 13.8 instead of 16. A mental age of 16 had been the base for the earlier studies which resulted in widespread findings of mental retardation among prisoners. The publication of the Army data stimulated a long, hard look at the earlier findings. Herman Adler and Myrtle Worthington found the average of scores of Illinois prisoners was actually higher than that of Army personnel at the time of World War I.[34] Goddard retreated from his earlier genetic view and acknowledged that everyone was a potential delinquent. And William Healy and Augusta Bronner, who had reported in 1926 that feeble-mindedness occurs from five to ten times more frequently among delinquents than in the general population, noted ten years later that their earlier conclusion was unwarranted. A great amount of carefully conducted and intensive psychological testing had resulted, "quite unexpectedly, in establishing no signs of differentiation between the mental equipment of the delinquents and the controls in our series."[35]

You will recall from Chapter 9 that it is now generally accepted that intelligence tests measure the degree to which individuals have assimilated middle-class values and concepts. The person born and raised in an urban slum tends to score below any innate capacity, as does the youngster reared in Appalachia or some other impoverished rural area. Both have been exposed to different values, stimuli, and life experiences from the test-maker. As we have become more aware of the limitations of intelligence testing, the differences between populations of convicted criminals and the rest of society have tended to disappear. If anything, we might anticipate that a mentally backward individual would find himself the victim of arrest and conviction procedures more readily than a brighter person. He would be less able, perhaps, to "talk himself out of" an incriminating situation and more likely to be the dupe of sophisticated criminal exploiters. Despite these factors, surprisingly few really feeble-minded people are convicted of crime.[36]

Personality   The man in the street would not hesitate to state that deep and serious personality differences exist between the criminal and himself. Psychologists have made many scientific efforts to determine if the personality characteristics of criminals differ significantly from those of the general population, almost always starting from a hypothesis in accord with prevailing common-sense notions. Here again, as in evaluative studies of biological and intellectual differences, the findings run counter to common-sense conceptions. The psychological approach to deviance is based on a pathological conception of deviance, seeking differences between individuals which account for the development of the undesirable condition of deviance in some and not in others.

Karl Schuessler and Donald Cressey made a careful survey of 113 studies in which the personality test scores for delinquents and adult criminals were compared with scores achieved by control groups.[37] Their main conclusions are:

1. As often as not, the evidence favors the view that personality traits are distributed in the criminal population in the same proportions a in the general population.

2. The results of the accumulated research fail to establish whether criminal behavior is the result of certain prior personality traits or the personality traits are the results of the criminal experience.

3. The majority of the criminals studied were drawn from prison populations. Conditions based on prison samples cannot be extended to the whole criminal population because prisoners are the failures in crime, those that got caught. Furthermore, the responses of prisoners on a paper and pencil test of personality may be unreliable because of the prison environment; there is an atmosphere of suspicion, hostility, and fear that pervades most detention facilities. Finally, the prison experience itself may well produce changes in the outlook, values, attitude, and overall personality of those who have spent extended periods behind bars.

Other methodological shortcomings noted by Schuessler and Cressey involved the comparison of scores on different types of personality tests and the tendency to group all criminals into one category regardless of the nature of the offenses. Not a single trait could be found which could be confidently stated as more characteristic of delinquents than nondelinquents.

Freudian Theory   The most widespread psychiatric theory of crime and deviance is derived from Freud's theories of human behavior.[38] The central argument is that there are three basic elements of personality that must be brought into balance if a person is to be "normal." These are the *id*, which contains the unconscious biological and psychological drives, urges, and impulses that underlie all behavior and threaten to disrupt organized social life; the *superego*, or the conscience, which reflects the moral ideas we derive from interaction with other people, particularly parents; the *ego*, which is the conscious, realistic, and rational part of the personality which the individual uses to control the demands of the id and the superego. According to Freud, the superego works on the ego to *repress* the id's socially unacceptable tendencies; this puts the superego and id in a continual conflict that the ego tries to resolve. The mechanism by which the ego shuts off the demands of the id is called *repression*, a mechanism that is rarely, if ever, fully efficient. The id continues to struggle for expression and gratification.

Criminal behavior, from the psychoanalytic orientation, is to be understood as a form of symbolic release of repressed complexes. These complexes are usually repressed ideas or impulses formed in early childhood which are put out of the conscious mind but evade the censorship of the superego and achieve indirect expression through criminal behavior. Kleptomania, a compulsive desire to steal, for example, might be seen by an adherent of psychoanalysis as a symbolic way to "steal" a parent's lost love.

The theoretical framework outlined above provides a basis for hypotheses about the nature and motivation of criminal and other deviant types of behavior. Individuals who fail to develop an adequate superego are thought to become criminal because of a deficiency of control over their instinctual drives, while other persons may become criminal because of the effects of overcontrol. Criminals of the first kind are said to have character disorders, that is, are deficient in character, and are sometimes classified as *psychopathic*. Offenders of the other type are called *neurotic* and *compulsive*.

An important component of the Freudian theoretical structure is the Oedipus complex, based on the premise that incest is a basic desire of human beings—every boy loves his mother and is jealous of his father because of the father's sex relations with the mother. If the id were to take command at that point, the father would be murdered and the mother raped. If the instincts are only partially repressed, the person may murder his father in some *symbolic* way, or the person may commit an act which is *symbolic* of the act of sex relations with the mother. In either case, a crime would be committed; he may "murder" the father by forging checks on his bank account or by becoming a drug addict. He may "rape" the mother by burglarizing a home or stealing a pocketbook.

Finally, the man may be sorry, on an unconscious level, because his id has gained some momentary dominance over the superego through unconscious wishes for possession of the mother. To get rid of the guilt feelings, the ego may seek punishment. Since punishment follows crime, he might, for example, commit a clumsy burglary, leading to his arrest and conviction.

Donald Cressey has pointed out that the major difficulty with Freudian theory is that the variables cannot be studied scientifically. There is no way to prove or disprove this theory because the elements of it cannot be observed or measured. To a nonbeliever, the symbolism is apparently more an exercise in imagination and fantasy than a fact of life. The analysts have no way of validly demonstrating the relation between the symbols and the objects they are supposed to represent. Moreover, one who contests the scientific base of psychoanalysis is sometimes accused by the defenders of the system of expressing some deeply hidden, unconscious emotional conflict. Finally, persons using the psychoanalytic approach to crime rarely use a control group of "normal" persons so that their explanations could be tested.

Summary The current theories that crime is an expression of inferior intelligence or of psychopathy appear no more justified than the original Lombrosian thesis that criminals constitute a distinct physical type. It is true that certain psychiatrists have claimed to have found a large proportion of criminals to be psychopathic. But it is agreed that a gross lack of standardization and objective features in their methods of diagnosis may account for the findings. An extreme form of the theory was presented in a report on the medical aspects of crime—a diagnosis of mental disease "is permissible even when the criminal has shown no evidence of mental disease other than his criminal behavior." According to that line of reasoning, the psychopathy that is to be used as the explanation of criminal behavior may be inferred from the criminal behavior it explains. Perhaps this circular line of reasoning enables another psychiatrist to state that "in all my experience I have not been able to find one single offender who did not show some mental pathology. The 'normal' offender is a myth."[39]

All of the psychological approaches we have reviewed have the common element of explaining the course of criminal behavior as a natural and necessary part of a basic personality orientation, with the specific criminal act taking on meaning and making sense in terms of the context of the particular individual's entire life history. Yet what stands out most clearly from organized research studies representing different schools of thought is that *no trait of personality* has been found to be closely associated with criminal behavior—no consistent differences between the personality traits of delinquents and of nondeliquents have been found. The explanation of criminal and much other deviant behavior, we therefore conclude, will be found in social interaction, in which both the behavior of a person and the overt or prospective behavior of other persons play their parts.[40]

The glib identification of criminality as a reflection of mental illness or psychopathy no longer goes unchallenged by psychiatrists, with the sharpest skepticism usually expressed by those in daily working contact with offenders. For example, Dr. Richard Jenkins comments that "the assertion that all or a major fraction of delinquency can be accounted for as neurotic behavior neither rings true nor makes sense . . . Usually, he has a certain earthy realism and is less, rather than more, inclined to be neurotic than is the non-delinquent.[41]

This accumulation of negative evidence suggests that perhaps psychological factors do not ordinarily determine *whether* a person becomes a criminal but, rather, *how he functions* as a criminal. Consider an assortment of barbers, lawyers, or television repairmen. Some are pleasant and prudent; others are aggressive and stupid; still others, passive and dependent—but all are barbers, lawyers, or television repairmen. Similarly, there are criminals who are skillful, pleasant, and prudent; criminals who are foolish and aggressive; and criminals who are kind and amiable.[42]

Sociological Approaches

Many different sociological theories of deviance have been advanced to explain the causes of deviant behavior and predict its occurrence. By somewhat oversimplifying, we might group these into the constraint, frustration, and subcultural conformity theories of deviance.

Constraint Theory

The constraint theory of deviance contends that a person becomes prone to commit deviant acts when his ties to the conventional order of society have been broken or are underdeveloped. If individuals are not integrated into traditional social groups, it is natural that they will become deviant from the norms of the wider society. The Chicago school of deviance, which flourished in the 1920's and 1930's, exemplifies this view. It held that the social disorganization that existed in many urban areas—broken homes, poor recreational facilities, lack of voluntary organizations, and the like—cut people off from participation in conventional activities. For children reared in such areas it becomes natural to turn to illegal activities frowned on by respectable members of society. Frederick Thrasher, in his study *The Gang*, argued that the street gang functioned as a substitute for the socialization agencies of the family, school, church, and others. When those institutions fail to attract and regulate the needs of youth, young people themselves form gangs as alternatives. These gangs, taking names such as the Dirty Dozen, the Vultures, and so on, are formed because of the absence of ties to larger social groups. In turn, they actively reject the values and activities of traditional society; their members get a sense of distinctiveness and identity from participating in criminal activities.[43]

Perhaps the most well known example of the constraint theory of deviance is Durkheim's theory of egoistic suicide. He found, among other things, that Protestants were more likely to commit suicide than Catholics and Jews, that single people were more likely to kill themselves than married persons,

Drawing by Dana Fradon; © 1971. The New Yorker Magazine, Inc.

"I can't say I like the looks of that bunch."

and that married persons without children had a higher suicide rate than those with children. He generalized those findings to the statement that the more integrated a person is into social groups such as the family, church, or state, the less likely he or she is to commit suicide. He saw Catholics and Jews, married people, and couples with children as being more integrated into social groups than Protestants, single persons, and childless couples. When people have an absence of group ties, their life loses its purpose and they become more prone to commit deviant acts such as suicide.[44]

Constraint theories of deviance are often used to explain why rates of deviant behavior increases with increasing urbanization and industrialization. Under those circumstances, people are seen as being torn from traditional group ties and left to themselves to form their own groups in opposition to the dominant society or to drift aimlessly and alone into suicide, mental illness, or alcoholism. Such a theory allows us to predict that rates of deviant behavior will be higher in urban areas than in rural areas, higher in slums than in suburban areas, and higher in industrialized than in agricultural nations. From the point of view of this approach, the establishment of social

If individuals are not integrated into traditional social groups, it is natural that they will become deviant from the norms of the wider society.

Crime and Deviance

332

mechanisms that attach individuals to stable groups should lessen the rate of deviant behavior and presumably make a "healthier" society.

Frustration Theory Frustration theory holds that when a person or social group cannot satisfy legitimate desires through conformity, they will likely resort to deviant behavior to achieve their goals. For example, the Black riots of the 1960's have been explained as the result of the frustration of many Blacks at being denied access to the decent jobs, housing, and education that are the major values in American society. Similarly, Albert Cohen has put forth the theory that the high rate of juvenile delinquency among lower class youths stems from their inability to measure up to middle-class standards in the school. They therefore become frustrated and rebel against those middle-class values of achievement.[45]

Those examples show that inherent in frustration theory is the belief that there is a tension between socially valued ends and the means available to individuals and groups to reach those ends. In American society, the ends would be a decent income, satisfying job, comfortable home, and the like. Members of the middle class have the educational and interpersonal skills necessary to reach those ends and presumably do not have to engage in deviant acts to attain them. Lower class people, on the other hand, are seen as having the same goals but lacking the means to reach them. The high rate of deviance among the lower class arises as a natural result of frustration at not being able to achieve the goals that society values most. Both the middle-class and the lower-class person desire the same ends, but one is able to reach these ends through conformity while the other is forced to deviate to achieve them.

Robert Merton's *theory of anomie* is the best known attempt to formalize frustration theory.[46] Merton attempts to show how deviant behavior may be the natural result of the pressures of the social structure on various social groups. The same forces that produce conformity—the desire to achieve cultural goals—also produce deviance. Those social groups that are unable to achieve success through conformity will be naturally led into deviant activities. Merton's theory of anomie contains five possible adaptations to cultural means and cultural goals, as shown in Table 10-1. The first adaptation, conformity, means that an individual has accepted both the cultural goals and the prescribed means to reach them, and so is unlikely to deviate. Innovation occurs when the cultural goals are accepted but the means to reach them are not, such as when a student cheats to gain a high grade on an exam or a person commits a crime for material gain. Ritualism occurs when a person has failed to achieve the cultural goals but nonetheless continues to religiously abide by the rules of the game. The low-level bureaucrat who has not been able to advance himself but who pedantically demands that his

Theories of Crime and Deviance

333

Table 10-1   Adaptations to cultural means and goals

Method of Adaptation	Culturally Prescribed Means	Culturally Prescribed Goals
Conformity	Acceptance	Acceptance
Innovation	Rejection	Acceptance
Ritualism	Acceptance	Rejection
Retreatism	Rejection	Rejection
Rebellion	Substitution of new means	Substitution of new goals

clients abide by every rule of the organization would be a ritualist. Retreatism means that a person has rejected both the goals and the means to reach them, such as a skid row alcoholic or a suicide. The final adaptation, rebellion, occurs when persons reject cultural means and goals but substitute new means and goals. Revolutionary movements are the primary example of that type of adaption.

Merton's typology, and frustration theories in general, show how deviance may be the natural product of access, or a lack of it, to cultural goals. Those who deviate, with the exception of the rebellious, do so because they have been taught the same values as those who conform. Deviance occurs as the result of the tension produced when the balance between means and goals is upset. Those groups most subject to deviance will be the lower class, and particularly ethnic minorities, who do not have the ability to achieve valued social ends.

Subcultural Conformity Theory   The final major sociological theory of deviance we will discuss is the subcultural conformity theory, which holds that deviant behavior is behavior that conforms to the standards of a group the supposed deviant is a member of. It rejects the idea of any abnormality in deviant behavior and stresses that in deviating the individual is merely acting the way he is expected to act in terms of the norms of his own social group. Deviance is seen as learned behavior, like any other form of activity, peculiar only in its conflict with the prevailing morality of groups with different standards of behavior. For instance, the lower class juvenile delinquent is conforming with the values of his own culture, which stresses such things as toughness, troublemaking, excitement, and exaggerated masculine behavior.[47] We should not be surprised that many lower class youths become delinquent but, indeed, should expect it in light of their culture. Similarly, college youths who smoke marihuana are only conforming to the values of their environment and certainly are not deviant in the eyes of their peers.

The theory of *differential association* developed by Sutherland is the most systematic presentation of subcultural conformity theory.[48] Sutherland's theory is fundamentally a form of learning theory which stresses that criminal behavior is behavior learned in interaction with other people. The basic statement of Sutherland's ideas is outlined below.

1. *Criminal behavior is learned.* It is not inherited nor invented but learned as other skills and procedures are learned.

2. *Criminal behavior is learned in interaction with other persons by the process of communication.* The communication is mostly verbal, but gestures and writing may be involved in the learning process.

3. The principal part of the learning of criminal behavior takes place within *intimate personal groups*, such as street gangs or by following criminal role models. Sutherland indicates that the impersonal agencies of communication, such as the mass media, movies, newspapers, and television, play a relatively unimportant role in the development of criminal behavior.

4. When criminal behavior is learned, it includes (a) *techniques of committing the crime*, which are sometimes complicated, sometimes very simple; and (b) *the specific direction of motives, drives, rationalizations, and attitudes toward criminal behavior.*

5. *The specific direction of motives and drives is learned from definitions of the legal codes as favorable or unfavorable.* If a person is constantly surrounded by people who look on laws as ideas to be respected and obeyed, he will find it hard to learn how to become a criminal from them. But if his companions are favorable to breaking the law, then the likelihood of his also becoming a lawbreaker is greater.

6. *A person becomes delinquent because of an excess of definitions favorable to violation of law over definitions unfavorable to violation of law.* This is *the* key statement of differential association. It refers to both criminal and anti-criminal associations. It suggests that when a person becomes criminal, he does so because of contacts with criminal patterns along with relative isolation from noncriminal patterns.

7. *Differential associations may vary in frequency, duration, priority, and intensity.*

8. The process of learning criminal behavior by association with criminal and anticriminal patterns involves *all the mechanisms* that are involved in any other learning process.

9. While criminal behavior is an expression of general needs and values, it is not explained by those general needs and values because *noncriminal behavior may be an expression of the same needs and values.* Thieves steal to secure money; honest laborers work for the same goal. That is the trouble with attempts by many scholars to explain criminal behavior in terms of drives and values, striving for social status, the money motive, frustration, and so on. The *identical* drives explain lawful behavior just as well, and explanations of this type fail to differentiate criminal from noncriminal behavior.

Summary   At first glance, any of those theories may seem too simple to explain so complex a phenomenon. Surely, there are a great number of other factors involved in the production of deviant behavior. However, it should be remembered that none of those theories pretends to include every single item that has something to do with deviant behavior. Instead, each attempts to identify certain essential variables that help us to explain and predict certain aspects of deviance. And those three sociological theories are not necessarily in conflict with one another, although they do have different emphases. For example, because of a lack of ties to conventional groups (constraint theory), lower class youths cannot measure up to middle class standards of achievement and become frustrated (frustration theory). As a result, they establish groups with their own norms and conform to these (subcultural conformity theory).

There seems to be no end of theories that attempt to explain crime and deviant behavior. We have briefly reviewed a small number of the outstanding formulations of a theoretical nature and must conclude that theories accounting for the existence of deviant behavior in general do not explain the appearance of deviance in any particular person. All the theories stop short of explaining why one person steals but his neighbor does not. Nevertheless, the sociological theories do allow us to explain why one social group has a higher *rate* of deviance than another group, which is a significant step in understanding and explaining deviant behavior.

The heart of the difficulty in explaining individual deviance seems to be that a social condition—a series of circumstances—no matter how universal within the community, does not fall with the same impact on all members of the community. As studies of identical twins raised in the same family have shown, a universal social condition does not imply a universal adjustment or a universal motivation. The failure of general theories to predict individual deviance may be traced to their inability to account for differential impact. A central dilemma of psychological theory is to account for the manner in which personality traits result in criminal behavior. Similarly, a major problem of any sociological theory of crime and deviance is to explain why social factors that impel certain persons into crime do not have the same effect on other individuals exposed to the same factors.[49]

SOCIAL CONTROL

The expression "social control" is employed to refer to social processes and structures that attempt to reduce deviance. Culture not only defines deviant behavior, largely on the basis of a labeling process, but also suggests appropriate responses to the deviant behavior. In the most general sense, any way by which society secures conformity to its norms is a type of social control. In a more specific sense, social control refers to the agencies whose explicit duty it is to enforce norms. Social control operates through formal agencies, such as the police, prisons, mental hospitals, and through such informal, everyday mechanisms as gossip, ostracism, or stares. Indirectly, families, schools, churches, and the like also have a major effect in controlling deviant behavior.

Social Control and Theories of Deviant Behavior

Each of the different theories of deviance we reviewed has different implications for social control. Whichever theory one chooses to explain the origins of deviance will affect the type of social control seen to be most able to reduce the rate of deviant behavior. For example, if one feels that deviant behavior stems from hereditary defects or physiological factors, the possibilities for controlling deviance are bleak. Sterilization of individuals considered as carriers of criminal traits would be possible but somewhat unacceptable in terms of prevailing cultural norms. And, as there is little reason to believe that biology plays a major role in the acquisition of deviant traits, such programs would probably have little effect in reducing the rate of deviant behavior.

Theories stressing personality defects, failures to control instinctual drives, unconscious conflicts, and so on, as causes of deviant behavior imply forms of control that will tend to change those psychological traits of individuals. Most psychological approaches logically prescribe individual treatment for offenders in order to reduce their tendencies toward deviance. However, such methods are costly. And in the absence of conclusive evidence that psychological variables account for a major fraction of most forms of deviance, such efforts at control appear unjustified.

Each of the three sociological theories has a different implication for theories of social control. A constraint theory would emphasize the need to set up social mechanisms to attach persons to groups. Family subsidies and income maintanance programs, which would stabilize families in ghetto areas, and the establishment of youth groups, such as the Boy Scouts or police athletic leagues, would be the most efficient ways of reducing deviance from this point of view. A frustration theorist would emphasize the need to eliminate the frustrating conditions that tend to produce deviant behavior. This would mean expanding educational and job opportunities for deprived groups and increasing the rate of upward mobility for such persons. From the point of view of subcultural conformity theory, it would be necessary to change the conceptions of right and wrong held by groups whose values differed from the dominant society. Destroying lower class culture and socializing all persons to believe in middle-class norms would be the logical control strategy.

However, societies generally do not attempt to reduce deviance by upgrading schools, opening up job opportunities, or guaranteeing adequate incomes to all its members. Instead, reliance is on specific agencies of control, such as prisons and mental hospitals, to deal with deviants. At first glance it may seem that the effect of formal social control agencies is to reduce deviance. Yet these agencies may not operate in a manner that reduces the rate of deviance but may actually work to increase the rate of deviant behavior by locking persons into deviant careers.

Self-fulfilling Prophecy

Common sense tells us that being punished for a deviant act will reduce the likelihood that we will commit the same act in the future. Persons incarcerated in prisons, for example, are not able to commit crimes during this period (at least against the society outside prisons) and we may feel that their experience will lead them to go "straight" when they return to the community. However, the prison as a social control device may actually increase the rate of subsequent criminal activity once the prisoner is released. This tendency of an offender to repeat the same offense after he has been caught the first time is called *recidivism*. Authorities estimate that up to 70 percent of inmates will return to prison after committing new crimes. It is not surprising that the recidivism rate for many types of crime, especially property crimes, is so high given the nature of the prison itself. In prison, the first-time offender is forced into constant interaction with other offenders and may actually learn to improve his skills in criminal activity. Once he is released, a person who has been in jail will find it difficult to find a respectable job, and the only alternative often open to him is further criminal behavior. In addition, once a person has been labeled a criminal, the word carries a number of connotations specifying auxiliary traits characteristic of anyone bearing the label. A man convicted of burglary and labeled criminal is presumed to be a person likely to break into other houses. Certainly the police operate on that principle when they round up suspects for investigation after a crime has been committed. Furthermore, in the eyes of the police and of a considerable segment of the public, he is considered likely to commit other kinds of crimes as well. He has, after all, proven himself to be without respect for law and property.[50]

Treating a person as though he were generally, rather than specifically, deviant produces the *self-fulfilling prophecy* effect. It sets in motion a number of mechanisms which conspire to shape the person in the image other people have of him. After being labeled deviant, the person is effectively cut off from participation in the activities of more conventional groups, even though the specific consequences of the particular activity might never of themselves have created the isolation. What makes a great deal of difference here is public knowledge and reaction. Being a homosexual, for example, does not affect a man's ability to do office work or his skill as a carpenter. But to become known as a "fag" may make it impossible for him to continue on his job. The homosexual who is deprived of a "respectable" job by discovery of his deviance may drift into marginal, unconventional occupations where his status is a matter of little concern. The drug addict, similarly, finds himself forced into other illegitimate activity, such as shoplifting and housebreaking, by the refusal of cautious employers to have him around.[51]

Thus, being caught and branded as deviant has important consequences for one's further social participation and self-image. The most significant consequence is a drastic change in the individual's public identity; engaging in the improper act and being caught at it places him in a new status. He emerges from the experience as a different person from the one he used to be. He is stuck with a label—pothead, lunatic, burglar, rapist, faggot, retarded— and is treated accordingly. Possession of one alleged deviant trait often has a generalized symbolic value, and people in the deviant's environment auto- matically assume that its bearer has other associated undesirable traits.[52]

Moral Entrepreneurs

Social control may, in fact, insure that a person who has been caught and labeled as deviant remains in a deviant career. But before going any further, we should determine what behaviors a society feels it necessary to control. Behaviors such as murder, rape, or robbery, which involve violence against other persons or property, seem obvious. Yet many types of deviance that do not constitute behaviors harmful toward others, such as marihuana smoking, homosexuality, or prostitution, are not so readily apparent. Here, the role of a special type of social control agent, what Howard Becker calls the *moral entrepreneur*, becomes crucial.[53] Moral entrepreneurs are persons with special interests and convictions who attempt to institute rules banning certain forms of behavior. For that reason they can also be referred to as *rule creators*.

The crusading reformer is the prototype of the rule creator; the existing rules do not satisfy him because there is some evil he wishes to correct. He is not necessarily a meddling busybody interested only in forcing his own moral code on others; many crusades have had strong humanitarian overtones. Early prohibitionists, for example, felt they were attempting to provide the conditions for a better way of life for people who would otherwise be ruined by alcohol.

Daniel Glaser has shown how the moral entrepreneur must persuade others to define as a criminal act something they would otherwise only see as atypical or eccentric.[54] The task of moral entrepreneurs is to portray the act they are crusading against as a threatening one. Glaser states that this usually involves three contentions: (1) the deviant injures himself through participation in the activity; (2) the deviance is contagious and will spread to other persons; (3) the deviance is conducive to the development of other, more harmful, forms of deviance. An example of a crusade of the moral entrepreneur is the passage of the Marihuana Tax Act in 1937. Largely through the efforts of one man, Henry Anslinger, the commissioner of the Federal Bureau of Narcotics, a scare campaign was launched using distorted accounts of the effects of the drug. Marihuana users were seen as destroying their own sanity and as developing serious forms of mental illness. They enticed others into partaking of their deviance. Finally, under the influence of the drug, they were pictured as being liable to commit other, more heinous, crimes. What had previously been considered only atypical behavior suddenly became a criminal activity.

Those moral crusades that succeed, by promulgating a new set of rules and regulations, manage in the process to lay the foundation for a new population of deviants. Some crusaders discover they have a taste for crusades and seek new problems to attack and conquer. Other crusaders fail in their attempt to achieve a specific goal and talk the organization they have created into dropping their distinctive mission. Some of those crusaders become outsiders themselves. They continue to espouse a doctrine that sounds increasingly strange with each passing year, as seems to have happened to the "little old ladies in tennis shoes" who were once pillars of the Women's Christian Temperance Union.[55]

Rule Enforcers

Once an activity comes to be defined as deviant there is still the problem of punishing those who participate in the activity. A successful moral crusade results in the creation of new sets of rules and also enlists rule enforcers who usually maintain a more detached and objective view of the whole business than the entrepreneur. The fervor of the original moral crusader leaves the enforcement agent, usually a policeman, cold and unconcerned. He is not so much involved with the content of any particular rule as he is with the fact that it is his job to enforce the laws. When the rules are changed, he arrests deviants for what was once acceptable behavior just as he ceases to interfere with those whose behavior may have been made legitimate by an act of the legislature. Since the enforcement of rules is central to his profession, the policeman develops two interests that condition his enforcement activity: he must justify the existence of his position, and he must win the respect of those with whom he deals.[56]

William Westley's study of policemen in a small industrial city furnishes a good example of how the police cope with those two problems. He asked,

"When do you think a policeman is justified in roughing a man up?" He found that at least 37 percent of the police questioned believed it was legitimate to use violence to coerce respect. He provided some illuminating quotations from his interviews:

Well, there are cases. For example, when you stop a fellow for a routine questioning, say a wise guy, and he starts talking back to you and telling you you are not good and that sort of thing. You know you can take a man in on a disorderly conduct charge, but you can practically never make it stick. So what you do in a case like that is to egg the guy on until he makes a remark where you can justifiably slap him and, then, if he fights back, you can call it resisting arrest.[57]

The point being made is that enforcers respond to the pressures of their own work situation and their own self-image, and they tend to enforce rules by way of those considerations. Thus, whether a person commits a deviant act and is in fact labeled as a deviant depends on many factors extraneous to his actual offense. For instance, Irving Piliavin and Scott Briar, in their observations of police interaction with juvenile offenders, found that there were distinct differences in the way police handled different youths stopped for the same offenses.[58] Those youths who were defiant to the policeman and who wore their hair and clothes in a way associated with a delinquent manner were more likely to be treated severely; youths who appeared contrite and who spoke politely to the policeman were more likely to be treated with leniency. The response of the control agent was not only determined by the offense of the deviant but also by the attitude of the deviant toward the agent himself. Whether someone who has been caught for a criminal violation will actually be arrested may depend on whether the enforcement official feels he must make a show of doing his job in order to justify his position, whether the culprit shows proper deference to the enforcer, whether a "fix" has been interposed, and whether the kind of act he has committed stands high on the enforcer's list of priorities.[59]

It is interesting that most research as well as speculation on deviance concerns itself with the people who break rules rather than with those who make and enforce them; the two possible foci of inquiry should be brought into balance. We should begin to see deviance and the human beings who carry the label "deviant" as a consequence of a process. This process includes interaction between people, some of whom, in the service of their own interests, make and enforce rules to catch others who, in the service of *their* own interests, have committed acts that cause them to be labeled as outsiders.[60] Social control and deviant behavior are intimately linked and we should not consider one process as independent of the other.

CONCLUSION

In this chapter we have attempted to highlight some of the difficulties in the study of deviant behavior. Even to define the term "deviance" raises a host of problems. For some, deviance may be the activities of a minority; for others, a dangerous disease; for another group, a positive force for society; and for a final group, only a label used to condemn persons for activities more powerful persons do not like. When we examined the major ways of explaining the causes of deviant behavior, we found that some theorists search for biological origins of deviance, others look to psychological predispositions, and a third group looks to social conditions conducive to the development of deviant behavior. None of those theories, we concluded, is fully adequate as an explanation of deviant behavior, although they do increase our understanding of certain aspects of the phenomenon. When we turned to the study of social control, we found that it is intimately related to the study of deviant behavior. Social control systems not only work to punish deviants but also may produce the very behavior they are supposed to eliminate or reduce. Both rule creators, or moral entrepreneurs, and rule enforcers play an active role in defining who the deviants actually are and selectively punish those who violate the rules.

Implicit in this chapter has been the theme that lawbreakers cannot be turned into law-abiding citizens only through fear of detection and punishment. The simplistic solution implied by the "law and order" concept is no real solution at all. A reasonably orderly society cannot be realized if responsibility for order rests solely with the constituted authorities—police and courts. Such responsibility is much broader. And that means that the great majority of the members of any given society must follow the rules willingly, as we strongly emphasized in Chapter 4. Not only punishment but also wide-ranging social reforms are necessary if rates of deviant behavior are to be substantially reduced.

Furthermore, deviance qua deviance is not automatically "bad." Some deviance seems essential for constructive social change. Indeed, in reasonable quantities and under certain conditions, deviance makes important contributions to the vigor and efficiency of social life. For example, on the political scene, those attempting to reform certain political processes are often described as deviants by others; simultaneously, the would-be reformers are labeling as evil what the professional politicians consider to be normative behavior, for politicians. In modern, complex societies any definition of what really constitutes deviance becomes more and more difficult as societies become more pluralistic, with the various subgroups and even subcultures having definitions for both deviance and normality that are not congruent with those of the dominant society.

Critics of sociology are often scornful of the theory that deviance is largely a function of society and that those labeled as deviant or criminal are often not much different from the rest of society. Based on that, the critics assume that sociology advocates that society be punished (clearly impossible) and the "criminals" and "deviants" turned loose to continue their antisocial or asocial behavior. Few sociologists would argue that society should not or does not have the right to deal in some ways with those violating its mores, norms, and laws. The principal point, made not merely by sociologists, psychologists, criminologists, and those concerned with the courts and the penal system, is that while current methods of punishing criminals may indeed do just that, the function of sending people to prison to reform them is simply a pretense, and a dangerous one. Prisons and penitentiaries are often schools for crime of all kinds, especially for young first offenders. Furthermore, because of the increasingly elaborate systems of record keeping, it is becoming not merely difficult but also impossible for someone convicted of a crime to conceal that fact from a potential employer; a high proportion of employers are reluctant to employ anyone with a "record." Thus, the dynamics of deviance involves the recognition of two principal processes. First, the structure of society, its values, its norms, and so forth, function in such a way as to produce a certain proportion of deviant behavior, some of which will be observed and punished. Second, many of the ways and means society has for dealing with deviants who are apprehended causes even more deviance, particularly recidivism.

We would emphasize that laws themselves function to create criminals— some will disobey them, be observed, apprehended, and punished. When laws are passed that do not have the support of a substantial proportion of the public, they will be disobeyed and they will be enforced differentially— Prohibition provides an excellent example. In addition to attempting to make jails and prisons more rehabilitative, a decrease in deviance can be brought about immediately simply by removing from the books laws that are regularly broken by a significant part of the population—laws against certain kinds of sexual behavior, for instance.

Chapter 11, "Population," involves some interesting possibilities for the creation of deviance where none existed before. For example, not too many years ago, large families were viewed with considerable approbation. In the decade of the 1970's, this particular norm appears to be changing. A significant question to be kept in mind while reading Chapter 11 is whether family size will remain a strictly private matter between husband and wife or will become society's business in the future.

REVIEW QUESTIONS

10.1 Because of space limitations, no discussion of prisons was made in this chapter. However, it seems worthwhile to ask: What functions do prisons really perform in general? In other words, do prisons serve any function in terms of reducing serious deviance? If not, how might prisons be changed?

10.2. It has been emphasized that deviance is immanent in all societies. But for the purposes of discussion, try to imagine a society in which there was no deviance. What *would* such a society be like, and would you really like to live in such a society? Indeed, is such a society possible?

10.3. There are many "rules for breaking rules." Although murder is proscribed by most societies, there are circumstances under which murder is considered justifiable and proper. Can you think of other examples of rules for breaking rules?

10.4. Psychologists and others have attempted to explain deviance on the basis of individual characteristics. Taking a sociological position, what, in general, is wrong with such explanations?

10.5. Keeping in mind question 10.4, recall the discussion in this chapter on the various psychological means of treating individuals who have been judged deviant. Do you perceive any inconsistency in assigning the causes of most deviance to society and attempting to change deviant behavior by psychological methods?

10.6. Numerous cases have been cited of men and women who became great successes in life even though they came from environments seen as producing delinquency and crime. Are there good sociological explanations for this, or should we look for the answers in individual psychological characteristics? Why or why not?

10.7. Although the use of alcohol is still considered by some to be deviant, reasonable alcohol consumption is not so viewed. It would be instructive to list some of the circumstances under which the use of alcohol *is* viewed as deviant. Also reflect on the changing public attitude toward alcoholism, which is tending toward the opinion that it is a form of illness. Does this change in public attitude have any implications for other forms of deviant behavior?

NOTES

[1] D. L. Rosenhan, "On Being Sane in Insane Places," *Science* 179 (19 January 1973), pp. 250–258.

[2] James S. Wallerstein and Clement J. Wyle, "Our Law-abiding Lawbreakers," *Probation* 25 (March-April 1947), pp. 107–112, 118.

[3] Fred J. Murphy, Mary M. Shirley, and Helen L. Witmer, "The Incidence of Hidden Delinquency," *National Probation and Parole Association Yearbook*, 1945;

and Maynard L. Erickson and LaMar T. Empey, "Court Records, Undetected Delinquency, and Decision Making," *Journal of Criminal Law, Criminology, and Police Science* 54 (1963), pp. 456–469.

[4] Wallerstein and Wyle, "Law-abiding Lawbreakers," p. 114.

[5] Howard S. Becker, *Outsiders* (New York: Free Press, 1963), p. 3.

[6] Ibid., pp. 3–8.

[7] Alfred C. Kinsey et al., *Sexual Behavior in the Human Male* (Philadelphia: Saunders, 1948).

[8] Becker, *Outsiders*, p. 6.

[9] Thomas Szasz, *The Myth of Mental Illness* (New York: Hoeber, 1961), pp. 44–45.

[10] Troy Duster, *The Legislation of Morality: Law, Drugs, and Moral Judgment* (New York: Free Press, 1970).

[11] Ned Polsky, *Hustlers, Beats, and Others* (New York: Doubleday, Anchor, 1969), pp. 183–200.

[12] Albert K. Cohen, *Deviance and Control* (Englewood Cliffs, N.J.: Prentice-Hall, 1966), p. 8.

[13] George Herbert Mead, "The Psychology of Punitive Justice," in *Sociological Theory: A Book of Readings*, 2d ed., ed. Lewis A. Coser and Bernard Rosenberg (New York: Macmillan, 1964), p. 596.

[14] Becker, *Outsiders*, p. 9.

[15] James F. Short, Jr., "The Study of Juvenile Delinquency by Reported Behavior: An Experiment in Method and Preliminary Findings," (Paper delivered at the Annual Meeting of the American Sociology Society, 1955); quoted in Cohen, *Deviance and Control*, p. 25.

[16] See Albert K. Cohen and James F. Short, Jr., "Juvenile Delinquency," in *Contemporary Social Problems*, ed. Robert K. Merton and Robert A. Nisbet (New York: Harcourt, Brace, Jovanovich, 1961), p. 87.

[17] See Harold Garfinkel, "Research Notes on Inter- and Intra-Racial Homicides," *Social Forces* 27 (May 1949), pp. 369–381.

[18] See Edwin H. Sutherland, *White Collar Crime* (New York: Dryden, 1949); idem, "White Collar Criminality," *American Sociological Review* 5 (February 1940), pp. 1–12; idem, "Is the White Collar Crime, Crime?" *American Sociological Review* 10 (April 1945), pp. 132–139.

[19] Becker, *Outsiders*.

[20] F. K. Heussenstamm, "Bumper Stickers and the Cops," *Transaction*, February 1971, pp. 32–33.

[21] Becker, *Outsiders*, p. 14.

[22] Kingsley Davis, "Prostitution," in *Contemporary Social Problems*, ed. Robert K. Merton and Robert A. Nisbet (New York: Harcourt, Brace, Jovanovich, 1961), pp. 262–288.

[23] Cohen, *Deviance and Control*, p. 49; pp. 49–52, especially pertinent to this discussion of biological theories of criminal behavior, are drawn on liberally.

[24] Charles Goring, *The English Convict* (London: His Majesty's Stationery Office, 1913).

[25] Edwin A. Hooton, *Crime and the Man* (Cambridge, Mass.: Harvard University Press, 1939).

[26] William H. Sheldon, *Atlas of Men: A Guide for Somatotyping the Adult Male at All Ages* (New York: Harper & Row, 1954).

[27] Cohen, *Deviance and Control*, p. 52.

[28] Sheldon Glueck and Eleanor Glueck, *Physique and Delinquency* (New York: Harper & Row, 1956), p. 9.

[29] Cohen, *Deviance and Control*, p. 52.

[30] Edwin H. Sutherland and Donald R. Cressey, *Principles of Criminology*, 6th ed. (Philadelphia: Lippincott, 1960), p. 55.

[31] R. Pintner, *Intelligence Testing: Method and Results* (New York: Holt, Rinehart and Winston, 1923).

[32] Edwin H. Sutherland, "Mental Deficiency and Crime," in *Social Attitudes,* ed. Kimball Young (New York: Holt, Rinehart and Winston, 1931), pp. 357–375.

[33] Henry Goddard, *Juvenile Delinquency* (New York: Dodd, Mead, 1921), p. 22.

[34] Herman M. Adler and Myrtle R. Worthington, "The Scope of the Problem of Delinquency and Crime as Related to Mental Deficiency," *Journal of Psycho-Asthanics* 30 (1925), pp. 47–57.

[35] William Healy and Augusta F. Bronner, *New Lights on Delinquency and Its Treatment* (New Haven, Conn.: Yale University Press, 1936), p. 61.

[36] Martin R. Haskell and Lewis Yablonsky, *Crime and Delinquency* (Skokie, Ill.: Rand McNally, 1970), p. 72.

[37] Karl K. Schuessler and Donald R. Cressey, "Personality Characteristics of Criminals," *American Journal of Sociology* 55 (March 1950), pp. 476–484.

[38] For a review of Freudian theory, see Charles Brenner, *An Elementary Textbook of Psychoanalysis* (Garden City, N.Y.: Doubleday, Anchor, 1957).

[39] David Abrahamsen, *Who Are the Guilty? A Study of Education and Crime* (New York: Holt, Rinehart and Winston, 1952), p. 125.

[40] Sutherland and Cressey, *Principles of Criminology,* p. 135.

[41] Richard L. Jenkins, "Adaptive and Maladaptive Delinquency," *The Nervous Child* 2 (October 1955), pp. 10–11.

[42] Adapted from Richard R. Korn and Lloyd W. McCorkle, *Criminology and Penology* (New York: Holt, Rinehart and Winston, 1959), p. 272.

[43] Frederick M. Thrasher, *The Gang* (Chicago: University of Chicago Press, 1927).

[44] Emile Durkheim, *Suicide: A Study in Sociology,* trans. John A. Spaulding and George Simpson (New York: Free Press, 1951).

[45] Albert K. Cohen, *Delinquent Boys: The Culture of the Gang* (New York: Free Press, 1955).

[46] Robert K. Merton, *Social Theory and Social Structure* (New York: Free Press, 1949), chapter on social structure and anomie.

[47] Walter B. Miller, "Lower-Class Culture as a Generating Milieu of Gang Delinquency," *Journal of Social Issues* 14 (1958), pp. 5–19.

[48] Sutherland and Cressey, *Principles of Criminology,* especially pps. 77–79.

[49] Korn and McCorkle, *Criminology and Penology,* p. 301.

[50] Becker, *Outsiders,* p. 33.

[51] Ibid., p. 34. See also Marsh Ray, "The Cycle of Abstinence and Relapse among Heroin Addicts," *Social Problems* 9 (Fall 1961), pp. 132–140.

[52] Becker, *Outsiders,* p. 31.

[53] Ibid., chap. 8.

[54] Daniel Glaser, *Social Deviance* (Chicago: Markham, 1971), p. 94.

[55] Sheldon Messinger, "Organizational Transformation: A Case Study of a Declining Social Movement," *American Sociological Review* 20 (February 1955), pp. 3–10.

[56] Becker, *Outsiders,* p. 156.

[57] William A. Westley, "Violence and the Police," *American Journal of Sociology* 59 (July 1953), p. 39.

[58] Irving Piliavin and Scott Briar, "Police Encounters with Juveniles," *American Journal of Sociology* 70 (September 1964), pp. 206–215.

[59] Becker, *Outsiders,* p. 161.

[60] Ibid., p. 162.

ANNOTATED BIBLIOGRAPHY

Becker, Howard S. *Outsiders.* New York: Free Press, 1963. These studies in the sociology of deviance provide a happy combination of fascinating reading and good sociology. The author develops his theory of the labeling process as it is applied to the marihuana user and the dance musician (paperback). *The Other Side*. New York: Free Press, 1964. A collection of essays dealing with a variety of deviant behaviors but employing the labeling perspective to explain the deviance.

Clinard, Marshall B. *Sociology of Deviant Behavior*. Rev. ed. New York: Holt, Rinehart and Winston, 1963. A pioneer text that is full of useful general observations. It contains excellent chapters on many of the particular kinds of deviance that were accorded only passing notice in this chapter because of space limitations.

Cohen, Albert K. *Deviance and Control*. Englewood Cliffs, N.J.: Prentice-Hall, 1966. A compact and scholarly review of the field for the serious student. Little space is devoted to treatment and rehabilitation of the offender and other deviants (paperback). *Delinquent Boys: The Culture of the Gang*. New York: Free Press, 1955. A provocative and highly readable little volume. It outlines and supports the view that much lower class delinquency is a response to status frustration by the youth who is unable to extract the material benefits of middle-class existence from his immediate environment.

Dodge, David L. *Social Stratification and Deviant Behavior*. New York: Random House, 1970. Dodge presents a self-esteem theory to explain the pathway linking deviance and social equality.

Erikson, Kai. *Wayward Puritans*. New York: Wiley, 1966. Modern theories of deviant behavior are applied by Erikson to the seventeenth-century Puritans of Massachusetts Bay. An analysis of historical documents reveals that deviant behavior in those days served to define social boundaries and maintain social order.

Glasser, William. *Reality Therapy: A New Approach to Psychiatry*. New York: Harper & Row, 1965. The former psychiatric consultant to the Ventura School for (delinquent) Girls presents a readable exposition for officers, teachers, social workers, and mental health staff. It is now widely accepted as a useful tool in rehabilitation and social control of deviant behavior.

Goffman, Erving. *The Presentation of Self in Everyday Life*. New York: Doubleday, 1959. A readable and interesting analysis of the self concept. Goffman uses the language of the stage to describe how we all present ourselves to others and manipulate the impression we attempt to create (paperback).

Haskell, Martin R. and Yablonsky, Lewis. *Crime and Delinquency*. Skokie, Ill.: Rand McNally, 1970. An up-to-date review of criminological theory and practice with a particularly useful section on treatment and rehabilitation, including an extended discussion of Synanon.

Hazelrigg, Lawrence, ed. *Prison within Society*. New York: Doubleday, Anchor Books, 1969. A collection of important recent articles by a wide range of interesting people who examine the personality-changing aspects of the prison experience. The Cressey paper on changing criminals is included in the collection (paperback).

Humphreys, Laud. *Tearoom Trade: Impersonal Sex in Public Places*. Chicago: Aldine, 1970. An astonishing report by a sociologist who gathered data for his dissertation by acting as lookout at public restrooms (called "tearooms") while his homosexual subjects engaged in fellatio.

Korn, Richard R. and McCorkle, Lloyd W. *Criminology and Penology*. New York: Holt, Rinehart and Winston, 1959. An outstanding text in terms of the clarity of exposition of theoretical frameworks and research problems encountered in the quest for scientific knowledge.

Milton, Ohmer, and Wahler, Robert G., eds. *Behavior Disorders: Perspectives and Trends*. 2d ed. New York: Lippincott, 1969. Two general themes permeate this volume: (1) the "disease" and "illness" view of disorders of thought and behavior is too restrictive, and (2) evidence against application of the "medical model" continues to mount and mount (paperback).

Mowrer, O. Hobart, ed. *Morality and Mental Health*. Skokie, Ill.: Rand McNally, 1967. A collection of seventy-five readings suggesting that morality, mental health, and concepts of deviance are all closely related and require scientific examination and exploration.

Simmons, Jerry L. *Deviants*. Berkeley, Calif.: Glendessary Press, 1969. A sprightly presentation of the thesis that perhaps the widespread labeling of deviants takes place because it lets the rest of us off the hook by directing attention to a defined culprit (paperback).

Sutherland, Edwin H. *White Collar Crime*. New York: Holt, Rinehart and Winston, 1961. The classic study of white-collar crime containing Sutherland's strictures against psychiatric interpretations of criminal behavior. Donald R. Cressey's introduction is a balanced rebuttal of many of the critics of Sutherland's positions.

Sutherland, Edwin H., and Cressey, Donald R. *Principles of Criminology*. 7th ed. Philadelphia: Lippincott, 1970. The most widely used of all criminology texts, it is an indispensable reference for the serious student of crime and deviance.

Strupp, Hans R. *Psychotherapy and the Modification of Abnormal Behavior*. New York: McGraw-Hill, 1971. An introduction to major theories of psychotherapy and to empirical research methods in the field, with a good chapter on behavior therapy (paperback).

Sykes, Gresham M., and Drabek, Thomas E., eds. *Law and the Lawless: A Reader in Criminology*. New York: Random House, 1969. A well rounded collection of essays, articles, and parts of books divided into three sections: "What is crime?"; "What causes crime?"; "What can be done?" (paperback).

Whyte, William F. *Street Corner Society*. Chicago: University of Chicago Press, 1955. Revision of a first-hand, participant-observer account of life in a white working-class section of Boston, Massachusetts. Operation of organized crime at a neighborhood level is minutely described.

11

Population and Population Growth: The World Is Only So Big

INTRODUCTION

Unchecked population growth threatens to be one of mankind's most critical problems in the decades to come. Population growth has presented only small-scale problems to human societies over the span of human history. But in today's world, events in South Asia or Sub-Saharan Africa can influence the quality of life in North America; human crises in any part of the world affect the course of events and may determine the consequences in other parts of the world. The two years 1970 and 1971 witnessed major human suffering and starvation. While often produced by natural disasters and political upheavals, they assumed disastrous proportions owing to the vast overpopulation of the societies in which those calamities occurred. In one case, a tropical cyclone in the Bay of Bengal claimed almost 1 million lives. The death toll was attributed to the extreme overpopulation in an area that was prone to such storms and virtually unable to defend itself against their effects. In another case, over 1 million Bangladesh refugees faced starvation in India. India's resources, barely enough to insure survival for her own population of over 500 million, could not accommodate the wave of immigrants. Those two examples of overpopulation and starvation are drawn from Asian nations long plagued by too rapid population growth. But they suggest what could happen in Western nations if population growth *continues unchecked* and if man's ability to provide resources for the population is strained beyond the limits of human capacity, available resources, or both.

POPULATION PROJECTIONS

In presenting projections of any sort of data on a temporal scale—that is, in terms of the future—it is necessary to exercise caution. Such projections are historically based and depend upon the future continuing to change at the same rate as the past. In discussing population trends, both in the United States and in the world, projections are based upon population growth during some period of time, as for example the decade of the 1960's. These projections, *should they be realized*, depict a world much different from what now exists—except in those already overpopulated areas. The following discussion is deliberately couched in pessimistic terms for a good reason. If these demographic projections are not to be realized, a substantial proportion of the world's population must realize the gravity of the situation and act on it.

A glance at the former, present, and future population estimates suggests that the problem of substantial overpopulation—such as that currently faced by many Asian, African, and Latin American nations—will confront the technologically advanced nations. Population forecasters ominously expect,

11

Population and Population Growth: The World Is Only So Big

U.S. Population Projections

Sex	1975	1980	1985	1990	2000
Male	106,256,000	114,322,000	123,433,000	132,249,000	150,196,000
Female	111,119,000	119,476,000	128,660,000	137,424,000	154,915,000
Total	217,375,000	233,798,000	252,093,000	269,673,000	305,111,000

NOTE: These projections are based on census assumptions that, on the average, women beginning childbearing after July 1, 1969, will bear 2.78 children during their lifetime, and that for the rest, fertility will remain the same as it had been in the U.S. in 1966. Estimates are for the 50-state area and the District of Columbia, and include the armed forces. Data are projected as of July 1 for each year.
SOURCE: U.S. Department of Commerce, Bureau of the Census.

given the *present rate* of increase alone (and not allowing for an acceleration in that rate of increase), severe worldwide overcrowding. Philip Hauser is one of America's leading experts on population. He predicts that, if the 1945–1960 rate of increase persisted without change, in 800 years each person would have only one square foot of available space.[1] If the present world population of about 3.75 billion increases at the same rate as between 1945 and 1960, by A.D. 2000 there should be about 6 billion people. If the rate should increase slightly, there could easily be a doubling of the world's population by the end of this century. Projecting still further, the world's population would double again by about A.D. 2020; in less than fifty years, there will be four persons for every one in the 1970's. If the present rate of increase is extended, the time taken to produce a doubling of the world's population would continue to decrease.

PROBLEMS OF PRODUCTIVITY

Underdeveloped Nations

While these projections are frightening enough, one must consider what consequences such growth will have for the composition of the population. For example, in many Latin American societies birth rates are among the highest in the world. With a high birth rate and increasing control over infant mortality, there will be a continuing increase in numbers of children. That will produce a great strain on the productive segment of those nations; in numerical terms, if a country has a median age of 17, over half of the population is nonproductive. Allowing for the presence of a substantial segment of elderly persons and adults who may be unproductive because of illness or other reasons, the actual proportion of productive persons in the population may be as low as 10 or 15 percent. That 10 or 15 percent of the population must be highly productive in order to support such a vast dependent population. In many of the nations of Latin America which have an agrarian base and are just beginning to industrialize, such productivity does not exist.

Even if rapid technological advances could cope with the present problems of productivity, sheer population increase would wipe out those gains in ten years. The growth in population within such societies will serve merely to reduce already low standards of living for much of the population.

Technologically Advanced Nations

The problems posed by the continuing strain on productivity produced by an increase in the size of the nonproductive segments of the population are not limited to the developing nations with high birth rates. In those nations that are technologically advanced, such as the United States, the trend toward falling birth rates in the 1960's could have damaging consequences. If that trend continues for any extended period, it will produce an appreciable increase in the proportion of elderly persons in the population. This results in the relative enlargement of a nonproductive sector of the population for which services, particularly health care, housing, and welfare support, must be provided. Complicating the problem for technologically advanced societies is the fact that many industrial occupations require long periods of training or apprenticeship or both. That pattern of preparation prolongs the period of nonproductivity for a substantial segment of the youthful population.

There are three factors operating to shrink the productive capacity of modern societies—at least insofar as manpower is concerned.

1. With the increased life span characteristic of modern societies, more and more people are living well beyond the retirement age. Although retirement brings an individual's contributions to the economy to an end, his (or her) needs continue.

2. With the increase in automation in modern societies, there are fewer and fewer low-skilled jobs available. More and more time must be spent by young people in acquiring knowledge and skills in order to fill available jobs. During the period of education and training, young people are not contributing to the economy but, rather, are consumers. The effects of the prolonging of formal education and training is to reduce the productive working years of the population.

3. Indications are that in the United States the birth rate has fallen below zero population growth (ZPG). In the coming years, that will reduce the input of young workers into the working force. That will further accelerate the process of lowering the proportion of the society engaged in productive work.

Those three factors do not necessarily involve serious consequences for modern societies in terms of standard of living. Over recent years, the trend has been toward shorter work weeks, somewhat relaxed rest periods, and generous vacations. Clearly, that trend is a function of increased per capita productivity. Indeed, the quite likely shift in the age composition of modern

Copyright © 1972 by Saturday Review/World, Inc.
Reprinted by permission from the publisher and Mort Gerberg.

"Congratulations! They just announced it: Human beings have made the list of endangered species."

Despite all the evidence that the predicted population growth rates can have disastrous consequences, overpopulation is recognized as a major problem by only some segments of the population.

societies including the United States may serve to solve current unemployment and underemployment problems. The essential requirement, if the standard of living is to be maintained or even improved, is increased productivity per individual during those years when they are active members of the work force. Technologically, modern societies should be capable of meeting such demands.

The fact remains that on a worldwide basis, and considering the productive capacity of all societies, there are too many people in the world. And the absolute numbers will continue to increase for the foreseeable future. One might, then, logically pose this question: If the short-run consequences of population are so inimical to human welfare, why weren't they foreseen earlier? As we shall see in the next section, there were ominous warnings almost two hundred years ago. Unfortunately, they went unheeded until recently. Even today, despite all the evidence that the predicted population growth rates can have disastrous consequences, overpopulation is recognized as a major problem by only some segments of the population. Some of the reasons might be found in the slowness of most governments to recognize and deal with their population problems because of economic convenience or

Problems of Productivity

ideological opposition to any form of population control. Such reasons, because they ignore the import of population growth trends, reflect the tendency of many to ignore the problem until it reaches such proportions that a solution cannot be worked out in time. Nations such as India are facing that situation now; few have had the vision to cope with the population problem before it affected the quality of life and the environment.

HISTORICAL SURVEY OF WORLD POPULATION GROWTH

Accurate estimates of world population size early in world history are difficult to calculate. Often it must be inferred from what little is known about rates of population growth in ancient and medieval societies. One fact remains, however: the rate of population growth during prehistoric and ancient times was exceptionally small. High mortality rates were due to such controlling factors as intersocietal conflict, famine, high infant death rates, short life spans (20-25 years), and widespread disease. It required thousands of years for the worldwide population to reach the 250 million persons who are thought to have existed at the time of the birth of Christ. Some societies, however, did attain substantial size. It is estimated that the population of the Roman Empire at the time of Christ was about 50 million; that of China reached 60 million under the Han dynasty.[2] With these exceptions, most ancient societies were small.

Partly because of increasing economic and commercial activity in Europe and partly because of the emergence of large-scale monarchies and nation-states, population grew rapidly at the close of the Middle Ages; world population approached 545 million by A.D. 1650. Asia is thought to have experienced the early stages of rapid population growth during the last few centuries of the Middle Ages. The population division of the United Nations Department of Social Affairs estimates that in 1650 Asians comprised about 60 percent of the world's total population.[3] The proportion of Asians relative to the world's entire population continued to increase, reaching about 66 percent in 1800. At that time the proportion began to decline because of the rapid increases in population elsewhere, notably the Americas and Europe. While Europeans comprised only 19 percent of the world's people in 1650, that figure increased to 27 percent by 1900 and now stands at approximately 25 percent. After 1650, the major population growth took place in North and South America. North America contained two-tenths of 1 percent of the earth's population in 1650 prior to major colonization. That figure has now risen to 7 percent of the total. Latin America experienced substantial growth, although not quite so pronounced, from just over 2 percent of the world's total in 1650 to about 7 percent in the early 1970's.

The only relative decline in population growth after 1650 occurred in

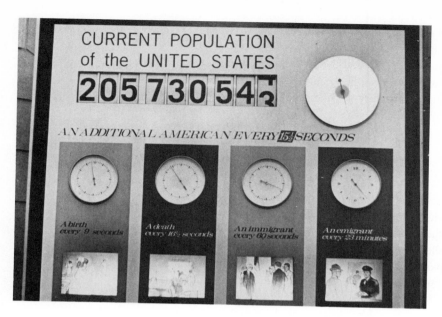

CURRENT POPULATION
of the UNITED STATES
205 730 54☐

AN ADDITIONAL AMERICAN EVERY 15¼ SECONDS

A birth
every 9 seconds

A death
every 16½ seconds

An immigrant
every 60 seconds

An emigrant
every 23 minutes

Africa, largely as a result of the slave trade. It has been estimated that at least 30 million African slaves were brought to the Americas. That accounts, in part, for the fact that, while Africa had about 19 percent of the world's total population in 1650, today it contains only 8 percent of the 1961 total. However, since the cessation of the slave trade, population growth rates in Africa have increased dramatically and are approaching and exceeding those in Latin America and South Asia.

Evidence provided by population specialists suggests that projections made of future population on the basis of present growth rates may grossly underestimate upcoming trends. Between 1650 and 1900 the average annual increase in world population was about one-half of 1 percent per year over the total period, although the rate of increase per year in the nineteenth century far exceeded that of the late seventeenth century. Now the estimated annual rate of growth is 1.8 percent, and some feel that this figure is far too conservative. Despite the controversy over the accuracy of that estimate, the fact remains that during 1971 world population increased by 67,500,000 persons, roughly one-third of the population of the United States.

Rapid increases in the United States population have occurred only recently. When the initial European colonists arrived, the native, or aboriginal, population of the continental United States was probably just under 1 million. The population climbed slowly from the initial 1790 census figure of almost 4 million (not including about 1 million Indians) to 50 million by 1880. At that time, immigration and industrialization swelled the growth rate so that by 1915 the population was 100 million. Only thirty-five more years were required to add 50 million more people to the population in 1950; only twenty additional years were needed for the population to reach and exceed 200 million. While Americans regard themselves as relatively free of the horrors of overpopulation, those statistics confirm that the growth rate has been rapid indeed. It approaches an annual increase of between 2.5 and 3 million persons per year (about the size of the central city population of Chicago), which is close to the overall world annual rate of increase.

DEMOGRAPHY

Now that we have considered the historical trends and future projections of population growth, we will discuss some of the variables employed in the study of population and of the consequences of population growth. The study of human populations is called *demography*. The characteristics of a population, such as the distribution of age groups, sex, race and ethnic groups, rural and urban populations, are called its *demographic characteristics*. Demography is closely related to other sciences (such as biology, geography, and human ecology), to the agricultural sciences, and to the social sciences, such as sociology, anthropology, political science, and so on. The concerns of demographers often overlap substantially with these allied fields, and specialists from related disciplines often are called upon to participate in studies on the present and long-range effects of population growth.

The first major contribution to the study of population was made by the English clergyman Thomas Malthus (1766–1834), who predicted the catastrophic consequences of unrestricted population growth.[4] Basically, Malthus argued that population tends to increase geometrically, while the food supply increases arithmetically. He observed that the rate of annual population increase had risen and would continue to do so, while the food supply available would grow at a constant rate. Eventually, the rate of population increase would exceed the rate of increase in the food supply. Since, he argued, annual rates of population would continue to rise, there would be a greater discrepancy each succeeding year between the rate of population growth and the increment in available resources. These gloomy predictions stimulated much interest in the problem of population outstripping resources; many nations began keeping accurate records of population growth as a matter of public policy.

Demographic Variables

Birth and Death Rates   The two major variables determining the rate of world population growth are *birth rates* (population fertility) and *death rates* (population mortality). In order to provide some proof regarding the forecasts of impending doom made by Malthus, nations began to keep track of the relationship between births and deaths. For purposes of comparison, demographers have agreed on some standardization. Rates are expressed according to the number of births and deaths per 1,000 people in the population at the beginning of any given year. A birth rate of 15 indicates that there were 15 births during a specific year for every 1,000 people who comprised the population at the beginning of that year. Death rates express the number of deaths per 1,000 residents at the beginning of a similar period. Using these two indices, the rate of natural increase in a population can be computed by finding the difference between the birth and death rates. For example, if the birth rate for any given year was 22 per 1,000 and the death rate was 8 per 1,000, the rate of natural increase would be 14 per 1,000. In order to find the percentage increase, the rate of natural increase is divided by 10. This produces a figure expressed against a total of 100 instead of 1,000. Using that example, dividing 14 by 10 gives a figure of 1.4 percent for the rate of natural increase in a population for that given year.

Birth and Death Rates

	Birth	*Death*
1940	79.9	10.8
1945	85.9	10.6
1950	106.2	9.6
1954	118.1	9.2
1958	120.2	9.5
1960	118.0	9.5
1962	112.1	9.5
1964	104.8	9.4
1966	91.3	9.5
1968	85.7	9.7

SOURCE: U.S. Department of Commerce, Bureau of the Census.

Migration Patterns   Two other factors must be considered in order to gain an understanding of the processes of population growth. While the difference between the birth and death rates gives the rate of natural increase, it must be taken into account that human populations are somewhat mobile. Populations will experience gains and losses due to *migration patterns*. Movement of persons *into* a specific population, or *immigration*, adds to population growth; movement *out* of the population, or *emigration*, subtracts from it. The net effect of migration can be calculated by noting the difference between the rates of immigration and emigration. As in the case of birth and death rates, immigration and emigration rates can be easily computed. To obtain the rate of immigration, find the total number of persons moving into a population in a given year and express that figure in terms of the proportion of immigrants per 1,000 residents in the population at the beginning of that year. A figure of 5 for an immigration rate would indicate that the population had received 5 immigrants during that year per 1,000 residents at the beginning

Demography

of that year. Similarly, an emigration rate of 3 signifies that for every 1,000 residents at the beinning of a given year, 3 persons left the population during that year. The difference between the rates is 2, giving the total contribution of migration to population growth as 2 persons added per 1,000 residents.

By employing the measures of natural increase and migration, the actual rate of population increase can be determined. Adding the rate of natural increase and the rate of migration provides the figure. Thus, the rate of population growth for any given population in any year can be expressed as follows:

$$\text{net increase} = (\text{birth rate} - \text{death rate}) + (\text{immigration} - \text{emigration})$$

Let us apply that formula to our example. The net increase of the hypothetical population in one year would be

$$\text{net increase} = \left(\frac{22 \text{ births}}{\text{per } 1{,}000} - \frac{8 \text{ deaths}}{\text{per } 1{,}000} \right) + \left(\frac{5 \text{ immigrants}}{\text{per } 1{,}000} - \frac{3 \text{ emigrants}}{\text{per } 1{,}000} \right)$$

or

$$\text{net increase} = 14 + 2 = 16$$

Convert that figure to a percentage—16 divided by 10—and the total increase of that population would be 1.6 percent.

Now substitute the 1968 United States figures for each of the demographic variables: birth rate 17.2 per 1,000; death rate, 9.2; immigration rate, approximately 2 per 1,000; emigration rate, negligible, less than 0.1 per 1,000. That would give a *net increase* of

$$(17.2 - 9.2) + (2 - 0.1) = 8 + 1.9 = 9.9$$
$$9.9 \div 10 = 0.99$$

or just under 1 percent per year.

Although America is experiencing rather rapid annual population growth relative to the base population of 205 million, certain societies in Asia and Latin America are experiencing far more acute problems. Comparable birth rate figures for selected societies include: Costa Rica, birth rate 45, death rate 7; Mexico, 43 and 9, respectively; Ceylon, 32 and 8; Malaya, 36 and 7. To indicate the significance of these figures, Costa Rica's population will double in eighteen years, provided the rate of growth does not change. However, for reasons to be discussed later, it now seems unlikely that population increases will be quite as large as projected.

Patterns of Birth and Death Rates

We have noted that the major force controlling the size and rate of world population growth is the relationship between birth and death rates. That relationship can fall into one of four different patterns. *High birth and death rates* produce slow rates of population growth. This was the dominant pattern through medieval times; in many areas of the world in which famine and disease still persist and modern medicine is absent, this trend in population change still lingers. A second relationship exists when *birth rates are high* and *death rates low*. Under such conditions, there would be rapid increases in population as a result of the excess of births over deaths. That kind of population growth pattern was noted earlier in such nations as Costa Rica, Mexico, Ceylon, and Malaya. It would not take too many decades for such a pattern of population growth to reach disastrous proportions. A third pattern has *low birth rates* and *high death rates*. That kind of growth trend, if sufficiently long, would result in the extermination of the population. Such an excess of death over birth rates occurs when contagious diseases, such as measles, are brought by Western colonizers to non-Western populations who possess no natural immunities against the diseases. *Low birth and death rates* is the fourth pattern; it produces virtually no population growth. Maintaining that relationship between birth and death rates is the goal of organizations, such as Zero Population Growth, that are concerned with the problem of manipulating population size and controlling the rate of growth.

Demographic Transition   Demographers have proposed that the history of world population growth follows a particular pattern of relationship between birth and death rates. This theory describing the stages followed by world population growth has been called the theory of the *demographic transition*.[5] It proposes that world population growth proceeds from a baseline of high birth and death rates. High rates of infant mortality and low incidence of longevity produce high death rates; high birth rates persist either because of the need to replace the population lost on account of the high death rate or because of the lack of any effective birth control technology. This is a stage of *high potential growth*, since eventually the increasing contacts with other societies are likely to result in the importation of some techniques to reduce the death rate. Even a slight alteration in the death rate will produce a substantial gain in population, since the birth rate remains so high. Population grows rapidly in a short period of time owing to the application of control that reduces the death rate. Population growth will proceed unchecked unless some attempts are made to bring the birth rate in line with the lowered death rate. Once this is done, the pattern of population growth gradually settles into a balance of birth and death rates. What has occurred, then, is a demographic *transition* from high birth and death rates to low birth and death rates; that transition is accompanied by rapid population growth in the period falling between the two periods when birth and death rates were in balance.

Some research suggests that population growth patterns may not always follow the stages predicted by the theory of the demographic transition.[6]

Recall that the period of rapid population growth was ushered in by a reduction in the death rate while birth rates remained unaltered at a high level. William Peterson, using the population of the Netherlands as an example, found that population increase could be traced to an increase in the birth rate following a change in the family and agricultural economic system, which promoted the expansion of the farm system and the development of independent, nuclear families. Changes in the birth rate may also be produced as a result of war. Following World War II, the birth rate in the United States jumped sharply as returning soldiers established families. And such other factors as industrialization, improved standard of living, better housing, and the density of population have potential influences on the birth rate. It appears, then, that while the theory of the demographic transition may be applicable to certain societies, it may have to be modified to account for the population growth patterns of others.

The theory of the demographic transition is an optimistic one since it predicts that the ultimate population growth pattern will be one characterized by low birth *and* death rates. And eventually birth control technology will be applied in those countries experiencing rapid growth because of recent reduction in high death rates and the maintenance of high birth rates. Time is not on the side of such nations. The decision to apply population controls might well be too late to insure even minimal sustenance levels for their populations.

Factors Affecting American Population Growth

Fertility   The term *fertility* refers to the actual rate of reproduction and is measured by the birth rate. *Fertility* is always limited by *fecundity*—the potential rate of reproduction in a population. Fertility would equal fecundity only if every woman in the society had as many children as she was capable of producing during the span of years in which she could bear children. That could hardly happen because of the societal limits on the type of sexual behavior allowed females. Examples of these are the taboos directed at premarital, extramarital, and exogamous sexual contact. When these are applied from puberty to menopause, they function to restrict fecundity. Other limits on fecundity derive from social, cultural, and personal sources, the last of these being limitations imposed by individuals themselves for preferential or economic reasons.

Differential fertility rates   Relative to such other societies as Costa Rica, Mexico, Malaya, and Ceylon, the United States has had a low birth rate. However, within the population of the United States there are considerable variations in fertility. These variations are known as *differenital fertility rates*. We shall discuss the most important of these—racial, religious, and socioeconomic differentials and the rural-urban differential. *Social class* (or socioeconomic) *differentials* in fertility continue to persist, with the working class having consistently higher birth rates than the middle and upper classes. Some view this persistent fertility differential with alarm, arguing that the most educated and competent segments of society are those that are under-reproducing. However, it appears that fears regarding the disappearance of the middle class are unfounded. Working-class fertility shows signs of decreasing for a variety of reasons. In addition, as a result of relative affluence, middle-class fertility shows signs of increasing but not at a significant rate. The affluence of the middle class is well known to members of the working class; they are aware that small families make for greater prosperity and an ability to provide more for each family member, thus insuring some chance for mobility for the children. The decline in working class fertility can be traced in part to the increase in the availability of birth control information and birth control devices, which have been provided by clinics and programs designed to educate poorer people to help themselves out of poverty by limiting the family size. Declines in the working-class fertility rate have been observed among rural and urban populations, indicating the extent to which birth control programs have spread throughout that society. However, it is essential to indicate that any alarm over the disappearance of the middle class appears to be based on the notion that social strata are, to some considerable extent, a function of inherited differences in talent. Should any significant fertility differences be maintained between the middle and so-called working class, it seems likely that quite adequate (and upwardly mobile) replacements would be available from the working class. The seeming differences between middle- and working-class persons are for the most part acquired, not inherited, characteristics. With any substantial decline in the numbers of middle-class persons, there would be ample numbers of individuals with substantial abilities (if not the acquired skills and education) to replace them.

Agrarian patterns of life favor the maintenance of high birth rates because children are regarded as economic assets on farms. This *rural-urban fertility differential* has historical antecedents and is widespread throughout human societies. In developing societies, for example, not only are children an important source of farm labor but they may also constitute their parents' only genuine form of "social security." As the United States continues to urbanize and as rural birth rates continue to decrease and approach the urban rates, overall declines in the national birth rate can be predicted in subsequent decades.

There continue to be substantial differentials in fertility among the various religious groups. Catholics retain the highest overall birth rates of any major religious group. That *religious fertility differential* occurs at each socioeconomic level; both working-class and middle-class Catholics each have higher birth rates than their Protestant or Jewish counterparts. Among Catholics, social class differences in fertility result in higher birth rates among working-class Catholics than among middle-class Catholics. But the overall high birth rate

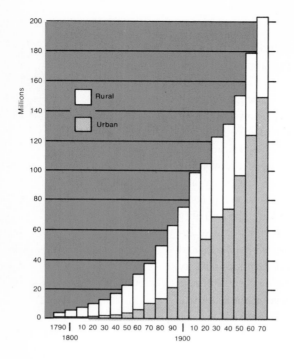

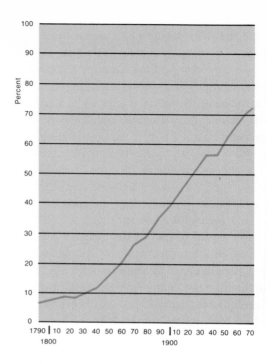

**Urban and Rural
Population: 1790–1970**

**Percent of Population—
Urban: 1790–1970**

may decline if the trend toward liberalization of official Catholic views on birth control takes effect.

Racial birth-rate differentials have persisted in the United States. Among Blacks, birth rates have always exceeded those among whites at all socio-economic levels. Although birth rates among urban Blacks were less than those among rural Blacks, relative to the birth rates among whites, both rates

Birth Rates by Race in the U.S.

Race	Rates 1940	1950	1960[1]
White	18.6	23.0	22.7
Negro	26.5	33.1	31.9
Indian	42.0	45.8	40.3
Japanese	15.0	24.5	28.0
Chinese	14.5	43.9	24.6
Other	22.0	19.1	37.8
All Races	19.4	24.1	23.7

SOURCE: National Center for Health Statistics, Public Health Service, U.S. Department of Health, Education, and Welfare. Rates per 1,000 population in each specified group, enumerated as of April 1, for 1940, 1950, and 1960. Rates for 1940 and 1950 based on

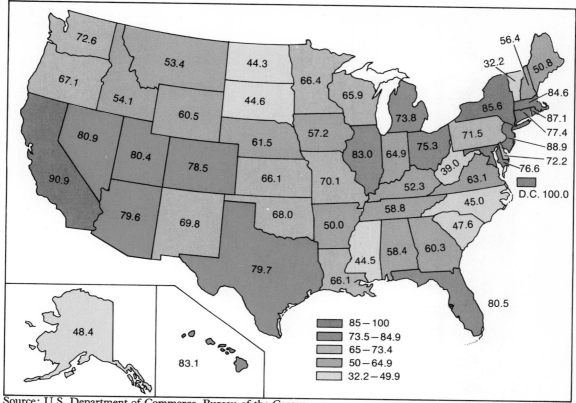

Source: U.S. Department of Commerce. Bureau of the Census.

births adjusted for underregistration; data for 1960, registered births.
[1] Based on a 50 percent sample of births. Includes Alaska and Hawaii for 1960.

Percent of Population—
Urban by States: 1970

are fairly high. Within the Black population, fertility differentials are similar to those that have been observed for the population as a whole, with social class, religion, and residential factors emerging as important variables. There appears to be a trend toward convergence of birth rates developing between the Black and white populations. Up to now, the reduction in the Black birth rate has been observed primarily within the middle class.

Overall national birth rate Fertility trends suggest that the overall national birth rate, which has been declining since the 1960's from the peak of the post-World-War-II "baby boom," may be leveling off at a fairly low rate. The growing popularity of birth control is aided in part by the emergence of such movements as Zero Population Growth and Planned Parenthood, which stress the immorality of having children who cannot be cared for adequately and who might contribute to a severe future overpopulation problem. Economic considerations also play an important role in the declining

Demography

Economic deprivation is reflected in the shorter life spans and higher infant mortality of poor Blacks and whites. The mortality rate among Blacks substantially exceeds that among whites.

birth rate. The extended period of education and training for young people so characteristic of modern societies very probably functions as a brake on fertility. Barbara Ward writes that "when people see more opportunities for better education . . . they begin to consider whether a smaller family might not be better for themselves and their children . . . Lower birth-rates are more likely to be a consequence than a cause of economic expansion."[7]

It also seems probable that one effect of the mass media is to depress fertility rates. Information on such things as family planning, ready access to birth control devices and information on their use and the inculcation of

Population and Population Growth

attitudes of disapproval against large families are all functions, to some considerable extent, of the mass media. Finally, a characteristic of modern societies—that is, rationality—tends to cause people to consider the pros and cons of having children and decide to limit their families.

If women decide against having large families on rational grounds, they consider economic factors among others. For example, over 35 percent of the current American labor force is composed of women. The obvious difficulties of a woman continuing to work during the latter stages of pregnancy and for at least a short while after giving birth are sharp restraints on family size; indeed, there seems to be a larger proportion of what used to be something of a rarity, childless couples. In agrarian and subsistence-level societies, on the other hand, the sexual division of labor is in large part based on the fact that women do bear children. Thus the kind of work women do in such societies places no check on fertility rates. In modern societies, the situation is reversed.

Mortality   Major *mortality differentials* in the United States exist between the sexes, racial groups, and socioeconomic segments. Economic deprivation is reflected in the shorter life spans and higher infant mortality of poor Blacks and whites. The mortality rate among Blacks substantially exceeds that among whites, particularly within the working classes. Sex differences in mortality continue to favor greater longevity for women. Although the rigors of the adult male occupational role have been used as an argument to explain the sex differential, mortality differentials favor females at all age levels. Occupational roles and the strain associated with them apparently do not account sufficiently for the reduced longevity of men; it appears evident that females are genetically favored for longer life.

As social change proceeds and the barriers that kept Blacks from taking advantage of opportunities continue to fall, the mortality differential between the races should continue to decrease. If, for example, adequate housing is provided on a large scale in urban ghettos so that the medical problems created by overcrowding in unsanitary conditions are reduced, there should be substantial declines in the mortality rates among urban Blacks. As opportunities for upward mobility continue to open up and Black males gain access to positions that do not involve occupational hazards or other noxious conditions, then the high mortality rate among Black males should show a marked decline. Future predictions about the fluctuation of the mortality rate among selected segments of the population are tied closely to the speed and success of that kind of social change, which can eradicate many of the conditions producing differentially high mortality among the poor and deprived segments of the population.

Immigration and Emigration   The role *immigration* has played in producing population growth will be minimal in the future, because the base population of the United States is currently so high. In the late nineteenth century, particularly the 1880's and 1890's, vast waves of immigration from Europe swelled the population dramatically. Because of the reaction of the host population, chiefly those descendants of Northern and Western European immigrants who entered the United States prior to 1820, extensive controls on immigration were imposed. Charges were made that the immigration quotas assigned yearly to various countries discriminated against Catholic countries and those with substantial Jewish populations, particularly the Southern and Eastern European nations. These quotas have been abolished, ending the blatant discrimination against certain nations. But a ceiling has been placed on the volume of immigration in any given year, thus placing a substantial restriction on the total number of immigrants allowed to enter the United States. The limit, which is subject to alteration in some situations, such as the airlift of Cuban refugees to Miami, is around 155,000 immigrants in any one year. The contribution immigration makes to population growth is meager indeed.

Immigration to and Emigration from the U.S., 1911–1971

Period	Immigrants	Emigrants
1911–1915	4,459,831	1,444,530
1916–1920	1,275,980	702,464
1921–1925	1,538,913	697,397
1926–1930	1,468,296	347,679
1931–1935	220,209	323,863
1936–1940	308,222	135,875
1941–1945	170,952	42,696
1946–1950	864,087	113,703
1951–1955	1,087,638	134,220
1956–1960	1,427,841	(1)
1961–1965	1,450,312	(1)
1966–1969	1,498,039	(1)
1970	373,326	(1)
1971	370,480	(1)

SOURCE: U.S. Immigration and Naturalization Service.

Emigration from the United States has been so small as to have virtually no effect upon population growth patterns. Aside from the much publicized emigration of individuals opposed to conditions within the United States or to governmental policies on such issues as the conflict in Vietnam and race relations, no substantial emigration of Americans has been observed as of the end of 1973. While emigration has solved many population problems, such as those occurring in western Europe prior to the great Atlantic migration to America, emigration does not appear to have any appreciable affect on reducing overpopulation in the United States.

While migration patterns may have little influence on the overall population growth rate, the pattern of movement of people within the confines of the United States has had profound effects—on life styles, overcrowding, housing density, environmental population, and so on. In the 1960's, the following trends in *internal migration* have been observed:

1. heavy migration toward metropolitan areas from rural regions, resulting in a rapid depopulation of small towns in traditionally farm states such as Kansas, Nebraska, and the Dakotas

2. heavy migration from low-income to high-income areas, with rural counties losing population disproportionately

3. heavy migration to states with warmer climates, such as Pacific coast states, Arizona, and the metropolitan areas of the southern states, particularly Florida

4. increased migration of Blacks to the metropolitan areas of the Pacific Coast, with little abatement in the rate of movement from the rural South to the urban North

5. heavy migration of middle and upper income groups from the central cities to the suburbs, with the suburbs of northern cities in particular becoming disproportionately "white", and the central cities predominately "Black" and "ethnic" (Spanish-American and other minority groups)

6. some indication of a trend among Blacks of moving out of central cities to suburbs as housing becomes available.[8]

Major redistributions of population were predicted for the 1970's, based on trends noted in the 1970 census. Although the validity of the predictions can't be known for some time, let us see what they are. There should be an increasing suburbanization of the population, resulting in strip cities spanning the distance between metropolitan areas. Such large urban and suburban regions, called *megalopolises* by demographers, are already forming in the Northeast between Washington, D.C. and Boston, Massachusetts; along the shores of the Great Lakes between Erie, Pennsylvania, and Milwaukee, Wisconsin; in the Southeast in the Piedmont regions of North and South Carolina; along the Pacific coast between San Francisco and San Diego, California; and in Florida along the east coast, particularly in the West Palm Beach—Miami region. Suburbs will merge so that the space between central cities will be filled by housing clusters serving as dormitory communities for people who derive their economic subsistence from those cities.

States with favorable climates, most notably Florida, California, and Arizona, are likely to face the problem of an increasing immigration of retired persons. Since many of these people exist on fixed incomes, they often require supplementary income, such as public welfare. In addition, health care centers will have to be provided to care for the special medical needs of the elderly. Because retired people are usually no longer productive, they will place a strain on the resources of communities in states with attractive climates.

Other Demographic Characteristics of American Population

Education   In the 1960's, the average level of education attained rose consistently among all major segments of the American population.[9] Comparing 1970 and 1960 on the basis of the number of persons in the 20–29 age group who were high school graduates, the total increased from 15 to 80 percent. The median number of school years completed for the entire population was 12.6 in 1968, reflecting the size of the population attaining post-high-school education.

The increase in the educational level of the entire population has had significant social impact. It has produced an increase in competition for jobs, particularly among high school graduates, although even among college graduates, the pressure of competition for available jobs has increased dramatically. Without a high school education at the very least, a person is at a disadvantage when attempting to earn a living.

Income Level   The median family income for the population of the United States as a whole is just under $10,000 per year. The median income among white families, slightly higher than the median for the whole population, exceeded the median income among Black families by about $4,000 as of 1968.[10] During the 1960's, nonwhite income relative to white income continued to improve slowly, undoubtedly a result of the gradual lessening of discrimination in hiring. Still, applying the United States government standard of poverty (a family income of less than $4,000 annually) and analyzing distribution of poverty in the United States, we find that three times as many nonwhite families are poor (roughly 30 percent) as compared to white families (10 percent).

Sex   The sex composition of the population is expressed through *sex ratios*. They indicate the number of males per 100 females in the population. They are calculated as follows:

$$\text{sex ratio} = \frac{\text{males}}{\text{females}} \times 100$$

While the sex ratio of the United States as a whole has been declining gradually, reaching 95.4 in 1968, there are variations in different regions. For example, in frontier regions such as Alaska, the sex ratio is high (Alaska's is 132). Cities, on the other hand, have low sex ratios (Washington, D.C.'s is 88).

Males tend to migrate in large numbers to frontier type regions, while females cluster disproportionately in bureaucratic and industrial centers.

Age Examining the age composition of the United States, we find that the dependent population—children and elderly people—is quite large, although not overwhelmingly so. The baby boom of the late 1940's has had its effect on enrollments in colleges and universities. Some demographers predict a slow-down in the growth in enrollment rates, which will lessen the pressure somewhat on those institutions. Indeed, in 1972, it appeared that this process had begun. However, as those "war babies" emerge into young adulthood, they will be taking their place in society in such numbers that a great strain will be placed on the nation's ability to provide jobs, housing, and the various amenities to which their life styles have accustomed them.

SOLVING THE POPULATION PROBLEM: BIRTH CONTROL

In the eighteenth century Malthus argued that population growth would be restricted by two sets of limits.[11] The first of these he called *positive checks*—famine, disease, violent death, and so on. The second set, because it is more subject to the control of man, he labeled *preventive checks*. Examples are infanticide, killing of the aged and infirm, and voluntary birth control. Since the first two examples are measures that may be undertaken only when survival is at stake, the third alternative, birth control, appears to be a rational, nonviolent solution to the problem of overpopulation. However, as we shall see, there are substantial obstacles to overcome if population growth is to be checked in time.

Proposals for birth control programs have emphasized a wide range of activities, from voluntary birth control to governmental regulation of family size. In the United States some have suggested that incentives for birth control be built into the tax structure, such as giving small families tax breaks. Others argue that a major overhaul of values and of the social structure is necessary before effective birth control can be implemented. Population specialists hope that their predictions of worldwide catastrophes due to unrestricted population growth will deter families from producing too many children.

Opposition

There are many obstacles to programs of voluntary birth control. One problem is how to enlist the cooperation of various segments of the population. For example, if wealthier families feel that they can afford the economic burden of a large family, how can a program of voluntary birth control be directed at convincing them that a small family would be in their long-run self-interest? Then there is the opposition to birth control based on religious conviction, which is extremely difficult to counter effectively. If some feel that the problem of overpopulation is not the proper concern of man, how can a program of birth control be developed to convince such people that overpopulation was not God's will? Moreover, many people feel that their private decisions on family size are purely matters of individual control. They would oppose any program of imposed birth control on the basis of their endorsement of individual freedom in such matters.

Some of the opposition to birth control is actually to specific methods of control rather than a rejection of the overall purpose of population control. Recently, adverse publicity about the side effects of oral contraceptives led many to discontinue using the "pill." Intrauterine devices are opposed because, if improperly installed, they can cause physical harm. Programs featuring voluntary sterilization encounter resistance on a wide scale. Many fear that a decision for sterilization may be regretted later on, when it would be too late to reverse the effects of the operation. The most emotional opposition to a birth control procedure is directed against abortion. Arguments against it are usually based on the presumption that life begins when the human egg is fertilized by the sperm. According to such a definition, abortion is murder. Additional sentiment against abortion rests on the assertion that such procedures have dangerous psychological and medical effects; they stress that such operations are risky for the patient and often are followed by depression and guilt. Other arguments emphasize the possible effects that readily available abortion would have on weakening family ties, moral standards, and patterns of sexual permissiveness. Opposition has, perhaps, been intensified by a United States Supreme Court ruling in 1973. It is now unconstitutional for any legislative body to pass legislation banning abortion in the first six months of pregnancy, provided the abortion is performed in a hospital by a qualified physician.

Since, as we have already suggested, there are prevailing sources of resistance to voluntary programs of birth control, it is hard to imagine acceptance of mandatory requirements on family size enforced by external authority. Against such a background of opposition to any such governmental interference in personal affairs, it appears unlikely that programs of mandatory regulation of family size will attract enough supporters to produce legislation.

Implementing Programs

The immediate prospects for success in implementing birth control programs apparently lie on the voluntary level. These would involve the operation of voluntary sterilization programs; the establishment of birth control clinics to dispense birth control information and devices; and the spread of legislation permitting legal, voluntary abortion. Substantial support is emerging for laws allowing any woman of majority age the right to decide to terminate a pregnancy for any reasons. Laws already exist that permit abortion in the event that the health of the mother is threatened. New York State passed a liberalized abortion law which has served as a model for other states. Much of the effectiveness of the clinics and the information and devices they dispense will depend on whether knowledge of their existence and availability becomes widespread. Many potential users of birth control devices and information are unaware that such agencies even exist in their localities. Another problem hinges on the ability of the clinics to communicate effectively to the potential user the exact procedures to be followed for successful birth control. Often, too technical directions will confuse the prospective user, because of educational inadequacies or lack of familiarity with medical procedure. Oral contraception, for example, is effective only if the patient can keep track of the normal monthly fertility cycle. This requires a level of sophistication that may be beyond the capacity of some people. There are, for example, parts of the world in which clocks and watches are virtually nonexistent and interest in calendars is largely a matter of seasons of the year. Gearing birth control techniques to the needs of all people and simplifying the procedures so they can be easily carried out will insure more effective population control.

If meaningful incentives can be developed to reward family-size limitations, the effectiveness of birth control programs would be aided considerably. Encouragement of life styles in which large families were discouraged and viewed with disfavor could set the stage for widespread acceptance of the value of birth control. As noted earlier, economic incentives for small families are one way. Cash payments, credits for government-supported educational training for children, and state-subsidized bonuses are a few alternatives to encourage birth control. Before such schemes could be legalized into policy, however, opposition to the state having anything to do with birth control would have to be effectively countered. And there would be arguments that such policies were discriminatory, placing an economic burden on the families of the poor, of the uneducated, of those who opposed birth control on religious grounds, and of those who resented the government's interference in what they regard as a purely private matter.

International Level

At an international level, birth control programs face substantial obstacles. One major factor is the resistance of a nation against any attempts by other nations to deal with their internal affairs. In many agrarian societies, besides reasons cited earlier, a man's worth is measured by his fertility—that is, the cult of *machismo*. Needless to say, birth control programs do not enjoy wide appeal in such societies. It often is very difficult to convince people that it is in their self-interest and in the interest of mankind at large to limit the size of their families. These cultural differences in attitudes toward fertility make it much harder to introduce the *idea* of birth control, much less to convince people to use birth control devices.

It might be argued that nations that resist birth control programs could be coerced by threats of economic sanction such as the withdrawal of aid, boycott, and so on. However, causing people in these countries further suffering because of their beliefs on birth control might seem stern and inhumane. Still, such procedures may be suggested in the future, particularly if the predictions about overpopulation in developing countries turn out to be accurate.

An alternative method of controlling population would specify an increase in the death rate, an option that, for most people, would be totally unacceptable. While some societies have employed this procedure—Hitler's program to exterminate Jews and other ethnic groups is an example—rarely in history has such a purposive increase in the death rate been carried out on a large scale.

It may be possible that technological breakthroughs will develop some radically different method of food production in order to forestall, for a short while, the inevitable depletion of resources owing to overpopulation. Malthus did not consider the possibility that technological advances might keep pace with population growth. However, almost two hundred years have passed since he made his predictions, and it is possible that the rate of population growth may already be outstripping the rate of food production more substantially than we yet realize.

Evidence to support this contention can be found in abundance by referring to Oscar Harkavy's study of the economic problems of population growth, which was reviewed by James Vander Zanden.[12] Recalling that Malthus predicted that population tended to increase geometrically while the food supply increased arithmetically, Harkavy's study provides support that this discrepancy between population growth and food supply has just begun to become critical. For example, in 1965, while the population of the world grew by the present rate of about 2 percent (adding roughly 60 million people to the world's total), food production increased only 1 percent. That means that in Asia, Africa, and Latin America, food production is declining and so must food consumption per capita. By 1977, projecting the 1965 rates of increase for food production and population, daily per capita food consumption of the population of the world would be cut by *half*, provided that food resources were *equally divided* among the nations and peoples of the world. Since it is obvious that serious inequities exist in resource distribution both between and within nations, the effect of this disparity will fall disproportionately on the shoulders of those who are already near starvation.

It has been argued by some that increased technology will provide the means to avoid disaster before it is too late. There are a number of handicaps to agricultural productivity—some technical, some cultural—which might serve to challenge this argument. Widespread illiteracy places many of the technological innovations out of the reach of some agriculturalists, as do fear and suspicion of the motives of those trying to introduce such aids to production. Even if those innovations were known, the low per capita income of many farmers prevents them from taking advantage of the developments. The economies of many agrarian nations often do not provide the agricultural sector with much more than mere subsistence. In addition, in some agrarian societies the producing farmer sees little of the product of his labor in the way of profits, as much is claimed by land-owners in the form of rental.

Even if the so-called advanced nations possessed the technology, manpower, and incentive to spread major agricultural innovations on a grand scale to underdeveloped nations, and provided massive food-supply programs, the results on the local economy could be just as disastrous as the famine such aid would be trying to alleviate. Providing a country with large, free quantities of agricultural commodities produced locally could result in a collapse in the local price system, which would bankrupt marginal farmers and cause economic depression among the very segments of the population toward which the aid programs were directed. Even if major breakthroughs could be tailored to the structure of the local economies, it is highly unlikely that, in countries with annual growth rates of 3 percent or more, the ratio of food production to population would be restored in a few years. In short, it appears that even modern technology would be unable to cope with *unrestricted* population growth.

A balance between birth and death rates (zero population growth) seems unlikely in the near future on any worldwide basis. As Durand points out, "the expansion of world population is not likely to spend its momentum very shortly. It is apparent that the twenty-first century might well surpass the twentieth for [the] magnitude of its addition to the number of the earth's inhabitants . . ."[13]

Vast, continued expansion in the world's population will occur if current trends continue into the future, as we have noted before. But there is some evidence that even in the so-called developing countries, neither the government nor the people are fully oblivious to the dangers of overpopulation. India, Pakistan, Malaysia, Korea, Hong Kong, Ceylon, Barbados, Taiwan, the United Arab Republic, the People's Republic of China, and other nations have instituted programs designed to reduce fertility rates within their borders.[14] Some of the programs are only in the beginning stage. Others are

Solving the Population Problem: Birth Control

375

well established and show signs of having the desired effects, with Malaysia having one of the most successful in the world.[15]

But the important point with respect to the developing nations is that population, or, rather, excess population, has become a social problem—it is recognized as a problem about which something can be done through collective action. On a mildly sanguine note, then, it can be speculated with more than a little historical support that the grim extrapolations of some demographers showing a catastrophic increase in the world's population may prove to be overly pessimistic. There are two principal reasons for this.

1. As we have just noted, some developing nations are taking steps to reduce fertility, even though, in many cases, these steps are less vigorous than might be considered desirable.

2. It is essential to keep in mind that the cause of present population increases is not so much a higher fertility rate but, rather, a lower death rate—particularly lower infant mortality. Although people are tending to live much longer, eventually the death rate will tend to draw closer to the birth rate. And, as noted in the first point, active measures are being taken to accelerate that process by reducing fertility rates.

If technology, particularly medical technology, has done much to bring about a population increase of a worrisome magnitude, then technology will assist in alleviating it.

CONCLUSION

This chapter has, in the main, deliberately presented a somewhat pessimistic picture of the world's future based on projections of population growth figures and the resultant excessive strain placed on the earth's resources by too many humans. Were these projections to prove accurate, it would be a real catastrophe for future generations. But sociological projections depend upon something more than extensions of lines on graphs. They depend on an analysis of human behavior, particularly group behavior and estimates based on expectations of how humans may or may not tend to behave in given situations.

While there is much constancy and predictability in human behavior, that constancy and predictability include a certain measure of flexibility—the ability and willingness to alter behavioral patterns when such patterns can be seen to be detrimental. Although there are many exceptions, a good deal of human behavior persists even when such behavior can be clearly demonstrated to be dysfunctional, as all social scientists recognize. Nonetheless, wide publicity has been given to the so-called population explosion. The mass media all over the world have carried much information not merely regarding the dangers inherent in the continuation of this explosion but also ways of averting it. If people do react to information and if values can change under the impact of altering situations, then we might expect that the current fertility rate will be lower than it was in the mid-1960's. In other words, under the stimulus of information regarding the population explosion, as well as other factors cited earlier, it could be anticipated that birth rates in modern, complex societies would have begun to drop to a lower level. The United States provides an excellent example. Between 1960 and 1970 the total population went from approximately 180,000,000 persons to a figure in excess of 200,000,000, an increase of some 10.1 percent. When we compare the age groups for 1960 and 1970 we find that in only three were there larger numbers in 1960 than in 1970. Two of those age groups—30–34 and 35–39— are clearly a function of the Great Depression when the birth rate dropped considerably. The other is the 0–4 age group, which shows 17.2 million persons in that range in 1970 compared with 20.3 million in 1960. That is a decrease of 15.6 percent in the very youngest age group, an interesting statistic in view of the fact that the overall population in 1970 was 10.1 percent greater than in 1960. On a rough estimate, there were approximately 41.6 million women of childbearing age in 1970, as compared with 35.4 in 1960. Yet the *fertility rate* has not only decreased but has done so dramatically.[16] Describing that as well as other developments, Donald Bogue has stated that "recent developments in the worldwide movement to bring runaway birth rates under control are such that it is now possible to assert with considerable confidence that the prospects for success are excellent." But, keeping in mind the grim possibilities inherent in any demographic projection of great population increases that turns out to be correct, we will conclude with another quotation from Bogue:

These optimistic assertions are not intended to detract from the seriousness of the present population situation . . . My optimistic remarks [are certainly not] intended to cause the participants in an international fertility control program to be lulled into complacency. The successful outcome anticipated . . . is not one that will come automatically . . .[17]

If we can afford to be cautiously optimistic about the serious population problem, which is likely to continue for some time, we can also afford to be cautiously optimistic about another problem endemic in most human societies—prejudice and discriminatory practices directed at minorities. In the following chapter we will consider the sociological aspects of minority groups and of structural changes, ongoing as well as possible, that may serve to alleviate or do away with prejudice and discrimination.

11.1. To what extent can the theory of the *demographic transition* be employed to account for population growth patterns in the United States? What additional examples, such as the Netherlands, can be cited that contradict the phases predicted by the theory? What phase most accurately describes present population trends in America, as compared with other developed nations and selected underdeveloped ones?

11.2. Evaluate some of the moral, legal, political, and religious implications involved in the proposal that governments adopt policies about birth control.

11.3. Which of the various theories of city growth and planning best describes your home community? Which best describes the community in which the university or college you attend is located? What socioeconomic factors might be cited as possible causes of such a pattern of spatial organization?

11.4. Evaluate some of the social and economic problems that may emerge and intensify in the coming decade if the trends in internal migration continue. What are some of the possible political ramifications at the local, state, and national levels? What present political problems could be traced to these migration patterns within the United States?

11.5. Evaluate the possibility of mankind being able to cope with the immediate food crisis predicted by Harkavy. What are the social, political, and economic problems that might arise in nations facing such food shortages; what possible effects might there be on the character of international relations?

11.6. In recent history there have been several large-scale wars, acts of genocide, and natural disasters that are examples of what Malthus called *positive checks* on population growth. Discuss the relationship between ecological factors and such events as the Biafran war (Nigeria), the intertribal war in the Southern Sudan, the Bangladesh revolution, the anticipated Chinese expansion into Southeast Asia, and any others you can think of.

NOTES

[1] Philip M. Hauser, *Population Perspectives* (New Brunswick, N.J.: Rutgers University Press, 1960), p. 7. Hauser makes a number of population projections based on the world's growth rate up to 1960.

[2] Irene Taeuber, "Population and Society," in *Handbook of Modern Sociology*, ed. Robert E. L. Faris (Skokie, Ill.: Rand McNally, 1964), pp. 83–126.

[3] United Nations Department of Social Affairs, *The Determinants and Consequences of Population Trends* (New York: United Nations, 1953), p. 11, table 2.

[4] Thomas R. Malthus, *Population: The First Essay* (Ann Arbor, Mich.: The University of Michigan Press, 1959), chap. 5.

[5] Kingsley Davis, "The World's Population Crisis," in *Contemporary Social Problems,* 2d ed., ed. Robert K. Merton and Robert A. Nisbet (New York: Harcourt, Brace, Jovanovich, 1966), p. 378.

[6] William Peterson, "The Demographic Transition in the Netherlands," *American Sociological Review* 25 (1960), pp. 334–347. In a study of the validity of the theory of the demographic transition, Peterson found that, in the Netherlands, population growth was produced by a growth in the birth rate rather than by a decrease in the death rate. His findings contradicted the predictions of the theory.

[7] Barbara Ward, *The Rich Nations and the Poor Nations* (New York: Norton, 1962), p. 93.

[8] Donald J. Bogue, "Population Growth in the United States," in *The Population Dilemma,* ed. Philip M. Hauser (Englewood Cliffs, N.J.: Prentice-Hall, 1963), pp. 74–75. This reference contains projections of future United States population growth based on available data.

[9] *Digest of Education Statistics* (Washington, D.C.: U.S. Government Printing Office, 1968), p. 4, table 4.

[10] *Statistical Abstract of the United States, 1969* (Washington, D.C.: U.S. Government Printing Office, 1969), table 323.

[11] Malthus, *Population.*

[12] James W. Vander Zanden, *Sociology: A Systematic Approach* (New York: Ronald, 1970), pp. 555–590. See also Oscar Harkavy, *Economic Problems of Population Growth* (New York: Ford Foundation, 1964), p. 3.

[13] John D. Durand, "The Modern Expansion of World Population," in *Population and Society,* ed. Charles B. Nam (Boston: Houghton Mifflin, 1968), p. 119. Nam's book is a scholarly and complete account of demography in general; it provides several articles on a wide range of concerns for demographers and sociologists alike.

[14] In 1973 the Indian government announced the suspension of their birth control program, which appeared to have been sporadic and largely uncoordinated. The program had been based on such procedures as offering cash payments to males submitting voluntarily to a vasectomy and on attempts to educate women and men about the advantages of using known birth control procedures. Even though the program was far from successful in terms of meeting somewhat ambitious goals, the long-range effect of abandoning the program may be very serious in a nation already seriously overpopulated and lacking even minimal resources to feed its large population.

[15] Dorothy Nortman, "Population Policies in Developing Countries and Related International Attitudes," in *Population and Society,* ed. Charles B. Nam (Boston: Houghton Mifflin, 1968), pp. 651–665.

[16] U.S. Department of Commerce, Bureau of the Census, *General Population Characteristics* (Washington, D.C.: U.S. Government Printing Office, 1972), pp. 1–259.

[17] Donald J. Bogue, "The End of the Population Explosion," in *Studies in the Sociology of Social Problems,* ed. Paul B. Horton and Gerald R. Leslie (New York: Appleton, 1971), pp. 276 and 277.

ANNOTATED BIBLIOGRAPHY

Boskoff, Alvan. *The Sociology of Urban Regions.* New York: Appleton, 1962. A review of important aspects of urban social organization.

Childe, V. Gordon. *Man Makes Himself.* rev. ed. London: Watts and Co., 1941. This volume provides a thorough review of the Neolithic revolution in technology, which allowed for the development of permanent settlements and the beginnings of urbanization. Extremely well written and highly readable.

Cowgill, Donald O. "Transition Theory as General Population Theory." *Social Forces* 41 (1963), pp. 270–274. This article contains a general statement on population theory in general as well as the theory of the demographic transition.

Gist, Noel P. and Halpert, L. A. *Urban Society*. New York: Crowell, 1956. An important text reviewing topics such as the growth of cities, urban ecology, migration, and urban planning.

Hawley, Amos O. *Human Ecology: A Theory of Community Structure*. New York: Ronald, 1950. Although somewhat dated, this is still a major work on human ecology. Hawley proposes a broad-based theory of the relationship between ecology and community structure.

Sjoberg, Gideon. *The Preindustrial City*. New York: Free Press, 1960. The most substantial work existing on the history and growth patterns of pre-industrial cities. An essential work for an understanding of the process of urbanization in developing nations.

WHITE ONLY

$5.00 FINE FOR SPITTING
IN THE FOUNTIAN

12

Race and Ethnic Relations: Some are More Equal than Others

INTRODUCTION

The study of race and ethnic relations focuses on aspects of social inequality that result from differential treatment accorded to groups solely on the basis of ascribed characteristics. The treatment that members of certain racial and ethnic groups receive and the life chances they experience depend heavily on whether those ascribed characteristics are highly valued or not. In the case of racial groups, members are identified mostly by physical characteristics; members of ethnic groups are discerned largely through cultural means—the type of behavior, life style, beliefs, and attitudes they overtly display. Race relations, then, focus upon the *social significance of physical characteristics*. Ethnic relations deal with the *social significance of cultural patterns*. Both areas of study are concerned with determining the social processes through which physical and cultural differences result in social inequality among groups. And it is critical to ascertain the consequences that such social inequality has for all groups in societies.

Race and Ethnic Relations: Some are More Equal than Others

DEFINING TERMS

There is considerable confusion regarding the use of the terms "race" and "ethnic group." Often the two terms are used synonymously and sometimes in conjunction with "nationality." A *race* may be defined as a group of people who possess inherited *physical* characteristics that are visibly different from those of other groups. For the term "race" to have sociological meaning, however, we must understand that the concept has relevance for social relations *only when social importance is attached to these inherited physical differences.* Social importance can be given to very minute differences between groups, and for this reason there has been little agreement on exactly what criteria should be used to define race. There is a bit more consensus on the definition of *ethnic group*, which is a concept employed generally to refer to a group that is visibly different in terms of purely *cultural criteria*. Again, the concept has importance for sociologists *only when ethnic differences produce patterns of social relations in which social inequality is a dominating factor.* We use the word "visible" to emphasize that significant differences—racial or ethnic—are those that can easily be seen.

Misuse of the term "race" has been associated with some of the most violent sequences of intergroup relations ever observed, particularly in modern times. Confusion of learned, cultural traits with inherited physical characteristics has been common in such instances. Notable examples are the "traditional" Southern Black-white relations in the United States and the Jewish-Gentile relations in Germany in the 1930's. Genetic explanations are extended to explain daily habits, modes of living, language patterns, physical

Copyright © 1973 by Saturday Review/World, Inc.
Reprinted by permission of the publisher and Henry R. Martin.

"I'm fond of you, Maynard, but your stripes run the wrong way."

Race has been defined largely in terms of inherited physical differences among groups to which are accorded social significance. The concept has little meaning for sociologists if social significance is not attached to such differences.

demeanor, and a host of other behavior patterns clearly related to learning, not to heredity. As a result, great social importance is attached to minor aspects of daily interaction that are supposed to reflect genetic traits. In Nazi Germany, this assignment of social importance to insignificant behavior patterns was used as the major justification for a program of systematic genocide directed at the Jewish population, which became more identifiable to other groups and, as a result, more vulnerable to persecution and attempted annihilation.

CONCEPT OF RACE

Attempts at a Scientific Definition

Partly because of the historic use of the concept *race* as a part of social policy, the concept must be examined in terms of its use by the scientific community. It is also essential to identify the sources of controversy over the employment of the term in order to define the concept separately from notions of nationality or ethnicity.

Race has been defined largely in terms of inherited physical differences among groups to which are accorded social significance. The concept has little meaning for sociologists if social significance is not attached to such differences. Among scientists in general, there is little agreement about just what differences are *biologically* significant for categorizing *Homo sapiens* into race groupings. There are several schools of thought regarding the subject of human races, the most important of which shall be reviewed briefly.

Skin color, hair color and texture, amount and distribution of body hair, general body form, head contour, nasal shape, lip form, and eye fold are, generally, the physical criteria through which scientists have classified the species *Homo sapiens* into races. Using these physical characteristics as the primary basis, scientists divide the species into three main categories—*Negroid*, *Caucasoid*, and *Mongoloid*. A fourth but seldom used category is *Australoid*, by which is meant the original inhabitants of Australia. While the existence of hybrid, or mixed, populations is recognized, many have argued that those three groups comprise the basic variations in man. They assert that the existence of the three groups can be traced back almost to the point when *Homo sapiens* emerged as a primate species. An example of this approach can be found in the works of Coon. He argued for the existence of three basic ancestral categories, which he called "pure" races.[1] He contended that mixed populations emerged through migration and intergroup mating and marriage. Differentiation between such "pure" races occurred due to isolation, mutation, and other genetic factors. However, such a classification scheme is inadequate to account for the categorization of *admixtures*, that is groups possessing traits common to two or more major racial groups. As knowledge of the significance and distribution of physical traits expanded, more and more limitations and inadequacies of the various racial classification schemes became apparent. Moreover, recent evidence suggests that races, as traditionally classified, using schemes such as Coon's, may have emerged much later than previously suspected. The findings contradict earlier contentions that the three major races comprise three early variations in man. They suggest that physical differentiation in *Homo sapiens* may have been a recent phenomenon.

For the most part, science has not been successful in classifying man by using physical criteria. More current efforts aimed at determining the existence of racial groups have focused on such things as the analysis of the distribution of blood types. The goal of such research is to identify groups that have certain genetic tendencies, such as the prevalence of certain blood types and other genetic factors as, for example, sickle-cell anemia. Once this has been accomplished, scientists attempt to discern what observable physical traits are characteristic of these groups. By integrating the earlier physical-trait approach with more sophisticated techniques, it is hoped that a more accurate knowledge of race differences might result. In a study employing a combination of these techniques, Dobzhansky was able to classify man into thirty-four different groups.[2] This newer typology is far more exhaustive and is based on more inclusive genetic evidence than were earlier attempts. However, it must be emphasized that research into race and racial differences is in its infancy, and what data now exist are essentially descriptive.

Definitions of race, therefore, depend heavily on the type, number, and character of traits employed. The scientific community lacks consensus on the issue of both the number of races which exist and the criteria that should be used to define them. Regardless of this continuing controversy, race assumes importance for the social scientist when it is a factor producing, or associated with, social inequality. While there remains considerable disagreement among scientists regarding the usage of the term, there is agreement on one point: racial differences relate to *physical*, not cultural or behavioral, criteria. When those differences assume importance in social relations, however, the race factor becomes highly relevant for the social scientist. As Thomas noted in his observation on the self-fulfilling prophecy: "If people believe certain things to be real, then they are real in their consequences," [3] particularly for others. And the self-fulfilling prophecy can be seen to operate very clearly in race relations.

Misuse of the Concept

A Case in Point: Jewish-Gentile Relations

Jewish-Gentile relations present an example of a pattern of social interaction which can be explained, in part, by the misuse of the concept of race and the operation of the self-fulfilling prophecy. Further it will serve as an illustration of the consequences of such misuse. A great many people still insist that the Jews constitute a race. They support their argument by claiming that Jews are easily recognizable by shared physical characteristics, such as "hooked" noses, swarthy complexions, dark hair, and relatively short stature. Some carry that argument so far as to assert that certain behavior patterns, such as a predilection for making money and a strong consciousness of kind (identification with others who are similar to oneself), are genetically transmitted from generation to generation and comprise major elements of "Jewishness." There is no scientific evidence to support the idea that Jews constitute a racial group. Within the world's Jewish population there is a substantial variation in most of the major physical traits used to identify races. Jews coming from North Africa and the Arab nations of the Middle East are physically indistinguishable from their Arab neighbors; European Jews share most of the physical characteristics of European populations in general.

There also is no scientific evidence to support the contention that cultural traits can be transmitted genetically. Different groups of Jews may exhibit certain identifiable cultural traits as a result of similar historical experiences with non-Jews. For example, the concern with economic mobility and success may result from their centuries-long experiences of discrimination and harassment. And their consciousness of kind, may be a common reaction to deprivation and discrimination, as some race relations scholars assert.[4] Consequently, any argument that Jews constitute a race, and that certain cultural traits among Jews comprise a set of genetic factors, has no support from scientific sources.

Despite scientific evidence to the contrary, Jews, as well as many other groups, often are accorded differential treatment by others, who justify their actions on racial and genetic grounds. Such beliefs are extremely difficult to change, because the use of the language and genetic arguments in support of a pattern of discrimination and persecution provide a powerful-sounding and seemingly accurate argument. The tendency to equate cultural traits with hereditary factors is very often behind the misuse of the concept of race, which continues to be a major factor justifying social inequality among racial and ethnic groups.

RACISM

Because of the lack of agreement regarding what criteria should be used to define races, and because sophisticated scientific research into race and racial differences is in its infancy, there continues to be a great deal of controversy over the presence of, and significance of, racial differences. That controversy has centered on the issue of racial differences in ability, particularly mental ability. The argument has considerable historical antecedents, and some of the issues involved are critically related to the social significance given to the race factor in intergroup relations. There is much speculation about whether racial differences in intellectual ability do exist, and if so, what *kinds* of differences prevail. A review of the development and present state of the controversy suggests the importance of the issues involved and reflects the social significance of those issues.

Controversy Over Racial Differences

The controversy over the possibility that racial differences in innate abilities do exist was generated by the development and spread of racist ideologies, particularly in the United States. Racism is not a new phenomenon, nor is it limited to the United States or the Western world. Racist ideologies emerged in the Western world during the nineteenth century, and the central theme supported the idea of European racial superiority. For example, Joseph Gobineau took the position that the peoples of central and northern Europe, whom he labeled the "Aryan" race, were superior to all others both racially and culturally. He argued that racial admixture would bring about the degeneration of civilization.[5] Another nineteenth-century writer, Houston S. Chamberlain, contended that Teutonic peoples were the bearers of modern civilization and that all progress and development could be attributed to them.[6] He also stressed the importance of maintaining racial purity; he was highly critical of intermarriage between Teutons and other groups, particularly Jews, which he felt would result in the downfall of European civilization.

Concept of Racial Superiority Western racism spread rapidly from Europe to the United States when the expansion of capitalism in the New

World and the operation of the slave trade required some justification. In particular, the Judeo-Christian ideas of freedom and equality clashed sharply with the cruelty of the slave trade and the ownership of humans by other humans. Racism in the United States emerged initially as an attempt to rationalize the slave trade by defining Black Africans as sub-human. The Nazi rationalization for exterminating millions of Jews and sending thousands of Czechs, Poles, Russians, and others into forced labor was based on identical grounds. That particular type of racism is not peculiar to the United States but often is found in what Pierre van den Berghe calls *Herrenvolk* democracies,[7] those that are democratic for a master race but are tyrannical for subordinate races. In the case of the United States, racism was coincidental with the spread of Darwinist ideas about the evolution of man. As a result, many radical views on race were cast in pseudo-scientific language and were supported by logic based on hypotheses about evolution. Gradually, pseudo-theories developed to justify the exploitation of Africans on the premise that Blacks were at an earlier stage of evolution than whites; therefore they had to be controlled until they "evolved." This brand of racist evolutionary theory also allowed for the postponement of the problem of granting civil rights to Blacks for the foreseeable future, since evolutionary processes take millenia rather than decades. The eventual form of American racism rested upon the assumption that Blacks were biologically inferior to whites; accordingly, the lowest-status white man was superior to the highest-status Black.[8] Traditional Southern racial orthodoxy dictated that any extensive education for biologically inferior persons was useless, and Blacks should be educated only in those ways that would enable them to better serve whites and white interests. Such contentions supported the idea that Blacks could be educated only at a minimal level and led, after the abolition of slavery, to the establishment of the traditional Southern "separate but equal" school system. However, it is well known that schools for Blacks were markedly inferior.

Concept of Racial Purity   Another cornerstone of American racism that paralleled developments in Europe was the idea that racial purity must be maintained at all costs and that "mixed" races undergo degeneration and decay. In Europe the racist theorists directed their attention to the Jewish population as the source of degeneration and as a "pariah" population with which intermarriage was to be avoided at all costs. In the United States such racist ideas were aimed at the Black population. Such notions were couched in pseudo-scientific language with strong genetic overtones, using terms such as "Negro blood" and "white blood" to refer to genetic makeup. In most southern states persons were defined socially as Black if it could be proved that they had a Black great-grandparent; in Mississippi, a person was considered as Black if he or she had a Black great-great-great-grandparent. It should be noted that greater importance was placed on whether a person had any ancestors of the subordinate race, not on whether a person had ancestors of the dominant race. That indicates the extent to which social importance was attached to the assumed biological superiority of one race and to the maintaining of racial purity within the dominant race.

Mental Ability and Intelligence Tests   As a result of the worldwide consequences of racism for subordinated populations, social scientists and other investigators have devoted much time and effort to providing scientific refutation of racist ideologies. Those efforts have centered upon studying the question of whether there are any really significant biologically determined racial differences, particularly in mental ability. With the development of intelligence testing, there appeared to be some means through which the scientific study of racial differences could be undertaken.

The initial evidence showed that racial and ethnic groups did differ on intelligence tests. Immigrants from Northern and Central Europe and from the British Isles performed best on the tests; those from Southern and Eastern Europe, American Indians, Mexican-Americans, and Black Americans had lower average scores. More recent testing carried out as part of a survey of educational opportunities in the United States, which was summarized in the Coleman Report, corroborates the earlier findings.[9] The later tests were designed to measure mechanical ability, spatial ability, vocabulary, and mathematical ability; in each of these areas substantial differences continue to be observed.

Attempts have been made to account for those variations in intelligence-test scores, particularly for the higher scores observed among whites and the substantial difference in scores between blacks and whites. A number of scientists have argued that there may be some race-related difference in the *type* of intelligence possessed by different racial groups, and the presence of this difference in type might account for the Black-white score differentials. Arthur Jensen, an educational psychologist at the University of California at Berkeley, has argued that the observed average score difference of 15 points between Blacks and whites on IQ tests might reflect a deficiency in "cognitive" learning (abstract ability and reasoning) among Blacks; IQ tests primarily measure that type of intelligence.[10] Blacks, he argued, are likely to perform better on "rote" tasks or on those involving repetitive activity. He suggested that education that stressed cognitive learning would not be geared to the learning skills of Blacks. He proposed altering educational methods of teaching in order to take these race-related differences into account.

It is doubtful that any intelligence test can be developed that would be entirely independent of social and cultural factors. Although some developers of psychological tests claim that they measure intelligence free of environmental influences, considerable evidence indicates that measured intelligence can be altered quite dramatically when there are changes in environment. As we mentioned in an earlier discussion, intelligence testing on a mass scale was done for the first time during World War I. Over a million recruits took those tests.[11] The findings disclosed that Blacks from the South did more poorly than did Blacks from the North, thus reflecting the influence of the more advantageous northern environment. Moreover, Blacks from some northern states performed better than did whites from some southern states, which showed dramatically the influence of environment, particularly quality of formal education, relative to the supposed influence of heredity.

Further evidence confirming the influence of environment on measured intelligence was provided by Otto Klineberg. He tried to determine whether the superior scores made on those Army tests by northern Blacks reflected a "selective migration" of more intelligent Blacks to the North or whether the score differentials were indicative of the influence of environment.[12] Based on a comparison of Black migrants to the North with those who stayed in the South, Klineberg could find no evidence that there was a difference in intellectual ability between migrants and nonmigrants. Further study of the influence of environment on intelligence over time showed there were consistent gains in IQ with length of residence in the North among Black migrants from the South. Later research confirms his basic conclusions about the beneficial effect of environment in producing changes in the measured intelligence among Blacks and further strengthens the argument that environment exercises a powerful influence on intelligence test scores.[13] There is, as we have said before, no such thing as a "culture-free" intelligence test. The majority of questions and test items are based on middle-class experiences and expectations. Many lower class individuals who take such tests never have the chance to demonstrate what they have learned from *their* life experiences. Survival in a ghetto environment, for example, requires quite different skills from those needed to exist in a middle-class milieu.

Those studies cast considerable doubt on the validity of intelligence tests as accurate measures of racial differences in ability. In order to assess the influence of genetic factors alone, the *entire* environment of groups of Blacks and whites would have to be standardized for such a test to produce valid results. Moreover, it may be impossible to measure genetic factors alone, since the organism itself can be substantially modified by environment. Physical factors are heavily dependent upon external influences such as nutrition; physical differences among races may reflect disadvantaged or, at least, different environments and their effects on physical development and functioning.

Recent research does suggest that some race differences may exist and may be significant. But they are unrelated to ability. An example of these is the susceptibility of a small percentage of the American Black population to sickle-cell anemia, a relatively rare debilitating blood disorder. Identification of this disease has led to a massive research program designed to control this disorder and eventually to eradicate it. In this instance, research into racial differences may lead to the improvement of life chances for thousands of Black Americans. With this research as an example, further inquiry into the presence of race differences can lead to a better understanding of genetic makeup, and such knowledge should contribute to the decline of unscientific racist thought. Interestingly, sickle-cell anemia is also found in West African populations residing in malaria-infested areas where it is a physiological defense against malaria.

In spite of the scientific evidence to the contrary, racism still persists in the United States and in many other parts of the modern world. The white government of the Republic of South Africa, for example, maintains that there are inherent biological differences among the races that compel it to pursue a policy of segregation and "separate development." Those directing that policy, better known as *apartheid*—an "apartness" or segregation—feel that this policy is dictated by natural law rather than by expediency.[14] Separate ghettos in the urban centers and vast reserves in rural South Africa have been designated as residence areas for the Black African population, and racial segregation extends into virtually all aspects of social life in that society.

In light of the fact that racism persists, it is necessary to examine some of the factors accounting for that persistence in order to gain a more thorough understanding of this social phenomenon.

Group-Related Factors

Since racism can have disastrous consequences for those against whom it is directed, social scientists have long been interested in the processes that both produce and sustain racism. That interest has led to the study of long-term historic sequences of intergroup relationships in order to determine what the basic variables are that lead to the development and maintenance of racism.

Ethnocentrism One of the most significant factors producing racism in social relations was identified by William Graham Sumner. He applied the term "ethnocentrism" to refer to the tendency to judge other groups on the basis of the standards of one's own group.[15] According to Sumner, ethnocentrism involves two distinct facets. First, there is a tendency to regard the standards of one's own group very highly, so much so that those standards are regarded as *the sole possible criteria by which other groups should be judged*. Secondly, there is a tendency to regard the culture of other groups negatively and to perceive those groups as "out" groups. This aspect of ethnocentrism often leads to the emergence of what is called *prejudice*. Prejudice can be defined as a set of negative concepts, feelings, beliefs, and action orientations directed at members of another group or at other groups who are regarded as out groups. That results in individuals "prejudging" others on the basis of the characteristics attributed to the out group to which they belong.

Often prejudice will lead to the emergence of an additional negative perspective on "out" groups. Members of such groups and the behavior they exhibit and the culture they possess come to be perceived as *deviant*. When members of out groups are thought to be deviating from norms regarded as critical, it is likely that members of the group having the prejudicial perspectives will act to suppress the supposedly deviant behavior. Examples can be found throughout European history—the Spanish Inquisition, for example—and American history—acts of terrorism against the Black population in the South. It appears that the development of ideas defining members of an out group as being deviant, when they are already regarded negatively on the basis of ethnocentric judgments, is a critical stage in social relations that may, and often does, culminate in violence.

There is an additional aspect of ethnocentrism that represents a curious phase in social relations—that which occurs when highly valued behavior displayed by a member of an out group arouses hostility and fears of competition.[16] In such an instance, conformity by members of an out group to the highly regarded standards of the "in" group may threaten the privileged position of that in group. Accordingly, members of that in group may try to suppress the behavior in members of the out group to reinforce the in group's advantage. Examples of that are common in intergroup relations in the United States. Jews are often negatively regarded because they demonstrate academic success, upward mobility, materialism, and aggressiveness, all of which are highly valued characteristics in American culture. Blacks were called "uppity" in the South when they displayed ambition and concern with status at the same time that they were being looked down upon for supposedly lacking those very values. Currently such minority groups as Mexican-Americans and American Indians are experiencing prejudice because they have successfully organized to press for redress of their grievances and for improvements in their life chances. Historically they have been regarded negatively because they were believed to be apathetic, happy-go-lucky, lazy, and without interest in their own welfare.

Perceived Competition   It is apparent that ethnocentrism is very closely related to *perceived* competition, another major factor that produces and sustains racism. Particularly when resources are scarce, and when the groups competing for those resources possess the actual or potential ability to succeed, racism is likely to be a major factor in social relations. There are several factors underlying a group's ability to compete successfully for resources. There is some indication that the relative population size of competing groups is a factor related to racism. Even though the Black population in the pre–Civil War South did not realistically compete with whites for economic resources, due to the large Black population whites feared that they potentially might compete. As a result, whites used racist rationales for keeping Blacks out of most craft occupations, and denied them access to the formal or occupational education necessary for high-status jobs. Jews, on the other hand, did have more economic and social resources with which to compete successfully. Accordingly, even though they comprised a very small percentage of the population, universities and colleges had Jewish "quotas" which were set up to insure that not too many Jews gained access to the higher status occupations through higher education. Similarly much of the prejudice and discrimination directed at Japanese-Americans is based on the fact that they have been very successful in academic and occupational competition. The underlying mechanism involved in sustaining racism in these instances is the fear on the part of a dominant group that potential or actual competition for resources with members of subordinated groups will threaten the dominant group's advantaged position.

Visibility Another factor closely related to both ethnocentrism and perceived competition, which is conducive to the emergence and maintenance of racism, can be referred to as *visibility*. It includes all of the identifying aspects of group membership. The importance of visibility in intergroup relations will depend to a great degree on how those identifying signs of group membership are regarded by members of other groups. Visibility is related to perceived competition since it is the means through which the potential or actual competitor is identifiable. When the potential competitor is identified on the basis of physical or cultural characteristics that are held in low esteem by members of an "in" group, they may make additional attempts to restrict the "out" group's ability to compete.

Examples of the interrelationship of ethnocentrism (including discrimination and prejudice), perceived competition for resources, and visibility can be found by studying patterns of intergroup relations in the United States. Skin color traditionally has been a factor associated with the visibility of Black Americans. American English is replete with examples that indicate the negative connotation assigned to the color black. Examples found in *Webster's New Collegiate Dictionary* include blackball, black-letter, blackmail, black sheep, and blacklist, to name but a few.[17] Lee Rainwater, writing about problems of color and identity in Black America, intimates that there is even a strong correlation within Black communities between skin color and prestige. Persons with darker complexions suffer internal community discrimination.[18] In many instances, having a lighter complexion will afford more opportunities for Black Americans, both inside and outside predominately Black communities. That illustrates the relationship between visibility and the ability to compete successfully for resources with other groups (as well as within one's own group). Here the ethnocentric and prejudicial standards of the whites have diffused into the Black community and the negative evaluations of visibility have been accepted by many Blacks themselves.

Since Blacks regard skin color as a highly significant factor in determining visibility, it is no mere accident that the recent Black protest movements have used the slogan "Black Power." Within those movements, blackness is extolled as a virtue. In reaction to the linguistic and cultural tendencies toward giving a negative connotation to blackness, there are firm ideological dictates regarding the beauty of blackness and the need for racial purity through the preservation of blackness and Black culture. As a result, these movements strongly emphasize the importance of African cultural heritage. Many of the members of Black Power movements have adopted African modes of dress and African names. As the influence of those movements spreads, the negative attitudes of many Blacks toward blackness is changing and will continue to do so.

Possession of Power   Inequalities in the possession of power among groups is another factor closely associated with the presence of racism. Such inequalities enable more powerful groups to manipulate and exploit less powerful ones using racism as a justification for differential treatment.[19] Racism, as we have noted, developed in Western Europe partially in order to justify the slave trade and European expansion into areas of the world peopled by nonwhites. In the case of European expansion, racism served to legitimate colonialism, in which native populations were subjugated by European colonial powers. In the United States, racism was used to support not only the subjugation of the native Indian population but also the domination of immigrant populations. The native Indian population resisted subjugation often violently through armed attacks. In the long run, however, despite occasional successes such as the victory over Custer at the Battle of the Little Big Horn, Indian military power proved ineffective.

Immigrants, unlike the American Indians, did not resort to force or, in general, struggle to maintain their accustomed ways of life. Instead—and this was particularly true of their sons and daughters—they became socialized into the ways of the dominant culture and, by losing the characteristics that identified them as immigrants, rendered the dominant group relatively powerless to discriminate against them.

Ethnocentrism, perceived competition, visibility, and inequalities in the distribution of power appear to be closely associated with the emergence and maintenance of racism. These, however, are group-related factors that support racism. There is a considerable body of evidence suggesting that there are personality-related factors that play an important part in producing and maintaining racism in human relations. These will be considered in some detail.

Ethnocentrism, perceived competition, visibility, and inequalities in the distribution of power appear to be closely associated with the emergence and maintenance of racism.

Copyright © 1973 by Saturday Review/World, Inc.
Reprinted by permission from the publisher and Mort Gerberg.

"Only eight classes at the French Institute and already he hates Americans."

Personality Factors

Most psychological approaches to the study of personality factors that are supportive of racism stress the importance of the mechanisms of *frustration*, *aggression*, *displacement*, and *projection*. According to these formulations, all persons experience in daily life some frustration due to their inability to satisfy various needs.[20] *Frustration* is likely to lead individuals to commit aggressive acts that serve to vent or release frustration-induced hostility. However, in many social situations, people may be unable to vent their anger directly at the source of their frustrations. Such a source may, for example, be too powerful, and any direct expression would result in unpleasant consequences for the individual. What occurs (or may occur) under such circumstances is *displacement*—hostility is vented on another object or person incapable of fighting back effectively. This alternative is referred to as a "scapegoat." Often, the displacement of aggression to an object other than the source is justified on the basis of a personality mechanism that psychologists call *projection*. Projection involves the tendency of people to attribute to others those characteristics or traits they are afraid to recognize in themselves. Displacement of aggression from the source to another object is regarded as highly appropriate if that other object possesses traits and characteristics that are despised; by doing so the person is punishing the other object for having those qualities. That is a far easier course of action than punishing one's own self for having the detested attributes.

Displacement and Projection of Aggression Racist ideologies play an important role in reinforcing those personality attributes. They provide the

Copyright © 1973 by G. B. Trudeau. Distributed by Universal Press Syndicate.

justification for displacing aggression to certain groups and serve to identify those characteristics that are held in low esteem. There is a close association between racism on the group level and the presence of those personality characteristics in individuals in racist societies. When groups are labeled as inferior, often the most despised characteristics are attributed to them. Racist ideologies of this type can be employed to reinformce prejudice and ethno-centrism. Under such conditions, the likelihood that projection and displace-ment of aggression (or "scapegoating") will occur is very great.

Examples of the character such projection and displacement of aggression may assume when justified on the basis of racism abound in American society. Taboos regarding sexual relations between whites and Blacks derive largely from the projection of excessive sexuality to blacks. Historically those taboos were often enforced through the lynching of Black males accused of violating them. Economic and social discrimination against Jews has been based pri-marily on projection of unethical business activities, excessive sexuality, and bizarre religious practices. Many other groups have experienced projection of undesirable qualities upon them, with racism or ethnicity often providing the rationale for such feelings and actions.

Recent research suggests that there may be a personality complex composed of a group of characteristics which might be called a "prejudiced personality."

Authoritarian Personality   There appears to be a number of important factors that will determine whether persons will tend to displace aggression and project unwanted qualities upon other groups. Recent evidence indicates that highly prejudiced persons are more likely to displace aggression than nonprejudiced persons when confronted with equal levels of frustration.[21] In addition, frustration which is produced by situations in which one's status or the status of one's own group is threatened are more likely to culminate in displaced aggression.[22] When a highly prejudiced person is presented with a situation in which his status is threatened, the racist ideologies identify the group against which he holds prejudice as the source of that threat. Then it is highly likely that he will displace aggression against members of that group.

Recent research suggests that there may be a personality complex composed of a group of characteristics which might be called a "prejudiced personality." In a comprehensive attempt to study that type, a group of researchers labeled it the "authoritarian personality." They believe that it is composed of a certain clearly identifiable set of traits: (1) *conventionalism*, or the tendency to adhere strictly to traditional values; (2) *projectivity*, indicating a tendency to project bizarre characteristics to the external world and to other groups; (3) *sex*, meaning an exaggerated concern with sexual matters; (4) *authoritarian aggression*, or the disposition to search out and punish those who violate conventional standards; (5) *power and toughness*, involving a strong emphasis on the role of dominance and power in social relations; (6) *destructiveness and cynicism*, entailing a hostile perspective on human relations and human weakness; (7) *superstition and stereotypic thinking*; (8) *authoritarian submission*, or a strong emphasis on submission to authority and to the literal dictate of values; and (9) *anti-intraception*, which involves a strong distaste for subjective perspectives and "tender-minded" characteristics. Those nine characteristics were shown by individuals who scored high on a questionnaire called the F-scale ("F" refers to a variable called "potentiality for fascism"). Persons scoring high on the F-scale were likely to score high on the three other scales employed in the research: the Ethnocentrism scale, the Political and Economic Conservatism scale, and the Anti-Semitism scale. While those were not found to be essential personality characteristics in order for a person to hold prejudice, highly prejudiced people were more likely to have at least a few of these attributes.[23]

There has been some criticism of this research, as well as of the whole concept of the authoritarian personality type. Most critics focus upon the contention that the authoritarian personality type is a unified personality syndrome. They argue that factors such as education, intelligence, and social class influence the extent to which those characteristics are present in persons. The more highly intelligent persons, those drawn from the higher socioeconomic groups, and the most educated are the least likely to be authoritarian.[24] Another criticism of the research contends that the authoritarian personality reflects right-wing political perspectives, ignoring the possibility of authoritarianism among those with left-wing political sympathies. Stili others believe that the researchers did not pay enough attention to regional variations in the incidence of prejudice, emphasizing that culture plays the critical role in accounting for racism and ethnocentrism. Despite those criticisms, the research was a major, landmark project attempting to study prejudice and its personality correlates. And it provided considerable insight into the personality characteristics that support prejudiced beliefs and are conducive to the development and maintenance of racism.

Reducing Racism

Owing to the pervasiveness of the group and personality factors that are supportive of racism, racism is highly resistant to attempts aimed at eradicating and changing essential belief components. Since the 1950's the United States has witnessed attempts to reduce racism through legal means. Those changes, in turn, allow for a wider range of contact among racial and ethnic groups. Through such increasing contact, people are given the opportunity to test the reality of their racist beliefs, and their irrationality may, possibly, be exposed. There is mounting evidence that, even among highly prejudiced persons, increasing intergroup contact has the result of lessening prejudice. In a recent study of the effects of integration in housing on interracial attitudes, there is clear evidence that increased interracial contact may, in certain conditions, result in a lessening of prejudice and leads to the erosion of negative inter-racial stereotypes.[25] However, there is considerable opposition to those legal means designed to increase intergroup contact. Such opposition is usually couched in such terms as, "the government can't legislate morality," and so on. Additional evidence suggests that increased education alone serves to provide more accurate knowledge about other groups but does not necessarily lead to *social* acceptance.[26] More recently, such activities as encounter groups and group therapy sessions have been tried as means of lowering the barriers between members of different groups. However, short-term attitude change is highly subject to decay, and it is questionable whether changes in levels of prejudice will persist significantly over the years. Individually initiated attitude change is also very difficult because most people are totally unaware of the scope and depth of their prejudiced attitudes. There are those who are conscious of their prejudice but regard it as entirely appropriate since they see separation of groups as desirable. As a result of those social and personal factors, it is evident that attempts aimed at reducing racism must take into account many factors and will encounter many obstacles. Further, as was observed in the Preface, mere propinquity does not *automatically* lessen prejudice.

In order to determine the consequences of racism in the social relations of the United States, it is necessary to consider the historical and contemporary experiences of groups against whom racism has been directed. That will require an investigation of patterns and sequences of intergroup relations. It will have to focus on how certain groups were regarded and treated; how racism affected their life chances; and how they responded to racism and dominance. The next few sections of this chapter will be devoted to that investigation.

MINORITY GROUPS IN AMERICA

One of the key concepts in the study of race and ethnic relations in the United States is that of "minority group." Robin Williams has provided a short, yet comprehensive definition:

> *Minorities . . . are any culturally or physically distinctive and self-conscious social aggregates, with hereditary membership and a high degree of endogamy, which are subject to political, or economic, or social discrimination by a dominating segment of an environing political society.*[27]

It should be emphasized that no notion of statistical minority is implied; minorities are defined on the basis of power differentials and the experience of disadvantage at the hands of other groups. Persons are born into minority groups, and minority group status is exceedingly difficult to change. Minority groups, as a reaction to disadvantage and discrimination, are highly self-conscious social groups and, as a result, tend to marry within their own group. They are, however, often prevented legally from marrying outside their group, as was the case in the South until only recently. Minority group status depends greatly on visibility, particularly when the treatment accorded minority groups is justified on the basis of physical or cultural traits that the dominant group or groups holds in low esteem. Minority group status has a relative aspect; that is, persons may be in a minority group in one society and not in another. In fact, migration to another society may be the only means available for a person to change his minority group status.

Minority groups may be classified according to the prevailing aspects of intergroup relations between themselves and dominant groups. Louis Wirth provided a perspective on minority-dominant intergroup relations by distinguishing four different types of minorities.[28] There are *pluralistic* minorities who desire to maintain their cultural identity in a nation composed largely of minority groups. The Chinese in many societies in the world, for example, seek to retain their cultural identity and folkways, asking only tolerance of their presence and freedom to pursue daily activities undisturbed. The *assimilationist* minority seeks to be blended into or absorbed by the dominant culture thus losing its minority identity. Most European immigrant groups would fit that description. *Secessionist* minorities are oriented toward political independence from the society at large. The French-speaking Canadians in Quebec, who call themselves Separatists, are an example. *Militant* minorities have as their goal not equality but superiority over other groups. Arabs in territories held by Israel may be representative of that type of minority group.

Minority group status may depend largely on race, ethnic status, or religion. However, certain minority groups may be classified by two or more of those criteria. Practicing Asiatic Buddhists residing in the United States would represent a racial, ethnic, and religious minority group. Attempts by such groups to fully assimilate are likely to encounter difficulty if their minority status depends on two or more highly visible factors. The experience of the principal minority groups in the United States, which will be reviewed in the next few pages, reflects to a substantial degree the importance accorded to race, ethnic group status, and religion as factors defining minority group status.

Blacks

The first Blacks reached America in Jamestown in 1619, and they came as indentured servants. Shortly thereafter, Blacks were imported to the Americas as slaves. With the growth of the plantation economy in the South, the rate of importation increased. After the Revolution there was no mention of giving citizenship to Black slaves. By the late 1700's racist notions of Black inequality were firmly entrenched, reinforced by the visibility of physical and cultural differences. The new nation was an example of a *Herrenvolk* democracy, with full citizenship rights extended to whites and none to Blacks. By the mid-1800's, a vigorous abolitionist movement emerged in the North. During this period arguments over the ethical merits of slavery contributed causally to the American Civil War of 1861–1865.

Emancipation   When Lincoln issued the Emancipation Proclamation on January 1, 1863, almost 90 percent of all Blacks in the United States were still enslaved. When the slaves were legally freed at the end of the Civil War, the vast majority had few, if any, of the skills and knowledge necessary for a successful adjustment to freedom. There was widespread chaos as thousands of hungry, homeless, and unemployed slaves wandered in search of support. Congress created the Freedmen's Bureau in 1865, whose activities involved setting up a system of public education and allocating land to freedmen. But few former slaves were able to retain land ownership after Reconstruction. While the Thirteenth, Fourteenth, and Fifteenth Amendments to the Constitution granted full citizenship and franchise to them, most Blacks had no experience with civil processes of any sort. Often newly enfranchised ex-slaves were manipulated by white politicians. But the decade after emancipation was a trying time for ex-slaves in other aspects of life as well. Evidence from that period indicates that the death rate among Blacks exceeded that of the late slavery period, showing the extent of the crisis brought on by sudden freedom for which the ex-slaves were almost totally unpre-pared.[29]

Following the end of Reconstruction, some influential northern whites who had shown interest in the plight of freedmen in the South withdrew their support for many of the activities intended to facilitate adjustment to freedom. Gradually white southerners were able to restore white supremacy. The franchise was withdrawn from Blacks, initially by terror tactics and later by quasi-legal poll taxes, literacy tests, and "white" primaries in which only white property holders could vote. New forms of discrimination and segregation emerged in the form of "Jim Crow" laws. Those effectively segregated the races in areas of public accommodation and transportation and provided legal justification for an "etiquette" of race relations that established taboos on much behavior between the racial groups. By 1900 Blacks had been fully segregated and disenfranchised, aided by two Supreme Court decisions: *Plessy* v. *Ferguson* (1896), which established legal credibility for the "separate but equal" principle establishing dual school systems; and *Williams* v. *Mississippi* (1898), which approved Mississippi's plan for depriving blacks of the right to vote. Intimidation increased dramatically during the last two decades of the nineteenth century, reaching a peak in the early 1900's, when over 160 Blacks were lynched in a single year. And that figure reflects only reported lynchings; it is not known how many blacks were lynched or otherwise murdered.

White Supremacy   There are a number of explanations accounting for why segregation and disenfranchisement were imposed so rapidly upon the Black population in the South following the end of Reconstruction and for the erosion of interest in freedmen by Northern whites. C. Vann Woodward believes that increased discrimination against Blacks was due largely to a need for a scapegoat to help reconcile the North and the South and to resolve class conflicts within the southern white population.[30] It is also possible that incentives to discriminate became greater as the educational status of Blacks began to improve and they changed from a potential competitive economic threat into an actual one. Moreover, it is possible that, as northern whites viewed the chaotic situation that accompanied freedom, they began to accept the southern contention of white supremacy and the necessity for a "paternalistic" policy toward Blacks. Whatever the causes of the successful restoration of white supremacy, by 1900 it was a firm social reality in the South.

American Dilemma   Gunnar Myrdal, the Swedish-born author of the classic study of American race relations, *The American Dilemma*, has described in detail the character of relations between the races following imposition of white supremacy. He summarizes them in what he called the "rank order of discrimination";[31] that is, the rank order of discrimination as perceived by the white population. *Rank 1,* the most important level of discrimination for the white population, is the bar against intermarriage and sexual intercourse between the races involving white women. *Rank 2* deals with the etiquette and discrimination that involves behavior in personal relations, such as barriers against dancing, eating, bathing, and drinking together, and general social relations. Also included at this level are rules regarding avoidance of handshaking; the mandatory use of formal titles when whites are addressed and the familiar when blacks are; forms of salutation; and so on. *Rank 3* comprises rules regarding segregation and discrimination in the use of public facilities and transportation. At *rank 4* is political disenfranchisement. *Rank 5* concerns discrimination in the courts, by police, and by other public servants. *Rank 6,* the least level of importance according to the white population, concerns discrimination in securing land, obtaining credit, getting a job, and in public relief and social welfare activities. Myrdal suggests that southern whites were most amenable toward granting to Blacks credit rights and means of earning a living, were somewhat less inclined to grant them the vote (rank 4), were definitely not disposed toward changing etiquette rules (2), and abhorred any change in interracial sex codes (1).

Myrdal also pointed out that, while this rank ordering of discrimination in traditional southern race relations reflected the importance according to the view of the white population, the rank ordering of importance among the Black population was likely to have been the reverse. Blacks were unlikely to regard interracial sexual avoidance codes as crucial for their daily lives. They were very likely to resent discrimination at rank 6, which would relate directly to their day-to-day lives and to economic opportunity in general. As a result, the Black and white populations of the South of the early 1900's misunderstood each other drastically on the issue of race relations, with blacks regarding as unimportant those very factors that formed the core of southern white racism.

The Church   Within the context of slavery and later segregation, social institutions developed and took shape. Religious institutions reflect the degree of social isolation in American race relations. Initially, white slave owners favored spreading Christianity to the slave population. But the whites soon became more and more reluctant, feeling that a formidable moral dilemma was posed by Christians enslaving fellow Christians. The dilemma had been "resolved" earlier in 1667 when the Virginia Assembly enacted a law, which was reaffirmed by the English Crown in 1729, that Christian baptism in no way altered the status of slaves. That allowed for massive missionary activities among the slave population; by 1863, the date of emancipation, the vast majority of the slave population was at least nominally Christian. Gradually, most of the slaves formed their own church bodies as whites became increasingly resistant to worshiping with Blacks in the same congregation.

Whites had permitted Blacks to set up separate church bodies within the structure of white denominations during slavery. But after the Civil War, Blacks were expelled entirely from white denominations. They formed their own denominations, most of which were variations of the Baptist and Methodist churches. With freedom and expulsion from white churches, the church gradually became the dominant social institution in Black communities. Often the minister was the most literate person in the community and, as such, was regarded perhaps with a sense of awe and certainly with profound respect. However, it should be emphasized that many of those churches existed because of white sufferance and tacit support. As a result, in the first few decades of freedom, Black churches fostered an "accommodationist" view of race relations in which the dominant theme was acquiescence to the existing social structure.

After World War I, and coincidental with mass Black migration to the North, the character of the Black churches began to change. More congregations departed from the accommodationist perspective and pursued welfare and other programs designed to aid in the advancement of Blacks. More and more, they became concerned with improved housing, health care, morality, education; by the mid-1940's, some had adopted announced goals of social protest. One such group was the congregation of the Reverend Adam Clayton Powell, Jr. He was pastor of the large Abyssinian Baptist Church in Harlem, New York, and started a political career as a congressman to U.S. House of Representatives from New York in November 1945. During his years in office, he began organizing social protest. More recently, Black churches have produced many of the major leaders of Black social protest. The most notable examples include the Reverend Dr. Martin Luther King, Jr.; the Reverend Ralph Abernathy; and the Reverend Jesse Jackson. The change in the role of the Black church in race relations has paralleled changes in the mood of Black America as a whole. While the relative dominance of the church as the major social institution has declined recently, mostly owing to competition for resources and personnel from other organizations—for example, CORE—the church still retains a central position in Black communities. Whether it will continue to do so depends in large part on the ability of Black churches to adjust to the changing currents of social protest.

Black Muslim Movement   Recently, the traditional Black church has had to come to grips with an unexpected challenge. Since the 1950's a new religious movement has expanded rapidly in both membership and influence. And it has as its major premise the total rejection of Christianity as the "white man's" religion, substituting the "Nation of Islam." It is more popularly known as the Black Muslim movement. Its founder, Elijah Muhammad, produced a program that embodied many of the protest demands of Black Americans. But it went well beyond other protest movements by advocating Black nationalism and calling for the founding of a Black nation composed of five southern states. Estimates of membership vary, with 50,000 as the highest figure. However, the influence of the movement was and is out of proportion to its numerical strength. The ideology of the Nation of Islam is highly racist, with many of the derogatory characteristics imputed to Blacks by whites—innate inferiority, "devil" status, cunning, deception— now being directed at whites. It is a powerful force directing social change, particularly in the urban ghettos. By pointing out the racist nature of Western society and Christianity in general and of American society in particular, many of Muhammad's assertions evoke a great deal of sympathy among many segments of the Black population. The movement has presented a substantial threat to the role of the present Black churches in guiding social protest, and it is likely to continue to do so.

Family Structure and Function   Family structure and function in Black America reflects the historical background of Blacks and possesses certain distinctive and important influences. Evidence indicates that a large percentage of Black families are matriarchal or "matricentric," with the mother serving as the central family figure and the basis for family stability and economic support.[32] In such families, fathers may be present irregularly or not all and therefore do not always assume responsibility for the care, rearing, and support of their children. Such marriages, often of the "common law" variety, frequently terminate in separation, divorce, or desertion. That kind of family structure and family life is most commonly observed in lower socioeconomic groups within Black America. The middle-class Black family very closely resembles families of other major groups in terms of structure and function.

There are conflicting explanations about why such a family type is found so often within the lower socioeconomic segments of Black America. Some argue that the widespread presence of that family type can be traced to a "survival" of culture patterns that existed in West Africa at the time of the slave trade. But the most plausible explanation places strong emphasis upon the background of slavery itself in accounting for Black family instability.[33] The social controls over family life and sexual behavior were deliberately destroyed by slave owners, who often went to considerable lengths to break up tribal and familial groups among the slave population. No new and consistent norms were provided, and those that emerged within the context of slavery were not conducive to family stability. Through sale and the breakup of plantations, families often were divided. The operation of the slave system did not encourage the development of strong family ties and stable marriage patterns. Moreover, since Black males were subservient to whites in the role of slavery, it was difficult for them to assert any real authority in the family setting (or in *any* role, for that matter). Accordingly, the role of slave encouraged the development and exercise of a weak authority role for the Black male; that pattern apparently has persisted past emancipation to the immediate present in the lower classes in Black America.

Other factors have served to perpetuate the matricentric family type. Black females are often better educated than males within the lower socioeconomic groups and, accordingly, are able to find more stable employment. In addition, Black females generally encounter somewhat less occupational discrimination than do males. As these factors persist, the matricentric character of Black families is likely to remain a major factor in lower class family life.

Changes in Black family life will depend partly upon the growth and influence of the Black middle class. That, in turn, will depend upon removal of discrimination and residual segregation as well as upon improved educational opportunities for Black Americans. Family size is an important factor in improving the quality of family life. And improvements in the nature of family life will depend to some degree on the acceptance and usage of birth control techniques to limit family size. Smaller families are more likely to enjoy a level of living more characteristic of the middle class. Controls exercised on family life can influence the growth of the middle class by making middle-class life styles more attainable and can serve to reduce the level of deprivation.

There are substantial sources of resistance to programs aimed at spreading birth control information and techniques among Black Americans. Many Black nationalists fear that birth control would eventually weaken the political power of the Black population by reducing their relative numerical representation in the population. Similar arguments are also encountered in developing nations, as we have discussed. In Brazil, for example, it is a commonplace argument that population growth and economic expansion are inseparable and desirable. In the United States, arguments against birth control are often based on the premise that birth control might be the first step in a program aimed at eventual genocide of the Black population. Such opinions provide the basis for the reluctance of some Black Americans to adopt birth control and family planning procedures.

Life Conditions Table 12-1 depicts some of the major life conditions within the Black population relative to the white. It indicates to a considerable degree the demographic consequences of domination and discrimination over the centuries. In particular, the relatively high rates of illiteracy among the older Black population reflect the legacy of segregation. The statistics on life expectancy and infant mortality point out the physiological effects of deprivation. While Table 12-2 shows that the occupational status of nonwhites relative to whites has improved in recent years, the gap remains substantial, as the figures in Table 12-1 indicate. Without considerable and rapid improve-

Table 12-1 Some Life Conditions of Blacks and Whites (percent)

Condition	Blacks	Whites
14–24-year-olds finishing eighth grade	85.6	92.6
25–29-year-olds finishing high school	60.5	79.5
illiteracy among 45–64-year-olds	5.5	0.7
illiteracy among over-65-year-olds	16.7	2.3
extent of fatherless households	29.0	9.0
infant mortality rates (per 1000)	37.5	19.5
life expectancy in years at birth	64.6	71.3
poverty-stricken families	29	8
families with income below $5000 per year	46.9	19.9
families with income over $8000 per year	29.5	57.6
mean family income per year (in dollars)	$6191.00	$9794.00
nonwhite income as percentage of white	63.0	
degree of unemployment	7.0	3.8
extent of home ownership	38.0	64.0
families with male head living in poverty	18.0	6.0
families with female head living in poverty	54.0	25.0
median income, families with male head (in dollars)	$7816.00	$10723.00
median income, families with female head (in dollars)	$3576.00	$5754.00

SOURCE: *Statistical Abstract of the United States, 1971,* p. 112; Education figures are drawn from "Characteristics of American Youth, 1971," *Current Population Reports, Special Studies,* series P-23, no. 40 (Washington, D.C.: Bureau of the Census, 1972).

ment in the available life chances for Blacks in American society, the obvious and persistent differences in life conditions will continue to be the focus for strain and conflict.

The Black population is rapidly becoming an urban one, with a consistent pattern of rural-urban migration in all parts of the nation. Along with the influx of Blacks into the major urban centers, there has been a heavy migration of middle and upper class whites from the cities to suburban areas. Those trends have produced large, predominately Black slum areas in the cities, ringed by affluent, predominately white suburbs. While there has been some Black migration to suburbs, most of this has been to older, less affluent, suburbs and to specially constructed low-cost housing enclaves in suburban areas. Often, these areas assume the character of suburban Black ghettos.

A number of factors can be determined in studying patterns of exclusion of Blacks from the suburbs. Restrictive covenants have been employed to keep them and other minority groups out. Intimidation by white real estate agents and suburban residents has contributed to the reluctance of many Blacks to press for access to those communities. The high cost of suburban housing is another factor excluding blacks from suburbs; many Blacks simply can not afford to pay for suburban housing. Moreover, many Blacks apparently feel that the social ostracism they would have to bear in living within predominately white communities would not justify whatever gains they would make in

Table 12-2   Ratio of Actual to Expected Proportion of Nonwhite Workers in Each Occupation, 1965 and 1970[a]

Category	1965	1970
white-collar		
professional, technical	0.55	0.64
managers, officials, and proprietors, except farm	0.25	0.33
clerical	0.53	0.76
sales workers	0.29	0.34
blue-collar		
craftsmen, foremen	0.52	0.64
operatives	1.15	1.34
laborers, except farm and mine	2.40	2.18
service workers		
service workers, except private household	1.94	1.77
private household workers	4.10	3.89
farm		
farmers and farm managers	0.58	0.45
farm laborers and foremen	2.25	1.68

SOURCE: *Monthly Labor Review* and *Employment and Earnings Report on the Labor Force* (Washington, D.C.: Bureau of Labor Statistics, 1971).

[a] The "expected" proportion of nonwhites in each occupational category is the proportion of all workers in that category. If, in 1965, 12.3 percent of all workers were professionals, we would expect the same percentage of nonwhite workers to be professional. If, however, only 6.8 percent of the nonwhite workers were professional, as was the case in 1965, we would compare the observed rate with the expected rate, which would produce a ratio of .55, indicating underrepresentation of nonwhites in the professional category. Ratios in excess of 1.0 would indicate overrepresentation of nonwhites.

standard of living and neighbourhood quality. It would seem to be preferable to remain in largely Black communities. Those are just a few of the factors contributing to the "ghettoization" of Blacks in America and perpetuating the racial isolation that has been prevalent in the character of American Black-white relations.

Chicanos

The Mexican-American minority group has assumed increasing importance in recent years, largely owing to the publicizing of economic grievances through labor movements. Such movements have served to focus attention on problems that Americans of Mexican descent share, and they have increased the visibility of the group in American life. In much the same way that the term "Black" has gained in popularity among Blacks, the name "Chicano," once a term of derision, is a label used by Mexican-Americans themselves. It embodies notions of ethnic pride, solidarity, consciousness of kind, and identity.

Annexation Mexican-Americans became a minority group when the land owned by Spanish-speaking persons was annexed by the United States at the end of the Mexican-American War of 1848. In addition, the rebellion in Texas and the Gadsden Purchase of 1853 allowed the United States to acquire the present states of Texas, New Mexico, Arizona, Utah, Nevada, California, and part of Colorado. Before annexation, Mexican colonists had settled those areas sparsely, with only about 80,000 Spanish-speaking persons of Mexican descent. Most of them lived no more than 150 miles north of the present boundary with Mexico. Much of the present Chicano population is still concentrated in the lower Southwest.

Migrant Labor Early in the twentieth century a pattern of seasonal migration began within the Chicano population. It was based on demand for unskilled and semiskilled labor in agricultural regions, particularly in the Eastern portions of the country. Mexican-Americans became a highly important labor source; to this day, a substantial portion of the Chicano population participates in seasonal labor migration. While the bulk of the Chicano population remains clustered in the southwestern cities and towns, many spend much of the year residing in labor camps following the demand for agricultural labor.

Life Conditions Presently, the Mexican-American population numbers about 5 million. While fertility rates are much higher among Chicanos than among "Anglos," (the term applied by Chicanos to white Americans of non-Spanish descent), much of the rapid growth of this population can be attributed to the steady immigration of workers from Mexico, both legally and illegally. Table 12-3 shows that the Mexican-American population is younger than the United States population as a whole, with a median age of 18.6 compared to the national median of 28.0 years. Chicano families are larger than the national mean, with an average size of 4.4 persons compared with a 3.5 national mean. Table 12-4 shows that the Mexican-Americans are considerably undereducated, particularly the older segment, only 0.6 percent of those over 65 having completed four years of high school, compared to the national figure of 32 percent. Tables 12-5 and 12-6 indicate the occupational distribution and income statistics for the Chicano population. Chicanos tend to be concentrated in the lower paying, manual, blue-collar occupations. The consequences of undereducation and low-status employment are borne out in the income data summarized in Table 12-7. Those demographic data attest to the degree of deprivation experienced by most of the Mexican-American population. In 1971, over 30 percent in the five southwestern states (Arizona, California, Colorado, New Mexico, and Texas) were subsisting on poverty-level annual incomes.

Table 12-3 Age Distribution of Spanish-American Population, March 1972 (percent)

Age	Total U.S. population	Spanish origin			
		Mexican	Puerto Rican	Cuban	Total[a]
under 5	8.5	13.4	14.0	4.9	12.7
5–9	9.2	15.0	14.7	11.6	13.8
10–17	16.0	20.2	21.5	13.4	19.4
18 and 19	3.6	4.3	2.6	3.8	3.8
20–24	8.4	8.3	8.0	3.7	7.8
25–34	12.9	13.3	14.8	13.8	14.2
35–44	11.0	10.8	12.6	15.4	11.8
45–54	11.4	7.5	5.3	14.4	8.0
55–64	9.2	3.9	4.6	12.1	5.0
65 and over	9.7	3.2	2.0	6.8	3.5
total (thousands)	204,840	5,254	1,518	629	9,178
median age	28.0	18.6	17.9	34.1	20.1

SOURCE: "Spanish-American Survey," *Current Population Reports*, Series P-20, no. 238 (Washington, D.C.: Bureau of the Census, 1972).

[a] Includes other persons of Spanish origin.

Table 12-4 Extent of Education of Spanish-American 25-Year-Olds and Over, March 1972 (percent)

Age	Total U.S. population	Spanish origin		
		Mexican	Puerto Rican	Total[a]
Less than 5 years of school				
25–29	0.8	7.3	5.8	5.5
30–34	1.4	12.6	8.7	8.4
35–44	2.5	21.0	19.9	15.9
45–54	3.4	33.1	39.9	25.1
55–64	5.6	47.9	[b]	30.8
65 and over	12.2	74.8	[b]	51.3
total	4.6	26.7	20.2	19.3
4 or more years of high school				
25–29	79.8	42.9	30.9	47.6
30–34	73.9	40.1	22.6	42.7
35–44	66.8	28.0	27.2	35.2
45–54	59.8	14.2	21.3	24.9
55–64	46.7	8.8	[b]	20.6
65 and over	32.0	0.6	[b]	12.1
total	58.2	25.8	23.7	33.0

SOURCE: "Spanish-American Survey," *Current Population Reports*, Series P-20, no. 238 (Washington, D.C.: Bureau of the Census, 1972).

[a] Includes other persons of Spanish origin.
[b] Base less than 75,000.

Table 12-5   Family Income of Spanish-American Population, March 1972

Total dollar income	Total U.S. population	Spanish origin			
		Mexican	Puerto Rican	Cuban	Total[a]
under 3,000	8.3	14.9	16.9	7.9	13.8
3,000–3,999	4.8	9.2	11.0	3.2	8.2
4,000–4,999	5.4	7.1	10.6	11.3	8.4
5,000–5,999	5.7	8.3	10.2	8.0	8.1
6,000–6,999	5.5	7.0	7.7	3.5	7.2
7,000–7,999	6.2	7.1	12.8	7.6	8.0
8,000–9,999	12.3	15.1	9.9	11.8	13.8
10,000–11,999	12.5	11.8	10.6	15.1	11.9
12,000–14,999	14.4	10.2	5.1	10.2	10.4
15,000–24,999	19.5	8.6	4.5	20.6	9.4
25,000 and over	5.3	0.5	0.8	0.8	0.9
median income	$10,285	$7,486	$6,185	$9,371	$7,548
number of families (thousands)	53,296	1,100	363	170	2,057
head, year-round, full-time worker					
median family income	$12,436	$9,472	$8,235	$11,296	$9,596
percent of all families	63.5	57.5	50.7	61.8	57.0

SOURCE: "Spanish-American Survey," *Current Population Reports*, Series P-20, no. 238 (Washington, D.C.: Bureau of the Census, 1972).
[a] Includes other persons of Spanish origin.

Chicanos are primarily urban residents, with estimates of the degree of urbanization running from 75 to 80 percent. In major southwestern cities and towns, Chicanos are clustered in separate ghettos. As is the case in predominately Black ghettos, overcrowding and poor housing are characteristic. Most Chicano males are employed in blue-collar occupations in the cities, and occupational advancement into professions and higher status occupations has been very slow. In terms of income and level of living, the quality of life afforded most urban Mexican-Americans exceeds that experienced by lower class blacks. But in most cases, the Chicanos are decidedly worse off than the Anglo population.

There are a number of problems characteristic of life for the Chicano population. Educational advancement is very difficult in a school system in which English is likely to be the sole language used. The level of formal education found in the Chicano population is low relative to the Anglos. There is a pattern of educational segregation of Chicano children in southwestern states into what are called "Mexican" schools, which are usually inferior in terms of instruction and facilities. Other problems include restriction of free access to higher quality housing through the operation of many of the same procedures used to restrict Blacks. In addition, there is a strong sense of

Table 12-6 Employed Spanish-American Men 16 Years Old and Over by Occupation Category, March 1972 (percent)

Occupation	Total U.S. population	Spanish origin		
		Mexican	Puerto Rican	Total[a]
white-collar				
professional, technical	14.1	4.8	2.7	6.9
managers, administrators, except farm	13.2	5.6	6.7	6.5
sales	6.3	2.6	2.2	2.9
clerical	6.9	4.5	9.9	6.9
total	40.5	17.5	21.5	23.2
blue-collar				
craftsmen, foremen	20.7	20.9	15.1	19.7
operatives, including transportation	18.7	27.3	36.8	27.2
laborers, except farm	7.2	14.3	7.2	11.5
total	46.6	62.4	59.1	58.4
farm				
farmers and farm managers	3.0	7.9		5.3
farm laborers and foremen	1.6	0.4	1.9	0.4
total	4.6	8.3	1.9	5.7
service	8.2	11.7	17.5	12.7
total (thousands)	49,401	1,088	262	1,890

SOURCE: "Spanish-American Survey," *Current Population Reports*, Series P-20, no. 238 (Washington, D.C.: Bureau of the Census, 1972).
[a]Includes other persons of Spanish origin.

Table 12-7 Median Income of Spanish-Americans by Years of School Completed for Males 25 Years Old and Over, March 1972

Years of school completed	Total U.S. population	Spanish origin	
		Mexican	Total[a]
	$8,243	$6,150	$6,384
elementary school			
0–4	2,945	3,956	4,110
5–7	4,241	5,648	5,407
8	5,472	6,136	5,941
high school			
1–3	7,571	7,132	6,919
4	9,091	8,421	7,980
college			
1 year or more	11,887	9,154	9,114

SOURCE: "Spanish-American Survey," *Current Population Reports*, Series P-20, no. 238 (Washington, D.C.: Bureau of the Census, 1972).
[a]Includes other persons of Spanish origin.

identity and community within the Chicano population, a feeling that is summed up in the term they often employ when referring to themselves, as well as to other Spanish-speakers: "La Raza" (the race). That serves to make many Mexican-Americans unwilling to leave their communities and settle in predominately Anglo areas. And the pattern of voluntary self-segregation is reinforced by language. That is likely to be a major factor contributing to the continuing vitality as well as to the separation from the dominant culture of Mexican-American life, culture, and language.

American Indians

At the time of the discovery of the New World, there may have been as many as 1 million Indians residing in what is now the continental United States.[34] As colonies expanded from the East Coast, the Indian population was either annihilated or driven westward. Indian tribes were compelled by force and fraud to cede more and more land to white colonists. Temporary treaties were negotiated and then violated consistently, forcing the Indian population to choose between bowing to the wishes of the colonists or resorting to short-term wars, which they could not win owing to the military superiority of the colonists. The early history of white-Indian relations was characterized by defeat for the Indian and expropriation of what they regarded as their land by the colonist.

Forced Assimilation   In the nineteenth century, there was a change in official policy from one that bordered on genocide to one of "forced assimilation." Indians were given the status of "wards" of the government and were resettled on reservations. The new policy proposed to integrate Indians into the total national life—a process that was to be accomplished by entirely obliterating the indigenous Indian culture. Indian children were to be educated according to the model of white schools, thus stripping them of their own culture and language. Through a program of land redistribution decreed by the Dawes Act of 1887, tribal holdings were divided among individual Indians. Although some tribal holdings were maintained by members of the tribes, the policy resulted in the loss of 86 million acres of Indian holdings to non-Indian settlers. It ignored the fact that *collective ownership* was a major cornerstone of many Indian tribal cultures. When faced with a forced pattern of individual ownership, many Indian holdings fell into decay and unproductivity, and many Indian small land holders became extremely poor. The massive poverty led to poor health conditions, which, in turn, kept the death rate high and, accordingly, the Indian population small.

Recent Official Policies   Official policy toward American Indians continues to vary from an emphasis on forced assimilation to one favoring the development of separate institutions within the context of traditional Indian

Table 12-8   Comparison of Employed Indians and Total Employed Population, California, by Occupation, 1960 (percent)

Occupation	Total population employed	Indian population employed	Difference
professional, technical, proprietors, managers, officials	24.0	8.0	−16.0
clerical and sales	30.0	10.0	−20.0
craftsmen, operatives	24.0	27.0	+3.0
domestics, service	11.0	18.0	+7.0
laborers, farm laborers	5.5	17.0	+11.5
no occupation reported	5.5	20.0	+14.5

SOURCE: "Minority Groups in California," *Monthly Labor Review* (Washington, D.C.: Bureau of Labor Statistics, 1966.)

culture. During the 1930's and 1940's, Indians were encouraged to re-emphasize their traditional culture; many aspects of the assimilationist policy were terminated. In the 1950's, the federal government took steps to remove the Indian population from the status of wards of the government. But there were also policies designed to eliminate tribalism as a factor in Indian life. Along with other minority groups, Indians were to be integrated into American life. Self-determination was reemphasized during the 1960's by both the Kennedy and Johnson administrations, while the Nixon administration showed a tendency to return to an assimilationist policy. Shifts in emphasis by the federal government have caused disruption in Indian communities and in Indian life, and the issue of self-determination continues to be a major one.

Life Conditions   Indians share many problems with other American minority groups: undereducation (the average Indian male has a fifth-grade education); underemployment; unemployment (over 40 percent on reservations); extreme poverty (75 percent of Indian families have incomes of less than $3,000 per year, with the average annual family income standing at $1,500 in 1969); high infant mortality; low life expectancy (only 44 years); high disease rates among adults. All those contribute to making the Indian the most deprived minority group in America today. They are subject to considerable prejudice and discrimination in the regions immediately surrounding reservations. Most Indians who do migrate to urban areas obtain low-status occupations, and high rates of unemployment persist within urban Indian communities, as Table 12-8 suggests. Most young Indians have few skills that would enable them to adapt successfully to urban life. Apparently, many who do try return to the reservation eventually; about 55 percent of the estimated Indian population of 800,000 is rural.

Protest Movements   In reaction to these facts of Indian life, more militant tactics are emerging as elements of Indian social protest. There has been a resurgence in emphasis on Indian culture and on self-determination among the various Indian tribes. "Pan-Indian" social movements have found considerable popularity among younger Indians. They have employed civil rights protest techniques pioneered by Blacks as a model through which to express demands for redress of their grievances—for example, the events at Wounded Knee. There is increasing resistance on the part of Indians to encroachment upon their culture and ways of life. That increased consciousness of their minority group status may result in a greater role for the Indians in their own affairs and more participation in the mainstream of American life.

Puerto Ricans

Following the conclusion of the Spanish-American War in 1898, the United States acquired Puerto Rico. An island in the Greater Antilles in the Caribbean, it was given commonwealth status. In 1917 Puerto Ricans were extended citizenship, but they do not vote in United States presidential elections. The population of the island is about 2.5 million and is growing rapidly, with an annual growth rate close to 3 percent. Puerto Rico is more densely populated than any Latin American country, and that has contributed to low standards of living and persistent unemployment.

Migration to the Mainland   Puerto Ricans began migrating en masse to the American mainland after the end of World War II, initially concentrating in the East Harlem section of Manhattan in New York City. Since then they have dispersed throughout many urban areas, particularly in the East. Most of the migrants were white, with only about 20 percent being classified as Black.[35] The majority of them had lived for some time in urban areas and had some experience with urban life before reaching the mainland urban centers. The motivation to migrate from Puerto Rico can be traced primarily to the underdeveloped economy of the island and to the lure of employment at wages far greater than those attainable on the island. Presently, the Puerto Rican population on the mainland numbers just over 1.5 million.

Life Conditions   Housing in predominately Puerto Rican ghettos is generally very poor and extremely overcrowded. In most instances, the housing is old and dilapidated, and most slum landlords do little to improve quality. High rents plus exorbitant security deposits are demanded of tenants by slum landlords because in an apartment housing ten or more persons, it is likely that there are multiple sources of income. The monthly rents charged for the inadequate facilities are often comparable to rents prevailing in middle-class suburban areas. Even though several members of a family may be employed, it does not mean there is a substantial rate of income. For example, available evidence suggests that Puerto Rican families have substantially less income than Black families in New York City.[36]

Social Definition of Race   While the bulk of Puerto Rican migrants to the mainland can be considered "white," their darker complexion has served to support prejudice and discrimination, most of it being justified on racial grounds. Often the Puerto Rican and Black populations are discriminated against equally by the host white population. For many Puerto Rican migrants, race is of little consequence, as there is little race-based discrimination on the island. However, race is a major factor in the social life of the mainland; often for the first time, white Puerto Ricans find themselves classified as Black. They are then confronted with all the restrictions imposed on Blacks by whites, and that understandably elicits hostile reactions. Accordingly, many Puerto Ricans see themselves as being discriminated against on all sides, with both whites and Blacks discriminating against them on the basis of race, culture, and language. As a result, most urban Puerto Ricans on the mainland are clustered in ghettos in which the culture is intensely Puerto Rican and residents virtually exclusively so.

Language   In addition to the problems related to the social definition of race on the mainland, Puerto Ricans have a great many problems that are traceable to language. A significant proportion of migrants possesses little or no facility in English upon arrival, and many Puerto Rican school children enter public schools lacking adequate command of that language. The school systems in most urban centers are not flexible enough to accommodate bilingual programs. Puerto Rican students often learn little in school but are nevertheless socially promoted until the age of permissible dropout. Accordingly, the level of formal education within their group tends to be very low, as Table 12-4 shows. And language problems continue to be substantial for Puerto Rican adults even though educated in American schools. These educational problems persist in preventing the upward mobility of the Puerto Rican population and represent a serious obstacle to their socioeconomic advancement. Puerto Ricans are concentrated, by and large, in low-status occupations (see Table 12-6), and median income levels per family are the lowest among any major Spanish-speaking minority. Many Puerto Rican families are headed by females (28.9 percent compared with a national average of 11.6 percent) and tend to be larger in size than the national mean (almost 20 percent of Puerto Rican families include 4 or more children compared with the national average of 8.6 percent). Such factors magnify the effect of educational disadvantage and compound the degree of deprivation experienced by many Puerto Ricans on the mainland.

Jews

The almost 6 million Jewish-Americans represent a diverse group. Predominately of European origin, they have experienced prejudice and discrimination in many countries of the world as well as the United States. They have been discriminated against because of their nationality as, for example, happened to Jewish immigrants from southern and eastern Europe. Owing to misuse of the term "race," Jews were and are subject to differential treatment because of characteristics that are thought to be hereditary but actually are cultural. Moreover, because of notions held by some Christians about the role of Jews in the crucifixion of Christ, Jews have experienced prejudice and discrimination as a religious minority. Over the centuries, Jews have been regarded as a racial, ethnic, and religious minority group. And the depth of prejudice and degree of discrimination has been substantial.

Many of the same restrictive measures applied to other minority groups in America are also directed against Jews. Many Jews find difficulty in gaining access to facilities and housing in high-status areas. Social clubs, fraternal groups, and country clubs discriminate against Jews, with the result that all-Jewish, parallel social institutions have been formed. But discrimination against Jews is gradually lessening in most areas of social life; they have enjoyed more economic success, particularly younger Jews, than have other minorities. And, in general, Jewish-Americans have been able to assimilate to a greater extent than other groups. Part of the reason lies in the fact that whether one is Jewish or not cannot be determined by merely looking at the person concerned. "Jewishness" is not visible in the way that being Black or Asian is. In addition, Jewish culture greatly values education. And many Jews, as a result of their education, have attained positions of considerable power and responsibility. While it is possible to be prejudiced against such individuals, active discrimination is difficult.

Nevertheless, Jews are essentially in a marginal position in American society, enjoying most of the advantages but being restricted in certain areas. They see themselves as being considered partly Americans—as Americans in nationality but as Jewish in a Christian nation. That dilemma can involve some serious crises in identification, particularly when Jewish traditions go virtually unrecognized—for example, not being paid when taking time off to observe important holy days. Jews, then, face the necessity of having to choose among priorities in their lives—between the demands of life in a predominately Christian nation and the dictates of their religion. Many have sought to resolve the dilemma by practicing Reform Judaism, which is far more flexible and liberal in its requirements than the orthodox traditions. But the very existence of this form of Judaism bears substantial testimony to the extent of Jewish-American marginality.

Asians

Chinese   Chinese immigrants first came to the West Coast of the United States in large numbers around 1850, during the period of westward expansion. As a source of cheap labor they at first encountered a warm reception; they were, in fact, actively recruited. However, as the Chinese began to compete with the white population for employment, the reception turned decidedly sour. Another factor related to the eventual prejudice and discrimination the Chinese experienced was visibility. Chinese were very different from the host white population in physical and cultural characteristics. Those differences were used to justify the severe violence that was eventually directed at the Chinese population. Many Chinese responded to this persecution by returning to China, but still others moved eastward through the country. Today most of America's major urban centers, particularly in the western United States, have some Chinese residents. An additional wave of Chinese immigrants entered America during and after the Communist takeover of mainland China in the mid-twentieth century.

Chinese-Americans are a highly urban population, with most of them living in ghettos called Chinatowns. Chinese-Americans evidence a strong pattern of voluntary self-segregation, traceable largely to their desire to preserve traditional clan and kin ties and cultural traditions and practices and to avoid hostile reactions from the larger society. As is the case with other minority groups, Chinese-Americans are vulnerable to restrictions placed on housing. Also, many families live close to the poverty level, and suburban housing is overpriced for them.

Owing to internal growth and the relaxation of immigration laws, the Chinese-American population is rising and now stands at about 435,000. Their communities, particularly those in New York City and San Francisco, are expanding quite rapidly, with resulting increases in overcrowding. Those factors are forcing the younger members to seek a livelihood elsewhere. The result has been that many have rejected the traditional home-based occupations in favor of higher status occupations and the professions. The trend should result in a greater dispersion of the Chinese-American population throughout all social levels, which will eventually produce substantial gains in life chances among the group.

Japanese   Japanese migrants came to the West Coast in considerable numbers a few decades after the Chinese, principally around the beginning of the twentieth century. They encountered a substantial amount of prejudice and discrimination, which was already being directed at the Chinese. Anti-Japanese movements grew rapidly and in 1924 reached such proportions that Congress was moved to bar further Japanese immigration. By that time, many Japanese had settled in largely Japanese urban ghettos. But a substantial number were involved in agricultural and urban small-business activities. They were quite successful in those enterprises, and were viewed as competitive, aggressive, and cunning by the host population.

In light of such stereotypes, and following Pearl Harbor, the Japanese-American population was the target of intense anti-Japanese feeling. Whether a person of Japanese ancestry was Japanese-born (an *Issei*) or American-born (a *Nisei*) was of no consequence; either was liable to be concentrated by the government in "relocation centers" in the West and Midwest. Thousands of people were relocated, and two-thirds of them were American citizens. The policy was clearly the result of racism, as no German-Americans or Italian-Americans were sent to relocation camps. The ultimate result was economic ruin for thousands of Japanese businessmen and small farmers. Before being relocated, they were permitted time to sell their businesses and properties. But prospective buyers took advantage of their need to sell and offered much less than the properties were actually worth.

After the war, most Japanese and Japanese-Americans returned to western states to resume their lives, and the reaction of other groups to their plight was generally favorable. Accordingly, their economic recovery was rapid, although most of the small farms and businesses were not reestablished. Rather, Japanese-Americans dispersed throughout all levels of the occupational structure. The youngest generation of Japanese-Americans (the *Sansei*) is found in middle- and high-status occupations, largely reflecting their strong commitment to middle-class values of achievement and occupational success. There were almost 600,000 Americans of Japanese descent in 1970.

Interestingly, the Supreme Court recently declared that the relocation of Japanese-Americans during World War II was unconstitutional. Accordingly, the court granted reparations, but full economic restitution was never made.

Other Minorities

In addition to the Jewish minority already mentioned, there are other Caucasian minority groups in the United States. The two most notable are the inhabitants of Appalachia and the Cajuns of southwestern Louisiana, although it is not unreasonable to include such groups as the Hutterites, polygynous Mormons, and Amish.[37] In all these cases, it is difficult to

Minority Groups in America

419

establish any pattern of discrimination or prejudice specifically aimed at members of the groups. Rather, they represent distinctive subcultures that, for various historical and ideological reasons, have become separated or even alienated from the general American culture although not completely.

Whether any of these subcultures truly represents a minority group in the sense that differential treatment is accorded on the basis of ascribed characteristics is difficult to say. The Cajuns come closest to representing a minority group in the sense that the term has been used in this chapter. The Cajuns have been described as "good-natured but hopelessly lazy, if not outright stupid, country bumpkins,"[38] and so forth. The people of Appalachia are thought of as isolated, given to intermarriage with close kin, and prone to blood feuds.[39]

The Cajuns may be moving toward changing their minority status in some ways. There have been, in recent years, attempts to create pride in the Cajun subculture and to increase the use of French as their primary language. While that may, of course, tend to perpetuate the status of the Cajuns as a recognizable subculture, it could at the same time reduce discriminatory practices against them, particularly politically. A factor militating against a distinctive Cajun subculture has been the increase in educational opportunities for young Cajuns, although much remains to be done. For example, early in the 1970's, "the median school years completed by persons over twenty-five years of age in the Cajun parishes was about 6.8 as compared with 11.8 for Louisiana and 10.6 for the country as a whole."[40]

In Appalachia the most severe problem is extreme poverty, brought on to some extent by a decrease in coal mining in the region. But the energy crisis of the 1970's could mean an eventual increase in coal production, which would alleviate some of the economic problems of that area. Such an economic revival would, then, alter the status of the people as a minority group.

The Amish and the Hutterites appear to represent exceptionally stable subcultures, and any dramatic changes in these groups appear unlikely. Further, it is difficult to perceive these subcultures as truly minority groups, although certainly they are regarded by some with suspicion and even dislike. Such discrimination as there is takes the form of obliviousness; both subcultures tend to be largely ignored by the larger society. That they do not participate fully in the mainstream of American life is a matter of group consensus and not the function of any active discrimination.

Responses to Dominance

James Vander Zanden has suggested that minority groups react to dominance in four distinct ways.[41] By *responding by acceptance*, a minority group fails to resist dominance exercised by another group. Such a pattern was observed among Japanese-Americans, who did not resist internment during World

War II. And after Reconstruction, when white supremacy was restored, many Blacks in the South had no alternative but acceptance. *Responding by aggression* involves vigorous social protest, or even violence, designed to redress grievances. Much recent social protest among minority groups has assumed that character. When *responding by avoidance*, a minority group, through insulation, migration, and the advocation of separatism, reacts by attempting to remove itself psychologically, spatially, or both, from the dominant group. Chinese-Americans have adopted that mode of reaction through voluntarily segregating themselves into urban ghettos. Black nationalists propose this alternative as the only viable response to white domination. In *responding by assimilation*, a minority group changes cultural characteristics so as to reduce the differences between itself and the dominant group. That pattern of response often includes a strong emphasis on integration and was characteristic of the civil rights movement between 1955 and 1965. Most European immigrant minority groups respond in such a manner by making determined efforts to become "Americanized" in all respects.

There are certain factors that will have a substantial influence on whether responding by assimilation will be a course of action permitted members of minority groups in America. Warner and Srole, on the basis of their research into such questions, suggest three propositions that can be used to predict rates of assimilation for minority groups.[42] And these factors may determine whether assimilation is an option open to certain minority groups.

1. The greater the differences between the host and the immigrant cultures, the greater will be the subordination. The greater the strength of the ethnic social systems, the longer the period necessary for the assimilation of the ethnic group.

2. The greater the visible racial differences between the populations of the immigrant and host societies, the greater the subordination of the immigrant group, the greater the strength of the social subsystem, and the longer the period necessary for assimilation.

3. When the combined cultural and biological traits are highly divergent from those of the host society, the subordination of the group will be very great, their subsystem strong, the period of assimilation long, and the processes slow and usually painful.

Generalizing from those propositions, Warner and Srole believe that the possibilities for assimilation in America are best for light Caucasoids, which would include populations of North and Central Europe and the British Isles. Dark Caucasoids, for example, Puerto Ricans, would fare somewhat less well. Groups that are Mongoloid-Caucasoid mixtures with Caucasoid appearance, such as some Spanish-speaking populations of the American Southwest and much of the mixed population of Latin America, would have poorer possibilities. Those groups that are Mongoloid, and those mixed groups with a predominately Mongoloid appearance, such as Malaysians, would follow with even lesser chances. Finally, those groups that are Negroid or mixed-Negroid would have the poorest life chances of all.

Accordingly, in predicting changes in dominant-minority relations in the United States, we would expect that dominance and racism will continue to exist as major factors in Black-white relations. The probability that opportunities for assimilation for Mexican-Americans and Puerto Ricans will continue to improve is fairly high, since most of these groups could be classified as Dark Caucasoid. The assimilation opportunities afforded Mongoloid and Mongoloid-mixture groups, such as Asian-Americans and American Indians, should continue to be greater than those afforded to Blacks.

The alternatives to assimilation are social and cultural pluralism. If Warner and Srole are correct in their thinking, race relations in the next few decades are likely to conform more closely to a model of pluralism in which, while economic barriers continue to fall, other forms of discrimination will remain as the essential fact of *social* life. The critical question is whether this pluralism will be "equal status" pluralism; one in which racial and ethnic groups are relatively equal economically but discriminate socially; or one in which race relations will continue to evolve in a separate but increasingly unequal direction.

CONCLUSION

Minority groups, as we have defined them in this chapter, suffer from a number of disabilities. Active discriminatory practices, legal and extra-legal, function to prevent members of minority groups not only from full participation in their parent society but from access to significant rewards available in such a society. It should be emphasized that discrimination and its handmaiden, prejudice, were not the result of any planned program; they are an outgrowth, or function, of the way societies and other groups tend to organize and function. To members of any group, all others not belonging to the group tend to be objects of suspicion, fear, and dislike. This is accentuated in the case of many minority groups by the factor of visibility. As we have observed, discrimination cannot easily be practiced or prejudice aroused unless those feeling prejudice or practicing discrimination can recognize that certain others are not members of the in-group.

Certain immigrants who initially are identifiable as minority group members cease to be objects of prejudice and discrimination when they learn the language and adopt the customs and dress of the host society; they assume what might be called protective coloration. But for those of different racial stock than the host society, learning the language and adopting the dress and customs of the host society is not enough. Since they can be easily identified by observation as minority group members, they are more subject to prejudice and discriminatory treatment.

We have also seen that distinguishable racial physical traits are unrelated to the potential ability of individuals to learn or to function capably as members of any society. And the long-range solution to minority group problems may lie in the field of education. As members of both minority and dominant groups are educated to the fact that physical differences are irrelevant, physical differences between the various races of mankind will come, in time, to be ignored.

REVIEW QUESTIONS

12.1 How has the Black Power movement influenced recent ethnic movements among Chicanos, Italian-Americans, and Indians? What are some of the similarities and differences in goals and tactics?

12.2 What are some of the most common stereotypes associated with the major minority groups? How have these evolved? Which relate to physical and which to cultural characteristics? How accurate are they in describing physical and cultural characteristics of these groups? Which are the most offensive, and which are essentially harmless? What stereotypes can be applied to dominant groups?

12.3 Examine patterns of racial and ethnic segregation in the community in which your educational institution is located. What is the intensity of racial or ethnic segregation? Where are the minority neighborhoods located relative to other sections of the city?

12.4 Consider some of the procedures designed to reduce racism. Which have you encountered? What media efforts have you observed that are designed to reduce racism and intergroup prejudice? What kinds of roles do you find minority group members play in media productions? Do these tend to erode or reinforce stereotypes?

12.5. When are members of minority groups likely to experience marginality? On what basis? How are they likely to resolve strains imposed by marginality?

12.6. What factors can be cited to support or to refute contentions that minority group life is improving in the United States? How effective has recent legislation actually been in reducing discriminatory barriers?

12.7. Compare the history of race and ethnic relations in the United States with other countries in the Western Hemisphere—Brazil, Caribbean nations, and so on. Where are the major similarities or differences? What is the essential character of race relations in other societies in the Western Hemisphere? What historical factors might account for these differences?

NOTES

[1] Carleton S. Coon, *The Origin of Races* (New York: Scribner, 1912).

[2] Theodosius Dobzhansky, *Mankind Evolving: The Evolution of the Human Species* (New Haven, Conn.: Yale University Press, 1962), p. 266.

[3] W. I. Thomas, *The Child in America: Behavior Problems and Programs* (New York: Knopf, 1928), p. 81. For a further discussion, see Robert K. Merton, *Social Theory and Social Structure*, rev. ed. (New York: Free Press, 1957), pp. 421–434.

[4] W. Lloyd Warner and Leo Srole, *The Social Systems of American Ethnic Groups* (New Haven, Conn.: Yale University Press, 1945), pp. 285–286.

[5] Joseph Arthur de Gobineau, "Essai sur l'inegalité des races humaines," cited in *Race: A History of Modern Ethnic Theories*, ed. Louis Snyder (London: Longmans, 1939).

[6] Houston S. Chamberlain, "Foundations of the Nineteenth Century," in *Race: A History of Modern Ethnic Theories,* ed. Louis Snyder (London: Longmans, 1939), pp. 103–161.

[7] Pierre van den Berghe, *Race and Racism: A Comparative Perspective* (New York: Wiley, 1967), p. 15.

[8] Thomas P. Bailey, *Race Orthodoxy in the South* (New York: Neale, 1914), pp. 92–115.

[9] James S. Coleman et al., *Equality of Educational Opportunity* (Washington, D.C.: U.S. Government Printing Office, 1966).

[10] Arthur Jensen, "How Much Can We Boost IQ and Scholastic Achievement?" *Harvard Educational Review* 39 (1969), pp. 1–123.

[11] Robert M. Yerkes, "Psychological Examining in the United States Army," *National Academy of Sciences Memoirs* 15 (1921), p. 870.

[12] Otto Klineberg, *Negro Intelligence and Selective Migration* (New York: Columbia University Press, 1935).

[13] Everett S. Lee, "Negro Intelligence and Selective Migration: A Philadelphia Test of the Klineberg Hypothesis," *American Sociological Review* 16 (1951), pp. 227–233.

[14] William M. Hailey, *An African Survey* (London: Oxford University Press, 1957), p. 434.

[15] William Graham Sumner, *Folkways* (Boston: Ginn, 1906), p. 13.

[16] Robert K. Merton, *Social Theory and Social Structure,* rev. ed. (New York: Free Press, 1957), p. 428.

[17] Simon Podain, "Language and Prejudice toward Negroes," *Phylon* 17 (1956), pp. 390–394.

[18] Lee Rainwater, "Crucible of Identity: The Negro Lower-Class Family," in *The Negro American,* ed. Talcott Parsons and Kenneth B. Clark (Boston: Beacon, 1966), pp. 160–199.

[19] Stanley Lieberson, "A Societal Theory of Race and Ethnic Relations," *American Sociological Review* 26 (1961), pp. 902–910.

[20] John Dollard et al., *Frustration and Aggression* (New Haven, Conn.: Yale University Press, 1939).

[21] Leonard Berkowitz, *Aggression: A Social Psychological Analysis* (New York: McGraw-Hill, 1962), chap. 6.

[22] Russell Eisenman, "Scapegoating and Social Control," *Journal of Psychology* 61 (1965), pp. 203–209.

[23] T. W. Adorno et al., *The Authoritarian Personality* (New York: Harper & Row, 1950).

[24] Robin M. Williams, *Strangers Next Door* (Englewood Cliffs, N.J.: Prentice-Hall, 1964).

[25] Morton Deutsch and Mary Evan Collins, *Interracial Housing* (Minneapolis: University of Minnesota Press, 1951).

[26] Charles H. Stember, *Education and Attitude Change* (New York: Institute of Human Relations, 1961).

[27] Williams, *Strangers Next Door,* p. 304.

[28] Louis Wirth, "The Problem of Minority Groups," in *The Science of Man in the World Crisis,* ed. Ralph Linton (New York: Columbia University Press, 1945), pp. 347–372.

[29] E. Franklin Frazier, *The Negro in the United States,* rev. ed. (New York: Macmillan, 1957), p. 568.

[30] C. Vann Woodward, *The Strange Career of Jim Crow* (New York: Galaxy, 1957).

[31] Gunnar Myrdal, *An American Dilemma* (New York: Harper & Row, 1944).

[32] *The Negro Family: The Case for National Action* (Washington, D.C.: United States Department of Labor, 1965); and Lee Rainwater and William L. Yancey, *The Moynihan Report and the Politics of Controversy* (Cambridge, Mass.: M.I.T. Press, 1967).

[33] Melville J. Herskovits, *The Myth of the Negro Past* (New York: Harper & Row, 1941); and E. Franklin Frazier, *Negro in the United States.*

[34] Alfred L. Kroeber, "Demography of the American Indians," *American Anthropologist* 36 (1934), pp. 1–25.

[35] C. Wright Mills, Clarence Senior, and Rose Kohn Goldsen, *The Puerto Rican Journey* (New York: Harper & Row, 1950), pp. 3–6.

[36] Nathan Glazer and Daniel P. Moynihan, *Beyond the Melting Pot* (Cambridge, Mass.: M.I.T. Press and Harvard University Press, 1963), pp. 116–117.

[37] A brief description of the Cajuns is contained in Jerah Johnson, "The Cajuns—Louisiana's French Minority," in *Viewpoints: The Majority Minority*, ed. Drew McCord Stroud (Minneapolis: Winston Press, 1973), pp. 51–53. A full and scholarly account of the Hutterites is to be found in John A. Hostetler and Gertrude E. Huntington, *The Hutterites in North America* (New York: Holt, Rinehart and Winston, 1967). Information on the Amish is contained in John A. Hostetler, *Amish Society* (Baltimore: Johns Hopkins Press, 1963).

[38] Johnson, "Cajuns," p. 53.

[39] Gerald R. Leslie, Richard F. Larson, and Benjamin L. Gorman, *Order and Change* (New York: Oxford University Press, 1973), p. 174.

[40] Johnson, "Cajuns," p. 53.

[41] James W. Vander Zanden, *American Minority Relations,* 3d ed. (New York: Ronald, 1972).

[42] Warner and Srole, *Social Systems.*

ANNOTATED BIBLIOGRAPHY

Adorno, T. W.; Frenkel-Brunswik, Else; Levinson, Daniel; and Sanford, Nevitt. *The Authoritarian Personality.* New York: Harper & Row, 1950. This important study into the "prejudiced personality" concludes that such a personality type does exist, and can be identified by a wide range of factors. It supposes that those factors compose a definite personality syndrome.

Bailey, Thomas P. *Race Orthodoxy in the South.* New York: Neale, 1914. Bailey analyzes southern race relations in depth, focusing on detailed characteristics of racism and the "etiquette" of race relations.

Berkowitz, Leonard. *Aggression: A Social Psychological Analysis.* New York: McGraw-Hill, 1962. Berkowitz suggests the importance of psychological mechanisms that produce and sustain prejudice, emphasizing the importance of projection.

Chamberlain, Houston S. "Foundations of the Nineteenth Century." Cited in *Race: A History of Modern Ethnic Theories*, edited by Louis Snyder. London: Longmans, 1939. Chamberlain was an influential racial theorist, and his assertions regarding the superiority of Teutonic peoples influenced Adolf Hitler. Many Third Reich policies reflect attempts to carry out many of Chamberlain's proposals regarding the subjugation of "inferior" races.

Coleman, James S., et al. *Equality of Educational Opportunity.* Washington, D.C.: U.S. Government Printing Office, 1966. This research, often called the Coleman Report, was a survey of educational opportunities for all groups in a sample of 4,000 schools. Particular attention was given to minority group students and their levels of achievement.

Coon, Carleton S. *The Origin of Races*. New York: Scribner, 1962. Coon provided early material on the origin of races and on the evolution of man.

Deutsch, Morton, and Collins, Mary Evan. *Interracial Housing*. Minneapolis: University of Minnesota Press, 1951. This study of the effect of integration on interracial attitudes found clear evidence that residential integration led to a reduction in intergroup hostility and racial prejudice.

Dobzhansky, Theodosius. *Mankind Evolving: The Evolution of The Human Species*. New Haven, Conn.: Yale University Press, 1962. Dobzhansky, using a combination of blood group analysis with schemata for classifying on the basis of physical traits, attempted to construct an exhaustive classification of race groups.

Dollard, John, et al. *Frustration and Aggression*. New Haven, Conn.: Yale University Press, 1939. This was Dollard's primary statement on the hypothesized relationship between aroused frustration and expressed aggression.

Eisenman, Russell. "Scapegoating and Social Control." *Journal of Psychology* 61 (1965), pp. 203–209. Eisenman proposes that scapegoating enforces social control and often has positive consequences, as well as disruptive influences, on society.

Frazier, E. Franklin. *The Negro in the United States*. Rev. ed. New York: Macmillan, 1957. In this exhaustive work on Blacks in the United States, Frazier cites the importance of the slave background in accounting for facets of life in Black communities and within Black institutional contexts.

Glazer, Nathan, and Moynihan, Daniel P. *Beyond the Melting Pot*. Cambridge, Mass., M.I.T. Press and Harvard University Press, 1963. Glazer and Moynihan devoted this work to a survey of the major American minority groups.

de Gobineau, Joseph Arthur. "Essai sur l'inegalité des races humaines." Cited in *Race: A History of Modern Ethnic Theories*, edited by Louis Snyder. London: Longmans, 1939. Gobineau asserted in this essay on racial inequality that European ethnic and racial groups were inherently superior to all others and warned against the consequences of racial mixing. His thought was representative of racist thinking in the nineteenth century.

Hailey, William M. *An African Survey*. London: Oxford University Press, 1957. Hailey notes that the official policy of the South African government is based on beliefs that biological differences exist between the races and that these factors justify practices of separate development and segregation.

Herskovits, Melville J. *The Myth of the Negro Past*. New York: Harper & Row, 1941. Herskovits believed strongly that the structure and functioning of Black American institutions could be explained by studying them as "survivals" of the African background. He contended specifically that Black family life and religious patterns were traceable to the African past.

Jensen, Arthur. "How Much Can We Boost IQ and Scholastic Achievement?" *Harvard Educational Review* 39 (1969), pp. 1–123. Jensen suggests there may be genetic differences between the races which call for adjustments in programs designed to compensate for "deprived" environments.

Klineberg, Otto. *Negro Intelligence and Selective Migration.* New York: Columbia University Press, 1935. Klineberg attempts to determine whether IQ differences between northern and southern Blacks could be accounted for by a "selective migration" of smarter Blacks to the North, or whether they were produced by environment. His evidence supports the contention that environment is the main factor producing the differences in intelligence.

Kroeber, Alfred L. "Demography of the American Indian." *American Anthropologist* 36 (1934), pp. 1–25. Kroeber attempts to determine the relative size of Indian populations at various points in time, suggesting how thorough the genocide of that population has been until recently.

Lee, Everett S. "Negro Intelligence and Selective Migration: A Philadelphia Test of the Klineberg Hypothesis." *American Sociological Review* 16 (1951), pp. 227–233. Lee found confirmation for Klineberg's findings when Lee made similar tests of the importance of environmental influences on intelligence among Blacks in Philadelphia.

Lieberson, Stanley. "A Societal Theory of Race and Ethnic Relations." *American Sociological Review* 26 (1961), pp. 902–910. Lieberson points out the importance of differential power among groups, particularly the importance those differentials play in race and ethnic relations.

Merton, Robert K. *Social Theory and Social Structure.* Rev. ed. New York: Free Press, 1957. This discusses many aspects of social life, among them the processes associated with stereotyping and intergroup relations.

Mills, C. Wright; Senior, Clarence; and Goldsen, Rose Kohn. *The Puerto Rican Journey.* New York: Harper & Row, 1950. This study was devoted to many aspects of life among Puerto Rican migrants, particularly to factors impelling migration and to racial and cultural characteristics of the migrants.

Myrdal, Gunnar. *An American Dilemma.* New York: Harper & Row, 1944. This "classic" work on race relations in America emphasizes the point that American race relations represent a fundamental contradiction between egalitarian ideologies and the realities of life.

The Negro Family: The Case for National Action. Washington, D.C.: United States Department of Labor, 1965. This study, often called the Moynihan Report, concluded that instability in the family structure of Black America was traceable to "pathologies" in Black family life.

Podain, Simon. "Language and Prejudice Toward Negroes." *Phylon* 17 (1956), pp. 390–394. This shows the importance of visibility by showing how language and meaning reflect the social significance of physical attributes.

Rainwater, Lee. "Crucible of Identity: The Negro Lower-Class Family." in *The Negro American,* edited by Talcott Parsons and Kenneth B. Clark, pp. 160–196. Boston: Beacon, 1966. Rainwater illustrates the importance of skin color and related traits in the lives of many Blacks.

———— and Yancey, William L. *The Moynihan Report and the Politics of Controversy*. Cambridge, Mass.: M.I.T. Press, 1967. Rainwater and Yancey review the varieties of reaction from various sources to the conclusions of the Moynihan report, pointing out the controversial nature of those conclusions.

Stember, Charles H. *Education and Attitude Change*. New York: Institute of Human Relations, 1961. Stember provides evidence that there is substantial prejudice among many educated persons, indicating that education alone will not result in the loss of prejudice.

Sumner, William Graham. *Folkways*. Boston: Ginn, 1906. This early American sociologist coined many of the terms common in sociological literature today, among them "ethnocentrism."

Thomas, W. I. "The Relation of Research to the Social Process." *Essays on Research in the Social Sciences*. Washington, D.C.: Brookings, 1931. Thomas produced the formulation now termed the "self-fulfilling prophecy," and he discussed its significance in social relations.

van den Berghe, Pierre. *Race and Racism: A Comparative Perspective*. New York: Wiley, 1967. van den Berghe's work on race relations and racism has been very influential. His distinction between "paternalistic" and "competitive" characters of race relations has been a useful tool in analyzing the historical sequences of race relations in the United States.

Vander Zanden, James W. *American Minority Relations*. 3d ed. New York: Ronald, 1972. In an updated text on minority group relations, Vander Zanden suggests a typology of response to dominance by minority groups.

Williams, Robin. *Strangers Next Door*. Englewood Cliffs, N.J.: Prentice-Hall, 1964. Williams studied the importance of social class and social mobility on prejudice and authoritarianism, and he concluded that both of those traits are widespread in the deprived segments of society.

Warner, W. Lloyd, and Srole, Leo. *The Social Systems of American Ethnic Groups*. New Haven, Conn.: Yale University Press, 1945. This work is one of the "Yankee City" series, summarizing extensive research into the importance of socioeconomic factors in the life of a medium-sized New England community.

Wirth, Louis. "The Problem of Minority Groups." In *The Science of Man in the World Crisis*, edited by Ralph Linton. New York: Columbia University Press, 1945. Wirth classified minority groups on the basis of goals and on the nature of social interaction between minority and dominant groups.

Woodward, C. Vann. *The Strange Career of Jim Crow*. New York: Galaxy, 1957. An historian, C. Vann Woodward traces the origin and development of segregation codes and practices in the South.

Yerkes, Robert M. "Psychological Examining in the United States Army." *National Academy of Sciences Memoirs* 15 (1921). Yerkes uses data provided by the intelligence testing of soldiers during World War I to conclude that the tests show clear evidence of racial differences and white superiority.

Social Change:
The Bad Old
Good Old Days

Social change is a fact of life. Individuals change, groups change, societies change and, indeed, the entire world changes. And the process of change has accelerated enormously in recent years. In 1666, Christian Huygens suggested an organized investigation of steam power in France. From that suggestion to George Stephenson's steam railroad (1825) there was a gap of 159 years. In 1948, the first transistor was developed at the Bell Laboratories. Just 10 years later transistors had greatly altered the electronics industry and were responsible for tremendous strides in computer technology. In 1958 experiments in light amplification through stimulated emission of radiation (Laser) were begun. Only 7 years later, there was wide medical, scientific, commercial, industrial, and artistic use of Laser techniques. And since the beginning of the twentieth century, the automobile, telephone, and airplane have made considerable changes in the life styles of many people throughout the world.

However, many people object to such rapid change, and that will be discussed at some length later in this chapter. To some people, the "good old days" have great appeal, and they presume that people led happier, less stressful, and more "fulfilled" lives. For example, there was little real concern over such degenerative conditions as cancer and heart disease, which tend to occur after forty years of age. Since the average life expectancy a hundred years ago was about forty years in the United States, people tended to die from causes other than cancer and heart attacks. As of 1975, the expectation of life in the United States was somewhat above seventy years.

But arguments, pro or con, about social change represent the values and attitudes of the debaters. Even in isolated, preliterate societies, some social change takes place. The problem facing humanity, then, is not to pass judgments on social change per se. The problem is to learn something about the dynamics of change so that some control over its speed and direction can be exerted.

For some time now, nations, individually and in concert, have attempted to control social change. The United Nations, for example, represents an effort to channel disputes between nations into settlement by peaceful means and to coordinate national behavior when and where international interests are involved. Many nations are concerned over the so-called population explosion and are making serious efforts to reduce the fertility rate and reduce or stop population increases. But if social change is to be directed at all, some knowledge of the processes underlying this dynamic process is necessary. And it appears useful to examine some of the various arguments with respect to modern societies and the effects modern societies have on their individual members. We should note that much discussion about the direction of modern society has its genesis in values and value systems. While this is

13

Social Change:
The Bad Old Good Old Days

perfectly legitimate, we suggest that some knowledge of the dynamics of change would make such discussion and argument more fruitful. In this chapter, we will (1) consider some of the factors of social change; (2) discuss some of the value positions concerning rapid recent change and modern societies; and (3) examine change-producing variables that exist outside of society but cause changes within. We turn now to some considerations basic to the study and understanding of social change.

PERSPECTIVES ON SOCIAL STRUCTURAL CHANGE

Karl Marx

Any overview of the writing on social structural change is materially assisted by turning to the work of Karl Marx for many of the most relevant and contemporary ideas. Some current authors are again emphasizing Marx's work by taking new perspectives on it and by using his interpretations in combinations with others on the same set of social issues.[1] But what must be considered most relevant today is Marx's basic model of society.

Marx was in error about the necessary polarization of class interests in society and inaccurate in his view that all history is the story of class struggles. But one great contribution was his concept that societies are dynamic, not static, entities. "Marx, of course, emphasized the ubiquity of conflict and its systemic relationship to all social structures; without conflict, no progress; this is the law which civilization has followed to the present day."[2]

But Marx quite correctly took no pessimistic view of conflict within societies. He saw that the tensions existing between groups could serve the useful purpose, in his estimation, of ultimately and drastically changing the social structure to a classless society. He was correct in principle but wrong in prediction. Conflict can and does serve to alter existing social structures. But the direction in modern societies has been more toward formalizing and managing conflict, although there are still somewhat abortive efforts to suppress it when conflict reaches a stage of open violence and violates the rules. Although the criminal code, in terms of sheer size, has grown considerably since the early 1900's, the civil code has shown the greatest increase in sheer volume—laws and regulations concerning corporations, labor unions, business contracts, voting and other political matters, and education including busing. Nearly all of those laws, regulations, and court decisions have the effect of constraining and regulating conflict but not eliminating it, which seems impossible in a pluralistic modern society. However, society is essentially a tension-management system.[3] The extremely complex social structure of society functions, in part, to maintain social control by keeping conflict and tension at some reasonable level. Furthermore, the ideal result of the changing social structure in modern societies is to channel conflict and tension in directions that are beneficial or, at least, not harmful to society.

For his basic view on the mechanisms that produced structural changes, Marx drew heavily on the German philosopher Hegel. Hegel's idea was that for each philosophical idea there will be one opposite to it; through the discussion and acting out of those opposing ideas a synthesis would develop that reflected the most useful aspects of both. Marx applied Hegel's basic theories not to ideas but to social structure.

Marx's model of how structural change occurred maintained that for each set of interests in society there was an opposing set. Given the fact that each set of interests tried to further its own cause at the expense of others, some sort of solution had to be worked out. He called one set of interests the *thesis*, the other set, its *antithesis*, and the resulting solution, the *synthesis*.

In Marx's original writings, the owners of the tools of production, the bourgeoisie, were in direct conflict with another set of interests in society represented by the proletariat, who were to finally overthrow the bourgeoisie and set up a communist state. After an unspecified but short period, that state would also wither away leaving a utopia built on Marx's famous dictum "From each according to his ability to each according to his needs."

Ralf Dahrendorf

Ralf Dahrendorf[4] recognized that the social classes, which Marx saw as large-scale phenomena, could in fact be broken down into smaller conflicting interest groups. Dahrendorf recognized that the communist revolution did not occur in Western society as Marx predicted. While conflict has continued, it is essentially institutionalized, with both management and workers constrained by laws, regulations, and precedent. Briefly, what has happened is: (1) the greatly enlarged middle class has become a buffer between management and worker; (2) material prosperity has greatly increased; (3) largely because of union activity, the relative income of workers has reached the highest point in the history of Western nations; (4) there has been a general blurring of the old class distinctions. Dahrendorf further modifies Marx by arguing that those conflicting interest groups are basically political and not economic in nature and that all relationships in society are determined by political priorities. Interestingly, Dahrendorf's conceptions of society were developed during the Nazi regime in his native Germany when political priority was undoubtedly a fact of life. In addition, Dahrendorf draws heavily from writers who live in the Soviet bloc countries, where politics is thought to be the "primary" insitution. In this sense, Dahrendorf reinforces the correctness of Marx's view of society that where one fits into the social structure very much determines one's consciousness of what is happening in that society.

Alienation and the Breakdown in Community

Serious problems often arise out of social change. In order for us to gain a fuller understanding of the nature of social change, we will examine some of those problems and review several different concepts of them.

Alienation, defined as a feeling of detachment from and hostility toward society, was first discussed in the context of social change by Marx. It was his idea that change deeply alienated men from each other. He blamed the contemporary situation he witnessed on the fact that the worker no longer owned the tools with which he worked and did not begin a piece of work and see it through to completion. As a result, the workers no longer took real pride in their work and derived no satisfaction from it. Marx, of course, was interested in alienation because he saw it as the fuel for revolution. But more recent concern has focused on the relationship between the breakdown in the sense of community and alienation.

Theodore Roszak: Technocracy   Theodore Roszak holds that the in-increasingly materialistic nature of society, while giving people great abundance, also creates a kind of emptiness and loneliness that they sense but do not understand. He attributes this alienation in part to the same kinds of problems Marx noted. Roszak has coined the word *technocracy* to describe a superindustrialized state in which the directions of the society, its prime values, and the relations between people are decided primarily on the grounds of technological efficiency. Technocracy

is the ideal men usually have in mind when they speak of modernizing, up-dating, rational planning. Every aspect of [American] society is organized by experts who are technically well trained and competent and know better than the average citizen. Around the central core of experts who deal with large scale public necessities there is a circle of subsidiary experts who, battening on the general social prestige of technical skill in the technocracy, assume authoritative influence over even the most seemingly personal aspects of life: sexual behavior, child-rearing, mental health, recreation, etc. In the technocracy everything aspires to become purely technical, the subject of professional attention. The technocracy therefore is the regime of experts—or of those who can employ the experts.[5]

According to Roszak, technocracy no longer has any ends, goals, or values other than those that are technocratically determined. Life often has a one-dimensionality in which people plan their lives around the technically possible or even merely possible.

Both long-range, idealized efforts and short-range, expediency behavior may and do contribute to social change. If we take the stand that many business decisions are essentially short-range and directed at immediate profits, we can see that some reactions to this kind of behavior may produce social change. Roszak, for example, sees one reaction to many of the problems created by the technocracy in the "dropping out" of sufficient numbers of American youth and in their alternative life styles. The communes, coops, and so on, are the beginnings of a counterculture, one based on a close *sense of community* among people, something very much lacking in a technocracy.

Ferdinand Tonnies: Gemeinschaft and Gesellschaft That presumed "breakdown" in the sense of community has been claimed by many writers to be the prime cause of mass alienation. Among the first to talk about the changing nature of the community was Ferdinand Tonnies, who published *Gemeinschaft und Gesellschaft* in 1887. He was attempting to show that

man was . . . by his very nature a social being who would unfold his essence only by living in communities (Gemeinschaft) of kinship, space (neighborhoods), and spirit, but who was also capable of forming and, at certain stages of history, compelled to form new kinds of associations by agreements—associations which could be understood as instruments for the attainment of certain ends (Gesellschaft)—whereas those "older" communities were taken as ends in themselves.[6]

Tonnies assumed that men choose their associates on the basis of two very different kinds of will: *rational will* (Gesellschaft) and *natural*, or *integral*, *will* (Gemeinschaft). Natural will is always irrational to some degree, and communities based on it are based on such things as liking or habit. Associations are not created primarily on that basis but, rather, are outgrowths of rationality in which a person carefully selects means to accomplish certain ends. Tonnies was concerned with where man's rational will had carried him in the creation of society. He held that, through creating society based on rational calculations of individual advantage, the human condition had deteriorated to a state of isolated individuals alienated from each other. Great cities had been built that were essentially Gesellschaft in nature and where the exploitation of the workers took place as part of the normal process of life. Tonnies recognized the need for each form of social organization and believed the best life to be composed of some blend of the two. But he often did seem to wonder if the process of the shift of social relations from Gemeinschaft to Gesellschaft had gone too far, a question that certainly plagues some people today.

Normative and functional integration When contemporary sociologists talk about Tonnies's Gemeinschaft and Gesellschaft, they often use the concepts of *normative* and *functional integration*. We recognize that while all social groups are integrated to some extent, the degree and manner of their integration varies widely. Every social group contains a blend of rules (the norms) that tie the members together with (1) some rules applying to all members of the group equally and (2) other rules applying only to certain members of subgroups within the larger context. Those rules that apply to all members give it a degree of normative integration (Gemeinschaft); those rules that apply only to some members are the basis for functional integration (Gesellschaft). In the case of functional integration, the ties that bind members together can be very real even though many rules that govern their conduct may not be the same. For example, in large metropolitan areas people are dependent on the men who have a monopoly over the collection and disposal of garbage. As has been demonstrated by several garbage strikes in places such as New York City, garbage collection has become a highly specialized task requiring licenses, trucks, and routes, so that people cannot dispose of their own garbage; because of the nature of the work involved, garbage men are not expected to be bound by the same set of behavioral codes as, for example, are society matrons. Yet it is recognized that a great deal of inter-dependency exists in large metropolitan areas over the issue of garbage collection. As long as some degree of community concern is maintained by the garbage men—as long as they continue to pick up garbage on a regular basis—they are largely free to act and talk as they desire. Only when essential services stop, do we recognize that America is a functionally interdependent society and each part depends on the other.

Without getting bogged down in the garbage analogy, the point is that the level and kind of integration American society has today becomes an issue when we study social change. The total integration of a group is always the combination of the two subtypes, functional and normative. Not only have some authors noted that the total amount of integration may generally be less, but they also have claimed that the basis for social integration is shifting rapidly from the normative to a more functional basis involving an extreme division and specialization of labor.

Many groups today are being formed in an effort to try to reinstitutionalize rules that apply to everyone.[7] The arts are seeking to dramatize this shift through films such as *Midnight Cowboy*, where in one scene no one pays attention to a dead executive lying on the sidewalk because it is rush hour, and *Easy Rider*, where the two main characters are violently shot to death because their beliefs, systems, and actions are not in accord with locally established norms. Many of the most widely acclaimed contemporary films are morality plays that reflect a growing concern with what is viewed by their makers as a breakdown of community. Such films raise the very real question of how far we can tolerate a breakdown in the normative system. People react strongly, even violently, to such problems as the draft dodgers, war protesters, and peace marchers prevalent during the Vietnam involvement, because these groups were breaking rules that were once considered to apply to everyone in the community. Today many more individuals are questioning the basis of

Today many more individuals are questioning the basis of the American social order by asking "Do these rules and laws apply to me?" Their answer often is no, and confrontations in the streets and courts over differing definitions of the law have become increasingly frequent since the 1960's.

the American social order by asking "Do these rules and laws apply to me?" Their answer often is no, and confrontations in the streets and courts over differing definitions of the law have become increasingly frequent since the 1960's.[8]

Emile Durkheim The question of how the law reflects changes in the social structure is an important aspect of contemporary social change. Durkheim felt that the law does and must continue to mirror the changing nature of relationships between people if it is to be respected.[9] He observed that the law no longer compels people to conform in all aspects of their behavior, with cruel and inhumane punishments likely if they do not. His mechanistic type of society demands a high degree of conformity, and it is clearly akin to Tonnies's concept of Gemeinschaft. Durkheim contrasted his mechanistic society with his organic type, in which relationships were more functionally interrelated, as we discussed in Chapter 1.

Maurice Stein: Artificial communities Various community studies have, since the 1950's updated some of the ideas and demonstrated further extensions of the trends we have been discussing. Maurice Stein has attempted to pull some of these ideas together.[10] It is his thesis that social life in America is changing rapidly in response to the forces of industrialization, urbanization, and bureaucratization. Without now going deeply into the dimesnions of those three factors, let us examine what Stein sees as happening to interpersonal relationships in America. He notes that American society is no longer composed of what have been called genuine communities[11] but, rather, consists of somewhat artificial ones. The word "artificial" mirrors for Stein the sense of community that is found in the modern suburbs. There the interaction between people, while being visible, is not motivated by real concern for the welfare of the group. It is, rather, concerned with keeping up appearances. Ceremonies that once helped pull a community together on a periodic basis are largely, if not totally, lacking. The result is that people are unsure of the outer boundaries of the community in which they live and of whom they may turn to for help in an emergency. Interpersonal relationships at all levels call for masking true emotions without effectively releasing them. This leads Stein to contrast modern communities with those within a preliterate society, where there are well established, customary methods of dealing with the common human problems of emotional adjustment by which feelings are externalized, publicly accepted, and given treatment in terms of ritual release. Stein is much disturbed by the demands currently made upon adults to be committed to putting on a status front where they must continually relate to significant others and to their children with "proclamations of success and happiness." A whole network of unresolved emotional feelings has been set up whose control becomes necessary for the maintenance of the suburban social order, while the modern suburb permits few of the benefits offered by earlier communities.

David Riesman: Search for identity Given increasingly rapid technological change and the changing forms of social organization, such as the suburb, through which Americans deal with and direct this change, certain authors have noted that many individuals become unsure of where to turn for the development of a durable and lasting identity. One's identity is derived

THE NOW SOCIETY

One's identity is derived from the ways significant others expect one to perform and from the roles one plays in different social groups.

© Chronicle Publishing Co. 1973   4-13

Reprinted by permission from Chronicle Publishing Company.

"Are you really mad, Georgie-Porgie, or are you just role-playing?"

from the ways significant others expect one to perform and from the roles one plays in different social groups. How can there be a sure sense of personal identity in a world built on the quicksand of social change? David Riesman recognized this problem in his most famous work *The Lonely Crowd.*[12] According to Riesman, people once knew where to turn for guidance when rates of change were much slower: *tradition* provided answers about how things should be done because what had worked in the past would work in the present. He sees whole generations of people in earlier times being able to be what he calls *tradition-directed*—able to use their ancestors as a reference group in coping with current social realities. But once significant change begins in a society, the ancestral solutions may not work well. Parents, there-fore, attempt to give their children a set of principles, an "internal gyroscope," to keep them on course throughout their lives. This internal gyroscope Riesman equates with a sense of *inner-direction.* That group is able to rely on principles that their parents had taught them were acceptable as solutions to problems they would face. While the tradition-directed individual would feel

Social Change

440

a sense of shame if he had betrayed his traditional community, the inner-directed person would feel guilty because he had not accomplished goals that were deeply ingrained in him from childhood.

As social change become ever more rapid, the internal gyroscope, like tradition, has to be discarded for another mode of response, that which Riesman calls *other-direction*. Given the diversity of the normative structure existing in contemporary society—the result of a growing tolerance and fewer norms that apply "across the board"—the individual finds it difficult to insist that the traditions of his ancestors, or the things he learned as a child, are the way things *must* be done. Since many different groups have their own distinctive sets of norms to govern social interaction, people who want to be mobile must first find out about the differing standards of behavior and then make an effort to fit themselves to it. What is distinctive about the other-directed person is that his source of direction is his contemporaries, not only those known personally but also those known indirectly through the mass media. If we accept Riesman's model (which is, as is the case with models in general, greatly oversimplified), it follows that other-directed persons do not feel guilty about having to adapt and conform to diverse, often conflicting, sets of rules. But they do feel a certain anxiety over not being able to find out quickly enough what the rules are and may therefore appear to be offensive. People find themselves in a rapidly shifting social network of group expectations where no single reference group can be used as the sole basis for judgment about how one is supposed to act. Other-direction in an extreme form seems to involve a lack of fixed identity, with emphasis on a chameleonlike ability to become whatever the situation calls for. Riesman holds that an individual is alone and lonely, even in a crowd.

Philip Slater: America at the breaking point   In his book *The Pursuit of Loneliness*, Philip Slater has expanded Riesman's ideas.[13] According to Slater, America faces the predicament of no longer having a totally viable society because three basic desires have been frustrated by the current way of life: the desire for (1) community, (2) engagement, and (3) dependence. Those three desires should come as no surprise in light of our discussions of Tonnies, Marx, Stein, and Reisman. When talking about the desire for community, Slater is referring to the need of an individual to have stable social groups in which he can cooperate with his peers on a trusting and total basis:

Technological change, mobility, and the individualistic ethos combine to rupture the bonds that tie each individual to a family, a community, a kinship network, a geographical location—bonds that give him a comfortable sense of himself. As this sense of himself erodes, he seeks ways of affirming it. But his efforts at self-enhancement automatically accelerate the very erosion he seeks to halt.

That highly pessimistic view of modern society, which in itself may engender both change and resistance to change, sees competition as responsible for building contemporary society. Slater holds that competition has crept more and more into all aspects of man's relation with his fellow men. It is, of course, obvious that there are kinds of competition today not known in the past—for space on crowded highways, in picnic areas, on the beach, in the city, and so on. Slater has summed up his view of the changes that have occurred with industrialization:

As the few vestiges of stable and familiar community life erode, the desire for a simple cooperative life style grows in intensity. The most seductive appeal of radical ideologies for Americans consists of the fact that all, in one way or another, attack the competitive foundations of our society.

If Slater and others of similar persuasion were correct, American and other modern societies would be on the verge of dissolution. But social change, to be understood, must be seen through many eyes. And we have attempted to present a somewhat pessimistic view of change to illustrate not merely that modern society is viewed by highly intelligent individuals (with great persuasive powers) as essentially antihuman but also that change has always been and will always be opposed by some. Slater, Riesman, and others of similar beliefs consider themselves to be radicals. But they are more likely ultraconservatives who wish not merely to stop social change but also to return to a way of living they believe was characteristic of earlier times. In a peculiar way, Riesman *has* grasped some essentials of social change which occur as societies move from developing to developed status. Things are more complex. Coupled with a highly mobile population, such complexity does render the community of the past exactly that—a thing of the past. And any notion that the community of a hundred or a thousand years ago was more satisfying is not borne out by historical evidence.

Before moving on to a discussion of a different view on social change, we should understand that those who favor change, oppose it, or seek some idealized form of society *all contribute to change*. We shall discuss this in more detail in the section on conflict and change.

Daniel Bell   For a long time students of society, beginning with Marx, have thought that men were becoming more and more isolated from each other with the result that communities were breaking down. The phrase "mass society" was coined to describe what had resulted. But we must be careful in reaching the conclusion that America is a society composed of masses of isolated, alienated, and unmotivated men. One sociologist, well known for objecting to describing America as a "mass society," is Daniel Bell.[14] He points out five different connotations of the word "mass": (I) a heterogeneous and undifferentiated audience, as in *mass communications;* (2) a low quality of life, as in *mass culture;* (3) a mechanical society in which the individual is reduced to his technical function, as in *mass production;* (4) the overorganization of life where people are manipulated by monolithic bureaucracies; and (5) the elimination of differences through an emphasis on uniformity.

Bell feels strongly that the emphasis on the concept "mass" does not recognize or acknowledge the enormous amount of interaction going on in society between different groups, each with their own values, or that new forms of interaction are always being created to replace those no longer functioning effectively. "Such new forms may be trade unions whose leaders rise from the ranks—there are 50,000 trade locals in the country that form little worlds of their own." If we look further, we see at least 200,000 voluntary associations that include clubs and societies to which 80 million people in our "nation of joiners" belong. "In no other country in the world, probably, is there such a high degree of voluntary activity. It often provides real satisfaction for real need." Bell presents further evidence that there are a lot of facts that the writers who use the term "mass society" neglect to mention. One example to which he refers is Morris Janowitz's study of community newspapers, whose numbers have jumped 165 percent since 1910 and whose circulation has jumped 770 percent. Bell presents Janowitz's own important comment on the notion of the mass disorganized society:

If society were as impersonal, as self-centered and barren as described by some who are preoccupied with the one-way shift from Gemeinschaft to Gesellschaft seem to believe, the levels of criminality, social disorganization, and psychopathology which social science seeks to accept for what would have to be viewed as very low rather than (as viewed now) alarmingly high.[15]

Bell's greatest contribution lies in his recognition that in many ways the quality of life in contemporary American society is better than at any time in its past and that social relations are conducted on a more humane basis. For example, those who condemn the loss of moral virtues as the divorce rate rises often fail to see that the new families being formed operate on a freer, more individualistic basis of choice, which is now called the "companionate marriage pattern." Bell pointed out that social change has created a real mixed set of problems, issues, and prospects; solutions to those are not going to be easy to find in most cases. However, it is Bell's basic belief that, through using objective, sociological analysis to determine what the realities of a situation are, people can adapt themselves to an ever-changing world in ways that minimize the meeting of shared and felt needs. And Bell feels this can be done in ways that maximize an individual's freedom to act, adding immeasurably to the quality of his life.

Summary   Having now read some of the views on social change as held by Slater on one hand and Bell on the other, the reader may well ask: Which is right? We have presented Slater along with Riesman and Stein to bring into focus feelings that some in modern society have with respect to the way they live. But Slater, Stein, and Riesman all differ from Bell in one very significant way: they write from a strongly held value position apparently without perceiving that those values shape and, indeed, distort their perceptions.[16] It must be understood that, with the exception of Bell, those writers rarely use any research data in support of their arguments. Bell's analysis of modern society and, in particular, social change is clearly sociological whereas those of Slater, Stein, and Riesman are not. We will end this particular discussion by indicating that (ideally at least) the sociologist should describe society as he or she sees it but *not* as he or she wants it to be or fears that it is. To the extent that values and attitudes prevent that kind of objectivity, the description will be flawed. Since complete objectivity is impossible in all the social sciences, our descriptions are not going to be fully congruent with reality.

FACTORS AFFECTING SOCIAL STRUCTURAL CHANGE

The preceding discussion focused on different views of social structural change and its effect on modern societies. Our next task will be to conceptualize the factors that cause change to take place. There are, briefly, two major views of the sources of change in a society. One sees changes occurring because of stresses and strains within the structure of society itself. The other contends that "events" external to the system are the root cause of structural change.

"Events"

Robert Nisbet develops the idea that "events," which by their very nature are often unpredictable and more or less random, are the key ingredient in causing social change. Nisbet feels that "from Aristotle on there has been a marked unwillingness in the history of social thought to deal with the problem of social change in terms of events."[17] Two main reasons for this are (1) events are so unpredictable as to be beyond scientific analysis and (2) events do not really grow out of structure itself. Nisbet is not alone in his reasoning. Weber developed the concept of *charisma* in order to discuss changes in structure. Charisma was an attribute of individuals; thus, it was a force in the change process that was an outside influence on the social system.

But the view of "events" and "charisma" as being external to social systems is not widespread. It does not, for example, make sense to view

Adolph Hitler as a charismatic leader whose personality was an "event" external to the realities of Germany in the 1930's. Thirty years of historical evidence indicates that Hitler was not alone in the feelings he voiced, and his actions were supported by an uncomfortably large proportion of the German nation until it became apparent that they had lost World War II. And the unique "event" of landing a man on the moon was the result of an enormous number of small, day-to-day decisions made by people in science, politics, economics, technology, and research. If anything, the contemporary view sees events more and more as the result of social processes. Sociologists reject the argument that the cause of World War I was the assassination of Arch-duke Ferdinand in July 1914. Surely, the large standing armies in Hungary, Germany, France, and so on, had something to do with the outbreak of the war. Events like the assassination can no longer be seen as being isolated from the social structures of the time; in large measure, they have a structural basis.

The appeal of Nisbet's argument is that we must recognize some slippage in social determinism. Social structures cannot, in fact, control or determine all the human behavior that occurs within them. People are real and they have unique personalities that do cause them to deviate from structural norms in varying degrees. But, while acknowledging this to be true, we must not fail to note that these unique personalities were also produced through interaction with others in the social structure. This is the import of the whole field of the "sociology of knowledge," which clearly tells us that the "great man" view of history is incorrect. Great men, after all, mirror, reflect, and embellish the needs of their times—not completely, to be sure, but enough so that we must be cautious in accepting a view that events outside the structure determine the nature of change within it.

What we are suggesting is that it is not easy to determine whether influences come from outside a social system, from within it, or both: almost all social systems in the world are in contact with other social systems. Therefore, it would seem that change in a social system might be caused by various factors in the environment or in other social systems: (1) technology, (2) values, (3) demography, (4) physical environment, and (5) conflict and dissensus.

Technology

Medium is the Message Currently in vogue are several writers who talk about the enormous change that is going to occur because of rapidly accelerating *technology*. So let us begin this discussion by looking at the work of a few of these writers. A man whose name is associated with communications, Marshall McLuhan, has become one of the most vocal and listened-to spokesmen of the unique effects of technology on our lives. McLuhan rejects an idea that David Sarnoff developed a few years ago: "We are too prone to make technological instruments the scapegoats for the sins of those who wield them. The products of modern science are not in themselves good or bad; it is the way they are used which determines their value."[18]

McLuhan criticizes Sarnoff for ignoring the nature of the media apart from its more apparent effects—a way of looking at communications phenomena which has become McLuhan's stock in trade. When McLuhan asserts his now famous phrase "The medium is the message," he is stating that, regardless of the encoded message that a medium presents, *the medium itself* is exerting an influence on people's consciousness. That represents quite a departure from more traditional ways of thinking about communication and has led McLuhan to make a series of statements about some media as being *hot* while others are *cool*. A hot medium is one that allows little participation by its audience because the data it presents need to be decoded and one is totally absorbed in it. Television drama is an example of a hot medium. A cool medium allows for a great deal of audience participation because the number of messages given to the audience are considerably less. A classroom discussion, for example, is a cool medium. McLuhan feels that understanding the media is helpful in understanding all technological change where computers, electronic devices, and the like are involved. Such technology speeds the pace of modern society to such an extent that there is a great "heating up" of the temperature of modern life. Much of McLuhan's writing is hard to follow and his analysis is often obscure. Nevertheless, he is considered by some to be a leading theorist on the effect of one aspect of technology—communication—on contemporary American society. McLuhan is very much concerned with making apparent the subtle effects of technology in terms of their meaning for social life. He has done a great service by pointing out a whole series of effects that had hardly been recognized before.

Future Shock Another author known for his ideas on the effects of technology is Alvin Toffler, who wrote the best seller *Future Shock*. We have already mentioned his view that people are dismayed and threatened by change. While his book does make that point, it also presents a view that likens mankind to the mindless automatons that were part of Orwell's *1984*. According to Toffler, people live in a society where novelty is automatically accepted, where the past is vanishing at an increasingly rapid rate, and where rapid turnover of material goods has created what he calls a "throw-away society." It is an age of transience where people no longer own the cars they drive or the homes in which they live (they finance such items through bank loans and mortgages); where marriages are of short duration; and where jobs are changed with great regularity by a large number of people.

Behind such prodigious economic facts lies that great growling engine of change— technology. This is not to say that technology is the only source of change in society. Social upheavals can be touched off by a change in the chemical composition of the atmosphere, by alteration in climate, by changes in fertility, and by many other factors. Yet technology is indisputably a major force behind the acceleration thrust.[19]

Toffler's book offers a closer examination of a series of trends which the reader can recognize more clearly after they are discussed. But, again, one gets the feeling that technology is managing society and that we are all just going along with the changes with little or no chance to review and redirect the course of events.

Industrialization, Urbanization, and Bureaucratization Technology has many facets and dimensions, as we have already seen from our discussion of Toffler and McLuhan. Three major dimensions that raise complicated problems in their own right are industrialization, urbanization, and bureaucratization. *Industrialization* involves the substitution of inanimate machines for animal power; *urbanization* involves the grouping of people together into cities that generate distinctive forms of social interaction based on the size, heterogeneity, and density of urban areas; and *bureaucratization* involves the separation of duties and responsibilities within an organization and relies on rules and a form of hierarchical grouping in order to maintain control. Each of these factors is part of the technological revolution that looms large in Maurice Stein's work *The Eclipse of Community*, which we discussed earlier.

Stein reviews a half century of urban research to demonstrate that the city has been broken into "natural areas." Each has a specialized usage and a particular standard of behavior which no longer cuts across the whole community but only affects subgroups within it. In his discussion of the structural changes brought about by industrialization, Stein updates Marxist ideas by noting that as a result of mass production, the symbols of status increase in importance. That has resulted in a situation where "life plans, whatever they may have been, had to be reoriented around the pursuit of station through money and commodity display."[20] Industrialization means that business values increasingly hold sway over community life; with mass production comes mass distribution systems and a simultaneous reorganization of status placement based on the competitive acquisition of mass-produced goods. Bureaucratization, with its emphasis on a separation of duties and responsibilities within an organization, makes it possible for the owners to live outside the community and to make decisions deeply affecting the lives of those in the community on the basis of factors that are no longer local but either national or international in scope.

Advancing technology has become the basis upon which modern forms of social life are built; those forms have had effects upon the individual which have changed him significantly over the past quarter century.

The work of Stein is a collection and synthesis of research by important students of community dynamics—Lloyd Warner, Robert Parks, and others—who were concerned with the different aspects of technology that we have been discussing. Stein's work is important because it shows that, regardless of the authors upon whom he draws, the effects of technology on people's lives are very nearly the same. Advancing technology has become the basis upon which modern forms of social life are built; those forms have had effects upon the individual which have changed him significantly over the past century and very significantly over the past quarter century.

Prospects for the Future In moving past Stein's review of the changes that technology has brought to American society in the last fifty years, we can begin to think about the kind of future that technology holds in store for the American way of life.

The work of Donald Fabun is typical of those who are concerned with the look of the future in terms of the acting out and continuation of current trends. In *The Dynamics of Change* he details in an imaginative way the possibilities technology presents: increased life span; new energy sources; substitution of manufactured and synthetic for natural products; the increasing gap between rich and poor; accelerated use of automated factories controlled by computers; and so on. His book draws from a wide range of thinkers in the field, and it implies that current life styles as we know them may well cease to exist. Even though one gets the feeling that Fabun is intrigued with the new technology, he communicates the unnerving notion that man may not really understand the nature of the challenge that technological changes will present to him. Fabun argues that man must again exert control over his technology if he is to survive:

It is only the future that is amenable to our plans and actions. Knowing this we can draw a broad general outline of the kind of future we feel we would be most happy in. And because we have now arrived at a stage in our development, or shortly will arrive there, where our most pressing problems are not technological but political and social—we can achieve the world we want by working together to get it.[21]

One may agree with Fabun's point that technology is not the real problem; but does the history of mankind in coping with change lead to the kind of unbridled optimism which is so much a part of this statement? In light of our discussions about the problems of alienation and malaise within modern society, such optimism must be tempered with a better recognition of problems than is inherent in Fabun's work. But he is probably right in noting that technology as a variable was created through the actions of man and will be changed and directed in ways we hardly think possible today.

While technology does have a momentum of its own, it is subject to the desire of human will. That is the position of Joseph Krutch. He violently reacts against statements like this one made in the book *The Year* 2000:

Practically all of the major technological changes since the beginning of industrialization have resulted in unforeseen consequences. Our very power over nature threatens to become itself a source of power that is out of control. Choices are posed that are too large, too complex, uncertain or uncomprehensible to be left to fallible humans.[22]

Weiner and Kahn are clearly implying that any attempts by man to control or plan his future are becoming more and more unrealistic because matters are becoming too complex for man's limited abilities. But one cannot, as they suggest, focus exclusively on the steady, unremitting continuation of all current trends. The creation of stress and strain by certain factors may, as awareness of such pressures grows, force man to decelerate the growth of many of the forces central to Weiner and Kahn's analysis. In addition, certain perceived trends will inevitably clash with ones not yet readily apparent, to nullify perhaps both sets of effects. Krutch presents a more rational picture of the future when he admits that, while he does not know what the future holds, he does know that mankind has the power to control events:

Conscious determination to resist the trend(s) can be effective though most of the prophets leave that out of consideration . . . The quality of life in the year 2000 may depend as much upon beliefs, attitudes, and values as it does upon the trends recognized by most people. There seems little reason for wanting to know what the future threatens to be like unless there is some possibility of changing it and some willingness to assume that some futures would be better than others.[23]

We must not neglect the fact that values and beliefs will help to determine the future, not in a simple-minded sense, but in real terms. And in the context of that statement, we would do well to ask the question "Where did the existing state of technology in America come from and what factors caused it to grow so rapidly in the last 100 years?" The answers to that question can provide an understanding of what will be necessary to bring about the desired kind of future for American society.

Values

For many years scholars have debated whether Weber's analysis of the consequences of the Protestant Ethic, or value system, was truly related to the rise of capitalism. Recent evidence seems to indicate that he was essentially correct. In the early 1950's Robert Bellah tested Weber's thesis by studying the rapid industrialization of Japan.[24] Japan, like the United States, had industrialized in a very short period, between 1865 and 1920. If Weber's thesis about the relation of values to social change and the growth of technology was correct, elements of the same type of value system discussed by Weber should be found among the Japanese. Using the same kind of analysis as Weber, Bellah looked for the values upon which changes in the economy of Japan were based. He found that values in Japan did indeed seem to have a considerable effect on the ability of the Japanese to restructure their society and that those values were similar to the ones discussed by Weber.

From those works and a multitude of others, students of society must conclude that values play a central part in producing social structural change. Here the humanist finds himself most at home with the sociologist as both conclude that what people think, feel, and believe is very important in determining the kind of world in which they live. But sociologists have also shown that people's behavior in terms of their value system often produces changes in society that were not intended by them. Thus, we must keep in mind that values often interact with other factors in complex and subtle ways in our model of social change. Values are, as you will remember, discussed in greater detail in Chapter 4.

Demography

While we can never answer the question of what is the real and ultimate cause of social change, we can suggest that demographic factors exert an influence on social structures regardless of the factors that may have caused demographic changes to take place. The demographic variables within a given society include, among other things, birth and death rates, size and density of a population, and life expectancy. While those variables are amenable to quantitative measurement, their effect in producing social change is not well understood because they have often been regarded as being dependent of other variables and not important in their own right.

Technological Advancement One author who makes demographic changes virtually synomous with the measurement of social change itself is V. Gordon Childe.[25] As a social scientist, Childe is very concerned with being able to measure "progress" in terms that do not involve making numerous value judgments. He uses the increase in the number of people living in an area as an indicator of the progress a civilization has made. His careful analysis links increases in numbers of people to certain technological changes occurring simultaneously within the same society. During the Neolithic period, for example, the cultivation of plants, a surplus of food, the settling of people into agricultural communities, and the increased trade between societies resulted in an increase in population density leading to the growth of ancient cities. In the cities, men lived, exchanged goods and ideas among themselves, and fostered the growth of knowledge. Childe, through his archeological research, presents good evidence that population density made the technological revolutions of antiquity possible. Many of the elements that constitute contemporary American culture, such social inventions as mathematics and written language, were not always available to Man. The basis for our modern civilization, developing out of the interaction of men with each other, was possible only as the result of a certain density of population.

Division of Labor Childe is not alone in recognizing that great changes in societies originated in the urban centers of antiquity as the result of vastly increased interaction between people. One of these changes, stratification, was discussed in Chapter 6. Durkheim, to whose work we have referred frequently, also makes this point central in his writing on the division of labor in society. It is Durkheim's thesis that the increased interaction allowed a certain specialization and division of labor to occur, something virtually impossible before men lived in cities. The division of labor, which we closely associate with a great number of changes in American technology, is seen by both Childe and Durkheim as the result of interaction with demographic changes that occurred when it became possible for population density to increase in a given area.[26]

Demographic Revolution and Social Character A more recent statement on the role of population density is provided by Riesman. His observations of certain demographic changes that have occurred in Western society drew heavily on the work of the demographer Notestein, who formulated a model of population growth called the S-curve, based, in part, on the influence of medicine in determing the size of a population.[27] For purposes of analysis, Notestein distinguishes three stages in the demographic revolution that societies go through as they develop a full-fledged medical technology. In the first stage, with minimal medical knowledge, both birth rates and death rates are very high. In stage two, the death rate begins to drop rapidly through the adoption of preventive health and sanitary measures, including the purification of water and the hygienic disposal of sewage and garbage. The preventive medical techniques greatly affect the infant mortality rate, causing it to drop sharply and accounting for a period of rapid population growth. Stage two lasts from fifty to perhaps several hundred years. During that time population density increases rapidly because there is no alteration in the birth rate to compensate for the lowering of the death rate. After that rather long period, society begins to respond to the problem of increased population density. Through a change in values, which is reflected by behavioral changes, the birth rate begins to decline. The result is the third stage—incipient population decline characterized by low birth and death rates. Riesman, using Notestein's model, distinguishes three types of societies to account for changes in social character. Type One Society, with little population growth, results in people being tradition-directed. Type Two Society, characterized by rapid population growth and a breakdown in traditional norms and values, tends to produce people who are inner-directed. Type Three Society, in which population density is greatly increased, produces some need for people to be other-directed:

A change in the relatively stable ratio of births to deaths which characterizes the period of high growth potential (Stage II) is both the cause and consequence of other profound social changes . . . The imbalance of births and deaths puts pressure on societies' customary ways. A new slate of character structures is called for or finds its opportunity in coping with the rapid changes—and the need for still more changes—in the social organization.[28]

Changes in Family Structure   Riesman has been criticized for paying too little attention to the role social structure plays in cushioning the effects of demographic changes on character structure. However, his analysis of the role of demography in producing social change agrees with the work of another leading theorist, Marion J. Levy.[29] He is concerned with changes in family structure that the demographic revolution has brought about, and he seems to avoid some of the pitfalls of Riesman's analysis. Using a population model much like Notestein's, Levy presents evidence that actual family structures have probably always been nuclear in composition, regardless of the ideal family model each society may have as part of its culture. In the first stage of his population model, with its very high birth and death rates, people do not live long enough to put into practice their ideals of a large extended family. However, as life expectancy increases the ideals become attainable, and there is increasing conflict within the family. Over time, the ideal is changed to correspond to new demographic realities. And in a highly developed society, the nuclear family becomes both the ideal and actual form of family life. Levy's work has also been criticized because it is based heavily on demographic factors. But additional research testing his hypotheses indicates that his line of reasoning is basically sound.[30]

Summary   For a complete understanding of how demographic changes may affect social interaction patterns, let us turn to the work of Georg Simmel. He was an acute observer of how the density associated with city life has affected the behavior of people who live in the city. With so many people coming into contact with each other every day, some sort of protective device must be sought that help a person to avoid being overwhelmed by the sheer numbers that characterize a large urban area: "With each crossing of the street, with the tempo and multiplicity of economic, occupational, and social life, the city sets up a deep contrast with small town and rural life with reference to the sensory foundations of psychic life."[31]

Childe's measure of progress as simply an increase in population implies that such progress is measured by success in not only maintaining a species but increasing its numbers. However, from the sociological perspective, particularly in reference to social change, more people means more interaction. And it is partly out of interaction that change arises, with interaction a necessary but not sufficient condition for change. Populations do not increase indefinitely without the fact of such increase resulting in social change. In the United States, for example, the decade of the 1960's was marked by an increasing acceptance of birth control and the removal of legal barriers to the dissemination of information regarding birth control. It appears that the decade of the 1970's will be equally marked by a concern with abortion as an additional means of population control.

At the present time demographic changes, particularly those concerned with population increases, are much less significant in terms of increasing interaction than in the past. Modern technology makes possible human interaction over the entire earth without the necessity of face-to-face contact. Even if the world population declines sharply over the next century or two, it seems reasonable to predict that interaction will continue to increase. Thus any marked decrement in population will not slow down the process of social change. Population, as an independent variable of social change, will probably function as a stimulus for population control along with a considerable number of so-called intervening variables, such as available resources, pollution, and values and value systems. Apropos of values and value systems and how they change with changing circumstances, the president of I. E. DuPont noted that

in the very abundance of swelling human numbers, the poverty of most of mankind is rooted. This truth, in the short arc of a dozen years, has etched itself deeply into the minds of scholars and physicians, priests and presidents, leaders of industry and science. I confess, like many others, I once took for granted the notion that a rapidly growing population almost automatically meant rising profits and better life for more people. I have learned that for the world as a whole this is not so. And for America, it will not be so much longer. [32]

It becomes clear that demographic variables are closely related to desires for a better future, just as they have been shown by many authors to have determined, in a different fashion, the course of social events in the past.

Physical Environment

The effect of changing environmental conditions is perhaps even less direct than those of the others, but it, too, is very real. Man's development of a culture, meaning in part his technology and value system, makes it possible for him to negate many direct effects of the environment upon his way of life. As the level of technology rises, Man is able to alter his environment in a variety of ways. For example, the Eskimos' way of life, their social institutions and patterns of behavior, originally developed as a response to the harsh environment. The introduction of rifles, helicopters, and snowmobiles into that environment produced a greater variety of social behaviors than was possible before. That observation does not, however, discount the effect that environment has in the development and change of social institutions. Even though a high level of technology mitigates the immediate impact of the environment, this extremely important variable still sets outer limits on the

American way of life. The current outrage over the damage to the American environment is based in large part on the recognition that, if that environment changes drastically in ways harmful to the ecological chain of life on which we depend, those changes will very quickly imperil our way of life.

But environmental damage is no new thing. We have mentioned before that over the course of time there was a shift from nomadic foodgathering and hunting to more stable, primarily agricultural communities. That shift was made possible in the fertile area of the Nile, for example, only because the richness of the soil in the valleys was replenished by annual floodings. Farmers no longer had to move about from area to area in search of adequate farm land and were able to establish permanent settlements. But even though the river valleys produced abundant food stuffs to establish an agricultural surplus, there was great need for raw materials that were not plentiful in the area, such as stone and timber for building. So the early farmers traded their excess food stuffs to others in exchange for raw materials. At that point, the early cities growing up in those rich agricultural lands became trading centers where not only goods but also ideas were exchanged. It is that exchange and diffusion of ideas, along with their constant refinement, that became the basis for rapid advances in technology and science. The foundations of Western civilization can be traced back to the people who lived in those river valleys and who profited from the geographical and environmental uniqueness of those areas.[33]

What, then, happened to the great civilizations that existed in those extremely fertile areas? Such areas as the Tigris-Euphrates and Nile valleys are today noted not for their abundant farm land but for their hot and dry deserts. People are leaning more and more toward the idea that the inhabitants of these areas neglected or were ignorant of the influence of the environment on their way of life. When the soil became less fertile through improper use, less food could be produced and the population could not be adequately fed. Eventually those great civilizations began to decay. It is becoming apparent that the transformation of the areas from the fertile "cradle of civilization" into a vast wasteland was not the result of natural forces but of misuse of the land by the people. We must not forget this lesson when thinking about the relation of changes in the environment to its impact on bringing about social change. Should the plankton of the ocean, one of the chief producers of oxygen in the atmosphere, become unable to survive due to massive pollution, changes of enormous magnitude in all human societies would automatically follow. Those who are optimistic about the fact that technology can overcome any environmental problem must take into account the fact that technology may not, in a short period, be able to reverse natural processes that have been taking place over long periods. The environment may not be able to respond quickly to man's attempts at superficial repair:

One of the reasons our unplanned use of land has been so destructive both in [America] and elsewhere is that man's horizons have been so limited, both by terrain and the curvature of the earth, that he could not see himself as a major force at work upon his environment. What he did was expedient and local, but its cumulative effect has been, all too often, disastrous.[34]

In looking more directly at the changes that have been brought about in the American social system as the result of the environment, the work of the historian Frederick Turner is important. Turner was widely criticized for being an environmental determinist to the exclusion of other factors, but in a balanced approach to the sources of change, his work cannot be neglected. He was concerned with the effect a wide-open frontier had on American social institutions, and he concludes that its effect was enormous:

The existence of an area of free land, its continuous recession, and the advancement of American settlement westward explains American development . . . The peculiarity of American institutions is the fact that they have been compelled to adapt themselves to the changes of an expanding people.[35]

Turner carefully examined the effects of pushing back the frontier by 300 years of settlement. Yet, while the physical frontier may now be closed, one suspects that America's fascination with putting a man on the moon is derived in part from a search for new frontiers, which can be exploited as were the frontiers of old. The mentality of the nation is far different from that of Europe, where people have, in part, already come to grips with the problem of running out of land.

In trying to make use of Turner's ideas without overstating the case for the frontier hypothesis, David Potter has written: "Do we really mean the influence of the frontier or do we mean the influence of a factor that was equally conspicuous in the frontier situation but that also operated apart from it upon many other parts of American experience?" Potter is referring to the abundant natural resources that presented "the greatest free gift that was ever spread out before civilized man."[36] It is Potter's thesis that the abundance found in America, such as the presence of oil in many parts of the country, had a great deal to do with the functioning of American social institutions. In reviewing the development of American institutions, there seems little evidence to contradict his ideas. The only criticism one could level at Potter is that he should have analyzed the changes in American social institutions in terms not only of the abundance provided by the environment but also of the other factors, such as the growth of technology, which we discussed earlier. Nevertheless, Potter does further our understanding of how an abundant environment can influence social institutions. And that represents a significant contribution to an adequate theory of social change.[37]

Utopias   There are two highly active and vocal groups with respect to change: those who abhor it and would turn the clock back if they could; those who favor it and welcome change with open arms. But the contrast between these two groups becomes somewhat blurred as they begin to resemble each other in one important aspect—conflict. Each group envisions an ideal society organized on their terms in which there is a complete *absence of dissensus or conflict*—that is, a utopia. Referring to ideal societies, Dahrendorf comments that "all utopias from Plato's Republic to George Orwell's brave new world of 1984 have had one element of construction in common, they are all societies from which change is absent."[38] In any hypothetical society from which change is absent, conflict too would tend to be either absent or at a minimum. It can be doubted that any such society could possibly exist. Francis Allen believes that "conflicts are not only common but they are virtually intrinsic to the social process; and they are . . . the source of much social change."[39]

As we have said, the structural-functionalists view societies as being basically concerned with maintaining equilibrium. From that perspective, conflict is seen as disruptive to equilibrium and, thus, dysfunctional. In the main, it is probably fair to described the structural-functionalist perspective as optimistic: everything works out for the best. But, as Neil Smelser inquires, "if the main focus of functional analysis is on the positive contributions of activities and structures to the current functioning of a social system, why . . . should we ever expect anything to change in that system?"[40]

Three Types of Social Change   Utopian arguments are, however, essentially moot and have little relevance for the real world in which conflict does exist. What, then, is the relationship between conflict and social change? Before exploring that question further let us review the definition of "conflict." Conflict is a process whereby two or more individuals or groups compete under circumstances where the outcome will, in all probability, be that one competitor will end up with more of some valued resource (tangible or intangible) than the other. It should be clear that conflict among humans is complex and ranges from war to subtle exchanges of glances between husband and wife at the bridge table. Indeed, a form of conflict which has become a significant political factor relatively recently has been nonviolent action: "Nonviolence is not to be equated with passive yielding to superior force or with working only through established channels. It is a positive, active, and in fact militant strategy designed to produce thorough-going changes in social patterns."[41]

Insofar as social change of widespread significance is concerned, Dahrendorf has noted that structural changes resulting from conflict tend to be of three types.[42]

Revolutionary change in power positions A sudden revolution in which one group of leaders is exchanged for another is a classic example of a total or almost total exchange of personnel in positions of power. Ordinarily, as history shows, change of this type has been the result of extremely violent conflict. But it is possible under other less violent circumstances, such as an election in which the party in power is largely superseded by another political party. To some extent, that was the case in the United States when Franklin Delano Roosevelt was victorious over Herbert Hoover in the presidential elections of 1931. That considerable social change followed the exchange of personnel in positions of power is well documented by events during Roosevelt's presidency.

Barring unforeseen events, it seems probable that in the developed industrial nations of the world such complete exchanges of persons in power will become less and less likely. Even the substantial plurality gained by Roosevelt in the 1931 presidential election did not result in a House of Representatives or a Senate in which only the Democratic Party was represented.

Evolutionary exchanges in power positions A partial exchange of personnel that might be termed "evolutionary" is a familiar process in modern societies. Conflict in the political arena is in accordance with norms that regulate such conflict. Some individuals do succeed in ousting incumbents, and others seeking office fail of election. This kind of conflict is not confined to politics; it goes on throughout any modern society where men and women compete, or are in conflict, for scarce societal rewards. The fact that business competitors do not go forth with their retainers to slay competitors or drive them from the society is evidence that conflict has been made normative in modern societies; that is, limits have been set on what the parties to a conflict may or may not do. These normative limits tend to encourage evolutionary changes in power and discourage revolution in the violent sense.

Changes in policy In some instances there is no exchange (or significant exchange) of persons in power. But ideas having their origin in various sectors of the society are incorporated into the policies and behaviors of those in power, and structural changes result. In many ways, Dahrendorf's third type of structural change brought about by conflict implies that, under specified conditions, conflict is at a minimum and responsiveness at a maximum. For those in power to change their views and incorporate ideas originating in sectors below them (using power as the criteria for ranking in this case), ideas must be, to a very large degree, judged on their merit as ideas and *not* on the power or influence or both of proponents of the ideas. However, it seems probable that changes of policy by those in power are in response to what might be called "political realities" rather than to the intrinsic worth of ideas, although "worth" does enter into such changes. It must be plain that if proponents of ideas simply presented them to those in power and had them either rejected or accepted purely on the basis of their merit as ideas (and any rejections were accepted without protest), there would be no real conflict. What does happen is that acceptance or rejection or partial acceptance (which involves some rejection), is probably predicated both on the intrinsic merit of ideas and proposals and the perceived power of the proponents.

Summary Briefly, we have attempted to provide some idea of the functions served by conflict with respect to social change and the close relationship between the two processes. It has been emphasized that any contentions that conflict is purely dysfunctional are both irrelevant and in error: irrelevant because conflict is endemic in all societies; in error because conflict has significant positive functions. We have also implied that the nature of conflict is changing, particularly with respect to industrialized modern societies, toward an increase in the overt expression of conflict that is channeled by norms. The importance of this trend is well stated by Coser:[43]

Rigid systems which suppress the incidence of conflict exert pressure toward the emergence of radical cleavages and violent forms of conflict. More elastic systems, which allow the open and direct expression of conflict within them and which adjust to the shifting balance of power that these conflicts both indicate and bring about, are less likely to be menaced by basic and explosive alignments within their midst.

Coser is referring to conflict that is normative, conflict that is conducted within the norms established in the society concerned and without serious violence. But does violence, the epitome of conflict, serve any useful purpose? Again Coser presents a useful statement:

Violence whether acted out or threatened serves to symbolize to those in power and to the community at large that aggrieved groups and individual actors are willing to forgo the gratifications that flow from peaceful acceptance and internalization of existing norms and to launch themselves on the uncharted seas of rebellion.

Violent conflict, then, indicates that certain of the actors see normative avenues of protest blocked and perceive no alternatives to the use of violence to bring about the changes they desire. We might also observe that even violent conflict tends to be in accordance with some norms, as Ralph Turner claims in his so-called emergent norm theory.[44]

That conflict can be and often is dysfunctional is perhaps too obvious to require elaboration. A dramatic case, which has dragged on for some years, is the conflict been the Protestant majority and the Catholic minority in Northern Ireland. At the individual level are the farmers over whose land warring armies contend in Vietnam. Even normative conflict, as in the

"market place," is clearly dysfunctional for those driven into bankruptcy by more successful rivals. But our problem is not how to stop conflict but how to contain it. As we have emphasized, conflict, and social change arising out of conflict, is endemic in human societies. We perhaps should not even desire to do away with conflict, as utopian concepts suggest. As Dahrendorf points out, "the difference between utopia and a cemetry is that occasionally some things do happen in utopia."[45]

CONCLUSION

We conclude our discussion of social change while recognizing that an enormous amount of relevant material has had to be omitted from an introductory text. We have examined some of the actual changes in social structure which have occurred in the United States since the 1920's, and we have tried to relate them to changes in five factors: technology, values, demography, environment, and conflict. Quite possibly the picture presented seems overly complex in terms of the causes of social change because of the emphasis on multiple factors in connection with the dynamics of modern society. Yet social reality is much more complex than has been indicated here. What must be kept in mind is the importance of those factors we know to have been influential in the past which we believe will determine the shape of the future. Much more directly than is realized at present, those factors can be brought under Man's control and direction if he is wise enough to act:

To take seriously the new developments in the technological revolution means to see the new possibilities and threats to human life which are latent in it. Thus a deep moral passion is a major element in the revolutionary posture. To be realistic cannot mean to limit ones self to what now seems politically possible, but to undertake the impossible in an attitude of daring and trust.[46]

If Man is to exercise at least some conscious, planned control over social change in the future, it is mandatory that he have some understanding of the dynamics of social change, not to mention an understanding of change processes in the past.

This chapter has noted that social change is proceeding at a much more rapid pace than in the past. Various of those factors are particularly significant because the independent variables of social change are coming increasingly under normative control but are, at the same time, freer because there is increasingly open expression of not only conflict but also ideas. These developments in social change are of considerable relevance. The last few decades have seen considerable changes in the area of international behavior not merely with respect to the control (or attempts to control) serious conflict but also in the area of mutual cooperation. It is not inconceivable that social changes of the greatest significance to mankind will take place in the coming years in the area of international behavior.

REVIEW QUESTIONS

13.1. Marx predicted as inevitable the revolution of the proletariat; as we know, there has been no such revolution. What did Marx fail to take into account in making his predictions?

13.2. Moore refers to society as "a tension-management system." Can you think of some ways society provides for draining off or releasing everyday tensions?

13.3. Read carefully Roszak's definition of a "technocracy" (p. 435). Does American society or any modern society fit that definition? If so, how good is the fit?

13.4. According to Roszak, men make plans on the basis of the "possible" rather than the "desirable." In effect, he is saying that men in modern societies no longer hold any ideals. Does this seem to be accurate? Why or why not?

13.5. To what extent have modern societies reached a stage where integration is almost entirely functional? Even in modern societies, are there not some rules that apply to all? Compile a list of examples of normative integration in contemporary American society.

13.6. Stein claims that American society is no longer composed of "genuine" communities. How would you define a "genuine" community? Having defined genuine community, do you think it is likely that any such communities ever really existed? Where and when?

13.7. Slater lists what he calls three basic desires that have been frustrated by the American way of life. You might ask yourself where or how Slater found out about these "desires." If we grant that these desires are genuine (for the sake of discussion), is Slater correct or incorrect in his assumption that American society does not satisfy them?

13.8. There are some people who consider technology to be *the* significant cause of social change. Assume, for the moment, that you do not agree with so sweeping a statement. What arguments can you muster to demonstrate that technology, while obviously involved in social change, is not the *significant* cause?

13.9. Weber's thesis that certain values can result in industrialization and the rise of capitalism has been well demonstrated. Can you think of a value or values that might tend to prevent or, at least, inhibit such changes?

NOTES

[1] See, for example, Theodore Roszak, *The Making of a Counter Culture* (New York: Doubleday, Anchor, 1969), pp. 84–123.

[2] Applebaum, *op. cit.,* p. 7.

[3] See W. Moore and A. Feldman, "Society as a Tension-Management System" in

Behavioral Science and Civil Defense Disaster Research Group, ed. G. Baker and L. Cottrell, Study no. 16 (Washington, D.C.: National Research Council, 1962).

[4] Ralf Dahrendorf, *Class and Class Conflict in Industrial Society* (Stanford, Calif.: Stanford University Press, 1959).

[5] Roszak, *Counter Culture,* p. 5–6.

[6] Ferdinand Tonnies, *Community and Society* (New York: Harper & Row, 1963). See introduction by P. Herbele, pp. ix–x.

[7] The work of John Gardner in his organization Common Cause is a good example of attempts in this direction.

[8] For more information on the issues behind this type of conflict, see Irving L. Horowitz, *Three Worlds of Development* (New York: Oxford University Press, 1966).

[9] Emile Durkheim, *The Division of Labor in Society* (New York: Free Press, 1949).

[10] M. Stein, *The Eclipse of Community* (New York: Harper & Row, 1964), p. 286 *passim.*

[11] See E. Sapir, "Culture, Genuine and Spurious," in D. Mandlebaum, *Selected Writings of Edward Sapir* (California Press, 1949).

[12] David Riesman, *The Lonely Crowd* (New Haven, Conn.: Yale University Press, 1969).

[13] Philip Slater, *The Pursuit of Loneliness* (Boston: Beacon, 1970), pp. 5, 7, 10.

[14] Daniel Bell, pp. 76, 80.

[15] As cited in Bell, p. 81.

[16] Is it, then, worthwhile reading those authors who are clearly taking a value position and who do not offer viable research data in support of their arguments? The answer is that writers such as Riesman, Stein, and Slater offer many useful insights and provide compelling evidence of some of the forces that operate to inhibit or stimulate social change. It is, however, important to exercise caution and not accept any sweeping generalizations that lack empirical evidence.

[17] R. Nisbet, *The Social Bond* (New York: Knopf, 1970), p. 323.

[18] Marshall McLuhan, *Understanding the Media* (New York: McGraw-Hill, 1964), pp. 11, 13.

[19] Alvin Toffler, *Future Shock,* p. 25.

[20] Stein, *Eclipse of Community,* p. 54.

[21] Donald Fabun, *The Dynamics of Change* (Englewood Cliffs, N.J.: Prentice-Hall, 1967), p. 5.

[22] As cited in Joseph Wood Krutch, "What the Year 2000 Won't Be Like," in *U.S.A. from Where We Stand,* ed. L. Ryan (Belmont, Calif.: Fearon, 1970), p. 236.

[23] Ibid., p. 233.

[24] Robert Bellah, *Tokugawa Religion* (New York: Free Press, 1957).

[25] V. Gordon Childe, *Man Makes Himself* (New York: New American Library, 1951).

[26] Durkheim, *Division of Labor.*

[27] As cited in Riesman, *Lonely Crowd,* p. xlii.

[28] Ibid., p. 14.

[29] Marion J. Levy, ed., *Aspects of the Analysis of Family Structure* (Princeton, N.J.: Princeton University Press, 1965).

[30] See L. Fallers, "The Range of Variation in Actual Family Size," in Levy, ed., *Analysis of Family Structure,* pp. 70–83; and T. Burch, "The Size and Structure of Families," *American Sociological Review* 32 (June 1967).

[31] G. Simmel, *The Sociology of Georg Simmel,* trans. K. Wolff (New York: Free Press, 1950), p. 410.

[32] As quoted in Fabun, *Dynamics of Change,* p. 5.

[33] See Childe, *Man Makes Himself.*

[34] Fabun, *Dynamics of Change,* p. 9.

[35] Frederick Turner, *The Frontier in American History* (New York: Holt, Rinehart and Winston, 1921), pp. 1–2.

[36] David Potter, *People of Plenty* (Chicago: University of Chicago Press, 1954), pp. 143 and 144.

[37] For a fuller examination of the role environment can play in interacting with social institutions, see A. Vayda, *Environment and Cultural Behavior* (New York: Natural History Press, 1969).

[38] Ralf Dahrendorf, "Out of Utopia: Toward a Reorientation of Sociological Analysis," in *Change and Conflict,* ed. N. J. Demerath III and Richard Peterson (New York: Free Press, 1967), p. 465.

[39] Francis R. Allen, *Sociocultural Dynamics: An Introduction to Social Change* (New York: Macmillan, 1971), p. 107.

[40] Neil J. Smelser, ed., *Sociology: An Introduction* (New York: Wiley, 1967), p. 707.

[41] Herbert C. Kelman, "The Relevance of Nonviolent Action," in *Readings in Sociology,* 4th ed., ed. Edgar A. Schuler et al. (New York: Crowell, 1971), p. 254.

[42] Ralf Dahrendorf, *Class and Class Conflict in Industrial Society* (Stanford, Calif.: Stanford University Press, 1959), chaps. 5 and 6.

[43] Lewis A. Coser, *Continuities in the Study of Social Conflict* (New York: Free Press, 1967), pp. 29 and 97.

[44] Ralph Turner, "Collective Behavior," in *Handbook of Modern Sociology,* ed. Robert E. L. Faris (Skokie, Ill.: Rand-McNally, 1965), pp. 389–392.

[45] Dahrendorf, "Out of Utopia," p. 467.

[46] Richard Shaull, "The Search for a New Style of Life," in *Containment and Change,* ed. C. Oglesby and Richard Shaull (New York: Macmillan, 1967), p. 187.

ANNOTATED BIBLIOGRAPHY

Allen, Francis R. *Sociocultural Dynamics: An Introduction to Social Change.* New York: Macmillan, 1971. This scholarly, well written book provides a complete introduction to the growing field of social change. It is lucid, objective, and well documented. As an illustration of the sociological perspective applied to social change, Allen's book provides a welcome antidote to reading endless complaints and criticisms of social change and highlights what social change really is from the scientific standpoint.

Childe, V. Gordon. *Man Makes Himself.* New York: New American Library, 1951. The book represents the careful piecing together of archeological evidence and provides the best statement of how Man first developed the basis for civilization.

Etzioni, Amitai, and Etzioni, Eva. *Social Change.* New York: Basic Books, 1964. A careful work that contains the contributions of many authors of great significance, which we were forced to leave out of this chapter.

Fabun, Donald. *The Dynamics of Change.* Englewood Cliffs, N.J.: Prentice-Hall, 1967. Filled with glimpses into the future by way of photographs, charts, figures, and so on, the book makes up, in beauty of presentation, for what it lacks in the way of theoretical insights.

Riesman, David. *The Lonely Crowd.* New Haven, Conn.: Yale University Press, 1969. The issues the book raises are contemporary, and it provides a good historical background for more recent works on loneliness and alienation in modern society.

Roszak, Theodore. *The Making of a Counter Culture*. New York: Doubleday, Anchor, 1969. The book, which has captured the imagination of contemporary youth, deals with the relevant subject of where the youth rebellion came from, the issues it faces in being effective, and its suggestions for needed direction changes in American society.

Slater, Philip. *The Pursuit of Loneliness*. Boston: Beacon, 1970. The book has good insight into the kinds of problems America as a society faces in the 1970's. Beautiful analogies and a gift for writing characterize Slater's work, making it interesting reading for those who are concerned with issues raised by this chapter.

Stein, Maurice. *The Eclipse of Community*. New York: Harper & Row, 1964. The book serves as an excellent review of the work that has been done on the community in America. It tries to synthesize and "zero in on" the changes that have occurred as America has gone from a land of small towns to a country where the vast majority of people live in urban areas.

In addition to including words that have different connotations for sociologists than for the general public, the glossary provides definitions of words commonly found in the sociological literature and attempts to reflect the meaning given words in the sociological context. For those desiring a more complete listing of social science terms, see George Theodorson and Achilles Theodorson, *A Modern Dictionary of Sociology* (New York: Crowell, 1969).

Accommodation A process or technique whereby two or more antagonistic groups (or individuals) work out a modus vivendi (way of life) that not only maintains reasonably amicable relationships between the groups or individuals concerned but also permits them to maintain their separate identities. Contracts, arbitration, truces, and so forth, are all forms of accommodation.

Acculturation Can be used as a synonym for socialization but is more generally used to indicate that a culture or cultures becomes modified through the acquisition of a trait or traits from another or other cultures. *See also* Assimilation, Socialization.

Achieved Position, see Position, achieved.

Action System An action system focuses on action rather than behavior; the distinction between the two is that action has meaning for the actors concerned whereas behavior may not, for example, instinctive behavior.

Adaptation Generally, a problem-solving approach to the dilemmas of adjusting to the environment, difficult conditions, and so forth. Broadly speaking, adaptation implies that problems arise which require a modification or change in behavior (permanent or temporary) in order to deal with them adequately.

Aggregate A human group of any size in close physical proximity under conditions where interaction, particularly any symbolic interaction, is minimal—people passing in the street, gathered in an airline waiting room, and so forth. This is in contrast to a group of people who are engaged on some continuing basis in interaction that is symbolic. *See also* Group.

Alienation A feeling state in which the individual experiences a sense of detachment from other people, groups, or society. It often accompanies a loss of personal identity as, for example, when an individual retires from a lifetime occupation.

Alteration A relatively minor innovation that involves some change in an aspect of culture but no really new information or unique combinations of existing information. *See also* Discovery, Invention.

Analogue Anything that is similar to something else in the functional sense. An example would be a computer and the human brain.

Animism The belief that inanimate objects are endowed with life. A form of animism in modern societies occurs when people who do not actually believe that inanimate objects are actually endowed with life refer, for example, to a ship as "she."

Anomie A state of normlessness where the individual has lost touch with the customary roles and norms of his or her society. Anomie can be a function of societal breakdowns or ambiguity of norms or norm conflict. It is sometimes experienced by persons who have moved either upward or downward in social class and are having difficulty in relating to the norms and roles of their new position. Most forms of anomie arise from the person not knowing what norms should guide his behavior within a specific social setting, such as entering a group for the first time.

Anticipatory Socialization Behaviors and learning undertaken by persons in anticipation of a change of status or class position or membership in some reference group in which membership is desired. What is involved is practice in a role or roles that the individual hopes or expects to fill at some future time.

Anxiety Fear or dread of a person, situation, or things which is generally out of proportion to the actual situation. Anxiety usually has its genesis either in a feeling of helplessness to avert or cope with something or a sort of "free-floating anxiety," by which is meant that the suffering individual does not know the source or cause of the fear or fears.

Ascribed Position, see Position, ascribed.

Assimilation The merging of two or more groups with differing cultures into a single culture in which the resultant single culture combines traits from all cultures included. The United States represents an excellent example, for the general culture of this country represents the assimilation of many diverse cultures into one general culture. *See also* Acculturation.

Association A formally organized group having limited objectives that are specifically spelled out or well understood. Armies, industrial plants, and clubs are examples. *See also* Voluntary Association.

Attitudes Learned tendencies to react in some characteristic or typical way to persons, situations, or things. Attitudes can be considered as specific representations having their origin in the more general values or value systems.

Audience Groups or individuals to whom messages are addressed, or individuals gathered together for the purpose of being entertained in some fashion.

Authority Legitimized power that is hedged in or restricted by the norms that made it legitimate.

Autocracy Rule by one person such as a king or dictator.

Autonomous Free or self-directing. There are varying degrees of autonomy: very young children have relatively little autonomy; as they grow older, they become more autonomous. Yet they never become completely autonomous.

Band An anthropological term describing a small group of people, generally nomadic, who subsist by hunting, fishing, and gathering. Bands are smaller than tribes and lack tribal organization with control being largely highly informal.

Behavior Pattern In humans, a learned, well-established way of behaving in response to various stimuli including situational stimuli. Considered to be the smallest unit of culture.

Belief A statement about the nature of the world or reality in general which is accepted by the believer or believers as true and accurate. Beliefs may or may not, in fact, be true. *See also* Self-fulfilling Prophecy.

Bureaucracy A large organization characterized by impersonality, hierarchical patterns of authority, emphasis on rules and regulations, universalism, and the location of authority not in individuals but in offices. Characterized by Max Weber as the most efficient way yet devised by man of successfully dealing with large-scale projects. In real life, bureaucracies do not function in quite the idealized manner noted but are marked by informal subgroups and diffusion of individual and group goals.

Caste A social status or category assigned by birth. Societies marked by caste systems have very little mobility. With few exceptions, one remains a member for life of the caste into which one is born.

Centralization A process whereby the density of the production of goods, services, political power, population, and so forth, tends to become maximized in urban centers; for example, the automobile industry in Detroit, Michigan, or the federal government in Washington, D.C.

Charisma Personal qualities attributed to some leaders which enable them to influence their followers and which represents a form of power. Examples of charismatic leaders in fairly recent times are Martin Luther King, Jr.; General George S. Patton, Jr.; Winston Churchill; and Franklin D. Roosevelt.

Civilization Difficult to define because all peoples consider themselves as civilized. Generally used ethnocentrically to mean a certain level of cultural and technological development. Frequently used to mean that the peoples so described are highly cultured which, by inference, means that those with differing values, norms, and folkways are uncultured and, thus, less civilized. High levels of organizational and technological development are probably inadequate as criteria because other values such as ethical conduct are unrelated to them.

Clan A human group in which descent is traced either patrilineally or matrilineally. Clans usually practice exogamy and have various other functions—political, economic, and so forth.

Class Class is associated with stratified social systems and implies an ordering from lower to higher based principally on economic criteria—the more wealth one possesses, the higher one's social class. Although class is ascriptive in the sense that one is born into a social class, the inference is that there are opportunities for vertical mobility (both upward and downward) in a class system.

Clique A small group characterized by very strong in-group feelings based upon the sharing of common values, norms, and goals. The word sometimes has an invidious connotation in that there is the assumption that cliques operate strictly on the basis of self-interest to the detriment of outsiders.

Club A formally organized group, the goals of which are usually but not always recreational. For example, there are political clubs whose goals may be partially recreational but which may have additional goals of obtaining or holding political power. Exclusive clubs with rigid membership criteria may function partly for purely social or recreational reasons but serve the added function of emphasizing prestige.

Collective Behavior A general term used to describe behavior not under the control of specific norms and which is relatively unstructured although behavior is interrelated and similar. Examples are fads, spontaneous crowds such as those gathered around a traffic accident, audiences at sporting events, and so forth.

Communication The process of exchanging ideas, attitudes, opinions, knowledge, and so forth, by symbolic means.

Community Ordinarily considered to be a collectivity of humans living largely within a delimited geographical area, marked by some continuous interaction, and satisfying a large number of the needs of those persons involved through what amounts to a system of interdependent relationships.

Competition The act of striving for some goal that is being simultaneously sought for by others with the qualification that all cannot attain or gain the goal; that is, there must be some losers.

Concentration An ecological process in which increasing numbers of individuals tend to settle in a given area. Also used to designate patterns of population density, that is, the average number of persons per square mile.

Concept A mental construct that focuses on certain aspects of some phenomenon for the purpose of classification and ordering. For example, the various breeds of dogs differ greatly in size, color, strength, and utility. Yet we call all of these "dogs" because they all possess what might best be described as "dogginess" even though in arriving at this concept it was necessary to overlook some rather considerable differences, such as those between a wolfhound and a dachshund.

Conflict A process whereby individuals and groups strive for scarce societal rewards either material or nonmaterial. Competition where competitors seek to eliminate or destroy each other. Conflict should be considered as falling on a continuum from the friendliest rivalry to the most savage warfare.

Conflict, role A situation wherein an individual is required to perform two or more incompatible roles which produce internal ambivalence or paradox. An example would be an individual living in a nation-state at war with some other nation-state who was both an ardent nationalist and a pacifist.

Conformity   Behavior on the part of members of a society or group which is in accord with the values, norms, and folkways of that group or society.

Conjugal Family, see Family, nuclear

Consensus   Agreement on something. Consensus is essential for the orderly functioning of any society; there must be at least some consensus on values, norms, and folkways. In addition, there must be a high level of consensus with respect to language including grammar, syntax, and the definitions of words and terms.

Cooperation   A form of interaction in which groups or individuals engage in behavior designed to attain some commonly agreed-upon goal. Cooperation should be thought of as a continuum ranging from a bare minimum to the most involved and efficient goal-seeking behavior.

Correlation   A measurement of the degree to which changes in one variable are associated with or accompanied by changes in another variable. Correlation ranges from − 1.00 through zero (no correlation) to + 1.00. It must be remembered that the establishment of some correlation between two variables does not necessarily mean that there is also a causal relationship.

Counterculture   A subculture existing within a larger culture which, while holding some of the values, norms, and folkways of the dominant culture, has values and norms of its own that are at variance or even in conflict with those of the dominant culture. *See also* Subculture.

Craze   Any behavior that becomes an all-consuming passion and upon which individuals spend an inordinate amount of time. Crazes are usually of short duration, for example, the hula hoop. *See also* Fad.

Crowd   A large number of persons in close physical proximity but whose interaction is superficial and largely unorganized, although the attention of crowd members may be directed at some activity such as a sporting event. Crowds usually remain crowds only for short periods of time. A crowd may become a mob when some leadership emerges and the attention of some crowd members is directed, usually destructively, at some objects, things, or persons.

Cultural Alternatives   A situation in a society where several appropriate alternative behaviors may be used.

Cultural Complex   A functionally integrated culture unit composed of a number of cultural elements; there is a cultural complex with respect to automobiles, spectator sports, and many other things.

Cultural Lag   A term, coined by the late William F. Ogburn, that was taken to mean that changes in nonmaterial culture lag behind those in material culture.

Cultural, or Social, Pluralism   A society organized in such a way that the existence, side-by-side in an amicable relationship, of diverse ethnic, racial, and religious groups and values is not merely permitted but encouraged.

Cultural Relativism   A concept that holds that members of one culture should not pass judgment on other cultures and that any cultural trait can be evaluated only in terms of the culture of which that trait is a part.

Cultural Universals   Behaviors or behavioral complexes that are universal to *Homo sapiens* wherever found in organized groups ranging from bands to societies. While certain functions must be performed by all human groups in order to survive, it is difficult to find any behaviors or behavior complexes that are, in fact, clearly universal.

Culture   It is difficult to arrive at a satisfactory, concise definition of culture but one of the better ones is "that complex whole which includes knowledge, belief, art, morals, law, custom, and any other capabilities acquired by man as a member of society."

Custom   A well established folkway or habitual way of doing things peculiar to a group or society. Violations of customs are rarely dealt with by formal sanctions or severely punished. However, violations of customs may be and often are subjected to mild informal sanctions. For example, an individual with poor table manners may not often be invited out for dinner. *See also* Folkways.

Demography   The statistical study of populations, including such things as births, deaths, fertility ratios, increases and decreases in population, and so forth.

Dependent Variable   A variable (usually labeled Y) in which changes are associated with antecedent changes in some other variable, called the independent variable (usually labeled X). In terms of cause and effect, the dependent variable is the effect. *See also* Independent Variable.

Determinism   A position that holds that all behavior is purely cause and effect and rejects any idea of free will or free choice. On a broader scale, the deterministic point of view sees certain factors as critical in determining broad social and cultural events, as technological determinism holds that technology is *the* causal factor in social change.

Deviance   Behavior that departs significantly from the values, norms, and folkways of a society.

Diffusion   The spread, by whatever means, of cultural traits from one society to another or others.

Discovery   The perception of something already in existence, such as relationships or previously unobserved phenomena. A discovery is purely a matter of perceiving, but it may involve extensive activity on the part of the discoverer as, for example, when new stars or planets are discovered because, on the basis of accrued information, such stars or planets must be in a certain place at a certain time. *See also* Innovation, Invention.

Discrimination   A condition present in a society in or by which members of a minority group or groups are dealt with in such a way as to reduce their individual and collective opportunities to participate fully in the society and to gain the various societal rewards available. Discrimination can and usually does involve both formal norms (laws and regulations) and informal norms with accompanying sanctions. Discrimination is the active component of prejudice, although it is possible for there to be discrimination without prejudice and vice versa. *See also* Prejudice.

Division of Labor   A process whereby the production of goods and services utilized in a society is divided among a number of individuals, with each contributing some element to the total. Because of certain factors, such as a reduction in the training period and so forth, a division of labor enables a society to produce much more than under conditions where individuals supply all or nearly all of their own needs and wants.

Dysfunction   Any process, behavior, or action the end results of which (either manifest or latent) are judged as inimical to individuals, groups, or entire societies. What may be dysfunctional for some individuals or groups within a society may be highly functional for others. For example, a high-profit industry is functional for those realizing the profit, but it may be seriously polluting the air or water adjacent to the plant.

Ecology   An area of study that deals with the mutual and interactional relationship between living organisms and their environment. Human ecology is concerned with the distribution of human populations as these are affected by such factors as centralization, dispersion, succession, invasion, and so forth.

Economy   The social institution that is concerned with the regulation of the production and distribution of goods and services within any given society. *See also* Social Institution.

Education   The social institution that regulates the accumulation of knowledge and is responsible (along with the institution of the family) for passing on this accumulated knowledge to the members of societies. This institution is also partly responsible for inculcation of social values and norms in societies. *See also* Social Institution.

Elite   High prestige bearing and receiving groups within societies. The sociological connotations of this term are that those defined as elite belong to the highest social stratum within a society or, by virtue of some characteristic, quality, or attainment, are viewed with special approbation and accorded great honors and prestige.

Empiricism   A method of acquiring primary knowledge from direct observation of the phenomena concerned. Commonly called the "empirical method," it is also concerned with controlled experimentation in order to test hypotheses and to construct theories.

Enculturation   Used by anthropologists to mean much the same as "socialization" is used by sociologists. In general, enculturation refers to the process by which new members of a society acquire the cultural traditions of that society. On occasion, the term is used to mean the acquiring of new cultural patterns by adults, but this use is not frequent and can ordinarily be understood in context. *See also* Socialization.

Endogamy   The requirement that marriage partners be sought within some socially defined group; for example, approved marriage only between members of a certain clan, tribe, or religion. *See also* Exogamy, Homogamy.

Environment   Anything and everything external to a group which influences, directly or indirectly, the behavior of group members.

Esteem   A quality assigned to individuals on the basis of the way in which they carry out the requirements of their positions and roles. For example, the late Albert Einstein was accorded high esteem. It should be thought of as an assigned and earned attribute of specific individuals.

Ethnic Group   Any group with a common cultural tradition which exists within a larger society. The implications of the term are that an ethnic group manages to maintain some distinctive identity that differentiates members of that group from others in the larger society—for example, matters of dress, custom, language, religion, and so forth.

Ethnocentricism   A belief common in virtually all human groups that the members of the group are in some way superior to all who are members of other groups. The general effect of ethnocentricism is that the members of each group judge all other groups and members of other groups by the standards of their own group.

Ethnography   Description of individual cultures based on close and generally continuing observation of a particular society. Ethnography is generally considered a branch of cultural anthropology.

Ethos   A qualitative aspect of a culture which distinguishes it from other cultures—the "know-how" attributed to Americans, the tenacity attributed to the British, and so on.

Exogamy   The requirement that marriage partners be sought outside some socially defined group. *See also* Endogamy, Homogamy.

Extended Family, see Family, extended.

Fad   A behavior introduced into a society that spreads rapidly among some proportion of that society but persists for only a relatively short period. *See also* Craze.

Family   A social institution that is concerned with reproduction, socialization of children, and related matters in societies. From the sociological perspective, the family can be regarded as comprising specific functions—the family is a process by which certain functions necessary to the continuance of a society are carried out. It should be noted that the family assumes widely diverse forms in human societies.

Family, conjugal, see Family, nuclear.

Family, extended   Generally considered to be a family that includes three or more generations, with the assumption that the entire family either lives under one roof or in very close geographical proximity. Extended families are usually based on blood relationships—they tend to be consanguine rather than conjugal.

Family, nuclear A family form found largely in industrialized societies, it consists of a man, his wife, and their dependent children. Sometimes referred to as "conjugal family."

Fashion A folkway or trait that endures for a relatively short period but does have general acceptance in a given society during that period.

Fecundity The capacity or potential for reproduction.

Fertility The actual reproduction rate of a society as measured by the births occurring on some temporal basis (usually annually) per thousand of the population.

Folk Society Used to characterize relatively small societies marked by adherence to traditional ways and usually subsisting at a marginal level. The term "folk society" is to be preferred to the term "primitive society," unless one is actually referring to a prehistoric society. *See also* Gemeinschaft.

Folkways The customs, habits, and so forth, of a society the observance or nonobservance of which is not deemed of particular importance, although persistent violators of folkways may be subject to mild, informal sanctions. Folkways are a type of norm. *See also* Mores, Norms.

Function The consequences of the operations or actions of any social variable. For example, a function of the institution of education in modern societies is to prepare members of a society for competent performance in the various pertinent roles in the society concerned. The foregoing is an ideal, or manifest, function. It should be remembered that there are also latent functions; the adolescent subculture, which is a latent function of the educational system, may socialize its members in ways that are not congruent with the values and norms of the larger society. *See also* Function, latent; Function, manifest.

Function, latent The actual consequences of any societal action or series of actions when they differ from those intended. Robert K. Merton, who coined the term, uses it also to mean that these actual consequences are unrecognized as well as unintended. *See also* Function; Function, manifest.

Function, manifest The intended or ideal consequence of any societal action or series of actions.

Functionalism A procedure or process whereby researchers concentrate on analyzing cultural and social phenomena in terms of the functions they serve in society. Functionalists conceive of a society as a system of interrelated parts, all of which have a mutual and reciprocal relationship with one another.

Gemeinschaft Used to describe a society (usually a folk society) that is small, based on tradition, and with close individual ties on kinship and friendship. *See also* Folk Society, Gesellschaft.

Generalized Other Information acquired by individuals about other individuals and groups, including values, roles, expectations, and so forth, which is utilized in the development of the self-concept and is essential to individual socialization. Coined by George Herbert Mead, the term also implies that it is through the development of the generalized other that individuals are able to see themselves as objects.

Gesellschaft A type of society epitomized by modern industrial societies in which relations between individual members are presumed to be secondary, that is, based on contractual relationships and mutual interdependence rather than on kinship and friendship. In actual fact, modern societies are not fully Gesellschaft; there are relationships based on kinship and friendship. *See also* Gemeinschaft.

Goals Attainments defined by the value system of a society, group, or individuals as worthy, good, desirable, and so forth.

Group A plurality of persons (three or more) who have certain things in common—a shared identity, common values, norms, goals, and so forth. Implied by the word "group" is the existence of a social structure. It can be assumed that there is some measure of interaction and interdependence between group members. Social groups can be quite small to very large, ranging from three persons to an entire society.

Group, interest, see Interest Group.

Group, primary Any small group marked by continuous close interaction of a highly personal and emotionally supportive nature. *See also* Group, secondary.

Group, reference, see Reference Group.

Group, secondary Any group in which the interaction tends to be segmental, impersonal, and utilitarian, such as groups found in the world of work and business.

Heredity A biological process whereby the general characteristics of a species and the specific characteristics of biological parents are transmitted to their offspring.

Hierarchy An ordering from lesser to greater. In human societies, hierarchies are based upon evalutions of various statuses with some statuses being assigned more prestige and, hence, a higher position in the hierarchy than others.

Homeostasis Originally a physiological concept that holds that the body functions to maintain some kind of internal equilibrium. In sociology, early functionalists assumed that societies functioned in much the same way, that is, to maintain some kind of internal balance or stability.

Homogamy Marriage between people possessing similar traits either social, physical, or both. *See also* Endogamy, Exogamy.

Hypothesis A tentative statement of the relationship between two or more variables. Hypotheses are conjectural; they are intended to be subjected to empirical testing. *See also* Theory.

Ideology A system of values and beliefs which serves to explain the past, interpret the present, predict the future, and, in general, justify behavior.

Independent Variable A variable (usually labeled X) whose appearance or changes causes changes to occur in another variable (usually labeled Y). In terms of cause and effect, the independent variable is the cause. *See also* Dependent Variable, Variable.

Industrialization A process whereby a society develops inanimate sources of power, shows an increasing division of labor, and develops a highly complex social organization which is characterized by what Durkheim called "organic solidarity," by which he means the cohesion that stems from interdependence of individuals and groups rather than from tradition and kinship. *See also* Gesellschaft.

In-group A human group, either primary or secondary, which is characterized by a strong sense of belongingness, identification, and loyalty to the group on the part of its membership. An accompanying characteristic is a sense of exclusiveness toward nonmembers. *See also* Group; Group, primary; Group, secondary; Out-group.

Innovation Changes in current behavior within a society which have their genesis in the development or recognition of new elements or patterns. *See also* Discovery, Invention.

Instinct A complex pattern of inherited, involuntary behavior that is species specific (characteristic of each member of any species) and is evoked fully operational upon the initial presentation of the relevant stimulus.

Institution, Social, see Social Institution.

Institutionalization The process whereby values, norms, and roles become stabilized and generally formalized, as do the sanctions, positive and negative, which encourage adherence to those values, norms, and roles.

Integration The process of producing a single unit from separate parts. In modern American, the term specifically refers to the on-going process that is designed to make racial and ethnic criteria irrelevant to the equal exercise of the rights of citizenship.

Interaction In the social sense, relationships between two or more persons which have some meaning to those concerned.

Interest Group A group organized for the express purpose of advancing some specific goal or goals of its members. Interest groups can be temporary or longlasting.

Internalize A process whereby persons come to accept values and norms as their own and, thus, right and proper.

Invention Any combinations of existing elements to form something new and unique; for example, the steamboat involved the combination of the hull of a boat with a steam engine, thus producing something new. *See also* Discovery, Innovation.

Language   A system of arbitrary symbols and a set of rules for combining these symbols so as to transmit different and varied meanings. By "abitrary symbols" is meant that the combination of vowels and consonants used to express some meaning or refer to some thing are a matter of consensus and that the symbols used do not have some basic or natural relationship with the meaning they are used to express.

Latent Functions, see Functions, latent.

Law   A collection and system of standardized norms constituting a codification of traditional practices. Ordinarily, law can be considered to represent some formalization of rules for behavior. The responsibility for enforcing laws lies with government, and formal sanctions are provided as one means of enforcement.

Learning   A change in behavior as a result of behavior (or experience). A process that manifests itself through or by changes in behavior based on prior experience. Deviant behavior is acquired by the same process and in the same way as socially approved behavior.

Legitimacy, see Legitimate.

Legitimate   That which is accepted by the majority of the members of any given society as proper, moral, right, and so forth. Legitimacy is conferred by consensus; nothing is inherently legitimate or illegitimate.

Leisure   Time used for purposes not connected with work or the demands of providing subsistence.

Life Cycle   A sequence of stages in the career of an individual, group, or society. Generally regarded as typical, sequential stages through which some entity progresses during its lifetime. When used with reference to societies, the assumption is that societies resemble living organisms in that they have birth, adolescence, maturity, old age, and death.

Life Expectancy   A demographic concept referring to the average number of years of life remaining to an individual at various ages from birth onward. Life expectancy conveys information with respect to the quality of life in a given society relative to other societies.

Looking-glass Self   An expression coined by Cooley to mean that one's conception of one's self is primarily a reflection or feedback from others, that is, one's self-concept comes about through information received about oneself from others.

Magic   Behavior based on the fallacious assumption that natural forces or other persons can be controlled by acts that have no actual relationship to such forces or persons.

Manifest Functions, see Functions, manifest.

Marginality   A condition of individuals who participate in two cultures without actually being a member of either. Modern examples are Chinese and Indians who live in societies having different cultures, performing useful services for those other societies but, nonetheless, being accepted neither by the parent society nor the one to which they have emigrated.

Marriage   A contractual arrangement or agreement between two persons of the opposite sex by which certain rights, privileges, and responsibilities are undertaken as these are set forth by the norms of the society in which the parties concerned live. All societies regulate sexual behavior, and marriage is a commonly found way by which many societies legitimize sexual access and provide for the care and socialization of offspring resulting from the marriage.

Mass   A term based on the assumption that large numbers of persons in a society are responding or could be brought to respond in roughly identical ways to the same stimuli. Another assumption is that this mass is relatively undifferentiated and highly pliable, being easily manipulated by the mass media. *See also* Mass Culture.

Mass Culture   Properly used, this can be taken to mean those values, norms, folkways, and so forth, which are habitual to large groups of people and with respect to which there is considerable and widespread consensus. Improperly used by those who are proponents of the mystique of the mass society to mean low tastes, lack of appreciation for the arts, failure of discernment, and being easily led and controlled by the mass media.

Mass Society, see Society, mass.

Matrilineal   A family form in which descent is traced through the mother's lineage. *See also* Clan, Patrilineal.

Mean   The sum of two or more quantities (numbers) divided by the number of these quantities or numbers. Often referred to as the average. *See also* Median, Mode.

Median   If all the numbers in a series of numbers are arranged in order from the lowest to the highest, the median is that value that precisely divides the series into an upper and lower half in terms of frequencies. *See also* Mean, Mode.

Migration   A change of residence from one locality to another.

Minority   A term used to designate groups, the individual members of which are denied full participation in the society of which they are a part. Somewhat paradoxically, minority groups are not necessarily inferior in the numerical sense as in, for example, South Africa or Rhodesia, where the whites are fewer in number but rule the native Black populations.

Mob   An emotionally aroused crowd, the goal of which is or appears to be some kind of violence or destruction.

Mode   A value that occurs most frequently in any series of numbers. A distribution may have two or more modes. *See also* Mean, Median.

Monogamy   A form of marriage in which the norm is the union of one man with one woman. *See also* Polygamy, Polyandry, Polygyny.

Mores   Norms that are considered to be obligatory and are highly valued or held sacred by a society. Deviation from mores is viewed as being more serious, and is more likely to be negatively sanctioned, than deviation from other norms. The singular form of mores is "mos". *See also* Folkways, Norms.

Mortality   Often referred to as "mortality rate," it refers to the numbers of deaths per one thousand population which occur during a given interval of time, usually one year.

Mos   The singular form of "mores."

Myths   Usually taken to mean traditional stories that serve to explain something of concern to a society, for example, its origin, the nature of man, or various practices. In sociology, the term "legitimating myths" is sometimes used to indicate largely fictitious stories or legends that serve to buttress the status quo, examples of which would be the story of George Washington and the cherry tree, Moses in the bulrushes, and so on.

Nation   A political entity usually governed by full-time leaders, which claims an internal monopoly of violence. Membership in nations is usually a matter of birth but most nations have provision for making citizens out of individuals who voluntarily seek to be members. Nations also claim full authority over all members (citizens).

Norms   A rule for behavior. There are gradations among norms, with mores being held as sacred and folkways defined as customs that may be violated with considerable impunity. *See also* Folkways, Mores.

Nuclear Family, see Family, nuclear.

Oligarchy   Political control exercised by very few persons or a small clique.

Opinion   A conclusion or conviction with respect to something which is not necessarily based upon sound, empirically derived evidence. An individual act of judgment. *See also* Belief.

Organization   A group of people functioning in accordance with values and norms for the purpose of achieving some goal or goals. Organizations are deliberately formed for some conscious purpose or purposes.

Out-group   Any group or society toward which a person or a group feels a sense of avoidance or opposition. *See also* In-group.

Participant-Observer   An individual who mingles with or joins a group for the purpose of studying that group and, as a result, participates to some extent in the activities of the group.

Particularism   Applied to efforts to explain complex events on the basis of some single independent variable.

Patrilineal   A family form in which descent is traced through the lineage of the father. *See also* Clan, Matrilineal.

Pattern   Recurrent regularities in behavior upon which prediction is based and from which such things as social structure, values, norms, roles, and so forth, are deduced.

Personality Totality of attitudes, ideas, values, habits, and characteristics of an invididual which grow or develop out of the continuing interplay between an individual's inherited physical traits and his or her environmental experiences.

Pluralism, see Cultural Pluralism.

Polity The political system or beliefs of a group. The term is usually applied to the political system of a society.

Polyandry A form of marriage in which one woman has two or more husbands at the same time. *See also* Monogamy, Polygamy, Polygyny.

Polygamy A form of marriage in which one spouse has two or more spouses at the same time. *See also* Monogamy, Polyandry, Polygyny.

Polygyny A form of marriage in which one man has two or more wives at the same time. *See also* Monogamy, Polyandry, Polygamy.

Population An inclusive term that refers to all organisms of any particular species inhabiting a given area at the same time and obtaining their sustenance therefrom.

Position A socially defined role, location, or status within a society with a concomitant set of norms defining the expectations of behavior for individuals occupying it as well as behavioral expectancies of others toward its occupants. *See also* Position, achieved; Position, ascribed.

Position, achieved A social role, location, or status that is attained through or by the efforts of the individual occupying it. In general, an individual occupying an achieved position has gained that position through his or her own efforts and merit. *See also* Position; Position, ascribed.

Position, ascribed A social role, location, or status that is assigned to an individual by others usually on the basis of some characteristic or trait that is not under the control of the individual so assigned. For example, "man" or "woman." *See also* Position; Position, achieved.

Power Ability to make and implement one's own decisions in the face of opposition or resistance from others.

Power Structure A pattern of orderly arrangement, allocation, and use or exercise of authority and power within any given social system.

Prejudice Unfavorable attitudes toward individuals or groups (usually minority groups) based on undesirable traits attributed to them. Prejudices are covert. Overt behavior stemming from prejudice is called discrimination. *See also* Discrimination.

Pressure Group Any organized group the goal or goals of which is to advance, protect, or reinforce some interest of the group's members.

Prestige The deference, honor, and so forth, accorded to individuals by others. Prestige is an ascribed personal quality awarded to individuals by others on the basis of such criteria as their accomplishments, position, class, or status.

Primary Group, see Group, primary.

Primitive The word has connotations of simple, crude, and so forth, and should not be applied to any contemporary society however undeveloped its technology.

Probability An assumption generally made by scientists that random events and chance factors function in many relationships in the natural world and, hence, that these causal relations are not predictable in any precise way but rather in terms of the probabilities of their occurrence. The odds given on sporting events constitute a common example of probability, or probabilistic thinking. The social sciences are probabilistic sciences.

Propaganda The dissemination (by whatever means) of information, whether true or not, designed to influence individuals to think, believe, or behave in some desired manner.

Public A collectivity of persons not necessarily interacting with one another who are, nonetheless, identifiable on the basis of sharing some common interest or interests and who, as individuals or in groups, may be expressing this interest through unilateral communications to those in power. The word can be used in a general way to refer to a collectivity of individuals who are assumed to be characterized by some common interest or interests.

Race Subdivisions of *Homo sapiens* determined on the basis of physiological and inherited traits.

Random The general meaning "by chance," or "haphazard." In science, random is usually taken to refer to an absence of any bias. For example, a "random sample" means a sample taken from a population in which all members of the population under study had an equal chance of being selected for the sample.

Reference Group Any group whose values, norms, or goals are utilized by an individual, whether an actual member of the group or not, as standards for guiding his or her own conduct and behavior.

Religion A social institution that functions to organize and regulate certain values, beliefs, attitudes, and practices with respect to what is regarded as sacred and morally imperative in a given group, including entire societies. In general, the beliefs basic to religion are concerned with explanations for questions or problems of importance which cannot be answered by empirical methods—for example, the question of life after death, and so forth. *See also* Social Institution.

Revolution In ordinary usage, revolution is taken to mean an attempt to overthrow an existing political system and to take power. If successful, this kind of revolution may not involve any significant social changes. A *social* revolution refers to some discernible and large-scale change in the social structure of a society and implies that the change has been both relatively swift and dramatic, such as the Industrial Revolution.

Rite of Passage   Any ritual that marks a profound and consequential change in the life history of individuals; for example, ceremonies marking such events as birth, puberty, marriage, and death.

Role   A pattern of behavior organized around specific rights and duties that are associated with a particular status or social position. This behavior involves two sets of expectations known to both the role-player and those associated with the playing of the role: (1) expectations on the part of others with respect to the behavior of the role-player; (2) expectations on the part of the role-player with respect to the reciprocal behavior of others.

Role Conflict, see Conflict, role.

Sanctions   The rewards (positive sanctions) and punishments (negative sanctions) used to enforce the values, norms, and folkways of a society.

Secondary Group, see Group, secondary.

Secularization   The process whereby the sacred or religious is changed or converted to the rational, utilitarian, or experimental.

Segregation   The formal or informal, forced or voluntary clustering together of individuals possessing some visible characteristic that defines them as different from the larger population of a society. Implied by the term is that (1) the group concerned is a minority group usually in terms of numbers and certainly in terms of power; (2) the separation (or clustering) is usually not voluntary but enforced by formal and informal norms; (3) this separation is based upon a desire to prevent or minimize equal-status social interaction between the members of the dominant group and the members of the minority group.

Self   The concept of personal identity held by each individual based upon information gained from others with respect to oneself.

Self-fulfilling Prophecy   This concept of Robert K. Merton's is based on W. I. Thomas's definition of the situation—if men define situations as real, they are real in their consequences. For example, if someone believes that another individual is dishonest, it is relatively easy to demonstrate it by interpreting various acts of the individual so defined as dishonest. Or, if one believes that others are hostile, the belief will cause the believer to behave in hostile ways toward these others and these others, in turn, will behave in hostile ways thus fulfilling the prophecy.

Social Institution   An interrelated system of values, norms, and roles organized around some function deemed of critical importance to society.

Social Movement   A voluntary and somewhat loosely organized association of persons engaged in some joint effort to achieve some social goal or goals. Women's Lib and Zero Population Growth are examples.

Social Stratification   Division of a society into two or more internally homogeneous groups with respect to certain criteria, such as occupation, source and amount of wealth, type of dwelling, and area in which dwelling is located.

Social Structure   Organized pattern of interrelated obligations, duties, and rights of persons and groups in a system of on-going interaction which is marked by some degree of stability and continuity. Social structure is determined through observations of persons and an analysis from which is deduced such parts of a social structure as institutions, values, mores, norms, folkways, roles, and so forth.

Socialization   That process whereby individuals learn the values, norms, roles, and so forth, of their society. Inherent in this term is the concept that the process involves the internalization of social learning so that the individual comes to accept as his own (and, thus, as right and proper) the values and other characteristics of the social structure of the society in which he or she lives. *See also* Acculturation, Internalize.

Society   A group of people with a common culture who generally occupy some delimited territory and who possess some feelings of unity and regard themselves as different from members of other groups.

Society, mass   A hypothetical construct that regards modern societies as being characterized by secondary rather than primary group interaction, marked by anomie, and generally characterized by a dulling homogeneity with respect to life styles. The term is often used by those who hold that life in small, agricultural societies is preferable to life in modern societies.

Status   A social category with behavioral or role implications, for example, male, female, young, old, and so forth. Status is not synonymous with prestige, although statuses have socially determined degrees of prestige attached to them. *See also* Class, Position, Prestige.

Stereotype   A simplistic flattering or unflattering description of the members of other groups within a society or other societies.

Subculture   A distinct and identifiable group within a larger culture which while similar in some ways to the larger culture is, nonetheless, marked by values, mores, norms, roles, and role-sets peculiar to the subculture. *See also* Counterculture.

Symbol   Anything that through consensus has come to stand for something else. In human societies, symbol has come to refer, for the most part, to language, which consists of arrangements of sound (oral or written) that have meanings understood by the members of a society in which the symbols and language are used as a means of communication.

Taxonomy   Any system of descriptive classification.

Theory   A set of interrelated propositions, principles, and definitions which serve to organize certain aspects of the objectively determined world in some systematic manner. Theories are based upon a set of assumptions and axioms with the theory itself being composed of empirically verified and interrelated propositions that are logical. Theories are subject to further and continuous empirical testing and verification. Theories attempt to explain a wide range of phenomena in a logical and parsimonious manner.

Universals, see Cultural Universals.

Urbanization   A change or transition from rural living to urban life.

Utopia   The ideal society as, for example, the society Plato presented in *The Republic.*

Value   A hypothetical, inferred construct assumed to exist on the basis of observable positive or negative behavior toward objects or symbolic representations of objects, persons, and situations. Values, further, are learned, social in origin, enduring, variable in intensity, and noninstinctive, and provide socialized individuals with bases for making judgments or selections from or on a wide range of objects, persons, situations, and behaviors.

Variable   Anything that varies. *See also* Dependent Variable, Independent Variable.

Voluntary Association   Any association in which membership is voluntary. *See also* Association.

Weltanschauung   The "world view" or underlying philosophy of life of a society.

Xenophobia   A fear or hatred of strangers or foreigners.

Birth rate, 359
  decline in advanced nations, 354,
    376–378
  factors affecting, 362–365
  patterns, 361–362, 365, 367
  See also Demography
Black Americans, 104, 384
  assimilation, 421–422
  birth-rate differentials, 365
  and education, 270, 290
  family patterns, 405–406
  historical summary, 401–406
  IQ test differences, 390–391
  and law, inequalities, 320
  life conditions, 406–408
  migration patterns (within U.S.),
    369, 391
  and poverty, 285–286
  and prejudice, 393–395
  religious groups, 300, 403–404
  sickle-cell anemia, 386, 391–392
  standard of living, 283–285
  status, 187, 189
  See also Slavery
Black Muslim movement, 404–405
Black nationalism, 404–406
Black Panther party, 320
Black Power, 395
Bourgeoisie, 175
  See also Marxism
British social system, 104, 171,
    184–185, 206
Bureaucracy, 19, 264–267
  and deviance, 317
Bureaucratization and social change,
    439, 447–448
Bushmen, Kalahari, 214
Business, 209–210
  advertising and marketing, 112
  competition, 110–111, 458, 460–
    461
  government control, 274–275
  market mechanisms, 260–261
  monopoly power, 274

Cajuns, 419–420
Calvinism (*see* Protestant Ethic)
Campus unrest, 14, 109, 148
Capitalism, 12, 16–18, 117
Caste, 190–191
  See also Ascription; Stratification
Cathars, 213–214
Catholic Church, Roman, 18
  view on birth control, 299, 363,
    365
Change, social (*see* Social change)
Charisma, 444–445
Chicanos (*see* Mexican-Americans)
Childhood
  Freudian view, 135–136, 137
  prolonged dependency, 69, 74
  See also Mother-child relation-
    ship; Socialization
China, 278
Chinese–Americans, 418, 422
Cities, 447, 453
  class divisions in, 181
  riots, urban, 283–284, 333
  social change and urbanization,
    439, 447–448, 453
  social services, 437
  See also Rural and urban com-
    munities
Civilization (*see* Culture)
Civil rights, 318
  See also Minority groups
Class, social, 13, 75–76, 183–186,
    285
  and birth-rate differentials, 362–
    363
  conflict, class, 14–15, 269
  definition, 183–184
  and deviance, 333–335
  distinctions blurred, 179, 191
  economic basis, 185–186
  endogamy, 241
  inherent in all societies, 76
  law, inequalities, 319–320
  and life style, 184–185

Class, (*continued*)
  and occupation, 271
  and prestige, 191
  social policy for equality, 186
  status, distinct from, 183, 186–188
  and upward mobility, 237–238
  visibility, 184–185
  See also Standard of living; Status; Stratification
Closed societies, 190
Colleges and universities, 291–292, 371
  See also Campus unrest; Education
Colonialism, 395
Common sense and science, 39–40, 42
Communes, 243–244, 302
  See also Group marriage; Kibbutz
Communication, 36
  See also Mass media
Communism, 10, 297, 302, 434
  See also Russia; Socialism
Competition, 111–112, 163–164
  in business, 176, 458, 460–461
  control, governmental, 288
  in economic institution, 271–275
  perceived competition and ethnocentrism, 393–394
  and social change, 441–442
  status, 190, 273–274
  value in American society, 104, 157
  See also Conflict
Complex societies (*see* Modern societies)
Conditioning, 138–139
Conflict, 109, 111–112, 163–164
  in business competition, 458, 460–461
  deprivation of status, 163–165
  Emergent Norm Theory, 459

"every man against every man," 164
  in family, 229
  inherent in all societies, 48, 54, 114, 115, 459
  inherent in competitive situations, 110–111
  institutions, conflict in and between, 213
  intergroup and intragroup, 22, 52–53, 165–166, 277–278
  learned behavior, 49
  normative in nature, 54, 273–275, 458
  and political power, 458–459
  positive functions, 459
  and social change, 457–461
  and socialization, 49–50
  and status quo, 171–172
  structural-functionalist view, 273, 457
  See also Aggression; Competition; Value Conflict
Conflict theory of sociology, 21–25
  and functional theory, 172–174
  social change, 48
  stratification, 163–167, 172–174
  See also Competition; Value conflict
Conformity, 144–145, 209–211, 439
  See also Subcultural conformity
Conjugal family (*see* Family, nuclear)
Conscience, 47–48, 297–298, 329
  collective conscience, 7–8
  form of negative sanctions, 50
Consensus, importance in functional theory, 48
  See also Value consensus
Conspicuous consumption, 168, 271–272
Constraints, 49
  deviance, constraint theory of, 331–333, 336, 337

Dress and social class, 184
Drugs and drug subculture, 80, 334
   illegality of drug use, 339–340
   and youth culture, 147
Dusun, people of Borneo, 46, 297
Dynamic solidarity, 46–48

Economic determinism, 14–15, 175
Economic institution, 205
   and class, 185–186
   comparative perspectives, 260–262
   credit and installment buying, 284–285
   and family, 231, 236–237, 367
   functionalist approach, 261–262
   geographic mobility, 236–237
   goals of society, 261
   governmental controls, 261
   historical development, 258–259
   integration and conflict, 271–275
   market economy, 260–261
   Marxian view, 11–15
   and political institution, 176, 274–275, 280–281
   and population, 362
   poverty, 268–272
   power, economic, 12–15
   progress, as a value, 108
   property, private, 272
   reciprocative distribution, 167–168
   and religious institutions, 206, 213
   stock ownership, 280–281, 282–283
   See also Standard of living
Economics (discipline), 36–37, 261
Ectomorph, 324–325
Education, 219, 289–295, 337, 370
   achievement as a norm, 78, 144–145, 291
   adults, continuing education, 295
   and business, 21–22
   and class, 186, 190–191

community control of schools, 219, 290
   economic importance, 178–179, 183
   extended period of, in modern societies, 149, 233, 238, 354, 365
   goals, 148
   influence on reducing prejudice, 399
   influence on value change, 115
   minority-group programs, 270
   political issue, 289–290
   radical perspective, 294–295
   school environment, 143–144
   and social change, 289–290
   and socialization, 239, 290
   and stratification, 206, 290–291, 292–293
   and upward mobility, 185, 189, 238
   value of, in American society, 110–111, 189–190
   See also Colleges and universities
Egalitarian ideal, 176, 212
Egypt, ancient, 168–170
Elderly (*see* Old age)
Elitism, 212
Emigration, 359–360, 368
Endogamy, 172, 241
Endomorph, 324–325
England (*see* British social system)
Environment, natural, 454–456
   protection, 96, 166, 455
Environment, social, 32, 204
Equilibrium, social, 21–22
   between institutions, 208
   structural-functional theory, 48, 457
Eskimos, 454
Ethnic groups
   definition, 384
   distinct from race, 384, 387–388
   IQ test differences, 390–391
Ethnocentrism, 205, 243–244
   definition, 83–84

Ethnocentrism, (*continued*)
  deviance, response to, 85–86
  and fear of competition, 393
  and perceived competition, 393–
    394
  phenomenal absolutism, 85–86
  positive features, 86
  and racism, 392–393
  religious groups, 299–300
  See also Prejudice
Ethnology, 35, 228
Ethos of a society, 103–104
Eugenics, 324, 337
Events and social change, 444–445
Evolution
  of man, 67, 70
  of society, 4
Exogamy, 241, 245
Exploitation, 284–285
Extended family (*see* Family, ex-
    tended)

Familism, 239–240
Family, 205, 213, 218, 443
  approaches to study of, 228–230
  changes in structure, 362
  cross-cultural view, 242–249
  definition, 226–228
  developmental approach, 229
  extended, 232, 238, 272, 453
  household structure, 232–233
  influence of, 238–239
  interactional approach, 228
  joint, 232, 238
  nuclear, 228, 232, 236–243, 246–
    247, 272, 453
  and population patterns, 362
  in preliterate societies, 228
  roles within, 218
  sexual access within, 227, 230–232
  size of, 367
  and social change, 453
  socializing agent, 214, 215, 239,
    249–250

structural-functional approach,
    229–230
  structure of, 230–233
  See also Marriage; Sexual be-
    havior
Fatalism, 159, 267
"Fear of the state," 7
Fecundity, 362
Fertile Crescent, 455
Fertility rate, 362, 377–378
  differential rates, 362–365
Folkways, 32, 77–78
  informal sanctions, 80–81
  See also Norms
Food production, 374–375
  See also Surpluses; Technology
Frontier settlement, 456
Frustration, 333–334, 336, 337,
    396–398
Functional integration of institu-
    tions, 272–273
Functional prerequisites of institu-
    tions, 204–205
Functional theory of sociology,
    21–25
  conflict, approach to, 273, 457
  and conflict theory, 172–174
  definition, 22
  deviance, approach to, 317–319,
    321, 343
  economic institution, approach
    to, 261–262
  equilibrium, view of, 48, 208
  family, approach to, 229
  political institution, approach to,
    277
  stratification, approach to, 159–
    163
  See also Value consensus
Future shock, 446–447

Gangs, street, 331, 335
Gemeinschaft and Gesellschaft,
    436–437

Insurance, 21
Integration, 21–22
 normative and functional, 436–437
Intelligence, 71
 behavioral context, 71
 and deviance, 326–327
 ethnic and racial differences, 388, 390–391
 problem-solving, 72
 See also IQ tests
Interaction, 43
 intergroup, 443
 and language, 74–75
 in urban life, 453
Interactional approach to study of family, 228
Interdependence, 77–78
 of groups, 8, 272–273
Intergenerational conflict (*see* Generation gap)
Internalization of norms and rules, 48–49, 141–142
 of values, 9–11, 83
International relations, 432, 461–462
IQ tests, 192, 326–327
 culturally weighted, 293, 390–391
 and expectations, 293
Israel (*see* Kibbutz)

Japan, 107, 450
Japanese-Americans, 418–419
 assimilation, 422
 prejudice, 394
Jesus Movement, 302–303
Jews, 83
 assimilation, 417
 in Germany, 384–385
 race concept misused, 387–388
 Reform Judaism, 417–418
 religious prejudice, 417–418
 social institutions, 417
 See also Antisemitism
Jim Crow laws, 402–403

Joint family (*see* Family, joint)
Juvenile delinquency, 146–147, 333, 334–335
 and police, 341
 See also Crime; Deviance

Kibbutz, 214
 and family, 227, 247–249
"Killer instinct" (*see* Aggression)
Kinship system, 233
 See also Family

Labeling approach (*see* Deviance)
Labor unions, 166
 as power elites, 176–177
Laissez-faire system, 274
Language, 62, 68, 72–73
 and interaction, 74–75
 and self-development, 133
 as social class indicator, 184–185
Law, 49–50, 315
 drugs, illegality of, 339–340
 equality and inequality, 156, 319–320
 racial discrimination, laws supporting, 402–403
 repressive and restitutive, 10
 and social control, 49, 277
 test cases, 318
 See also Police; Social control
Law of inertia (*see* Value change)
Leadership, development of, 170–171, 173
Learned behavior, 49
 culture, 62
 deviance, 334–335
Learning and intelligence, 71
 and socialization, 138–142
 See also Education; Modeling
Learning theory, 138–142
 developmental approach, 141–142
 instrumental theory, 138–139
 social theory, 139–141

"Pentagon papers," 180
Personality
    authoritarian type, 397–399
    and deviance, 328
    and prejudice, 396–399
Peru, ancient, 259
Phenomenal absolutism (*see* Ethno-
    centrism)
Physical anthropology, 35
Pluralism, 14, 286, 288, 400
    and conflict over norms, 80
    and conflict theory, 24–25
    and functional theory, 24
    and other-direction, 441
    in race and ethnic relations, 400,
        422
    and religious institutions, 302
Police, 49, 137
    See also Social control
Political economy, 276–277
Political institution, 276–288
    and armed forces, 278, 286–288
    authority and high status, 188–189
    conflict with economic institu-
        tion, 274–275
    corruption, 180, 275, 279
    decision-making, 285–286, 288
    and economic institution, 176,
        260, 274–277, 280–281
    functionalist view, 277
    legitimacy of government, 278–
        279
    liberalism and sociology, 23
    and mass media, 179–180
    and poverty, relief of, 286
    radicalism and sociology, 23
    taxation, 282
    See also Democracy; Power,
        political
Political science, 37
Pollution, 96, 166, 455
Polyandry (*see* Polygamy)
Polygamy, 230, 232
Polygyny (*see* Polygamy)
Population

age distribution, 371
growth, 352
    advanced nations, 354–355
    birth control, 371–377
    checks, 371
    factors in American pattern,
        362–368
    and food production, 170,
        374–376
    historical survey, 356–358
    measurement, 360
    and productivity, 353–356
    projections for future, 352–
        353, 357–358
    technological change, effects of,
        374–375, 451–452
    underdeveloped nations, 353–
        354, 373–377
    young population, 354
income levels, 370
and poverty, 454
sex ratios, 370–371
and social structure, 259
    See also Demography
Poverty, 268–272
    and minority groups, 370
    and population size, 454
    relief of, 286
    statistics, 268–269
Power elites, 174–175, 177–178,
    207, 281, 286–288
    See also Aristocracy
Power, political, 158, 175, 193,
    260, 277–278
    social, 22–23, 277–280
    and stratification, 158, 163, 165–
        166
    See also Revolutions
Predictability of behavior, 105–106
Prehistoric societies, 44, 236, 356
    neolithic, 258–259, 451
    paleolithic, 258–259
Prejudice, 392–399
    authoritarian personality type
        397–399

Rebellion, 333–334
See also Deviance
Reciprocative distribution, 167
Reinforcement, 142
in early childhood, 132
instrumental learning theory, 138–139
random reinforcement, 52
reinforcers, primary and secondary, 51
See also Sanctions
Relativism (*see* Deviance, labeling approach
Religious groups, birth-rate differentials, 363, 365
suicide rates, 331–332
Religious institutions, 295–303
Black churches in America, 300, 403–404
dysfunctions, 299–300
and economic institution, 298–299
enforcement of values and norms, 297–298
functional utility, 296–297, 303
future prospects, 302–303
influence, declining, 298–300
in modern societies, 298–301
in prehistoric societies, 295–296
Protestantism, 17–18
psychological functions, 296
and science, 301–302
societal functions, 297
subcultures, religious, 302–303, 420
and value conflict, 112–114
youth, appeals to, 300
See also Catholic Church, Roman; Jesus Movement; Jews; Protestant Ethic
Religious prejudice (*see* Antisemitism; Prejudice)
Religious values, 105, 117, 118, 297–298
See also Protestant Ethic
Retirement, socialization in, 150

Revolutions, 175, 183, 334, 458
Rewards, 157
stratification, 162, 165
See also Competition; Reinforcement; Sanctions
Roles, social, 204
adolescence, 149–150
childhood role-playing, 133–134
family, roles within, 218
and groups, 76
and institutions, 218
and norms, 78–79
predictability, 105–106
and rules, social, 135
socialization, 133–134, 137, 149–150
and status, 76
Rule-breaking behavior, 320–321
See also Deviance
Rules, social, 137
childhood, acceptance of rules in, 141–142
"rules for breaking rules," 48
in self-development, 135
and social order, 7
and stratification, 164
Ruling class (*see* Aristocracy; Class, social)
Rural and urban communities
birth-rate differentials, 363–364
migration, 407
population patterns, 396
Russia, 434
American attitude to, 84
prehistoric peoples, 236
stratification in, 175–176
See also Communism

Sanctions, 50–51, 79–81
definitions, 50–51
and deviant behavior, 77, 79–81
formal, 79–80
informal, 80–81
moral, 50
negative, 50–51

Sanctions, *(continued)*
　positive, 50–51
　in preliterate and modern societies, 79
　religious, 299
　See also Reinforcement; Rewards
Sciences, natural
　and religion, 301–302
　and social sciences, 20
　and society, 32–33
　and values, 105, 117, 118, 302
　See also Technology
Scientific method, 38–42
Scientific progress, 14
　See also Technology
Secessionist minorities, 400, 404–405, 406
Segregation (*see* Racism)
Self-awareness, 129–138
Self-definition, 439–441
Self-fulfilling prophecy, 338–339
Self-identity and culture, 63–64
Sexual behavior
　adolescence, 145–146
　changing patterns, 145–146
　courtship, 240–241
　deviance, 316, 317, 319, 339
　homosexuality, 339
　and instincts, 66–67
　in kibbutz, 248
　roles, sex, 145–146
　taboos, 362, 403
　unwritten law, 78
　See also Family; Marriage
Sickle-cell anemia, 386, 391–392
Simple societies (*see* Preliterate societies)
Slavery, 389, 393–394, 401–402, 403, 405–406
Slum environments, 146–147
　See also Ghettos
Social change
　alienation, 435, 436–438
　artificial communities, 439

causes and factors, 444–461
and competitive values, 441–442
and conflict and dissensus, 457–461
conflict theory, 48
demographic factors, 451–454
dynamics of change, 3, 432–433
economic factors, 117, 451–452
and environment, 454–456
and "events," 444–445
family structure, 453
future shock, 446–447
Gemeinschaft and Gesellschaft, 436–437
identity and social character, 439–441, 452–453
and institutionalized conflict, 434
international perspectives, 432, 461–462
and law, 438–439
Marxian view, 433–434
and mass media, 445–446
Mass Society, 442–443
normative and functional integration, 436–437
norms, changing, 81
radical ideologies, 439–442
resistance of societies to, 117, 118, 172, 206–207
in stratification systems, 174–183
synthesis of opposed interests, 433–434
and technocracy, 435–436
and technology, 181–183, 441–442, 445–450
theories of, 433–443
and urbanization, 439, 447–448, 453
and values, 117, 450–451
　See also Tradition
Social control, 48–54, 205
　childhood, early, 132–133
　definition, 336–337
　moral entrepreneurs, 339–340, 342

Social control, (*continued*)
  police and prisons, 338, 340–343
  rule creators, 339–340, 342
  See also Sanctions
Social facts, 9–11, 104
Socialism, 16, 247
  See also Communism
Socialization, 205, 290, 337
  and adaptability, 151
  adolescence, 143–149
  of adults, 149–150
  anticipatory, 150
  conformity to existing institutions, 209–211
  continuity of society, 129
  definition, 128
  and ethnocentrism, 83
  gangs, street, 331
  importance challenged, 49
  of individual, 9–11
  in kibbutz, 247–248
  and religion, 297–298
  self-awareness, development of, 129–138
  See also Education; Learning
Social order, 3, 6–7
  and alienation, 437–438
  challenges to, 437–438
  "fear of the state," 7
  and instincts, 65
  institutions, order maintained by, 215
  and power, 22–23
  problem of order, 6–8, 65
  See also Deviance; Social control
Social psychology, 35
Social sciences and society, 32–34
  See also Sciences, natural
Society, continuity of, 103, 129
  necessarily self-correcting, 53
  prehistoric, 44
  structure of, 43–48, 54
Sociology (discipline), 36–37, 43, 444
  early, 3–21

Somatotypes, 324–325
South Africa, Republic of, 392
  resistance to value change, 116, 117
Soviet Union (*see* Russia)
Space program, 261, 289, 445
Spanish-Americans (*see* Mexican-Americans; Puerto Ricans)
Specialization (*see* Division of labor)
Specificity, 212
Sports, 156
  competition, 110–111
  and random reinforcement, 52
Standard of living, 283–285
  nonfunctional goods, 179
  population growth, effects of, 354–355
  and surpluses, 182–183
Statistical analysis, 38, 41–42
Status
  achieved, 75, 117, 165, 273–274
  ascribed, 75, 165, 187, 384
  competition for high status, 273–274
  distinct from class, 183, 186–188
  in employment, 267
  and institutions, 218
  and racism, 389
  retirement, effects of, 150
  and rewards, 209
  and roles, 76, 149–150
  "status front," 439
  inconsistency, 24, 187–188
  "status panic," 188–189
  and stratification, 156–157
  symbols, 447
  wealth confers high status, 188
  See also Class; Stratification
Stimulus and response (*see* Reinforcement)
Stratification, 160
  in business, 161
  closed systems, 173
  compared in different societies, 159–160, 167

Stratification, (*continued*)
conflict theory, 23–25, 163–167, 172–174
definition, 156–157
in democracy, 279–280
distributive theory, 168–169
eclectic approach, 167–174
and education, 206, 290–291
egalitarian ideal, 176, 212
functional theory, 23–25, 159–163, 172–174
inherent in all societies, 159–160, 192
institutionalized inequality, 25, 279–280
Marxian view, 25
and power, 158, 163
problem, social, 157–159
in simple societies, 167
rules, social, 164
and surpluses, 193
value consensus, 107–108
See also Class; Status
Structural-functional theory (*see* Functional theory of sociology)
Subcultural conformity theory of deviance, 334–335, 336, 338
Subcultures, 52, 54
See also Drugs; Youth culture
Success, as a value, 105, 108, 174, 212
See also Achievement; Competition
Suicide, 331–332
Supernatural, 297–298
See also Religious institutions; Religious values
Surpluses and standard of living, 182–183
and stratification, 167–168, 172–173, 193
Survival of societies, 213–215, 216–217
Symbols, 72, 297
See also Language

Taboos, definition of, 46
racial, 319, 402–403
sexual, 241, 362
Technocracy, 435–436
Technology
and agriculture, 168–170
and bureaucratic organizations, 265–266
and cultural change, 53
and developing countries, 260
and environment, 455–456
future prospects and importance of, 449–450, 461–462
and material culture, 82
and military research, 287
rate of change, 432–439
and social change, 14–15, 181–183, 439, 441–442, 445–450
and value change, 117, 118
See also Sciences, natural
Technostructure (*see* Managerial class)
Tension-management system, 272, 433–434
Territorial imperative (*see* Aggression)
Tool-making, 68–69
Tradition, 77–78
conformity to, 209
and institutions, 206–207
and values, 101
Tradition-direction, 440–441, 452–453
Tristan da Cunha, 116, 117, 167
Trobriand Islands, 46

Underdeveloped nations, population growth in, 353–354, 373–376
Universalism, 212
Upper class, 283
See also Aristocracy; Ascription
Upward mobility, 170–171, 173, 237–239, 337
contest mobility, 191

Upward mobility, (*continued*)
  and education, 185, 189–190
  and higher education, 292
  value, regarded as, 174, 273–274
Urbanization (*see* Cities)
Urban riots (*see* Cities)
USSR (*see* Russia)
Utopias, 163, 457, 461

stability, source of, 116, 118–119, 120
  and stratification, 107–108
  and tradition, 101
  and war, 96
  See also Norms
Vasilika, Greece, 45–46
Vietnam war, 96, 437, 460
Visibility, 184–185, 394
Volstead Act (*see* Prohibition)

Value change, 114–118
  complex societies, greater change in, 116–117
  education, influence of, 115–116
  homeostasis, 115–116
  law of inertia, 115–116
  resistance to, 115–117
  and social change, 117, 118
  and stability, 118–120
  and technology, 117,118
Value conflict, 22–23, 109–115
Value consensus, 22–23, 104, 107–108
Values, 96, 211–212
  characteristics and definitions, 97–103, 204
  as causes of conflict, 109
  dysfunctions, 107–109
  functions, 103–106
  ideal, 102
  interpretations within a society, 112
  norms determined by, 101–104
  norms distinguished from, 100
  and personal desires, 116, 117
  pragmatic, 102
  and private property, 271
  relativity of, 97–99, 100–101, 108
  and religion, 117, 297–298
  science, value system of, 302
  and sexual behavior, 145–146
  and social change, 450–451

War on Poverty, 268–272
  assessment of, 269–271
  statistics, 269
WASPs (White Anglo-Saxon Protestants), 283
Watergate affair, 180, 275, 279
Wealth, 188, 279–283
Welfare programs (*see* War on Poverty)
Women, rights of, 191
Work, alienation from, 262–267, 435–437
Working class, 175
  attitudes, 269
  in capitalist system, 13
  See also Labor unions

Youth culture, 111, 146–148, 300, 436
  conformity within peer group, 146–147
  disenchantment with power structure, 158
  and drug use, 147
  and Jesus Movement, 302–303
  See also Campus unrest; Drugs and drug subculture; Generation gap

Zweckrational action, 18–19

Cantril, Hadley, 124
Cardwell, J. D., 99; 101; 122 nn.5, 11; 123 n.25
Carter, Roy E., Jr., 124
Catlin, George E. G., 57 n.21, 58
Catton, William R., Jr., 115, 123 n.42, 124
Centers, Richard, 199 n.48
Chamberlain, Houston S., 388, 425 n.6, 426
Chance, Norman A., 197 n.11
Childe, V. Gordon, 44; 57 n.15; 296; 306 nn.2, 4; 309 n.76; 380–381; 451–452; 453; 464 nn.25, 33; 465
Chinoy, Eli, 266, 307 n.20
Chomsky, Noam, 74, 91 n.48
Clark, Kenneth B., 425 n.18
Clarke, Burton, 292, 309 nn.68–69
Clausen, John A., 146, 152–153 n.10
Clinard, Marshall B., 253 n.32, 347
Cloward, Richard A., 307 n.23
Cohen, Albert K., 319–320; 324–325; 333; 345 nn.12, 15–16, 23, 27, 29; 346 n.45; 347
Cohen, Ronald, 197 n.11
Cohen, Yehudi A., 89 n.3
Coleman, James S., 390, 425 n.9, 426
Collins, Mary Evan, 425 n.25, 427
Comte, Auguste, 3–4, 12, 27 nn.2–3
Conant, James, 289
Conot, Robert, 308 n.59
Cooley, Charles Horton, 132–133, 136–137, 142, 152 n.2, 478
Coon, Carleton S., 44–45; 57 nn.14, 17; 73; 90 nn.41, 43; 386; 424 n.1; 427
Coser, Lewis A., 27 n.2, 28, 345 n.13, 459, 465 n.43
Coser, Rose, 253 n.37
Cottrell, L., 307 n.32, 463–464 n.3
Cowgill, Donald O., 381
Cox, Frank D., 254
Cox, Harvey, 309 n.84

Cressey, Donald R., 328; 330; 345 n.30; 346 nn.37, 40, 48; 347–348
Crutchfield, R. S., 123 n.40
Cuzzort, R. P., 57 n.12, 214, 222 n.18

Dahrendorf, Ralf, 23–25; 27–28 n.11; 197 n.20; 252 n.6; 308 n.44; 434; 457–458; 461; 464 n.4; 465 nn.38, 42, 45
Dalton, Melville, 310
Davis, Kingsley, 50; 57 n.25; 100; 122 n.9; 159–163; 192; 197 nn.10, 12–14; 208; 221 n.6; 345 n.22; 380 n.5
Demereth, N., 222 n.8, 310, 465 n.38
Deutsch, Morton, 425 n.25, 427
Devereux, Edward C., Jr., 87, 92 n.85
Diebold, John, 38, 57 n.6, 58, 198 nn.38–39, 295, 309 n.74
Doby, John T., 69; 71; 74; 90 nn.27, 36; 91 n.48
Dobzhansky, Theodosius, 53; 58 nn.28, 31; 92–93; 386; 424 n.1; 427
Dodge, David L., 347
Dodson, Dan, 289
Dollard, J., 152 n.6, 425 n.20, 427
Domhoff, G. William, 281; 282; 308 nn.47, 52; 310
Dorjahn, Vernon, 252 n.12
Drabek, Thomas E., 348
Dreger, R. M., 152 n.9
Duncan, Otis D., 252 n.20
du Nouy, Pierre Lecomte, 40, 57 n.9
Durand, John D., 375, 380 n.13
Durkheim, Emile, 5–11; 20; 22; 26; 27 nn.5, 7–8; 28; 32; 46–47; 57 n.21; 58; 65; 77; 81; 86; 91 nn.57–58; 104; 153; 237; 262; 272; 296–298; 307 n.33;

Durkheim, Emile, (*continued*)
309 n.79; 318; 331–332;
346 n.44; 438–439; 452;
464 nn.9, 26; 477
Duster, Troy, 345 n.10
Dynes, Robert, 308 n.57

Edwards, Allen L., 116, 123 n.46,
199 n.57
Eisenman, Russell, 425 n.22, 427
Eisenstadt, S. N., 124–125
Empey, LaMar T., 344–345 n.3
Engels, Friedrich, 11, 124 n.55
Erickson, Maynard L., 344–345 n.3
Erikson, Kai, 211, 222 n.14, 347
Etkin, William, 92
Etzioni, Amitai, 196–197 n.6, 223,
252 n.6, 465
Etzioni, Eva, 223, 252 n.6, 465

Fabun, Donald, 449; 464 nn.21,
32, 34; 465
Fallers, L., 464 n.30
Faris, Robert E. L., 57 n.25,
122 n.9, 251 n.3, 254, 379
n.2, 465 n.44
Feldman, A., 307 n.32, 463–464
n.3
Fest, Joachim C., 200 n.59
Fillol, T. R., 108, 123 n.29
Flacks, Richard, 286–287, 308 n.61
Foote, Nelson, 239–240, 252 n.24
Fortune, Reo, 253 n.37
Frazier, E. Franklin, 425 n.29, 426
n.33, 427
Frenkel-Brunswik, Else, 426
Freud, Sigmund, 49, 57 n.23,
64–65, 122 n.13, 135–136,
137, 138, 142, 152 n.4, 197
n.17, 328–330, 346 n.38
Friedl, Ernestine, 57 n.18
Fullerton, Gail Putney, 254
Fusfeld, Daniel R., 112, 123 n.36

Galbraith, John Kenneth, 57 n.4,
176, 198 n.31, 310
Gardner, John, 464 n.7
Gardner, Martin, 58
Garfinkel, Harold, 345 n.17
Garn, Stanley M., 90 n.37, 92
Gaviglio, G., 307 nn.17, 21–22;
308 n.47; 310
Geertz, Clifford, 62; 66; 68; 89
nn.3, 13; 90 n.21
Geger, A. Kent, 253 n.42
Gehlen, Arnold, 209, 222 n.10
Gerth, H. H., 199 n.44
Gilmore, Kenneth O., 307 n.27
Gist, Noel P., 381
Gittell, Marilyn, 308 n.63
Glaser, Daniel, 339–340, 346 n.54
Glasser, William, 347
Glazer, Nathan, 426 n.36, 427
Glidewell, John G., 106, 123 n.24
Glueck, Eleanor, 324, 345 n.28
Glueck, Sheldon, 324, 345 n.28
Glynn, James A., 115, 123 n.43
de Gobineau, Joseph Arthur, 388,
424 n.5, 427
Goddard, Henry, 327, 346 n.33
Goffman, Erving, 347
Goldschmidt, Walter, 99; 101; 117;
122 nn.4, 12; 124 n.50; 125;
183–184; 199 n.41
Goldsen, Rose Kohn, 426 n.35,
428
Goode, William, 226, 233, 249–250,
251 nn.1–2, 252 n.17, 254
n.47, 254–255
Goring, Charles, 323, 326, 345 n.24
Gorman, Benjamin L., 426 n.39
Goulden, Joseph C., 311
Gouldner, A., 222 n.8
Green, Arnold W., 81, 91 n.68,
92 n.84
Gross, Neal, 308 n.64
Guthrie, Edwin., 62, 89 n.2, 216,
222 n.24, 252 n.23
Gutkind, Peter C. W., 116, 123 n.45

Hacker, A., 221 n.1
Hagen, Everett E., 117, 124 n.49
Hailey, William M., 425 n.14, 427
Halpert, L. A., 381
Halsey, A. H., 199 n.55
Hansen, Donald, 228, 252 n.5
Hare, A. Paul, 57 n.13, 199 n.56
Harkavy, Oscar, 374, 380 n.12
Harrington, Michael, 268, 307 nn.21–22
Haskell, Martin R., 346 n.36, 347
Hauser, Philip M., 379 n.1, 380 n.8
Havemann, Ernest, 57 n.27, 71, 90 n.34
Hawley, Amos O., 381
Hayden, Thomas, 287–288, 308 n.62
Hazelrigg, Lawrence, 347–348
Healy, William, 327, 346 n.35
Heilbroner, Robert, 260, 282, 307 n.5, 308 n.53
Heisenberg, Werner K., 57 n.10
Heller, Celia, 252 n. 20
Henry, Jules, 123 n.37, 239, 252 n.22
Herbele, P., 464 n.6
Herskovits, Melville J., 123 n.41, 252 n.12, 426 n.33, 427
Hertzler, J. O., 222 n.28, 222–223
Heussenstamm, F. K., 320, 345 n.20
Hilgard, Ernest R., 57 n.26, 152 n.5
Hill, Reuben, 228, 252 n.5
Himes, Joseph S., 91 n.73
Hirsch, W., 221 n.4
Hobbes, Thomas, 6–8, 57 n.23, 65, 89 n.10, 164, 197 n.17
Hodge, Robert W., 199 n.47
Hoebel, Adamson E., 62–63; 68; 77–78; 89 nn.1, 14; 90 nn.22, 45; 91 nn.59, 69
Hoffer, Eric, 319
Hoffman, Abbie, 6, 27 n.6

Hoffman, L. W., 153
Hoffman, M. L., 153
Hofstadter, Richard, 125, 274, 308 n.35, 311
Hoijer, Harry, 56 n.2; 70; 72; 90 nn. 19, 32–33, 40; 198 n.23; 222 n.19; 231; 252 nn.9, 11, 13; 271; 303; 307 n.28; 309 nn.75, 87
Hollinshead, August B., 197 n.19, 290
Homans, George C., 78, 91 n.62
Hooton, Ernest A., 323–324, 345 n.25
Horowitz, Irving L., 197 n.19, 464 n.8
Horton, Paul B., 157; 196 nn.1, 4; 197 nn.7, 18; 380 n.17
Hoselitz, Bert F., 198 n.34, 199–200 n.58
Hostetler, John A., 426 n.37
Hovland, C. I., 123 n.40
Howell, F. Clark, 236, 252 n.18
Hughes, Everett, 199 n.46
Hull, Clark L., 152 n.5
Humphreys, Laud, 348
Hunt, J. McVey, 122 n.13
Huntington, Gertrude E., 426 n.37
Hyman, Herbert, 199 n.45
Hyman, J., 123 n.40

Inkeles, Alex, 28
Iscoe, I., 152 n.6

Jacobson, Lenore, 309 n.71
Janowitz, Morris, 443
Jay, Antony, 90 n.42
Jay, Phyllis C., 90 n.20
Jenkins, Richard L., 330–331, 346 n.41
Jensen, Arthur, 390, 425 n.10, 427–428

Johnson, Jerah, 426 nn.37–38, 40
Jolly, Allison, 90 n.23

Kagan, Jerome, 57 n.27, 71, 90 n.34
Kahl, Joseph, 237–238, 252 n.19
Keesing, Felix M., 92
Keesing, Robert M., 92
Kelly, William, 89 n.4
Kelman, Herbert C., 122 n.7, 123
    n.33, 465 n.41
Keyserling, Leon, 282, 308 n.50
Kinch, John W., 78, 91 n.63
Kinsey, Alfred C., 316, 319, 345 n.7
Kirsch, A. Thomas, 200–201
Kisburg, Nicholas, 269
Klein, Richard G., 252 n.18
Klemer, Richard H., 255
Klineberg, Otto, 391, 425 nn.12–13,
    428
Kluckhohn, Clyde, 57 n.16; 62;
    89 n.4; 96; 99–100; 122
    nn.1, 6, 8; 125
Knebel, Fletcher, 308 n.56
Kohlberg, L., 153
Komarovsky, Mirra, 153 n.12
Korn, Richard R., 346 nn.42, 49;
    348
Kozol, Jonathan, 289, 292, 309 n.66
Krech, David, 73, 91 n.46, 123 n.40
Kroeber, Alfred L., 426 n.34, 428
Krutch, Joseph Wood, 449–450,
    463 nn.22–23
Kuhn, H. J., 90 n.25

Lampman, Robert, 308 n.51
Lang, Gladys Engel, 222 n.26
Lang, Kurt, 222 n.26
Larson, Richard F., 426 n.39
Lasswell, Thomas E., 122 n.20,
    199 n.53, 222 n.21
Leach, Edmund R., 89 n.17
Lee, Everett S., 57 n.8, 425 n.13,
    428
Lenski, Gerhard, 92; 102; 122 n.14;
    167–168; 198 nn.22, 28

Leslie, Gerald R., 157; 196 nn.1, 4;
    197 nn.7, 18; 380 n.17;
    426 n.39
Levine, Robert A., 91 n.77
Levinson, Daniel, 426
Levy, Marion J., 453, 464 nn.29–30
Lewin, Kurt, 189, 199 n.52
Lieberson, Stanley, 425 n.19, 428
Lindesmith, Alfred R., 74, 91 n.47
Lindzey, G., 123 n.40
Link, Arthur S., 308 n.36
Linton, Ralph, 57 n.16; 78; 83;
    89 n.4; 91 nn.60, 75; 123
    n.41; 246; 252 nn.16, 41;
    425 n.28; 429
Lipset, Seymour Martin, 199 n.45;
    211–213; 222 nn.16–17;
    279–280; 300; 308 nn.42,
    45–46; 311
Locke, John, 156
Lombroso, Cesare, 323, 324, 325,
    326, 330
Loomis, Charles, 28
Lorenz, Konrad, 67, 85, 89 n.16,
    91 n.78, 123 n.31, 130
Lowie, Robert H., 92, 252 n.8,
    253 n.28, 259, 306 n.3
Lowry, Ritchie P., 91 n.54
Luckey, Eleanor B., 240–241

Madge, John, 28
Malcolm X, 277–278, 308 n.40
Malthus, Thomas R., 358; 371;
    374; 380 nn.4, 11
Mandlebaum, D., 464 n.11
Mannheim, Karl, 123 n.47
March, James G., 198 nn.32–33
Marquis, Donald G., 71, 90 n.35
Martindale, Donald, 28; 205; 209;
    221 nn.3, 5
Marx, Karl, 11–15, 16, 18, 19, 21,
    25, 26, 28, 117, 124 n.55,
    163, 175, 176, 186, 191,
    197 n.9, 204, 213, 285
Maslow, Abraham, 125

Mayer, Albert J., 105, 122 n.20, 298, 309 n.83

McClelland, David C., 117, 124 nn.53–54, 298, 309 n.83

McCorkle, Lloyd W., 346 nn.42, 49; 348

McDougall, William, 67, 89 n.18

McGee, Reece, 58; 62–63; 76; 89 n.5; 91 nn.52–53, 55, 76

McKee, James B., 200, 242, 253 n.31, 255, 311

McLuhan, Marshall, 445–446, 447, 464 n.18

Mead, George Herbert, 81, 133–135, 137, 142, 152 n.3, 153, 318, 345 n.13, 476

Melman, Seymour, 307 n.7

Mencher, Joan P., 253 n.40

Mendel, Gregor Johann, 325

Merrill, Francis E., 91 n.72, 200, 296, 306 n.1, 309 n.77

Merton, Robert K., 57 n.4; 333–334; 345 nn.16, 22; 346 n.46; 380 n.5; 424 n.3; 425 n.16; 428; 475; 483

Merz, Charles, 91 n.65

Messinger, Sheldon, 346 n.55

Meyer, John W., 123 n.27

Michels, Robert, 171, 198 n.27

Middleton, Russell, 244–245, 253 n.38

Miller, Daniel R., 255

Miller, Herman, 308 n.49

Miller, N. E., 152 n.6

Miller, K. S., 152 n.9

Miller, Walter B., 346 n.47

Mills, C. Wright, 2; 14; 27 nn.1, 9; 28; 188–189; 199 nn. 44, 50; 262–263; 282; 307 nn.9–10, 14; 308 n.54; 426 n.35; 428

Milton, Ohmer, 348

Miner, Horace, 223

Miyadi, D., 90 n.25

Montagu, Ashley, 89 n.17, 123 n.32

Moore, Barrington, 214, 222 n.20, 249–250, 254 n.45

Moore, Wilbert E., 159–163; 192; 197 nn.10, 12–14; 198 n.34; 199–200 n.58; 272; 307 n.32; 463–464 n.3

Morgan, Clifford T., 39, 57 n.7, 89 n.8, 114–115, 123 n.38

Morgan, Henry Lewis, 181, 198 n.36

Morison, Samuel Eliot, 199, n.42

Morris, Desmond, 69, 90 n.26, 123 n.31

Morris, Richard T., 122 n.10

Mosca, Gaetano, 198 n.25

Mowrer, O. Hobart, 348

Mowry, George E., 91 nn.65–66

Moynihan, Daniel P., 425 n.32, 426 n.36, 427, 428, 429

Munch, Peter A., 123–124 n.48, 197–198 n.21

Murdock, George P., 58 n.29, 197 n.8

Murphy, Fred J., 344–345 n.3

Myrdal, Gunnar, 37, 57 n.5, 402–403, 425 n.31, 428

Nam, Charles B., 309–310; 380 nn.13, 15

Napier, John, 92–93

Nef, John, 49

Newcomb, Theodore M., 123 n.39, 199 n.52

Nimkoff, M. F., 253 n.40

Nisbet, Robert A., 57 n.4; 80; 91 n.67; 123 n.30; 345 nn.16, 22; 380 n.5; 444–445; 464 n.17

Nolan, James, 303, 309 n.86

Nortman, Dorothy, 380 n.15

Oden, Melita H., 56 n.1

Oelfke, William O., 90 n.31

Ogburn, William F., 91 n.74, 471

Oglesby, Carlo, 307 n.8, 464 n.46

Opler, Morris E., 92 n.83

Orshansky, Mollie, 268
Orwell, George, 446, 457

Pareto, Vilfredo, 173–174, 198 n.26
Parkr, Robert, 448
Parsons, Talcott, 23–25; 27 nn.3, 5, 10; 27–28 n.11; 28; 89 n.9; 92 n.85; 115; 117; 122 n.8, 16; 123 n.44; 124 nn. 51–52; 199–200 n.58; 211–213; 221 n.1; 242; 245; 253 nn.33, 39; 255; 296; 308 n.38; 309 n.78; 425 n.18
Pauling, Harold G., 123 n.23
Pavalko, Ronald M., 199 n.54, 271, 307 n.29
Payne, Robert, 198 n.30
Peacock, James L., 200–201
Peterson, Richard, 222 n.8, 310, 465 n.38
Peterson, William, 362, 380 n.6
Phillips, Bernard S., 122 n.10
Piaget, Jean, 65, 89 n.11, 141–142, 143, 144, 151, 152 n.8
Piliavin, Irving, 341, 346 n.58
Pilisuk, Marc, 287–288, 308 n.62
Pintner, R., 327, 345, n.31
Pitts, Jesse R., 122 n.16
Pivan, F., 307 n.23
Plato, 163, 227, 247, 252 n.4, 457
Podain, Simon, 425 n.17, 428
Polsky, Ned, 345 n.11
Popenoe, David, 105, 122 n.21, 201
Potter, David, 456, 465 n.36
Powdermaker, Hortense, 199 n.43

Quarantelli, Ernest, 308 n.57

Rafferty, Max, 289
Rainwater, Lee, 394; 425 nn.18, 32; 428; 429
Rankin, Robert P., 91 n.54
Ray, Marsh, 346 n.51

Raye, David, 307 nn.17, 21–22; 308 n.47; 310
Redfield, Robert, 243, 253 n.35
Redlich, E. C., 197 n.19
Rensch, Bernard, 72, 90 n.38
Rescher, Nicholas, 122 n.3
Revel, Jean-François, 286, 308 n.60
Rex, John, 28–29
Rickover, Hyman, 289
Riesman, David, 36–37; 57 n.4; 439–441; 442; 444; 452–453; 464 nn.12, 16, 27–28; 465
Rimmer, Robert H., 252 n.10
Roach, Jack L., 197 n.20
Roe, Anne, 64; 68–69; 89 n.7; 90 nn.24, 29; 92–93
Rose, Arnold M., 85; 86; 91 nn.70, 80; 92 n.82; 190; 199 n.53
Rose, Caroline B., 85; 86; 91 nn. 70, 80; 92 n.82
Rose, Peter I., 252 n.17
Rosenberg, Bernard, 125, 264–265, 307 n.15–16, 345 n.13
Rosenfeld, Eva, 197 n.15
Rosenhan, D. L., 314, 344 n.1
Rosenthal, Robert, 309 n.71
Roslansky, J. D., 91 n.48
Ross, H. Laurence, 223
Ross, Robert, 260–261, 307 n.6
Roszak, Theodore, 435–436, 463 n.1, 464 n.5, 466
Rousseau, Jean-Jacques, 45, 65, 278, 308 n.41

de Saint Simon, Henri, 3
Sanford, Nevitt, 426
Sapir, Edward, 464 n.11
Sarnoff, David, 446
Schellenberg, James A., 91 n.64
Schneider, R., 90 n.25
Schrag, Peter, 269, 307 nn.24–25
Schuessler, Karl K., 328, 346 n.37
Schuler, Edgar A., 253 n.35, 465 n.41
Schwartz, Richard D., 197 n.15